READINGS IN CONTEMPORARY ETHICAL THEORY

READINGS IN CONTEMPORARY ETHICAL THEORY

EDITED BY

Kenneth Pahel & Marvin Schiller

Department of Philosophy
Knox College

Department of Philosophy
Southern Methodist University

PRENTICE-HALL, INC., Englewood Cliffs, New Jersey

36285

13-755819-8

Library of Congress Catalog Card Number: 78–87265

Printed in the United States of America

Current printing (last number):

10   9   8   7   6   5   4   3   2   1

PRENTICE-HALL INTERNATIONAL, INC., *London*
PRENTICE-HALL OF AUSTRALIA, PTY. LTD., *Sydney*
PRENTICE-HALL OF CANADA, LTD., *Toronto*
PRENTICE-HALL OF INDIA PRIVATE LIMITED, *New Delhi*
PRENTICE-HALL OF JAPAN, INC., *Tokyo*

Preface

The idea of publishing a collection of readings in contemporary ethical theory grew out of our planning together a course in contemporary ethics and then discovering that no existing text began to do justice to the numerous developments in ethical theory from around 1950 to the present. While including enough material from the first half of the century to provide a sense of continuity, our aim has been both to bring up to date the main controversies in twentieth-century ethical theory and to include new controversies which have come into focus only in recent years. Rather than offer a sample of every current problem on which work is being done, we have chosen to include several essays on a few of the most important of these problems. Our aim has been to include papers sufficient in number to involve the reader in the ongoing dialogue that is taking place within each of these problem areas.

In our introductions to each section, we have sought to illuminate the issues and indicate the direction in which an author moves without detailed reconstructions of his argument. Occasionally we have raised questions that may be useful for the reader to keep in mind while examining a certain essay.

Nearly all of the papers in the volume are uncut and are reprinted in their original form (except for corrections of typographical errors). The exceptions are as follows: (1) the first chapter of G. E. Moore's *Principia Ethica* is terminated after Section 17; (2) at Professor Stevenson's request, we are using the modified version of "The Emotive Meaning of Ethical Terms," which appeared as Chapter Two in *Facts and Values*; (3) we have selected substantial excerpts from the relevant chapters of Professor Toulmin's *The Place of Reason in Ethics* for Section Four of the collection; and finally, (4) Professor Smart has made a number of minor corrections and has substituted one extensively revised paragraph in his "Extreme and Restricted Utilitarianism."

We are happy to be able to include two previously unpublished papers, which were written for this volume. For our section "Moral Reasoning and the Is-Ought Controversy,"

John Searle has written a reply to R. M. Hare's "The Promising Game," which is itself a critique of Searle's "How to Derive 'Ought' from 'Is'." For our section "Rules, Principles, and Utilitarianism," B. J. Diggs has written a reply to Richard Brandt's "A Defense of One Form of Rule Utilitarianism," and Brandt's paper contains several critical remarks pertaining to Diggs's "Rules and Utilitarianism." In both cases the replies add greatly to the dialogue of the section, and we are indeed grateful to Professors Searle and Diggs.

We wish to thank: Knox College and Southern Methodist University for providing secretarial services, Knox College for a grant which has covered much of the expense of preparing the manuscript, our reviewers for many valuable suggestions, and our typists Ginger Lyne and Martha Denault.

K. P.

M. S.

Contents

READINGS IN CONTEMPORARY ETHICAL THEORY

Section One
Moral Reasoning and the Is-Ought Controversy

What sorts of relations are there between evaluative and factual statements? Can evaluative statements be logically derived from factual statements alone? What are the purposes for which we use value words and how is *reasoning* involved in accomplishing these purposes? Does this reasoning differ in important respects from that employed in the sciences? The general issue which is raised in one way or another by each of these questions is the possible objectivity of our moral or ethical judgments. After a brief sketch of the predominant metaethical views in the first half of the twentieth century, we shall focus on some of the features of each of the essays in this section which are pertinent to the analysis of moral reasoning and the "is-ought" controversy.

Perhaps the most instructive division of the earlier metaethical views is into cognitivism and noncognitivism: that is, into theories which uphold the claim that there is some basis for objective moral knowledge or "true" ethical judgments, and those theories which deny that there is an objective basis for moral knowledge and believe it to be either mistaken of misleading to assert that ethical judgments are "true" or "false." On the cognitivist side we find Ethical Naturalism and Intuitionism, and on the noncognitivist side we find Emotivism.[1] These labels must be used with caution, for there are many different theses proffered within each of the types of view, and occasionally, there are overlapping theses among the types.

COGNITIVE THEORIES

One basic aim of Ethical Naturalists has been to establish a type of empirical or "scientific" reasoning by means of which moral or practical questions may be answered.

---

1 In his *Ethics* (Prentice-Hall, Inc., Foundations of Philosophy Series, 1963), William K. Frankena notes that "many existentialists likewise regard basic ethical and value judgments, particular or general, as arbitrary commitments or decisions for which no justification can be given." P. 88.

1

To accomplish this aim the Ethical Naturalist has tried to do one or both of the following: (1) He may define moral words in terms of nonmoral or strictly "descriptive" words, which then function as the criteria of application of the moral word. For instance, R. B. Perry defines "good" in terms of "object of interest" and "right" in terms of being conducive to "harmonious happiness." (2) He may construct an argument for the reasonableness or even necessity of adopting certain ultimate principles of conduct based entirely upon factual and theoretical considerations about human nature and society. In practice, the two projects just mentioned are interrelated, for the ultimate principles of conduct mentioned in (2) will typically be the definitions of value words mentioned in (1). Given a naturalistic definition of "right," one may decide a moral question in the same manner as one decides some factual questions, by observation, e.g., Is doing X conducive to harmonious happiness? It would be a mistake to charge that the Naturalist has failed to derive a value judgment from descriptive premises alone because his definition functions as a principle of conduct, since he need not claim to derive an evaluative conclusion from descriptive premises at this level. When we turn to the justification of the definition-principle, however, the Ethical Naturalist has more often than not baffled the critics by his logic.

Not the least of the problems involved in understanding and assessing this logic has been that of clarifying the nature of the Naturalist's definitions. Should they be thought of as reportive of ordinary usage, or merely stipulative, or in some way reformative of ordinary usage? It is suggested that regardless of how closely a particular Naturalist believes his definition coincides with some context of ordinary usage, he will rest the case for his definition-principle primarily upon considerations which are extralinguistic, for instance, on psychological theories claiming a universal desire for happiness, or on general explanations of the ultimate sources of value.[2]

---

2 See the discussion of Jeremy Bentham in W. T. Blackstone's "Are Metaethical Theories Normatively Neutral?" reprinted in Section Five. Blackstone maintains that Bentham's normative commitment to the principle of utility led to the metaethical claim about the meanings of moral words, not vice versa. Hence, the grounds for the combined definition-principle would have to be extralinguistic.

What is the nature of the inference that the Ethical Naturalist makes from his facts and psychological theories to his definition-principle? Is it deductive, inductive, or is it, as some have suspected, seductive? Ethical Naturalists have not been clear about this logic, although some, like John Stuart Mill, have explicitly disclaimed that the inference could be deductive. Mill speaks of a broader sense of "proof" in which considerations of various kinds may be presented in order to gain the assent of the intellect. Thus the Naturalist is probably most convincing when he constructs an argument (in Mill's broader sense) in which his definition-principle is shown to be not only compatible, but, in some sense, required by the facts of human nature and society.

G. E. Moore, in the pages reprinted here from his *Principia Ethica,* charges that all of these definitions commit the "Naturalistic Fallacy." However, the account that Moore gives of this fallacy, although it has been extremely influential, is subject to various interpretations. William K. Frankena explores a number of these in "The Naturalistic Fallacy," and finds neither a logical fallacy nor a logical confusion in Moore's so-called fallacy. For the present, we shall concentrate on aspects of the Naturalistic Fallacy which are not discussed in Prof. Frankena's paper.

Moore believed that if the naturalistic definition identified "good," for example, with "being desired," all that we need to do in order to refute it is to point out that we can still ask significantly whether being desired is good. We have not simply asked the empty question whether good is good, or being desired is being desired. Regardless of how the definition is revised, it appears that we can go on indefinitely asking the same meaningful question (but note P. H. Nowell-Smith's excellent comment in his paper on "Good"). This interpretation of the Naturalistic Fallacy is commonly referred to as the "open question" argument. Insofar as the argument hangs merely on the intelligibility of asking the question "Is having X good?" it is a fruitless attack against the Naturalist whose definition is reformative, or taken to be applicable in only one of many possible practical contexts.

To some, notably philosophers of ordinary language, the most illuminating interpretation of the Naturalistic Fallacy is that it is the typical empiricist error of confusing the meaning of a word with the grounds one has for using it. If we suppose that the meaning of a value word is exhausted in the specification of its "descriptive" criteria of application (assuming that these *could* be specified), then we have dispensed with the unique nondescriptive function of the value word when it is used to advise, prescribe, commend, or appraise, etc. Although it may be fair to charge the Naturalist with neglecting to take account of the "normative" or "prescriptive" use of a value word in his definition, it is important to note that even a linguistically enlightened Naturalist would not exchange his definition for one in which the *definiens* was a synonymous expression precisely capturing the "prescriptive force" of the word (e.g., defining "desirable" in terms of "worthy of being desired"). No definition or analysis such as this could yield the "descriptive" criteria upon which the Ethical Naturalist's conception of moral reasoning depends. Thus there is a fundamental difference between an Ethical Naturalist and a "definist," i.e., one who would apparently be content with any type of definition of a moral term.[3] Furthermore, insofar as the Naturalist *uses* his definition as a normative principle, it may be argued that he has not dispensed with the nondescriptive functions of the value word. Ethical Naturalists have had a bad press for many years now, and to some extent this has been due to misconstruing their intentions, with the result that they have been practically defined out of contention.

The other cognitivist view mentioned was Intuitionism. Moral reasoning, for the Intuitionist, finally rests upon a direct awareness of intrinsic value, which gives the word "good" its meaning for us, or of duty and obligation which give the word "right" its meaning for us. G. E. Moore insisted only on the basic intuition of goodness, as a unique, nonnatural, and indefinable property, and argued that "right" means "productive of the greatest possible good." Other Intuitionists, e.g., Ross and Prichard reprinted in this volume, have vigorously rejected all attempts at giving such teleological (goal oriented) accounts of duty and obligation. For them, "right" is as basic and irreducible as is "good," so we must rely on the immediate awareness of our obligations in particular situations, or our "prima facie" duty, i.e., our actual duty unless another duty takes precedence.

The principal weakness of Intuitionism lies in the dubi-

---

[3] Cf. Prof. Frankena's account in the "Naturalistic Fallacy" in Section One.

ous conviction that objectivity in morals may be achieved via a private experience ("intuition") which by definition excludes public confirmation. Beyond reviewing the facts and relations of a given situation, one merely "sees" the rightness or fittingness of a certain action. Since we could not suppose that there would be universal agreement even when the facts and relations were known, it was feared that the Intuitionist's only recourse would be to charge his adversary with moral blindness or perversity. Instead of a special infallible sixth sense for perceiving moral properties, some critics prefer to account for the "intuitions" in terms of a highly developed sensitivity to the promptings of an acquired, fallible, and culturally dependent moral conscience. Nevertheless, the epistemological weaknesses in the views of the Intuitionists are independent of many of their other principal theses. We may, for instance, reject Intuitionism as a theory of justification and yet find considerable merit in the deontological (nonpurposive or rule oriented) emphasis of Ross or Prichard.

NONCOGNITIVE THEORIES

Opposing the cognitive theories of the Ethical Naturalists and the Intuitionists are a number of noncognitive theories which normally go by the label "Emotivism." The early Emotivists sounded much like Hume when he argued for the ultimate dependence of moral judgments upon our feelings of approval or disapproval (but without his thesis regarding a universal sentiment of "humanity"). They bolstered this argument with theses about the meaning and functions of moral discourse. Whereas the Cognitivists tended to emphasize the similarities between descriptive-factual sentences and practical-moral sentences, the Emotivists emphasized their differences. That there were overstatements on both sides is part of the story of this anthology.

The earliest forms of Emotivism completely rejected the possibility of rational justification of uniquely ethical judgments. The indicative form of many moral judgments was believed to be misleading, for they are not empirically verifiable statements. Rather, they are more like ejaculations, e.g., "Hurrah for honesty" or "Boo, lying." At times, they were construed on the model of imperatives, e.g., "Stealing is wrong" would become "Do not steal." In any case, moral judgments were simply references to or expressions of the feelings and attitudes of the speaker. Moreover, as is illustrated in the Stevenson paper "The Emotive Meaning of Ethical Terms," they were usually aimed at evoking a similar response in the person addressed. Disagreements in *belief* may be settled in a straightforward empirical manner ("Did he stab her or did she fall on the knife?"), but disagreements in attitude may require more persuasive measures for their settlement ("I agree that Negroes are not inherently inferior to whites, nevertheless I find them repulsive.") It is the use of these more persuasive measures that uniquely characterizes moral reasoning for Emotivists like Ayer and Stevenson. For them, reasons are good ones insofar as they are effective instruments for altering attitudes, in short, for achieving agreement in attitude.

By giving an exclusively "causal" analysis of good reasons, the early Emotivists thereby placed moral reasoning outside the sphere of rational justification or conventions of correctness and incorrectness. However, from around midcentury on and from a variety of sources, there have been renewed efforts to find logically more significant roles for reason in ethics. These efforts are represented in all sections of this book, while the present section stresses problems of a more general nature. There are inevitable difficulties in classifying the recent views on moral reasoning by philosophers in the analytic tradition. On the one hand, they could be called Contemporary Noncognitivists, in that most of them are critical of both Naturalism and Intuitionism, and further stress the multiple nondescriptive functions of ethical discourse, e.g., that it is used to express approval, give advice, appraise, or evaluate, etc. On the other hand, they could be called Neo-Cognitivists because they strive to make moral reasoning as fully rational as possible, while avoiding the pitfalls of Naturalism, Intuitionism, and early Emotivism. In order to determine which of these labels is more appropriate for a given author, we could apply what may be a sufficient condition for being an Emotivist: If in the last analysis moral reasoning is shown to depend upon a decision for which no justification can be given beyond a personal "I just do" statement (e.g., I just do prefer this way of life to any other), then that author is an Emotivist and so primarily a Noncognitivist. However, since the efforts of Cognitivists and

Noncognitivists alike are aimed at exploring the limits of reason in ethics, the more philosophically illuminating question to ask about each author is: To what extent has he been successful in eliminating or minimizing nonrational elements in his characterization of moral reasoning?

W. D. Falk is concerned with, in the words of the late Prof. Everett Hall, "going beyond the view that moralistic persuasion is confined to crude, direct goading to seeing that one can guide, can teach appreciation, can be eminently reasonable in one's methods of influencing others."[4] His aim is to locate more reliably the place of moral speech on the logical map by exploring the differences between rational vs. nonrational methods of persuasion. His analysis of the differences between "goading" and "guiding" serves to illustrate that moral language is neither always nor typically used to reach "agreement in attitude." Moreover, Falk contends, to say "you ought to" is to make an objective claim, i.e., one which may be confirmed or falsified.

In his chapter entitled "Good," P. H. Nowell-Smith describes the many functions of a value word such as "good." Of particular significance to the subject of moral reasoning is his attempt to list the uses of "good" in a progression from the fundamental use of expressing or explaining a preference to uses in which the contextual background of impersonal facts, criteria, or standards looms larger and larger. It is surely the case that some of the debate between subjectivists and objectivists, or noncognitivists and cognitivists, results from taking as a model uses which are located at opposite ends of Nowell-Smith's list. Also, in his discussion of natural and conventional aspects of "criteria" for appraising or grading, Nowell-Smith appears to leave the door ajar for further naturalistic explanations (justifications?) of the criteria that we normally employ in moral judgments.

Kurt Baier, in "Good Reasons," attempts to show that certain facts are reasons for and certain others reasons against doing certain things, quite irrespective of the purposes, wishes, plans, desires, and passions of the person concerned. He explores the problem of the conventionality of reason giving, and attempts to answer the skeptic who wants

---

4 "Practical Reasons and the Deadlock in Ethics," *Mind*, LXIV (1955), 319–32.

(and doesn't expect to get) a proof that the reasons which are recognized to be good reasons or the best reasons really are so.

Marcus Singer examines a version of the familiar generalization argument—What would happen if everyone did that?—and tries to determine the conditions under which it is valid. The paper illustrates well some of the perplexing obstacles to eliminating the irrational residue in moral reasoning. In addition to restricting the argument in light of various counter-examples, Singer deals with such problems as "How does one decide that one has a reasonable ground for difference of treatment?" and "What does it mean to say 'similar persons in similar circumstances'?"

R. M. Hare, who has been a persistent critic of naturalistic deductions of moral conclusions from nonmoral premises, also finds objectionable the suggestion that the transition to moral conclusions is made by means of some other type of nondeductive inference peculiar to morals. By drawing upon a parallel of falsifiability in the philosophy of science and two features of moral judgments called prescriptivity and universalizability, Hare develops, in "A Moral Argument," a theory of moral reasoning. It is particularly interesting to ask about this theory: How is it possible to develop a theory which is at once morally neutral, which Hare claims his theory to be, and morally relevant, i.e., helpful to persons faced with difficult moral problems, which Hare also claims his theory to be? Further, just how wide is the escape route provided by the "freedom" of possibly wanting *anything,* which curiously exempts the fanatic from moral argumentation?

Phillipa Foot opposes the view that moral arguments must always break down, at least for the reasons usually cited by Noncognitivists such as Ayer, Stevenson, and Hare. If there are objective relations between facts and values, and she believes that there are, they could be of two kinds: descriptive or factual premises might *entail* evaluative conclusions, or they might count as *evidence* for them. Although she would be satisfied with the latter sort of relation, she argues that the noncognitivists have not even shown that the stronger relationship cannot exist. She concludes that moral terms do lose their meaning (or an essential part of it) when they are divorced from their criteria of application, just as the word "rude" loses its meaning when the criterion of offensiveness is dropped. If this is true, then at least some inferences from descriptive to evaluative conclusions are entailments warranted by relations of meaning. For many philosophers this is an objectionable employment of "meaning." Nevertheless, it is clear that Mrs. Foot is talking about some sort of discoverable conventions connecting facts and values (perhaps of the same sort that account for "good reasons"), and the ordinary meanings of "meaning" are sufficiently inclusive to lend some credence to calling them linguistic conventions.

The lively exchange between John Searle and R. M. Hare is also concerned with the possibility of logically deriving an evaluative statement from a set of descriptive statements. The dispute hinges on whether or not engaging in the practices of an institution, like making promises, involves commitment to or approval of a synthetic moral principle. If it does, then Hare may be right in contending that Searle's derivation of an "ought" from an "is" fails, for the descriptive premises will contain a disguised or implicit prescription. If, on the other hand, Searle is correct in his claim that the way of subscribing to rules which is involved in uttering "I hereby promise" is no more evaluative or prescriptive than any undertaking to use words literally, then he may have successfully derived an "ought" from an "is."

Actually, the stakes in this promising game are considerably higher than the success of a single counter-example to the supposed logical gulf between "is" and "ought." At issue is what Searle describes as the traditional empiricist picture of the way words relate to the world. In his opinion, it is a picture that fails to distinguish between brute facts and institutional facts that are understood in terms of systems of constitutive rules. At the very least, Searle is right in calling for a reexamination of the distinction between descriptive and evaluative words.

The Subject Matter of Ethics

G. E. MOORE

PREFACE TO *Principia Ethica*

It appears to me that in Ethics, as in all other philosophical studies, the difficulties and disagreements, of which its history is full, are mainly due to a very simple cause: namely to the attempt to answer questions, without first discovering precisely *what* question it is which you desire to answer. I do not know how far this source of error would be done away, if philosophers would *try* to discover what question they were asking, before they set about to answer it; for the work of analysis and distinction is often very difficult: we may often fail to make the necessary discovery, even though we make a definite attempt to do so. But I am inclined to think that in many cases a resolute attempt would be sufficient to ensure success; so that, if only this attempt were made, many of the most glaring difficulties and disagreements in philosophy would disappear. At all events, philosophers seem, in general, not to make the attempt; and, whether in consequence of this omission or not, they are constantly endeavoring to prove that 'Yes' or 'No' will answer questions, to which *neither* answer is correct,, owing to the fact that what they have before their minds is not one question, but several, to some of which the true answer is 'No,' to others 'Yes.'

I have tried to distinguish clearly two kinds of question, which moral philosophers have always professed to answer, but which, as I have tried to show, they have almost always confused both with one another and with other questions. These two questions may be expressed, the first in the form: What kind of things ought to exist for their own sakes? the second in the form: What kind of actions ought we to perform? I have tried to show exactly what it is that we ask about a thing, when we ask whether it ought to exist for its own sake, is good in itself or has intrinsic value; and exactly what it is that we ask about an action, when we ask whether we ought to do it, whether it is a right action or a duty.

But from a clear insight into the nature of these two questions, there appears to me to follow a second most important result: namely, what is the nature of the evidence, by which alone any ethical proposition can be proved or disproved, confirmed or rendered doubtful. Once we recognize

From G. E. Moore, *Preface and Chapter 1, Sections 1–17,* Principia Ethica *(Cambridge: Cambridge University Press, 1903), pp. vii–x, 1–37. Reprinted by permission of the publisher.*

the exact meaning of the two questions, I think it also becomes plain exactly what kind of reasons are relevant as arguments for or against any particular answer to them. It becomes plain that, for answers to the *first* question, no relevant evidence whatever can be adduced: from no other truth, except themselves alone, can it be inferred that they are either true or false. We can guard against error only by taking care that, when we try to answer a question of this kind, we have before our minds that question only, and not some other or others; but that there is great danger of such errors of confusion I have tried to show, and also what are the chief precautions by the use of which we may guard against them. As for the *second* question, it becomes equally plain, that any answer to it *is* capable of proof or disproof—that, indeed, so many different considerations are relevant to its truth or falsehood, as to make the attainment of probability very difficult, and the attainment of certainty impossible. Nevertheless the *kind* of evidence, which is both necessary and alone relevant to such proof and disproof, is capable of exact definition. Such evidence must contain propositions of two kinds and of two kinds only: it must consist, in the first place, of truths with regard to the results of the action in question—of *causal* truths—but it must *also* contain ethical truths of our first or self-evident class. Many truths of both kinds are necessary to the proof that any action ought to be done; and any other kind of evidence is wholly irrelevant. It follows that, if any ethical philosopher offers for propositions of the first kind any evidence whatever, or if, for propositions of the second kind, he either fails to adduce both causal and ethical truths, or adduces truths that are neither, his reasoning has not the least tendency to establish his conclusions. But not only are his conclusions totally devoid of weight: we have, moreover, reason to suspect him of the error of confusion; since the offering of irrelevant evidence generally indicates that the philosopher who offers it has had before his mind, not the question which he professes to answer, but some other entirely different one. Ethical discussion, hitherto, has perhaps consisted chiefly in reasoning of this totally irrelevant kind.

One main object of this book may, then, be expressed by slightly changing one of Kant's famous titles. I have endeavored to write 'Prolegomena to any future Ethics that can possibly pretend to be scientific.' In other words, I have endeavored to discover what are the fundamental principles of ethical reasoning; and the establishment of these principles, rather than of any conclusions which may be attained by their use, may be regarded as my main object. I have, however, also attempted to present some conclusions, with regard to the proper answer of the question 'What is good in itself?' which are very different from any which have commonly been advocated by philosophers. I have tried to define the classes within which all great goods and evils fall; and I have maintained that very many different things are good and evil in themselves, and that neither class of things possesses any other property which is both common to all its members and peculiar to them.

In order to express the fact that ethical propositions of my *first* class are incapable of proof or disproof, I have sometimes followed Sidgwick's usage in calling them 'Intuitions.' But I beg it may be noticed that I am not an 'Intuitionist,' in the ordinary sense of the term. Sidgwick himself seems never to have been clearly aware of the immense importance of the difference which distinguishes his Intuitionism from the common doctrine, which has generally been called by that name. The Intuitionist proper is distinguished by maintaining that propositions of my *second* class—propositions which assert that a certain action is *right* or a *duty*—are incapable of proof or disproof by any enquiry into the results of such actions. I, on the contrary, am no less anxious to maintain that propositions of *this* kind are not 'Intuitions,' than to maintain that propositions of my *first* class *are* Intuitions.

Again, I would wish it observed that, when I call such propositions 'Intuitions,' I mean *merely* to assert that they are incapable of proof; I imply nothing whatever as to the manner or origin of our cognition of them. Still less do I imply (as most Intuitionists have done) that any proposition whatever is true, *because* we cognize it in a particular way or by the exercise of any particular faculty: I hold, on the contrary, that in every way in which it is possible to cognize a true proposition, it is also possible to cognize a false one.

THE SUBJECT MATTER OF ETHICS

1. It is very easy to point out some among our everyday judgments, with the truth of which Ethics is undoubtedly concerned. Whenever we say, 'So and so is a good man,' or 'That fellow is a villain'; whenever we ask, 'What ought I to do?' or 'Is it wrong for me to do like this?'; whenever we hazard such remarks as 'Temperance is a virtue and drunkenness a vice'—it is undoubtedly the business of Ethics to discuss such questions and such statements; to argue what is the true answer when we ask what it is right to do, and to give reasons for thinking that our statements about the character of persons or the morality of actions are true or false. In the vast majority of cases, where we make statements involving any of the terms 'virtue,' 'vice,' 'duty,' 'right,' 'ought,' 'good,' 'bad,' we are making ethical judgments; and if we wish to discuss their truth, we shall be discussing a point of Ethics.

So much as this is not disputed; but it falls very far short of defining the province of Ethics. That province may indeed be defined as the whole truth about that which is at the same time common to all such judgments and peculiar to them. But we have still to ask the question: What is it that is thus common and peculiar? And this is a question to which very different answers have been given by ethical philosophers of acknowledged reputation, and none of them, perhaps, completely satisfactory.

2. If we take such examples as those given above, we shall not be far wrong in saying that they are all of them concerned with the question of 'conduct'—with the question, what, in the conduct of us, human beings, is good, and what is bad, what is right, and what is wrong. For when we say that a man is good, we commonly mean that he acts rightly; when we say that drunkenness is a vice, we commonly mean that to get drunk is a wrong or wicked action. And this discussion of human conduct is, in fact, that with which the name 'Ethics' is most intimately associated. It is so associated by derivation; and conduct is undoubtedly by far the commonest and most generally interesting object of ethical judgments.

Accordingly, we find that many ethical philosophers are disposed to accept as an adequate definition of 'Ethics' the statement that it deals with the question what is good or bad in human conduct. They hold that its enquiries are properly confined to 'conduct' or to 'practice'; they hold that the name 'practical philosophy' covers all the matter with which it has to do. Now, without discussing the proper meaning of the word (for verbal questions are properly left to the writers of dictionaries and other persons interested in literature; philosophy, as we shall see, has no concern with them), I may say that I intend to use 'Ethics' to cover more than this—a usage, for which there is, I think, quite sufficient authority. I am using it to cover an enquiry for which, at all events, there is no other word: the general enquiry into what is good.

Ethics is undoubtedly concerned with the question what good conduct is; but, being concerned with this, it obviously does not start at the beginning, unless it is prepared to tell us what is good as well as what is conduct. For 'good conduct' is a complex notion: all conduct is not good; for some is certainly bad and some may be indifferent. And on the other hand, other things, beside conduct, may be good; and if they are so, then, 'good' denotes some property, that is common to them and conduct; and if we examine good conduct alone of all good things, then we shall be in danger of mistaking for this property, some property which is not shared by those other things: and thus we shall have made a mistake about Ethics even in this limited sense; for we shall not know what good conduct really is. This is a mistake which many writers have actually made, from limiting their enquiry to conduct. And hence I shall try to avoid it by considering first what is good in general; hoping, that if we can arrive at any certainty about this, it will be much easier to settle the question of good conduct: for we all know pretty well what 'conduct' is. This, then, is our first question: What is good? and What is bad? and to the discussion of this question (or these questions) I give the name of Ethics, since that science must, at all events, include it.

3. But this a question which may have many meanings. If, for example, each of us were to say 'I am doing good now' or 'I had a good dinner yesterday,' these statements would each of them be some sort of answer to our question, although perhaps a false one. So, too, when A asks B what school he ought to send his son to, B's answer will certainly be an ethical judgment. And similarly all distribution of praise or blame to any personage or thing that has existed, now exists, or will exist, does give some answer to the question 'What is good?' In all such cases some particular thing is judged to be good or bad: the question 'What?' is answered by 'This.' But this is not the sense in which a scientific Ethics asks the question. Not one, of all the many million answers of this kind, which must be true, can form a part of an ethical system; although that science must contain reasons and principles sufficient for deciding on the truth of all of them. There are far too many persons, things, and events in the world, past, present, or to come, for a discussion of their individual merits to be embraced in any science. Ethics, therefore, does not deal at all with facts of this nature, facts that are unique, individual, absolutely particular; facts with which such studies as history, geography, astronomy, are compelled, in part at least, to deal. And, for this reason, it is not the business of the ethical philosopher to give personal advice or exhortation.

4. But there is another meaning which may be given to the question 'What is good?' 'Books are good' would be an answer to it, though an answer obviously false; for some books are very bad indeed. And ethical judgments of this kind do indeed belong to Ethics; though I shall not deal with many of them. Such is the judgment 'Pleasure is good'—a judgment, of which Ethics should discuss the truth, although it is not nearly as important as that other judgment, with which we shall be much occupied presently—'Pleasure *alone* is good.' It is judgments of this sort, which are made in such books on Ethics as contain a list of 'virtues'—in Aristotle's 'Ethics' for example. But it is judgments of precisely the same kind, which form the substance of what is commonly supposed to be a study different from Ethics, and one much less respectable—the study of Casuistry. We may be told that Casuistry differs from Ethics, in that it is much more detailed and particular, Ethics much more general. But it is most important to notice that Casuistry does not deal with anything that is absolutely particular—particular in the only sense in which a perfectly precise line can be drawn between it and what is general. It is not particular in the sense just noticed, the sense in which this book is a particular book, and A's friend's advice particular advice. Casuistry may indeed be *more* particular and Ethics *more* general; but that means that they differ only in

degree and not in kind. And this is universally true of 'particular' and 'general,' when used in this common, but inaccurate, sense. So far as Ethics allows itself to give lists of virtues or even to name constituents of the Ideal, it is indistinguishable from Casuistry. Both alike deal with what is general, in the sense in which physics and chemistry deal with what is general. Just as chemistry aims at discovering what are the properties of oxygen, *wherever it occurs*, and not only of this or that particular specimen of oxygen; so Casuistry aims at discovering what actions are good, *whenever they occur*. In this respect Ethics and Casuistry alike are to be classed with such sciences as physics, chemistry, and physiology, in their absolute distinction from those of which history and geography are instances. And it is to be noted that, owing to their detailed nature, casuistical investigations are actually nearer to physics and to chemistry than are the investigations usually assigned to Ethics. For just as physics cannot rest content with the discovery that light is propagated by waves of ether, but must go on to discover the particular nature of the ether waves corresponding to each several color; so Casuistry, not content with the general law that charity is a virtue must attempt to discover the relative merits of every different form of charity. Casuistry forms, therefore, part of the ideal of ethical science: Ethics cannot be complete without it. The defects of Casuistry are not defects of principle; no objection can be taken to its aim and object. It has failed only because it is far too difficult a subject to be treated adequately in our present state of knowledge. The casuist has been unable to distinguish, in the cases which he treats, those elements upon which their value depends. Hence he often thinks two cases to be alike in respect of value, when in reality they are alike only in some other respect. It is to mistakes of this kind that the pernicious influence of such investigations has been due. For Casuistry is the goal of ethical investigation. It cannot be safely attempted at the beginning of our studies, but only at the end.

5. But our question 'What is good?' may have still another meaning. We may, in the third place, mean to ask, not what thing or things are good, but how 'good' is to be defined. This is an enquiry which belongs only to Ethics, not to Casuistry; and this is the enquiry which will occupy us first.

It is an enquiry to which most special attention should be directed; since this question, how 'good' is to be defined, is the most fundamental question in all Ethics. That which is meant by 'good' is, in fact, except its converse 'bad,' the *only* simple object of thought which is peculiar to Ethics. Its definition is, therefore, the most essential point in the definition of Ethics; and moreover a mistake with regard to it entails a far larger number of erroneous ethical judgments than any other. Unless this first question be fully understood, and its true answer clearly recognized, the rest of Ethics is as good as useless from the point of view of systematic knowledge.

True ethical judgments, of the two kinds last dealt with, may indeed be made by those who do not know the answer to this question as well as by those who do; and it goes without saying that the two classes of people may lead equally good lives. But it is extremely unlikely that the *most general* ethical judgments will be equally valid, in the absence of a true answer to this question: I shall presently try to show that the gravest errors have been largely due to beliefs in a false answer. And, in any case, it is impossible that, till the answer to this question be known, any one should know *what is the evidence* for any ethical judgment whatsoever. But the main object of Ethics, as a systematic science, is to give correct *reasons* for thinking that this or that is good; and, unless this question be answered, such reasons cannot be given. Even, therefore, apart from the fact that a false answer leads to false conclusions, the present enquiry is a most necessary and important part of the science of Ethics.

6. What, then, is good? How is good to be defined? Now, it may be thought that this is a verbal question. A definition does indeed often mean the expressing of one word's meaning in other words. But this is not the sort of definition I am asking for. Such a definition can never be of ultimate importance in any study except lexicography. If I wanted that kind of definition I should have to consider in the first place how people generally used the word 'good'; but my business is not with its proper usage, as established by custom. I should, indeed, be foolish, if I tried to use it for something which it did not usually denote: if, for instance, I were to announce that, whenever I used the word 'good,' I must be understood to be thinking of that object which is usually denoted by the word 'table.' I shall, therefore, use the word in the sense in which I think it is ordinarily used; but at the same time I am not anxious to discuss whether I am right in thinking that it is so used. My business is solely with that object or idea, which I hold, rightly or wrongly, that the word is generally used to stand for. What I want to discover is the nature of that object or idea, and about this I am extremely anxious to arrive at an agreement.

But, if we understand the question in this sense, my answer to it may seem a very disappointing one. If I am asked 'What is good'? my answer is that good is good, and that is the end of the matter. Or if I am asked 'How is good to be defined?' my answer is that it cannot be defined, and that is all I have to say about it. But disappointing as these answers may appear, they are of the very last importance. To readers who are familiar with philosophic terminology, I can express their importance by saying that they amount to this: That propositions about the good are all of them synthetic and never analytic; and that is plainly no trivial matter. And the same thing may be expressed more popularly, by saying that, if I am right, then nobody can foist upon us such an axiom as that 'Pleasure is the only good' or that 'The good is the desired' on the pretence that this is 'the very meaning of the word.'

7. Let us, then, consider this position. My point is that 'good' is a simple notion, just as 'yellow' is a simple notion; that, just as you cannot, by any manner or means, explain to any one who does not already know it, what yellow is, so you cannot explain what good is. Definitions of the kind that I was asking for, definitions which describe the real nature of the object or notion denoted by a word, and which do not merely tell us what the word is used to mean, are only possible when the object or notion in question is something complex. You can give a definition of a horse, because a horse has many different properties and qualities, all of which you can enumerate. But when you have enumerated them all, when you have reduced a horse to his simplest terms, then you can no longer define those terms. They are simply something which you think of or perceive, and to any one who cannot think of or perceive them, you can never, by any definition, make their nature known. It may perhaps be objected to this that we are able to describe to others, objects which they have never seen or thought of. We can, for instance, make a man understand what a chimera is, although he has never heard of one or seen one. You can tell him that it is an animal with a lioness's head and body, with a goat's head growing from the middle of its back, and with a snake in place of a tail. But here the object which you are describing is a complex object; it is entirely composed of parts, with which we are all perfectly familiar—a snake, a goat, a lioness; and we know, too, the manner in which those parts are to be put together, because we know what is meant by the middle of a lioness's back, and where her tail is wont to grow. And so it is with all objects, not previously known, which we are able to define: they are all complex; all composed of parts, which may themselves, in the first instance, be capable of similar definition, but which must in the end be reducible to simplest parts, which can no longer be defined. But yellow and good, we say, are not complex: they are notions of that simple kind, out of which definitions are composed and with which the power of further defining ceases.

8. When we say, as Webster says, 'The definition of horse is "A hoofed quadruped of the genus Equus,"' we may, in fact, mean three different things. (1) We may mean merely: 'When I say "horse," you are to understand that I am talking about a hoofed quadruped of the genus Equus.' This might be called the arbitrary verbal definition: and I do not mean that good is indefinable in that sense. (2) We may mean, as Webster ought to mean: 'When most English people say "horse," they mean a hoofed quadruped of the genus Equus.' This may be called the verbal definition proper, and I do not say that good is indefinable in this sense either; for it is certainly possible to discover how people use a word: otherwise, we could

never have known that 'good' may be translated by 'gut' in German and by 'bon' in French. But (3) we may, when we define horse, mean something much more important. We may mean that a certain object, which we all of us know, is composed in a certain manner: that it has four legs, a head, a heart, a liver, etc., etc., all of them arranged in definite relations to one another. It is in this sense that I deny good to be definable. I say that it is not composed of any parts, which we can substitute for it in our minds when we are thinking of it. We might think just as clearly and correctly about a horse, if we thought of all its parts and their arrangement instead of thinking of the whole: we could, I say, think how a horse differed from a donkey just as well, just as truly, in this way, as now we do, only not so easily; but there is nothing whatsoever which we could so substitute for good; and that is what I mean, when I say that good is indefinable.

9. But I am afraid I have still not removed the chief difficulty which may prevent acceptance of the proposition that good is indefinable. I do not mean to say that *the* good, that which is good, is thus indefinable; if I did think so, I should not be writing on Ethics, for my main object is to help towards discovering that definition. It is just because I think there will be less risk of error in our search for a definition of 'the good,' that I am now insisting that *good* is indefinable. I must try to explain the difference between these two. I suppose it may be granted that 'good' is an adjective. Well 'the good,' 'that which is good,' must therefore be the substantive to which the adjective 'good' will apply: it must be the whole of that to which the adjective will apply, and the adjective must *always* truly apply to it. But if it is that to which the adjective will apply, it must be something different from that adjective itself; and the whole of that something different, whatever it is, will be our definition of *the* good. Now it may be that this something will have other adjectives, beside 'good,' that will apply to it. It may be full of pleasure, for example; it may be intelligent: and if these two adjectives are really part of its definition, then it will certainly be true, that pleasure and intelligence are good. And many people appear to think that, if we say 'Pleasure and intelligence are good,' or if we say 'Only pleasure and intelligence are good,' we are defining 'good.' Well, I cannot deny that propositions of this nature may sometimes be called definitions; I do not know well enough how the word is generally used to decide upon this point. I only wish it to be understood that that is not what I mean when I say there is no possible definition of good, and that I shall not mean this if I use the word again. I do most fully believe that some true proposition of the form 'Intelligence is good and intelligence alone is good' can be found; if none could be found, our definition of *the* good would be impossible. As it is, I believe *the* good to be definable; and yet I still say that good itself is indefinable.

10. 'Good,' then, if we mean by it that quality which we assert to belong to a thing, when we say that the thing is good, is incapable of any definition, in the most important sense of that word. The most important sense of 'definition' is that in which a definition states what are the parts which invariably compose a certain whole; and in this sense 'good' has no definition because it is simple and has no parts. It is one of those innumerable objects of thought which are themselves incapable of definition, because they are the ultimate terms by reference to which whatever *is* capable of definition must be defined. That there must be an indefinite number of such terms is obvious, on reflection; since we cannot define anything except by an analysis, which, when carried as far as it will go, refers us to something, which is simply different from anything else, and which by that ultimate difference explains the peculiarity of the whole which we are defining: for every whole contains some parts which are common to other wholes also. There is, therefore, no intrinsic difficulty in the contention that 'good' denotes a simple and indefinable quality. There are many other instances of such qualities.

Consider yellow, for example. We may try to define it, by describing its physical equivalent; we may state what kind of light vibrations must stimulate the normal eye, in order that we may perceive it. But a moment's reflection is sufficient to show that those light vibrations are not themselves what we mean by yellow. *They* are not what we perceive. Indeed we should never have been able to discover their existence, unless we had first been struck by the patent difference of quality between the different colors. The most we can be entitled to say of those vibrations is that they are what corresponds in space to the yellow which we actually perceive.

Yet a mistake of this simple kind has commonly been made about 'good.' It may be true that all things which are good are *also* something else, just as it is true that all things which are yellow produce a certain kind of vibration in the light. And it is a fact, that Ethics aims at discovering what are those other properties belonging to all things which are good. But far too many philosophers have thought that when they named those other properties they were actually defining good; that these properties, in fact, were simply not 'other,' but absolutely and entirely the same with goodness. This view I propose to call the 'naturalistic fallacy' and of it I shall now endeavor to dispose.

11. Let us consider what it is such philosophers say. And first it is to be noticed that they do not agree among themselves. They not only say that they are right as to what good is, but they endeavor to prove that other people who say that it is something else, are wrong. One, for instance, will affirm that good is pleasure, another, perhaps, that good is that which is desired; and each of these will argue eagerly to prove that the other is wrong. But how is that possible? One of them says that good is nothing

but the object of desire, and at the same time tries to prove that it is not pleasure. But from his first assertion, that good just means the object of desire, one of two things must follow as regards his proof:

(1) He may be trying to prove that the object of desire is not pleasure. But, if this be all, where is his Ethics? The position he is maintaining is merely a psychological one. Desire is something which occurs in our minds, and pleasure is something else which so occurs; and our would-be ethical philosopher is merely holding that the latter is not the object of the former. But what has that to do with the question in dispute? His opponent held the ethical proposition that pleasure was the good, and although he should prove a million times over the psychological proposition that pleasure is not the object of desire, he is no nearer proving his opponent to be wrong. The position is like this. One man says a triangle is a circle: another replies 'A triangle is a straight line, and I will prove to you that I am right: *for*' (this is the only argument) 'a straight line is not a circle.' 'That is quite true,' the other may reply; 'but nevertheless a triangle is a circle, and you have said nothing whatever to prove the contrary. What is proved is that one of us is wrong, for we agree that a triangle cannot be both a straight line and a circle: but which is wrong, there can be no earthly means of proving, since you define triangle as straight line and I define it as circle.' —Well, that is one alternative which any naturalistic Ethics has to face; if good is *defined* as something else, it is then impossible either to prove that any other definition is wrong or even to deny such definition.

(2) The other alternative will scarcely be more welcome. It is that the discussion is after all a verbal one. When A says 'Good means pleasant' and B says 'Good means desired,' they may merely wish to assert that most people have used the word for what is pleasant and for what is desired respectively. And this is quite an interesting subject for discussion: only it is not a whit more an ethical discussion than the last was. Nor do I think that any exponent of naturalistic Ethics would be willing to allow that this was all he meant. They are all so anxious to persuade us that what they call the good is what we really ought to do. 'Do, pray, act so, because the word "good" is generally used to denote actions of this nature': such, on this view, would be the substance of their teaching. And in so far as they tell us how we ought to act, their teaching is truly ethical, as they mean it to be. But how perfectly absurd is the reason they would give for it! 'You are to do this, because most people use a certain word to denote conduct such as this.' 'You are to say the thing which is not, because most people call it lying.' That is an argument just as good!—My dear sirs, what we want to know from you as ethical teachers, is not how people use a word; it is not even, what kind of actions they approve, which the use of this word 'good' may certainly imply: what we want to know is simply what *is* good. We may indeed agree that what most people do think good, is actually so; we

shall at all events be glad to know their opinions: but when we say their opinions about what *is* good, we do mean what we say; we do not care whether they call that thing which they mean 'horse' or 'table' or 'chair,' 'gut' or 'bon' or '*αγαθος*'; we want to know what it is that they so call. When they say 'Pleasure is good,' we cannot believe that they merely mean 'Pleasure is pleasure' and nothing more than that.

12. Suppose a man says 'I am pleased'; and suppose that is not a lie or a mistake but the truth. Well, if it is true, what does that mean? It means that his mind, a certain definite mind, distinguished by certain definite marks from all others, has at this moment a certain definite feeling called pleasure. 'Pleased' *means* nothing but having pleasure, and though we may be more pleased or less pleased, and even, we may admit for the present, have one or another kind of pleasure; yet in so far as it is pleasure we have, whether there be more or less of it, and whether it be of one kind or another, what we have is one definite thing, absolutely indefinable, some one thing that is the same in all the various degrees and in all the various kinds of it that there may be. We may be able to say how it is related to other things: that, for example, it is in the mind, that it causes desire, that we are conscious of it, etc., etc. We can, I say, describe its relations to other things, but define it we can *not*. And if anybody tried to define pleasure for us as being any other natural object; if anybody were to say, for instance, that pleasure *means* the sensation of red, and were to proceed to deduce from that that pleasure is a color, we should be entitled to laugh at him and to distrust his future statements about pleasure. Well, that would be the same fallacy which I have called the naturalistic fallacy. That 'pleased' does not mean 'having the sensation of red,' or anything else whatever, does not prevent us from understanding what it does mean. It is enough for us to know that 'pleased' does mean 'having the sensation of pleasure,' and though pleasure is absolutely indefinable, though pleasure is pleasure and nothing else whatever, yet we feel no difficulty in saying that we are pleased. The reason is, of course, that when I say 'I am pleased,' I do *not* mean that 'I' am the same thing as 'having pleasure.' And similarly no difficulty need be found in my saying that "pleasure is good' and yet not meaning that 'pleasure' is the same thing as 'good,' that pleasure *means* good, and that good *means* pleasure. If I were to imagine that when I said 'I am pleased,' I meant that I was exactly the same thing as 'pleased,' I should not indeed call that a naturalistic fallacy, although it would be the same fallacy as I have called naturalistic with reference to Ethics. The reason of this is obvious enough. When a man confuses two natural objects with one another, defining the one by the other, if for instance, he confuses himself, who is one natural object, with 'pleased' or with 'pleasure' which are others, then there is no reason to call the fallacy naturalistic. But if he confuses 'good,' which is not in the same sense a

natural object, with any natural object whatever, then there is a reason
for calling that a naturalistic fallacy; its being made with regard to 'good'
marks it as something quite specific, and this specific mistake deserves a
name because it is so common. As for the reasons why good is not to be
considered a natural object, they may be reserved for discussion in another
place. But, for the present, it is sufficient to notice this: Even if it were a
natural object, that would not alter the nature of the fallacy nor diminish
its importance one whit. All that I have said about it would remain quite
equally true: only the name which I have called it would not be so
appropriate as I think it is. And I do not care about the name: what I
do care about is the fallacy. It does not matter what we call it, provided
we recognize it when we meet with it. It is to be met with in almost every
book on Ethics; and yet it is not recognized: and that is why it is necessary
to multiply illustrations of it, and convenient to give it a name. It is a
very simple fallacy indeed. When we say that an orange is yellow, we do
not think our statement binds us to hold that 'orange' means nothing else
than 'yellow,' or that nothing can be yellow but an orange. Supposing the
orange is also sweet! Does that bind us to say that 'sweet' is exactly the
same thing as 'yellow,' that 'sweet' must be defined as 'yellow'? And
supposing it be recognized that 'yellow' just means 'yellow' and nothing
else whatever, does that make it any more difficult to hold that oranges
are yellow? Most certainly it does not: on the contrary, it would be
absolutely meaningless to say that oranges were yellow, unless yellow did
in the end mean just 'yellow' and nothing else whatever—unless it was
absolutely indefinable. We should not get any very clear notion about
things, which are yellow—we should not get very far with our science, if
we were bound to hold that everything which was yellow, *meant* exactly
the same thing as yellow. We should find we had to hold that an orange
was exactly same thing as a stool, a piece of paper, a lemon, anything
you like. We could prove any number of absurdities; but should we be
the nearer to the truth? Why, then, should it be different with 'good'?
Why, if good is good and indefinable, should I be held to deny that
pleasure is good? Is there any difficulty in holding both to be true at
once? On the contrary, there is no meaning in saying that pleasure is
good, unless good is something different from pleasure. It is absolutely
useless, so far as Ethics is concerned, to prove, as Mr. Spencer tries to do,
that increase of pleasure coincides with increase of life, unless good *means*
something different from either life or pleasure. He might just as well try
to prove that an orange is yellow by showing that it always is wrapped up
in paper.

13. In fact, if it is not the case that 'good' denotes something simple
and indefinable, only two alternatives are possible: either it is a complex,
a given whole, about the correct analysis of which there may be disagree-

ment; or else it means nothing at all, and there is no such subject as Ethics. In general, however, ethical philosophers have attempted to define good, without recognizing what such an attempt must mean. They actually use arguments which involve one or both of the absurdities considered in §11. We are, therefore, justified in concluding that the attempt to define good is chiefly due to want of clearness as to the possible nature of definition. There are, in fact, only two serious alternatives to be considered, in order to establish the conclusion that 'good' does denote a simple and indefinable notion. It might possibly denote a complex, as 'horse' does; or it might have no meaning at all. Neither of these possibilities has, however, been clearly conceived and seriously maintained, as such, by those who presume to define good; and both may be dismissed by a simple appeal to facts.

(1) The hypothesis that disagreement about the meaning of good is disagreement with regard to the correct analysis of a given whole, may be most plainly seen to be incorrect by consideration of the fact that, whatever definition be offered, it may be always asked, with significance, of the complex so defined, whether it is itself good. To take, for instance, one of the more plausible, because one of the more complicated, of such proposed definitions, it may easily be thought, at first sight, that to be good may mean to be that which we desire to desire. Thus if we apply this definition to a particular instance and say 'When we think that A is good, we are thinking that A is one of the things which we desire to desire,' our proposition may seem quite plausible. But, if we carry the investigation further, and ask ourselves 'Is it good to desire to desire A?' it is apparent, on a little reflection, that this question is itself as intelligible, as the original question 'Is A good?'—that we are, in fact, now asking for exactly the same information about the desire to desire A, for which we formerly asked with regard to A itself. But it is also apparent that the meaning of this second question cannot be correctly analyzed into 'Is the desire to desire A one of the things which we desire to desire?': we have not before our minds anything so complicated as the question 'Do we desire to desire to desire to desire A?' Moreover any one can easily convince himself by inspection that the predicate of this proposition—'good'—is positively different from the notion of 'desiring to desire' which enters into its subject: 'That we should desire to desire A is good' is *not* merely equivalent to 'That A should be good is good.' It may indeed be true that what we desire to desire is always also good; perhaps, even the converse may be true: but it is very doubtful whether this is the case, and the mere fact that we understand very well what is meant by doubting it, shows clearly that we have two different notions before our minds.

(2) And the same consideration is sufficient to dismiss the hypothesis that 'good' has no meaning whatsoever. It is very natural to make the mistake of supposing that what is universally true is of such a nature that

its negation would be self-contradictory: the importance which has been assigned to analytic propositions in the history of philosophy shows how easy such a mistake is. And thus it is very easy to conclude that what seems to be a universal ethical principle is in fact an identical proposition; that, if, for example, whatever is called 'good' seems to be pleasant, the proposition 'Pleasure is the good' does not assert a connection between two different notions, but involves only one, that of pleasure, which is easily recognized as a distinct entity. But whoever will attentively consider with himself what is actually before his mind when he asks the question 'Is pleasure (or whatever it may be) after all good?' can easily satisfy himself that he is not merely wondering whether pleasure is pleasant. And if he will try this experiment with each suggested definition in succession, he may become expert enough to recognize that in every case he has before his mind a unique object, with regard to the connection of which with any other object, a distinct question may be asked. Every one does in fact understand the question 'Is this good?' When he thinks of it, his state of mind is different from what it would be, were he asked 'Is this pleasant, or desired, or approved?' It has a distinct meaning for him, even though he may not recognize in what respect it is distinct. Whenever he thinks of 'intrinsic value,' or 'intrinsic worth,' or says that a thing 'ought to exist,' he has before his mind the unique object—the unique property of things— which I mean by 'good.' Everybody is constantly aware of this notion, although he may never become aware at all that it is different from other notions of which he is also aware. But, for correct ethical reasoning, it is extremely important that he should become aware of this fact; and, as soon as the nature of the problem is clearly understood, there should be little difficulty in advancing so far in analysis.

14. 'Good,' then, is indefinable; and yet, so far as I know, there is only one ethical writer, Prof. Henry Sidgwick, who has clearly recognized and stated this fact. We shall see, indeed, how far many of the most reputed ethical systems fall short of drawing the conclusions which follow from such a recognition. At present I will only quote one instance, which will serve to illustrate the meaning and importance of this principle that 'good' is indefinable, or, as Prof. Sidgwick says, an 'unanalyzable notion.' It is an instance to which Prof. Sidgwick himself refers in a note on the passage, in which he argues that 'ought' is unanalyzable.[1]

'Bentham,' says Sidgwick, 'explains that his fundamental principle "states the greatest happiness of all those whose interest is in question as being the right and proper end of human action"'; and yet 'his language in other passages of the same chapter would seem to imply' that he *means*

---

[1] *Methods of Ethics*, Bk. 1, Chap. III, §1 (6th edition).

by the word 'right' 'conducive to the general happiness.' Prof. Sidgwick
sees that, if you take these two statements together, you get the absurd
result that 'greatest happiness is the end of human action, which is conducive to the general happiness'; and so absurd does it seem to him to call
this result, as Bentham calls it, 'the fundamental principle of a moral
system,' that he suggests that Bentham cannot have meant it. Yet Prof.
Sidgwick himself states elsewhere[2] that Psychological Hedonism is 'not
seldom confounded with Egoistic Hedonism'; and that confusion, as we
shall see, rests chiefly on that same fallacy, the naturalistic fallacy, which
is implied in Bentham's statements. Prof. Sidgwick admits therefore that
this fallacy is sometimes committed, absurd as it is; and I am inclined to
think that Bentham may really have been one of those who committed it.
Mill, as we shall see, certainly did commit it. In any case, whether Bentham
committed it or not, his doctrine, as above quoted, will serve as a very
good illustration of this fallacy, and of the importance of the contrary
proposition that good is indefinable.

Let us consider this doctrine. Bentham seems to imply, so Prof.
Sidgwick says, that the word 'right' *means* 'conducive to general happiness.'
Now this, by itself, need not necessarily involve the naturalistic fallacy. For
the word 'right' is very commonly appropriated to actions which lead to
the attainment of what is good; which are regarded as *means* to the ideal
and not as ends in themselves. This use of 'right,' as denoting what is good
as a means, whether or not it be also good as an end, is indeed the use to
which I shall confine the word. Had Bentham been using 'right' in this
sense, it might be perfectly consistent for him to *define* right as 'conducive
to the general happiness,' *provided only* (and notice this proviso) he had
already proved, or laid down as an axiom, that general happiness was *the*
good, or (what is equivalent to this) that general happiness alone was
good. For in that case he would have already defined *the* good as general
happiness (a position perfectly consistent, as we have seen, with the contention that 'good' is indefinable), and, since right was to be defined as
'conducive to *the* good,' it would actually *mean* 'conducive to general
happiness.' But this method of escape from the charge of having committed
the naturalistic fallacy has been closed by Bentham himself. For his fundamental principle is, we see, that the greatest happiness of all concerned is
the *right* and proper *end* of human action. He applies the word 'right,'
therefore, to the end, as such, not only to the means which are conducive
to it; and, that being so, right can no longer be defined as 'conducive to
the general happiness,' without involving the fallacy in question. For now
it is obvious that the definition of right as conducive to general happiness

2 *Methods of Ethics*, Bk. 1, Chap. IV, §1.

can be used by him in support of the fundamental principle that general happiness is the right end; instead of being itself derived from that principle. If right, by definition, means conducive to general happiness, then it is obvious that general happiness is the right end. It is not necessary now first to prove or assert that general happiness is the right end, before right is defined as conducive to general happiness—a perfectly valid procedure; but on the contrary the definition of right as conducive to general happiness proves general happiness to be the right end—a perfectly invalid procedure, since in this case the statement that 'general happiness is the right end of human action' is not an ethical principle at all, but either, as we have seen, a proposition about the meaning of words, or else a proposition about the *nature* of general happiness, not about its rightness or goodness.

Now, I do not wish the importance I assign to this fallacy to be misunderstood. The discovery of it does not at all refute Bentham's contention that greatest happiness is the proper end of human action, if that be understood as an ethical proposition, as he undoubtedly intended it. That principle may be true all the same; we shall consider whether it is so in succeeding chapters. Bentham might have maintained it, as Prof. Sidgwick does, even if the fallacy had been pointed out to him. What I am maintaining is that the *reasons* which he actually gives for his ethical proposition are fallacious ones so far as they consist in a definition of right. What I suggest is that he did not perceive them to be fallacious; that, if he had done so, he would have been led to seek for other reasons in support of his Utilitarianism; and that, had he sought for other reasons, he *might* have found none which he thought to be sufficient. In that case he would have changed his whole system—a most important consequence. It is undoubtedly also possible that he would have thought other reasons to be sufficient, and in that case his ethical system, in its main results, would still have stood. But, even in this latter case, his use of the fallacy would be a serious objection to him as an ethical philosopher. For it is the business of Ethics, I must insist, not only to obtain true results, but also to find valid reasons for them. The direct object of Ethics is knowledge and not practice; and any one who uses the naturalistic fallacy has certainly not fulfilled this first object, however correct his practical principles may be.

My objections to Naturalism are then, in the first place, that it offers no reason at all, far less any valid reason, for any ethical principle whatever; and in this it already fails to satisfy the requirements of Ethics, as a scientific study. But in the second place I contend that, though it gives a reason for no ethical principle, it is a *cause* of the acceptance of false principles—it deludes the mind into accepting ethical principles, which are false; and in this it is contrary to every aim of Ethics. It is easy to see that if we start with a definition of right conduct as conduct conducive to general happiness; then, knowing that right conduct is universally conduct conducive to the good, we very easily arrive at the result that the good is general happiness. If, on the other hand, we once recognize that we must start our Ethics without a definition, we shall be much more apt to look about us, before we adopt any ethical principle whatever; and the more we look about us, the less likely are we to adopt a false one. It may be replied to this: Yes, but we shall look about us just as much, before we settle on our definition, and are therefore just as likely to be right. But I will try to show that this is not the case. If we start with the conviction that a definition of good can be found, we start with the conviction that good *can mean* nothing else than some one property of things; and our only business will then be to discover what that property is. But if we recognize that, so far as the meaning of good goes, anything whatever may be good, we start with a much more open mind. Moreover, apart from the fact that, when we think we have a definition, we cannot logically defend our ethical principles in any way whatever, we shall also be much less apt to defend them well, even if illogically. For we shall start with the conviction that good must mean so and so, and shall therefore be inclined either to misunderstand our opponent's arguments or to cut them short with the reply, 'This is not an open question: the very meaning of the word decides it; no one can think otherwise except through confusion.'

15. Our first conclusion as to the subject matter of Ethics is, then, that there is a simple, indefinable, unanalyzable object of thought by reference to which it must be defined. By what name we call this unique object is a matter of indifference, so long as we clearly recognize what it is and that it does differ from other objects. The words which are commonly taken as the signs of ethical judgments all do refer to it; and they are expressions of ethical judgments solely because they do so refer. But they may refer to it in two different ways, which it is very important to distinguish, if we are to have a complete definition of the range of ethical judgments. Before I proceeded to argue that there was such an indefinable notion involved in ethical notions, I stated (§4) that it was necessary for Ethics to enumerate all true universal judgments, asserting that such and such a thing was good, whenever it occurred. But, although all such judgments do refer to that unique notion which I have called 'good,' they do not all refer to it in the same way. They may either assert that this unique property does always attach to the thing in question, or else they may assert only that the thing in question is *a cause or necessary condition* for the existence of other things to which this unique property does attach. The nature of these two species of universal ethical judgments is extremely different; and a great part of the difficulties, which are met with in ordinary ethical speculation, are due to the failure to distinguish them clearly. Their difference has, indeed, received expression in ordinary language by the contrast between the terms 'good as means' and 'good in itself,' 'value as

a means' and 'intrinsic value.' But these terms are apt to be applied correctly only in the more obvious instances; and this seems to be due to the fact that the distinction between the conceptions which they denote has not been made a separate object of investigation. This distinction may be briefly pointed out as follows.

16. Whenever we judge that a thing is 'good as a means,' we are making a judgment with regard to its causal relations: we judge *both* that it will have a particular kind of effect, *and* that that effect will be good in itself. But to find causal judgments that are universally true is notoriously a matter of extreme difficulty. The late date at which most of the physical sciences became exact, and the comparative fewness of the laws which they have succeeded in establishing even now, are sufficient proofs of this difficulty. With regard, then, to what are the most frequent objects of ethical judgments, namely actions, it is obvious that we cannot be satisfied that any of our universal causal judgments are true, even in the sense in which scientific laws are so. We cannot even discover hypothetical laws of the form 'Exactly this action will always, under these conditions, produce exactly that effect.' But for a correct ethical judgment with regard to the effects of certain actions we require more than this in two respects. (1) We require to know that a given action will produce a certain effect, *under whatever circumstances it occurs.* But this is certainly impossible. It is certain that in different circumstances the same action may produce effects which are utterly different in all respects upon which the value of the effects depends. Hence we can never be entitled to more than a *generaliza-tion*—to a proposition of the form 'This result *generally* follows this kind of action'; and even this generalization will only be true, if the circumstances under which the action occurs are generally the same. This is in fact the case, to a great extent, within any one particular age and state of society. But, when we take other ages into account, in many most important cases the normal circumstances of a given kind of action will be so different, that the generalization which is true for one will not be true for another. With regard then to ethical judgments which assert that a certain kind of action is good as a means to a certain kind of effect, none will be *universally* true; and many, though *generally* true at one period, will be generally false at others. But (2) we require to know not only that *one* good effect will be produced, but that, among all subsequent events affected by the action in question, the balance of good will be greater than if any other possible action had been performed. In other words, to judge that an action is generally a means to good is to judge not only that it generally does *some* good, but that it generally does the greatest good of which the circumstances admit. In this respect ethical judgments about the effects of action involve a difficulty and a complication far greater than that involved in the establishment of scientific laws. For the latter we need only consider a single

effect; for the former it is essential to consider not only this, but the effects of that effect, and so on as far our view into the future can reach. It is, indeed, obvious that our view can never reach far enough for us to be certain that any action will produce the best possible effects. We must be content, if the greatest possible balance of good seems to be produced within a limited period. But it is important to notice that the whole series of effects within a period of considerable length is actually taken account of in our common judgments that an action is good as a means; and that hence this additional complication, which makes ethical generalizations so far more difficult to establish than scientific laws, is one which is involved in actual ethical discussions, and is of practical importance. The commonest rules of conduct involve such considerations as the balancing of future bad health against immediate gains; and even if we can never settle with any certainty how we shall secure the greatest possible total of good, we try at least to assure ourselves that probable future evils will not be greater than the immediate good.

17. There are, then, judgments which state that certain kinds of things have good effects; and such judgments, for the reasons just given, have the important characteristics (1) that they are unlikely to be true, if they state that the kind of thing in question *always* has good effects, and (2) that, even if they only state that it *generally* has good effects, many of them will only be true of certain periods in the world's history. On the other hand there are judgments which state that certain kinds of things are themselves good; and these differ from the last in that, if true at all, they are all of them universally true. It is, therefore, extremely important to distinguish these two kinds of possible judgments. Both may be expressed in the same language: in both cases we commonly say 'Such and such a thing is good.' But in the one case 'good' will mean 'good as means,' i.e. merely that the thing is a means to good—will have good effects: in the other case it will mean 'good as end'—we shall be judging that the thing itself has the property which, in the first case, we asserted only to belong to its effects. It is plain that these are very different assertions to make about a thing; it is plain that either or both of them may be made, both truly and falsely, about all manner of things; and it is certain that unless we are clear as to which of the two we mean to assert, we shall have a very poor chance of deciding rightly whether our assertion is true or false. It is precisely this clearness as to the meaning of the question asked which has hitherto been almost entirely lacking in ethical speculation. Ethics has always been predominantly concerned with the investigation of a limited class of actions. With regard to these we may ask *both* how far they are good in themselves *and* how far they have a general tendency to produce good results. And the arguments brought forward in ethical discussion have always been of both classes— both such as would prove the conduct in question to be good in itself and

such as would prove it to be good as a means. But that these are the only questions which any ethical discussion can have to settle, and that to settle the one is *not* the same thing as to settle the other—these two fundamental facts have in general escaped the notice of ethical philosophers. Ethical questions are commonly asked in an ambiguous form. It is asked 'What is a man's duty under these circumstances?' or 'Is it right to act in this way?' or 'What ought we to aim at securing?' But all these questions are capable of further analysis; a correct answer to any of them involves both judgments of what is good in itself and causal judgments. This is implied even by those who maintain that we have a direct and immediate judgment of absolute rights and duties. Such a judgment can only mean that the course of action in question is *the* best thing to do; that, by acting so, every good that *can* be secured will have been secured. Now we are not concerned with the question whether such a judgment will ever be true. The question is: What does it imply, if it is true? And the only possible answer is that, whether true or false, it implies both a proposition as to the degree of goodness of the action in question, as compared with other things, and a number of causal propositions. For it cannot be denied that the action will have consequences: and to deny that the consequences matter is to make a judgment of their intrinsic value, as compared with the action itself. In asserting that the action is *the* best thing to do, we assert that it together with its consequences presents a greater sum of intrinsic value than any possible alternative. And this condition may be realized by any of the three cases:— (a) If the action itself has greater intrinsic value than any alternative, whereas both its consequences and those of the alternatives are absolutely devoid either of intrinsic merit or intrinsic demerit; or (b) if, though its consequences are intrinsically bad, the balance of intrinsic value is greater than would be produced by any alternative; or (c) if, its consequences being intrinsically good, the degree of value belonging to them and it conjointly is greater than that of any alternative series. In short, to assert that a certain line of conduct is, at a given time, absolutely right or obligatory, is obviously to assert that more good or less evil will exist in the world, if it be adopted than if anything else be done instead. But this implies a judgment as to the value both of its own consequences and of those of any possible alternative. And that an action will have such and such consequences involves a number of causal judgments.

Similarly, in answering the question 'What ought we to aim at securing?' causal judgments are again involved, but in a somewhat different way. We are liable to forget, because it is so obvious, that this question can never be answered correctly except by naming something which *can* be secured. Not everything can be secured; and, even if we judge that nothing which cannot be obtained would be of equal value with that which can, the possibility of the latter, as well as its value, is essential to its being a proper end of action. Accordingly neither our judgments as to what actions we ought to perform, nor even our judgments as to the ends which they ought to produce, are pure judgments of intrinsic value. With regard to the former, an action which is absolutely obligatory *may* have no intrinsic value whatsoever; that it is perfectly virtuous may mean merely that it causes the best possible effects. And with regard to the latter, these best possible results which justify our action can, in any case, have only so much intrinsic value as the laws of nature allow us to secure; and they in their turn *may* have no intrinsic value whatsoever, but may merely be a means to the attainment (in a still further future) of something that has such value. Whenever, therefore, we ask 'What ought we to do?' or 'What ought we to try to get?' we are asking questions which involve a correct answer to two others, completely different in kind from one another. We must know *both* what degree of intrinsic value different things have, *and* how these different things may be obtained. But the vast majority of questions which have actually been discussed in Ethics—*all* practical questions, indeed—involve this double knowledge; and they have been discussed without any clear separation of the two distinct questions involved. A great part of the vast disagreements prevalent in Ethics is to be attributed to this failure in analysis. By the use of conceptions which involve both that of intrinsic value and that of causal relation, as if they involved intrinsic value only, two different errors have been rendered almost universal. Either it is assumed that nothing has intrinsic value which is not possible, or else it is assumed that what is necessary must have intrinsic value. Hence the primary and peculiar business of Ethics, the determination what things have intrinsic value and in what degrees, has received no adequate treatment at all. And on the other hand a *thorough* discussion of means has been also largely neglected, owing to an obscure perception of the truth that it is perfectly irrelevant to the question of intrinsic values. But however this may be, and however strongly any particular reader may be convinced that some one of the mutually contradictory systems which hold the field has given a correct answer either to the question what has intrinsic value, or to the question what we ought to do, or to both, it must at least be admitted that the questions what is best in itself and what will bring about the best possible, are utterly distinct; that both belong to the actual subject matter of Ethics; and that the more clearly distinct questions are distinguished, the better is our chance of answering both correctly.

The Naturalistic Fallacy

WILLIAM K. FRANKENA

The future historian of 'thought and expression' in the twentieth century will no doubt record with some amusement the ingenious trick, which some of the philosophical controversialists of the first quarter of our century had, of labeling their opponents' views 'fallacies'. He may even list some of these alleged fallacies for a certain sonority which their inventors embodied in their titles: the fallacy of initial predication, the fallacy of simple location, the fallacy of misplaced concreteness, the naturalistic fallacy.

Of these fallacies, real or supposed, perhaps the most famous is the naturalistic fallacy. For the practitioners of a certain kind of ethical theory, which is dominant in England and capably represented in America, and which is variously called objectivism, nonnaturalism, or intuitionism, have frequently charged their opponents with committing the naturalistic fallacy. Some of these opponents have strongly repudiated the charge of fallacy, others have at least commented on it in passing, and altogether the notion of a naturalistic fallacy has had a considerable currency in ethical literature. Yet, in spite of its repute, the naturalistic fallacy has never been discussed at any length, and, for this reason, I have elected to make a study of it in this paper. I hope incidentally to clarify certain confusions which have been made in connection with the naturalistic fallacy, but my main interest is to free the controversy between the intuitionists and their opponents of the notion of a logical or quasi-logical fallacy, and to indicate where the issue really lies.

The prominence of the concept of a naturalistic fallacy in recent moral philosophy is another testimony to the great influence of the Cambridge philosopher, Mr. G. E. Moore, and his book, *Principia Ethica*. Thus Mr. Taylor speaks of the 'vulgar mistake' which Mr. Moore has taught us to call 'the naturalistic fallacy',[1] and Mr. G. S. Jury, as if to illustrate how well we have learned this lesson, says, with reference to naturalistic definitions of value, 'All such definitions stand charged with Dr. Moore's "naturalistic fallacy" '.[2] Now, Mr. Moore coined the notion of the naturalistic fallacy in his polemic against naturalistic and metaphysical systems of ethics. 'The naturalistic fallacy is a fallacy', he writes, and it 'must not be committed'. All naturalistic and metaphysical theories of ethics, however, 'are *based* on

From Mind, *XLVIII (1939). Reprinted by permission of the author and* Mind.
[1] A. E. Taylor, *The Faith of a Moralist*, I, 104 n.
[2] *Value and Ethical Objectivity*, p. 58.

the naturalistic fallacy, in the sense that the commission of this fallacy has been the main cause of their wide acceptance.'[3] The best way to dispose of them, then, is to expose this fallacy. Yet it is not entirely clear just what is the status of the naturalistic fallacy in the polemics of the intuitionists against other theories. Sometimes it is used as a weapon, as when Miss Clarke says that if we call a thing good simply because it is liked we are guilty of the naturalistic fallacy.[4] Indeed, it presents this aspect to the reader in many parts of *Principia Ethica* itself. Now, in taking it as a weapon, the intuitionists use the naturalistic fallacy as if it were a logical fallacy on all fours with the fallacy of composition, the revelation of which disposes of naturalistic and metaphysical ethics and leaves intuitionism standing triumphant. That is, it is taken as a fallacy in advance, for use in controversy. But there are signs in *Principia Ethica* which indicate that the naturalistic fallacy has a rather different place in the intuitionist scheme, and should not be used as a weapon at all. In this aspect, the naturalistic fallacy must be proved to be a fallacy. It cannot be used to settle the controversy, but can only be asserted to be a fallacy when the smoke of battle has cleared. Consider the following passages: (a) 'the naturalistic fallacy consists in the contention that good *means* nothing but some simple or complex notion, that can be defined in terms of natural qualities'; (b) 'the point that good is indefinable and that to deny this involves a fallacy, is a point capable of strict proof'.[5] These passages seem to imply that the fallaciousness of the naturalistic fallacy is just what is at issue in the controversy between the intuitionists and their opponents, and cannot be wielded as a weapon in that controversy. One of the points I wish to make in this paper is that the charge of committing the naturalistic fallacy can be made, if at all, only as a conclusion from the discussion and not as an instrument of deciding it.

The notion of a naturalistic fallacy has been connected with the notion of a bifurcation between the 'ought' and the 'is', between value and fact, between the normative and the descriptive. Thus Mr. D. C. Williams says that some moralists have thought it appropriate to chastise as the naturalistic fallacy the attempt to derive the Ought from the Is.[6] We may begin, then, by considering this bifurcation, emphasis on which, by Sidgwick, Sorley, and others, came largely as a reaction to the procedures of Mill and Spencer. Hume affirms the bifurcation in his *Treatise*: 'I cannot forbear adding to these reasonings an observation, which may, perhaps, be found of some importance. In every system of morality which I have hitherto met with, I

---

[3] *Principia Ethica*, pp. 38, 64.

[4] M. E. Clarke, 'Cognition and Affection in the Experience of Value', *Journal of Philosophy* (1938).

[5] *Principia Ethica*, pp. 73, 77. See also p. xix.

[6] 'Ethics as Pure Postulate', *Philosophical Review* (1933). See also T. Whittaker, *The Theory of Abstract Ethics*, pp. 19 f.

have always remarked, that the author proceeds for some time in the ordinary way of reasoning, and establishes the being of a God, or makes observations concerning human affairs; when of a sudden I am surprised to find, that instead of the usual copulations of propositions, *is,* and *is not,* I meet with no proposition that is not connected with an *ought,* or an *ought not.* This change is imperceptible; but is, however, of the last consequence. For as this *ought,* or *ought not,* expresses some new relation or affirmation, it is necessary that it should be observed and explained; and at the same time that a reason should be given, for what seems altogether inconceivable, how this new relation can be a deduction from others, which are entirely different from it. But as authors do not commonly use this precaution, I shall presume to recommend it to the readers; and am persuaded, that this small attention would subvert all the vulgar systems of morality, and let us see that the distinction of vice and virtue is not founded merely on the relations of objects, nor is perceived by reason'.[7]

Needless to say, the intuitionists *have* found this observation of some importance.[8] They agree with Hume that it subverts all the vulgar systems of morality, though, of course, they deny that it lets us see that the distinction of virtue and vice is not founded on the relations of objects, nor is perceived by reason. In fact, they hold that a small attention to it subverts Hume's own system also, since this gives naturalistic definitions of virtue and vice and of good and evil.[9]

Hume's point is that ethical conclusions cannot be drawn validly from premises which are nonethical. But when the intuitionists affirm the bifurcation of the 'ought' and the 'is', they mean more than that ethical propositions cannot be deduced from nonethical ones. For this difficulty in the vulgar systems of morality could be remedied, as we shall see, by the introduction of definitions of ethical notions in nonethical terms. They mean, further, that such definitions of ethical notions in nonethical terms are impossible. 'The essential points', says Mr. Laird, 'is the irreducibility of values to nonvalues'.[10] But they mean still more. Yellow and pleasantness are, according to Mr. Moore, indefinable in nonethical terms, but they are natural qualities and belong on the 'is' side of the fence. Ethical properties, however, are not, for him, mere indefinable natural qualities, descriptive or expository. They are properties of a different *kind*— nondescriptive or nonnatural.[11] The intuitionist bifurcation consists of three statements:—

---

7 Book III, part ii, section i.
8 See J. Laird, *A Study in Moral Theory*, pp. 16 f.; Whittaker, op. cit., p. 19.
9 See C. D. Broad, *Five Types of Ethical Theory*, ch. iv.
10 *A Study in Moral Theory*, p. 94 n.
11 See *Philosophical Studies*, pp. 259, 273 f.

(1) Ethical propositions are not deducible from nonethical ones.[12]

(2) Ethical characteristics are not definable in terms of nonethical ones.

(3) Ethical characteristics are different in kind from nonethical ones.

Really it consists of but one statement, namely, (3), since (3) entails (2) and (2) entails (1). It does not involve saying that any ethical characteristics are absolutely indefinable. That is another question, although this is not always noticed.

What, now, has the naturalistic fallacy to do with the bifurcation of the 'ought' and the 'is'? To begin with, the connection is this: many naturalistic and metaphysical moralists proceed as if ethical conclusions can be deduced from premises all of which are nonethical, the classical examples being Mill and Spencer. That is, they violate (1). This procedure has lately been referred to as the 'factualist fallacy' by Mr. Wheelwright and as the 'valuational fallacy' by Mr. Wood.[13] Mr. Moore sometimes seems to identify it with the naturalistic fallacy, but in the main he holds only that it involves, implies, or rests upon this fallacy.[14] We may now consider the charge that the procedure in question is or involves a fallacy.

It may be noted at once that, even if the deduction of ethical conclusions from nonethical premises is in no way a fallacy, Mill certainly did commit a fallacy in drawing an analogy between visibility and desirability in his argument for hedonism; and perhaps his committing *this* fallacy, which, as Mr. Broad has said, we all learn about at our mothers' knees, is chiefly responsible for the notion of a naturalistic *fallacy*. But is it a fallacy to deduce ethical conclusions from nonethical premises? Consider the Epicurean argument for hedonism which Mill so unwisely sought to embellish: pleasure is good, since it is sought by all men. Here an ethical conclusion is being derived from a nonethical premise. And, indeed, the argument, taken strictly as it stands, *is* fallacious. But it is not fallacious because an *ethical* term occurs in the conclusion which does not occur in the premise. It is fallacious because any argument of the form "A is B, therefore A is C" is invalid, if taken strictly as it stands. For example, it is invalid to argue that Crœsus is rich because he is wealthy. Such arguments are, however, not intended to be taken strictly as they stand. They are enthymemes and contain a suppressed premise. And, when this suppressed premise is made explicit, they are valid and involve no logical fallacy.[15] Thus the Epicurean inference from psychological to ethical hedonism is valid when the suppressed premise

12 See J. Laird, op. cit., p. 318. Also pp. 12 ff.

13 P. E. Wheelwright, *A Critical Introduction to Ethics*, pp. 40–51, 91 f.; L. Wood, 'Cognition and Moral Value', *Journal of Philosophy*, (1937), p. 237.

14 See *Principia Ethica*, pp. 114, 57, 43, 49. Whittaker identifies it with the naturalistic fallacy and regards it as a 'logical' fallacy, op. cit., pp. 19 f.

15 See ibid., pp. 50, 139; Wheelwright, loc. cit.

is added to the effect that what is sought by all men is good. Then the only question left is whether the premises are true.

It is clear, then, that the naturalistic fallacy is not a logical fallacy, since it may be involved even when the argument is valid. How does the naturalistic fallacy enter such 'mixed ethical arguments'[16] as that of the Epicureans? Whether it does or not depends on the nature of the suppressed premise. This may be either an induction, an intuition, a deduction from a 'pure ethical argument', a definition, or a proposition which is true by definition. If it is one of the first three, then the naturalistic fallacy does not enter at all. In fact, the argument does not then involve violating (1), since one of its premises will be ethical. But if the premise to be supplied is a definition or a proposition which is true by definition, as it probably was for the Epicureans, then the argument, while still valid, involves the naturalistic fallacy, and will run as follows:—

(a) Pleasure is sought by all men.

(b) What is sought by all men is good (by definition).

(c) Therefore, pleasure is good.

Now I am not greatly interested in deciding whether the argument as here set up violates (1). If it does not, then no 'mixed ethical argument' actually commits any factualist or valuational fallacy, except when it is unfairly taken as complete in its enthymematic form. If it does, then a valid argument may involve the deduction of an ethical conclusion from non-ethical premises and the factualist or valuational fallacy is not really a fallacy. The question depends on whether or not (b) and (c) are to be regarded as ethical propositions. Mr. Moore refuses so to regard them, contending that, by hypothesis, (b) is analytic or tautologous, and that (c) is psychological, since it really says only that pleasure is sought by all men.[17] But to say that (b) is analytic and not ethical and that (c) is not ethical but psychological is to prejudge the question whether 'good' can be defined; for the Epicureans would contend precisely that if their definition is correct then (b) is ethical but analytic and (c) ethical though psychological. Thus, unless the question of the definability of goodness is to be begged, (b) and (c) must be regarded as ethical, in which case our argument does not violate (1). However, suppose, if it be not nonsense, that (b) is nonethical and (c) ethical, then the argument will violate (1), but it will still obey all of the canons of logic, and it is only confusing to talk of a 'valuational logic' whose basic rule is that an evaluative conclusion cannot be deduced from nonevaluative premises.[18]

---

16 See C. D. Broad, The *Mind and Its Place in Nature*, pp. 488 f.; Laird, loc. cit.

17 See op. cit., pp. 11 f.; 19, 38, 73, 139.

18 See L. Wood, loc. cit.

For the only way in which either the intuitionists or postulationists like Mr. Wood can cast doubt upon the conclusion of the argument of the Epicureans (or upon the conclusion of any parallel argument) is to attack the premises, in particular (b). Now, according to Mr. Moore, it is due to the presence of (b) that the argument involves the naturalistic fallacy. (b) involves the identification of goodness with 'being sought by all men', and to make this or any other such identification is to commit the naturalistic fallacy. The naturalistic fallacy is not the procedure of violating (1). It is the procedure, implied in many mixed ethical arguments and explicitly carried out apart from such arguments by many moralists, of defining such characteristics as goodness or of substituting some other characteristic for them. To quote some passages from *Principia Ethica*:—

> (a) '. . . far too many philosophers have thought that when they named those other properties [belonging to all things which are good] they were actually defining good; that these properties, in fact, were simply not "other", but absolutely and entirely the same with goodness. This view I propose to call the "naturalistic fallacy". . . .'[19]
>
> (b) 'I have thus appropriated the name Naturalism to a particular method of approaching Ethics. . . . This method consists in substituting for "good" some one property of a natural object or of a collection of natural objects. . . .'[20]
>
> (c) '. . . the naturalistic fallacy [is] the fallacy which consists in identifying the simple notion which we mean by "good" with some other notion'.[21]

Thus, to identify 'better' and 'more evolved', 'good' and 'desired', etc., is to commit the naturalistic fallacy.[22] But just why is such a procedure fallacious or erroneous? And is it a fallacy only when applied to good? We must now study Section 12 of *Principia Ethica*. Here Mr. Moore makes some interesting statements:—

> '. . . if anybody tried to define pleasure for us as being any other natural object; if anybody were to say, for instance that pleasure *means* the sensation of red. . . . Well, that would be the same fallacy which I have called the naturalistic fallacy. . . . I should not indeed call that a naturalistic fallacy, although it is the same fallacy as I have called naturalistic with reference to Ethics. . . . When a man confuses two natural objects with one another, defining the one by the other . . . then there is no reason to call the fallacy naturalistic.

---

[19] P. 10.
[20] P. 40.
[21] P. 58, cf. pp. xiii, 73.
[22] Cf. pp. 49, 53, 108, 139.

> But if he confuses "good", which is not . . . a natural object, with
> any natural object whatever, then there is a reason for calling that
> a naturalistic fallacy. . . .'[23]

Here Mr. Moore should have added that, when one confuses 'good',
which is not a metaphysical object or quality, with any metaphysical object
or quality, as metaphysical moralists do, according to him, then the fallacy
should be called the metaphysical fallacy. Instead he calls it a naturalistic
fallacy in this case too, though he recognizes that the case is different
since metaphysical properties are nonnatural[24]—a procedure which has
misled many readers of *Principia Ethica*. For example, it has led Mr. Broad
to speak of 'theological naturalism'.[25]

To resume: 'Even if [goodness] were a natural object, that would
not alter the nature of the fallacy nor diminish its importance one white'.[26]

From these passages it is clear that the fallaciousness of the procedure
which Mr. Moore calls the naturalistic fallacy is not due to the fact that it is
applied to good or to an ethical or nonnatural characteristic. When Mr.
R. B. Perry defines 'good' as 'being an object of interest' the trouble is not
merely that he is defining *good*. Nor is the trouble that he is defining an
ethical characteristic in terms of *nonethical* ones. Nor is the trouble that he
is regarding a *nonnatural* characteristic as a *natural* one. The trouble is
more generic than that. For clarity's sake I shall speak of the definist fallacy
as the generic fallacy which underlies the naturalistic fallacy. The naturalistic fallacy will then, by the above passages, be a species or form of the
definist fallacy, as would the metaphysical fallacy if Mr. Moore had given
that a separate name.[27] That is, the naturalistic fallacy, as illustrated by
Mr. Perry's procedure, is a fallacy, not because it is naturalistic or confuses
a nonnatural quality with a natural one, but solely because it involves the
definist fallacy. We may, then, confine our attention entirely to an understanding and evaluation of the definist fallacy.

To judge by the passages I have just quoted, the definist fallacy is the
process of confusing or identifying two properties, of defining one property
by another, or of substituting one property for another. Furthermore, the
fallacy is always simply that two properties are being treated as one, and it
is irrelevant, if it be the case, that one of them is natural or nonethical and
the other nonnatural or ethical. One may commit the definist fallacy without
infringing on the bifurcation of the ethical and the nonethical, as when one
identifies pleasantness and redness or rightness and goodness. But even when

---

23 P. 13.
24 See pp. 38–40, 110–12.
25 *Five Types of Ethical Theory*, p. 259.
26 P. 14.
27 As Whittaker has, loc. cit.

one infringes on that bifurcation in committing the definist fallacy, as when one identifies goodness and pleasantness or goodness and satisfaction, then the *mistake* is still not that the bifurcation is being infringed on, but only that two properties are being treated as one. Hence, on the present interpretation, the definist *fallacy* does not, in any of its forms, consist in violating (3), and has no essential connection with the bifurcation of the 'ought' and the 'is'.

This formulation of the definist fallacy explains or reflects the motto of *Principia Ethica,* borrowed from Bishop Butler: 'Everything is what it is, and not another thing'. It follows from this motto that goodness is what it is and not another thing. It follows that views which try to identify it with something else are making a mistake of an elementary sort. For it *is* a mistake to confuse or identify two properties. If the properties really are two, then they simply are not identical. But do those who define ethical notions in nonethical terms make this mistake? They will reply to Mr. Moore that they are not identifying two properties; what they are saying is that two words or sets of words stand for or mean one and the same property. Mr. Moore was being, in part, misled by the material mode of speech, as Mr. Carnap calls it, in such sentences as 'Goodness is pleasantness', 'Knowledge is true belief', etc. When one says instead, 'The word "good" and the word "pleasant" mean the same thing', etc., it is clear that one is not identifying two things. But Mr. Moore kept himself from seeing this by his disclaimer that he was interested in any statement about the use of words.[28]

The definist fallacy, then, as we have stated it, does not rule out any naturalistic or metaphysical definitions of ethical terms. Goodness is not identifiable with any 'other' characteristic (if it is a characteristic at all). But the question is: *which* characteristics are other than goodness, which names stand for characteristics other than goodness? And it is begging the question of the definability of goodness to say out of hand that Mr. Perry, for instance, is identifying goodness with something else. The point is that goodness is what it is, even if it is definable. That is why Mr. Perry can take as the motto of his naturalistic *Moral Economy* another sentence from Bishop Butler: 'Things and actions are what they are, and the consequences of them will be what they will be; why then should we desire to be deceived?' The motto of *Principia Ethica* is a tautology, and should be expanded as follows: Everything is what it is, and not another thing, unless it is another thing, and even then it is what it is.

On the other hand, if Mr. Moore's motto (or the definist fallacy) rules out any definitions, for example of 'good', then it rules out all definitions of any term whatever. To be effective at all, it must be understood to

---

[28] See op. cit., pp. 6, 8, 12.

mean, 'Every term means what it means, and not what is meant by any other term'. Mr. Moore seems implicitly to understand his motto in this way in Section 13, for he proceeds as if 'good' has no meaning, if it has no unique meaning. If the motto be taken in this way, it will follow that 'good' is an indefinable term, since no synonyms can be found. But it will also follow that no term is definable. And then the method of analysis is as useless as an English butcher in a world without sheep.

Perhaps we have misinterpreted the definist fallacy. And, indeed, some of the passages which I quoted earlier in this paper seem to imply that the definist fallacy is just the error of defining an indefinable characteristic. On this interpretation, again, the definist fallacy has, in all of its forms, no essential connection with the bifurcation of the ethical and the nonethical. Again, one may commit the definist fallacy without violating that bifurcation, as when one defines pleasantness in terms of redness or goodness in terms of rightness (granted Mr. Moore's belief that pleasantness and goodness are indefinable). But even when one infringes on that bifurcation and defines goodness in terms of desire, the *mistake* is not that one is infringing on the bifurcation by violating (3), but only that one is defining an indefinable characteristic. This is possible because the proposition that goodness is indefinable is logically independent of the proposition that goodness is nonnatural: as is shown by the fact that a characteristic may be indefinable and yet natural, as yellowness is; or nonnatural and yet definable, as rightness is (granted Mr. Moore's views about yellowness and rightness).

Consider the definist fallacy as we have just stated it. It is, of course, an error to define an indefinable quality. But the question, again, is: which qualities are indefinable? It is begging the question in favor of intuitionism to say in advance that the quality goodness is indefinable and that, therefore, all naturalists commit the definist fallacy. One must know that goodness is indefinable before one can argue that the definist fallacy *is* a fallacy. Then, however, the definist fallacy can enter only at the end of the controversy between intuitionism and definism, and cannot be used as a weapon in the controversy.

The definist fallacy may be stated in such a way as to involve the bifurcation between the 'ought' and the 'is'.[29] It would then be committed by anyone who offered a definition of any ethical characteristic in terms of nonethical ones. The trouble with such a definition, on this interpretation, would be that an *ethical* characteristic is being reduced to a *nonethical* one, a *nonnatural* one to a *natural* one. That is, the definition would be ruled out by the fact that the characteristic being defined is ethical or nonnatural and therefore cannot be defined in nonethical or natural terms.

---

[29] See J. Wisdom, *Mind* (1931), p. 213, note 1.

But on this interpretation, too, there is danger of a *petitio* in the intuitionist argumentation. To assume that the ethical characteristic is exclusively ethical is to beg precisely the question which is at issue when the definition is offered. Thus, again, one must know that the characteristic is nonnatural and indefinable in natural terms before one can say that the definists are making a mistake.

Mr. Moore, McTaggart, and others formulate the naturalistic fallacy sometimes in a way somewhat different from any of those yet discussed. They say that the definists are confusing a universal synthetic proposition about *the good* with a definition of *goodness*.[30] Mr. Abraham calls this the 'fallacy of miscontrued proposition'.[31] Here again the difficulty is that, while it is true that it is an error to construe a universal synthetic proposition as a definition, it is a *petitio* for the intuitionists to say that what the definist is taking for a definition is really a universal synthetic proposition.[32]

At last, however, the issue between the intuitionists and the definists (naturalistic or metaphysical) is becoming clearer. The definists are all holding that certain propositions involving ethical terms are analytic, tautologous, or true by definition, e.g., Mr. Perry so regards the statement, 'All objects of desire are good'. The intuitionists hold that such statements are synthetic. What underlies this difference of opinion is that the intuitionists claim to have at least a dim awareness of a simple unique quality or relation of goodness or rightness which appears in the region which our ethical terms roughly indicate, whereas the definists claim to have no awareness of any such quality or relation in that region, which is different from all other qualities and relations which belong to the same context but are designated by words other than 'good' and 'right' and their obvious synonyms.[33] The definists are in all honesty claiming to find but one characteristic where the intuitionists claim to find two, as Mr. Perry claims to find only the property of being desired where Mr. Moore claims to find both it and the property of being good. The issue, then, is one of inspection or intuition, and concerns the awareness or discernment of qualities and relations.[34] That is why it cannot be decided by the use of the notion of a fallacy.

If the definists may be taken at their word, then they are not actually confusing two characteristics with each other, nor defining an indefinable characteristic, nor confusing definitions and universal synthetic propositions

---

[30] *See Principia Ethica*, pp. 10, 16, 38; *The Nature of Existence*, II, p. 398.

[31] Leo Abraham, 'The Logic Intuitionism', *International Journal of Ethics*, (1933).

[32] As Mr. Abraham points out, loc. cit.

[33] See R. B. Perry, *General Theory of Value*, p. 30; cf. *Journal of Philosophy*, (1931), p. 520.

[34] See H. Osborne, *Foundations of the Philosophy of Value*, pp. 15, 19, 70.

—in short they are not committing the naturalistic or definist fallacy in any of the interpretations given above. Then the only fallacy which they commit—the real naturalistic or definist fallacy—is the failure to descry the qualities and relations which are central to morality. But this is neither a logical fallacy nor a logical confusion. It is not even, properly speaking, an error. It is rather a kind of blindness, analogous to color blindness. Even this moral blindness can be ascribed to the definists only if they are correct in their claim to have no awareness of any unique ethical characteristics and if the intuitionists are correct in affirming the existence of such characteristics, but certainly to call it a 'fallacy', even in a loose sense, is both unamiable and profitless.

On the other hand, of course, if there are no such characteristics in the objects to which we attach ethical predicates, then the intuitionists, if we may take them at their word, are suffering from a corresponding moral hallucination. Definists might then call this the intuitionistic or moralistic fallacy, except that it is no more a 'fallacy' than is the blindness just described. Anyway, they do not believe the claim of the intuitionists to be aware of unique ethical characteristics, and consequently do not attribute to them this hallucination. Instead, they simply deny that the intuitionists really do find such unique qualities or relations, and then they try to find some plausible way of accounting for the fact that very respectable and trustworthy people think they find them.[35] Thus they charge the intuitionists with verbalism, hypostatization, and the like. But this half of the story does not concern us now.

What concerns us more is the fact that the intuitionists do not credit the claim of the definists either. They would be much disturbed, if they really thought that their opponents were morally blind, for they do not hold that we must be regenerated by grace before we can have moral insight, and they share the common feeling that morality is something democratic even though not all men are good. Thus they hold that 'we are all aware' of certain unique characteristics when we use the terms 'good', 'right', etc., only due to a lack of analytic clearness of mind, abetted perhaps by a philosophical prejudice, we may not be aware at all that they are different from other characteristics of which we are also aware.[36] Now, I have been arguing that the intuitionists cannot charge the definists with committing any fallacy unless and until they have shown that we are all, the definists included, aware of the disputed unique characteristics. If, however, they were to show this, then, at least at the end of the controversy, they could accuse the definists of the error of confusing two characteristics, or of the error of defining an indefinable one, and these errors might, since

---

[35] Cf. R. B. Perry, *Journal of Philosophy* (1931), pp. 520 ff.
[36] *Principia Ethica*, pp. 17, 38, 59, 61.

the term is somewhat loose in its habits, be called 'fallacies', though they are not logical fallacies in the sense in which an invalid argument is. The fallacy of misconstrued proposition depends on the error of confusing two characteristics, and hence could also on our present supposition, be ascribed to the definists, but it is not really a logical confusion,[37] since it does not actually involve being confused about the difference between a proposition and a definition.

Only it is difficult to see how the intuitionists can prove that the definists are at least vaguely aware of the requisite unique characteristics.[38] The question must surely be left to the inspection or intuition of the definists themselves, aided by whatever suggestions the intuitionists may have to make. If so, we must credit the verdict of their inspection, especially of those among them who have read the writings of the intuitionists reflectively, and, then, as we have seen, the most they can be charged with is moral blindness.

Besides trying to discover just what is meant by the naturalistic fallacy, I have tried to show that the notion that a logical or quasi-logical fallacy is committed by the definists only confuses the issue between the intuitionists and the definists (and the issue between the latter and the emotivists or postulationists), and misrepresents the way in which the issue is to be settled. No logical fallacy need appear anywhere in the procedure of the definists. Even fallacies in any less accurate sense cannot be implemented to decide the case against the definists; at best they can be ascribed to the definists only after the issue has been decided against them on independent grounds. But the only defect which can be attributed to the definists, *if* the intuitionists are right in affirming the existence of unique indefinable ethical characteristics, is a peculiar moral blindness, which is not a fallacy even in the looser sense. The issue in question must be decided by whatever method we may find satisfactory for determining whether or not a word stands for a characteristic at all, and, if it does, whether or not it stands for a unique characteristic. What method is to be employed is, perhaps, in one form or another, the basic problem of contemporary philosophy, but no generally satisfactory solution of the problem has yet been reached. I shall venture to say only this: it does seem to me that the issue is not to be decided against the intuitionists by the application *ab extra* to ethical judgments of any empirical or ontological meaning dictum.[39]

---

[37] But see H. Osborne, op. cit., pp. 18 f.

[38] For a brief discussion of their arguments, see ibid., p. 67; L. Abraham, op. cit. I think they are all inconclusive, but cannot show this here.

[39] See *Principia Ethica*, pp. 124 f., 140.

The Emotive Meaning
of Ethical Terms

C. L. STEVENSON

1

Ethical questions first arise in the form "is so and so good?" or "is this alternative better than that?" These questions are difficult partly because we don't quite know what we are seeking. We are asking, "is there a needle in the haystack?" without even knowing just what a needle is. So the first thing to do is to examine the questions themselves. We must try to make them clearer, either by defining the terms in which they are expressed or by any other method that is available.

The present essay is concerned wholly with this preliminary step of making ethical questions clear. In order to help answer the question "is X good?" we must *substitute* for it a question that is free from ambiguity and confusion.

It is obvious that in substituting a clearer question we must not introduce some utterly different kind of question. It won't do (to take an extreme instance of a prevalent fallacy) to substitute for "is X good?" the question "is X pink with yellow trimmings?" and then point out how easy the question really is. This would beg the original question, not help answer it. On the other hand, we must not expect the substituted question to be strictly "identical" with the original one. The original question may embody hypostatization, anthropomorphism, vagueness, and all the other ills to which our ordinary discourse is subject. If our substituted question is to be clearer it must remove these ills. The questions will be identical only in the sense that a child is identical with the man he later becomes. Hence we must not demand that the substitution strike us, on immediate introspection, as making no change in meaning.

Just how, then, must the substituted question be related to the original? Let us assume (inaccurately) that it must result from replacing "good" by some set of terms that define it. The question then resolves itself to this: How must the defined meaning of "good" be related to its original meaning?

From Mind, *XLVI (1937), with modifications as in C. L. Stevenson,* Facts and Values *(New Haven: Yale University Press, 1963), Chapter 2. Reprinted by permission of the author and* Mind.

I answer that it must be *relevant*. A defined meaning will be called "relevant" to the original meaning under these circumstances: Those who have understood the definition must be able to say all that they then want to say by using the term in the defined way. They must never have occasion to use the term in the old, unclear sense. (If a person did have to go on using the word in the old sense, then to this extent his meaning would not be clarified and the philosophical task would not be completed.) It frequently happens that a word is used so confusedly and ambiguously that we must give it *several* defined meanings, rather than one. In this case only the whole set of defined meanings will be called "relevant," and any one of them will be called "partially relevant." This is not a rigorous treatment of *relevance*, by any means, but it will serve for the present purposes.

Let us now turn to our particular task—that of giving a relevant definition of "good." Let us first examine some of the ways in which others have attempted to do this.

The word "good" has often been defined in terms of *approval*, or similar psychological attitudes. We may take as typical examples: "good" means *desired by me* (Hobbes); and "good" means *approved by most people* (Hume, in effect).[1] It will be convenient to refer to definitions of this sort as "interest theories," following R. B. Perry, although neither "interest" nor "theory" is used in the most usual way.[2]

Are definitions of this sort relevant?

It is idle to deny their *partial relevance*. The most superficial inquiry will reveal that "good" is exceedingly ambiguous. To maintain that "good" is never used in Hobbes' sense, and never in Hume's, is only to manifest an insensitivity to the complexities of language. We must recognize, perhaps, not only these senses, but a variety of similar ones, differing both with regard to the kind of interest in question and with regard to the people who are said to have the interest.

But that is a minor matter. The essential question is not whether interest theories are *partially* relevant, but whether they are *wholly* relevant. This is the only point for intelligent dispute. Briefly: Granted that some

---

[1] The definition ascribed to Hume is oversimplified, but not, I think, in a way that weakens the force of the observations that I am about to make. Perhaps the same should be said of Hobbes.

A more accurate account of Hume's Ethics is given in *Ethics and Language* (New Haven, 1944), pp. 273–76.

[2] In *General Theory of Value* (New York, 1926) Perry used "interest" to refer to any sort of favoring or disfavoring, or any sort of disposition to be for or against something. And he used "theory" where he might, alternatively, have used "proposed definition," or "proposed analysis of a common sense meaning."...

senses of "good" may relevantly be defined in terms of interest, is there some *other* sense which is *not* relevantly so defined? We must give this question careful attention. For it is quite possible that when philosophers (and many others) have found the question "is X good?" so difficult, they have been grasping for this *other* sense of "good" and not any sense relevantly defined in terms of interest. If we insist on defining "good" in terms of interest, and answer the question when thus interpreted, we may be begging *their* question entirely. Of course this *other* sense of "good" may not exist, or it may be a complete confusion; but that is what we must discover.

Now many have maintained that interest theories are *far* from being completely relevant. They have argued that such theories neglect the very sense of "good" that is most typical of ethics. And certainly, their arguments are not without plausibility.

Only—what *is* this typical sense of "good"? The answers have been so vague and so beset with difficulties that one can scarcely determine.

There are certain requirements, however, with which the typical sense has been expected to comply—requirements which appeal strongly to our common sense. It will be helpful to summarize these, showing how they exclude the interest theories:

In the first place, we must be able sensibly to *disagree* about whether something is "good." This condition rules out Hobbes' definition. For consider the following argument: "This is good." "That isn't so; it's not good." As translated by Hobbes, this becomes: "I desire this." "That isn't so, for *I* don't." The speakers are not contradicting one another, and think they are only because of an elementary confusion in the use of pronouns. The definition, "good" means *desired by my community*, is also excluded, for how could people from different communities disagree.[3]

In the second place, "goodness" must have, so to speak, a magnetism. A person who recognizes X to be "good" must ipso facto acquire a stronger tendency to act in its favor than he otherwise would have had. This rules out the Humian type of definition. For according to Hume, to recognize that something is "good" is simply to recognize that the majority approve of it. Clearly, a man may see that the majority approve of X without having, himself, a stronger tendency to favor it. This requirement excludes any attempt to define "good" in terms of the interest of people *other* than the speaker.[4]

In the third place, the "goodness" of anything must not be verifiable solely by use of the scientific method. "Ethics must not be psychology." This restriction rules out all of the traditional interest theories without

---

[3] See G. E. Moore, *Philosophical Studies* (New York, 1922), pp. 332–34.
[4] See G. C. Field, *Moral Theory* (London, 1921), pp. 52, 56–57.

exception. It is so sweeping a restriction that we must examine its plausibility. What are the methodological implications of interest theories which are here rejected?

According to Hobbes' definition a person can prove his ethical judgments with finality by showing that he is not making an introspective error about his desires. According to Hume's definition one may prove ethical judgments (roughly speaking) by taking a vote. *This* use of the empirical method, at any rate, seems highly remote from what we usually accept as proof and reflects on the complete relevance of the definitions that imply it.

But are there not more complicated interest theories that are immune from such methodological implications? No, for the same factors appear; they are only put off for a while. Consider, for example, the definition: "X is good" means *most people would approve of X if they knew its nature and consequences.* How, according to this definition, could we prove that a certain X was good? We should first have to find out, empirically, just what X was like and what its consequences would be. To this extent the empirical method as required by the definition seems beyond intelligent objection. But what remains? We should next have to discover whether most people would approve of the sort of thing we had discovered X to be. This could not be determined by popular vote—but only because it would be too difficult to explain to the voters, beforehand, what the nature and consequences of X really were. Apart from this, voting would be a pertinent method. We are again reduced to counting noses as a *perfectly final* appeal.

Now we need not scorn voting entirely. A man who rejected interest theories as irrelevant might readily make the following statement: "If I believed that X would be approved by the majority, when they knew all about it, I should be strongly *led* to say that X was good." But he would continue: "*Need* I say that X was good, under the circumstances? Wouldn't my acceptance of the alleged 'final proof' result simply from my being democratic? What about the more aristocratic people? They would simply say that the approval of most people, even when they knew all about the object of their approval, simply had nothing to do with the goodness of anything, and they would probably add a few remarks about the low state of people's interests." It would indeed seem, from these considerations, that the definition we have been considering has presupposed democratic ideals from the start; it has dressed up democratic propaganda in the guise of a definition.

The omnipotence of the empirical method, as implied by interest theories and others, may be shown unacceptable in a somewhat different way. G. E. Moore's familiar objection about the open question is chiefly pertinent in this regard. No matter what set of scientifically knowable properties a thing may have (says Moore, in effect), you will find, on careful introspection, that it is an open question to ask whether anything having these properties is *good*. It is difficult to believe that this recurrent question is a totally confused one, or that it seems open only because of the ambiguity of "good." Rather, we must be using some sense of "good" which is not definable, relevantly, in terms of anything scientifically knowable. That is, the scientific method is not sufficient for ethics.[5]

These, then, are the requirements with which the "typical" sense of "good" is expected to comply: (1) goodness must be a topic for intelligent disagreement; (2) it must be "magnetic"; and (3) it must not be discoverable solely through the scientific method.

2

I can now turn to my proposed analysis of ethical judgments. First let me present my position dogmatically, showing to what extent I vary from tradition.

I believe that the three requirements given above are perfectly sensible, that there is some *one* sense of "good" which satisfies all three requirements, and that no traditional interest theory satisfies them all. But this does not imply that "good" must be explained in terms of a Platonic Idea, or of a categorical imperative, or of a unique, unanalyzable property. On the contrary, the three requirements can be met by a *kind* of interest theory. *But we must give up a presupposition that all the traditional interest theories have made.*

Traditional interest theories hold that ethical statements are *descriptive* of the existing state of interests—that they simply *give information* about interests. (More accurately, ethical judgments are said to describe what the state of interests is, was, or will be, or to indicate what the state of interests *would* be under specified circumstances.) It is this emphasis on description, on information, which leads to their incomplete relevance. Doubtless there is always *some* element of description in ethical judgments, but this is by no means all. Their major use is not to indicate facts but to *create an influence*. Instead of merely describing people's interests they *change* or *intensify* them. They *recommend* an interest in an object, rather than state that the interest already exists.

For instance: When you tell a man that he ought not to steal, your object is not merely to let him know that people disapprove of stealing. You are attempting, rather, to get *him* to disapprove of it. Your ethical judgment has a quasi-imperative force which, operating through suggestion

---

[5] See G. E. Moore, *Principia Ethica* (Cambridge, 1903), ch. 1. I am simply trying to preserve the spirit of Moore's objection and not the exact form of it.

and intensified by your tone of voice, readily permits you to begin to *influence*, to *modify*, his interests. If in the end you do not succeed in getting *him* to disapprove of stealing, you will feel that you have failed to convince him that stealing is wrong. You will continue to feel this, even though he fully acknowledges that you disapprove of it and that almost everyone else does. When you point out to him the consequences of his actions—consequences which you suspect he already disapproves of—these *reasons* which support your ethical judgment are simply a means of facilitating your influence. If you think you can change his interests by making vivid to him how others will disapprove of him, you will do so, otherwise not. So the consideration about other people's interest is just an additional means you may employ in order to move him and is not a part of the ethical judgment itself. Your ethical judgment does not merely describe interests to him, it directs his very interests. The difference between the traditional interest theories and my view is like the difference between describing a desert and irrigating it.

Another example: A munitions maker declares that war is a good thing. If he merely meant that he approved of it, he would not have to insist so strongly nor grow so excited in his argument. People would be quite easily convinced that he approved of it. If he merely meant that most people approved of war, or that most people would approve of it if they knew the consequences, he would have to yield his point if it were proved that this was not so. But he would not do this, nor does consistency require it. He is not *describing* the state of people's approval; he is trying to *change* it by his influence. If he found that few people approved of war, he might insist all the more strongly that it was good, for there would be more changing to be done.

This example illustrates how "good" may be used for what most of us would call bad purposes. Such cases are as pertinent as any others. I am not indicating the *good* way of using "good." I am not influencing people but am describing the way this influence sometimes goes on. If the reader wishes to say that the munitions maker's influence is bad—that is, if the reader wishes to awaken people's disapproval of the man, and to make him disapprove of his own actions—I should at another time be willing to join in this undertaking. But this is not the present concern. I am not using ethical terms but am indicating how they *are* used. The munitions maker, in his use of "good," illustrates the persuasive character of the word just as well as does the unselfish man who, eager to encourage in each of us a desire for the happiness of all, contends that the supreme good is peace.

Thus ethical terms are *instruments* used in the complicated interplay and readjustment of human interests. This can be seen plainly from more general observations. People from widely separated communities have different moral attitudes. Why? To a great extent because they have been subject to different social influences. Now clearly this influence does not operate through sticks and stones alone; words play a great part. People praise one another to encourage certain inclinations and blame one another to discourage others. Those of forceful personalities issue commands which weaker people, for complicated instinctive reasons, find it difficult to disobey, quite apart from fears of consequences. Further influence is brought to bear by writers and orators. Thus social influence is exerted, to an enormous extent, by means that have nothing to do with physical force or material reward. The ethical terms facilitate such influence. Being suited for use in *suggestion*, they are a means by which men's attitudes may be led this way or that. The reason, then, that we find a greater similarity in the moral attitudes of one community than in those of different communities is largely this: ethical judgments propagate themselves. One man says "this is good"; this may influence the approval of another person, who then makes the same ethical judgment, which in turn influences another person, and so on. In the end, by a process of mutual influence, people take up more or less the same attitudes. Between people of widely separated communities, of course, the influence is less strong; hence different communities have different attitudes.

These remarks will serve to give a general idea of my point of view. We must now go into more detail. There are several questions which must be answered: How does an ethical sentence acquire its power of influencing people—why is it suited to suggestion? Again, what has this influence to do with the *meaning* of ethical terms? And finally, do these considerations really lead us to a sense of "good" which meets the requirements mentioned in the preceding section?

Let us deal first with the question about *meaning*. This is far from an easy question, so we must enter into a preliminary inquiry about meaning in general. Although a seeming digression this will prove indispensable.

3

Broadly speaking, there are two different *purposes* which lead us to use language. On the one hand we use words (as in science) to record, clarify, and communicate *beliefs*. On the other hand we use words to give vent to our feelings (interjections), or to create moods (poetry), or to incite people to actions or attitudes (oratory).

The first use of words I shall call "descriptive," the second, "dynamic." Note that the distinction depends solely upon the *purpose* of the *speaker*.

When a person says "hydrogen is the lightest known gas," his purpose *may* be simply to lead the hearer to believe this, or to believe that the speaker believes it. In that case the words are used descriptively. When a person cuts himself and says "damn," his purpose is not ordinarily to record, clarify, or communicate any belief. The word is used dynamically. The two ways of using words, however, are by no means mutually exclusive. This is obvious from the fact that our purposes are often complex. Thus when one says "I want you to close the door," part of his purpose, ordinarily, is to lead the hearer to believe that he has this want. To that extent the words are used descriptively. But the major part of one's purpose is to lead the hearer to *satisfy* the want. To that extent the words are used dynamically.

It very frequently happens that the same sentence may have a dynamic use on one occasion and not on another, and that it may have different dynamic uses on different occasions. For instance: A man says to a visiting neighbor, "I am loaded down with work." His purpose may be to let the neighbor know how life is going with him. This would *not* be a dynamic use of words. He may make the remark, however, in order to drop a hint. This *would* be dynamic usage (as well as descriptive). Again, he may make the remark to arouse the neighbor's sympathy. This would be a *different* dynamic usage from that of hinting.

Or again, when we say to a man, "of course you won't make those mistakes any more," we *may* simply be making a prediction. But we are more likely to be using "suggestion," in order to encourage him and hence *keep* him from making mistakes. The first use would be descriptive, the second, mainly dynamic.

From these examples it will be clear that we can not determine whether words are used dynamically or not merely by reading the dictionary —even assuming that everyone is faithful to dictionary meanings. Indeed, to know whether a person is using a word dynamically we must note his tone of voice, his gestures, the general circumstances under which he is speaking, and so on.

We must now proceed to an important question: What has the dynamic use of words to do with their *meaning*? One thing is clear—we must not define "meaning" in a way that would make meaning vary with dynamic usage. If we did, we should have no use for the term. All that we could say about such "meaning" would be that it is very complicated and subject to constant change. So we must certainly distinguish between the dynamic use of words and their meaning.

It does not follow, however, that we must define "meaning" in some nonpsychological fashion. We must simply restrict the psychological field. Instead of identifying meaning with *all* the psychological causes and effects that attend a word's utterance, we must identify it with those that it has a *tendency* (causal property, dispositional property) to be connected with. The tendency must be of a particular kind, moreover. It must exist for all who speak the language; it must be persistent and must be realizable more or less independently of determinate circumstances attending the word's utterance. There will be further restrictions dealing with the interrelations of words in different contexts. Moreover, we must include, under the psychological responses which the words tend to produce, not only immediately introspectable experiences but *dispositions* to react in a given way with appropriate stimuli. I hope to go into these matters in a subsequent essay.[6] Suffice it now to say that I think "meaning" may be thus defined in a way to include "propositional" meaning as an important kind.

The definition will readily permit a distinction between meaning and dynamic use. For when words are accompanied by dynamic purposes, it does not follow that they *tend* to be accompanied by them in the way mentioned above. E.g., there need be no tendency realizable more or less independently of the determinate circumstances under which the words are uttered.

There will be a kind of meaning, however, in the sense above defined, which has an intimate relation to dynamic usage. I refer to "emotive" meaning (in a sense roughly like that employed by Ogden and Richards).[7] The emotive meaning of a word is a tendency of a word, arising through the history of its usage, to produce (result from) *affective* responses in

---

[6] The "subsequent essay" became, instead, Chapter 3 of *Ethics and Language*, which among other points defends those that follow:

(1) When used in a generic sense that emphasizes what C. W. Morris calls the *pragmatic* aspects of language, the term "meaning" designates a tendency of words to express or evoke states of mind in the people who use the words. The tendency is of a special kind, however, and many qualifications are needed (including some that bear on syntax) to specify its nature.

(2) When the states of mind in question are cognitive, the meaning can conveniently be called *descriptive*; and when they are feelings, emotions, or attitudes, the meanings can conveniently be called *emotive*.

(3) The states of mind (in a rough and tentative sense of that term) are normally quite complicated. They are not necessarily images or feelings but may in their turn be further tendencies—tendencies to respond to various stimuli that may subsequently arise. A word may have a constant meaning, accordingly, even though it is accompanied, at various times that it is used, by different images or feelings.

(4) Emotive meaning is sometimes more than a by-product of descriptive meaning. When a term has both sorts of meaning, for example, a change in its descriptive meaning may not be attended by a change in emotive meaning.

(5) When a speaker's use of emotive terms evokes an attitude in a hearer (as it sometimes may not, since it has only a *tendency* to do so), it must not be conceived as merely adding to the hearer's attitude in the way that a spark might add its heat to the atmosphere. For a more appropriate analogy, in many cases, we must think rather of a spark that ignites tinder.

[7] See C. K. Ogden and I. A. Richards, *The Meaning of Meaning* (2nd ed. London, 1927). On p. 125 there is a passage on ethics which is the source of the ideas embodied in this essay.

people. It is the immediate aura of feeling which hovers about a word.[8] Such tendencies to produce affective responses cling to words very tenaciously. It would be difficult, for instance, to express merriment by using the interjection "alas." Because of the persistence of such affective tendencies (among other reasons) it becomes feasible to classify them as "meanings."

Just *what* is the relation between emotive meaning and the dynamic use of words? Let us take an example. Suppose that a man tells his hostess, at the end of a party, that he thoroughly enjoyed himself, and suppose that he was in fact bored. If we consider his remark an innocent one, are we likely to remind him, later, that he "lied" to his hostess? Obviously not, or at least, not without a broad smile; for although he told her something that he believed to be false, and with the intent of making her believe that it was true—those being the ordinary earmarks of a lie—the expression, "you lied to her," would be emotively too strong for our purposes. It would seem to be a reproach, even if we intended it not to be a reproach. So it will be evident that such words as "lied" (and many parallel examples could be cited) become suited, on account of their emotive meaning, to a certain kind of dynamic use—so well suited, in fact, that the hearer is likely to be misled when we use them in any other way. The more pronounced a word's emotive meaning is, the less likely people are to use it purely descriptively. Some words are suited to encourage people, some to discourage them, some to quiet them, and so on.

Even in these cases, of course, the dynamic purposes are not to be identified with any sort of meaning; for the emotive meaning accompanies a word much more persistently than do the dynamic purposes. But there is an important contingent relation between emotive meaning and dynamic purpose: the former assists the latter. Hence if we define emotively laden terms in a way that neglects their emotive meaning, we become seriously confused. *We lead people to think that the terms defined are used dynamically less often than they are.*

---

[8] In *Ethics and Language* the phrase "aura of feeling" was expressly repudiated. If the present essay had been more successful in anticipating the analysis given in that later work, it would have introduced the notion of emotive meaning in some such way as this:

The emotive meaning of a word or phrase is a strong and persistent tendency, built up in the course of linguistic history, to give direct expression (quasi-interjectionally) to certain of the speaker's feelings or emotions or attitudes; and it is also a tendency to evoke (quasi-imperatively) corresponding feelings, emotions, or attitudes in those to whom the speaker's remarks are addressed. It is the emotive meaning of a word, accordingly, that leads us to characterize it as *laudatory* or *derogatory*—that rather generic characterization being of particular importance when we are dealing with terms like "good" and "bad" or "right and wrong." But emotive meanings are of great variety: they may yield terms that express or evoke horror, amazement, sadness, sympathy, and so on.

4

Let us now apply these remarks in defining "good." This word may be used morally or nonmorally. I shall deal with the nonmoral usage almost entirely, but only because it is simpler. The main points of the analysis will apply equally well to either usage.

As a preliminary definition let us take an inaccurate approximation. It may be more misleading than helpful but will do to begin with. Roughly, then, the sentence "X is good" means we *like* X. ("We" includes the hearer or hearers.)

At first glance this definition sounds absurd. If used, we should expect to find the following sort of conversation: A. "This is good." B. "But I *don't* like it. What led you to believe that I did?" The unnaturalness of B's reply, judged by ordinary word usage, would seem to cast doubt on the relevance of my definition.

B's unnaturalness, however, lies simply in this: he is assuming that "we like it" (as would occur implicitly in the use of "good") is being used descriptively. This will not do. When "we like it" is to take the place of "this is good," the former sentence must be used not purely descriptively, but dynamically. More specifically, it must be used to promote a very subtle (and for the nonmoral sense in question, a very easily resisted) kind of *suggestion*. To the extent that "we" refers to the hearer it must have the dynamic use, essential to suggestion, of leading the hearer to *make* true what is said, rather than merely to believe it. And to the extent that "we" refers to the speaker, the sentence must have not only the descriptive use of indicating belief about the speaker's interest, but the quasi-interjectory, dynamic function of giving direct expression to the interest. (This immediate expression of feelings assists in the process of suggestion. It is difficult to disapprove in the face of another's enthusiasm.)

For an example of a case where "we like this" is used in the dynamic way that "this is good" is used, consider the case of a mother who says to her several children, "one thing is certain, *we all like to be neat.*" If she really believed this, she would not bother to say so. But she is not using the words descriptively. She is *encouraging* the children to like neatness. By telling them that they like neatness, she will lead them to *make* her statement true, so to speak. If, instead of saying "we all like to be neat" in this way, she had said "it's a good thing to be neat," the effect would have been approximately the same.

But these remarks are still misleading. Even when "we like it" is used for suggestion, it is not quite like "this is good." The latter is more subtle. With such a sentence as "this is a good book," for example, it would be practically impossible to use instead "we like this book." When the latter is used it must be accompanied by so exaggerated an intonation, to prevent its becoming confused with a descriptive statement, that the force of suggestion becomes stronger and ludicrously more overt than when "good" is used.

The definition is inadequate, further, in that the definiens has been restricted to dynamic usage. Having said that dynamic usage was different from meaning, I should not have to mention it in giving the *meaning* of "good."

It is in connection with this last point that we must return to emotive meaning. The word "good" has a laudatory emotive meaning that fits it for the dynamic use of suggesting favorable interest. But the sentence "we like it" has no such emotive meaning. Hence my definition has neglected emotive meaning entirely. Now to neglect emotive meaning serves to foster serious confusions, as I have previously intimated; so I have sought to make up for the inadequacy of the definition by letting the restriction about dynamic usage take the place of emotive meaning. What I should do, of course, is to find a definiens whose emotive meaning, like that of "good," simply does *lead* to dynamic usage.

Why did I not do this? I answer that it is not possible if the definition is to afford us increased clarity. No two words, in the first place, have quite the same emotive meaning. The most we can hope for is a rough approximation. But if we seek for such an approximation for "good," we shall find nothing more than synonyms, such as "desirable" or "valuable"; and these are profitless because they do not clear up the connection between "good" and favorable interest. If we reject such synonyms, in favor of nonethical terms, we shall be highly misleading. For instance "this is good" has something like the meaning of "I *do* like this: do so as well." But this is certainly not accurate. For the imperative makes an appeal to the conscious efforts of the hearer. Of course he cannot like something just by trying. He must be led to like it through suggestion. Hence an ethical sentence differs from an imperative in that it enables one to make changes in a much more subtle, less fully conscious way. Note that the ethical sentence centers the hearer's attention not on his interests but on the object of interest, and thereby facilitates suggestion. Because of its subtlety, moreover, an ethical sentence readily permits counter-suggestion and leads to the give and take situation that is so characteristic of arguments about values.

Strictly speaking, then, it is impossible to define "good" in terms of favorable interest if emotive meaning is not to be distorted. Yet it is possible to say that "this is good" is *about* the favorable interest of the speaker and the hearer or hearers, and that it has a laudatory emotive meaning which fits the words for use in suggestion. This is a rough description of meaning, not a definition. But it serves the same clarifying function that a definition ordinarily does, and that, after all, is enough.

A word must be added about the moral use of "good." This differs from the above in that it is about a different kind of interest. Instead of being about what the hearer and speaker *like*, it is about a stronger sort of approval. When a person *likes* something, he is pleased when it prospers and disappointed when it does not. When a person *morally approves* of something he experiences a rich feeling of security when it prospers and is indignant or "shocked" when it does not. These are rough and inaccurate examples of the many factors which one would have to mention in distinguishing the two kinds of interest. In the moral usage, as well as in the nonmoral, "good" has an emotive meaning which adapts it to suggestion.

And now, are these considerations of any importance? Why do I stress emotive meanings in this fashion? Does the omission of them really lead people into errors? I think, indeed, that the errors resulting from such omissions are enormous. In order to see this, however, we must return to the restrictions, mentioned in Section 1, with which the typical sense of "good" has been expected to comply.

5

The first restriction, it will be remembered, had to do with disagreement. Now there is clearly some sense in which people disagree on ethical points, but we must not rashly assume that all disagreement is modeled after the sort that occurs in the natural sciences. We must distinguish between "disagreement in belief" (typical of the sciences) and "disagreement in interest." Disagreement in belief occurs when A believes *p* and B disbelieves it. Disagreement in interest occurs when A has a favorable interest in X and when B has an unfavorable one in it. (For a full-bodied disagreement, neither party is content with the discrepancy.)

Let me give an example of disagreement in interest. A. "Let's go to a cinema tonight." B. "I don't want to do that. Let's go to the symphony." A continues to insist on the cinema, B on the symphony. This is disagreement in a perfectly conventional sense. They cannot agree on where they want to go, and each is trying to redirect the other's interest. (Note that imperatives are used in the example.)

It is disagreement in *interest* which takes places in ethics. When C says "this is good," and D says "no, it's bad," we have a case of suggestion and counter-suggestion. Each man is trying to redirect the other's interest. There obviously need be no domineering, since each may be willing to give ear to the other's influence; but each is trying to move the other none the less. It is in this sense that they disagree. Those who argue that certain interest theories make no provision for disagreement have been misled, I believe, simply because the traditional theories, in leaving out emotive meaning, give the impression that ethical judgments are used descriptively only; and of course when judgments are used purely descriptively, the only disagreement that can arise is disagreement *in belief*. Such disagreement may be disagreement in belief *about* interests, but this is not the same as disagreement *in* interest. My definition does not provide for disagreement in belief about interests any more than does Hobbes'; but that is no matter, for there is no reason to believe, at least on common sense grounds, that this kind of disagreement exists. There is only disagreement *in* interest. (We shall see in a moment that disagreement in interest does not remove ethics from sober argument—that this kind of disagreement may often be resolved through empirical means.)

The second restriction, about "magnetism," or the connection between goodness and actions, requires only a word. This rules out only those interest theories that do *not* include the interest of the speaker in defining "good." My account does include the speaker's interest, hence is immune.

The third restriction, about the empirical method, may be met in a way that springs naturally from the above account of disagreement. Let us put the question in this way: When two people disagree over an ethical matter, can they completely resolve the disagreement through empirical considerations, assuming that each applies the empirical method exhaustively, consistently, and without error?

I answer that sometimes they can and sometimes they cannot, and that at any rate, even when they can, the relation between empirical knowledge and ethical judgments is quite different from the one that traditional interest theories seem to imply.

This can best be seen from an analogy. Let us return to the example where A and B could not agree on a cinema or a symphony. The example differed from an ethical argument in that imperatives were used, rather than ethical judgments, but was analogous to the extent that each person was endeavoring to modify the other's interest. Now how would these people argue the case, assuming that they were too intelligent just to shout at one another?

Clearly, they would give "reasons" to support their imperatives. A might say, "but you know, Garbo is at the Bijou." His hope is that B, who admires Garbo, will acquire a desire to go to the cinema when he knows what film will be there. B may counter, "but Toscanini is guest conductor tonight, in an all-Beethoven program." And so on. Each supports his imperative (*"let's* do so and so") by reasons which may be empirically established.

To generalize from this: disagreement in interest may be rooted in disagreement in belief. That is to say, people who disagree in interest would often cease to do so if they knew the precise nature and consequences of the object of their interest. To this extent disagreement in interest may be resolved by securing agreement in belief, which in turn may be secured empirically.

This generalization holds for ethics. If A and B, instead of using imperatives, had said, respectively, "it would be *better* to go to the cinema," and "it would be better to go to the symphony," the reasons which they would advance would be roughly the same. They would each give a more thorough account of the object of interest, with the purpose of completing the redirection of interest which was begun by the suggestive force of the ethical sentence. On the whole, of course, the suggestive force of the ethical statement merely exerts enough pressure to start such trains of reasons, since the reasons are much more essential in resolving disagreement in interest than the persuasive effect of the ethical judgment itself.

Thus the empirical method is relevant to ethics simply because our knowledge of the world is a determining factor to our interests. But note that empirical facts are not inductive grounds from which the ethical judgment problematically follows. (This is what traditional interest theories imply.) If someone said "close the door," and added the reason "we'll catch cold," the latter would scarcely be called an inductive ground of the former. Now imperatives are related to the reasons which support them in the same way that ethical judgments are related to reasons.

Is the empirical method *sufficient* for attaining ethical agreement? Clearly not. For empirical knowledge resolves disagreement in interest only to the extent that such disagreement is rooted in disagreement in belief. Not all disagreement in interest is of this sort. For instance: A is of a sympathetic nature and B is not. They are arguing about whether a public dole would be good. Suppose that they discovered all the consequences of the dole. Is it not possible, even so, that A will say that it is good and B that it is bad? The disagreement in interest may arise not from limited factual knowledge but simply from A's sympathy and B's coldness. Or again, suppose in the above argument that A was poor and unemployed and that B was rich. Here again the disagreement might not be due to different factual knowledge. It would be due to the different social positions of the men, together with their predominant self-interest.

When ethical disagreement is not rooted in disagreement in belief, is there *any* method by which it may be settled? If one means by "method" a *rational* method, then there is no method. But in any case there is a "way." Let us consider the above example again, where disagreement was due to A's sympathy and B's coldness. Must they end by saying, "well, it's just a matter of our having different temperaments"? Not necessarily. A, for instance, may try to *change* the temperament of his opponent. He may pour out his enthusiasms in such a moving way—present the sufferings of the poor with such appeal—that he will lead his opponent to see life through different eyes. He may build up by the contagion of his feelings an influence which will modify B's temperament and create in him a sympathy for the poor which did not previously exist. This is often the only way to obtain ethical agreement, if there is any way at all. It is persuasive, not empirical or rational; but that is no reason for neglecting it. There is no reason to scorn it, either, for it is only by such means that our personalities are able to grow, through our contact with others.

The point I wish to stress, however, is simply that the empirical method is instrumental to ethical agreement only to the extent that disagreement in interest is rooted in disagreement in belief. There is little reason to believe that all disagreement is of this sort. Hence the empirical method is not sufficient for ethics. In any case, ethics is not psychology, since psychology does not endeavor to *direct* our interests; it discovers facts about the ways in which interests are or can be directed, but that is quite another matter.

To summarize this section: my analysis of ethical judgments meets the three requirements for the typical sense of "good" that were mentioned in Section 1. The traditional interest theories fail to meet these requirements simply because they neglect emotive meaning. This neglect leads them to neglect dynamic usage, and the sort of disagreement that results from such usage, together with the method of resolving the disagreement. I may add that my analysis answers Moore's objection about the open question. Whatever scientifically knowable properties a thing may have, it *is* always open to question whether a thing having these (enumerated) qualities is good. For to ask whether it is good is to ask for *influence*. And whatever I may know about an object, I can still ask, quite pertinently, to be influenced with regard to my interest in it.

6

And now, have I really pointed out the "typical" sense of "good"?

I suppose that many will still say "no," claiming that I have simply failed to set down *enough* requirements that this sense must meet, and that my analysis, like all others given in terms of interest, is a way of begging the issue. They will say: "When we ask 'is X good?' we don't want mere influence, mere advice. We decidedly don't want to be influenced through persuasion, nor are we fully content when the influence is supported by a wide scientific knowledge of X. The answer to our question will, of course, modify our interests. But this is only because a unique sort of truth will be revealed to us—a truth that must be apprehended a priori. We want our interests to be guided by this truth and by nothing else. To substitute for this special truth mere emotive meaning and mere factual truth is to conceal from us the very object of our search."

I can only answer that I do not understand. What is this truth to be *about*? For I recollect no Platonic Idea, nor do I know what to *try* to recollect. I find no indefinable property nor do I know what to look for. And the "self-evident" deliverances of reason, which so many philosophers have mentioned, seem on examination to be deliverances of their respective reasons only (if of anyone's) and not of mine.

I strongly suspect, indeed, that any sense of "good" which is expected both to unite itself in synthetic a priori fashion with other concepts and to influence interests as well, is really a great confusion. I extract from this meaning the power of influence alone, which I find the only intelligible part. If the rest is confusion, however, then it certainly deserves more than the shrug of one's shoulders. What I should like to do is to *account* for the confusion—to examine the psychological needs which have given rise to it and show how these needs may be satisfied in another way. This is *the* problem, if confusion is to be stopped at its source. But it is an enormous problem and my reflections on it, which are at present worked out only roughly, must be reserved until some later time.

I may add that if "X is good" has the meaning that I ascribe to it, then it is not a judgment that professional philosophers and only professional philosophers are qualified to make. To the extent that ethics predicates the ethical terms of anything, rather that explains their meaning, it becomes more than a purely intellectual study. Ethical judgments are social instruments. They are used in a cooperative enterprise that leads to a mutual readjustment of human interests. Philosophers have a part in this; but so too do all men.

Goading and Guiding

W. D. FALK

1

Some years ago, it was said 'we are now happy about ethics'. The thanks were due to the emotive theory. There are signs now of a more reflective mood. The new therapy has revived the patient, but he is still too unlike his once boisterous self. What then has gone wrong?

Hume said of moral judgments that they 'are supposed to influence our passions and actions, and go beyond the calm and indolent judgments

From Mind, *LXII (1953). Reprinted by permission of the author and* Mind.

of the understanding'. Much of the merit of the modern approach lies, I think, in the development of his observation. What is stressed is the similarity between moral and other kinds of prescriptive speech. 'You ought not to smoke here' is more like 'Don't smoke here' than like 'Smoking is expensive here'. It is typically said for direction, as a way of telling someone to *do* something; not just for *instruction*, 'calmly' as a piece of gossip or information. We cannot say 'you ought' and deny that we meant to influence, or be surprised at having said something evocative. Hence, we shall not get to the bottom of moral speech unless we treat the study of it as part of a study of language as an instrument of persuasion and practical direction, rather than one purely of the dissemination of knowledge.

Observations like these have given a fresh impulse to enquiry; and so far so good. But there are bigger claims; they are also said to entail a new solution. 'You ought to' plays a practical role like 'do'; hence it also shares its logical properties; it is another and specialized way of using the imperative mood. There are good reasons why this suggestion should have been welcomed. Ethical theory of the recent past has culminated in what to many appears a dilemma. If moral statements were to assert moral truths, these would allow in principle of only two interpretations: such as are 'naturalistic' and false, and such as are nonnaturalistic and, except to the initiated, mystifying. To me, this disjunction is neither unambiguous, nor convincing. But, if accepted, it may well appear a dilemma; and the emotive theory has the merit of evading it without having to deny it. Its welcome has been proportionate to the hope of relief it raised. But this welcome would not be justified purely on the ground that if true the theory would dispose of an embarrassment. It will not dispose of anything unless it is true; and the test for this must be in its conformity with linguistic usage. This conformity is being claimed for it; I shall try to show on insufficient grounds.

I shall press here only one point. It is not contended that moral statements are *simply* imperatives. Stevenson calls them 'quasi-imperatives', stressing that they are different from ordinary ones. And this is as well, for plainly 'you ought to' has at best a similar use, not the same use as 'do'. 'You ought not to smoke here' cannot be replaced by 'anyway, don't' without a drastic change of tune. But, then, is it safe to say that 'you ought to' *is* only a special way of saying 'do'? Surely not, unless the dissimilarities have been scrutinized as well as the resemblances. What is the special work which 'you ought to' does and 'do' does not do? There is evasion on this point, covered by remarks about the dangers of pressing language too hard. But language, though flexible, is not without definite shapes which pressing, and only hard pressing, can reveal; and there can be no assurance that 'you ought to' is logically like 'do', unless the dissimilarities have been pressed, and shown to be irrelevant to the issue. The emotive theory lies open to attack on this point.

It may be said 'but we are agreed "you ought to" tells someone to *do* things, and not just *about* things; what else then should it be but a way of saying "do"?' It often seems that there is implicit reliance on this. If 'you ought' serves to change 'attitudes', that it should also serve to impart some elusive species of moral belief is treated as a plain case for Ockham's razor. Yet might 'you ought to' not also play its practical role not by being a kind of ordering, but the communicating of a special evocative truth? This alternative receives scanty consideration; there are even suggestions that it can be in principle ruled out. I shall try to show that complacency on this point is as unjustified as on the previous one.

2

As a preliminary, two slogans need disposing of which have all too easily gained currency.

One is that moral statements cannot be assertions, since we are agreed to call them 'normative,' and a normative statement is one like 'keep off the grass', one which gives an order, 'prescribes a norm'. This short way with dissenters turns on an unsettled point of language. One can grant that, 'normative statement' tends to suggest 'statement that prescribes a norm'. But the term is not one of ordinary language, and there are no settled rules for using it; and it is certain that if there were no other use, there would be no general agreement about using it of moral statements. In fact, it is obvious how it has been used in the past. Moral statements have been treated as an analogue of statements *reporting* that some law is in force, the sort of statements *about* the state of the law that are made by solicitors, jurists, and legal commentaries; they were called 'normative' in the sense of a 'statement about a norm, or prescription'. And this is a defensible alternative to the use of 'normative statement' for one which *issues* a prescription, or *enunciates* a law, like the statements found in legal statutes or public notices. The point of the present controversy is whether moral statements are more properly conceived as being in type like a 'normative' statement in the one or in the other sense. This issue cannot be prejudged by reference to the unsettled usage of a technical term.

Confusions of greater interest are contained in another argument. 'You ought to', it is said, cannot be an assertion about a kind of law because of its admitted practical role. It serves to tell others to do things; hence it does not serve to tell them *that* something is the case, whether the state of some law or anything else. Professor Barnes, in a paper on Ethics without Propositions, has made the point by asking rhetorically 'how *can* a statement both assert a fact and prescribe a norm?' It is assumed that it is plain that it cannot. And, in a sense, this is correct. One can ask: what is the *point,* the characteristic objective, of a prescriptive utterance, a command, entreaty, warning, admonition? It is proper to reply, to induce people to *do* things, and *not* to tell them a story; to be evocative, and *not* to be informative. In this sense, a statement used to 'prescribe a norm' is obviously not one used to 'assert a fact'. But also, this is trivial, and to let the matter rest here misleading. One could not say either that 'to fish' *is* 'to sit by the water holding a rod'; for the point about fishing is not this, but to try and catch fish. But one could not use this as an argument to show that one cannot both fish and sit by the water holding a rod. On the contrary, the latter, though it *is* not to fish, may yet be the way we fish, or part of the way, or one way among others. The same applies when one says that to speak prescriptively *is* not to tell a story. This does not entail in the slightest that one cannot speak prescriptively by way of telling a story, or that this cannot be part of how it is done, or be one way among others.

In fact, quite evidently, the contrary is the case. It is commonly said that orders are not used to tell that something is the case, and certainly 'get out' is not meant to *state* a fact. But 'I want you to leave' may also be an order; and, among other things, it uses as a means of being evocative a statement about the speaker's wishes. An order becomes 'unconvincing', among other things, when we think the speaker is untruthful or in error in what he communicates about his wishes. Orders in the imperative mood do not of course make *statements* about the speaker's wishes; and they are the paradigm of an utterance which is purely presciptive without being assertive. But the imperative mood is only one way of giving orders, a point too commonly overlooked; moreover, orders in the imperative mood rely also, as a rule, on communicating some matter of fact. 'Leave me alone' is not *saying* 'I want you to leave me' but we use it to *convey* this, by the use of descriptive terms together with a conventional grammatical sign, as surely as if we had said it. A story may be told by hinting at it, as well as by expressly stating it; and the imperative mood is, among other things, a conventional formula for giving a hint.

Moreover, it is onesided to refer to orders as the only way in which we can prescribe to others. 'You will burst if you don't stop eating' is not an order; but it may do the work of 'stop eating'. In either case, you cannot complain that you had not been warned. But 'you will burst if . . . ' obviously relies for being a warning on making a statement of fact. As a warning, its point is to influence, and not to tell a story; but also it is the type of warning that depends for effect primarily on telling a deterrent story, and on having it believed. A statement like this may be as manifestly evocative in tone and manner as an order, but it aims at 'changing attitudes' only by way of 'imparting beliefs'. One can ask 'what did it say?' and 'was it true?'

The case is of special interest for our problem. For plainly there may also be warnings which rely for effect on a statement *about* a prescription. 'Smoking is forbidden here' may be used to restrain a fellow traveler, as well as 'you are making me cough', or 'don't'. Here the state of some law is reported, not however for information, as in a lecture on railway by-laws, but for direction, as a way of telling someone to stop doing something. A report on anyone's order or plea may be so used. Father's 'don't be home after ten' will be a prescription, manifestly evocative in purpose and manner. Mother's 'father says don't' may report this, and the reporting may be no less prescriptive and in purpose and manner manifestly evocative. So far then from it being the case that a statement cannot both be prescriptive and assert a fact, it may well be *prescriptive by way of asserting a fact about a prescription*; and if orders can perform a practical role, so can reports about them.

The new observations about the evocative character of saying 'you ought' should not therefore lead to premature conclusions. They may imply that 'you ought not to smoke here' is a way of saying 'don't'; but they need not. They could also be compatible with the traditional view that it is a way of saying 'smoking is forbidden here'. All that they demand is that moral speech should be accounted for in a way that explains how it has the pre-eminently prescriptive capacity which its use exhibits. The candidates are to be looked for either in a specially evocative way of speaking, or in a way of saying something specially fit to be evocative. Whether the case for the one or the other is the stronger, must depend on further considerations.

3

If one were to treat the matter purely as one of tracking down a quarry from the traces left by it here and there, how should one proceed? There is, I think, an approach which has not yet sufficiently been tried out. We are agreed that 'you ought to' is prescriptive; we are in doubt whether it is so after the manner of 'do', or 'the law says'. Both forms are, or may be, used to direct others, but they differ in type; 'do' goes about directing others in one way, 'the law says', or 'you are making me cough' in another. The differences extend to the logic, the methods, and the evocative attitudes typical of each form.

These differences have not passed unnoticed; they are referred to in recent discussions as the differences between 'nonrational' and 'rational' methods of persuasion. But they have not been explored sufficiently, and there has been bias in the treatment of 'rational methods' as largely a way of 'supporting' nonrational methods of persuasion by other means. With a clearer view of these two types of approach it will become possible to locate more reliably the place of moral speech on the logical map.

Let me illustrate what I mean. If one says 'do', 'please do', 'I want you to', 'I should be glad if you did', one will not deny that one is telling or asking someone to do something; and this is one type of evocative address. But if one merely says pointedly 'smoking is forbidden here', or 'heavy smokers die early', and the other retorts, with a touch of indignation, 'are you telling or asking me to stop?', then one *might* reply, 'not at all, I was merely pointing out a fact, I was making no demand'. But the denial would be thin. It would be met by 'surely, you were not saying this merely to let me know, but to make me *do* something'. And the fair reply would be 'well, then, I was *indirectly* telling or asking you to do something; but still not straightout or directly'. One would have used an evocative address, but of different type.

The two types may be referred to respectively as 'direct' and 'indirect' performances of telling or asking. The first comprises most, though not all, speech in the imperative mood, and any other statement which can be said to be a way of *straightout* making a demand. The other comprises any statement, used evocatively, on which one can comment by saying 'I was not directly telling or asking you to do anything, I was merely saying so and so'. The distinction is logically basic to prescriptive speech, and cuts across its grammatical forms. The imperative mood is not always used for a direct telling or asking; it is not in 'my advice is, do this', or in 'take ten eggs'. Mrs. Beeton is not telling us to cook, but how to cook; and to make recommendations is incompatible with making demands. Conversely, all three of 'I want you to go', 'your bus is about to leave', 'if you don't leave, I shall show you the door', use a statement of fact or prediction, and all may be prescriptive. But the first, as a rule, tells directly, and is used like 'go'; the second tells indirectly; and the third, a threat, is characteristically in between the two.

Furthermore, there are striking differences in detail. A policeman may warn 'parking is forbidden here', or order 'I want you to move on.' One would say that one complied with the warning 'because of what was said', with the order 'because one was told to'. People are good at indirect pleading when they are apt at convincing others; good at direct pleading when they know how to speak with firmness, charm, or pathos. One would call some-one rude, disobedient, or disobliging if 'do stop smoking' met with no response; but not rude, only perverse, weakminded, or difficult to convince, if 'heavy smokers die early' met the same fate. There is some measure of coercion in every direct telling or asking, even the mildest 'please'; one feels one is being *goaded* into responding. But coercive intention can be denied of every indirect plea; the speaker can claim that he is only trying to *guide,* not to *goad;* he is not himself doing the urging, he is only 'letting the facts speak' for him. 'I am not saying "go", only your bus is about to leave'; 'not saying "don't play with matches"', only people burn their fingers if they do'; 'not saying "don't drive so fast"', only it is against the law'. One will bring up one's children quite differently whether one favors the one or the other approach. Their comparative merits, as ways of directing other people, are a matter for debate among educationalists, moralists, and politicians.

Here are tests which should help to settle to what family of utterance 'you ought to' belongs. Is it compatible, or not, with the disclaimer 'I am not telling or asking you to, I am only saying you ought to'? Can one say 'you ought to' and claim one is only seeking to guide, not at all to goad? Does one comply because it was said impressively, or because one was convinced of what it said? Would one be in tune in calling someone rude, disobliging or disobedient for being deaf to having been told 'you ought to'? Or should one only call him hard to convince, perverse, or weakminded? Tests like these should be of use. They will still not be enough to run down what exactly 'you ought to' is used to do. They will only show whether in type it does the work of a direct or indirect telling, is more like 'do', or like 'the law says'; and it is certain that, whichever of the two it resembles more, it does not exactly do the work of either, but one peculiar to itself. But there would have been a methodical narrowing down of the direction for further enquiry.

I shall take up the question of these comparisons in the last part of this paper. My first and main concern must be with the two prototypes and the contrast between them.

4

What is it to be directly prescriptive? In the first place, what is the method? It has been referred to as 'nonrational,' and contrasted with the 'rational method' of persuading by telling an evocative story. But this is too simple. Direct pleading *may* be entirely 'nonrational' in its methods, but it is not so as a rule, only in marginal cases. 'Shoo' if said to drive away the cat, or 'attention' on the parade ground, are orders which don't rely on telling any story. The cat could not grasp a story, the well-drilled soldier need not. Effect is sought here not by using speech to relate something evocative, but to make an evocative noise: one to which, one hopes, cats are constitutionally ill-disposed, and to which soldiers have been drilled to respond as the 'mere word of command'. But the more usual forms of direct pleading do not rely purely on the act of speaking and its manner. 'I want you to go', we have noted, states a fact, and 'go' signalizes what 'I want you to go' states. The speaker relies on a communication being understood and believed; and the same applies to threats or bribes which may support direct pleading. They either state or hint at matters of fact calculated to be evocative.

It is characteristic of direct pleas that, threats and bribes apart, what they put forward for persuasion are the speaker's own wishes, and never an impersonal fact like 'your bus is about to leave'. But the mere fact that they voice our wishes does not make them directly prescriptive either. I may say 'I want you to stay', and add, 'but please I am not telling or asking you to, and don't feel committed by my saying so; just bear it in mind'. Here I have voiced my wishes persuasively, but divested my doing so of being directly prescriptive.

What makes pleading direct is not therefore that it never relies on telling a story calculated to be evocative, but that this is never *all* that it relies on. Characteristically, when one is anxious to get one's way, one troubles to *voice* one's wishes, even when thinking them known. *That* one voices them, one thinks, will add to the impressiveness of the known fact one is voicing; and there is a familiar excuse for inaction in saying 'I guessed your wishes well enough, but after all you did not say so'. The force of an asking is in the saying, not only in what is said.

Much combines to make speaking impressive. I have mentioned the evocative impact of sounds; and no less hypnotic in effect may be gestures, facial expressions, and the whole impact of the speaker's personality. A telling or asking is more impressive in person than over the telephone or by letter.

Moreover, in addition to the story told and the mechanics of telling it, there is the force of the story that transpires from the telling. Saying 'I want you to' is something one does to influence someone; it is the display in action of the same desire one reports. The speaker is not, and could not, be saying that it is this: a statement cannot be used to comment upon itself. The speaker cannot report that he is ordering or asking in the same words in which he does so. But the story of one's purpose in speaking can transpire; the hearer can piece it together from one's tone of voice, the fact that one volunteers one's wants, the circumstances in which one does. One is not thought to have made a request when one says 'I want you to', or 'do this' in answer to a question about one's wishes. Any prescriptive utterance thus tends to manifest something about one's own mood and concern in speaking; and in direct pleading one relies for effect on what one's speaking makes manifest as much as on what it says.

Furthermore, merely because one has spoken, others will find it harder to resist one. One has shown one's hand and courted rebuff, created a situation which others may be too timid, too softhearted or too embarrassed to resist. One has committed them by what one is *doing* to give consideration to more than what one is *saying*.

Finally, some of these effects can also be bettered deliberately. One can vary the direct force, and the suggestiveness, of one's voice or bearing, or wear down others by sheer persistence. Direct pleading can be a skill, if not an art.

All this makes it direct. The act of relating one's wishes, complete with what it both says and shows about itself, its manner, and the situation it creates, is one's act of telling or asking; and persuasion is made dependent on the whole act: directly on what one is *doing,* and not merely indirectly on what one is *saying.* Hence the way people explain their compliance with direct pleas: 'because one was told to'; not just 'because one was told something'.

Hence also the catch in asking in relation to an order 'what did he tell you about?', and 'was it true?' This does not apply to a saying whose persuasive significance on the whole is in what it is trying on, not in what it is trying to say. But the present fashion is to oversimplify this. There is generally something which, in giving an order, is meant to be believed and understood; and this part can be challenged apart from the rest in the ordinary way. 'I don't ever want you to set foot in this house again' by 'I don't believe you; you don't speak the truth, or don't know your own mind'; 'I want you to buy me a horse' by 'what do you mean, a toy horse or a real one?'; 'I want you to lend me your brains' by 'don't talk nonsense'. It depends partly on what is said in the ordering whether an order is 'convincing' and 'clear'; and hence also whether it will be effective. Only this need not be all. Even an order expressed in terms which are unconvincing may carry weight by the sheer force of the giving.

More consideration must be given to the most telling feature of direct pleading, its peculiar coerciveness. Even the mildest 'please' and 'if you don't mind' seems intent on dragging someone where he had not intended to go; and, in complying *purely* on the ground of someone's pleading, one says 'I did it, but not at all voluntarily, only because I was asked to'. One may, of course, buy a child a toy not because of his asking, but thinking it anyway a good thing for him to have it. A telling or asking only coerces if one is made to yield by its own method of persuasion. But the method is intrinsically coercive, and contrasts with others which seek to make people do things, but not otherwise than 'voluntarily'.

This brings up the distinction between 'rational' methods and the 'nonrational' methods of direct pleading. Persuasion by 'rational methods', it is said, is 'purely by reasons' and not coercive. But when are methods 'rational' and when not? Direct pleading surely also provides reasons for doing things; orders, threats, bribes are referred to as supplying them. Why then not here speak of 'rational methods'?

The point is partially met by distinguishing 'reason' from 'cause'. One speaks of a 'reason' where one can ask for the consideration which induced someone to do something; but not all behavior has reasons. A shout makes one flinch, but it is the cause of one's flinching, not the consideration which induced one to flinch; and direct pleading partly *causes* behavior directly by what it does. One may succumb to the policeman's voice or bearing not from any considerations, but like the snake obeying its charmer. This much, direct pleading is the continuation of violence by other means. It is coercive in the sense of controlling others while bypassing, if not paralyzing, any kind of voluntary contribution to their own behavior.

But direct pleas are not always, or entirely obeyed in robot fashion. They are also obeyed for reasons supplied by themselves; by what the speaker says and shows about his wishes and mood, the situation he otherwise creates, and by threats and bribes, and compliance for such reasons is no enforced reflex. 'Ten days in jail if you keep resisting' will make one come 'off one's own bat' rather than be dragged. Surely, this is to yield to 'rational' methods, and 'voluntarily'.

There is a sense in which one persuades by 'rational methods' when one purely adduces or proffers a reason. This is *not* what 'I want you to leave' does. Instead of merely *adducing* a persuasive circumstance by what it says, it *imports* one into the situation by what it does. It does not *proffer,* it *creates* a reason. Threats and bribes, though less obviously so, do the same. 'If you don't leave, I shall show you the door', 'if you do, you can take what you want' does in form proffer a reason. It has the air of being indirectly prescriptive. 'I am not telling or asking, am I? I am merely saying so and so'. But the air is spurious, for the reason which is proffered is also imported. The situation would not contain it independently, as a preexisting feature; it only will for the speaker's deliberate intervention.

Compared with having force used on one's body or nervous system to yield to put up incentives is to yield to 'rational methods' and 'voluntarily'. But, in another use of these terms, this would be a travesty of the facts. A child is not taking its medicine 'purely of its own accord' if only because it was offered a sweet, or threatened to have to go without it; nor would this be the occasion to boast of how amenable to 'reason' it was. Had it taken the medicine on the ground that it would do it good, this would have been a different matter. Here, what is meant by 'rational methods' is to persuade purely by adducing reasons which preexist in the nature of the act and its circumstances; and by 'acting of one's own accord' to act purely from the consideration that there are such reasons. And, in this sense, telling, asking, threatening, or bribing are the negation of using rational methods, and a way of making people do things otherwise than of their own accord. One does not wait for them to consider a case on its merits, either because one knows there is no case, or does not trust them to appreciate it, or is just impatient to get results. Instead, one creates a case to goad them along, giving them a sense of unfreedom in succumbing. This unfreedom consists in dependence in action on the deliberate intervention of another's will; its contrary is 'doing things freely', not here in any absolute sense, but simply in the sense of depending in action not on anyone else, but purely on considerations relating to the merits of the case.

Not all *goading* however is *coercing.* One is goaded, or coaxed when one is offered a bribe or a tempting deal. But no one can claim that he was coerced by bribery. This is reserved for threats and direct pleas. The point is, the yoke of being goaded may be born willingly or not; and this involves another sense of 'voluntary' cutting across the two distinguished already. What is done to obtain something wanted is said to be done 'voluntarily' or 'willingly'; what is done to avoid something unwanted 'not voluntarily' or 'unwillingly'. Such is the time honored case of the sailor throwing his goods overboard to lighten the ship. There is no paradox in saying that he acted purely voluntarily (on the merits of the case alone, not just under captain's orders), and yet not at all voluntarily or willingly, only under compulsion. Actions from put up incentives may bear these same traits. A bribe solicits action for the sake of obtaining something wanted; a threat for the sake of avoiding something unwanted. Hence when bribed one responds willingly to being goaded, when threatened unwillingly. A threat adds insult to injury. It makes one act otherwise than of one's own accord and for no more than the avoidance of a *trumped-up* unpleasantness. Hence bribes only seduce and corrupt; threats coerce and break the will.

All direct pleading tends to coerce in this way, though with varying insistence. This is plain of tellings which rely for a great part on threats, but it applies also to askings which do not. An asking does not coerce like a threat by holding out a future unpleasantness to be avoided, but by creating a present one to be got rid of. One is called on to comply to escape a quandary put up for one: either to pay ransom, and be badgered no longer, or to make oneself unpleasant. The coercion one yields to is only less patent, but often more insidious, than that of any straight telling.

It has been said that the typical purpose manifested by prescriptive speech is to reach 'agreement in attitude'. One speaks in the first place to make others favor what one oneself desires, to get one's own way with them. I think that, as an account of the typical objectives of *all* prescriptive speech, this is either too vague to be of use, or, if taken at its face value, a travesty of the facts. But it does describe direct pleading. The evocative attitude it manifests is one of 'getting one's own way'.

Actually, in its full sense this notion is complex. It suggests that someone is trying to gain some purely personal, or at least capricious end; that he should be 'goading in aim'; and also an attitude of readiness to gain his end by a liberal use of means, by 'goading in method'. Plainly, must direct pleading is carried out fully in this spirit; it is the characteristic note one often senses in it. But there are variations on the theme. An asking does not display the same evocative attitude as a telling even if they are both goading in their aim. It is self-limiting in its attitude towards the means, and correspondingly in its insistence on gaining the end: one shows that one is restricting oneself to using some means, and not others (not threats or shouts), or is ready to withdraw in some circumstances (if one were to cause avowed inconvenience, as in 'please, if you don't mind'). Some direct pleas, again, may display an uncompromising determination to be goading in method while not being goading in aim. A parent who firmly orders his offspring about may claim he is not doing it for a purely personal or capricious end. Still, all direct pleading is getting one's own way at least by being goading in method; and, frequently, by being goading in aim as well. Nor should the last cause surprise. Direct pleading is exactly suited to the role. It is not restricted to preexisting incentives. It can liberally create them, and pile them up to enforce any end, however purely personal, or capricious. It is the open and natural method for the purpose, with no need either for making bones about it.

5

What is it, by contrast, to be indirectly prescriptive? In most ways, the reverse. One pleads indirectly when one puts forward a fact for consideration, like 'your bus is about to leave'; and the fact must belong to the situation as it is, and not be one of one's own importing. 'If you don't leave, I shall show you the door' resembles an indirect plea, but is none. Moreover, an indirect plea relies *purely* on what it says, on 'letting the facts speak for themselves'; and not also on being a 'telling'. It is a telling, and manifestly so. But it is not effective directly by being a telling, or by showing itself to be one; but indirectly by the story it tells. It is always in place to ask of an indirect telling 'what did it say?', and 'was it true?'

One may state one's own wishes, just as a feature of the situation to be borne in mind; one will then voice them without making a direct plea. But this is exceptional. 'I want you to' is normally part of a direct pleading, and will be so unless one desires otherwise, and takes special steps. One would have to say 'don't take this as a request', 'don't do anything merely because I say so; only if you want to of your own accord', 'just hear the fact in mind'; and one must take care not to spoil one's words by one's deeds, as by an insistent, pathetic, or agitated tone of voice. Otherwise, one will still be taken to be asking.

But as a rule one relates something impersonal of concern to others. Indirect pleading is the way to widen one's persuasive appeal beyond saying 'I want'; and, what is more, this widening of appeal is not logically possible except through pleading which is indirect. No one expects one to put forward one's wishes not 'tellingly', but just for consideration; if one does, it is one's own choice. But one is expected not to put forward impersonal facts, except purely for consideration. To add to 'your bus is about to leave' 'this is not to urge you to go, only to remind you' invites 'naturally, I should expect so'.

This is not to say that impersonal facts may not be related in a deliberately evocative or pleading manner, and the plea succeeds on this account.

People often put them forward not at all intending to give others the chance to be influenced purely 'by a reason', and to act of their own accord alone. They want to be able to appeal to impersonal facts with the aid of the same methods of goading by which one can aid the stating of one's wishes. The point is not that this cannot be done, but that there is an incongruity in doing it. The test is that a too emphatic speaker can here be held up for inconsistency; and an obstinate hearer can pretend that no more surely *could* have been intended than the proffering of a reason. 'Your bus is about to leave' you say firmly, ill-disguising a desire to see the last of me. 'Not yet, in another hour', I can reply uncooperatively; or 'never mind, I need not hurry, there are more buses later'; and you cannot rightly call me rude or disobliging for this. Of, if you do, referring to the pleadingness of your speaking, I can say 'but surely, considering what you *said*, this was neither here nor there. Why not be honest, and tell me to go straightout?' People sometimes act on an admonition or warning, not because the reasons were convincing, but quietly taking a hint, or being browbeaten by firm speaking. But one cannot reasonably expect this, or insist on it; nor should one here say that these were sufficient grounds for yielding.

Why is there a logical bar to stating impersonal facts 'tellingly', but not one's wishes? Because in the first case, what is said, and what is done by the saying diverge in their influence; in the other they converge.

'I want you to go' puts forward one's wishes, and shows and exercises them in the speaking. What is shown makes what is said more impressive, for it confirms and amplifies it; what is done by voice or manner is consistent with the purpose stated and shown. The hearer is subjected to influences all of a piece; if ready to yield to one, he will yield to all unless told not to.

'Your bus is about to leave' puts forward a fact other than one's wishes; and it gives one to understand that this fact alone is to count as incentive. To be precise, this is not *said*. Persuasive statements of this form *state* nothing except a fact about the situation. They don't state, what would be a distinct proposition, *that* the fact is sufficient to provide a reason. But this goes without saying. The story is manifestly told to persuade. Hence the speaker must wish to claim that it provides a reason and a decisive one; for otherwise why tell the story, or this story and not another? The hearer can certainly take him up on what he *said* as much as on what he *implied*: dispute the facts, or grant them and add 'but this is no reason'. And the speaker can expect the hearer to consider that much, but no more.

This is why any impersonal plea is logically indirect. A prescriptive statement manifests the speaker's concern; but the speaker's concern is here irrelevant to the fact on which persuasion has been openly made to turn. The hearer is not committed to consider it, since he was not invited to; nor could he do so without deserting the point openly at issue. An impersonal plea is a challenge to be influenced only by what is said about a feature of the situation, and suggested about it providing a reason. It is met to all in intents when both claims are considered, and as adequately by their honest acceptance or rejection. The speaker cannot therefore grumble if no heed was given to his own persuasive concern, which was shown but not mentioned. He has staked success on asserting something evocative, and impersonal; it is not then either here or there that the assertion should have been made evocatively. In any appeal to impersonal reasons, as distinct from direct pleading, the manifestly prescriptive purpose of the utterance does *not* logically figure as an instrument of persuasion.

Nor again would it here be consistent for the speaker even to *try* to be effective by a deliberately evocative manner. To be goading in method is to exercise one's wish for someone to do something. To exercise it when one has also put forward one's wishes is all of a piece; to do so for good measure when openly inviting someone to accept some impersonal fact as a good and sufficient reason is so to mix persuasive methods as to make nonsense of both. One can try to put up impersonal facts, and not 'let them speak for themselves', to turn impersonal pleading into the continuation of direct pleading by other means; but one cannot do so consistently. It invites the protest 'what are you after? trying to give me a reason for doing this? or badgering me into doing it? you can't have it both ways'. Nor is it any more becoming, instead of mixing the two methods, to let them succeed each other. 'You will cut your tongue with the knife, dear'. 'No, this is the blunt one.' 'Well, any way put it down' won't endear one to an intelligent child. It shows that the first plea had been insincere, or that one was just being muddled.

Where *goading* is a plain incongruity, impersonal pleading is confined to its own method, which by contrast I may call *guiding*. To influence by guiding is to influence without compulsion. One is not creating an evoca tive situation; one is merely using the situation as it is. One is trying to make others do only what they will acknowledge they have independently a reason for doing. While goading is intrinsically detrimental to producing actions 'purely on the merits of the case', and 'of people's own accord', guiding is intrinsically and purely in aid of producing such actions.

All this affects the evocative attitudes appropriate to this form of pleading. 'Get out' and 'your bus is about to leave' cannot *both* be simply 'aiming at agreement with one in attitude', 'bringing you round to favoring what I favor', 'getting my own way with you'. In their ordinary meaning these descriptions fit direct, but not indirect pleading. If they were meant to cover both, they would have to mean something different in each case.

For one thing, the ordinary notion of 'getting one's own way' carries the suggestion of *forcing* one's will on others; one is familiar with sensing the note of this being intended and tried in direct pleas. But the note is absent from an indirect prescription. One is being beckoned to do something in 'your bus is leaving' as in 'get out'; but here with no suggestion of dragging or harrowing, and with a note of deference to oneself as someone able to appreciate reasons, and quite unanxious to do things otherwise than of his own accord. To be addressed guidingly bears no resemblance to being addressed goadingly; and if it does it shouldn't.

Moreover, to be trying to get one's own way suggests that one is after some *purely* personal end; and this too is inconsistent with indirect pleading. This is not because one may not be both guiding in method and goading in aim. Commercial advertisers notoriously, but if moderately honest, quite properly, guide to goad by making evocative observations about their wares. The point is rather that the goading aim is perforce here qualified by the means chosen. Indirect pleading is intrinsically less well adapted to gaining purely personal ends than direct pleading. One is at the mercy of coincidence. There *need* be no reasons for others to do what one wants them to do for reasons of one's own; and even if one thinks there are, one is still dependent on finding them appreciated. At best, therefore, guiding as a method is only suited to a goading severely self-limited in aim: to try to make others do as one wants them to do, but no further than within the limits in which they are ready to do so for reasons of their own. 'Dentex will keep your dentures clean' shows someone intent on persuading for gain; but one takes it that he is not after more than can be achieved by leaving us free to buy only when we believe him, and need to. And not only is this in a restricted sense only to 'try and make others fall in with one's own ends'; it cannot be *purely* called this at all. For there is another side to it: it is also to 'try and make others fall in with what would be an *end for them*'. Wherever guiding is used as a method, persuasion has an other-regarding orientation: looking at actions from other people's point of view, trying to make others do what they would want, or would have an incentive to do, if they were not ignorant or obtuse. And where one is guiding to goad one is still trying to make them act as one wants *oneself* only by means of trying to make them act as they would want *themselves*. Surely then not all prescriptive speech aims purely and typically at bending the hearer's attitudes to those of the speaker. This language is more than misleading. It implies disregard of what is an outstanding characteristic of prescriptive speech: that it may have a dual orientation, egocentric as well as centered on others. It can serve both to make others favor what we favor; and to aid them in learning to favor what *they* do not favor but would, or might, for independent and acknowledged reasons of their own.

In fact, on occasions, the last may be the one and only object of prescriptive speech. Instead of *guiding to goad,* one may just be *guiding to guide.* I may give you the news about the timetable not in order to get rid of you without having to say so; but purely from a concern that you should not get into trouble for being late for supper. One may put facts to people purely so that they should not act rashly or in ignorance. The wheel here comes round full circle, and prescriptive speech loses the last vestige of an egocentric objective. To refer to its object one would have to say 'I am putting this to you, not to see you influenced by it for a personal reason; only to prevent you from acting rashly or in ignorance; or so that cogent reasons should prevail with you'. None of this is *said*. One only says 'your bus is about to leave'. But one would need words like these to explain one's persuasive attitude, or defend it against the charge of being purely interested. And other words might be used as well. 'I only want you to act sensibly, reasonably, rationally'; 'to show a rational attitude', 'to do what the situation requires', 'what it is desirable for you to do'. All these notions present familiar difficulties. But there seems here a natural soil for them to grow on. *They cannot be dispensed with if one is to describe one's characteristic aim in persuading others by giving them reasons.* It is plain then that these terms cannot be only formulae of direct pleading, conventional trumpet calls to press others into conformity with one's own attitudes. For they have a place in the description of the implicit intentions of a form of prescriptive speech which does not *use* them for persuasion at all, and has neither the aims nor employs the methods of direct pleading. One cannot call on prescriptive speech to account for them if they are needed, in some of its forms, to account for it.

Persuasion by rational methods has been treated as if it had none of these implications; and this raises a last point about it. The silence is due in some measure to a biased interest in its use in a special context: where it serves in support of 'nonrational' or direct methods of pleading. One says 'please take the evening off: come out with me. You need distraction; your work can wait'. Here a direct plea is supported by observations of evocative fact. In this context, it certainly does not follow that the evocative observations will be made genuinely to 'guide'. They may be made not to guide, but to misguide; they will serve their purpose as well if they successfully do the one or the other. In fact, evocative observations are a really useful tool for supporting direct pleading only if they are not used squeamishly. The facts as they are, or as one thinks them to be, need not be at all suitable for the purpose. But they can be taken in hand. One can allege that something is the case, knowing it is not; or quietly not mention what one knows is the case besides; or put forward what is the case knowing it would provide no good reason on dispassionate consideration. If Eve had said 'come on, eat', praising the apple knowing it to be rotten, and quietly ignoring the taboo, Adam would have fallen for all the wiles. The Eves are now joined by advertisers and politicians; and there are still Adams.

For an account of how *direct pleading is supported by evocative observations* it is therefore irrelevant whether they are used to guide or misguide, and the distinction can be suppressed. But this is not at all irrelevant to an account of *persuasion by rational methods.* It is not only significant that they can be used in either of two ways; what is more, only guiding and not misguiding can be properly described as using rational methods at all. One hesitates to say that an unscrupulous advertiser or friend, is using 'rational methods' on one; or that persuasion by a deliberately misguiding story is properly called 'warning someone,' or 'commending something'. Or else, one will distinguish between using rational methods in form, but not 'really'; and between an honest warning or recommendation, and a lying one. The point is that misguiding is not a *variant* of guiding, but its *corruption.* It is goading in method dressed up as guiding; a form of speech which is not what it gives out to be. The lie is not only in misstating the facts; they may be correct as far as they go. It is in the false claim, implicit in mentioning the facts for persuasion, that they provide good and sufficient reasons for a doing. When this claim is made dishonestly, or with wishful carelessness, just to make others think, or deceive themselves into thinking, that there is a good reason where there is none, pleading by evocative observations of fact does not aim at guidance; but it is not then either *persuading by rational methods.*

Recent discussions have bypassed or suppressed these distinctions by falsely treating the original and the fake under the same name.

6

I shall now return to moral speech, and try to locate its place on the logical map of prescriptive speech. There are two diametrically opposed prototypes. To which does 'you ought not to smoke here' or 'you ought to leave now' bear the greater resemblance? To 'don't smoke here' or 'smoking is forbidden here'? To 'leave now', or 'your bus is about to leave'?

There is often, no doubt, a resemblance to direct pleading. 'You ought to' may be said goadingly, crossly, entreatingly, peremptorily, insinuatingly, with the deployment of all coercive devices of a direct telling or asking.

But we have seen that whether in fact such methods are used does not decide whether an utterance is directly or indirectly prescriptive in *type.* The devices may have been used inconsistently; in spite of them, the utterance may logically be one to rely on saying something evocative, and not on being a form of evocative speaking. Here tests from the grammar of direct and indirect pleading must be used; and by these tests 'you ought to' is more like indirect than direct pleading. I shall enumerate a few.

(1) If I crossly say 'you ought not to smoke here', you can say 'what are you trying to do? Tell me that I ought not to? or ordering me not to

do it?' And I can answer apologetically 'sorry, I got excited; I am not telling or asking or begging you not to smoke here, I am only saying you ought not to.'

(2) It is proper to say 'I complied with him when he said I ought to, because I was convinced what he said was right'. If I said, 'I just complied because he said "you ought to" so firmly', one might remark, 'Surely, this was not a very adequate reason'.

(3) If I say 'you ought to', and you reply 'honestly, I don't see this at all, I don't think I need to', I shall feel, unless I can argue back that my plea has been properly met and disarmed, I have said something calculated to be evocative, and failed to carry conviction. I can say that you are 'difficult to convince', 'perverse', 'unreasonable'; but not 'how rude', 'how disobliging' of you to refuse me when I said 'you ought to' so firmly, so pathetically, or so nicely.

(4) 'You ought to leave now' is compatible with 'I have no personal interest in your going', I am not 'goading in aim'; and 'I am not trying to coerce you in any way'; I am not 'goading in method'. I am only trying to make you 'see reason'; 'to make you act in accord with the realities of the situation', 'to aid you to act as you would of your own accord if you were not ignorant or obtuse'. Moral pleading can claim for itself to be guiding in both aim and method.

None of this one could say if it were a special formula for being *directly* prescriptive by speaking evocatively. All of it fits in with saying that it is a way of being *indirectly* prescriptive by asserting some evocative truth.

All, at any rate, but one thing. 'You ought to' is like 'the law says' or 'your bus is leaving' indirectly prescriptive in grammar; but otherwise it is not like either.

It is familiar ground that the analogy with 'the law says' cannot be pressed. 'The law says' reports that one is being addressed commandingly by someone, like 'captain's orders: everyone to throw his goods overboard'. But 'you ought to', if used to report anything, is not used to report on the deliverances of any moral captain. If it were, what was done purely because one ought to would be done regardless of whether one also had cause for doing it of one's own accord, for reasons purely in the nature of the act or its circumstances; it would, once again, be done purely because someone had spoken coercively, though not here the speaker himself but the agent whose command he is reporting. But usage suggests the opposite. What is done purely because one ought to, one tends to say, is done purely from considerations relating to the nature of the act and its circumstances; it is precisely not what is done purely because one was told to. Moral persuasion consists no more in *reporting,* as an incentive, a feature imported *ad hoc* into the situation by someone, than in importing such a feature by 'telling' speaking. At the best one might say, as has been said, it consists in reporting that some doing is 'commanded' or 'demanded' by the nature of the act itself and its circumstances. But, whatever it may mean to say this, it only underlines further the failure of the analogy with 'the law says'. 'Commands' or 'demands', in their ordinary sense, can issue only from persons, capable of displaying their will impressively. Whatever 'the nature of the act and its circumstances' may be able to 'do', it is not this.

Is one to say then that 'you ought to' is more like 'your bus is leaving' than like 'the law says'? That it is used to persuade by reporting some evocative feature of the situation which naturally inheres in it? Strangely, this too has its difficulties. It is common ground that 'you ought to' cannot be said to report a feature of the situation of the same type as 'your bus is leaving'. If at all, it is said, it reports a 'nonnatural' feature, not a 'natural' one. But observations like these do not get down to the root of the difficulty. The trouble is not that 'you ought to' cannot be said to persuade by reporting as a reason for a doing the same *type* of feature of the situation as 'your bus is leaving'; but that what it reports does not seem to figure among the *reasons* put forward for any doing at all. One may put forward 'your bus is leaving' as an evocative feature of the situation; or, again, 'you are expected for dinner' as another such feature, either to add to the weight of the first, or in its place. But what about 'you ought to go now'? If it were also reported as a reason one would expect it to be put forward along with the others, either as an alternative, or in addition to them. But, plainly, it is not. I do not try to persuade you to go (alternatively) by saying either 'you ought to go' *or* 'your bus is leaving'; nor would 'you ought to go' be on a *par* with 'you are expected for dinner', to be mentioned in addition to 'your bus is leaving' as a further feature of the situation to count towards going. The fact is 'you ought to' is not used to *replace* or *supplement* any of the features of the situation ordinarily put forward in persuasion by rational methods. On the contrary, it only works in *conjunction* with them. 'You ought to go now' is incompletely persuasive by itself. It needs support from 'your bus is leaving', or 'you are expected for dinner', or any other natural feature of the situation which may count as a reason for going, the same features in fact which one might also have brought to the hearer's notice without saying expressly that he ought to go at all. In order to make moral persuasion as effective as it might be one will mention *any* feature of the situation *whatever* which may count in the circumstances in favor of the doing which one is trying to induce; and only then will one add, if one does, 'and so you ought'. It follows that 'you ought to' is not used either to persuade by reporting some evocative feature of the situation which pre-exists in it. It is not one *among* the features put forward as counting towards some particular doing; it is only said once *all* of these have been enumerated, and, as one says, 'on the strength of them'.

The oddity of this conclusion needs stressing. 'You ought to' seems part of the machinery of persuasion by 'rational methods'; it is used when they are used, seems to share the grammar of statements doing this work, and, apparently, is persuasive in its effects. 'And so you ought to go' seems to clinch what 'you are expected for dinner' has begun. But also it seems a logically redundant part of this machinery. One persuades by rational methods when one gives reasons, reports those features of the situation likely to count in favor of a doing. And, when *all* reasons have been given, one should expect, all that rational persuasion can *try* to do, should have been *done*. What else but another reason could add persuasive force to the reasons already given? But 'you ought to' is said *after* everything to count as a reason has been enumerated. It seems persuasive, and like adducing a reason, and yet it is not. It seems both to belong to persuasion by rational methods, and not to be part of it. Odd as this may seem, it needs facing. The oddity is the logical turning point for the understanding of the special function of moral and similar types of speech.

It is tempting to account for this by once more falling back on the imperative view. Moral persuasion, it has been suggested, is not purely either by rational methods or by direct pleading, but by a mixture of both. 'You ought to' is a way of saying 'come on, do' which one is prepared to support by rational methods, or which one uses in order to support them. One says, 'you ought to go, your bus is leaving': here it assists persuasion by reasons as a kind of imperative *hors-d'oeuvre*. Or one says 'your bus is leaving, and so you ought to go'; here it assists rational persuasion as a kind of imperative dessert. 'You ought to' is shown to belong to persuasion by rational methods without being part of it.

The suggestion is persuasive, but once again it won't pass the test of usage. It rests on taking it for granted that direct and indirect pleading can without hitch be used as *complementary* methods of persuasion. But there are logical incompatibilities between these two methods; and they also rule out any account of moral persuasion as consisting, in essentials, in a kind of *mixed pleading*.

'You ought to', it is said, expresses the speaker's desire to make the hearer conform with the speaker's wishes. Reasons are adduced in practical support of a pleading of this sort. The whole broadly is 'moral persuasion'. But if so, there is no assurance here that *misguiding* won't be used as well as *guiding*. For it is not specified that the aim of adducing reasons need be any other than 'goading'; and misguiding may serve this aim as well as or better than guiding. It may equally suit the speaker to support 'you ought to' by a truthful and complete as by a deliberately distorted presentation of the facts. But then this is implicitly to define moral persuasion so as to make using 'rational methods' not a *necessary*, but only an *incidental*, part of it; and to make it comprise indiscriminately both scrupulous guiding, and unscrupulous special pleading. And this plainly would be a travesty of the facts. Part of the common understanding of 'moral persuasion' is that it should be distinct from unprincipled goading; and it would not be necessarily distinct from this if its aim were to advance persuasive arguments simply for the sake of bending the hearer's will to the expressed will of the speaker.

Another example will underline this point. The notion of mixed pleading can be applied to aesthetics as well as to ethics. 'This picture is good', 'look at the coherence and assurance of the lines, the varied and balanced coloring, the unusual decorative design' can be taken as an invitation to the onlooker to share the speaker's sense of appreciation, followed up by deeds to get him into the right frame of mind. One may agree that the whole performance is correctly described as a way of trying to teach someone to appreciate something. But is it also correctly described as a way of *just* making the onlooker share the *speaker's* sense of appreciation? Surely, one needs a way of distinguishing between the manner appreciation is taught by a cunning dealer, and by a conscientious critic. If the theory were correct, both would be equally intent on making us appreciate things in the way *they* happen to desire; and 'this is good' should have prepared us for an assault of this kind and nothing else, by expressing no more than 'come on, like it as I do'. In fact, one thinks, 'this is good' no less than 'you ought to' *entitles* one to expect guiding and not goading in its support: a scrupulous attempt at least to convert one to an attitude, as it might be in response to a truthful and comprehensive appreciation of the relevant facts. One may agree that both announcements are properly followed up less by *proving* to someone that something which they state is the case, than by *converting* him to a novel attitude of appreciation, whether of a work of art, or of a line of conduct. But the procedure is surely hitched on to the wrong bandwagon if one describes it as consisting in the ill-assorted companionship of the use of rational methods in the service of the intentions of a purely personal plea.

It is also plain that there would here again be a case for the hearer to challenge the mixing of the rational appeal with coercion. 'You are expected for supper', sandwiched in between 'do go', and 'so be gone' is open to be challenged by 'make up your mind, are you leaving it to me to decide for myself, or have you decided for me?' When the issue is pressed, one cannot insist on persuading by a mixture of telling and arguing. One either says 'all right, I am not arguing, I am telling you'; or one is ready to rely on arguing, and to be done with telling.

There is one form of imperative speech which can be combined with persuasion by rational methods without being open to these objections; and it teaches a lesson of special interest. 'Do this' may be used in the sense of 'my advice to you is, do this'; it may express a *recommendation*. One might say, with some force, that this is what 'you ought to' is used to express. 'Do this', as advice, is not direct pleading, in spite of its grammatical form. One can say it, and deny that one is telling, or asking, or in any way trying to coerce; one is 'merely saying, my advice is, do this'; nor can one consistently take personal umbrage at having what was 'purely advice' rejected. It is also logically assured here that none but rational methods will be used in support. Advice can be 'good' or 'bad'; it has an implicit canon of achievement, defined in terms of what it is understood to set out to do. And this is purely to 'guide', to make people act as they would have valid and sufficient reasons for acting and not otherwise. 'My advice is, do this' can consistently only be supported by evocative observations of fact thought, and implicitly claimed, to constitute reasons of this kind; one cannot honestly say it without having formed an opinion concerning the facts of the situation all round, as well as concerning their relevance as reasons for the hearer. In fact, 'do this', as advice, may also be treated as the stating of an opinion to this effect. One can say 'my opinion is, do this' as if one were saying 'my opinion is that you have the best of reasons for doing this, the facts all round being so and so'; and one disarms advice by challenging either the facts or their alleged force as reasons. Hence 'do this', as advice, foots the bill of being an imperative expression necessarily, and not merely incidentally supported by 'guiding in method'. The imperative view would be free of inconsistencies if it claimed that 'you ought to' was used to express no more than precisely this.

But, if reduced to this, it would also then be too anaemic to survive. 'Do', as advice, is effective not as a *plea* but an account of the *opinion* it ventures. One follows advice when one thinks it sound, believing its claim that there are valid reasons for doing the thing suggested. One can give advice without stating this claim. 'Go; you are expected for supper' does not mention it. But, also, one might as well have explicitly made it, as certainly the hearer must take it to have been made for advice to be understood and to be effective as such. One might say 'go, there is the best of reasons, you are expected for supper'; and instead also 'go, it's reasonable ... ', or 'it's what the circumstances require ... '; or again, to someone with hesitations, 'go, it's what you ought to do ... '. The last is here of a type with the others, and is no way of saying 'go' any more than they. 'Go, you ought to go' is no more just repetitive than 'go, it's reasonable to go'; what would be repetitive, though there would be a shade of difference, is 'you ought to go, it's reasonable to go'.

Lastly one may give advice by using these expressions alone without the exhortative prefix 'go'.

The imperative view was called in to account for this type of expression. It turns out that the only imperative expression which would otherwise fit the requirements is one which for its description, and its effective understanding, presupposes an independent and descriptive use for the expressions which the imperative view had been devised to account for.

7

It is outside the scope of this paper to argue the use of these expressions in detail. I have attempted no more than to locate their place on the logical map of prescriptive speech. And this place should by now be reasonably assured. 'You ought to', 'it is reasonable to', 'desirable to' are expressions belonging to prescriptive speech purely in its capacity to guide; and they are of a type *to answer the need for making its implicit intentions and functions explicit.* What tends to obscure this is that 'persuading by giving someone a reason' is an ambiguous notion. It may mean 'by stating a fact calculated to act as a reason'; and also 'by stating such a fact *and* stating *that*, if considered, it will act as such a reason'. Prescriptive speech of the guiding type reaches a new level of concepts and propositions when it turns from purely stating persuasive facts to announcing the claim that they constitute reasons, 'good' reasons, 'valid' reasons, 'sufficient' reasons, 'reasons on the whole, or despite counter-reasons'. No wonder 'it is reasonable', 'it is desirable', 'you ought to' are not *among* the reasons one puts forward for persuasion. What one puts so forward are the preexisting features of the situation; claiming *that* they are reasons is not to put forward a reason, but claiming that this is what one is doing. Nevertheless the explicit claim or reminder that something put forward as a reason is one seems to have a persuasive function of its own; something seems to be capable of turning on emphasizing 'and so you ought to go' after 'you are expected for supper' has been said. But how this is so is another story.

Much more needs saying to reach final conclusions, but the position which emerges may be characterized as follows. 'You ought to go', 'this picture is good' *state* something, the one something like *that* there would be reasons for a doing if the facts of the situation were known and borne in mind; the other something like *that* there would be reasons for appreciation if the features of a work of art were all noted and attended to with discrimination. But the bare statement is vacuous here unless its claim is put to the test by a demonstration *ad oculos* not only *to* the hearer but *on* the hearer. What is more, it is not in order to *prove* what we say that we insist on the demonstration; but becuase we desire the hearer to have the benefit of *experiencing* what we claim. 'You ought to', 'this is good' are in this respect one of a type with 'you will like it if you try'. One does not say this just for information, but for *conversion*. One is making an objective claim, and the claim may be falsified or confirmed as things turn out. But one is not in the first place interested in what happens to the claim, but in that what was claimed should occur. 'You ought to go', 'this picture is good', followed up by relevant observations of fact, is an attempt *to teach someone to appreciate something,* a line of conduct, or a work of art. And 'teaching appreciation' is a type of activity of its own, different both from telling a story, and from exhorting or preaching, though related to both. It shares with the first that it involves making an *objective claim*; and with the second that it aims at *practical conversion*.

'Good'

P. H. NOWELL-SMITH

1

'Good' in the context of choice. We have seen that when 'good' is used in the context of choice there can be no logical gap between deciding that something is the best or better than its rivals and choosing it. This does not imply that there can be no discrepancy between the decision which is, on the face of it, not a performance of any kind but a judgment, and the choice; but it does imply that if there is such a discrepancy a special reason must be given for it. And we must now consider the role of such expressions as 'because it is a good one' and 'because it is the best' when they are used to explain why a man chose the thing he did.

The answer to the question 'Why did you choose that car?' might be a statement of fact ('because it has more leg room') or an A-sentence ('because it is more comfortable'); and I have already discussed the con-textual background in which such answers can be given and taken as logically complete explanations. In each case the car must have some A-property and some ordinary, empirical properties on which its A-property depends. While the factual answer says what the empirical properties are and contextually implies an A-property without specifying what it is, the A-sentence does the reverse. And each answer implies a pro-attitude towards the A-property concerned; otherwise it would not be an answer to the question.

The answer 'because it is the best' functions in a similar way, but with certain important differences. In the first place it does not just imply a pro-attitude; it expresses it. But it does not only do this. If this were all I wanted to do I should have to say 'because I happen to like it more than the others'. It contextually implies that I have reasons for my choice; but it does not say what they are and therefore does not explain my choice.

We are tempted to say that it gives the best possible reason. After

From P. H. Nowell-Smith, Ethics *(Harmondsworth: Penguin Books, 1954), pp. 160–82. Printed by permission of the author and the publisher.*

all, what better reason could there be for choosing a car than the fact that it was the best available or the best that I could afford? What better reason could there be for doing anything than the belief that it is the best thing to do?

The trouble is that the reason is *too* good. It is like saying that I was frightened because it was a terrifying experience; and, as an explanation, it operates in much the same way. Just as 'because it was terrifying' shows that my fear was not an unusual one and contextually implies that the object had certain unspecified properties by which people are usually frightened, so 'because it was the best' shows that my choice was no passing whim, that it was considered more or less carefully, that the object had certain unspecified 'good-making' properties, and that my choice was not a peculiar one. Any of these contextual implications could be expressly withdrawn, especially, as we shall see, the last; but in default of such withdrawal my audience would be entitled to assume them. Just as a G-sentence showed more plainly than an A-sentence that advice was being given but was less explicit about the reasons, so 'because it was the best' shows more plainly that I was choosing but says even less about the reasons.

In fact it says nothing about them at all; it only implies that I have reasons. The goodness of something is not one of the properties for which I choose it. If it were, it would make sense to ask why its superior goodness was a reason for choosing it. To ask a man who chose a car because it was faster or more economical or had more leg room why he chose it is to display ignorance of people's purchasing habits; to say to him "I know you thought it the best car; but why did you choose it?" is logically odd.

The same logical ties that bind goodness so closely to choosing bind it also to activities that are akin to choosing. A man who says that he voted for a certain proposal because he thought it good has not explained why he voted for it; he has merely guarded himself against accusations of flippancy, irresponsibility, or indulging in complicated machinations. And it is logically odd to say "I think it is an excellent proposal, but I shan't vote for it". As we saw, reasons could be given for this discrepancy, and the logical nexus between thinking good and voting comes out in the fact that we should feel entitled to infer that there must be a special reason. To call something good is, in a way, already to vote for it, to side with it, to let others know where I stand. But it does more than this; it implies that I have reasons for casting my vote as I do.

'Good' in the context of advice. The considerations that apply to 'good' in the context of choice apply equally in the context of advice. And here again the subjectivist is right in connecting 'this is good' with the pro-attitude of the speaker. There is the same sort of absurdity in 'This is good, but I don't advise you to do it' as there is in 'This is the best course;

but shall I take it?'. In the latter case the speaker both expresses a decision as to how he should act and in the same breath asks if he should; and in the former he gives advice and in the same breath retracts it. It would be equally odd if the hearer were to say "You have told me that it is the best course to take; but do you advise me to take it?".

The differences in the use of 'good' in advice and choice are due to the fact that the problem to be solved is now someone else's. The adviser is not making up his mind what to do, but helping someone else to make up his mind. And this difference brings with it another. The relevant pro-attitude is that of the audience. But in other respects the contextual implications are the same. To tell someone that something is the best thing for him to do is to advise him to do it, but not irresponsibly. The speaker implies that he has good reasons for his advice, that he knows what the problem is and that his advice is relevant. The same predictive and causal elements are present as in the case of A-sentences; and advice may, as before, be given disingenuously, improperly, mistakenly, or unfortunately if one or other of the contextual implications is absent.

2

Other uses of 'good'. I shall discuss the other uses of 'good' in the order in which they seem to diverge more and more from the fundamental use, which is to express or explain a preference.

(a) *Praising and applauding.* Like choosing, these are performances, not statements; and, although in primary uses they do express the speaker's pro-attitude, they have other contextual implications which will be examined later. They can be done with or without words; but the gestures, handclapping and the like, which are used for praising have conventional, symbolic meanings. They mean what they do in the way that words mean, not in the way that clouds mean rain or cobras in the garden mean trouble. Virtue words are words of praise; and relatively specific words like 'brave', 'honest', and 'generous' are also descriptive; for they describe a person's behavior and predict the way in which he can be relied upon to behave in certain sorts of situation. They both praise and give the reason, what the praise is *for*. But 'good' does not do this. In cases where there are recognized standards that man must reach to be worthy of praise they contextually imply that he has reached those standards; but they do not say what the standards are. 'Because it is a good one' does not explain why I praise something; but it does imply that the thing has certain unspecified properties for which I praise it. My praise was not casual or capricious.

(b) *Commending.* The verb 'to commend' is used in two ways. It may mean 'entrust to the care of'; but this sense is irrelevant, since 'good' is not used to commend in this sense. In the sense in which 'good' is used for commending it is akin to praising but has a more hortatory force. To commend something to someone is to advise him to choose it. *The Oxford Dictionary*, as we saw, calls 'good' "the most general adjective of commendation" in English; but it goes on to add "implying the existence in a high or at least satisfactory degree of characteristic qualities which are either admirable in themselves or useful for some purpose".

The form of this definition is interesting, since it brings out the difference between the job that the word is used for and the conditions limiting its use in way that philosophers' definitions of 'good' never do. The writer of the dictionary sees clearly that the word is used to do a job which is not 'stating' but commending and that the elements of objective fact which some philosophers insist on treating as part of its meaning are really part of the contextual background of its use. In the uses which follow this contextual background looms larger and larger, so that in some uses the word 'good' almost comes to be a descriptive word, though, as we shall see, it never quite does this and in moral contexts it can never wholly lose its gerundive force or its pro-force.

(c) *Verdicts and appraisals.* In chapter 1 [of *Ethics*] we saw that moral language is not only used for choosing and advising, but also for making moral judgments, which are not decisions to do something but verdicts or appraisals of something or somebody. Now appraisals are *judgments*, not just expressions of a man's own taste or preference; and it is this point that the Consequential Property Theory tries to bring out, but in a misleading way. When we judge something to be good we always judge it to be good in respect of some property, and it is a question of empirical fact whether is has this property or not. Thus to judge a wine to be good is not just to express a preference for it—and we shall see that it need not be to do this at all—; the judgment must be backed by my belief that it has a certain bouquet, body, and flavor, and these are objective qualities, since a man who found that he disagreed markedly from all the experts on these points would admit himself to be wrong. It is an essential feature of judgments that they are made by reference to standards or criteria; but it is necessary to be extremely careful in discussing the way in which the criteria are related to the verdict or appraisal.

Let us assume for the moment that the criteria used by experts at wine tastings, horse shows, beauty contests, and school examinations are agreed to be the proper criteria, though this will have to be questioned later. We might be tempted to say that if the criteria for being a good X are that the X must have properties a, b, and c in some specifiable degree, then 'good X' simply means 'X which has the properties a, b, and c in the requisite degree'. But this will not do. For it is possible to under-

_ H. Nowell-Smith_ 87

stand what 'good X' means without knowing what the criteria are. Thus, if I do not know the criteria used at Crufts I could not tell a good dog (in this sense of 'good') from a bad one or pick out the best dog from a group. But this does not mean that I cannot understand what 'good dog' means in the way that I could not understand what 'mangy dog' meant if I did not know what 'mangy' meant. For I do know that if it is a good dog it must have in a fairly high degree those properties which are mentioned in the list of criteria for judging dogs, although I do not know what these properties are or to what degree a dog must have them to rate as 'good'.

The next two uses are special cases of the appraising use.

(d) _Efficiency._ When 'good' is predicated of any object (natural or artificial, animate or inanimate) that is used for a purpose it implies the presence in a relatively high degree of those properties that the object must have to do its job. But again it would be a mistake to say that 'good knife' just _means_ 'knife that is sharp, easily handled, durable, etc.'. The connection between the properties which a knife must have to be efficient and its efficiency is an empirical one. We know from experience that a knife which has not got these properties at all just won't cut and that its relative efficiency at cutting depends on the degree to which it has these properties. Nor can we even say that 'good knife' means 'knife which cuts efficiently', because we could understand what 'good' means in the expression 'good knife' without knowing what knives were for. But 'good knife' (in this sense of 'good') does mean 'knife which has those properties (whatever they are) which a knife must have if it is to do its job efficiently (whatever that is)'.

(e) _Skill._ When we call a man a good lawyer, scholar, cricketer, or liar, the use is similar to the 'efficiency' use except for the fact that, since these are men, the purpose concerned is their purpose, not the purpose they are used for. Just as we could not use 'good' to imply efficiency unless we agreed about what the object concerned is for, so we could not use it to imply skill unless there was something that was agreed to constitute success at the activity concerned. But, just as we cannot say that 'good' means 'efficient' in the one sense, so we cannot say that it means 'successful' in the other. In activities involving skill there are rules for achieving success which are such that we know from experience that unless a man applies them he is unlikely to be successful. Thus, if we know the rules for success at bridge or cricket we can predict, in a very general way, what a good bridge player or cricketer will do; and in calling a man 'good' we imply that he applies or follows the rules. This implication can, of course, be expressly withdrawn because we know that people sometimes achieve success in very unorthodox ways. But 'good' never quite loses its gerundive force and if we call a man a good cricketer without intending to imply that his methods ought to be imitated we mislead our audience.

(f) *The descriptive use.* Like most words, 'good' can be used to mean 'what most people would call good'. A man who uses it may not be choosing, advising, defending a choice or piece of advice, or appraising, but referring to an object which he or others would call good if they were doing one of these. Thus I may call a wine good even if I am not competent to apply the criteria, just because I have heard the experts praise it.

This use belongs to descriptive discourse because it is a question of historical fact whether people do or do not call the object good, and that is what is being asserted. It is necessarily a secondary use, since it would be impossible to use 'good' to mean 'what people call good' unless people called things good in primary ways. And 'good' is hardly ever used with this descriptive force alone. The speaker implies that he himself sides with those who call the thing good unless this implication is expressly withdrawn or obviously inadmissible in the context.

3

We must now consider the ways in which these uses of 'good' are connected with each other. It is clearly not an accident that the same word is used in all these different ways nor could this fact be explained in a purely historical or philological way. 'Good' is *the* Janus word *par excellence*; it is often used to do more than one job on one occasion and the logical connections between the various jobs are what they are because the facts are what they are. It is also most emphatically an ordinary, nontechnical word and it is a consequence of this that the logic of its use reflects empirical truths that hold only for the most part and admit of exceptions. For ordinary language, unlike mathematics, is not deliberately constructed by men who have a keen eye for consistency and rigor; it is not deliberately constructed at all but grows and changes in an environment in which the exceptional case can be and must be ignored. The contextual implications of any use of 'good' are many and varied and, on occasion, any of them can be withdrawn, a point which should make us suspicious of counter-examples. It is impossible to understand the actual uses of 'good' by considering artificial and exceptional situations because the logic of ordinary language does not cater for such situations.

But there is one element which seems to be common to all cases. Although a man need have no comparisons in mind when he calls something 'good', such comparisons are always implied. He must, if challenged, be able to produce examples of descriptively similar things that he would call not so good. For example, we always praise something with a certain degree of warmth which lies somewhere on a scale between mild commendation and hysterical adulation. The word 'good' can be used to express almost any degree of warmth, but it must be less than that expressed in the same context by 'excellent' or 'superb' and greater than that expressed by 'fair' or 'tolerable'.

It is not difficult to understand the connections between the more obviously performatory uses, praising, applauding, and commending; nor is it difficult to appreciate their intimate connection with preference and choice. To praise is not to choose; but it is connected with choosing in that it would be odd for a man to choose the thing he was prepared to praise less highly or not at all. He must have special reasons for this, modesty for example, a sense of unworthiness to possess the 'better' thing or a desire that someone else should have it. Again, if a man habitually praises one pianist more highly than another we expect to find him attending the recitals of the former more regularly and to be more annoyed when he is prevented from going. But he might have been told that the second is really a better pianist and be trying to cultivate a taste for his performance. Explanations can be given of discrepancies between praising and choice; but in default of an explanation the connection is contextually implied.

If, on a particular occasion, I call a man brave it would be logically odd to ask if I was in favor of what he did; for 'brave' is a praising word and by using it I show that I am in favor. Similiarly, if I call courage a 'virtue' I show that I am, in a general way, in favor of courage, although I might not always want to praise a brave deed. It is an empirical fact that men are, for the most part, in favor of the modes of conduct that they call (descriptively) brave, honest, or generous. But this pro-attitude is so widespread that these words are not pure descriptive words; they are terms of praise and imply a pro-attitude unless this is expressly withdrawn.

Now praising and applauding are activities which are often performed with the special purpose of encouraging the person concerned to continue in the same style, and hissing and booing are used with the opposite intention. Although the words and gestures employed in praising owe their encouraging force to convention, they have, granted the convention, a natural effect on the people praised. For it is an empirical fact that, except in special circumstances—for example, if the praise is considered impertinent—people enjoy being praised and are therefore likely to go on doing what they are praised for. Praising is logically tied to approval; for if we heard a man praise something we could not wonder whether he approved of it or not unless we suspected him of being disingenuous or ironical; and it is logically tied in the same way to encouraging. But, although it is an empirical fact that men tend to encourage and try to promote that of which they approve, we must, as always, assume that men on the whole intend the natural consequences of their actions and therefore do not praise that which they would prefer to be otherwise. And this assumption is reflected in the fact that praising implies both approval and encouragement.

The same logical ties bind praising to advising; it would be logically odd to praise one candidate more highly than another and to go on to say that one was advising against his being given the job or the prize. Odd, but not impossible; for there might, as always, be special reasons for this.

The "characteristic qualities" which, according to the dictionary, are implied by the use of 'good' may be "either admirable in themselves or useful for some purpose". In contexts involving efficiency or skill it is the latter that we have in mind. In such contexts there need be no direct connection between the performatory uses, which are all variations of 'preferring' or 'being on the side of', and the usefulness implied by 'good'. We may have no pro-attitude whatsoever towards the purpose for which something is used or the activity at which a man is skillful, as when we speak of a 'good cosh' or a 'good liar'. But there is still an indirect link with the pro-attitudes since 'good' in these contexts implies success, and 'success' is a pro-word. A man is not a good liar unless he fairly consistently achieves his aim.

Preference and appraisal. But it is the connections between the performatory uses and the verdict giving, judging, or appraising use when the qualities on which the verdict is based are thought to be "admirable in themselves" that are the most important and the most difficult. I shall substitute 'preferable' for 'admirable', since admiration is itself a performance akin to praising and 'admirable' is therefore too narrow in scope to cover all appraisals other than those of efficiency or skill.

All the performatory uses contextually imply appraisal; for we have seen that it is improper to use 'good', at least in an impersonal formula, to express or defend a preference unless the preference is a considered one, based on reasons and not unusual. And to say that the preference is 'based on reasons' is to say that the speaker applied criteria or standards. It is not necessary that he should have done this deliberately; he may have done it automatically; but he must be able to defend his choice by an appeal to the standards which justify it.

But, although the performatory uses imply appraisal, it is not so clear that the converse is true. Indeed it is not true in any direct sense; appraisals often imply preference only in a roundabout way. For when 'good' is used to give a verdict it need neither express nor imply a pro-attitude on the part of the speaker. In such cases what a man is primarily doing with the word 'good' is *applying* those standards which are only contextually implied in the more subjective uses. Since 'good' is a Janus word, he may, of course, be expressing his preferences or advising as well; but he need not be. The embittered schoolmaster may have no interest in the work of the examination candidates at all; he may even prefer stupidity to intelligence or have a private belief that the usual criteria for intelligence are quite wrong. Nevertheless he may still apply the grading words 'good', 'fair', 'poor', and so on in accordance with the accepted criteria either from conscientiousness or from habit or from fear of losing his job.

In the same way a professional taster of wine may dislike all wine or prefer the less good to the better; his judgment is based solely on the presence of those "characteristic qualities" which, as an expert, he is able to detect and knows to be among the criteria for 'good wine'. But even in these cases there is an indirect reference to choosing and advising which comes out when we turn from the question "What are the criteria in fact used for grading X's?" to the question "Why do we have the criteria that we do?". Professional wine tasters are, after all, business men or the employees of business men and, though their job may be to taste wine, they only have this job because wine is to be bought and sold. It is no accident that the criteria for 'good X's' are connected with the X's that people prefer or approve of more highly. The professional wine taster may not *like* Chateau Laffitte; but he uses criteria for judging wine under which it gets high marks because people are prepared to pay highly for wine which rates highly under these criteria, and they do this because they like it.

4

Nature and convention. The dictionary's phrase "admirable in themselves" is unfortunately ambiguous. In its context it is clear that 'in themselves' is contrasted with 'for a purpose', and that what the author has in mind is the familiar contrast between good-as-means and good-as-an-end. But 'in itself' is often used in philosophy with at least three other meanings. (a) It is sometimes used as a synonym for 'really' or 'objectively' to imply independence of human opinion or judgment of value. But, in discussing Moore's 'two worlds' argument I have already suggested that it is doubtful whether any sense can be given to the idea of something being good if there was no one to judge it good.

(b) It is sometimes used with a gerundive force. What is admirable or preferable in itself is what people ought to admire or prefer. But to use it in this way is not to comment on the use of 'good' but to make a value judgment; and, if the author of the dictionary were thought to be using it in this way, he must be thought to subscribe himself to all the value judgments he cites as examples of 'good'. (c) But 'good-in-itself' could also be used to mean 'naturally good', to imply that the criteria or standards used for judging the goodness of something are not, like the criteria for a good postage stamp, dependent on human convention. It is this contrast that I propose to discuss.

We call a taste (or any other pro-attitude) a 'natural' one if (a) it is pretty general even among people of very different societies and if (b) most people do not have to learn to acquire it. It is important to notice that both these criteria for what is 'natural' are extremely vague and that they both admit of exceptions. A taste for strawberries does not cease to be natural because Jones happens not to like them or because Smith did not like them at first. Benevolence and love of life are natural pro-attitudes, even though there are misanthropes and suicides.

The criteria used for appraising are partly natural and partly conventional. In music, for example, the criteria which critics apply to a composition or performance are conventional in that they vary in different cultures and it is necessary to learn what they are; and musical taste is also partly conventional in that it is not natural to like or admire a Bach fugue in the way that it is natural to like sweets or to love one's children. It may well be that no criteria or tastes are wholly conventional. Correlations can be found between the criteria employed and the physiological facts of hearing; for example we know that the musical intervals and key relationships on which all western music is based and which enter into the criteria used for judging a musical composition are of a mathematically simple kind. And even in the case of the criteria used for judging dogs at Crufts, which are highly artificial, it is possible to trace historical connections between the criteria now used and the criteria that were used when dogs were used for practical purposes; and these last were natural criteria in that the purposes, such as hunting and protection from wild animals, were based on natural pro-attitudes.

But in many cases the criteria now used are connected to natural criteria only through a long process of change and have become modified to such an extent that their original connection with natural pro-attitudes has been entirely lost. And in such cases it often happens that we do not use the criteria we do because people have the pro-attitudes they have, but we have the pro-attitudes we have because the criteria are what they are. It may be that no one can now remember exactly why certain criteria were originally chosen to be the standards of judging something to be good or bad of its kind and that people are now prepared to admire, praise, and pay highly for objects because they conform to the accepted criteria, rather than accepting the criteria as 'proper' ones because, under them, the things that they admire rate highly. Taste is dictated by fashion, not fashion by taste.

But such cases must (logically) be secondary cases and it would therefore be a mistake to cite them in proof of the contention that criteria are logically prior to pro-attitudes. For unless there were primary cases in which we adopted criteria *because* we already had a pro-attitude towards the objects that in fact rate highly under them, it would be impossible to understand how the same set of words could be used both in applying criteria and for choosing, praising, and advising. It is only because 'good' is used in applying criteria in cases where we use the criteria we do because our desires, interests, and tastes are what they are that men can come to acquire a taste for what counts as 'good' under the accepted criteria even in cases where the original connection between the criteria and the taste has been lost. Advertisers and propagandists, arbiters of taste and leaders of fashion could not (logically) stimulate new tastes and attitudes by the reiterated use of criterion-applying language unless this language was also used for applying criteria in cases where there are preexisting tastes and attitudes. Without genuine enthusiasts there could be no snobs.

In many cases, therefore, the answer to the question 'Why do we use the criteria for judging so-and-so's that we do?' may be of a purely historical kind; the criteria are traditional; they have been concocted and molded by interested parties, and so on. But this sort of answer cannot be given in all cases; there must be some cases in which we use a set of criteria because, as an empirical fact, they give higher ratings to those objects which we prefer.

In discussing appraisals I assumed that there was no difficulty about saying what the proper criteria for judging X's are or about selecting the experts, leaders of fashion, or arbiters of taste; and it might seem that these assumptions involve a vicious circularity in the attempt to construe the grading scale of good, fair, poor, and bad in terms of the standards used by experts. But this is not so for two reasons. (a) In some cases there are tests of competence which are purely objective and empirical. Some men, for example, have perfect pitch, can detect minute musical intervals, can recognize and accurately reproduce long and complicated tunes and so on, while others cannot; and these are matters of fact. In judging their expertise we must, of course, rely on the ability of other experts to assess their competence; but the judgments of these experts is 'objective' because they fulfil the requirements for objective language discussed in chapter 4 [of *Ethics*]. It is possible that one man might have a finer ear than all other men, so that in a case in which he said that two notes were slightly different when everyone else said they were the same he would be right and they wrong. But if there were no indirect tests, such as the appeal to readings of scales and meters, for deciding whether he can really detect these differences or is only bluffing, and if those who honestly claimed to be able to make fine discriminations did not on the whole agree with each other, we could not call their judgments 'objective'.

Now from the fact that a man is able to make these fine discriminations or to perform better than others in these objectively testable ways, it does

not, of course, follow that he is a good judge. For to say that he is a good
judge is either to state that he is good at applying the accepted criteria for
what is good (which is different from being good at passing the objective
tests) or to express approval of his judgments, to praise him, to encourage
others to accept his judgments, and so on; and in most cases it is to do all
these things at once. But, once again, the reason why we allow that, in a
general way, the most technically competent people are the best judges
lies in the facts. A man who is tone deaf is unlikely to be able even to
distinguish one piece of music from another and his value judgments (if
he makes them), are not likely to be consistent with each other; so that his
value judgments would be useless as a guide to others. A man who knows
little Greek could not be a good judge of a piece of Greek prose. Consistency
and fine discrimination are not sufficient conditions of good taste or moral
insight, but they are necessary conditions if criteria are to be used for the
purposes for which they are used.

(b) Secondly, the person who rejects the criteria usually employed
or the verdict of the acknowledged experts may do so in two ways. He may
simply refuse to be guided by them on the grounds that he happens not to
like what is usually called good. But, if he goes further and says that the
usual criteria are not *good* criteria, he is not just rejecting them; he is
himself using criterion-applying language and he implies that he has
second order criteria for judging (and condemning) the usual first order
criteria.

To the questioning of criteria there is no end; but if we ask whether
the criteria for judging X's are *good* criteria we must, at whatever level
we have reached, use criteria for deciding whether they are good or not.
It is logically absurd to ask a question without knowing how the answers
to it are to be judged to be good or bad answers. The appeal to criteria
accepted by experts is not circular, but regressive; and the regress is not
a vicious one since, although we *can* always question the criteria, there is
no practical or logical necessity to do so. The self-guaranteeing criteria so
vainly sought by some moralists are neither possible nor necessary.

5

Nonpractical appraisals. We often make appraisals in contexts
where there is clearly no question of choosing or advising, for example
moral judgments about historical or fictional characters. And this seems to
involve a difficulty for theories which make appraisals logically dependent
on pro-attitudes. Hutcheson and Hume, for example, tried to reduce moral
judgments to expressions of feeling. They were not guilty of the Naturalistic
Fallacy, since they were prepared to allow that moral approval and
sympathy are special, moral feelings distinct from other types of feeling.
But even this concession to the peculiarity of the moral use of language

does not save them from an important objection that seems at first sight fatal to their case. Sentiments, as Hume noticed, seem to vary in rough proportion to the propinquity of their objects. We are not moved by the iniquity of remote historical characters as we are by those closer to us; and we feel more approval for and sympathy with those near to us than with those who are more remote. Yet our moral judgments do not vary in the same way. "We read Cicero now without emotion, yet we can still judge Verres to be a villain. According to Hume's theory our judgment must change as do our feelings. I do not feel indignation as strongly now about the German invasion of Czechoslovakia as I did at the time it happened; yet I do not judge the action to be less wrong than I did then, or the agents less criminal.... It is but a weak subterfuge to say we transport ourselves by the force of imagination into distant ages and countries, and consider the passions which we should have felt on contemplating these characters had we been contemporaries and had commerce with the persons.... I now feel completely indifferent to Verres, and know it. Yet, Hume tells me, when I judge Verres to have been a villain, I am so deceived by my imagination that I talk as if I felt a strong feeling of anger."[1]

Dr. Raphael's criticism is fatal to the theory that a man who makes a moral appraisal is always expressing a feeling; and a similar criticism could also be made of any theory which says that to appraise is always to praise, advise, commend, etc. On some occasions a man may be simply *applying* the criteria that he and others customarily use for these purposes. To call Verres a villain is to pass a verdict on him, to condemn him. Now the Moral Sense School were, I think, mistaken in construing moral approval and disapproval as *feelings*, since this suggests too strongly the analogy with itches, aches, and tickles. But they were right to connect moral appraisals and verdicts with approval and disapproval. For although a man who passes a verdict need not be expressing a pro- or con-attitude, we have seen that the criteria he uses are directly or indirectly linked with these attitudes; and in the case of moral judgments they must be linked in a special way that may be absent in other cases.

I said earlier that, although in other cases 'good' might lose its gerundive force, it cannot wholly do so when used to make moral appraisals. The reason is that, whatever may be the case with other types of appraisal, moral appraisals must be universal. Anyone who makes a moral appraisal even of a remote character must be willing to apply the same criteria universally. And it follows from this that he must be willing to apply them in practical contexts. If I am not prepared to condemn anyone whose behavior is like that of Verres in all relevant respects, then, in calling Verres a villain, I am not making a genuine moral judgment;

[1] D. D. Raphael: *The Moral Sense*, pp. 88 and 91.

and the relevant respects are all of an empirical, objective kind. It would, of course, be trivial to include among them an objective property of villainy or moral turpitude; all that is necessary is that I should be prepared to condemn anyone who did the sort of thing that Verres is called a villain for having done, anyone who oppressed the poor, robbed the rich, took bribes, and cheated the treasury, and all for his own personal profit.

Moral appraisals are therefore connected with choosing and advising in a way that nonmoral appraisals need not be. It is not logically odd to say "This is the better wine, but I prefer that"; but it is logically odd to say "This is the (morally) better course; but I shall do that".[2] And a man cannot be making a genuine moral judgment about Verres if he would himself be prepared to act on the same principles on which Verres acted and prepared to exhort others to do so. In condemning Verres he is not expressing any emotion; but he is affirming his own moral principles.

6

Objective-subjective. In chapter 6 [of *Ethics*] I said that the distinction between "For what job is the word '. . .' used?" and "Under what conditions is it proper to use that word for that job?" throws light on the objective-subjective dispute.

As we should expect, both parties are right. Just as the subjectivists are right in denying that A-words stand for special properties and explaining them in terms of people's reactions, so they are also right in connecting 'good' and 'bad' with people's desires, tastes, interests, approvals, and disapprovals. There is a logical absurdity about calling a play 'amusing' if the speaker believes that it never has amused anyone and never will; and there is the same logical absurdity in calling something 'good' without any direct or indirect reference to a pro-attitude. If the connection between 'good' and the pro-attitude that is contextually relevant were not a logical one, a gap would emerge between calling something good on the one hand and deciding to choose it, choosing it or advising others to choose it on the other which would make these activities unintelligible. Moreover, the subjectivists are also right in connecting 'good' with the pro-attitudes of the speaker, at least in moral cases.

But the objectivists are also right. They are mistaken in denying the points made by the subjectivists above and in thinking that goodness must be a unique, nonnatural property. It is sometimes argued that if there were no such property we could not account for the fact that we use the impersonal form 'this is good' rather than the personal form 'I approve

---

2 This may sound surprising. We all know what it is to take what we know to be the morally worse course. I . . . try to remove the air of paradox in chapter 18 [of *Ethics*].

of this', and those who use this argument are inclined to forget that we have an impersonal form 'this is nice' as well as the personal form 'I like it', so that niceness would have to be an objective property too.

It would indeed be puzzling to understand why we use these impersonal forms if we were just talking about or expressing our own approvals; but this argument does not show that we are talking about something else, still less that this must be a unique property. We can account for the objective formula, as we did in the case of 'nice', by saying (a) that 'X is good' is not only used in the context of choice and (b) that, when it is so used, it implies a great deal that is not implied by 'I approve of X' and is expressly denied by 'I happen to approve of X'. It implies that my approval is not an unusual one and that I could give reasons for it. It implies also—what is a matter of objective fact—that the object conforms to certain standards which are generally accepted.

It is sometimes argued that 'this is good' cannot just mean 'I approve of this' on the ground that we can say "I approve of this because it is good". Approval must therefore be an intellectual emotion which arises in us only when we recognize something to have the objective property 'goodness'. But it has never been clear what the connection between the approval and the recognition of the property is supposed to be. Is it logically necessary that anyone who recognizes the property should feel approval or is it just an empirical fact that people who notice the property, and only they, have the feeling? Each of these answers involves insuperable difficulties; but if neither is correct we must find some other way of explaining the 'because' in 'I approve of X because it is good'.

The need for such an explanation vanishes when we see that this is not a reason-giving 'because' like that in 'I approve of Jones because he is kind to children' but more like 'I like Jones because he is likeable'. It rebuts the suggestion that I just 'happen to' approve of X and it implies that X has certain properties which make it worthy of my approval and that it conforms to the known standards for X's.

The objectivist is right in drawing attention to the factual background which makes impersonal appraisals possible; but the facts which it contains are ordinary, empirical facts, not special, nonnatural facts. Unlike the subjectivist (who tends to ignore the background altogether), he tries to include the background in the meaning of the word; and this, combined with the mistake of confusing practical and descriptive discourse, leads him into the vain pursuit of a single ingredient to which we always refer when we call something good.

7

The Naturalistic Fallacy. We are now in a position to see why the moral philosophers of the past subordinated the critical or appraising uses of moral language to the practical uses. Each presupposes the other, but in a different way. The practical uses presuppose the appraising use in that we could not use 'good' as we do for choosing, advising, and praising if we did not employ criteria or standards; since we only use 'good' for these purposes *when* we are employing standards. Nevertheless people who did not know what standards were could do things recognizably like what we, who have standards, call choosing, advising, and praising. They would be very rudimentary performances, hardly deserving the names of choice, advice, and praise; but they could occur. We draw a distinction between 'good' and 'happen to like' which people without standards could not draw; and we, who have the distinction, would describe their activities in terms of what they 'happen to like', because they could not do anything that we would call 'choosing the best'. In this way the practical uses of 'good' imply the appraising use.

But the practical uses are logically prior to the appraising use in a much more fundamental way. Unless men had pro-attitudes, there could not be even rudimentary analogues of what we know as appraising, judging, or passing a verdict. For these involve the use of standards; and without pro-attitudes we should neither have any use for standards nor even be able to understand what a 'standard' was. We can imagine a world in which there was choosing, but no appraising and also a world in which there was classifying, sorting, and ordering (for example by size) but no choosing; but, in a world in which there was no choosing, there could be no such thing as appraising or grading.

Ethical Naturalism is the attempt to trace logical connections between moral appraisals and the actual pro- and con-attitudes of men, their desires and aversions, hopes and fears, joys and sorrows. One-track naturalistic theories always fail to do justice to the complexity both of the facts and of the logical connections, since they suggest that there is only one thing towards which men have a pro-attitude, pleasure, or that all pro-attitudes are desires. And these theories are both psychologically and logically misleading.

Opponents of the Naturalistic Fallacy have pointed out the logical errors. It is true that gerundive and deontological words cannot be defined in terms of pleasure, desire, or even purpose; and I shall try to show how they are connected with these teleological concepts later. It is also true that gerundive judgments and value judgments do not follow logically from descriptive statements about what men like, enjoy, and approve of. But the reason for this is not that gerundive words and value words refer to special entities or qualities, but that a person who *uses* them is not, except in certain secondary cases, describing anything at all. He is not doing what psychologists do, which is to describe, explain, and comment on what people like, enjoy, and approve of; and he is not doing what moral philosophers do, which is to describe, explain, and comment on the way in which people use moral words; he is himself using moral language, expressing approval, praising, advising, exhorting, commending, or appraising.

The attack on the Naturalistic Fallacy is thus far justified. But the conclusion which is commonly drawn, that moral concepts are a special sort of concept which must be purged of all association with the 'merely empirical or phenomenal' concepts of enjoying, wanting, and approval is not justified. Psychology is not as irrelevant to ethics as some modern philosophers insist; for, although moral judgments do not follow from psychological statements, we cannot understand what the terms used in moral judgments mean unless we examine them in the context of their use; and they are used either directly to express a pro- or con-attitude or to perform some other task which beings who had no pro- or con-attitudes could not perform or even understand. The various ways in which 'good' is used are unintelligible unless they are directly or indirectly connected with choice; and I shall try to show later that the same applies to 'ought'.

Moral philosophy does not, therefore, "rest on a mistake". For the great philosophers were not primarily interested in the question whether deontological words could be analyzed in terms of 'merely empirical' or 'natural' concepts. They believed that, human beings being what they are, there are certain types of activity that are in fact satisfactory to them and that it is possible empirically to discover what these are. No doubt they often made mistakes of fact, for example that of supposing that what is satisfactory to one man would be satisfactory to another; and they made mistakes of logic, for example that of supposing that 'good' could be extracted from its context and be said to mean the same as 'satisfactory'. But they do not seem to have been mistaken in their basic assumptions that the language of obligation is intelligible only in connection with the language of purpose and choice, that men choose to do what they do because they are what they are, and that moral theories which attempt to exclude all consideration of human nature as it is do not even begin to be moral theories.

Good Reasons

KURT BAIER

When we ask people why they did a certain thing, they are often able to tell us their reasons. We usually have no difficulty in telling whether their reasons are good or bad reasons. But when we ask ourselves on what grounds we call some of their reasons good reasons and others bad, we do not know. It is often said that reason can only tell us how our desires can best be satisfied, or how some of our desires can be satisfied without others being frustrated, or which of our aspirations and wishes are based on a correct judgment of the situation and which are not. Some have held that these are the only things that reason can do and that there is no question of whether some of the aims we are pursuing are themselves contrary to, or sanctioned by, reason. It is indeed admitted that some goals are widely held to be so, but this is said to be a serious mistake. In this paper, I wish to show that certain facts are good reasons for, and certain others good reasons against, doing certain things, quite irrespective of the purposes, wishes, plans, desires, and passions of the person concerned.

The first point to note is that usually when we claim that something is a good reason for doing a certain thing, we mean that it is so, *other things being equal*. When I smoke my fiftieth cigarette, my reason for doing so—if I have a reason at all—may be that it will satisfy a craving which interferes with my work.

Other things being equal, 'it will satisfy a craving' is a good reason for doing that which will have this effect. But in this case, other things are of course not equal. There are very many good reasons against my smoking my fiftieth cigarette. Smoking is very expensive. It is bad for my health. It keeps me from sleeping at night. It ruins my appetite. And so on. Thus, a good reason for doing something usually is not the only reason there is. It will have to compete with other reasons for and against doing the contemplated course of action. We call them considerations, or reasons other things being equal.

We must keep apart this sort of reason from a final or sufficient reason for doing something in the circumstances in question. Considerations are at hand for the prospective and deliberating agent, just as the weights are ready for the butcher weighing the meat. But the weights do not by themselves get the weighing done. Similarly, the agent must "weigh" the various courses of action against the various considerations ready at hand.

From Philosophical Studies, *IV (1953). Reprinted by permission of the author and* Philosophical Studies.

The butcher who has weighed the pieces of meat *in order to buy the heaviest* may, of course, take the lightest (or the medium one) after the weighing, but this would be more than strange. Similarly, the agent may after deliberation not enter upon the course of action which he finds favored by the weightiest considerations but this would be equally out of place unless the agent has good reasons for doing so, as when after the weighing he decides to make a personal sacrifice.

The weights which the butcher uses may be correct or incorrect. Customers and butchers alike (though for different reasons) have an interest in the correctness of the weight. In most countries, balances and weights are checked by authorized commissioners. In the case of considerations, there can, of course, be no such commissioners. All we have to go by are the common evaluations of considerations, and our own reason. When we weigh the various courses of action, we do better if we frequently check on the "weight" of the considerations we use. Our judgments, after the review of the considerations, may or may not be right. The final reason we arrive at will usually be the operative reason, i.e. that which determines our choice. But, of course, as in the case of the butcher, a check after we have made a choice may reveal the faultiness of our "balance" and our "weights." We may find that our final reason was not a sufficient reason. Our deliberation was faulty. Our final reason was not a good one.

Practical reasoning consists in surveying the situation, reviewing the courses of action open to the agent, reviewing the considerations, or reasons other things being equal, which bear on the issue, weighing and balancing them against one another, and then deciding. Philosophy can hope to improve our knowledge of what are considerations and what in general are better reasons. But it cannot hope to do all the practical thinking once and for all, any more than logic can do all the theoretical.

Another implication of saying that x is a reason for doing y, in this sense of 'reason', is that it is so only *presumptively*. That is to say, a fact when stated in one way may look like a reason for doing something, but when stated in another more complete way, it may be seen not to be a good reason for doing something. Thus 'it gives Jones pleasure' is a consideration in favor of doing something. It is a reason only prima facie, for in the circumstances there may be many reasons against the action in question. But it is not even a consideration, it is a reason merely presumptively. For if it turns out that what I do and what gives Jones pleasure is the flagellation of Smith, then my presumptive reason for doing it, namely, that it gives Jones pleasure, has been rebutted. That it gives Jones pleasure is seen, in this case, to be not even a consideration, or reason prima facie, as some philosophers would say.

The presumptive nature of reasons must not be confused with their prima facie nature. In any specific case, prima facie reasons, i.e. considerations, are additional to, or in competition with, other prima facie reasons. They either have cumulative weight or one overrides the other. In judging the relative weight of considerations we do not alter or annul them qua considerations. We say that smoking satisfies a craving but that it is bad for one's health. The fact that it satisfies a craving is a prima facie reason for or consideration in favor of, smoking. The fact that it is bad for one's health is a prima facie reason against it. Some people would judge the fact that it satisfies a craving a better reason *for* smoking than the fact that it is bad for one's health is a reason *against* smoking; others the reverse. But neither of these judgments in any way undermines the prima facie nature of either reason.

By contrast, to say of a reason that it is so only presumptively is to say that its character as a prima facie reason for doing something may be wiped out or rebutted. In order to see this let us return to the example above. Suppose a certain activity gives pleasure to Jones. Then this is for him a prima facie reason for doing it. But suppose the activity which gives him pleasure is inflicting pain on Smith; then it is more fully described as 'affording Jones pleasure at another man's pain.' It is not merely that Jones' pleasure is unavoidably linked with Smith's pain. It is the very pain of Smith which affords Jones pleasure. Contrast this case with that in which Jill decides to dance with Jack. In doing so she will unavoidably hurt John. But the pleasure of Jack is derived from the dance, not from John's anguish. In the first case, the fact that Jones' pleasure is at Smith's pain wipes out as a prima facie reason the fact that doing this sort of thing gives pleasure to Jones. That is to say, the fact that something gives pleasure to Jones is merely a presumptive prima facie reason for doing it. The presumption that it is a prima facie reason can be rebutted by showing that the pleasure is at another man's pain. This is quite different from the case of Jill and Jack. There two prima facie reasons compete: the fact that her dancing with Jack will give pleasure to Jack and that it will give anguish to John. She will have to judge the comparative weight of these two prima facie reasons. But the fact that her dancing with Jack will give anguish to John does not rebut the prima facie reason that it will also give pleasure to Jack. At best, it overrides it.

There is yet a further important logical feature of the use of 'reason' we are examining. It is self-contradictory to say 'x is a good reason for doing y and x is a good reason against doing y,' where 'reason' is used in the same sense both times it occurs. Hence what Jones says contradicts what Smith says, if Jones says 'x is a good reason for doing y' and Smith says 'x is a good reason against doing y,' if reason is used in the sense just elaborated, namely, prima facie presumptive reason. This has an important consequence. A tribe in which people gave as a reason *for* entering on a certain course of action that it caused the agent's death would be a tribe which regarded as a reason *for*, what we regard as a reason *against*, doing something. This cannot be accepted as just a "brute fact" about this tribe, in the way we accept the fact that different people enjoy doing different things. It follows from the feature of 'reason' just mentioned that what they say contradicts what we say, i.e. that we and they cannot both be right. It does not, of course, follow that we are right and they are wrong.

This point is incompatible with two views about the "logic" of 'reason' in this use: the view that what is regarded as a reason for doing something is just a matter of convention; and the view that what is so regarded is just a brute fact about the person so regarding it. That these views are wrong is shown by the point just made. For if it were a matter of convention or a brute fact about the person in question, then if one person regarded something as a reason for doing something and another regarded the same thing as a reason against doing it, this would be the end of the matter. But, as we have just seen, it is not. When Jones and Smith differ in this way we do not accept this as a difference in their upbringing or in their nature and leave it at that, but we say that one of them must be wrong.

It is of some importance to understand why this has been overlooked. It is thought that what people regard as a reason is a matter of convention because of the superficial similarity between giving reasons and going through a rigmarole (cf. Toulmin). People have noticed the formal, ritual character of the procedure of giving reasons. But, as we shall see, when we give reasons we are not giving conventional tokens. The other reason why this is overlooked is that it is thought that what is regarded as a reason by someone or by some group is just a brute fact about them. But this is equally mistaken, a confusion between two different sorts of fact: on the one hand, a fact like the fact that Jones enjoys fishing while Smith does not, and on the other hand a fact like the fact that Jones' enjoyment of fishing furnishes him with a good reason for fishing, whereas Smith's dislike of it furnishes him (Smith) with a good reason against fishing. The first sort is indeed a brute fact about Jones and Smith. The second is not.

Consider a parallel case. Suppose Jones *believes* that fishing is good fun but Smith believes it is boring. Now, these are brute facts about Jones and Smith. Similarly, if a whole society thinks fishing is good fun, or alternatively that it is boring, then that they have this belief is a brute fact about this society. But it is not *just* a brute fact. For in addition to the question whether they do in fact have these beliefs, we may ask whether these beliefs are true or false.

The situation is similar in the case we are considering. That Jones or a whole society enjoys fishing is a brute fact. That they regard this as a good reason for going fishing is also a brute fact about them but not merely a brute fact. We may also ask whether they really do so regard the fact that someone enjoys doing something, and *whether they are right* in so regarding it. When two people have contradictory beliefs, then the question which is true necessarily arises. Similarly, when two people or two societies regard one and the same fact, say, that someone enjoys doing something, the one as a prima facie presumptive reason *for*, the other as a prima facie presumptive reason *against* doing it, then the question who is right necessarily arises. We cannot simply leave the matter at that and be satisfied with their just being different, as we can with regard to the brute facts of their enjoyment of different things.

It is true that many people will come to regard this or that as a reason for doing something because of the conventions prevailing in the group, as when we learn to refrain from belching after meals. But there are many reasons for or against doing something which are not conventional in this sense at all. Even these reasons must be learned by members of the group. The children of the group will be taught that this or that is regarded as a good reason for or a good reason against doing something. Many members of the group will never challenge what is commonly so regarded. Nevertheless, it is possible to ask this question which many people never ask, namely, whether *what is regarded as* a good reason for doing something really is a good reason for doing it. The most obvious need for asking this question arises when two people give the same fact, one as a reason for, the other as a reason against, doing one and the same thing.

It remains to decide whether we can ever know about any fact that it is a prima facie presumptive reason for or against entering on a certain course of action. Can we ever say with absolute certainty that people are wrong who do not recognize a certain fact to be a good reason for (or against) doing something? Are there any paradigms of a good reason? The answer is, of course, Yes.

Take the following example. A prisoner of war is chained to a tree. One of his arms is free. He is unguarded. His only chance of escape is to cut off his arm above the handcuffs. He is contemplating doing so.

There are what would ordinarily be called excellent reasons against doing so. It would involve the loss of a hand. Lacking medical attention, he might bleed to death or die of gangrene. He would be too weak to get away. Even if he had the strength and was not caught again by the Japanese, he would not survive the trek across the jungle. But there are also what would ordinarily be called excellent reasons for cutting off the hand. The chances of survival as a prisoner of war with the Japanese are not good. The suffering in such a camp is appalling. And so on.

Every one of the reasons mentioned against cutting off the hand would ordinarily be said to be excellent. They are in fact typical cases by reference to which we learn what is a good reason against doing something. What better reasons could one give than the fact that doing a certain thing would probably cost the agent his life, or would involve the loss of a hand or very great suffering? When confronted with these facts, it would be pretty unreasonable to say that these were not very good reasons against doing something.

Yet, skeptics will not be appeased by this sort of remark. They will say that it is, of course, true that these are *recognized* reasons in our society, and that they are well aware of that. But, they will add, this only shows their conventional status and does not preclude the possibility of there being a tribe in which these reasons are not recognized as reasons against doing something, but where on the contrary they are recognized as reasons for doing it. It is then up to us to prove that we are right in recognizing them as reasons against, while they are wrong in recognizing them as reasons for, doing something.

In order to meet the skeptic's request, let us first be clear about the difference between, on the one hand, being dissatisfied with the reasons given and, on the other, wishing to have it proved that a certain fact constitutes a reason for or against doing something. Thus someone planning to have his antrums washed out may be warned by someone else that this operation hurts a little. He may reply 'I think I shall have to have it done unless there is some other better reason against it.' One may then add that the nose and throat specialist consulted is notoriously bad, and that this sort of operation usually leaves things worse than they were before. These further reasons would generally be regarded as better reasons than the mere fact that it hurts a little.

Clearly, our skeptic does not wish for this sort of improvement of the reasons given. He quite realizes that the reasons given against cutting off one's hand are the very best that can be given. He does not doubt that among the recognized reasons these are recognized to be the weightiest. He does not want other reasons which are recognized to be better. He wants something quite different. He wants a proof that the reasons which are recognized to be good reasons or recognized to be the best reasons really are so. How can we satisfy his demand?

To an ordinary doubter, we would simply point out what such a recognized reason involves or comes to. If we point out that the loss of a hand means that he will not be able to write, to drive, to engage in certain sports, to use a knife and fork, to compete with others for jobs, friends, and so on, then surely *the magnitude of the loss* will be brought home to the person. And what is true of the loss of a hand is true, *mutatis mutandis*, of the loss of any limb, faculty, or sense.

But the skeptic may not be convinced by this way of proving that these facts which are recognized to be good reasons really are good reasons. He may ask why the fact that one should not be able to play games, compete for jobs and friends, write, and so on, indeed why any loss whatever should constitute a reason against doing that which would involve such a loss. In reply to this, one may repeat the previous moves. One may set out in detail what is involved in not being able to play games, compete for jobs, and so on. But if the skeptic is not impressed by losses, then he will not be impressed by any considerations of this sort. The skeptic wants a different sort of thing altogether. He wants a *proof* that something or other is a good reason. I shall now attempt to provide such a proof.

Of course, from the nature of the case, this proof cannot have the form of a deductive proof. For if it had, the skeptic would only repeat his performance with regard to the premises from which such a proof sets out. In any case, a deductive proof is only one variety of proof. It is characterized by the fact that its premises are either undeniable or, at any rate, generally accepted and that acceptance of the premises and rejection of the conclusion would involve one in self-contradiction. Self-contradiction is a very strong sanction, but it is not the only one. The proof that I shall give is not of the deductive sort, but it shows that anyone denying that a certain fact is a good reason (prima facie and presumptively) against doing a certain thing is laying himself open to criticism of a sort just as serious as that he is contradicting himself, namely, that he is irrational.

The proof I want to give is interesting not only because it attempts to show that something or other is a good reason, but also because that which it shows to be a good reason is the fact that a certain course of action will cause the agent pain. In view of the importance of pain to moral philosophy, this particular proof is of more than logical interest. What I wish to prove, then, is that to say 'it will cause me pain' is to give a good reason (prima facie and presumptively) against doing "it," because the fact that it will cause me pain is a good prima facie presumptive reason against doing "it."

My proof will consist in examining a certain course of action which obviously causes pain to a man. I shall try to show that if this man denies that the fact that a certain course of action will cause him pain is a prima facie presumptive reason against doing what he does, he is laying himself open to criticism of such a sort that we must infer that what he denies (or by his behavior rejects) is clearly true.

Consider the following example. A man has laid out on the ground a bed of smoldering coal on which he is racing up and down barefoot. Suppose he treads firmly on the coal, does not flinch, does not scream or show the strain of holding back the manifestations of pain, does not perspire or twitch, etc. In such a case we shall be inclined to say that he does not feel pain. If he says he does not feel pain and if the soles of his feet are not burned, we shall be confirmed in our opinion. We shall be surprised at this, and perhaps admire his will power. But since walking up and down on burning coal does not appear to cause him pain, we have no reason to think that he does not regard 'it causes me pain' as a good prima facie presumptive reason against doing "it." Hence this is not yet the case we wish to examine.

But now suppose that he shows all the signs of intense pain and says that he experiences it. Suppose now that he says, in reply to the question why he does it, that it is good for his soul, or that he is training to become a spy and is practicing to stand up to torture, or that he is training to become a Yogi, or that being able to endure pain makes one an upright sort of person. Then we must say that he is in pain and that he thinks that there is a good reason why one should do things which cause one pain. But he does not think that 'it causes me pain' is itself a good prima facie reason for doing it. He has given other reasons why one should endure pain. He implies that 'it causes me pain' is *a reason against* doing it, but that *he has better reasons for* doing it. That is to say, he does not deny that 'it causes me pain' is a good prima facie presumptive reason against doing it. He thinks he can mention reasons which override it. This still is not the case we want.

But now suppose that he has no reasons, that in his case there are no reasons for walking on the burning coal. When asked why he does it, he says 'Why? How do you mean why? Don't you see, I am walking on burning coal and it causes me excruciating pain? Isn't that good enough?' What could this mean? What should we say about such a man?

Had he said 'exquisite pain,' we might have understood. Evidently he is a masochist. If, moreover, he thinks that everybody is like him in this respect, then we can understand why he should think an explanation unnecessary. For masochists are people who cannot be sexually stimulated or attain sexual gratification except by the infliction of pain in certain specific ways. What we should say in such cases is that the man was seeking sexual stimulation and gratification in the only manner which, in his case, could lead to success. But then he does not *really* think that 'it will cause me pain' is a good reason for doing it, but that 'it will give me sexual satisfaction' is. This latter, of course, really is a good prima facie presumptive reason for doing something. So, this would not be a case of a man rejecting 'it causes pain' as a prima facie presumptive reason.

However, our man is not a masochist, for he does not say 'exquisite pain,' but 'excruciating pain.' So what shall we say? Can we perhaps say that he just enjoys or likes having pain? Ryle seems to suggest (*Concept of Mind*, p. 109) that this a possible view, for he says "It should be mentioned that 'pain,' in the sense in which I have pains in my stomach, is not the opposite of 'pleasure.' In this sense, a pain is a sensation of a special sort, *which we ordinarily dislike having.*"

However, it does not make sense to say 'I enjoy pain.' For to say this is to take away with one hand what one has given with the other. To say that one enjoys being in a certain state, having something done to one, or doing something is to be wholeheartedly in it, to pursue it, to seek opportunities for it, to tend to prolong it, to be disappointed when it is ended, and so on. On the other hand, to say that one is in pain or that one has a pain is to imply the opposite.

The main reason why people overlook this is that they think of a pain as a sensation of a kind normally found painful—one, as Ryle puts it, "which we ordinarily dislike having." They think of pains as certain kinds of "sensation" which most people, but not necessarily all, dislike, and which we all ordinarily though not necessarily always dislike.

Nevertheless, this view is mistaken. A pain is not a sensation logically neutral to enjoyment and dislike. We mean by 'a pain' something about which it is natural to complain, natural to wish that it were to end, that it were never to return, and so on. This can be shown by attending briefly to the way in which we come to use the word 'pain.' A very young child cannot simulate or dissimulate the so-called manifestations of pain. Thus, if a baby cries when a certain spot is touched or pressed, winces, shrinks away from the pressing finger, shows signs of relief when ointments are applied, and so on, one would take this as conclusive evidence that the baby was in pain. On the other hand, if, on being touched, he snuggles up, smiles and gurgles and coos, cries when mother stops touching him, etc., then one would think that pressing the spot did not cause him pain but that, on the contrary, he enjoyed it.

It is in circumstances such as these that the normal child is introduced to the characteristic "pain talk." That the baby is in pain is first ascertained by its parents, and it is ascertained entirely, of course, on the basis of the so-called manifestations of pain. I am here interested only in the normal child, i.e. the child whose manifestations of pain are genuine. That is to say, the child who shows signs of pain *before* he can simulate them. I am not here concerned to refute the skeptical position that everyone other than the speaker may be a pain-simulator, or a person who because he never had a pain shows the signs of pain without understanding the difference between the pain-simulator and the person genuinely in pain.

Now, the normal baby is introduced to the characteristic "pain talk" when, by his behavior, his mother can tell that he is in pain. She then says things like "Poor baby has hurt himself, has a nasty big bad bruise. Oh, never mind, it will be better tomorrow" and so on. Thus when the baby is in a situation which is interpreted by adults around him as a case of baby in pain, he hears the characteristic "pain talk," and he becomes the object of attention, sympathy, commiseration, and pity. The child comes to understand that having a pain is something on account of which he gets and deserves to get sympathy, and something which one hopes will not last long. This helps him to identify correctly those feelings which we mean by 'pain,' namely, those which he himself hopes to avoid, to end as quickly as possible, and on account of which he feels miserable and sorry for himself. These, from the nature of the way we learn expressions like 'I am in pain,' 'he has a pain in his finger,' and so on, are logically necessary features of 'pain.' These are not features which are contingently connected with pain. A feeling *would not be a pain* if it did not have these features.

There is a further point which helps to obscure this. We have just seen that a pain by its nature has these negative features. But that certain happenings to the body are painful is not a logical necessity. Some people may not find it painful to have their ears tweaked or their teeth knocked out. Nevertheless, it is worth noting how uniform people in fact are in this respect. In any case, this is a causal matter, a matter of physiology. It is certainly not a matter of convention or accident. What we find painful is determined by the way we are built. No doubt, if we had different sorts of bodies, different things would be found painful or perhaps we would not feel pain at all. But as it is, human nature being what it is, we find very much the same sorts of treatment painful. And if we find something painful, then we have a good reason for avoiding it.

What about pleasant pains? Does not their existence show that the account above is wrong? Sometimes, after a visit to the dentist, I have in my tooth a feeling as if the filling were too big. The gums are a bit raw and there is a dull sort of pressure in the tooth. If the new filling is amalgam and it is near a gold filling, I get a peculiar sensation by passing my tongue over the amalgam while at the same time touching the gold. A mild electric shock shoots through the tooth. I find this quite pleasant, although the sensation itself must be described as a mild pain. Notice the circumstances in which we can speak of a pleasant pain. If the pain were intense and of very long duration, we could not possibly call it pleasant. Moreover, it must occur in a certain sort of context. I would not find it pleasant if I did not have that dull feeling of pressure in my tooth. The flash of pain relieves the dull monotony of this pressure. Hence I find these flashes pleasant. Conditions like these are not accidental. If there were no such context, I should regard the feeling merely as a pain but not as pleasant. And if it were not unpleasant, I might regard it as pleasant, but not as pain. Thus, what is pleasant is the whole experience of which the pain is an (unpleasant) part.

Alternatively, one may not find the pain really pleasant or enjoy it, but one may merely rejoice in the pain, as the martyr does whose willing agony testifies to the glory of God.

Thus, it won't do to say that the man walking on burning coal enjoys pain. For to say that something is a pain is to say that it is *a sort of thing one does not enjoy*. This is part of the meaning of pain. It is not an empirical matter. It is not to say that pain is the sort of thing most people, as a matter of empirical fact, do not enjoy. For if it is the latter, we must *first* come to know what pain is and *then* discover by empirical examination of people how they react to it, as we come to know what it is to dig in the garden or to drink gin before we know whether most people enjoy doing it. To say 'I enjoy a glass of gin after dinner' is to give information. To say 'I don't enjoy pain' is not even to mention what is common knowledge. To say 'I enjoy pain' is not to reveal peculiar or odd predilections. It is to make an incomprehensible remark. I do not of course mean that this remark could never be understood by anybody. All I mean is that it has no literal, no standard, no natural significance. It has no more significance than the remark 'I had a little girl brother yesterday.' This does not, of course, mean that the mother of male triplets who has just had a girl will not understand what one of her sons means when he makes that remark.

Thus, our fakir cannot be said to enjoy pain. This account of why he walks on burning coal will not do, for it is literally meaningless. Shall we perhaps say that he *likes* pain? For this does make sense. We can say that. It can be understood. One may like things which one does not enjoy and enjoy things which one does not like. Let us then examine briefly the differences between the uses of 'liking' and 'enjoying.'

In the first place, we can enjoy only the doing or undergoing of something or the being in a certain state. We cannot enjoy material objects. 'I enjoyed that steak' is elliptical for 'I enjoyed eating that steak.' On the other hand, we can like things as well as doing things. 'I like that picture' does not merely mean 'I enjoy or like looking at that picture,' 'I like Jones' does not mean merely 'I enjoy or like talking to Jones.' It involves things like the fact that this picture is skillfully painted, or that Jones has a good character.

This leads to the second difference. Enjoyment is not based on reason in the way liking is. It always makes sense to ask "Why do you like that?" though the person in question need not be able to answer. But while it often makes sense to ask "Why do you enjoy that?" this is really a different sort of question, and moreover, it is sometimes appropriate to answer "No reason at all. I just do enjoy it." Thus, I may ask "Why do you enjoy a hot bath?" However, this is never a question for *his reason for enjoying* it. It is a request for an explanation, i.e. the pointing to that feature in the whole thing which the person enjoys. He may say in reply "I enjoy a hot bath because I love that tingling warm feeling I have all over when I sit in the tub." But when I ask "Why do you enjoy having that warm tingling feeling?" he may say "No particular reason, I just enjoy it."

But while enjoyments are not based on reasons, we may ruin someone's enjoyment of something by telling him things about it. Sensitive ladies can no longer enjoy their steak when the story of the slaughterhouses is told. This story works in two ways. In the first place, it arouses their disgust and horror, just as the sight of the slaughter would. They certainly would not enjoy witnessing this spectacle. This is not, of course, *a reason for not enjoying steak*. It is *a reason why* they cannot any longer enjoy steak. The picture of cattle being slaughtered *interferes* with their enjoyment of eating steak. In addition, these ladies may also have a bad conscience about it. They may feel that eating steak helps to perpetuate this method of slaughter. They now also have *a reason for* not eating steak. This may further spoil their enjoyment of eating steak. It is notorious that some people cannot enjoy doing things that they do with a bad conscience. Some people, of course, derive extra enjoyment from doing what is forbidden but this is not usually so with this sort of enjoyment.

In the case of liking something, on the other hand, we can always ask 'why?' in the sense of asking for a reason *for* liking it, and not merely for an explanation of why he likes it. That I enjoy doing it is a reason for liking it. That I have been given a certain injection, or that I have been hypnotized or conditioned in a certain way, is no reason for liking it, though it may well be a *reason (explanation) why* I like it.

Thus enjoying and liking are comparatively independent of each other. There are plenty of things I do not enjoy doing, which nevertheless I like doing for one reason or another. I like paying my debts on time, I like to visit my mother's grave at least once a year, I like to have my cold shower and my run before breakfast every morning, and so on. Similarly, there are lots of things I enjoy doing though I dislike doing them for one reason or another. Thus I dislike picking a quarrel, talking about myself, taking out my best friend's best girl, and so on, though I would enjoy doing these things if I ever did do them.

It would, then, seem that while a man cannot say that he enjoys pain, he might well say that he likes pain in cases analogous to the ones we have just mentioned. What is characteristic of all these cases is that I have good reasons for my dislike of doing them although I enjoy doing them; or good reasons for my liking to do them in spite of finding them repugnant or painful.

But what would we say if someone maintained that he liked something which he found repugnant or painful and that he had no reason whatever for liking them. A man may, of course, say "I just like this. I have no particular reason for liking it." But what would we say if he added "and what's more, I find doing these things repugnant and painful"? We would be puzzled and would not know what he was getting at; we would want to know what was the matter with such a man. Our fakir is just that sort of case.

We might, in the first place, suspect that he did not know what he was saying. We might do our best for him, in the way of interpretation, as the mother does whose son said, "I had a little girl brother yesterday." Most naturally, we would think he meant perhaps that when he said he *liked* walking on burning coal and that he found it painful and repugnant, he did not really mean that he liked it. Perhaps he merely meant that he approved of it or thought it necessary or good or a duty, etc. In all these cases, of course, the man has an explanation, and while it may be a very bad explanation, we at least understand what he is getting at. Or alternatively, he may not really mean that he finds it repugnant and painful. Then again, we understand.

We may make sure that the man in question understands what he is saying and see whether his behavior supports what he says. If he drinks ink or eats live toads or drives hairpins through his cheeks and if disgust and revulsion and agony are plainly written on his face; if he always asks for ink and hairpins with his meals, advertises for live toads, and so on, then we have reason to think that he really means what he says and that it is true, namely, that in a way he likes doing these things although he finds them repugnant, disgusting, and painful, and has no reason at all for doing them.

But what must we say about such a man? Shall we say that he is odd, eccentric, different? Surely, that would not be right. For we reserve these words for cases of unusual and startlingly different enjoyments. A man who eats live toads with obvious relish or enjoys drinking ink would certainly be said to be odd or to have strange tastes, perhaps even perverse and unnatural tastes. But they are not irrational. Again, to derive enjoyment from collecting pavement stones or from getting up at 3 A.M. to watch birds, or from taking part in whist drives, may seem to some very odd indeed. But this is simply being different from the rest of us, having different tastes, getting enjoyment out of different things.

This is quite different from a second case where a man likes doing something which he finds repugnant or painful but has a good reason for doing. St. Elizabeth (presumably) did not indulge a perverted taste for kissing lepers. She overcame her natural aversion to doing so for the sake of showing affection to these poor creatures and thus bring them comfort and consolation. The fakir who dances on burning coal for a living, or because he thinks it will secure him a place in heaven, is not indulging odd tastes or deriving enjoyment from unusual practices.

These two groups of cases are different from the case we are considering. We are not considering people with odd tastes or people who, for one reason or another, have overcome their normal or unusual inclinations and tastes. We are considering the case of a man who, for no reason whatever, does what his organism revolts against. For this is the truth about a man who, without having a reason for doing so, does what he knows will cause him pain. Hence, it is not an explanation of our case to say that this man does only what he likes doing, since he likes doing what he knows will cause him pain. We know, of course, that there must be an explanation, a reason why he acts in this way. But the explanation (*the reason why*) will not be in terms of the man's *reasons for* doing it. He has no reason for doing it. There is no reason for doing it.

What do we say of a man who does this? Well, in the first place, it would be natural to suspect that he was insane. But if further investigation reveals that in all other fields of behavior he is normal, we cannot say that, but we call his behavior irrational, contrary to reason.

It is, of course, true that the man in question is not contradicting himself. He is saying something that we barely understand, namely, that he likes pain for its own sake. What he means we have described in detail: namely, he regularly goes in for doing something of which he knows that it will cause him pain, without having any reason for doing it. It is a conceivable case, but such behavior is the prototype of irrationality, of flying in the face of reason.

It may be said that this strong word, 'irrationality,' ought to be reserved for cases of self-contradiction. But this would be a mistake. For a man may contradict himself without therefore being irrational. People often contradict themselves either because they have forgotten what they previously said or because they do not realize that what they are now saying contradicts what they have previously said. This is to be inconsistent. Perfectly rational people do this. We can speak of irrationality only when someone, in the face of a detailed proof of the incompatibility of two claims, maintains the two claims, either because he refuses to admit that the two claims are contradictory although they plainly are, or in spite of the fact that he admits their contradictoriness (and we have good reason to think that he understands what this means).

But if it is admitted that a person who does what he knows will cause him pain and who has no reason for doing it, must be called irrational, then I have proved my original contention, that a person who offers 'it will cause me pain' as a reason against doing "it" has offered a good reason. For a person who behaves in the way described obviously rejects 'it will cause me pain' as a good reason against doing "it." Since rejecting this reason draws upon one the criticism that one is irrational in so doing, that one acts contrary to reason, that one flies in the face of reason, then, clearly, accepting it as a reason has the opposite consequence. In accepting it as a reason, one is on the side of reason, one has reason on one's side, one is supported by reason. But if in offering something as a reason one has reason on one's side, then what one has offered as a reason must be a good reason (prima facie and presumptively, of course).

Generalization in Ethics

MARCUS GEORGE SINGER

The question "What would happen if everyone did that?" is one with which we are all familiar. We have heard it asked, and perhaps have asked it ourselves. We have some familiarity with the sort of context in which it would be appropriate to ask it. For instance, we understand that it is either elliptical for or a prelude to saying, "If everyone did that, the consequences would be disastrous", and that this is often considered a good reason for concluding that one ought not to do that. The situations in which this sort of consideration might be advanced are of course exceedingly diverse. One who announces his intention of not voting in some election might be met by the question, "What would happen if no one voted?" If no one voted the government would collapse, or the democracy would be repudiated, and this is deemed by many to indicate decisively that everyone should vote. Again, one who disapproves of another's attempts to avoid military service might point out: "If everyone refused to serve, we would lose the war." The members of a discussion group, which meets to discuss papers presented by members, presumably all realize that each should take a turn in reading a paper, even if he does not want to and prefers to take part in the discussion only, because if everyone refused to read a paper the club would dissolve, and there would be no discussions. This sort of consideration would not be decisive to one who did not care whether the club dissolved. But it undoubtedly would be decisive to one who enjoys the meetings and wishes them to continue.

Each of these cases provides an example of the use or application of a type of argument which I propose to call the *generalization argument*: "If everyone were to do that, the consequences would be disastrous (or undesirable); therefore, no one ought to do that." Any argument of the form "The consequences of no one doing x would be undesirable; therefore every one ought to do x" is also, obviously, an instance of the generalization argument. Now the basic problem about this argument is to determine the conditions under which it is a good or valid one, that is to say, the conditions under which the fact that the consequences of everyone doing x would be undesirable provides a good reason for concluding that it is wrong for anyone to do x. I have formulated the problem in this way because there

From Mind, *LXIV (1955). Reprinted by permission of the author and* Mind. *The substance of this essay, in revised and considerably expanded form, is contained in Marcus George Singer,* Generalization in Ethics *(New York: Alfred A. Knopf, 1961).*

are conditions under which the generalization argument is obviously not applicable. Though the instances presented above are ones in which the consideration of the consequences of everyone acting in a certain way seems clearly relevant to a moral judgment about that way of acting, there are others in which this sort of consideration is just as clearly irrelevant. While "humanity would probably perish from cold if everyone produced food, and would certainly starve if everyone made clothes or built houses",[1] it would be absurd to infer from this that no one ought to produce food or build houses.

It might be thought that this is a counter-example, which proves the generalization argument to be invalid or fallacious generally, and that the fallacy consists in arguing from "not everyone" to "no one", or from "some" to "all". But this would be a mistake. It is not always a fallacy to argue from "some" to "all". The belief that it is is merely a prejudice arising out of a preoccupation with certain types of statements. It is true that the generalization argument involves an inference from "not everyone has the right" to "no one has the right", from "it would not be right for everyone" to "it would not be right for anyone". This inference, however, is mediated by what I shall call "the generalization *principle*", that *what is right (or wrong) for one person must be right (or wrong) for any similar person in similar circumstances.*

Since the generalization argument presupposes and thus depends on the generalization principle, and since the generalization principle is certainly of considerable interest in its own right, I shall devote the next section—the major portion—of this paper to an attempt to determine the meaning and importance of this principle. This will involve a consideration of the meaning and function of the qualification "similar persons in similar circumstances". Following this I shall take up the problem about the generalization argument mentioned above, by considering briefly certain fairly plausible objections to it and attempting to show that they are not decisive. This will go some distance towards the formulation of the conditions under which the generalization argument is valid.

1. THE GENERALIZATION PRINCIPLE

The basic question about the generalization principle, as I have already indicated, concerns the qualification "similar persons in similar circumstances". Now in his discussion of this principle, which he called the principle of justice or impartiality, Sidgwick pointed out:

> We cannot judge an action to be right for A and wrong for B,
> unless we can find in the natures or circumstances of the two some

---

[1] M. R. Cohen, *The Faith of a Liberal*, p. 86.

difference which we can regard as a reasonable ground for difference in their duties. If therefore I judge any action to be right for myself, I implicitly judge it to be right for any other person whose nature and circumstances do not differ from my own in certain important respects. . . .

If a kind of conduct that is right (or wrong) for me is not right (or wrong) for someone else, it must be on the ground of some difference between the two cases, other than the fact that I and he are different persons.[2]

This, however, does not seem to go very far towards meeting the basic objection that might be made against this principle, which might be put in this manner: "It is all very well to insist that what is right for one person must be right for any similar person in similar circumstances. But what does this mean? How can you tell in any particular case whether the natures or circumstances of the people involved are similar or not? Indeed, under what conditions could not two people be said to be similar? You can always find some similarities, and, since this is the case, this principle is so vague as to be useless. It will not help matters to say that 'similar persons in similar circumstances' are those persons 'whose natures and circumstances do not differ in some important respects'. For which respects are important ones? Obviously there will always be some differences. How can you tell in any particular case which differences are important and which are not?"

Though I think this objection rests on a confusion, it is an important one and must be met. (It was on this ground that C. D. Broad asserted that Sidgwick's principle, while "not absolutely verbal", is "extraordinarily trivial", while Bradley claimed that it is a "bare tautology".)[3] The questions it sets forth, so far as they are sensible, can be given satisfactory answers. These questions, however, are not, as they stand, altogether legitimate. They arise, to some extent, out of a confusion.

For this sort of objection to the generalization principle assumes that it pretends or is supposed to contain within itself the criteria for "similar persons in similar circumstances", while it most emphatically does not. The fact that it does not is not a defect in it. The occurrences of the term 'similar' in the statement of this principle do not make it vague or inapplicable. They ensure its generality. The expression 'similar persons in similar circumstances' is to be construed as a "place holder", to be filled in different ways in different contexts. In other words, the occurrences of the term 'similar' in the statement of this principle are to be regarded as blanks *to be filled* in different ways depending on the context. Different

2 Henry Sidgwick, *The Methods of Ethics* (7th ed., 1907), pp. 209, 379.
3 C. D. Broad, *Five Types of Ethical Theory*, p. 223; F. H. Bradley, "Mr. Sidgwick's Hedonism" in *Collected Essays*, I, 100.

applications of the principle, in which the term 'similar' does not occur, will result from different ways of filling in these blanks. Each of these applications may be regarded as a rule or principle on a lower level of generality than the generalization principle itself, or simply as a particular application of the general principle.

I realize that these brief remarks are in need of illustration. But I propose postponing giving illustrations of the applications of this principle until some further questions are disposed of. It is necessary first to answer the legitimate questions involved in the foregoing objection. While it is not a legitimate criticism of the generalization principle that it cannot by itself determine the concrete meaning of the phrase "similar persons in similar circumstances", it would be a legitimate criticism of it if there were no way at all of determining this. For if this were the case the principle would be inapplicable. Thus it is necessary to show that this is not the case.

One thing that gives rise to this sort of objection is the fact that things may be similar in different ways. A and B may be similar in one respect and not in another. And it holds trivially that given any two things it is possible to specify some respect in which they are alike as well as some respect in which they are different. But while some similarities (and differences) can always be specified, not all of them will be relevant ones. The generalization principle must be understood in the sense that what is right for one person must be right for every *relevantly* similar person in *relevantly* similar circumstances. While it is true that two things may be similar in one respect and not in another, it is also true that two things may be similar for one purpose and not for another. Whether A and B are to be regarded as similar in any nontrivial sense is thus dependent on the purpose or context. If we think of relevant and irrelevant similarities this should be obvious. For the notion of relevance has no meaning apart from some determinate context. A statement of the form "A is relevant" is, as it stands, incomplete. It is either elliptical for a statement of the form "A is relevant to B", where this further reference is determined from the context, or else it is nonsense. Now just as what is relevant to one thing may not be relevant to another, what is relevant in one context may not be relevant in another. Thus the phrase "(relevantly) similar persons in (relevantly) similar circumstances" cannot be translated or defined or made more specific in abstraction from any definite context. If a more definite term were substituted for it, we should have a particular application of the generalization principle, and not the principle itself. However, it is not impossible to formulate criteria or a general set of directions for determining whether or not certain persons or their circumstances are to be regarded as similar in various contexts. This I shall now proceed to do, constructing for this purpose some model cases which can appropriately serve as paradigms of the application of this phrase.

1. Consider the following case presented by Sidgwick, in which he mentions certain conditions under which lying might be justified.

> Suppose . . . a Utilitarian thinks it on general grounds right to answer falsely a question as to the manner in which he has voted at a political election where the voting is by secret ballot. His reasons will probably be that the Utilitarian prohibition of falsehood is based on (1) the harm done by misleading particular individuals, and (2) the tendency of false statements to diminish the mutual confidence that men ought to have in each other's assertions; and that in this exceptional case it is (1) expedient that the questioner should be misled; while (2) in so far as the falsehood tends to produce a general distrust of all assertions as to the manner in which a man has voted, it only furthers the end for which voting has been made secret. It is evident, that if these reasons are valid for any person, they are valid for all persons. . . .[4]

The particular reasons Sidgwick gives are not very important in this context. Neither is his reference to utilitarianism. What is important is his statement that *if these reasons are valid for any person, they are valid for all persons*. Sidgwick goes on to say (p. 486) that the principle of justice means "that an act, if right for any individual, must be right on general grounds, and therefore for some class of persons". Now the importance of these two statements is that they provide the clue to the proper interpretation of 'similar' as it appears in this principle. The criteria for "all similar cases" are contained in the "general grounds" or reasons on the basis of which an act is, or is said to be, right or wrong. These reasons determine who are similar and who are not in a certain context. All those to whom the reasons apply are similar to each other and relevantly different from those to whom the reasons do not apply.

Consider the following remarks on this point by A. K. Rogers.

> Although I may feel the force of my own rights as a passionate demand, and still decline to entertain those of others, I cannot make of them a *social concept*, cannot argue about them and present them to others for their recognition, without generalizing them, and so implicitly granting to the other man the right to use the same words with reference to himself. . . . Argument implies general principles as its basis; a rational right is therefore by definition something that can be made general. . . . What you claim for yourself, every man whatsoever has the right to claim for himself, *unless* you can show definite reasons, that a reasonable being is bound to admit, why the principle applies in the one instance and not in the other. And the reasons must be themselves general ones; it is not

---

4 Op. cit., p. 485.

enough to make the difference consist merely in the fact that I am
I, and that you are someone else.[5]

This last statement, of course, is essentially the same as one of Sidwick's
presented above: a difference in what is right for two individuals cannot
be justified simply on the ground that they are *two* individuals, that A is
A and B is B. The fact that I am I, or the person I am, cannot justify my
claim that my case is exceptional, that I have the right to do something
others do not have the right to do. But this is not because this purported
reason is not a general one, or does not have a general application. It
actually has *too general* an application. If I can say "I am I, and you are
someone else", *everyone* can say "I am I, and you are someone else". Thus
this cannot show that one case is different from another. The attempt to
use the fact that I am I to justify the claim that my case is exceptional
actually involves a contradiction. For since it is true of everyone that he is
he, since everyone can say "I am I", it would follow that every case is
exceptional, and this is self-contradictory.

The claim that "I am John Smith, while you are not", which is not
tautological, still could not justify one in holding that he is an exception.
Everyone can make a similar claim: "I am John Jones, while you are not",
or "I am Ignatz McGillicuddy III, while you are not". If the fact that
someone has a certain name could be used to show that his case is an
exception, it could be used to show that every case is an exception, which
is, again, self-contradictory. Nor can the attempt to justify oneself by
reference to a "rule" which refers to oneself by name (and which of course
would not be a general rule at all) work any better. If John Smith can say
"Everyone whose name is John Smith has the right to act in such and such
a way", Ignatz McGillicuddy III can say "Everyone whose name is Ignatz
McGillicuddy III has the right to act in such and such a way", and everyone else can invoke a similar "rule". If one could invoke the fact that he
has a certain name or is a certain person—is "someone special"—to justify
his acting in a certain way, he could invoke the same consideration to
justify his acting in any way he pleases under any circumstances whatever.
But so could everyone else. It would follow that everyone has the right to
act in any way he pleases. Now this is not just false—it is self-contradictory.
The fact that one has a certain name or is a certain person may be relevant
to the claim that one has the right to do something or is an exception to
some rule. But the point is that one has to show how it is relevant. To do
this is to show how one is genuinely different from others in the situation in
question. It is to show that one is an exception on the basis of considerations
which would not show everyone to be an exception.

While the statement of a reason certainly need not, as Rogers' state-

---

[5] A. K. Rogers, *The Theory of Ethics*, pp. 191–92.

ment seems to imply, be given in general or abstract terms, nevertheless it must be generalizable. The statement of a reason, that is to say, must imply a rule or general proposition. The reason given must be capable of applying beyond the particular person in the particular situation to a class of persons in a certain type of situation. Hence to give a reason in support of the judgment that a given individual, A, ought or has the right to do some act presupposes that anyone with the characteristics specified in the statement of the reason ought, or has the right, to do the same kind of act in a situation of the kind specified. If the statement of a reason does not imply this then it is not the statement of a reason at all, but merely the reiteration of the assertion. Now anyone (and everyone) who has these characteristics is *similar* to A in this context. Any set of circumstances with the characteristics described by the reasons offered is in this context similar to the circumstances in which it is right for A to do the act in question. If B meets these conditions then in this context B is similar to A. If C does not then there is an important difference in this context between C and A. This is quite consistent with the fact that A and B may be similar in one context and not in another. On the basis of the reasons justifying some act of some other kind, or the same sort of act in different circumstances (or for another kind of individual), A and B may be dissimilar, and if so it will be right for one of them to act in this way and wrong for the other.

2. In a speech in Parliament Macaulay once said, "Official appointments ought not to be subject to regulations purely arbitrary, to regulations for which no reason can be given but mere caprice, . . . those who would exclude any class from public employment are bound to show some special reason for the exclusion".[6] This is an obvious though implicit appeal to the generalization principle, and this should serve to provide us with our second model.

What sort of consideration could serve as a "reason for the exclusion"? What would justify excluding some class of persons from public employment, or more generally, from appointment to any sort of position? "Purely arbitrary" regulations would be those "for which no reason can be given but mere caprice", or simply those for which no reason can be given. It is relatively easy to see what would fall into this class. The fact that someone does not like people of a certain type would not, by itself, justify him in claiming that they ought to be excluded from some position. The fact that he does not like them would not be a reason, though he might think that it is. For suppose it were. Then the argument would be that people of type T ought not to be allowed to hold a certain type of position because A does not like people of type T. But this presupposes that anyone A does not like ought not to be allowed to obtain that position. This involves us in the

---

[6] T. B. Macaulay, speech on "Jewish Disabilities", April 17th, 1833.

situation discussed above. Anyone can argue in the same way. If there is anyone who does not like the people A does like (himself included), then these people ought to be excluded also. It is possible to maintain on these grounds that no one ought to hold any position, and this is absurd. How does A justify his claim to a privileged status for his likes and dislikes? It is possible for him to do so, but not on the ground that he is he, or is a person of "special importance". Nor could people of type T justifiably be excluded simply on the ground that they are people of type T. This also would apply to everybody: people of type U ought to be excluded because they are of type U, and so on. Perhaps no one would be persuaded by this sort of reasoning when it is set out in this abstract form. It does not follow that no one has ever argued in this way. I should say that this sort of "reasoning" is fairly common. If it were not there would have been no point to Macaulay's statement, and no one familiar with the context in which his speech was made could maintain this.

But now what would count as a reason for excluding a class of people from a certain type of employment? In order to justify the claim that a certain class or group of people ought to be excluded from a certain type of position, it would have to be shown that the members of that class have certain characteristics, *in virtue of their membership in that class*, which are such as to unfit them or make them incompetent to perform the duties of that position. But then this class of people must be defined by these characteristics. Identification of them in terms of some popular category, as say Negroes, or Poles, or Jews, will not be sufficient. It would have to be shown that because someone is a negro, or has certain characteristics commonly associated with negroes, he is incapable of carrying out the requirements of the position in question. Obviously the relevance of this consideration will vary with different offices or positions. The fact that a man has red hair may of course be sufficient to exclude him from being sent as an emissary to a land or region where red-headed people are regarded with ill-will. It is not sufficient to exclude him from being sent as an emissary to some other place. If the Erewhonians liked and respected only fair-haired people, and had a horror of physical weakness, then the fact that someone has dark hair or is sickly may be a good reason for excluding him from the class of those who are acceptable as emissaries to Erewhon. But the fact that someone has dark hair would be irrelevant in a situation in which someone has to be picked as an emissary to a place where people do not care about the color of one's hair. Furthermore, the fact that someone has dark hair would not justify excluding him from the class of possible emissaries to Erewhon unless *all* people with dark hair were thereby excluded. It is not simply that it would be unfair to exclude someone from the position on the ground that he has dark hair, while some other dark-haired person is not excluded. It *would* be unfair. But the reason why it is unfair is that in such a case the color of one's hair would not, and could not possibly, be the reason or ground for the exclusion. This is obvious from the form of argument involved: A would not be a good ambassador to Erewhon (and therefore ought not to be sent there) *because* he has dark hair and *because* the Erewhonians do not like people with dark hair. This statement would be senseless unless it were applicable not only to A but to B, C, ... in short, to everyone. It presupposes the proposition that no one with dark hair would make a good ambassador to Erewhon. To paraphrase a statement from Sidgwick quoted previously, a reason in one case is a reason in all cases—or else it is not a reason at all. This should make fairly obvious the connection between impartiality, generality, and consistency or rationality.

The relation of the generalization principle to this sort of case should be apparent. Let us state the application of the principle to it in easy stages. The principle is: what is right for one person must be right for every similar person in similar circumstances. In the first stage of its application to this case we have the proposition (a) it is right for A to be prevented from being an emissary to Erewhon if and only if it is right to prevent everyone similar to A from being sent. Now the class of persons similar to A in this context is determined by the reasons which justify, or are said to justify, this exclusion of A. It is right to prevent A from being sent as an emissary to Erewhon because A has dark hair and because the Erewhonians have a great distaste for dark-haired people. This consideration, to be a genuine reason, must apply to all people with dark hair. Hence we have (b) it is right to prevent A from being sent as an emissary to Erewhon, because he has dark hair and the Erewhonians do not like dark-haired people, if, and only if, it would be right to prevent any dark-haired person from being sent as an emissary to Erewhon. Or more simply, it is right to prevent one dark-haired person from being sent as an emissary to Erewhon (on the ground that he has dark hair) if, and only if, it would be right to prevent any dark-haired person from being sent. The term 'similar' does not occur here at all. But this is obviously an application of the more general principle in which it does occur.

It should be noticed that the fact that someone has dark hair, though it is a good reason for excluding him, is not a logically conclusive reason. Even this may be overridden in some cases. Hence a case may arise in which a dark-haired person may justifiably be sent, because *on other grounds* he is likely to make a good ambassador. "He has certain qualities to make up for the deficiency, etc." But then, if so, having dark hair is not, by itself, *the* reason for exclusion. We cannot say simply "A is excluded *because* he has dark hair". The ground for excluding A must be that he has dark hair and does not have other qualities to make up for this. Having dark hair

is then one reason, or a presumptive reason, for exclusion; it is not a conclusive reason.

This brings us to one further fact about the generalization principle
that must be elaborated. Sidgwick remarked about this principle that its
effect is to "throw a definite *onus probandi* on the man who applies to
another a treatment of which he would complain if applied to himself".[7]
This is in line with his statement (p. 209) that "we cannot judge an action
to be right for A and wrong for B, unless we can find in the natures or
circumstances of the two some difference which we can regard as a reasonable ground for difference in their duties". The generalization principle can
be regarded as specifying the conditions under which an act must be
justified, and as specifying abstractly the conditions that must be met by
a justification. Thus the generalization principle can be formulated in any
of the following ways. What is right for one person cannot be wrong for
another, unless there is some relevant difference in their natures or circumstances. Or, what is right (or wrong) for one person must be right (or
wrong) for everyone, if there is no reason for the contrary. Thus the claim
that something that would not be right for everyone is right for a given
person is one that must be justified. In the form peculiarly appropriate to
the generalization argument, the principle may be stated: *If not everyone
has the right to act in a certain way, then no one has the right to act in
that way without a reason.*

When it is formulated in some such way as this, it is clear that when
Macaulay said that "those who would exclude any class from public employment are bound to show some special reason for the exclusion", he was
appealing to the generalization principle.

3. I have said that the generalization principle implies that an act
which is right or wrong is right or wrong on "general grounds" and is
therefore right or wrong for a class of persons This class of persons is determined by the reasons in terms of which the act is right or wrong. This may
appear to conflict with the fact that there are some acts which would be
right for only one person. But there is really no conflict here. An act of this
sort is still right for a class of persons in the sense that it would be right for
anyone who meets certain conditions, even though these conditions may be
such that just one person can meet them. The act is still right as an act
of a certain *kind*, or as an instance of a certain class of acts. It may be right
for A and for no one else to do act d in certain circumstances. Yet if B were
similar to A in certain respects then it would be right for B to do d. (The
act may be described in such a way that this last statement may seem silly.
It would amount to saying "if B were A then ...". But this can be met by

---

[7] Op. cit., p. 380.

redescribing the act.) Furthermore, since d must be an act of a certain kind (if it were not it could not be described at all), it must be the case that it would be right for everyone similar to A to do an act of the same kind as d (to act in the same way) in similar circumstances.

The following example should make this clear. While it would not be wrong for Mr. Jones to have sexual relations with Mrs. Jones, it would (generally) be wrong for anyone else to do so, and certainly wrong for everyone else to do so. Here we have an act which is right for just one person. But there is no conflict with the generalization principle. This principle does not say that no one ought to do what not everyone ought to do. It says that no one ought to do what not everyone ought to do, without a reason or justification. Mr. Jones is justified in having sexual relations with Mrs. Jones by the fact that he is married to her. If he were not he would (presumably) not be justified in this, and anyone else who was married to Mrs. Jones would be justified in having sexual relations with her. Furthermore, this act is an act of a certain kind, and can be described in a more general way so as to bring this out. Instead of describing Mr. Jones' act as one of "having sexual relations with Mrs. Jones", it can be referred to as "having sexual relations with one's own wife". Everyone is justified in doing an act of this kind in similar circumstances—everyone has the right to have sexual relations with his own wife, though not with anyone else's. (This rule necessarily does not apply to women. This does not make it unfair or unjust. It can obviously be restated to cover this.) Mr. Jones is justified in having sexual relations with Mrs. Jones because she is his wife. This last statements is of course perfectly general. It can thus be seen to be a further application of the more general generalization principle.

2. THE GENERALIZATION ARGUMENT

The fact that the generalization principle is involved in the generalization argument removes the ground from the claim that the latter involves a formal fallacy, that of arguing from "some" to "all". It would be fallacious to argue that, since not everyone has red hair, no one has red hair. But it is not necessarily fallacious to argue that, since not everyone has the right to act in a certain way, no one has the right to act in that way. The difference is that in the latter case we are dealing with moral judgments; and this latter inference is mediated by the generalization principle. That this is so is probably obscured by the fact that in applications of the argument the qualification "all similar persons in similar circumstances" is left inexplicit. But in valid applications of the argument this restriction is either implicitly understood or is indicated by various linguistic devices. For example, the argument "everyone ought to vote because if no one voted the government would collapse" is evidently meant to apply only to those legally permitted to vote. This is taken as understood. It is a further consequence of the generalization principle that the conclusion "no one has the right to do x" is really elliptical for "no one has the right to do x without a reason or justification". One can justify his failing or refusing to vote. Hence the generalization argument provides only a presumptive, and not a conclusive, reason for its conclusion.

Another objection to the generalization argument which has already been mentioned is that "humanity would probably perish from cold if everyone produced food, and would certainly starve if everyone made clothes or built houses". Since the consequences of everyone producing food would be undesirable, on the pattern of the generalization argument it would seem to follow that it is wrong for anyone to do so. But this actually does not follow. For consider what would happen if no one produced food. If no one produced food, everyone would starve. Hence on the same line of reasoning it might be argued that everyone ought to produce food. The argument that no one ought to produce food because of what would happen if everyone did can thus be met by the counter-argument that everyone ought to produce food because of what would happen if no one did. But a valid application of the generalization argument cannot be met by such a counter-argument. The argument that everyone ought to vote because of what would happen if no one did cannot be rebutted in this way.

In a case in which the consequences of everyone acting in a certain way would be undesirable, while the consequences of no one acting in that way would also be undesirable, I shall say that the argument can be *inverted*. Thus the argument is invertible with respect to producing food, building houses, and making clothes. Now in order for the generalization argument to have a valid application with respect to some action it is necessary that it not be invertible with respect to that action.

Consider the following possible objection: "If everyone ate at six o'clock there would be no one to perform certain essential functions, things which must be attended to at all times, and so on, with the net result that no one would be able to eat at six or any other time, and with various other undesirable consequences." Does it follow that no one has the right to eat at six o'clock? It should be noted that this argument in no way depends on the exact time specified. If we could argue that no one has the right to eat at six, we could argue that no one has the right to eat at five, or at seven, or at three minutes past two, and so on. We could therefore argue that no one has the right to eat at any time, that is to say, that no one has the right to eat.

In such a case as this the argument may be said to be *reiteratable*. Note that there is no need to restrict ourselves to eating in order to obtain examples of a reiteratable argument. Any action, such as walking, talking, sleeping, or drinking—even doing nothing at all—when particularized in this way, will do as well. Now any instance of the generalization argument that is reiteratable is invalid. For any instance of the generalization argument that is reiteratable is also invertible. For example, the argument from "not everyone has the right to eat at six o'clock" to "no one has the right to eat at six o'clock", since it can be reiterated for any time, implies "no one has the right to eat". But if no one were to eat the consequences would be just as undesirable, presumably, as if everyone were to eat at the same time.

This last condition, that the argument be not reiteratable, is closely tied up with the procedure by which one can justify his acting in a way in which it would be undesirable for everyone to act. One can justify his acting in that way by showing that he is a member of a certain class of persons such that if every member of that class were to act in that way the consequences would not be undesirable, or by showing that the circumstances of his action are such that the consequences of everyone acting in that way in those circumstances would not be undesirable. But the argument must not be reiteratable with respect to the class of persons or circumstances selected. Otherwise the class in question would be "distinguished" by a characteristic in terms of which everyone would be an exception, and hence not really distinguished at all.

There is one other objection to the generalization argument, one which is, oddly enough, fairly popular, that must be disposed of. It is simply irrelevant to reply, "Not everyone *will* do it". It is irrelevant because the argument does not imply that everyone will. What the argument implies is that if A has the right to do something, then everyone else (or everyone similar to A in certain respects) has this same right in a similar situation; and therefore if it is undesirable for everyone to have this right, it is undesirable for A to have it. (This, incidentally, is not to say that if the consequences of everyone acting in a certain way would be undesirable, then the consequences of some particular individual acting in this way would be undesirable. The consequences of any particular act of this kind, considered by themselves, may be beneficial.) Thus what has to be shown is how A is an exception. One is not shown to be an exception by the fact that the consequences of his acting in a certain way would not be the same as the consequences of everyone acting in that way. Nor is one shown to be an exception by the fact that not everyone will act in that way. For what such facts would show is that everyone is an exception, which is strictly nonsense.

Finally, it should, perhaps, be made clear that the application of the generalization argument presupposes, and does not by itself determine, that the consequences of everyone acting in a certain way would be undesirable. I have not here been concerned with the question how to determine the desirability or undesirability of a certain set of consequences. It is sufficient to have shown the argument to be *valid*. The question of the *soundness* of any particular application of it, that is to say, the question whether its premises are true, is something else again.

A Moral Argument

R. M. HARE

And as ye would that men should do to you, do ye also to them likewise.   *St. Luke vi. 31*

6.1. Historically, one of the chief incentives to the study of ethics has been the hope that its findings might be of help to those faced with difficult moral problems. That this is still a principal incentive for many people is shown by the fact that modern philosophers are often reproached for failing to make ethics relevant to morals.[1] This is because one of the main tenets of many recent moral philosophers has been that the most popular method by which it was sought to bring ethics to bear on moral problems was not feasible—namely the method followed by the group of theories loosely known as 'naturalist'.

The method of naturalism is so to characterize the *meanings* of the key moral terms that, given certain factual premises, not themselves moral judgments, moral conclusions can be deduced from them. If this could be done, it was thought that it would be of great assistance to us in making moral decisions; we should only have to find out the nonmoral facts, and the moral conclusion as to what we ought to do would follow. Those who say that it cannot be done leave themselves the task of giving an alternative account of moral reasoning.

Naturalism seeks to make the findings of ethics *relevant* to moral decisions by making the former not morally *neutral*. It is a very natural assumption that if a statement of ethics is relevant to morals, then it cannot be neutral as between different moral judgments; and naturalism is a tempting view for those who make this assumption. Naturalistic definitions are not morally neutral, because with their aid we could show that state-

---

From R. M. Hare, Freedom and Reason *(Oxford: The Clarendon Press, 1963), pp. 86–111. Reprinted by permission of the author and the publisher.*
1 I have tried to fill in some of the historical background of these reproaches, and to assess the justification for them, in my article in *The Philosophy of C. D. Broad*, ed. P. Schilpp.

ments of nonmoral facts *entailed* moral conclusions. And some have thought that unless such an entailment can be shown to hold, the moral philosopher has not made moral reasoning possible.

One way of escaping this conclusion is to say that the relation linking a set of nonmoral premises with a moral conclusion is not one of entailment, but that some other logical relation, peculiar to morals, justifies the inference. This is the view put forward, for example, by Mr. Toulmin.[2] Since I have argued elsewhere against this approach, I shall not discuss it here. Its advocates have, however, hit upon an important insight: that moral reasoning does not necessarily proceed by way of *deduction* of moral conclusions from nonmoral premises. Their further suggestion, that therefore it makes this transition by means of some other, peculiar, nondeductive kind of inference, is not the only possibility. It may be that moral reasoning is not, typically, any kind of 'straightline' or 'linear' reasoning from premises to conclusion.

6.2. A parallel from the philosophy of science will perhaps make this point clear. It is natural to suppose that what the scientist does is to reason from premises, which are the data of observation, to conclusions, which are his 'scientific laws', by means of a special sort of inference called 'inductive'. Against this view, Professor Popper has forcibly argued that in science there are no inferences other than deductive; the typical procedure of scientists to propound hypotheses, and then look for ways of testing them— i.e. experiments which, if they are false, will show them to be so. A hypothesis which, try as we may, we fail to falsify, we accept provisionally, though ready to abandon it if, after all, further experiment refutes it; and of those that are so accepted we rate highest the ones which say most, and which would, therefore, be most likely to have been falsified if they were false. The only inferences which occur in this process are deductive ones, from the truth of certain observations to the falsity of a hypothesis. There is no reasoning which proceeds from the data of observation to the *truth* of a hypothesis. Scientific inquiry is rather a kind of *exploration*, or looking for hypotheses which will stand up to the test of experiment.[3]

We must ask whether moral reasoning exhibits any similar features. I want to suggest that it too is a kind of exploration, and not a kind of linear inference, and that the only inferences which take place in it are deductive. What we are doing in moral reasoning is to look for moral judgments and moral principles which, when we have considered their logical consequences and the facts of the case, we can still accept. As we shall see, this approach

---

[2] S. E. Toulmin, *The Place of Reason in Ethics*, esp. pp. 38–60. See my review in *Philosophical Quarterly*, I (1950–51), 372, and *Language of Morals* 3.4.

[3] K. R. Popper, *The Logic of Scientific Discovery* (esp. pp. 32 f.). See also his article in C. A. Mace, ed., *British Philosophy in the Mid-Century*, p. 155.

to the problem enables us to reject the assumption, which seemed so natural, that ethics cannot be relevant to moral decisions without ceasing to be neutral. This is because we are not going to demand any inferences in our reasoning other than deductive ones, and because none of these deductive inferences rely for their validity upon naturalistic definitions of moral terms.

Two further parallels may help to make clear the sense in which ethics is morally neutral. In the kind of scientific reasoning just described, mathematics plays a major part, for many of the deductive inferences that occur are mathematical in character. So we are bound to admit that mathematics is relevant to scientific inquiry. Nevertheless, it is also neutral, in the sense that no discoveries about matters of physical fact can be made with the aid of mathematics alone, and that no mathematical inference can have a conclusion which says more, in the way of prediction of observations, than its premises implicitly do.

An even simpler parallel is provided by the rules of games. The rules of a game are neutral as between the players, in the sense that they do not, by themselves, determine which player is going to win. In order to decide who wins, the players have to play the game in accordance with the rules, which involves their making, themselves, a great many individual decisions. On the other hand, the 'neutrality' of the rules of a game does not turn it into a game of chance, in which the bad player is as likely to win as the good.

Ethical theory, which determines the meanings and functions of the moral words, and thus the 'rules' of the moral 'game', provides only a clarification of the conceptual framework within which moral reasoning takes place; it is therefore, in the required sense, neutral as between different moral opinions. But it is highly relevant to moral reasoning because, as with the rules of a game, there could be no such thing as moral reasoning without this framework, and the framework dictates the form of the reasoning. It follows that naturalism is not the only way of providing for the possibility of moral reasoning; and this may, perhaps, induce those who have espoused naturalism as a way of making moral thought a rational activity to consider other possibilities.

The rules of moral reasoning are, basically, two, corresponding to the two features of moral judgments which I argued for in the first of this book [*Freedom and Reason*], prescriptivity and universalizability. When we are trying, in a concrete case, to decide what we ought to do, what we are looking for (as I have already said) is an action to which we can commit ourselves (prescriptivity) but which we are at the same time prepared to accept as exemplifying a principle of action to be prescribed for others in like circumstances (universalizability). If, when we consider some proposed action, we find that, when universalized, it yields prescriptions which we cannot accept, we reject this action as a solution to our moral problem—if we cannot universalize the prescription, it cannot become an 'ought'.

It is to be noticed that, troublesome as was the problem of moral weakness when we were dealing theoretically with the logical character of the moral concepts, it cannot trouble us here. For if a person is going to reason seriously at all about a moral question, he has to presuppose that the moral concepts are going, in his reasoning, to be used prescriptively. One cannot start a moral argument about a certain proposal on the basis that, whatever the conclusion of it, it makes no difference to what anybody is to do. When one has arrived at a conclusion, one may then be too weak to put it into practice. But *in arguing* one has to discount this possibility; for, as we shall see, to abandon the prescriptivity of one's moral judgments is to unscrew an essential part of the logical mechanism on which such arguments rely. This is why, if a person were to say 'Let's have an argument about this grave moral question which faces us, but let's not think of any conclusion we may come to as requiring anybody to *do* one thing rather than another', we should be likely to accuse him of flippancy, or worse.

6.3. I will now try to exhibit the bare bones of the theory of moral reasoning that I wish to advocate by considering a very simple (indeed oversimplified) example. As we shall see, even this very simple case generates the most baffling complexities; and so we may be pardoned for not attempting anything more difficult to start with.

The example is adapted from a well-known parable.[4] A owes money to B, and B owes money to C, and it is the law that creditors may exact their debts by putting their debtors into prison. B asks himself, 'Can I say that I ought to take this measure against A in order to make him pay?' He is no doubt *inclined* to do this, or *wants* to do it. Therefore, if there were no question of universalizing his prescriptions, he would assent readily to the *singular* prescription 'Let me put A into prison' (4.3). But when he seeks to turn this prescription into a moral judgment, and say, 'I *ought* to put A into prison because he will not pay me what he owes', he reflects that this would involve accepting the principle 'Anyone who is in my position ought to put his debtor into prison if he does not pay'. But then he reflects that C is in the same position of unpaid creditor with regard to himself (B), and that the cases are otherwise identical; and that if anyone in this position ought to put his debtors into prison, then so ought C to put him (B) into prison. And to accept the moral prescription 'C ought to put me into prison' would commit him (since, as we have seen, he must be using the word 'ought' prescriptively) to accepting the singular prescription 'Let C put me into prison'; and this he is not ready to accept. But if he is not, then neither can he accept the original judgment that he (B) ought to

---

[4] Matthew xviii. 23.

put A into prison for debt. Notice that the whole of this argument would break down if 'ought' were not being used both universalizably *and prescriptively*; for if it were not being used prescriptively, the step from 'C ought to put me into prison' to 'Let C put me into prison' would not be valid.

The structure and ingredients of this argument must now be examined. We must first notice an analogy between it and the Popperian theory of scientific method. What has happened is that a provisional or suggested moral principle has been rejected because one of its particular consequences proved unacceptable. But an important difference between the two kinds of reasoning must also be noted; it is what we should expect, given that the data of scientific observation are recorded in descriptive statements, whereas we are here dealing with prescriptions. What knocks out a suggested hypothesis, on Popper's theory, is a singular statement of fact: the hypothesis has the consequence that p; but not-p. Here the logic is just the same, except that in place of the observation statements 'p' and 'not-p' we have the singular *prescriptions* 'Let C put B into prison for debt' and its contradictory. Nevertheless, given that B is disposed to reject the first of these prescriptions, the argument against him is just as cogent as in the scientific case.

We may carry the parallel further. Just as science, seriously pursued, is the search for hypotheses and the testing of them by the attempt to falsify their particular consequences, so morals, as a serious endeavor, consists in the search for principles and the testing of them against particular cases. Any rational activity has its discipline, and this is the discipline of moral thought: to test the moral principles that suggest themselves to us by following out their consequences and seeing whether we can accept *them*.

No argument, however, starts from nothing. We must therefore ask what we have to have before moral arguments of the sort of which I have given a simple example can proceed. The first requisite is that the facts of the case should be given; for all moral discussion is about some particular set of facts, whether actual or supposed. Secondly we have the logical framework provided by the meaning of the word 'ought' (i.e. prescriptivity and universalizability, both of which we saw to be necessary). Because moral judgments have to be universalizable, B cannot say that he ought to put A into prison for debt without committing himself to the view that C, who is *ex hypothesi* in the same position *vis-à-vis* himself, ought to put *him* into prison; and because moral judgments are prescriptive, this would be, in effect, prescribing to C to put him into prison; and this he is unwilling to do, since he has a strong inclination not to go to prison. This inclination gives us the third necessary ingredient in the argument: if B were a completely apathetic person, who literally did not mind what happened to himself or to anybody else, the argument would not touch him. The three necessary ingredients which we have noticed, then, are (1) facts; (2) logic; (3) inclinations. These ingredients enable us, not indeed to arrive at an evaluative conclusion, but to *reject* an evaluative proposition. We shall see later that these are not, in all cases, the only necessary ingredients.

6.4. In the example which we have been using, the position was deliberately made simpler by supposing that B actually stood to some other person in exactly the same relation as A does to him. Such cases are unlikely to arise in practice. But it is not necessary for the force of the argument that B should *in fact* stand in this relation to anyone; it is sufficient that he should consider hypothetically such a case, and see what would be the consequences in it of those moral principles between whose acceptance and rejection he has to decide. Here we have an important point of difference from the parallel scientific argument, in that the crucial case which leads to rejection of the principle can itself be a supposed, not an observed, one. That hypothetical cases will do as well as actual ones is important, since it enables us to guard against a possible misinterpretation of the argument which I have outlined. It might be thought that what moves B is the *fear* that C will actually do to him as he does to A—as happens in the gospel parable. But this fear is not only irrelevant to the moral argument; it does not even provide a particularly strong nonmoral motive unless the circumstances are somewhat exceptional. C may, after all, not find out what B has done to A; or C's moral principles may be different from B's, and independent of them, so that what moral principle B accepts makes no difference to the moral principles on which C acts.

Even, therefore, if C did not exist, it would be no answer to the argument for B to say 'But in my case there is no fear that anybody will ever be in a position to do to me what I am proposing to do to A'. For the argument does not rest on any such fear. All that is essential to it is that B should disregard the fact that he plays the particular role in the situation which he does, without disregarding the inclinations which people have in situations of this sort. In other words, he must be prepared to give weight to A's inclinations and interests as if they were his own. This is what turns selfish prudential reasoning into moral reasoning. It is much easier, psychologically, for B to do this if he is actually placed in a situation like A's *vis-à-vis* somebody else; but this is not necessary, provided that he has sufficient imagination to envisage what it is like to be A. For our first example, a case was deliberately chosen in which little imagination was necessary; but in most normal cases a certain power of imagination and readiness to use it is a fourth necessary ingredient in moral arguments, alongside those already mentioned, viz. logic (in the shape of universalizability and prescriptivity), the facts, and the inclinations or interests of the people concerned.

It must be pointed out that the absence of even one of these ingredients may render the rest ineffective. For example, impartiality by itself is not enough. If, in becoming impartial, B became also completely dispassionate and apathetic, and moved as little by other people's interests as by his own, then, as we have seen, there would be nothing to make him accept or reject one moral principle rather than another. That is why those who, like Adam Smith and Professor Kneale, advocate what have been called 'Ideal Observer Theories' of ethics, sometimes postulate as their imaginary ideal observer not merely an impartial spectator, but an impartially *sympathetic* spectator.[5] To take another example, if the person who faces the moral decision has no imagination, then even the fact that someone can do the very same thing to him may pass him by. If, again, he lacks the readiness to universalize, then the vivid imagination of the sufferings which he is inflicting on others may only spur him on to intensify them, to increase his own vindictive enjoyment. And if he is ignorant of the material facts (for example about what is likely to happen to a person if one takes out a writ against him), then there is nothing to tie the moral argument to particular choices.

6.5. The best way of testing the argument which we have outlined will be to consider various ways in which somebody in B's position might seek to escape from it. There are indeed a number of such ways; and all of them may be successful, at a price. It is important to understand what the price is in each case. We may classify these maneuvres which are open to B into two kinds. There are first of all the moves which depend on his using the moral words in a different way from that on which the argument relied. We saw that for the success of the argument it was necessary that 'ought' should be used universalizably and prescriptively. If B uses it in a way that is either not prescriptive or not universalizable, then he can escape the force of the argument, at the cost of resigning from the kind of discussion that we thought we were having with him. We shall discuss these two possibilities separately. Secondly, there are moves which can still be made by B, even though he is using the moral words in the same way as we are. We shall examine three different sub-classes of these.

Before dealing with what I shall call the *verbal* maneuvres in detail, it may be helpful to make a general remark. Suppose that we are having a

---

5 It will be plain that there are affinities, though there are also differences, between this type of theory and my own. For such theories see W. C. Kneale, *Philosophy*, XXV (1950), 162; R. Firth and R. B. Brandt, *Philosophy and Phenomenological Research*, XII (1951–52), 317, and XV (1954–55), 407, 414, 422; and J. Harrison, *Aristotelian Society*, supp. vol. XXVIII (1954), 132. Firth, unlike Kneale, says that the observer must be 'dispassionate', but see Brandt, op. cit., p. 411 n. For a shorter discussion see Brandt, *Ethical Theory*, p. 173. Since for many Christians God occupies the role of 'ideal observer', the moral judgments which they make may be expected to coincide with those arrived at by the method of reasoning which I am advocating.

simple mathematical argument with somebody, and he admits, for example, that there are five eggs in this basket, and six in the other, but maintains that there are a dozen eggs in the two baskets taken together; and suppose that this is because he is using the expression 'a dozen' to mean 'eleven'. It is obvious that we cannot compel him logically to admit that there are not a dozen eggs, in *his* sense of 'dozen'. But it is equally obvious that this should not disturb us. For such a man only appears to be dissenting from us. His dissent is only apparent, because the proposition which his words express is actually consistent with the conclusion which we wish to draw; he *says* 'There are a dozen eggs'; but he *means* what we should express by saying 'There are eleven eggs'; and this we are not disputing. It is important to remember that in the moral case also the dissent may be only apparent, if the words are being used in different ways, and that it is no defect in a method of argument if it does not make it possible to prove a conclusion to a person when he is using words in such a way that the conclusion does not follow.

It must be pointed out, further (since this is a common source of confusion), that in this argument nothing whatever hangs upon our *actual* use of words in common speech, any more than it does in the arithmetical case. That we use the sound 'dozen' to express the meaning that we customarily do use it to express is of no consequence for the argument about the eggs; and the same may be said of the sound 'ought'. There is, however, something which I, at any rate, customarily express by the sound 'ought', whose character is correctly described by saying that it is a universal or universalizable prescription. I hope that what I customarily express by the sound 'ought' is the same as what most people customarily express by it; but if I am mistaken in this assumption, I shall still have given a correct account, so far as I am able, of that which I express by this sound.[6] Nevertheless, this account will interest other people mainly in so far as my hope that they understand the same thing as I do by 'ought' is fulfilled; and since I am moderately sure that this is indeed the case with many people, I hope that I may be of use to them in elucidating the logical properties of the concept which they thus express.

At this point, however, it is of the utmost importance to stress that the fact that two people express the same thing by 'ought' does not entail that they share the same moral opinions. For the formal, logical properties of the word 'ought' (those which are determined by its *meaning*) are only one of the four factors (listed earlier) whose combination governs a man's moral opinion on a given matter. Thus ethics, the study of the logical properties of the moral words, remains morally neutral (its conclusions neither are substantial moral judgments, nor entail them, even in conjunction with factual premises); its bearing upon moral questions lies in this, that it makes logically

---

[6] Cf. Moore, *Principia Ethica*, p. 6 [this volume, p. 13].

impossible certain combinations of moral and other prescriptions. Two people who are using the word 'ought' in the same way may yet disagree about what ought to be done in a certain situation, either because they differ about the facts, or because one or other of them lacks imagination, or because their different inclinations make one reject some singular prescription which the other can accept. For all that, ethics (i.e. the logic of moral language) is an immensely powerful engine for producing moral agreement; for if two people are willing to use the moral word 'ought', and to use it in the same way (viz. the way that I have been describing), the other possible sources of moral disagreement are all eliminable. People's inclinations about most of the important matters in life tend to be the same (very few people, for example, like being starved or run over by motorcars); and, even when they are not, there is a way of generalizing the argument . . ., which enables us to make allowance for differences in inclinations. The facts are often, given sufficient patience, ascertainable. Imagination can be cultivated. If these three factors are looked after, as they can be, agreement on the use of 'ought' is the only other necessary condition for producing moral agreement, at any rate in typical cases. And, if I am not mistaken, this agreement in use is already there in the discourse of anybody with whom we are at all likely to find ourselves arguing; all that is needed is to to think clearly, and so make it evident.

After this methodological digression, let us consider what is to be done with the man who professes to be using 'ought' in some different way from that which I have described—because he is not using it prescriptively, or not universalizably. For the reasons that I have given, if he takes either of these courses, he is no longer in substantial moral disagreement with us. Our apparent moral disagreement is really only verbal; for although, as we shall see shortly, there may be a residuum of substantial disagreement, this cannot be moral.[7]

Let us take first the man who is using the word 'ought' prescriptively, but not universalizably. He can say that he ought to put his debtor into prison, although he is not prepared to agree that his creditor ought to put *him* into prison. We, on the other hand, since we are not prepared to admit that our creditors in these circumstances ought to put us into prison, cannot say that we ought to put our debtors into prison. So there is an appearance of substantial moral disagreement, which is intensified by the fact that, since we are both using the word 'ought' prescriptively, our respective views will lead to different particular actions. Different *singular* prescriptions about what to do are (since both our judgments are prescriptive) derivable from what we are respectively saying. But this is not enough to

---

[7] Strictly, we should say 'evaluative'; but for the reason given on p. 130, we can ignore the nonevaluative moral judgments mentioned on pp. 26 f. [of *Freedom and Reason*] and in *Language of Morals* 11.3.

constitute a moral disagreement. For that, we should have to differ, not only about what *is* to be done in some particular case, but about some universal principle concerning what *ought* to be done in cases of a certain sort; and since B is (on the hypothesis considered) advocating no such universal principle, he is saying nothing with which we can be in moral or evaluative disagreement. Considered purely as prescriptions, indeed, our two views are in substantial disagreement; but the moral, evaluative (i.e. the *universal prescriptive*) disagreement is only verbal, because, when the expression of B's view is understood as he means it, the view turns out not to be a view about the morality of the action at all. So B, by this maneuvre, can go on prescribing to himself to put A into prison, but has to abandon the claim that he is justifying the action morally, as we understand the word 'morally'. One may, of course, use any word as one pleases, at a price. But he can no longer claim to be giving that sort of justification of his action for which, as I think, the common expression is 'moral justification'.

I need not deal at length with the second way in which B might be differing from us in his use of 'ought', viz. by not using it prescriptively. If he were not using it prescriptively, it will be remembered, he could assent to the singular prescription 'Let not C put me into prison for debt', and yet assent also to the nonprescriptive moral judgment 'C ought to put me into prison for debt'. And so his disinclination to be put into prison for debt by C would furnish no obstacle to his saying that he (B) ought to put A into prison for debt. And thus he could carry out his own inclination to put A into prison with apparent moral justification. The justification would be, however, only apparent. For if B is using the word 'ought' nonprescriptively, then 'I ought to put A into prison for debt' does not entail the singular prescription 'Let me put A into prison for debt'; the 'moral' judgment becomes quite irrelevant to the choice of what to do. There would also be the same lack of substantial moral disagreement as we noticed in the preceding case. B would not be disagreeing with us other than verbally, so far as the moral question is concerned (though there might be points of *factual* disagreement between us, arising from the *descriptive* meaning of our judgments). The 'moral' disagreement could be only verbal, because whereas we should be dissenting from the universalizable prescription 'B ought to put A into prison for debt', *this* would not be what B was expressing, though the words he would be using would be the same. For B would not, by these words, be expressing a prescription at all.

6.6 So much for the ways (of which my list may well be incomplete) in which B can escape from our argument by using the word 'ought' in a different way from us. The remaining ways of escape are open to him even if he is using 'ought' in the same way as we are, viz. to express a universalizable prescription.

We must first consider that class of escape routes whose distinguishing feature is that B, while using the moral words in the same way as we are, refuses to make positive moral judgments at all in certain cases. There are two main variations of this maneuvre. B may either say that it is indifferent, morally, whether he imprisons A or not; or he may refuse to make any moral judgment at all, even one of indifference, about the case. It will be obvious that if he adopts either of these moves, he can evade the argument as so far set out. For that argument only forced him to *reject* the moral judgment 'I ought to imprison A for debt'. It did not force him to assent to any moral judgment; in particular, he remained free to assent, either to the judgment that he ought not to imprison A for debt (which is the one that we want him to accept) or to the judgment that it is neither the case that he ought, nor the case that he ought not (that it is, in short, indifferent); and he remained free, also, to say 'I am just not making any moral judgments at all about this case'.

We have not yet, however, exhausted the arguments generated by the demand for universalizability, provided that the moral words are being used in a way which allows this demand. For it is evident that these maneuvres could, in principle, be practiced in any case whatever in which the morality of an act is in question. And this enables us to place B in a dilemma. Either he practices this maneuvre in *every* situation in which he is faced with a moral decision; or else he practices it only *sometimes*. The first alternative, however, has to be subdivided; for 'every situation' might mean 'every situation in which he himself has to face a moral decision regarding one of his own actions', or it might mean 'every situation in which a moral question arises for him, whether about his own actions or about somebody else's'. So there are three courses that he can adopt: (1) He either refrains altogether from making moral judgments, or makes none except judgments of indifference (that is to say, he either observes a complete moral silence, or says 'Nothing matters morally'; either of these two positions might be called a sort of amoralism); (2) He makes moral judgments in the normal way about other people's actions, but adopts one or other of the kinds of amoralism, just mentioned, with regard to his own; (3) He expresses moral indifference, or will make no moral judgment at all, with regard to *some* of his own actions and those of other people, but makes moral judgments in the normal way about others.

Now it will be obvious that in the first case there is nothing that we can do, and that this should not disturb us. Just as one cannot win a game of chess against an opponent who will not make any moves—and just as one cannot argue mathematically with a person who will not commit himself to any mathematical statements—so moral argument is impossible with a man who will make no moral judgments at all, or—which for practical purposes comes to the same thing—makes only judgments of indifference. Such a person is not entering the arena of moral dispute, and therefore it is impossible to contest with him. He is compelled also—and this is important—to abjure the protection of morality for his own interests.

In the other two cases, however, we have an argument left. If a man is prepared to make positive moral judgments about other people's actions, but not about his own, or if he is prepared to make them about some of his own decisions, but not about others, then we can ask him on what principle he makes the distinction between these various cases. This is a particular application of the demand for universalizability. He will still have left to him the ways of escape from this demand which are available in all its applications, and which we shall consider later. But there is no way of escape which is available in this application, but not in others. He must either produce (or at least admit the existence of) some principle which makes him hold different moral opinions about apparently similar cases, or else admit that the judgments he is making are not moral ones. But in the latter case, he is in the same position, in the present dispute, as the man who will not make any moral judgments at all; he has resigned from the contest.

In the particular example which we have been considering, we supposed that the cases of B and of C, his own creditor, were identical. The demand for universalization therefore compels B to make the same moral judgment, whatever it is, about both cases. He has therefore, unless he is going to give up the claim to be arguing morally, either to say that neither he nor C ought to exercise their legal rights to imprison their debtors; or that both ought (a possibility to which we shall recur in the next section) ; or that it is indifferent whether they do. But the last alternative leaves it open to B and C to do what they like in the matter; and we may suppose that, though B himself would like to have this freedom, he will be unwilling to allow it to C. It is as unlikely that he will *permit* C to put him (B) into prison as that he will *prescribe* it. We may say, therefore, that while move (1), described above, constitutes an abandonment of the dispute, moves (2) and (3) really add nothing new to it.

6.7. We must next consider a way of escape which may seem much more respectable than those which I have so far mentioned. Let us suppose that B is a firm believer in the rights of property and the sanctity of contracts. In this case he may say roundly that debtors ought to be imprisoned by their creditors whoever they are, and that, specifically, C ought to imprison him (B), and he (B) ought to imprison A. And he may, unlike the superficially similar person described earlier, be meaning by 'ought' just what we usually mean by it—i.e. he may be using the word prescriptively, realizing that in saying that C ought to put him into prison, he is prescribing that C put him in prison. B, in this case, is perfectly ready to go to prison for his principles, in order that the sanctity of contracts may be enforced. In real life, B would be much more likely to take this line if the situation in which he himself played the role of debtor were not actual but only hypothetical; but this, as we saw earlier, ought not to make any difference to the argument.

We are not yet, however, in a position to deal with this escape route. All we can do is to say why we cannot now deal with it, and leave this loose end to be picked up later. B, if he is sincere in holding the principle about the sanctity of contracts (or any other universal moral principle which has the same effect in this particular case), may have two sorts of grounds for it. He may hold it on utilitarian grounds, thinking that, unless contracts are rigorously enforced, the results will be so disastrous as to outweigh any benefits that A, or B himself, may get from being let off. This could, in certain circumstances, be a good argument. But we cannot tell whether it is, until we have generalized the type of moral argument which has been set out in this chapter, to cover cases in which the interests of more than two parties are involved. As we saw, it is only the interests of A and B that come into the argument as so far considered (the interests of the third party, C, do not need separate consideration, since C was introduced only in order to show B, if necessary fictionally, a situation in which the roles were reversed; therefore C's interests, being a mere replica of B's, will vanish, as a separate factor, once the A/B situation, and the moral judgments made on it, are universalized). But if utilitarian grounds of the sort suggested are to be adduced, they will bring with them a reference to all the other people whose interests would be harmed by laxity in the enforcement of contracts. This escape route, therefore, if this is its basis, introduces considerations which cannot be assessed until we have generalized our form of argument to cover 'multilateral' moral situations. At present, it can only be said that if B can show that leniency in the enforcement of contracts would really have the results he claims for the community at large, he might be justified in taking the severer course. This will be apparent after we have considered in some detail an example (that of the judge and the criminal) which brings out these considerations even more clearly.

On the other hand, B might have a quite different, nonutilitarian kind of reason for adhering to his principle. He might be moved, not by any weight which he might attach to the interests of other people, but by the thought that to enforce contracts of this sort is necessary in order to conform to some moral or other *ideal* that he has espoused. Such ideals might be of various sorts. He might be moved, for example, by an ideal of abstract justice, of the *fiat justitia, ruat caelum* variety. We have to distinguish such an ideal of justice, which pays no regard to people's interests, from that which is concerned merely to do justice *between* people's interests. It is very important, if considerations of justice are introduced into a moral argument, to know of which sort they are. Justice of the second kind can perhaps be accommodated within a moral view which it is not misleading to call utilitarian (7.4). But this is not true of an ideal of the first kind. It is characteristic of this sort of nonutilitarian ideals that, when they are introduced into moral arguments, they render ineffective the appeal to universalized self-interest which is the foundation of the argument that we have been considering. This is because the person who has whole-heartedly espoused such an ideal (we shall call him the 'fanatic') does not mind if people's interests—even his own—are harmed in the pursuit of it.

It need not be justice which provides the basis of such an escape route as we are considering. Any moral ideal would do, provided that it were pursued regardless of other people's interests. For example, B might be a believer in the survival of the fittest, and think that, in order to promote this, he (and everyone else) ought to pursue their own interests by all means in their power and regardless of everyone else's interests. This ideal might lead him, in this particular case, to put A in prison, and he might agree that C ought to do the same to him, if he were not clever enough to avoid this fate. He might think that universal obedience to such a principle would maximize the production of supermen and so make the world a better place. If these were his grounds, it is possible that we might argue with him factually, showing that the universal observance of the principle would not have the results he claimed. But we might be defeated in this factual argument if he had an ideal which made him call the world 'a better place' when the jungle law prevailed; he could then agree to our factual statements, but still maintain that the condition of the world described by us as resulting from the observance of his principle would be better than its present condition. In this case, the argument might take two courses. If we could get him to imagine himself in the position of the weak, who went to the wall in such a state of the world, we might bring him to realize that to hold his principle involved prescribing that things should be done to him, in hypothetical situations, which he could not sincerely prescribe. If, so, then the argument would be on the rails again, and could proceed on lines which we have already sketched. But he might stick to his principle and say 'If I were weak, then I ought to go to the wall'. If he did this, he would be putting himself beyond the reach of what we shall call 'golden rule' or 'utilitarian' arguments by becoming what we shall call a 'fanatic'. Since a great part of the rest of this book will be concerned with people who take this sort of line, it is unnecessary to pursue their case further at this point.

6.8. The remaining maneuver that B might seek to practice is probably the commonest. It is certainly the one which is most frequently brought up in philosophical controversies on this topic. This consists in a fresh appeal to the facts—i.e. in asserting that there are in fact morally relevant differences between his case and that of others. In the example which we have been considering, we have artificially ruled out this way of escape by assuming that the case of B and C is exactly similar to that of A and B; from this it follows *a fortiori* that there are no morally relevant differences. Since the B/C case may be a hypothetical one, this condition of exact similarity can always be fulfilled, and therefore this maneuvre is based on a misconception of the type of argument against which it is directed. Nevertheless it may be useful, since this objection is so commonly raised, to deal with it at this point, although nothing further will be added thereby to what has been said already.

It may be claimed that no two actual cases would ever be exactly similar; there would always be some differences, and B might allege that some of these were morally relevant. He might allege, for example, that, whereas his family would starve if C put him into prison, this would not be the case if he put A into prison, because A's family would be looked after by A's relatives. If such a difference existed, there might be nothing logically disreputable in calling it morally relevant, and such arguments are in fact often put forward and accepted.

The difficulty, however, lies in drawing the line between those arguments of this sort which are legitimate, and those which are not. Suppose that B alleges that the fact that A has a hooked nose or a black skin entitles him, B, to put him in prison, but that C ought not to do the same thing to him, B, because his nose is straight and his skin white. Is this an argument of equal logical respectability? Can I say that the fact that I have a mole in a particular place on my chin entitles me to further my own interests at others' expense, but that they are forbidden to do this by the fact that they lack this mark of natural preeminence?

The answer to this maneuvre is implicit in what has been said already about the relevance, in moral arguments, of hypothetical as well as of actual cases. The fact that no two actual cases are ever identical has no bearing on the problem. For all we have to do is to imagine an identical case in which the roles are reversed. Suppose that my mole disappears, and that my neighbor grows one in the very same spot on his chin. Or, to use our other example, what does B say about a hypothetical case in which he has a black skin or a hooked nose, and A and C are both straight nosed and white skinned? Since this is the same argument, in essentials, as we used at the very beginning, it need not be repeated here. B is in fact faced with a dilemma. Either the property of his own case, which he claims to be morally relevant, is a properly universal property (i.e. one describable without reference to individuals), or it is not. If it is a universal property, then, because of the meaning of the word 'universal', it is a property which might be possessed by another case in which he played a different role (though in fact it may not be); and we can therefore ask him to ignore the fact that it is he himself who plays the role which he does in this case.

This will force him to count as morally relevant only those properties which he is prepared to allow to be relevant even when other people have them. And this rules out all the attractive kinds of special pleading. On the other hand, if the property in question is not a properly universal one, then he has not met the demand for universalizability, and cannot claim to be putting forward a moral argument at all.

6.9. It is necessary, in order to avoid misunderstanding, to add two notes to the foregoing discussion. The misunderstanding arises through a too literal interpretation of the common forms of expression—which constantly recur in arguments of this type—'How would you like it if . . .?' and 'Do as you would be done by'. Though I shall later, for convenience, refer to the type of arguments here discussed as 'golden rule' arguments, we must not be misled by these forms of expression.

First of all, we shall make the nature of the argument clearer if, when we are asking B to imagine himself in the position of his victim, we phrase our question, never in the form 'What *would* you say, or feel, or think, or how *would* you like it, if you were he?' but always in the form 'What *do* you say (*in propria persona*) about a hypothetical case in which you are in your victim's position?' The importance of this way of phrasing the question is that, if the question were put in the first way, B might reply 'Well, of course, if anybody did this to me I should resent it very much and make all sorts of adverse moral judgments about the act; but this has absolutely no bearing on the validity of the moral opinion which I am *now* expressing'. To involve him in contradiction, we have to show that he *now* holds an opinion about the hypothetical case which is inconsistent with his opinion about the actual case.

The second thing which has to be noticed is that the argument, as set out, does not involve any sort of deduction of a moral judgment, or even of the negation of a moral judgment, from a factual statement about people's inclinations, interests, etc. We are not saying to B 'You are as a matter of fact averse to this being done to you in a hypothetical case; and from this it follows logically that you ought not to do it to another'. Such a deduction would be a breach of Hume's Law ('No "ought" from an "is" '), to which I have repeatedly declared my adherence (*Language of Morals* 2.5). The point is, rather, that because of his aversion to its being done to him in the hypothetical case, he cannot accept the singular *prescription* that in the hypothetical case it should be done to him; and this, because of the logic of 'ought', precludes him from accepting the moral judgment that he ought to do likewise to another in the actual case. It is not a question of a factual statement about a person's inclinations being inconsistent with a moral judgment; rather, his inclinations being what they are, he cannot assent sincerely to a certain singular prescription, and if he cannot do this, he cannot assent to a certain universal prescription

which entails it, when conjoined with factual statements about the circumstances whose truth he admits. Because of this entailment, if he assented
to the factual statements and to the universal prescription, but refused (as
he must, his inclinations being what they are) to assent to the singular
prescription, he would be guilty of a logical inconsistency.

If it be asked what the relation is between his aversion to being put in
prison in the hypothetical case, and his inability to accept the hypothetical
singular prescription that if he were in such a situation he should be put
into prison, it would seem that the relation is not unlike that between a
belief that the cat is on the mat, and an inability to accept the proposition
that the cat is not on the mat. Further attention to this parallel will perhaps
make the position clearer. Suppose that somebody advances the hypothesis
that cats never sit on mats, and that we refute him by pointing to a cat on
a mat. The logic of our refutation proceeds in two stages. Of these, the
second is: 'Here is a cat sitting on a mat, so it is not the case that cats
never sit on mats'. This is a piece of logical deduction! and to it, in the
moral case, corresponds the step from 'Let this not be done to me' to 'It is
not the case that I ought to do it to another in similar circumstances'. But
in both cases there is a first stage whose nature is more obscure, and different in the two cases, though there is an analogy between them.

In the 'cat' case, it is logically possible for a man to look straight at the
cat on the mat, and yet believe that there is no cat on the mat. But if a
person with normal eyesight and no psychological aberrations does this, we
say that he does not understand the meaning of the words, 'The cat is on
the mat'. And even if he does not have normal eyesight, or suffers from
some psychological aberration (such as phobia of cats, say, that he just *cannot* admit to himself that he is face to face with one), yet, if we can convince him that everyone else can see a cat there, he will have to admit that
there *is* a cat there, or be accused of misusing the language.

If, on the other hand, a man says 'But I *want* to be put in prison, if
ever I am in that situation', we can, indeed, get as far as accusing him of
having eccentric desires; but we cannot, when we have proved to him that
nobody else has such a desire, face him with the choice of either saying,
with the rest, 'Let this not be done to me', or else being open to the accusation of not understanding what he is saying. For it is not an incorrect use of
words to want eccentric things. Logic does not prevent me wanting to be
put in a gas chamber if a Jew. It is perhaps true that I logically cannot
want for its own sake an experience which I think of as *unpleasant*; for to say
that I think of it as unpleasant may be logically inconsistent with saying
that I want it for its own sake. If this is so, it is because 'unpleasant' is a
prescriptive expression. But 'to be put in prison' and 'to be put in a gas
chamber if a Jew', are not prescriptive expressions; and therefore these
things can be wanted without offense to logic. It is, indeed, in the logical

possibility of wanting *anything* (neutrally described) that the 'freedom' which is alluded to in my title essentially consists. And it is this, as we shall see, that lets by the person whom I shall call the 'fanatic'.

There is not, then, a complete analogy between the man who says 'There is no cat on the mat' when there is, and the man who wants things which others do not. But there is a partial analogy, which, having noticed this difference, we may be able to isolate. The analogy is between two relations: the relations between, in both cases, the 'mental state 'of these men and what they say. If I believe that there is a cat on the mat I cannot sincerely say that there is not; and, if I want not to be put into prison more than I want anything else, I cannot sincerely say 'Let me be put into prison'. When, therefore, I said above 'His inclinations being what they are, he cannot assent sincerely to a certain singular prescription', I was making an analytic statement (although the 'cannot' is not a logical 'cannot'); for if he were to assent sincerely to the prescription, that would entail *ex vi terminorum* that his inclinations had changed—in the very same way that it is analytically true that, if the other man were to say sincerely that there was a cat on the mat, when before he had sincerely denied this, he must have changed his belief.

If, however, instead of writing 'His inclinations being what they are, he cannot . . . ', we leave out the first clause and write simply 'He cannot . . . ', the statement is no longer analytic; we are making a statement about his psychology which might be false. For it is logically possible for inclinations to change; hence it is possible for a man to come sincerely to hold an ideal which requires that he himself should be sent to a gas chamber if a Jew. That is the price we have to pay for our freedom. But, as we shall see, in order for reason to have a place in morals it is not necessary for us to close this way of escape by means of a logical barrier; it is sufficient that, men and the world being what they are, we can be very sure that hardly anybody is going to take it with his eyes open. And when we are arguing with one of the vast majority who are not going to take it, the reply that somebody else *might* take it does not help his case against us. In this respect, all moral arguments are *ad hominem*.[8]

---

[8] The above discussion may help to atone for what is confused or even wrong in *Language of Morals* 3.3 (p. 42). The remarks there about the possibility or impossibility of accepting certain moral principles gave the impression of creating an impasse; I can, however, plead that in *Language of Morals* 4.4 (p. 69) there appeared a hint of the way out which is developed in this book.

Moral Arguments

PHILIPPA FOOT

Those who are influenced by the emotivist theory of ethics, and yet wish to defend what Hare has called "the rationality of moral discourse", generally talk a lot about "giving reasons" for saying that one thing is right, and another wrong. The fact that moral judgments need defence seems to distinguish the impact of one man's moral views upon others from mere persuasion or coercion, and the judgments themselves from mere expressions of likes and dislikes. Yet the version of argument in morals currently accepted seems to say that, while reasons must be given, no one need accept them unless he happens to hold particular moral views. It follows that disputes about what is right and wrong can be resolved only if certain contingent conditions are fulfilled; if they are not fulfilled, the argument breaks down, and the disputants are left face to face in an opposition which is merely an expression of attitude and will. Much energy is expended in trying to show that no skeptical conclusion can be drawn. It is suggested, for instance, that anyone who has considered all the facts which could bear on his moral position has *ipso facto* produced a 'well founded' moral judgment; in spite of the fact that anyone else who has considered the same facts may well come to the opposite conclusion. How 'x is good' can be a well founded moral judgment when 'x is bad' can be equally well founded it is not easy to see.

The statement that moral arguments 'may always break down' is often thought of as something that has to be accepted, and it is thought that those who deny it fail to take account of what was proved once for all by Hume, and elaborated by Stevenson, by Ayer, and by Hare. This article is an attempt to expose the assumptions which give the 'breakdown' theory so tenacious a hold, and to suggest an alternative view.

Looked at in one way, the assertion that moral arguments "may always break down" appears to make a large claim. What is meant is that they may break down in a way in which other arguments may not. We are therefore working on a model on which such factors as shortage of time or temper are not shown; the suggestion is not that A's argument with B may break down because B refuses for one reason or another to go on with it, but that their positions as such are irreconcilable. Now the question is: how can we assert that any disagreement about what is right and wrong may end like this? How do we know, without consulting the details of each argument, that there is always an impregnable position both for the man who says that x

From Mind, *LXVII (1958). Reprinted by permission of the author and* Mind.

is right, or good, or what he ought to do, and for the man who denies it? How do we know that each is able to deal with every argument the other may bring?

Thus, when Hare describes someone who listens to all his adversary has to say and then at the end simply rejects his conclusion, we want to ask "How can he?" Hare clearly supposes that he can, for he says that at this point the objector can only be asked to make up his mind for himself.[1] No one would ever paint such a picture of other kinds of argument—suggesting, for instance, that a man might listen to all that could be said about the shape of the earth, and then ask why he should believe that it was round. We should want, in such a case, to know how he met the case put to him; and it is remarkable that in ethics this question is thought not to be in place.

If a man making a moral judgment is to be invulnerable to criticism, he must be free from reproach on two scores: (a) he must have brought forward evidence, where evidence is needed; and (b) he must have disposed of any contrary evidence offered. It is worth showing why writers who insist that moral arguments may always break down assume, for both sides in a moral dispute, invulnerability on both counts. The critical assumption appears in different forms because different descriptions of moral arguments are given; and I shall consider briefly what has been said by Stevenson and by Hare.

1. Stevenson sees the process of giving reasons for ethical conclusions as a special process of nondeductive inference, in which statements expressing beliefs (R) form the premises and emotive (evaluative) utterances (E) the conclusion. There are no rules validating particular inferences, but only causal connections betwen the beliefs and attitudes concerned. "Suppose", he writes, "that a theorist should *tabulate* the 'valid' inferences from R's to E's. It is difficult to see how he could be doing anything more than specify what R's he thereby resolves to *accept* as supporting the various E's. . . . Under the name of 'validity' he will be selecting those inferences to which he is psychologically disposed to give assent, and perhaps inducing others to give a similar assent to them."[2] It follows that disputes in which each man backs up his moral judgment with "reasons" may always break down, and this is an implication on which Stevenson insists. So long as he does not contradict himself and gets his facts right, a man may argue as he chooses, or as he finds himself psychologically disposed. He alone says which facts are relevant to ethical conclusions, so that he is invulnerable on counts (a) and (b) : he can simply assert that what he brings forward is evidence, and can simply deny the relevance of any other. His argument may be

---

[1] *The Language of Morals*, p. 69.
[2] *Ethics and Language*, pp. 170–71.

ineffective, but it cannot be said to be wrong. Stevenson speaks of ethical "inference" and of giving "reasons", but the process which he describes is rather that of trying to produce a result, an attitude, by means of a special kind of adjustment, an alteration in belief. All that is needed for a breakdown is for different attitudes in different people to be causally connected to the same beliefs. Then even complete agreement in belief will not settle a moral dispute.

2. Hare gives a picture of moral reasoning which escapes the difficulties of a special form of inference without rules of validity. He regards an argument to a moral conclusion as a syllogistic inference, with the ordinary rules. The facts, such as "this is stealing", which are to back up a moral judgment are to be stated in a "descriptive" minor premise, and their relevance is to be guaranteed by an "evaluative" major premise in which that kind of thing is said to be good or bad. There is thus no difficulty about the validity of the argument; but one does arise about the status of the major premise. We are supposed to say that a particular action is bad because it is a case of stealing, and because stealing is wrong; but if we ask why stealing is wrong, we can only be presented with another argument of the same form, with another exposed moral principle as its major premise. In the end everyone is forced back to some moral principle which he simply asserts —and which someone else may simply deny. It can therefore be no reproach to anyone that he gives no reasons for a statement of moral principle, since any moral argument must contain some undefended premise of this kind. Nor can he be accused of failing to meet arguments put forward by opponents arguing from different principles; for by denying their ultimate major premises he can successfully deny the relevance of anything they say.

Both these accounts of moral argument are governed by the thought that there is no logical connection between statements of fact and statements of value, so that each man makes his own decision as to the facts about an action which are relevant to its evaluation. To oppose this view we should need to show that, on the contrary, it is laid down that some things do, and some things do not, count in favor of a moral conclusion, and that a man can no more decide for himself what is evidence for rightness and wrongness than he can decide what is evidence for monetary inflation or a tumor on the brain. If such objective relations between facts and values existed, they could be of two kinds: descriptive, or factual premises might *entail* evaluative conclusions, or they might count as *evidence* for for them. It is the second possibility which chiefly concerns me, but I shall nevertheless consider the arguments which are supposed to show that the stronger relationship cannot exist. For I want to show that the arguments usually brought forward do not *even* prove this. I want to say that it has not even been proved that moral conclusions cannot be entailed by factual or descriptive premises.

It is often thought that Hume showed the impossibility of deducing "ought", from "is", but the form in which this view is now defended is, of course, that in which it was rediscovered by G. E. Moore at the beginning of the present century, and developed by such other critics of "naturalistic" ethics as Stevenson, Ayer, and Hare. We need therefore to look into the case against naturalism to see exactly what was proved.

Moore tried to show that goodness was a nonnatural property, and thus not to be defined in terms of natural properties; the problem was to explain the concept of a "natural property", and to prove that no ethical definition in terms of natural properties could be correct. As Frankena[3] and Prior[4] pointed out, the argument against naturalism was always in danger of degenerating into a truism. A natural property tended to become one not identical with goodness, and the naturalistic fallacy that of identifying goodness with "some other thing".

What was needed to give the attack on naturalism new life was the identification of some deficiency common to the whole range of definitions rejected by Moore, a reason why they all failed. This was provided by the theory that value terms in general, and moral terms in particular, were used for a special function—variously identified as expressing feelings, expressing and inducing attitudes, or commending. Now it was said that words with emotive or commendatory force, such as "good", were not to be defined by the use of words whose meaning was merely "descriptive". This discovery tended to appear greater than it was, because it looked as if the two categories of fact and value had been identified separately and found never to coincide, whereas actually the factual or descriptive was defined by exclusion from the realm of value. In the ordinary sense of "descriptive" the word "good" is a descriptive word and in the ordinary sense of "fact" we say that it is a fact about so and so that he is a good man, so that the words must be used in a special sense in moral philosophy. But a special philosopher's sense of these words has never, so far as I know, been explained except by contrasting value and fact. A word or sentence seems to be called "descriptive" on account of the fact that it is *not* emotive, does *not* commend, does *not* entail an imperative, and so on according to the theory involved. This might seem to reduce the case against naturalism once more to an uninteresting tautology, but it does not do so. For if the nonnaturalist has discovered a special feature found in all value judgments, he can no longer be accused of saying merely that nothing is a definition of "good" unless it is a definition of "good" and not "some other thing". His part is now to insist that any definition which fails to allow for the

---

3 W. K. Frankena, "The Naturalistic Fallacy", *Mind* (1939) [reprinted above, pp. 32–43].

4 A. N. Prior, *Logic and the Basis of Ethics* (London: Oxford University Press, 1949), Chap. 1.

special feature of value judgments must be rejected, and to label as "naturalistic" all the definitions which fail to pass this test.

I shall suppose, for the sake of argument, that the nonnaturalist really has identified some characteristic (let us call it f) essential to evaluative words; that he is right in saying that evaluations involve emotions, attitudes, the acceptance of imperatives, or something of the kind. He is therefore justified in insisting that no word or statement which does not have the property f can be taken as equivalent to any evaluation, and that no account of the use of an evaluative term can leave out f and yet be complete. What, if anything, follows about the relation between premises and conclusion in an argument designed to support an evaluation?

It is often said that what follows is that an evaluative conclusion cannot be deduced from descriptive premises, but how is this to be shown? Of course if a descriptive premise is redefined, as one which does not entail an evaluative conclusion, the nonnaturalist will once more have bought security at the price of becoming a bore. He can once more improve his position by pointing to the characteristic f belonging to all evaluations, and asserting that no set of premises which do not entail an f proposition can entail an evaluation. If he takes this course he will be more like the man who says that a proposition which entails a proposition about a dog must be one which entails a proposition about an animal; he is telling us what to look out for in checking the entailment. What he is not so far telling us is that we can test for the entailment by looking to see whether the premise itself has the characteristic f. For all that has yet been shown it might be possible for a premise which is not f to entail a conclusion which is f, and it is obviously this proposition which the nonnaturalist wants to deny.

Now it may seem obvious that a nonevaluative premise could not entail an evaluative conclusion, but it remains unclear how it is supposed to be proved.

In one form, the theory that an evaluative conclusion of a deductive argument needs evaluative premises is clearly unwarrantable; I mention it only to get it out of the way. We cannot possibly say that at least one of the premises must be evaluative if the conclusion is to be so; for there is nothing to tell us that whatever can truly be said of the conclusion of a deductive argument can truly be said of any one of the premises. It is not necessary that the evaluative element should "come in whole", so to speak. If f has to belong to the premises it can only be necessary that it should belong to the premises *together*, and it may be no easy matter to see whether a set of propositions has the property f.

How in any case is it to be proved that if the conclusion is to have the characteristic f the premises taken together must also have it? Can it be said that unless this is so it will always be possible to assert the premises and yet deny the conclusion? I shall try to show that this at least is false, and in order to do so I shall consider the case of arguments designed to show that a certain piece of behavior is or is not rude.

I think it will be agreed that in the wide sense in which philosophers speak of evaluation, "rude" is an evaluative word. At any rate it has the kind of characteristics upon which nonnaturalists fasten: it expresses disapproval, is meant to be used when action is to be discouraged, implies that other things being equal the behavior to which it is applied will be avoided by the speaker, and so on. For the purpose of this argument I shall ignore the cases in which it is admitted that there are reasons why something should be done in spite of, or even because of, the fact that it is rude. Clearly there are occasions when a little rudeness is in place, but this does not alter the fact that "rude" is a condemnatory word.

It is obvious that there is something else to be said about the word "rude" besides the fact that it expresses, fairly mild, condemnation: it can only be used where certain descriptions apply. The right account of the situation in which it is correct to say that a piece of behavior is rude, is, I think, that this kind of behavior causes offense by indicating lack of respect. Sometimes it is merely conventional that such behavior does indicate lack of respect (e.g. when a man keeps his hat on in someone else's house); sometimes the behavior is naturally disrespectful, as when one man pushes another out of the way. (It should be mentioned that rudeness and the absence of rudeness do not exhaust the subject of etiquette; some things are not rude, and yet are "not done." It is rude to wear flannels at a formal dinner party, but merely not done to wear a dinner jacket for tennis.)

Given that this reference to offense is to be included in any account of the concept of rudeness, we may ask what the relation is between the assertion that these conditions of offence are fulfilled—let us call it O— and the statement that a piece of behavior is rude—let us call it R. Can someone who accepts the proposition O (that this kind of offense is caused) deny the proposition R (that the behavior is rude)? I should have thought that this was just what he could not do, for if he says that it is not rude, we shall stare, and ask him what sort of behavior would be rude; and what is he to say? Suppose that he were to answer "a man is rude when he behaves conventionally'", or "a man is rude when he walks slowly up to a front door", and this not because he believes that such behavior causes offense, but with the intention of leaving behind entirely the usual criteria of rudeness. It is evident that with the usual criteria of rudeness he leaves behind the concept itself; he may say the words "I think this rude", but it will not on that account be right to describe him as "thinking it rude". If I *say* "I am sitting on a pile of hay" and bring as evidence the fact that the object I am sitting on has four wooden legs and a hard wooden back, I shall hardly be described as thinking, even mistakenly, that I am sitting on a pile of hay; all I am doing is to use the *words* "pile of hay".

It might be thought that the two cases were not parallel, for while the meaning of "pile of hay" is given by the characteristics which piles of hay must possess, the meaning of "rude" is given by the attitude it expresses. The answer is that if "thinking a thing rude" is to be described as having a particular attitude to it, then having an attitude presupposes, in this case, believing that certain conditions are fulfilled. If "attitudes" were solely a matter of reactions such as wrinkling the nose, and tendencies to such things as making resolutions and scolding, then thinking something rude would not be describable solely in terms of attitudes. Either thinking something rude is not to be described in terms of attitudes, or attitudes are not to be described in terms of such things. Even if we could suppose that a particular individual could react towards conventional behavior, or to walking slowly up to an English front door, *exactly* as most people react to behavior which gives offense, this would not mean that he was to be described as thinking these things rude. And in any case the supposition is nonsense. Although he could behave in some ways as if he thought them rude, e.g. by scolding conventional or slow walking children, but not turning daughters with these proclivities out of doors, his behavior could not be just as if he thought them rude. For as the social reaction to conventional behavior is not the same as the social reaction to offensive behavior, he could not act in just the same way. He could not for instance apologize for what he would call his "rudeness", for he would have to admit that it had caused no offense.

I conclude that whether a man is speaking of behavior as rude or not rude, he must use the same criteria as anyone else, and that since the criteria are satisfied if O is true, it is impossible for him to assert O while denying R. It follows that if it is a sufficient condition of P's entailing Q that the assertion of P is inconsistent with the denial of Q, we have here an example of a nonevaluative premise from which an evaluative conclusion can be deduced.

It is of course possible to admit O while refusing to assert R, and this will not be like the refusal to say about prunes what one has already admitted about dried plums. Calling an action 'rude' is using a concept which a man might want to reject, rejecting the whole practice of praising and blaming embodied in terms such as 'polite' and 'rude'. Such a man would refuse to discuss points of etiquette, and arguments with him about what is rude would not so much break down as never begin. But once he did accept the question "Is this rude?", he would have to abide by the rules of this kind of argument; he could not bring forward any evidence he liked, and he could not deny the relevance of any piece of evidence brought forward by his opponent. Nor could he say that he was unable to move from O to R on this occasion because the belief in O had not induced in him feelings or attitudes warranting the assertion of R. If he had agreed to discuss rudeness he had committed himself to accepting O as evidence for R, and evidence is not a sort of medicine which is taken in the hope that it will work. To suggest that he could refuse to admit that certain behavior was rude because the right psychological state had not been induced, is as odd as to suppose that one might refuse to speak of the world as round because in spite of the good evidence of roundness a feeling of confidence in the proposition had not been produced. When given good evidence it is one's business to act on it, not to hang around waiting for the right state of mind. It follows that if a man is prepared to discuss questions of rudeness, and hence to accept as evidence the fact that behavior causes a certain kind of offense, he cannot refuse to admit R when O has been proved.

The point of considering this example was to show that there may be the strictest rules of evidence even where an evaluative conclusion is concerned. Applying this principle to the case of moral judgments, we see that —for all that the nonnaturalist has proved to the contrary—Bentham, for instance, may be right in saying that when used in conjunction with the principle of utility "the words *ought* and *right* and *wrong*, and others of that stamp, have a meaning: when otherwise they have none".[5] Anyone who uses moral terms at all, whether to assert or deny a moral proposition, must abide by the rules for their use, including the rules about what shall count as evidence for or against the moral judgment concerned. For anything that has yet been shown to the contrary these rules could be entailment rules, forbidding the assertion of factual propositions in conjunction with the denial of moral propositions. The only recourse of the man who refused to accept the things which counted in favor of a moral proposition as giving him a reason to do certain things or to take up a particular attitude, would be to leave the moral discussion and abjure altogether the use of moral terms.

To say what Bentham said is not, then, to commit any sort of "naturalistic fallacy". It is open to us to enquire whether moral terms do lose their meaning when divorced from the pleasure principle, or from some other set of criteria, as the word "rude" loses its meaning when the criterion of offensiveness is dropped. To me it seems that this is clearly the case; I do not know what could be meant by saying that it was someone's duty to do something unless there was an attempt to show why it mattered if this sort of thing was not done. How can questions such as "what does it matter?", "what harm does it do?", "what advantage is there in ... ?", "why is it important?", be set aside here? Is it even to be suggested that the harm done by a certain trait of character could be taken, by some extreme moral eccentric, to be just what made it a virtue? I suggest that such a man

---

[5] *Principles of Morals in Legislation*, Chap. I, x.

would not even be a moral eccentric, any more than the man who used the word "rude" of conventional behavior was putting forward strange views about what was rude. Both descriptions have their proper application, but it is not here. How exactly the concepts of harm, advantage, benefit, importance, etc., are related to the different moral concepts, such as rightness, obligation, goodness, duty, and virtue, is something that needs the most patient investigation, but that they are so related seems undeniable, and it follows that a man cannot make his own personal decision about the considerations which are to count as evidence in morals.

Perhaps it will be argued that this kind of freedom of choice is not ruled out after all, because a man has to decide for himself what is to count as advantage, benefit, or harm. But is this really plausible? Consider the man described by Hare as thinking that torturing is morally permissible.[6] Apparently he is not supposed to be arguing that in spite of everything torture is justifiable as a means of extracting confessions from enemies of the state, for the argument is supposed to be at an end when he has said that torturing people is permissible, and his opponent has said that it is not. How is he supposed to have answered the objection that to inflict torture is to do harm? If he is supposed to have said that pain is good for a man in the long run, rather than bad, he will have to show the benefits involved, and he can no more choose what shall count as a benefit than he could have chosen what counted as harm. Is he supposed perhaps to count as harm only harm to himself? In this case he is guilty of *ignoratio elenchi*. By refusing to count as harm anything except harm to himself, he puts himself outside the pale of moral discussion, and should have explained that this was his position. One might compare his case to that of a man who in some discussion of common policy says "this will be best thing to do", and announces afterwards that *he* meant best for himself. This is not what the word "best" does mean in the context of such a discussion.

It may be objected that these considerations about the evidence which must be brought for saying that one thing is good and another bad, could not in any case be of the least importance; such rules of evidence, even if they exist, only reflect the connection between our existing moral code and our existing moral terms; if there are no "free" moral terms in our language, it can always be supposed that some have been invented—as indeed they will have to be invented if we are to be able to argue with people who subscribe to a moral code entirely different from our own. This objection rests on a doubtful assumption about the concept of *morality*. It assumes that even if there are rules about the grounds on which actions can be called good, right, or obligatory, there are no rules about the grounds on which a principle which is to be called a moral principle may be asserted.

---

6 *Universalizability, Proceedings of the Aristotelian Society*, 1954–1955, p. 304.

Those who believe this must think it possible to identify an element of feeling or attitude which carries the meaning of the word "moral". It must be supposed, for instance, that if we describe a man as being for or against certain actions, bringing them under universal rules, adopting these rules for himself, and thinking himself bound to urge them on others, we shall be able to identify him as holding moral principles, whatever the content of the principle at which he stops. But why should it be supposed that the concept of morality is to be caught in this particular kind of net? The consequences of such an assumption are very hard to stomach; for it follows that a rule which was admitted by those who obeyed it to be completely pointless could yet be recognized as a moral rule. If people happened to insist that no one should run round trees left handed, or look at hedgehogs in the light of the moon, this might count as a basic moral principle about which nothing more need be said.

I think that the main reason why this view is so often held in spite of these difficulties, is that we fear the charge of making a verbal decision in favor of our own moral code. But those who bring that charge are merely begging the question against arguments such as those given above. Of course if the rules we are refusing to call moral rules can really be given this name, then we are merely legislating against alien *moral codes*. But the suggestion which has been put forward is that this could not be the right description for rules of behavior for which an entirely different defence is offered from that which we offer for our moral beliefs. If this suggestion is right, the difference between ourselves and the people who have these rules is not to be described as a difference of moral outlook, but rather as a difference between a moral and a nonmoral point of view. The example of etiquette is again useful here. No one is tempted to say that the ruling out, *a priori*, of rules of etiquette which each man decides on for himself when he feels so inclined, represents a mere verbal decision in favor of our kind of socially determined standards of etiquette. On what grounds could one call a rule which someone was allowed to invent for himself a rule of *etiquette?* It is not just a fact about the use of our words "rude", "not done", etc., that they could not be applied in such a case; it is also a fact about etiquette that if terms in another language did appear in such situations they would not be terms of etiquette. We can make a similar point about the terms "legal" and "illegal" and the concept of law. If any individual was allowed to apply a certain pair of terms expressing approval and disapproval off his own bat, without taking notice of any recognized authority, such terms could not be legal terms. Similarly it is a fact about etiquette and law that they are both conventional as morality is not.

It may be that in attempting to state the rules which govern the assertion of moral propositions we shall legislate against a moral system radically opposed to our own. But this is only to say that we may make a mistake. The remedy is to look more carefully at the rules of evidence, not to assume that there cannot be any at all. If a moral system such as Nietzsche's has been refused recognition as a moral system, then we have got the criteria wrong. The fact that Nietzsche was a moralist cannot, however, be quoted in favor of the private enterprise theory of moral criteria. Admittedly Nietzsche said "You want to decrease suffering; I want precisely to increase it" but he did not *just* say this. Nor did he offer as a justification the fact that suffering causes a tendency to absentmindedness, or lines on the human face. We recognize Nietzsche as a moralist because he tries to justify an increase in suffering by connecting it with strength as opposed to weakness, and individuality as opposed to conformity. That strength is a good thing can only be denied by someone who can show that the strong man overreaches himself, or in some other way brings harm to himself or other people. That individuality is a good thing is something that has to be shown, but in a vague way we connect it with originality, and with courage, and hence there is no difficulty in conceiving Nietzsche as a moralist when he appeals to such a thing.

In conclusion it is worth remarking that moral arguments break down more often than philosophers tend to think, but that the breakdown is of a different kind. When people argue about what is right, good, or obligatory, or whether a certain character trait is or is not a virtue, they do not confine their remarks to the adducing of facts which can be established by simple observation, or by some clear-cut technique. What is said may well be subtle or profound, and in this sort of discussion as in others, in the field of literary criticism for instance, or the discussion of character, much depends on experience and imagination. It is quite common for one man to be unable to see what the other is getting at, and this sort of misunderstanding will not always be resolvable by anything which could be called argument in the ordinary sense.

How to Derive "Ought" from "Is"

JOHN R. SEARLE

1

It is often said that one cannot derive an "ought" from an "is." This thesis, which comes from a famous passage in Hume's *Treatise*, while not as clear as it might be, is at least clear in broad outline: there is a class of statements of fact which is logically distinct from a class of statements of value. No set of statements of fact by themselves entails any statement of value. Put in more contemporary terminology, no set of *descriptive* statements can entail an *evaluative* statement without the addition of at least one evaluative premise. To believe otherwise is to commit what has been called the naturalistic fallacy.

I shall attempt to demonstrate a counter-example to this thesis.[1] It is not of course to be supposed that a single counter-example can refute a philosophical thesis, but in the present instance if we can present a plausible counter-example and can in addition give some account or explanation of how and why it is a counter-example, and if we can further offer a theory to back up our counter-example—a theory which will generate an indefinite number of counter-examples—we may at the very least cast considerable light on the original thesis; and possibly, if we can do all these things, we may even incline ourselves to the view that the scope of that thesis was more restricted than we had originally supposed. A counter-example must proceed by taking a statement or statements which any proponent of the thesis would grant were purely factual or "descriptive" (they need not actually contain the word "is") and show how they are logically related to a statement which a proponent of the thesis would regard as clearly "evaluative". (In the present instance it will contain an "ought".)[2]

From The Philosophical Review, *LXXIII (1964). Reprinted by permission of the author and* The Philosophical Review.

Earlier versions of this paper were read before the Stanford Philosophy Colloquium and the Pacific Division of the American Philosophical Association. I am indebted to many people for helpful comments and criticisms, especially Hans Herzberger, Arnold Kaufmann, Benson Mates, A. I. Melden, and Dagmar Searle.

[1] In its modern version. I shall not be concerned with Hume's treatment of the problem.

[2] If this enterprise succeeds, we shall have bridged the gap between "evaluative" and "descriptive" and consequently have demonstrated a weakness in this very terminology. At present, however, my strategy is to play along with the terminology, pre-

Consider the following series of statements:

(1) Jones uttered the words "I hereby promise to pay you, Smith, five dollars."

(2) Jones promised to pay Smith five dollars.

(3) Jones placed himself under (undertook) an obligation to pay Smith five dollars.

(4) Jones is under an obligation to pay Smith five dollars.

(5) Jones ought to pay Smith five dollars.

I shall argue concerning this list that the relation between any statement and its successor, while not in every case one of "entailment," is nonetheless not just a contingent relation; and the additional statements necessary to make the relationship one of entailment do not need to involve any evaluative statements, moral principles, or anything of the sort.

Let us begin. How is (1) related to (2)? In certain circumstances, uttering the words in quotation marks in (1) is the act of making a promise. And it is a part of or a consequence of the meaning of the words in (1) that in those circumstances uttering them is promising. "I hereby promise" is a paradigm device in English for performing the act described in (2), promising.

Let us state this fact about English usage in the form of an extra premise:

(1a) Under certain conditions C anyone who utters the words (sentence) "I hereby promise to pay you, Smith, five dollars" promises to pay Smith five dollars.

What sorts of things are involved under the rubric "conditions C?" What is involved will be all those conditions, those states of affairs, which are necessary and sufficient conditions for the utterance of the words (sentence) to constitute the successful performance of the act of promising. The conditions will include such things as that the speaker is in the presence of the hearer Smith, they are both conscious, both speakers of English, speaking seriously. The speaker knows what he is doing, is not under the influence of drugs, not hypnotized or acting in a play, not telling a joke or reporting an event, and so forth. This list will no doubt be somewhat indefinite because the boundaries of the concept of a promise, like the boundaries of most concepts in a natural language, are a bit loose.[3] But one

---

tending that the notions of evaluative and descriptive are fairly clear. At the end of the paper I shall state in what respects I think they embody a muddle.

[3] In addition the concept of a promise is a member of a class of concepts which suffer from looseness of a peculiar kind, viz. defeasibility. Cf. H. L. A. Hart, "The Ascription of Responsibility and Rights," *Logic and Language*, First Series, ed. A. Flew (Oxford, 1951).

thing is clear; however loose the boundaries may be, and however difficult it may be to decide marginal cases, the conditions under which a man who utters "I hereby promise" can correctly be said to have made a promise are straightforwardly empirical conditions.

So let us add as an extra premise the empirical assumption that these conditions obtain.

(1b) Conditions C obtain.

From (1), (1a), and (1b) we derive (2). The argument is of the form: If C then (if U then P): C for conditions, U for utterance, P for promise. Adding the premises U and C to this hypothetical we derive (2). And as far as I can see, no moral premises are lurking in the logical woodpile. More needs to be said about the relation of (1) to (2), but I reserve that for later.

What is the relation between (2) and (3)? I take it that promising is, by definition, an act of placing oneself under an obligation. No analysis of the concept of promising will be complete which does not include the feature of the promiser placing himself under or undertaking or accepting or recognizing an obligation to the promisee, to perform some future course of action, normally for the benefit of the promisee. One may be tempted to think that promising can be analyzed in terms of creating expectations in one's hearers, or some such, but a little reflection will show that the crucial distinction between statements of intention on the one hand and promises on the other lies in the nature and degree of commitment or obligation undertaken in promising.

I am therefore inclined to say that (2) entails (3) straight off, but I can have no objection if anyone wishes to add—for the purpose of formal neatness—the tautological premise:

(2a) All promises are acts of placing oneself under (undertaking) an obligation to do the thing promised.

How is (3) related to (4)? If one has placed oneself under an obligation, then, other things being equal, one is under an obligation. That I take it also is a tautology. Of course it is possible for all sorts of things to happen which will release one from obligations one has undertaken and hence the need for the *ceteris paribus* rider. To get an entailment between (3) and (4) we therefore need a qualifying statement to the effect that:

(3a) Other things are equal.

Formalists, as in the move from (2) to (3), may wish to add the tautological premise:

(3b) All those who place themselves under an obligation are, other things being equal, under an obligation.

The move from (3) to (4) is thus of the same form as the move from (1) to (2): If E then (if PUO then UO): E for other things are equal, PUO for place under obligation and UO for under obligation. Adding the two premises E and PUO we derive UO.

Is (3a), the *ceteris paribus* clause, a concealed evaluative premise? It certainly looks as if it might be, especially in the formulation I have given it, but I think we can show that, though questions about whether other things are equal frequently involve evaluative considerations, it is not logically necessary that they should in every case. I shall postpone discussion of this until after the next step.

What is the relation between (4) and (5)? Analogous to the tautology which explicates the relation of (3) and (4) there is here the tautology that, other things being equal, one ought to do what one is under an obligation to do. And here, just as in the previous case, we need some premise of the form:

(4a) Other things are equal.

We need the *ceteris paribus* clause to eliminate the possibility that something extraneous to the relation of "obligation" to "ought" might interfere.[4] Here, as in the previous two steps, we eliminate the appearance of enthymeme by pointing out that the apparently suppressed premise is tautological and hence, though formally neat, it is redundant. If, however, we wish to state it formally, this argument is of the same form as the move from (3) to (4): If E then (if UO then O); E for other things are equal, UO for under obligation, O for ought. Adding the premises E and UO we derive O.

Now a word about the phrase "other things being equal" and how it functions in my attempted derivation. This topic and the closely related topic of defeasibility are extremely difficult and I shall not try to do more than justify my claim that the satisfaction of the condition does not necessarily involve anything evaluative. The force of the expression "other things being equal" in the present instance is roughly this. Unless we have some reason (that is, unless we are actually prepared to give some reason) for supposing the obligation is void (step 4) or the agent ought not to keep the promise (step 5), then the obligation holds and he ought to keep the promise. It is not part of the force of the phrase "other things being equal" that in order to satisfy it we need to establish a universal negative proposi-

---

4 The *ceteris paribus* clause in this step excludes somewhat different sorts of cases from those excluded in the previous step. In general we say, "He undertook an obligation, but nonetheless he is not (now) under an obligation" when the obligation has been *removed*, e.g., if the promisee says, "I release you from your obligation." But we say, "He is under an obligation, but nonetheless ought not to fulfill it" in cases where the obligation is *overriden* by some other considerations, e.g., a prior obligation.

tion to the effect that no reason could ever be given by anyone for supposing the agent is not under an obligation or ought not to keep the promise. That would be impossible and would render the phrase useless. It is sufficient to satisfy the condition that no reason to the contrary can in fact be given.

If a reason is given for supposing the obligation is void or that the promiser ought not to keep a promise, then characteristically a situation calling for an evaluation arises. Suppose, for example, we consider a promised act wrong, but we grant that the promiser did undertake an obligation. Ought he too keep the promise? There is no established procedure for objectively deciding such cases in advance, and an evaluation (if that is really the right word) is in order. But unless we have some reason to the contrary, the *ceteris paribus* condition is satisfied, no evaluation is necessary, and the question whether he ought to do it is settled by saying "he promised." It is always an open possibility that we may have to make an evaluation in order to derive "he ought" from "he promised," for we may have to evaluate a counter-argument. But an evaluation is not logically necessary in every case, for there may as a matter of fact be no counter-arguments. I am therefore inclined to think that there is nothing necessarily evaluative about the *ceteris paribus* condition, even though deciding whether it is satisfied will frequently involve evaluations.

But suppose I am wrong about this: would that salvage the belief in an unbridgeable logical gulf between "is" and "ought"? I think not, for we can always rewrite my steps (4) and (5) so that they include the *ceteris paribus* clause as part of the conclusion. Thus from our premises we would then have derived "Other things being equal Jones ought to pay Smith five dollars," and that would still be sufficient to refute the tradition, for we would still have shown a relation of entailment between descriptive and evaluative statements. It was not the fact that extenuating circumstances can void obligations that drove philosophers to the naturalistic fallacy fallacy; it was rather a theory of language, as we shall see later on.

We have thus derived (in as strict a sense of "derive" as natural languages will admit of) an "ought" from an "is." And the extra premises which were needed to make the derivation work were in no case moral or evaluative in nature. They consisted of empirical assumptions, tautologies, and descriptions of word usage. It must be pointed out also that the "ought" is a "categorical" not a "hypothetical" ought. (5) does not say that Jones ought to pay up if he wants such and such. It says he ought to pay up, period. Note also that the steps of the derivation are carried on in the third person. We are not concluding "I ought" from "I said 'I promise,' " but "he ought" from "he said 'I promise.' "

The proof unfolds the connection between the utterance of certain words and the speech act of promising and then in turn unfolds promising into obligation and moves from obligation to "ought." The step from (1) to (2) is radically different from the others and requires special comment. In (1) we construe "I hereby promise..." as an English phrase having a certain meaning. It is a consequence of that meaning that the utterance of that phrase under certain conditions is the act of promising. Thus by presenting the quoted expressions in (1) and by describing their use in (1a) we have as it were already invoked the institution of promising. We might have started with an even more ground-floor premise than (1) by saying:

(1b) Jones uttered the phonetic sequence:/ai⁺hirbai⁺pramis⁺təpei⁺yu⁺ smiθ⁺faiv⁺dalərz/

We would then have needed extra empirical premises stating that this phonetic sequence was associated in certain ways with certain meaningful units relative to certain dialects.

The moves from (2) to (5) are relatively easy. We rely on definitional connections between "promise," "obligate," and "ought," and the only problem which arises is that obligations can be overridden or removed in a variety of ways and we need to take account of that fact. We solve our difficulty by adding further premises to the effect that there are no contrary considerations, that other things are equal.

2

In this section I intend to discuss three possible objections to the derivation.

First objection. Since the first premise is descriptive and the conclusion evaluative, there must be a concealed evaluative premise in the description of the conditions in (1b).

So far, this argument merely begs the question by assuming the logical gulf between descriptive and evaluative which the derivation is designed to challenge. To make the objection stick, the defender of the distinction would have to show how exactly (1b) must contain an evaluative premise and what sort of premise it might be. Uttering certain words in certain conditions just *is* promising and the description of these conditions needs no evaluative element. The essential thing is that in the transition from (1) to (2) we move from the specification of a certain utterance of words to the specification of a certain speech act. The move is achieved because the speech act is a conventional act; and the utterance of the words, according to the conventions, constitutes the performance of just that speech act.

A variant of this first objection is to say: all you have shown is that "promise" is an evaluative, not a descriptive, concept. But this objection again begs the question and in the end will prove disastrous to the original distinction between descriptive and evaluative. For that a man uttered certain words and that these words have the meaning they do are surely objective facts. And if the statement of these two objective facts plus a description of the conditions of the utterance is sufficient to entail the statement (2) which the objector alleges to be an evaluative statement (Jones promised to pay Smith five dollars), then an evaluative conclusion is derived from descriptive premises without even going through steps (3), (4), and (5).

Second objection. Ultimately the derivation rests on the principle that one ought to keep one's promises and that is a moral principle, hence evaluative.

I don't know whether "one ought to keep one's promises" is a "moral" principle, but whether or not it is, it is also tautological; for it is nothing more than a derivation from the two tautologies:

> All promises are (create, are undertakings of, are acceptances of) obligations,

and

> One ought to keep (fulfill) one's obligations.

What needs to be explained is why so many philosophers have failed to see the tautological character of this principle. Three things I think have concealed its character from them.

The first is a failure to distinguish external questions about the institution of promising from internal questions asked within the framework of the institution. The questions "Why do we have such an institution as promising?" and "Ought we to have such institutionalized forms of obligation as promising?" are external questions asked about and not within the institution of promising. And the question "Ought one to keep one's promises?" can be confused with or can be taken as (and I think has often been confused with or can be taken as) an external question roughly expressible as "Ought one to accept the institution of promising?" But taken literally, as an internal question, as a question about promises and not about the institution of promising, the question "Ought one to keep one's promises?" is as empty as the question "Are triangles three-sided?" To recognize something as a promise is to grant that, other things being equal, it ought to be kept.

A second fact which has clouded the issue is this. There are many situations, both real and imaginable, where one ought not to keep a promise, where the obligation to keep a promise is overridden by some further considerations, and it was for this reason that we needed those clumsy *ceteris paribus* clauses in our derivation. But the fact that obligations can be overridden does not show that there were no obligations in the first place. On the contrary. And these original obligations are all that is needed to make the proof work.

Yet a third factor is the following. Many philosophers still fail to realize the full force of saying that "I hereby promise" is a performative expression. In uttering it one performs but does not describe the act of promising. Once promising is seen as a speech act of a kind different from describing, then it is easier to see that one of the features of the act is the undertaking of an obligation. But if one thinks the utterance of "I promise" or "I hereby promise" is a peculiar kind of description—for example, of one's mental state—then the relation between promising and obligation is going to seem very mysterious.

Third objection. The derivation uses only a factual or inverted commas sense of the evaluative terms employed. For example, an anthropologist observing the behavior and attitudes of the Anglo-Saxons might well go through these derivations, but nothing evaluative would be included. Thus step (2) is equivalent to "He did what they call promising" and step (5) to "According to them he ought to pay Smith five dollars." But since all of the steps (2) to (5) are in *oratio obliqua* and hence disguised statements of fact, the fact-value distinction remains unaffected.

This objection fails to damage the derivation, for what it says is only that the steps can be reconstrued as in *oratio obliqua*, that we can construe them as a series of external statements, that we can construct a parallel (or at any rate related) proof about reported speech. But what I am arguing is that, taken quite literally, without any *oratio obliqua* additions or interpretations, the derivation is valid. That one can construct a similar argument which would fail to refute the fact-value distinction does not show that this proof fails to refute it. Indeed it is irrelevant.

3

So far I have presented a counter-example to the thesis that one cannot derive an "ought" from an "is" and considered three possible objections to it. Even supposing what I have said so far is true, still one feels a certain uneasiness. One feels there must be some trick involved somewhere. We might state our uneasiness thus: How can my granting a mere fact about a man, such as the fact that he uttered certain words or that he made a promise, commit *me* to the view that *he* ought to do something? I now want briefly to discuss what broader philosophic significance my attempted derivation may have, in such a way as to give us the outlines of an answer to this question.

I shall begin by discussing the grounds for supposing that it cannot be answered at all.

The inclination to accept a rigid distinction between "is" and "ought," between descriptive and evaluative, rests on a certain picture of the way words relate to the world. It is a very attractive picture, so attractive (to me at least) that it is not entirely clear to what extent the mere presentation of counter-examples can challenge it. What is needed is an explanation of how and why this classical empiricist picture fails to deal with such counter-examples. Briefly, the picture is constructed something like this: first we present examples of so-called descriptive statements ("my car goes eighty miles an hour," "Jones is six feet tall," "Smith has brown hair"), and we contrast them with so-called evaluative statements ("my car is a good car," "Jones ought to pay Smith five dollars," "Smith is a nasty man"). Anyone can see that they are different. We articulate the difference by pointing out that for the descriptive statements the question of truth or falsity is objectively decidable, because to know the meaning of the descriptive expressions is to know under what objectively ascertainable conditions the statements which contain them are true or false. But in the case of evaluative statements the situation is quite different. To know the meaning of the evaluative expressions is not by itself sufficient for knowing under what conditions the statements containing them are true or false, because the meaning of the expressions is such that the statements are not capable of objective or factual truth or falsity at all. Any justification a speaker can give of one of his evaluative statements essentially involves some appeal to attitudes he holds, to criteria of assessment he has adopted, or to moral principles by which he has chosen to live and judge other people. Descriptive statements are thus objective, evaluative statements subjective, and the difference is a consequence of the different sorts of terms employed.

The underlying reason for these differences is that evaluative statements perform a completely different job from descriptive statements. Their job is not to describe any features of the world but to express the speaker's emotions, to express his attitudes, to praise or condemn, to laud or insult, to commend, to recommend, to advise, and so forth. Once we see the different jobs the two perform, we see that there must be a logical gulf between them. Evaluative statements must be different from descriptive statements in order to do their job, for if they were objective they could no longer function to evaluate. Put metaphysically, values cannot lie in the world, for if they did they would cease to be values and would just be another part of the world. Put in the formal mode, one cannot define an evaluative word in terms of descriptive words, for if one did, one would no longer be able to use the evaluative word to commend, but only to describe. Put yet another way, any effort to derive an "ought" from an "is" must be a waste of time, for all it could show even if it succeeded would be that the "is" was not a real "is" but only a disguised "ought" or, alternatively, that the "ought" was not a real "ought" but only a disguised "is."

This summary of the traditional empirical view has been very brief, but I hope it conveys something of the power of this picture. In the hands of certain modern authors, especially Hare and Nowell-Smith, the picture attains considerable subtlety and sophistication.

What is wrong with this picture? No doubt many things are wrong with it. In the end I am going to say that one of the things wrong with it is that it fails to give us any coherent account of such notions as commitment, responsibility, and obligation.

In order to work toward this conclusion I can begin by saying that the picture fails to account for the *different types* of "descriptive" statements. Its paradigms of descriptive statements are such utterances as "my car goes eighty miles an hour," "Jones is six feet tall," "Smith has brown hair," and the like. But it is forced by its own rigidity to construe "Jones got married," "Smith made a promise," "Jackson has five dollars," and "Brown hit a home run" as descriptive statements as well. It is so forced, because whether or not someone got married, made a promise, has five dollars, or hit a home run is as much a matter of objective fact as whether he has red hair or brown eyes. Yet the former kind of statement (statements containing "married," "promise," and so forth) seem to be quite different from the simple empirical paradigms of descriptive statements. How are they different? Though both kinds of statements state matters of objective fact, the statements containing words such as "married," "promise," "home run," and "five dollars" state facts whose existence presupposes certain institutions: a man has five dollars, given the institution of money. Take away the institution and all he has is a rectangular bit of paper with green ink on it. A man hits a home run only given the institution of baseball; without the institution he only hits a sphere with a stick. Similarly, a man gets married or makes a promise only within the institutions of marriage and promising. Without them, all he does is utter words or makes gestures. We might characterize such facts as institutional facts, and contrast them with noninstitutional, or brute, facts: that a man has a bit of paper with green ink on it is a brute fact, that he has five dollars is an institutional fact.[5] The classical picture fails to account for the differences between statements of brute fact and statements of institutional fact.

The word "institution" sounds artificial here, so let us ask: what sorts of institutions are these? In order to answer that question I need to distinguish between two different kinds of rules or conventions. Some rules regulate antecedently existing forms of behavior. For example, the rules of polite table behavior regulate eating, but eating exists independently of these rules. Some rules, on the other hand, do not merely regulate but create or define new forms of behavior: the rules of chess, for example, do not merely

---

[5] For a discussion of this distinction see G. E. M. Anscombe, "Brute Facts," *Analysis* (1958).

regulate an antecedently existing activity called playing chess; they, as it were, create the possibility of or define that activity. The activity of playing chess is constituted by action in accordance with these rules. Chess has no existence apart from these rules. The distinction I am trying to make was foreshadowed by Kant's distinction between regulative and constitutive principles, so let us adopt his terminology and describe our distinction as a distinction between regulative and constitutive rules. Regulative rules regulate activities whose existence is independent of the rules; constitutive rules constitute (and also regulate) forms of activity whose existence is logically dependent on the rules.[6]

Now the institutions that I have been talking about are systems of constitutive rules. The institutions of marriage, money, and promising are like the institutions of baseball or chess in that they are systems of such constitutive rules or conventions. What I have called institutional facts are facts which presuppose such institutions.

Once we recognize the existence of and begin to grasp the nature of such institutional facts, it is but a short step to see that many forms of obligations, commitments, rights, and responsibilities are similarly institutionalized. It is often a matter of fact that one has certain obligations, commitments, rights, and responsibilities, but it is a matter of institutional, not brute, fact. It is one such institutionalized form of obligation, promising, which I invoked above to derive an "ought" from an "is." I started with a brute fact, that a man uttered certain words, and then invoked the institution in such a way as to generate institutional facts by which we arrived at the institutional fact that the man ought to pay another man five dollars. The whole proof rests on an appeal to the constitutive rule that to make a promise is to undertake an obligation.

We are now in a position to see how we can generate an indefinite number of such proofs. Consider the following vastly different example. We are in our half of the seventh inning and I have a big lead off second base. The pitcher whirls, fires to the shortstop covering, and I am tagged out a good ten feet down the line. The umpire shouts, "Out!" I, however, being a positivist, hold my ground. The umpire tells me to return to the dugout. I point out to him that you can't derive an "ought" from an "is." No set of descriptive statements describing matters of fact, I say, will entail any evaluative statements to the effect that I should or ought to leave the field. "You just can't get orders or recommendations from facts alone." What is needed is an evaluative major premise. I therefore return to and stay on second base (until I am carried off the field). I think everyone feels my claims here to be preposterous, and preposterous in the sense of logically

---

[6] For a discussion of a related distinction see J. Rawls, "Two Concepts of Rules," *Philosophical Review*, LXIV (1955).

absurd. Of course you can derive an "ought" from an "is," and though to actually set out the derivation in this case would be vastly more complicated than in the case of promising, it is in principle no different. By undertaking to play baseball I have committed myself to the observation of certain constitutive rules.

We are now also in a position to see that the tautology that one ought to keep one's promises is only one of a class of similar tautologies concerning institutionalized forms of obligation. For example, "one ought not to steal" can be taken as saying that to recognize something as someone else's property necessarily involves recognizing his right to dispose of it. This is a constitutive rule of the institution of private property.[7] "One ought not to tell lies" can be taken as saying that to make an assertion necessarily involves undertaking an obligation to speak truthfully. Another constitutive rule. "One ought to pay one's debts" can be construed as saying that to recognize something as a debt is necessarily to recognize an obligation to pay it. It is easy to see how all these principles will generate counter-examples to the thesis that you cannot derive an "ought" from an "is."

My tentative conclusions, then, are as follows:

1. The classical picture fails to account for institutional facts.
2. Institutional facts exist within systems of constitutive rules.
3. Some systems of constitutive rules involve obligations, commitments, and responsibilities.
4. Within those systems we can derive "ought's" from "is's" on the model of the first derivation.

With these conclusions we now return to the question with which I began this section: How can my stating a fact about a man, such as the fact that he made a promise, commit me to a view about what he ought to do? One can begin to answer this question by saying that for me to state such an institutional fact is already to invoke the constitutive rules of the institution. It is those rules that give the word "promise" its meaning. But those rules are such that to commit myself to the view that Jones made a

---

[7] Proudhon said: "Property is theft." If one tries to take this as an internal remark it makes no sense. It was intended as an external remark attacking and rejecting the institution of private property. It gets its air of paradox and its force by using terms which are internal to the institution in order to attack the institution.

Standing on the deck of some institutions one can tinker with constitutive rules and even throw some other institutions overboard. But could one throw all institutions overboard (in order perhaps to avoid ever having to derive an "ought" from an "is")? One could not and still engage in those forms of behavior we consider characteristically human. Suppose Proudhon had added (and tried to live by): "Truth is a lie, marriage is infidelity, language is uncommunicative, law is a crime," and so on with every possible institution.

promise involves committing myself to what he ought to do (other things being equal).

If you like, then, we have shown that "promise" is an evaluative word, but since it is also purely descriptive, we have really shown that the whole distinction needs to be reexamined. The alleged distinction between descriptive and evaluative statements is really a conflation of at least two distinctions. On the one hand there is a distinction between different kinds of speech acts, one family of speech acts including evaluations, another family including descriptions. This is a distinction between different kinds of illocutionary force.[8] On the other hand there is a distinction between utterances which involve claims objectively decidable as true or false and those which involve claims not objectively decidable, but which are "matters of personal decision" or "matters of opinion." It has been assumed that the former distinction is (must be) a special case of the latter, that if something has the illocutionary force of an evaluation, it cannot be entailed by factual premises. Part of the point of my argument is to show that this contention is false, that factual premises can entail evaluative conclusions. If I am right, then the alleged distinction between descriptive and evaluative utterances is useful only as a distinction between two kinds of illocutionary force, describing and evaluating, and it is not even very useful there, since if we are to use these terms strictly, they are only two among hundreds of kinds of illocutionary force; and utterances of sentences of the form (5)—"Jones ought to pay Smith five dollars"—would not characteristically fall in either class.

---

[8] See J. L. Austin, *How to Do Things with Words* (Cambridge, Mass., 1962), for an explanation of this notion.

The Promising Game

R. M. HARE

One of the most fundamental questions about moral judgments is whether they, and other value judgments, can be logically derived from statements of empirical fact. Like most important philosophical questions, this one has reached the stage at which its discussion is bound to proceed piecemeal, in terms of particular examples, arguments, and counterarguments. This article is intended as a contribution to one such controversy.

From Revue Internationale de Philosophie, *XVIII (1964). Reprinted by permission of the author and* Review Internationale de Philosophie, *Bruxelles.*

In a recent article, "How to derive 'ought' from 'is' "[1], Professor J. R. Searle attempts a feat which many before him have thought to perform. His argument, though it seems to me unsound, is set out with such clarity and elegance as amply to repay examination.

He asks us to consider the following series of statements:

(1) Jones uttered the words "I hereby promise to pay you, Smith, five dollars".

(2) Jones promised to pay Smith five dollars.

(3) Jones placed himself under (undertook) an obligation to pay Smith five dollars.

(4) Jones is under an obligation to pay Smith five dollars.

(5) Jones ought to pay Smith five dollars.

He then argues concerning this list that "the relation between any statement and its successor, while not in every case one of 'entailment', is nonetheless not just a contingent relation; and the additional statements necessary to make the relationship one of entailment do not need to involve any evaluative statements, moral principles, or anything of the sort" (p. 44).

Though there may be other steps in the argument that are open to question, I shall concentrate on those from (1) to (2) and from (2) to (3). One of the "additional statements" which Searle supplies between (1) and (2) is

(1a) Under certain conditions C anyone who utter the words (sentence) "I hereby promise to pay you, Smith, five dollars" promises to pay Smith five dollars.

This, he says, in conjunction with the further premise,

(1b) Conditions C obtain,

turns the step from (1) to (2) into an entailment (pp. 44 f.). Next, he similarly inserts between (2) and (3), in order to show that that step is an entailment, what he calls the "tautological"[2] premise,

---

[1] *Philosophical Review*, 1964. I must acknowledge the help I have received from an unpublished paper which Professor A. G. N. Flew kindly lent me, as well as from several enjoyable arguments with Professor Searle himself. Searle's argument, though I cannot accept it, is both more plausible, and sets a higher moral tone, than that recently supplied by Mr. MacIntyre and repeated in an unimportantly different form by Professor Black (*Phil. Rev.*, 1959 and 1964). While Searle seeks to demonstrate logically that we ought to keep our promises, Black and MacIntyre seek to demonstrate that we ought to do whatever is the one and only means to achieving anything that we happen to want, or avoiding *anything* that we want to avoid.

[2] "Analytic" seems to me preferable; but I will use Searle's term.

(2a) All promises are acts of placing oneself under (undertaking) an obligation to do the thing promised.

This premise is "tautological" because "No analysis of the concept of promising will be complete which does not include the feature of the promiser placing himself under an obligation" (p. 45).

Later, Searle puts what appears to be the same point in terms of what he calls "constitutive rules". There are some institutions which are not merely regulated but constituted by the rules governing them. Thus "the rules of chess, for example, do not merely regulate an antecedently existing activity called playing chess; they, as it were, create the possibility of or define that activity" (p. 55). The rules of chess and baseball are examples of constitutive rules, and so is "the constitutive rule that to make a promise is to undertake an obligation" (p. 56).

I wish to consider the relations between (1a) and (2a). In order to clarify them, I shall appeal to the "baseball" analogy with which Searle has helpfully provided us (p. 56). He describes a set of empirical conditions such that, if they obtain, a baseball player is out, and is obliged to leave the field. I will call these conditions "E", in order to conceal my ignorance of the rules of baseball in which they are specified. What correspond, in the "promising" case, to conditions E in the baseball case, are conditions C *together with* the condition that the person in question should have uttered the words "I promise, etc." Let us number the propositions in the "baseball" case to correspond with Searle's numbering in the "promising" case, distinguishing them by the addition of a "prime." There will then be a constitutive rule of baseball to the effect that

(1a′) Whenever a player satisfies conditions E, he is out.

And, since no analysis of the concept *out* will be complete which does not include the feature of the player who is out being obliged to leave the field, we can add the "tautological" premise,

(2a′) All players who are out are obliged to leave the field.

We can simplify the argument by combining (1a′) and (2a′) into the single constitutive rule,

(1a′*) Whenever a player satisfies conditions E, he is obliged to leave the field.

For, if the definition in virtue of which (2a′) is a tautology is applied direct to (1a′), it turns into (1a′*). And similarly in the "promising" case, the argument will be simplified if we combine (1a) and (2a) into the single constitutive rule,

(1a*) Under certain conditions C anyone who utters the words (sentence)

"I hereby promise to pay you, Smith, five dollars" places himself under (undertakes) an obligation to pay Smith five dollars.

The rule could be put in a general form, leaving out the reference to Smith; but we need not trouble with this.

What then is the status of (1a*)? Five answers seem plausible enough to merit discussion:

(a) It is a tautology;

(b) It is a synthetic empirical statement about English word usage;

(c) It is a synthetic prescription about word usage in English;

(d) It is a synthetic empirical statement about something other than word usage;

(e) It is, or implicitly contains, a synthetic evaluation or prescription, not merely about word usage.

Searle would appear to maintain (b). I shall argue for (e). Since the arguments which I shall use against (a), (b), and (c) are all the same, I shall not need to detail them separately for the three answers; (d) will require to be rebutted independently, but this will not take long.

Let us start by discussing the status of the analogous statement (1a′*). Is it a tautology? There certainly is a tautology with which it can be easily confused, namely

(1a′*⁺) *In (i.e. according to the rules of) baseball,* whenever a player satisfies conditions E, he is obliged to leave the field.

This is a tautology because a definition of "baseball" would have to run "a game with the following rules, viz. ...." followed by a list of rules, including (1a′*) or its equivalent. But this does not make (1a′*) itself, in which the italicized part is omitted, into a tautology. (1a′*) is a summary of part of the rules of baseball, and, although it may be that some of the rules of a game are tautologies, it is impossible that they should all be. For if they were, what we should have would be, not the rules for playing a game, but rules (or, more strictly, exemplifications of rules) for speaking correctly about the game. To conform to the rules of a game it is necessary to act, not merely speak, in certain ways. Therefore the rules are not tautologies.

For the same reasons, as we shall see, the rules of baseball (and in particular (1a′) and (1a′*)) cannot be treated as synthetic statements, or even as synthetic prescriptions, about word usage. They are about how a game is, or is to be, played.

Let us now apply all this to the "promising" case. By parity of reasoning it is clear that (1a*) is not a tautology, although it is easy to confuse it with another proposition (1a*⁺), which *is* a tautology. (1a*⁺) will consist of (1a*), preceded by the words "In the institution of promising"—we might say, if it were not liable to misinterpretation, "In the promising game".

This is a tautology, because it is expansible into "According to the rules of an institution whose rules say 'Under conditions C anyone who utters the words. . . (etc., as in (1a*))', under conditions C anyone who utters the words . . . (etc., as in (1a*))". But (1a*) itself is not a tautology. As before, the constitutive rules of an institution may contain some tautologies, but they cannot all be tautologies, if they are going to prescribe that people *act* in certain ways and not in others. And, as before, we must not be misled into thinking that, because it is a tautology that promising is an institution of which (1a*) is a constitutive rule, (1a*) itself is a tautology.

As before, and for analogous reasons, (1a*) is neither a synthetic statement nor a synthetic prescription about how English is, or ought to be, spoken. Just because it has the consequences which Searle claims for it, it is more than this.

There is one apparent disparity between the "promising" and "baseball" cases which might be a source of confusion. In the "baseball" case the word "baseball" does not occur in (1a'*); and therefore, though (1a'*) is in a sense definitive of "baseball", it is not thereby made tautologous. But in the "promising" case, (1a*) does contain the word "promise"; and this makes it much more plausible to suggest that (1a*), since it is in a sense explicative of the notion of promising, is a tautology. This plausibility is even stronger in the case of (1a). The answer to this objection may help to clarify the whole procedure of introducing a word like "promise" into the language. The word is introduced by means of such a proposition as (1a*). But we must not be misled into thinking that this makes (1a*) a tautology, or a mere statement about word usage. For as we shall see, it is a characteristic of words like "promise", which have meaning only within institutions, that they can be introduced into language only when certain synthetic propositions about how we should *act* are assented to. (1a*) is such a proposition. The word "promise" depends for its meaning upon the proposition, but the proposition is not true solely in virtue of the meaning of "promise". Similarly, a word like "out" is dependent for its meaning upon the rules of baseball or cricket; but those rules are not tautologies in virtue of the meaning of "out" and other such words.

However, this may not seem to go to the root of the objection. For Searle's argument could be stated without mentioning the word "promise" at all. He could simply, in (1a), substitute the words "place upon himself an obligation" for the word "promise" throughout. The proposition then becomes

> Under certain conditions C anyone who utter the words (sentence) "I hereby place upon myself an obligation to pay you, Smith, five dollars" places upon himself an obligation to pay Smith five dollars.

Surely, it might be said, I cannot deny that *this* is a tautology, or, alternatively, a statement about word usage. But this is just what I do wish to deny. For, to begin with, if the mere repetition of the words "place ... an obligation" in the proposition made it into a tautology, it is hard to see what the words "Under certain conditions C" are doing; one might think that under any conditions whatever a person who says "I hereby place upon myself an obligation, etc." must necessarily have thereby placed upon himself an obligation, etc. But once we have seen that this is not so (for example, the man might be under duress or mad), we see that the appearance of tautology is deceptive. It is not in general true (let alone tautologous) that the man who says "p" makes it the case that p. Something like this does happen in the case of what used to be called performative verbs; it happens in our present case with the verb "promise". The man who says "I promise", promises (under certain conditions). But it is not a tautology that he does so, nor is it a tautology that the man who says "I hereby place myself under an obligation" places himself under an obligation, even under certain (empirical) conditions. Nor are either of these merely remarks about word usage. For it is a necessary condition for the adoption of these performative expressions that certain synthetic constitutive (and not merely linguistic) rules be also adopted, thus creating the institution within which the expressions have meaning.

To make this clearer, let us suppose that we have already in our language the word "obligation" (and kindred words like "ought"), but that none of our obligations has been, as Searle puts it, "institutionalized" (p. 56). That is to say, we can speak of our having obligations (e.g. to feed our children) and even of our placing upon ourselves obligations (e.g., by having children we place upon ourselves the obligation to feed them); but we cannot yet speak of placing upon ourselves an obligation just by saying, merely, "I place upon myself the obligation, etc." Then suppose that some inventive person suggests the adoption of this useful expression (or rather its conversion to this new use). The other members of society may well stare at him and say "But we don't see how you can place upon yourself an obligation just by saying these words". What he will then have to say, in order to sell this device to them, and therewith the institution of which it is a part, is something like this: "You have to adopt the constitutive rule or moral principle that one has an obligation to do those things of which one has said 'I (hereby) place upon myself an obligation to do them'." When they have adopted this principle, or in adopting it, they can introduce the new use for the expression. And the principle is a synthetic one. It is a new synthetic moral principle, and not merely a new way of speaking, that is being introduced; this shows up in the fact that, if they adopt the principle, they will have acquired obligations to do things that they have not done before, not merely to speak in ways that they have not spoken before.

There may be, indeed, an interpretation on which (1a), (1a*), and their analogues could be said to be statements "about" the English language. They could be treated as statements which say, or imply, that the English have in their language the performative expression "I promise", or the performative expression "I place myself under an obligation", whose use is tied to the institution of promising (or undertaking obligations); and which therefore imply also that the English (or sufficient of them) subscribe to the rules of this institution. The latter half of this would be an anthropological statement about the English. But it is obvious that such a statement cannot generate the entailments which Searle requires. For the conclusions which will then follow will be, at most, of the type: "The English subscribe to the view that Jones is under an obligation"; "The English subscribe to the view that Jones ought", etc. For the required nonanthropological, moral (or at least prescriptive) conclusions to follow, (1a) must, interpreted in the light of (2a), be taken as expressing the speaker's own subscription to the rules of the institution of promising, i.e. to moral principles. I do not wish to argue which is the most natural way to take these statements; all I need to say is that *unless* they are taken in this way, the derivation will not work.

It is often the case that performative expressions cannot be introduced without the adoption of synthetic constitutive rules. Thus it would be impossible to introduce the expression "I stake a claim to this land" unless there were adopted, at the same time, a principle that by saying this, under the appropriate conditions, if the claimant has not been forestalled by somebody else, he acquires at least some claim to the land. In pioneering days in America one could do this; but try doing it in modern Siberia, where they do not have that principle.

Another way of showing that (1a*) is not a tautology, and is not made so by the fact that it is used for introducing the word "promise" into the language, is the following. If (1a*) were true in virtue of the meaning of the word "promise", and therefore tautologous, then both (1a) and (2a) would have to be tautologous. For (1a*) was arrived at by applying to (1a) the definition which made (2a) tautologous; and it is impossible to get a tautology out of a synthetic proposition by definitional substitution. But (1a) and (2a) cannot both be made tautologous without an equivocation on the word promise". For (2a) is tautologous, if it is, in virtue of *one* definition of "promise", and (1a) is tautologous, if it is, in virtue of *another* definition of "promise" (or, on the alternative suggestion that (1a) is a statement about language, it can be so only in virtue of *another* definition of "promise"). If we take (1a) as tautologous, or as a usage statement, it will have to be in virtue of some such definition as the following:

(D1) Promising is saying, under certain conditions C, "I hereby promise, etc."

But (2a), if it is tautologous, is so in virtue of a *different* definition, namely

Promising is placing oneself under an obligation. . . .

How the definition is completed does not matter; it has at any rate to start like this. To make (1a*) tautologous, or a usage statement, we have to take "promise" simultaneously in these two different senses. And the trouble cannot be escaped by completing the last definition thus:

(D2) Promising is placing oneself under an obligation by saying, under certain conditions C, "I hereby promise, etc."

This definition sounds attractive, and may be more or less correct; but it does not make (1a) a tautology, and would make it into more than a statement about word usage. According to (D2), a man who says "I hereby promise, etc." has satisfied only one of the conditions of promising, but may not have satisfied the other; he may have said the words, but may not have thereby placed upon himself any obligation. We can only say that he has succeeded in doing this if we assent to the *synthetic* principle (1a*). The necessity of assenting to this synthetic principle before the trick works may be concealed by taking (D2), not as a verbal definition of the modern type, but as that old device of synthetic a priorists, an "essential" or "real" definition of promising. But then it will be synthetic.

I conclude, for these reasons, that (1a*) cannot be tautologous or a statement about word usage, but must be a synthetic constitutive rule of the institution of promising. If the constitutive rules of the institution of promising are moral principles, as I think they are, then (1a*) is a synthetic moral principle. It follows that, if Searle sticks to it that (2a) is tautologous, he must allow that (1a) either is or implicitly contains a synthetic moral principle. But this would destroy his argument; and indeed he says that it is not; for, after introducing it, he says "As far as I can see, no moral premises are lurking in the logical woodpile" (p. 43). He says this, in spite of the fact that he is going on immediately to make (1a) by definition equivalent to (1a*), which we have seen to be a synthetic moral principle.

It might be suggested that (1a) is an empirical statement of some non-linguistic sort. I am assured by Searle that he does not think this; but the suggestion is worth examining. If it were true, it might save his argument, which is, essentially, that no moral or other nonempirical, nontautological, premises have to be included. He spends some effort in showing that conditions C, to which (1a) alludes, are empirical conditions—and this may be granted for the sake of argument. But, although this would make the proposition (1b), "Conditions C obtain", into an empirical statement, it by no means makes (1a) into one. For however empirical these conditions C may be, it is possible to construct nonempirical propositions, and even imperatives, of the form "Under conditions C, p"—e.g. "Under conditions C, switch off (*or* you ought to switch off) the motor". Nevertheless, it is easy to be misled into thinking that, if the conditions under which a man who utters "I hereby promise" can correctly be said to have made a promise are empirical conditions, this proves that (1a) is not a moral statement.

I said that I would concentrate my attack on steps (1) to (3) of Searle's argument. But I may mention here that an analogous attack could be made against steps (3) to (5). These too depend on a nontautologous rule of the institution of promising, or in general of (performatively) placing oneself under obligations. This nontautologous rule is as follows:

(3a) If anybody has placed himself under an obligation (in the past) he is (still) under an obligation, unless he has done already what he was obliged to do.

To find out whether this is a tautology, we should have, as before, to rewrite it with the aid of the definition or tautology which is required to make the step from (4) to (5) into an entailment, viz. the definition

(D3) For one to be under an obligation to do a thing is for it to be the case that one ought to do that thing

(I shall not enquire whether this definition is a sufficient one; it is probably not); or the tautology

(4a) All people who are under obligations to do things ought to do them.

(3a) then turns into

(3a*) If anybody has placed himself under an obligation (in the past), it is (still) the case that he ought to do the thing that he placed himself under an obligation to do, unless he has already done it.

That this is not a tautology (or for that matter a statement about word usage) could be shown, if it is not plain already, by an argument analogous to the preceding.

I will conclude with some general remarks about the nature of the mistake that Searle seems to me to have made in this paper. There are many words which could not have a use unless certain propositions were assented to by the users or a sufficient number of them. The possibility of using a word can depend on assent to synthetic propositions. This will apply especially to many words whose use is dependent upon the existence of institutions, though not only to them.[3] Unless there were laws of property, we could not speak of "mine" and "thine"; yet the laws of property are not

---

[3] What Kant was driving at, without the synthetic a priorism, might possibly be hinted at by pointing out that many words that we use in physics and in everyday life, such as "table", and in general "material object", would lack a use unless we made certain assumptions about the regularity of the universe.

tautologies. Unless there were a readiness to accept currency in exchange for goods, words like "dollar" and "pound" would pass out of use; yet to be ready to accept currency in exchange for goods is not to assent to a tautology or to a statement about language. In a community which did not play, or accept the rules of, baseball, the word "out", as it is used by umpires, would lack a use (though not as used by anthropologists, if they were discussing the ways of a community which did have the game) ; but this does not make the rules of baseball into tautologies or statements about word usage.

In the case of promising we have a similar phenomenon. Unless a sufficient number of people were prepared to assent to the moral principles which are the constitutive rules of the institution of promising, the word "promise" could not have a use. To take the extreme case: suppose that nobody thought that one ought to keep promises. It would then be impossible to make a promise; the word "promise" would become a mere noise (except, as before, in the mouths of anthropologists), unless it acquired some new use. But it does not follow from this that the moral principles, assent to which by a sufficient number of people is a condition for the remaining in use of the word "promise", are themselves analytic.

It is necessary, moreover, only that a sufficiently large number of people should assent to the constitutive rule. If they do so, and if the word in question comes into use, it is possible for people who do not assent to the rules to use the word comprehensibly. Thus an anarchist can use the word "property"; a man who for reasons of his own has no confidence in paper money, and is therefore not prepared to exchange goods for it, can still use the word "pound"; and a Machiavellian politician who recognizes no duty to keep promises can still use the word "promise". He can even use it to make promises, always provided that his moral opinions are not too well known.

Such people are, admittedly, parasites; but not all parasites are reprehensible. Let us suppose that somebody is opposed to fox hunting. This does not stop him engaging in fox hunting, in the sense of going to meets, following hounds, etc., and using all the terminology of the chase. He may think it his duty, whenever he can get away with it, to help the fox to escape (that may be why he goes fox hunting) ; but this does not involve him in any self-contradiction. It may be that to try to help foxes to escape is contrary to the constitutive rules for fox hunting[4]; for unless there were among these rules one which said that the object of the game was to kill the fox, it would not be fox *hunting*. But this does not stop our opponent of blood sports

[4] It might be objected that the rules of fox hunting are not constitutive but regulative. This would depend on establishing some relevant difference between the chasing of foxes and the chasing of cricket balls—a question into which I shall not go, but whose investigation might cast doubt on this distinction.

masquerading as a person who accepts this rule; nor does it mean that, by so masquerading, he lays upon himself any obligation to abide by it. And in just the same way the Machiavellian politician can, without self-contradiction, think it his duty to break some of the promises he makes (and think this even while he is making them). He could not have made them unless the word "promise" were in use; and it could not be in use unless a sufficient number of people assented to the moral principles governing promising; but this does not mean that a person who, while making promises, dissents, silently, from the principles contradicts himself. In using the word "promise" indeed, he is masquerading as one who thinks that one ought to keep promises, just as one who lies is masquerading as one who thinks that p, when he does not. But neither the liar nor the man who makes lying promises is contradicting himself. And when the lying promiser comes to break his promise, he is still not contradicting himself; he can say "I pretended to think, when I made the promise, that one ought to keep promises; but I don't really think this and never have."

Talking about "institutional facts", though it can be illuminating, can also be a peculiarly insidious way of committing the "naturalistic fallacy". I do not think that Searle actually falls into this particular trap; but others perhaps have. There are moral and other principles, accepted by most of us, such that, if they were not generally accepted, certain institutions like property and promising could not exist. And if the institutions do exist, we are in a position to affirm certain "institutional facts" (for example, that a certain piece of land is my property), on the ground that certain "brute facts" are the case (for example, that my ancestors have occupied it from time immemorial). But from the "institutional facts", certain obviously prescriptive conclusions can be drawn (for example, that nobody ought to deprive me of the land). Thus it looks as if there could be a straight deduction, in two steps, from brute facts to prescriptive conclusions *via* institutional facts. But the deduction is a fraud. For the brute fact is a ground for the prescriptive conclusion only if the prescriptive principle which is the constitutive rule of the institution be accepted; and this prescriptive principle is not a tautology. For someone (a communist for example) who does not accept this nontautologous prescriptive principle, the deduction collapses like a house of cards—though this does not prevent him from continuing to use the word "property" (with his tongue in his cheek).

Similarly with promising. It may seem as if the "brute fact" that a person has uttered a certain phonetic sequence entails the "institutional fact" that he has promised, and that this in turn entails that he ought to do a certain thing. But this conclusion can be drawn only by one who accepts, in addition, the nontautologous principle that one ought to keep one's promises. For unless one accepts this principle, one is not a subscribing member of the institution which it constitutes, and therefore cannot be compelled logically to accept the institutional facts which it generates in such a sense that they entail the conclusion, though of course one must admit their truth, regarded purely as pieces of anthropology.

If I do not agree with Searle's reasons for maintaining that we ought to keep our promises, what are my own reasons? They are of a fundamentally different character, although they take in parts of Searle's argument in passing. To break a promise is, normally, a particularly gross form of deception. It is grosser than the failure to fulfil a declaration of intention, just because (if you wish) our society has *pari passu* with the introduction of the word "promise", adopted the moral principle that one ought to keep promises, thus constituting the institution called "promising". My reason for thinking that I ought not to take parasitic advantage of this institution, but ought to obey its rules, is the following. If I ask myself whether I am willing that I myself should be deceived in this way, I answer unhesitatingly that I am not. I therefore cannot subscribe to any moral principle which permits people to deceive other people in this way (any general principle which says "It is all right to break promises"). There may be more specific principles which I could accept, of the form "It is all right to break promises in situations of type S". Most people accept some specific principles of this form. What anybody can here substitute for "S" he will determine, if he follows my sort of reasoning, by asking himself, for any proposed value of "S", whether he can subscribe to the principle when applied to all cases, including cases in which he is the person to whom the promise is made. Thus the morality of promise keeping is a fairly standard application of what I have called elsewhere[5] the "golden rule" type of moral argument; it needs no "is"–"ought" derivations to support it—derivations whose validity will be believed in only by those who have ruled out *a priori* any questioning of the existing institutions on whose rules they are based.

---

[5] *Freedom and Reason*, esp. pp. 86–125.

Reply to
"The Promising Game"

JOHN R. SEARLE

Hare's objection to my argument rests entirely on the assumption that it cannot be part of the meaning of such expressions as "I hereby promise" that the utterance of these expressions under certain conditions and with certain intentions places the speaker under an obligation. I think it is quite obviously a matter of the meaning of such expressions that they do precisely that, and that his arguments to the contrary are invalid as well as in conflict with certain other positions he holds.

His argument for the contrary view is that if it were a matter of meaning then the constitutive rule would be a tautology, but it cannot be a tautology because it prescribes behavior and tautologies cannot prescribe behavior. Therefore the rule cannot be a meaning rule.

This argument confuses rules and tautologies and confuses prescriptions of behavior with ascriptions of obligations. I argue that it is a matter of meaning that an appropriate utterance of "I hereby promise" counts as the making of a promise and hence as the undertaking of an obligation. My conclusion can be taken either as itself an expression of a rule or as an empirical statement about English invoking that rule. It cannot be taken as a tautology because the occurrence of the expression "I hereby promise" is in quotation marks. To use an old fashioned terminology, the expression is mentioned and not used. But for such meaning rules there are corresponding tautologies. In this case one such tautology is: All promises are undertakings of obligation. Qua rule the rule is not a tautology, qua tautology the tautology is not a rule. Rather, corresponding to meaning rules there are tautologies which use and do not mention the expressions mentioned in the rules.

But neither the rule nor the tautology prescribes behavior in Hare's sense. In his terminology, to prescribe behavior is to make an utterance which either is or entails an imperative—but the rule and the tautology do nothing of the sort. Furthermore, nor do statements of the form "X is under an obligation to do Y" or "X ought to do Y" prescribe behavior in that sense, since it is perfectly possible to make such assertions and, without any logical inconsistency, explicitly deny the intention to imply an imperative. The actual role that such utterances play is to state or express reasons for acting. But that is quite different from uttering imperatives to act.

Hare does not offer an analysis of the meaning of "promise", and, given his views, it is not easy to see how he could; since he denies any meaning connection between "promise" and concepts like obligation or commitment. But that there is such a connection is shown conclusively by the fact that it is inconsistent and indeed self-contradictory to say "He promised to do it but he didn't undertake any obligations or make any commitments to do it", or "I promise to do it but I am not committing myself or undertaking any obligation to do it". The only way to account for the obvious fact that these are internally inconsistent statements is to admit the definitional connection between "promise" and such notions as obligation and commitment. Hare is precluded from granting this connection by his views about "prescribing behavior".

It is a curious fact about Hare's writing that he is willing to make derivations of evaluative statements about commitments from descriptive statements about utterances when he is just doing philosophy and not discussing the "naturalistic fallacy". Consider the following fairly typical passage from his book *Freedom and Reason*, (p. 11). "If a person says that a thing is red he is *committed* to the view that anything which was like it in the relevant respects would likewise be red". And again on p. 15: "If I call a thing red I am *committed* to calling anything else like it red".[1] This he tells us is purely in virtue of the meaning of the words uttered. Leaving aside the question of whether what Hare says is true,[2] it is of exactly the same form as my argument. I say: if a person says he promises, he is committed to doing what he promises to do, and this is in virtue of the meaning of the word "promise". The only important difference is that the commitment in Hare's example is to future linguistic behavior and the commitment in mine is not restricted to linguistic behavior. Hare is puzzled by the question, How can it be a matter of meaning that saying "I promise" commits or obligates me? The answer is: in exactly the same way that it is a matter of meaning that saying "It is red" *commits* me, as he argues at some length in his book. Most types of speech acts do in fact involve commitments of one sort or another, and there is nothing mysterious about promising in this regard.

In the latter half of his article Hare presents me with a dilemma: either we have to take "promise", "obligate", etc. in an anthropological sense—as meaning "what the English call 'promises,' 'obligations' "—in which case my argument is invalid; or it depends on 'subscribing' to the rules of the institution, in which case it requires evaluative premises. Why does he suppose the second alternative requires an evaluative premise?

---

[1] My italics.
[2] The second formulation must have been a slip of Hare's pen. By calling a thing red I do not commit myself to *calling* similar things anything at all; I am free to pass them by in silence. He must have meant: "If I call a thing red I am committed to not calling things which I admit are relevantly like it not red."

Because he thinks that such subscriptions to the rules somehow involve approval of the rules, thinking that they are a good thing, or some such. But notice that in stating the rules for "the describing game", when he discusses the notion of describing something as red, he does not feel it necessary to declare himself a partisan of or an enthusiast for the institution of describing. What he points out, correctly in principle if not in detail, is that someone who undertakes to use words literally commits himself in ways that are determined by the meaning of the words. I want to argue that exactly the same holds for the promising game. If by "subscribing" to the rules all that is meant is that someone who says literally "I hereby promise" commits himself in ways that are determined by the rules, then uttering "I hereby promise" does require subscribing, but there is nothing evaluative about such subscribing. If on the other hand he thinks, as he plainly does, that such subscribing to the rules involves approval of the institution then he is quite mistaken. He makes much of the fact people may disapprove of promising or think it evil or exploit it for Machiavellian reasons, as if this had some relevance to the validity of the proof. It has exactly the same relevance to my proof as people who disapprove of geometry or think it evil or seek to exploit it have to the validity of geometrical proofs. There are two ways to take the notion of "subscribing" to the rules. One way is to undertake to use the words in accordance with their literal meanings; the second is to think the rules are good, or to approve of the rules. The first is crucial to my account of promising and his of describing, but is not evaluative. The second is evaluative, but is completely irrelevant to both promising and describing.

There are several misinterpretations of my argument that Hare makes which may be important.

First, he assumes I am trying to derive "morally ought" from "is". I am not. I am trying to derive "ought" from "is". The obligation to keep a promise is often a moral obligation, if the matter is serious enough, but it is not always or necessarily so.

Second, he assumes that I am trying to derive institutional facts from brute facts. I am not and I deny that it can be done. That is why incidentally (1a) has to be an empirical statement invoking a rule, and not a tautology.

Third, at the end of his paper he assumes I am giving reasons why we ought to keep our promises. I am not, and I think that internally the question is empty. Externally it is a question about the desirability of having such linguistic institutions as promising, a question which I do not discuss.

Section Two
Rules, Principles, and Utilitarianism

One of the most fundamental disputes in the history of ethics has been between deontologists and teleologists. The latter, exemplified by the many forms of Utilitarianism, stress that what is morally right or obligatory is a function of producing desirable consequences (avoiding undesirable consequences) for oneself, society, or possibly all mankind. The former deny that right and wrong are primarily a function of consequences, whether they are the production of intrinsic good or the avoidance of evil. "A promise is a promise," or "It is the only fair thing to do," or "It is what God requires of us," may be decisive considerations to a deontologist even when he knows that the greatest balance of good (pleasure, knowledge, happiness, etc.) over evil would result from acting otherwise.

W. D. Ross, in "What Makes Right Acts Right?", forcefully attacks the utilitarian conception of morality and develops his own deontological system of prima facie duties. His criticisms are aimed at a type of view which is currently referred to as "act-utilitarianism." The act-utilitarian believes that he may determine his duty by a direct application of the principle of utility to the particular situation in which an action is contemplated. The only consideration is whether doing this act in these circumstances will produce more good than any alternative act. However, such a theory, it is claimed, yields results which are "counter-intuitive," i.e., incompatible with our considered moral opinions. Whereas we should ordinarily respect and give due consideration to the "special relations" in which we stand to others—promisor to promisee, father to son, etc.—the act-utilitarian cannot do so apart from estimating the consequences of ignoring these relations in the present or in the long run. Thus, we can imagine cases in which the act-utilitarian would decide that it was his moral duty to break a promise, do away with his grandmother, or take advantage of an innocent bystander, on grounds of maximizing utility, all of which would normally be judged immoral.

Those who find such criticisms of act-utilitarianism convincing may yet resort to one of the forms of "rule-utilitarianism." The many varieties of rule-utilitarianism stress the idea of levels of justification. Particular acts are appropriately justified by or are obligatory because of a relevant rule or practice, while the rules and practices are determined to be acceptable or unacceptable by the estimation of the consequences of everyone's acting in the way prescribed (prohibited) by the rule. Hence, the principle of utility applies only indirectly to the determination of duty and obligation. The attractiveness of this view is that it appears to gain the best of two worlds by reconciling the long-standing feud between deontologists and teleologists. "Right" does not simply mean "productive of the best possible consequences," and yet human welfare is recognized to be relevant to morality. The reader will quickly discover, however, in the selections by Mabbott, Rawls, Diggs, and Brandt, that there are numerous obstacles to making a strong case for any of the many forms of rule-utilitarianism. Not the least of these is the possibility that, upon close examination, a form of rule-utilitarianism will collapse into act-utilitarianism and so be vulnerable to the very objections it was designed to avoid. This may happen either when the rules are shown to be "rules of thumb" or generalizations from experience, or when it is determined that more often than not the individual will need to appeal directly to the principle of utility in order to adjudicate cases of conflicting rules or to apply a rule in novel situations.

Prof. J. D. Mabbott's paper "Moral Rules" is a good illustration of the rule-utilitarian approach. In the first place, we find the typical insistence upon keeping clear the distinction between the utilitarian validation of a rule and the utilitarian account of the rightness of a particular action. In the second place, we find an argument in opposition to those who treat moral rules as empirical generalizations, which is a characteristic tendency of act-utilitarians. Prof. Mabbott's own solution amounts to employing a Kantian universalization test with a "utilitarian twist."

One of the intriguing theories which has sharpened the distinction between justifying a rule and justifying a particular action is developed by John Rawls in "Two Concepts of Rules." It is an essential feature of Rawls' "practice" conception of rules that the individual, for whom a rule of this type is applicable, is not entitled to appeal directly to the principle of utility, or, what is the same, to assume the different office of (moral) legislator. This is seen most clearly in examples of law and games. In the game of baseball, a player is not entitled to question the applicability of the "constitutive" rules like the one which designates that each player gets three strikes. He may, at most, attempt to get a new rule adopted by an authoritative baseball commission. Rawls argues convincingly that some moral practices are analogous to these constitutive rules of games. The point of having a practice of promising, he maintains, "is to abdicate one's title to act in accordance with utilitarian and prudential considerations in order that the future may be tied down and plans coordinated in advance." The notion that the individual is entitled to appeal to the principle of utility does not occur in every description of a form of rule-utilitarianism, and it appears that there is much yet to be done in the way of assessing the importance of the notion.

In Prof. J. J. C. Smart's "Extreme and Restricted Utilitarianism," we have a vigorous counter-argument for act-utilitarianism in opposition to deontologists and rule-utilitarians alike. For Prof. Smart, secondary rules such as "Keep your promises" are "rules of thumb" which do not in themselves justify any action. Furthermore, he sees no reason to treat ordinary moral opinions as sacred or as a final test of the adequacy of a theory. These opinions are frequently infested with superstition and logically confused elements, so that our act-utilitarian theory may well be correct even when results of applying it are "counter-intuitive."[1]

Yet another variation among types of rule-utilitarianism concerns whether or not the rules which determine duty and obligation are existing practices. Whereas J. D. Mabbott, J. Rawls, and B. J. Diggs appear to hold that a rule must be an existing practice, Prof. Richard Brandt, in "Some Merits of One Form of Rule-Utilitarianism," develops an Ideal Moral Code theory. An action is right, according to this theory, "if and only if it would not be prohibited by the moral code ideal for the society in which it occurs, where a moral code is taken to be 'ideal' if and only if its currency would produce at least as much good per person as the currency of

---

[1] See also P. H. Nowell-Smith's paper "Morality: Religious and Secular," for an interesting approach which also lends support to the act-utilitarian conception of morality. Reprinted in this book, Section Five.

any other moral code." It is unlike some forms of rule-utilitarianism in that the individual is entitled to formulate rules or a moral code for himself. He pretends, so to speak, to hold the office of moral legislator, but having no actual authority he legislates only for himself. The theory has the advantage, in common with act-utilitarianism, of being independent of (and so being in a position to criticize) the existing system of moral practices. However, the theory seems to be a hybrid showing features of act- and rule-utilitarianism and may collapse into act-utilitarianism if it is true that "one may freely disregard a rule if ever he discovers that action on the rule is not maximally felicific, and in this respect makes moral rules like 'practical maxims'."

Prof. B. J. Diggs, in "Rules and Utilitarianism," argues that there are objectionable features of rule-utilitarianism due to the use of a certain type of rule (instrumental), just as objectionable features of act-utilitarianism were shown to depend upon a certain conception of rules (summaries or generalizations from experience). "Instrumental" rules are adopted or followed as a means to an end, in order to "accomplish a purpose" or "get a job done." Consequently, they are designed to promote a goal that is logically independent of the rules and institutions. Prof. Diggs shows that Rawls' "practice" conception of rules fits the model of "instrumental" rules. When these rules are contrasted, then, with Diggs' alternative analysis of moral rules, he believes that rule-utilitarianism loses much of its appeal. His "Comment" on Prof. Brandt's paper contains valuable clarification of both his own and Brandt's views, and focuses on the following issue: Is the criterion of right acts a code or a set of rules which is ideal in the sense that its currency in a particular society *would* produce at least as much good as the currency of any other moral code?

The relations between act- and rule-utilitarianism are subtle and complex, and the reader should not expect a simple formula for distinguishing them. There is a fair amount of disagreement, if not confusion, in the contemporary literature on this subject. One of the theses merits special attention here: It is often said that the move from act- to rule-utilitarianism is made whenever we refer to a class of actions instead of to some particular action. Since any judgment that we make for certain "reasons" is "universalizable," i.e., commits us to (1) treating situations which are exactly alike or alike in all relevant respects in the same way, and (2) acknowledging that any other person would be justified in making the same judgment in those circumstances, it is impossible to make a judgment (or decision) about a single act. If we are always talking, then, about classes of acts rather than single acts, we can simply forget about act-utilitarianism and concentrate on the appraisal of rule-utilitarianism.

It is surely the case, however, that both act- and rule-utilitarians can affirm that their judgments (or decisions) are "universalizable" in this minimal sense without allowing that, in so affirming, significant differences between them are obliterated. It would seem that even the rule-utilitarian, who abides by "ideal" rules formulated by him after weighing the utilities of alternative acts, accepts an additional principle not shared by the act-utilitarian, viz., he must think of himself as formulating a public moral policy, or as acting on a rule which is possible and practicable when conceived as a rule having general currency. This is, perhaps, an implicit consent to the criterion of moral rules which Kurt Baier has called "universal teachability." However, the sense in which the act-utilitarian's judgments are "universalizable" does not commit him to the criterion of "universal teachability." The act-utilitarian could decide that making a lying promise was morally justified (the consequences of doing so would be maximally felicific in any situation like this one in relevant respects) in circumstances in which the act of making this promise would be "self-frustrating" or "self-defeating" if it were generally practiced or if his intentions were made public.

What Makes Right Acts Right?

W. D. ROSS

The real point at issue between hedonism and utilitarianism on the one hand and their opponents on the other is not whether 'right' means 'productive of so and so'; for it cannot with any plausibility be maintained that it does. The point at issue is that to which we now pass, viz. whether there is any general character which makes right acts right, and if so, what it is. Among the main historical attempts to state a single characteristic of all right actions which is the foundation of their rightness are those made by egoism and utilitarianism. But I do not propose to discuss these, not because the subject is unimportant, but because it has been dealt with so often and so well already, and because there has come to be so much agreement among moral philosophers that neither of these theories is satisfactory. A much more attractive theory has been put forward by Professor Moore: that what makes actions right is that they are productive of more *good* than could have been produced by any other action open to the agent.[1]

This theory is in fact the culmination of all the attempts to base rightness on productivity of some sort of result. The first form this attempt takes is the attempt to base rightness on conduciveness to the advantage or pleasure of the agent. This theory comes to grief over the fact, which stares us in the face, that a great part of duty consists in an observance of the rights and a furtherance of the interests of others, whatever the cost to ourselves may be. Plato and others may be right in holding that a regard for the rights of others never in the long run involves a loss of happiness for the agent, that 'the just life profits a man'. But this, even if true, is irrelevant to the rightness of the act. As soon as a man does an action *because* he thinks he will promote his own interests thereby, he is acting not from a sense of its rightness but from self-interest.

To the egoistic theory hedonistic utilitarianism supplies a much needed amendment. It points out correctly that the fact that a certain pleasure will be enjoyed by the agent is no reason why he *ought* to bring it into being

From W. D. Ross, The Right and the Good *(Oxford: The Clarendon Press, 1930), pp. 16–47. Reprinted by permission of the publisher.*

[1] I take the theory which, as I have tried to show, seems to be put forward in *Ethics* rather than the earlier and less plausible theory put forward in *Principia Ethica*. For the difference, cf. Ross, *The Right and the Good* (Oxford: 1930), pp. 8–11.

rather than an equal or greater pleasure to be enjoyed by another, though, human nature being what it is, it makes it not unlikely that he *will* try to bring it into being. But hedonistic utilitarianism in its turn needs a correction. On reflection it seems clear that pleasure is not the only thing in life that we think good in itself, that for instance we think the possession of a good character, or an intelligent understanding of the world, as good or better. A great advance is made by the substitution of 'productive of the greatest good' for 'productive of the greatest pleasure'.

Not only is this theory more attractive than hedonistic utilitarianism, but its logical relation to that theory is such that the latter could not be true unless *it* were true, while it might be true though hedonistic utilitarianism were not. It is in fact one of the logical bases of hedonistic utilitarianism. For the view that what produces the maximum pleasure is right has for its bases the views (1) that what produces the maximum good is right, and (2) that pleasure is the only thing good in itself. If they were not assuming that what produces the maximum *good* is right, the utilitarians' attempt to show that pleasure is the only thing good in itself, which is in fact the point they take most pains to establish, would have been quite irrelevant to their attempt to prove that only what produces the maximum *pleasure* is right. If, therefore, it can be shown that productivity of the maximum good is not what makes all right actions right, we shall *a fortiori* have refuted hedonistic utilitarianism.

When a plain man fulfills a promise because he thinks he ought to do so, it seems clear that he does so with no thought of its total consequences, still less with any opinion that these are likely to be the best possible. He thinks in fact much more of the past than of the future. What makes him think it right to act in a certain way is the fact that he has promised to do so—that and, usually, nothing more. That his act will produce the best possible consequences is not his reason for calling it right. What lends color to the theory we are examining, then, is not the actions (which form probably a great majority of our actions) in which some such reflection as 'I have promised' is the only reason we give ourselves for thinking a certain action right, but the exceptional cases in which the consequences of fulfilling a promise (for instance) would be so disastrous to others that we judge it right not to do so. It must of course be admitted that such cases exist. If I have promised to meet a friend at a particular time for some trivial purpose, I should certainly think myself justified in breaking my engagement if by doing so I could prevent a serious accident or bring relief to the victims of one. And the supporters of the view we are examining hold that my thinking so is due to my thinking that I shall bring more good into existence by the one action than by the other. A different account may, however, be given of the matter, an account which will, I believe, show itself to be the true one. It may be said that besides the duty of fulfilling promises I have and recognize a duty of relieving distress,[2] and that when I think it right to do the latter at the cost of not doing the former, it is not because I think I shall produce more good thereby but because I think it the duty which is in the circumstances more of a duty. This account surely corresponds much more closely with what we really think in such a situation. If, so far as I can see, I could bring equal amounts of good into being by fulfilling my promise and by helping some one to whom I had made no promise, I should not hesitate to regard the former as my duty. Yet on the view that what is right is right because it is productive of the most good I should not so regard it.

There are two theories, each in its way simple, that offer a solution of such cases of conscience. One is the view of Kant, that there are certain duties of perfect obligation, such as those of fulfilling promises, of paying debts, of telling the truth, which admit of no exception whatever in favor of duties of imperfect obligation, such as that of relieving distress. The other is the view of, for instance, Professor Moore and Dr. Rashdall, that there is only the duty of producing good, and that all 'conflicts of duties' should be resolved by asking 'by which action will most good be produced?' But it is more important that our theory fit the facts than that it be simple, and the account we have given above corresponds (it seems to me) better than either of the simpler theories with what we really think, viz. that normally promise keeping, for example, should come before benevolence, but that when and only when the good to be produced by the benevolent act is very great and the promise comparatively trivial, the act of benevolence becomes our duty.

In fact the theory of 'ideal utilitarianism', if I may for brevity refer so to the theory of Professor Moore, seems to simplify unduly our relations to our fellows. It says, in effect, that the only morally significant relation in which my neighbors stand to me is that of being possible beneficiaries by my action.[3] They do stand in this relation to me, and this relation is morally significant. But they may also stand to me in the relation of promisee to promisor, of creditor to debtor, of wife to husband, of child to parent, of friend to friend, of fellow countryman to fellow countryman, and the like; and each of these relations is the foundation of a *prima facie* duty, which is more or less incumbent on me according to the circumstances of the case. When I am in a situation, as perhaps I always am, in which more than

---

[2] These are not strictly speaking duties, but things that tend to be our duty, or *prima facie* duties. Cf. Ross, op. cit., pp. 19–20.

[3] Some will think it, apart from other considerations, a sufficient refutation of this view to point out that I also stand in that relation to myself, so that for this view the distinction of oneself from others is morally insignificant.

one of these *prima facie* duties is incumbent on me, what I have to do is to study the situation as fully as I can until I form the considered opinion (it is never more) that in the circumstances one of them is more incumbent than any other; then I am bound to think that to do this *prima facie* duty is my duty *sans phrase* in the situation.

I suggest '*prima facie* duty' or 'conditional duty' as a brief way of referring to the characteristic (quite distinct from that of being a duty proper) which an act has, in virtue of being of a certain kind (e.g. the keeping of a promise), of being an act which would be a duty proper if it were not at the same time of another kind which is morally significant. Whether an act is a duty proper or actual duty depends on *all* the morally significant kinds it is an instance of. . . .

There is nothing arbitrary about these *prima facie* duties. Each rests on a definite circumstance which cannot seriously be held to be without moral significance. Of *prima facie* duties I suggest, without claiming completeness or finality for it, the following division.[4]

(1) Some duties rest on previous acts of my own. These duties seem to include two kinds, (a) those resting on a promise or what may fairly be called an implicit promise, such as the implicit undertaking not to tell lies which seems to be implied in the act of entering into conversation (at any rate by civilized men), or of writing books that purport to be history and not fiction. These may be called the duties of fidelity. (b) Those resting on a previous wrongful act. These may be called the duties of reparation. (2) Some rest on previous acts of other men, i.e. services done by them to me. These may be loosely described as the duties of gratitude.[5] (3) Some rest on the fact or possibility of a distribution of pleasure or happiness (or of the means thereto) which is not in accordance with the merit of the persons concerned; in such cases there arises a duty to upset or prevent such a distribution. These are the duties of justice. (4) Some rest on the mere fact that there are other beings in the world whose condition we can make

---

[4] I should make it plain as this stage that I am *assuming* the correctness of some of our main convictions as to *prima facie* duties, or, more strictly, am claiming that we *know* them to be true. To me it seems as self-evident as anything could be, that to make a promise, for instance, is to create a moral claim on us in someone else. Many readers will perhaps say that they do *not* know this to be true. If so, I certainly cannot prove it to them; I can only ask them to reflect again, in the hope that they will ultimately agree that they also know it to be true. The main moral convictions of the plain man seem to me to be, not opinions which it is for philosophy to prove or disprove, but knowledge from the start; and in my own case I seem to find little difficulty in distinguishing these essential convictions from other moral convictions which I also have, which are merely fallible opinions based on an imperfect study of the working for good or evil of certain institutions or types of action.

[5] For a needed correction of this statement, cf. Ross, op. cit., pp. 22–23.

better in respect of virtue, or of intelligence, or of pleasure. These are the duties of beneficence. (5) Some rest on the fact that we can improve our own condition is respect of virtue or of intelligence. These are the duties of self-improvement. (6) I think that we should distinguish from (4) the duties that may be summed up under the title of 'not injuring others'. No doubt to injure others is incidentally to fail to do them good; but it seems to me clear that nonmaleficence is apprehended as a duty distinct from that of beneficence, and as a duty of a more stringent character. It will be noticed that this alone among the types of duty has been stated in a negative way. An attempt might no doubt be made to state this duty, like the others, in a positive way. It might be said that it is really the duty to prevent ourselves from acting either from an inclination to harm others or from an inclination to seek our own pleasure, in doing which we should incidentally harm them. But on reflection it seems clear that the primary duty here is the duty not to harm others, this being a duty whether or not we have an inclination that if followed would lead to our harming them; and that when we have such an inclination the primary duty not to harm others gives rise to a consequential duty to resist the inclination. The recognition of this duty of nonmaleficence is the first step on the way to the recognition of the duty of beneficence; and that accounts for the prominence of the commands 'thou shalt not kill,' 'thou shalt not commit adultery', 'thou shalt not steal', 'thou shalt not bear false witness', in so early a code as the Decalogue. But even when we have come to recognize the duty of beneficence, it appears to me that the duty of nonmaleficence is recognized as a distinct one, and as *prima facie* more binding. We should not in general consider it justifiable to kill one person in order to keep another alive, or to steal from one in order to give alms to another.

The essential defect of the 'ideal utilitarian' theory is that it ignores, or at least does not do full justice to, the highly personal character of duty. If the only duty is to produce the maximum of good, the question who is to have the good—whether it is myself, or my benefactor, or a person to whom I have made a promise to confer that good on him, or a mere fellow man to whom I stand in no such special relation—should make no difference to my having a duty to produce that good. But we are all in fact sure that it makes a vast difference. . . .

If the objection be made, that this catalogue of the main types of duty is an unsystematic one resting on no logical principle, it may be replied, first, that it makes no claim to being ultimate. It is a *prima facie* classification of the duties which reflection on our moral convictions seems actually to reveal. And if these convictions are, as I would claim that they are, of the nature of knowledge, and if I have not misstated them, the list will be a list of authentic conditional duties, correct as far as it goes though not necessarily complete. The list of *goods* put forward by the rival theory is

reached by exactly the same method—the only sound one in the circumstances—viz. that of direct reflection on what we really think. Loyalty to
the facts is worth more than a symmetrical architectonic or a hastily reached
simplicity. If further reflection discovers a perfect logical basis for this or
for a better classification, so much the better.

It may, again, be objected that our theory that there are these various
and often conflicting types of *prima facie* duty leaves us with no principle
upon which to discern what is our actual duty in particular circumstances.
But this objection is not one which the rival theory is in a position to bring
forward. For when we have to choose between the production of two
heterogeneous goods, say knowledge and pleasure, the 'ideal utilitarian'
theory can only fall back on an opinion, for which no logical basis can be
offered, that one of the goods is the greater; and this is no better than a
similar opinion that one of two duties is the more urgent. And again, when
we consider the infinite variety of the effects of our actions in the way of
pleasure, it must surely be admitted that the claim which hedonism sometimes makes, that it offers a readily applicable criterion of right conduct, is
quite illusory.

I am unwilling, however, to content myself with an *argumentum ad
hominem*, and I would contend that in principle there is no reason to an-
ticipate that every act that is our duty is so for one and the same reason.
Why should two sets of circumstances, or one set of circumstances, *not* possess
different characteristics, any one of which makes a certain act our *prima
facie* duty? When I ask what it is that makes me in certain cases sure that I
have a *prima facie* duty to do so and so, I find that it lies in the fact that
I have made a promise; when I ask the same question in another case, I
find the answer lies in the fact that I have done a wrong. And if on
reflection I find (as I think I do) that neither of these reasons is reducible
to the other, I must not on any *a priori* ground assume that such a reduction
is possible.

An attempt may be made to arrange in a more systematic way the main
types of duty which we have indicated. In the first place it seems self-
evident that if there are things that are intrinsically good, it is *prima facie*
a duty to bring them into existence rather than not to do so, and to bring
as much of them into existence as possible. . . . there are three main things
that are intrinsically good—virtue, knowledge, and, with certain limitations, pleasure. And since a given virtuous disposition, for instance, is
equally good whether it is realized in myself or in another, it seems to be
my duty to bring it into existence whether in myself or in another. So too
with a given piece of knowledge.

The case of pleasure is difficult, for while we clearly recognize a duty
to produce pleasure for others, it is by no means so clear that we recognize
a duty to produce pleasure for ourselves. This appears to arise from the

following facts. The thought of an act as our duty is one that presupposes a certain amount of reflection about the act; and for that reason does not normally arise in connection with acts towards which we are already impelled by another strong impulse. So far, the cause of our not thinking of the promotion of our own pleasure as a duty is analogous to the cause which usually prevents a highly sympathetic person from thinking of the promotion of the pleasure of others as a duty. He is impelled so strongly by direct interest in the well-being of others towards promoting their pleasure that he does not stop to ask whether it is his duty to promote it; and we are all impelled so strongly towards the promotion of our own pleasure that we do not stop to ask whether it is a duty or not. But there is a further reason why even when we stop to think about the matter it does not usually present itself as a duty: viz. that, since the performance of most of our duties involves the giving up of some pleasure that we desire, the doing of duty and the getting of pleasure for ourselves come by a natural association of ideas to be thought of as incompatible things. This association of ideas is in the main salutary in its operation, since it puts a check on what but for it would be much too strong, the tendency to pursue one's own pleasure without thought of other considerations. Yet if pleasure is good, it seems in the long run clear that it is right to get it for ourselves as well as to produce it for others, when this does not involve the failure to discharge some more stringent *prima facie* duty. The question is a very difficult one, but it seems that this conclusion can be denied only on one or other of three grounds: (1) that pleasure is not *prima facie* good (i.e. good when it is neither the actualization of a bad disposition nor undeserved), (2) that there is no *prima facie* duty to produce as much that is good as we can, or (3) that though there is a *prima facie* duty to produce other things that are good, there is no *prima facie* duty to produce pleasure which will be enjoyed by ourselves. . . . The second hardly admits of argument but seems to me plainly false. The third seems plausible only if we hold that an act that is pleasant or brings pleasure to ourselves must for that reason not be a duty; and this would lead to paradoxical consequences, such as that if a man enjoys giving pleasure to others, or working for their moral improvement, it cannot be his duty to do so. Yet it seems to be a very stubborn fact, that in our ordinary consciousness we are not aware of a duty to get pleasure for ourselves; and by way of partial explanation of this I may add that though, as I think, one's own pleasure is a good and there is a duty to produce it, it is only if we *think* of our own pleasure not as simply our own pleasure, but as an objective good, something that an impartial spectator would approve, that we can think of the getting it as a duty; and we do not habitually think of it in this way.

If these contentions are right, what we have called the duty of beneficence and the duty of self-improvement rest on the same ground. No different principles of duty are involved in the two cases. If we feel a special responsibility for improving our own character rather than that of others, it is not because a special principle is involved, but because we are aware that the one is more under our control than the other. It was on this ground that Kant expressed the practical law of duty in the form 'seek to make yourself good and other people happy'. He was so persuaded of the internality of virtue that he regarded any attempt by one person to produce virtue in another as bound to produce, at most, only a counterfeit of virtue, the doing of externally right acts not from the true principle of virtuous action but out of regard to another person. It must be admitted that one man cannot compel another to be virtuous; compulsory virtue would just not be virtue. But experience clearly shows that Kant overshoots the mark when he contends that one man cannot do anything to *promote* virtue in another, to bring such influences to bear upon him that his own response to them is more likely to be virtuous than his response to other influences would have been. And our duty to do this is not different in kind from our duty to improve our own characters.

It is equally clear, and clear at an earlier stage of moral development, that if there are things that are bad in themselves we ought, *prima facie*, not to bring them upon others; and on this fact rests the duty of non-maleficence.

The duty of justice is particularly complicated, and the word is used to cover things which are really very different—things such as the payment of debts, the reparation of injuries done by oneself to another, and the bringing about of a distribution of happiness between other people in proportion to merit. I use the word to denote only the last of these three. [Later] I shall try to show that besides the three (comparatively) simple goods, virtue, knowledge, and pleasure, there is a more complex good, not reducible to these, consisting in the proportionment of happiness to virtue. The bringing of this about is a duty which we owe to all men alike, though it may be reinforced by special responsibilities that we have undertaken to particular men. This, therefore, with beneficence and self-improvement, comes under the general principle that we should produce as much good as possible, though the good here involved is different in kind from any other.

But besides this general obligation, there are special obligations. These may arise, in the first place, incidentally, from acts which were not essentially meant to create such an obligation, but which nevertheless create it. From the nature of the case such acts may be of two kinds—the infliction of injuries on others, and the acceptance of benefits from them. It seems clear that these put us under a special obligation to other men, and that only these acts can do so incidentally. From these arise the twin duties of reparation and gratitude.

And finally there are special obligations arising from acts the very intention of which, when they were done, was to put us under such an obligation. The name for such acts is 'promises'; the name is wide enough if we are willing to include under it implicit promises, i.e. modes of behavior in which without explicit verbal promise we intentionally create an expectation that we can be counted on to behave in a certain way in the interest of another person.

These seem to be, in principle, all the ways in which *prima facie* duties arise. In actual experience they are compounded together in highly complex ways. Thus, for example, the duty of obeying the laws of one's country arises partly (as Socrates contends in the *Crito*) from the duty of gratitude for the benefits one has received from it; partly from the implicit promise to obey which seems to be involved in permanent residence in a country whose laws we know we are *expected* to obey, and still more clearly involved when we ourselves invoke the protection of its laws (this is the truth underlying the doctrine of the social contract); and partly (if we are fortunate in our country) from the fact that its laws are potent instruments for the general good.

Or again, the sense of a general obligation to bring about (so far as we can) a just apportionment of happiness to merit is often greatly reinforced by the fact that many of the existing injustices are due to a social and economic system which we have, not indeed created, but taken part in and assented to; the duty of justice is then reinforced by the duty of reparation.

It is necessary to say something by way of clearing up the relation between *prima facie* duties and the actual or absolute duty to do one particular act in particular circumstances. If, as almost all moralists except Kant are agreed, and as most plain men think, it is sometimes right to tell a lie or to break a promise, it must be maintained that there is a difference between *prima facie* duty and actual or absolute duty. When we think ourselves justified in breaking, and indeed morally obliged to break, a promise in order to relieve some one's distress, we do not for a moment cease to recognize a *prima facie* duty to keep our promise, and this leads us to feel, not indeed shame or repentance, but certainly compunction, for behaving as we do; we recognize, further, that it is our duty to make up somehow to the promisee for the breaking of the promise. We have to distinguish from the characteristic of being our duty that of tending to be our duty. Any act that we do contains various elements in virtue of which it falls under various categories. In virtue of being the breaking of a promise, for instance, it tends to be wrong; in virtue of being an instance of relieving distress it tends to be right. Tendency to be one's duty may be called a parti-resultant attribute, i.e. one which belongs to an act in virtue of some one component in its nature. *Being* one's duty is a toti-resultant attribute, one which belongs to an act in virtue of its whole nature and of nothing less than this.[6] . . .

_____

[6] But, cf. the qualification in n. 8.

Another instance of the same distinction may be found in the operation of natural laws. *Qua* subject to the force of gravitation towards some other body, each body tends to move in a particular direction with a particular velocity; but its actual movement depends on *all* the forces to which it is subject. It is only by recognizing this distinction that we can preserve the absoluteness of laws of nature, and only by recognizing a corresponding distinction that we can preserve the absoluteness of the general principles of morality. But an important difference between the two cases must be pointed out. When we say that in virtue of gravitation a body tends to move in a certain way, we are referring to a causal influence actually exercised on it by another body or other bodies. When we say that in virtue of being deliberately untrue a certain remark tends to be wrong, we are referring to no causal relation, to no relation that involves succession in time, but to such a relation as connects the various attributes of a mathematical figure. And if the word 'tendency' is thought to suggest too much a causal relation, it is better to talk of certain types of act as being *prima facie* right or wrong (or of different persons as having different and possibly conflicting claims upon us), than of their tending to be right or wrong.

Something should be said of the relation between our apprehension of the *prima facie* rightness of certain types of act and our mental attitude towards particular acts. It is proper to use the word 'apprehension' in the former case and not in the latter. That an act, *qua* fulfilling a promise, or *qua* effecting a just distribution of good, or *qua* returning services rendered, or *qua* promoting the good of others, or *qua* promoting the virtue or insight of the agent, is *prima facie* right, is self-evident; not in the sense that it is evident from the beginning of our lives, or as soon as we attend to the proposition for the first time, but in the sense that when we have reached sufficient mental maturity and have given sufficient attention to the proposition it is evident without any need of proof, or of evidence beyond itself. It is self-evident just as a mathematical axiom, or the validity of a form of inference, is evident. The moral order expressed in these propositions is just as much part of the fundamental nature of the universe (and, we may add, of any possible universe in which there were moral agents at all) as is the spatial or numerical structure expressed in the axioms of geometry or arithmetic. In our confidence that these propostions are true there is involved the same trust in our reason that is involved in our confidence in mathematics; and we should have no justification for trusting it in the latter sphere and distrusting it in the former. In both cases we are dealing with propositions that cannot be proved, but that just as certainly need no proof. . . .

Our judgments about our actual duty in concrete situations have none of the certainty that attaches to our recognition of the general principles of duty. A statement is certain, i.e. is an expression of knowledge, only in one or other of two cases: when it is either self-evident, or a valid conclusion from self-evident premises. And our judgments about our particular duties have neither of these characters. (1) They are not self-evident. Where a possible act is seen to have two characteristics, in virtue of one of which it is *prima facie* right, and in virtue of the other *prima facie* wrong, we are (I think) well aware that we are not certain whether we ought or ought not to do it; that whether we do it or not, we are taking a moral risk. We come in the long run, after consideration, to think one duty more pressing than the other, but we do not feel certain that it is so. And though we do not always recognize that a possible act has two such characteristics, and though there *may* be cases in which it has not, we are never certain that any particular possible act has not, and therefore never certain that it is right, nor certain that it is wrong. For, to go no further in the analysis, it is enough to point out that any particular act will in all probability in the course of time contribute to the bringing about of good or of evil for many human beings, and thus have a *prima facie* rightness or wrongness of which we know nothing. (2) Again, our judgments about our particular duties are not logical conclusions from self-evident premises. The only possible premises would be the general principles stating their *prima facie* rightness or wrongness *qua* having the different characteristics they do have; and even if we could (as we cannot) apprehend the extent to which an act will tend on the one hand, for example, to bring about advantages for our benefactors, and on the other hand to bring about disadvantages for fellow men who are not our benefactors, there is no principle by which we can draw the conclusion that it is on the whole right or on the whole wrong. In this respect the judgment as to the rightness of a particular act is just like the judgment as to the beauty of a particular natural object or work of art. A poem is, for instance, in respect of certain qualities beautiful and in respect of certain others not beautiful; and our judgment as to the degree of beauty it possesses on the whole is never reached by logical reasoning from the apprehension of its particular beauties or particular defects. Both in this and in the moral case we have more or less probable opinions which are not logically justified conclusions from the general principles that are recognized as self-evident.

There is therefore much truth in the description of the right act as a fortunate act. If we cannot be certain that it is right, it is our good fortune if the act we do is the right act. This consideration does not, however, make the doing of our duty a mere matter of chance. There is a parallel here between the doing of duty and of what will be to our personal advantage. We never *know* what act will in the long run be to our advantage. Yet it is certain that we are more likely in general to secure our advantage if we estimate to the best of our ability the probable tendencies of our actions in this respect, than if we act on caprice. And similarly we are more likely to do our duty if we reflect to the best of our ability on the *prima facie* rightness or wrongness of various possible acts in virtue of the characteristics we perceive them to have, than if we act without reflection. With this greater likelihood we must be content.

Many people would be inclined to say that the right act for me is not that whose general nature I have been describing, viz. that which if I were omniscient I should see to be my duty, but that which on all the evidence available to me I should think to be my duty. But suppose that from the state of partial knowledge in which I think act A to be my duty, I could pass to a state of perfect knowledge in which I saw act B to be my duty, should I not say 'act B was the right act for me to do'? I should no doubt add 'though I am not to be blamed for doing act A'. But in adding this, am I not passing from the question 'what is right' to the question 'what is morally good'? At the same time I am not making the *full* passage from the one notion to the other; for in order that the act should be morally good, or an act I am not to be blamed for doing, it must not merely be the act which it is reasonable for me to think my duty; it must also be done for that reason, or from some other morally good motive. Thus the conception of the right act as the act which it is reasonable for me to think my duty is an unsatisfactory compromise between the true notion of the right act and the notion of the morally good action.

The general principles of duty are obviously not self-evident from the beginning of our lives. How do they come to be so? The answer is, that they come to be self-evident to us just as mathematical axioms do. We find by experience that this couple of matches and that couple make four matches, that this couple of balls on a wire and that couple make four balls; and by reflection on these and similar discoveries we come to see that it is of the nature of two and two to make four. In a precisely similar way, we see the *prima facie* rightness of an act which would be the fulfillment of a particular promise, and of another which would be the fulfillment of another promise, and when we have reached sufficient maturity to think in general terms, we apprehend *prima facie* rightness to belong to the nature of any fulfillment of promise. What comes first in time is the apprehension of the self-evident *prima facie* rightness of an individual act of a particular type. From this we come by reflection to apprehend the self-evident general principle of *prima facie* duty. From this, too, perhaps along with the apprehension of the self-evident *prima facie* rightness of the same act in virtue of its having another characteristic as well, and perhaps in spite of the apprehension of its *prima facie* wrongness in virtue of its having some third characteristic, we come to believe something not self-evident at all, but an object of probable opinion, viz. that this particular act is (not *prima facie* but) actually right.

In this respect there is an important difference between rightness and mathematical properties. A triangle which is isosceles necessarily has two of its angles equal, whatever other characteristics the triangle may have—

whatever, for instance, be its area, or the size of its third angle. The equality of the two angles is a parti-resultant attribute.[7] And the same is true of all mathematical attributes. It is true, I may add, of *prima facie* rightness. But no act is ever, in virtue of falling under some general description, necessarily actually right; its rightness depends on its whole nature[8] and not on any element in it. The reason is that no mathematical object (no figure, for instance, or angle) ever has two characteristics that tend to give it opposite resultant characteristics, while moral acts often (as everyone knows) and indeed always (as on reflection we must admit) have different characteristics that tend to make them at the same time *prima facie* right and *prima facie* wrong; there is probably no act, for instance, which does good to anyone without doing harm to someone else, and *vice versa*.

Supposing it to be agreed, as I think on reflection it must, that no one *means* by 'right' just 'productive of the best possible consequences', or 'optimific', the attributes 'right' and 'optimific' might stand in either of two kinds of relation to each other. (1) They might be so related that we could apprehend *a priori*, either immediately or deductively, that any act that is optimific is right and any act that is right is optimific, as we can apprehend that any triangle that is equilateral is equiangular and *vice versa*. Professor Moore's view is, I think, that the coextensiveness of 'right' and 'optimific' is apprehended immediately.[9] He rejects the possibility of any proof of it. Or (2) the two attributes might be such that the question whether they are invariably connected had to be answered by means of an inductive inquiry. Now at first sight it might seem as if the constant connection of the two attributes could be immediately apprehended. It might seem absurd to suggest that it could be right for anyone to do an act which would produce consequences less good than those which would be produced by some other act in his power. Yet a little thought will convince us that this is not absurd. The type of case in which it is easiest to see that this is so is, perhaps, that in which one has made a promise. In such a case we all think that *prima facie* it is our duty to fulfill the promise irrespective of the precise goodness of the total consequences. And though we do not think it is necessarily our actual or absolute duty to do so, we are far from thinking that any, even the slightest, gain in the value of the total consequences will necessarily

---

[7] Cf. Ross, op. cit., pp. 28, 122–23.

[8] To avoid complicating unduly the statement of the general view I am putting forward, I have here rather overstated it. Any act is the origination of a great variety of things many of which make no difference to its rightness or wrongness. But there are always many elements in its nature (i.e. in what it is the origination of) that make a difference to its rightness or wrongness, and no element in its nature can be dismissed without consideration as indifferent.

[9] *Ethics*, p. 181.

justify us in doing something else instead. Suppose, to simplify the case by abstraction, that the fulfillment of a promise to A would produce 1,000 units of good[10] for him, but that by doing some other act I could produce 1,001 units of good for B, to whom I have made no promise, the other consequences of the two acts being of equal value; should we really think it self-evident that it was our duty to do the second act and not the first? I think not. We should, I fancy, hold that only a much greater disparity of value between the total consequences would justify us in failing to discharge our *prima facie* duty to A. After all, a promise is a promise, and is not to be treated so lightly as the theory we are examining would imply. What, exactly, a promise is, is not so easy to determine, but we are surely agreed that it constitutes a serious moral limitation to our freedom of action. To produce the 1,001 units of good for B rather than fulfill our promise to A would be to take, not perhaps our duty as philanthropists too seriously, but certainly our duty as makers of promises too lightly.

Or consider another phase of the same problem. If I have promised to confer on A a particular benefit containing 1,000 units of good, is it self-evident that if by doing some different act I could produce 1,001 units of good for A himself (the other consequences of the two acts being supposed equal in value), it would be right for me to do so? Again, I think not. Apart from my general *prima facie* duty to do A what good I can, I have another *prima facie* duty to do him the particular service I have promised to do him, and this is not to be set aside in consequence of a disparity of good of the order of 1,001 to 1,000, though a much greater disparity might justify me in so doing.

Or again, suppose that A is a very good and B a very bad man, should I then, even when I have made no promise, think it self-evidently right to produce 1,001 units of good for B rather than 1,000 for A? Surely not. I should be sensible of a *prima facie* duty of justice, i.e. of producing a distribution of goods in proportion to merit, which is not outweighed by such a slight disparity in the total goods to be produced.

Such instances—and they might easily be added to—make it clear that there is no self-evident connection between the attributes 'right' and 'optimific'. The theory we are examining has a certain attractiveness when applied to our decision that a particular act is our duty (though I have tried to show that it does not agree with our actual moral judgments even here). But it is not even plausible when applied to our recognition of *prima facie* duty. For if it were self-evident that the right coincides with the

---

[10] I am assuming that good is objectively quantitative, but not that we can accurately assign an exact quantitative measure to it. Since it is of a definite amount, we can make the *supposition* that its amount is so-and-so, though we cannot with any confidence *assert* that it is.

optimific, it should be self-evident that what is *prima facie* right is *prima facie* optimific. But whereas we are certain that keeping a promise is *prima facie* right, we are not certain that it is *prima facie* optimific (though we are perhaps certain that it is *prima facie* bonific). Our certainty that it is *prima facie* right depends not on its consequences but on its being the fulfillment of a promise. The theory we are examining involves too much difference between the evident ground of our conviction about *prima facie* duty and the alleged ground of our conviction about actual duty. . . .

There is one direction in which a fairly serious attempt has been made to show the connection of the attributes 'right' and 'optimific'. One of the most evident facts of our moral consciousness is the sense which we have of the sanctity of promises, a sense which does not, on the face of it, involve the thought that one will be bringing more good into existence by fulfilling the promise than by breaking it. It is plain, I think, that in our normal thought we consider that the fact that we have made a promise is in itself sufficient to create a duty of keeping it, the sense of duty resting on remembrance of the past promise and not on thoughts of the future consequences of its fulfillment. Utilitarianism tries to show that this is not so, that the sanctity of promises rests on the good consequences of the fulfillment of them and the bad consequences of their nonfulfillment. It does so in this way: it points out that when you break a promise you not only fail to confer a certain advantage on your promisee but you diminish his confidence, and indirectly the confidence of others, in the fulfillment of promises. You thus strike a blow at one of the devices that have been found most useful in the relations between man and man—the device on which, for example, the whole system of commercial credit rests—and you tend to bring about a state of things wherein each man, being entirely unable to rely on the keeping of promises by others, will have to do everything for himself, to the enormous impoverishment of human well-being.

To put the matter otherwise, utilitarians say that when a promise ought to be kept it is because the total good to be produced by keeping it is greater than the total good to be produced by breaking it, the former including as its main element the maintenance and strengthening of general mutual confidence, and the latter being greatly diminished by a weakening of this confidence. They say, in fact, that the case I put some pages back[11] never arises—the case in which by fulfilling a promise I shall bring into being 1,000 units of good for my promisee, and by breaking it 1,001 units of good for someone else, the other effects of the two acts being of equal value. The other effects, they say, never are of equal value. By keeping my promise I am helping to strengthen the system of mutual confidence; by breaking it I am helping to weaken this; so that really the first act produces

---

[11] Pp. 200–201.

1,000 + x units of good, and the second 1,001 − y units, and the difference between + x and − y is enough to outweigh the slight superiority in the *immediate* effects of the second act. In answer to this it may be pointed out that there must be *some* amount of good that exceeds the difference between + x and − y (i.e. exceeds $x + y$); say, $x + y + z$. Let us suppose the *immediate* good effects of the second act to be assessed not at 1,001 but at 1,000 + $x + y + z$. Then its *net* good effects are 1,000 + $x + z$, i.e. greater than those of the fulfillment of the promise; and the utilitarian is bound to say forthwith that the promise should be broken. Now, we may ask whether that is really the way we think about promises? Do we really think that the production of the slightest balance of good, no matter who will enjoy it, by the breach of a promise frees us from the obligation to keep our promise? We need not doubt that a system by which promises are made and kept is one that has great advantages for the general well-being. But that is not the whole truth. To make a promise is not merely to adapt an ingenious device for promoting the general well-being; it is to put oneself in a new relation to one person in particular, a relation which creates a specifically new *prima facie* duty to him, not reducible to the duty of promoting the general well-being of society. By all means let us try to foresee the net good effects of keeping one's promise and the net good effects of breaking it, but even if we assess the first at 1,000 + x and the second at 1,000 + $x + z$, the question still remains whether it is not our duty to fulfill the promise. It may be suspected, too, that the effect of a single keeping or breaking of a promise in strengthening or weakening the fabric of mutual confidence is greatly exaggerated by the theory we are examin- ing. And if we suppose two men dying together alone, do we think that the duty of one to fulfill before he dies a promise he has made to the other would be extinguished by the fact that neither act would have any effect on the general confidence? Anyone who holds this may be suspected of not having reflected on what a promise is.

I conclude that the attributes 'right' and 'optimific' are not identical, and that we do not know either by intuition, by deduction, or by induction that they coincide in their application, still less that the latter is the founda- tion of the former. It must be added, however, that if we are ever under no special obligation such as that of fidelity to a promisee or of gratitude to a benefactor, we ought to do what will produce most good; and that even when we are under a special obligation the tendency of acts to promote general good is one of the main factors in determining whether they are right.

In what has preceded, a good deal of use has been made of 'what we really think' about moral questions; a certain theory has been rejected because it does not agree with what we really think. It might be said that this is in principle wrong; that we should not be content to expound what our present moral consciousness tells us but should aim at a criticism of our existing moral consciousness in the light of theory. Now I do not doubt that the moral consciousness of men has in detail undergone a good deal of modification as regards the things we think right, at the hands of moral theory. But if we are told, for instance, that we should give up our view that there is a special obligatoriness attaching to the keeping of promises because it is self-evident that the only duty is to produce as much good as possible, we have to ask ourselves whether we really, when we reflect, *are* convinced that this is self-evident, and whether we really *can* get rid of our view that promise keeping has a bindingness independent of productiveness of maximum good. In my own experience I find that I cannot, in spite of a very genuine attempt to do so; and I venture to think that most people will find the same, and that just because they cannot lose the sense of special obligation, they cannot accept as self-evident, or even as true, the theory which would require them to do so. In fact it seems, on reflection, self-evident that a promise, simply as such is something that *prima facie* ought to be kept, and it does *not,* on reflection, seem self-evident that production of maximum good is the only thing that makes an act obligatory. And to ask us to give up at the bidding of a theory our actual apprehension of what is right and what is wrong seems like asking people to repudiate their actual experience of beauty, at the bidding of a theory which says 'only that which satisfies such and such conditions can be beautiful'. If what I have called our actual apprehension is (as I would maintain that it is) truly an apprehension, i.e. an instance of knowledge, the request is nothing less than absurd.

I would maintain, in fact, that what we are apt to describe as 'what we think' about moral questions contains a considerable amount that we do not think but know, and that this forms the standard by reference to which the truth of any moral theory has to be tested, instead of having itself to be tested by reference to any theory. I hope that I have in what precedes indicated what in my view these elements of knowledge are that are involved in our ordinary moral consciousness.

It would be a mistake to found a natural science on 'what we really think', i.e. on what reasonably thoughtful and well-educated people think about the subjects of the science before they have studied them scientifically. For such opinions are interpretations, and often misinterpretations, of sense experience; and the man of science must appeal from these to sense experience itself, which furnishes his real data. In ethics no such appeal is possible. We have no more direct way of access to the facts about rightness and goodness and about what things are right or good, than by thinking about them; the moral convictions of thoughtful and well-educated people are the data of ethics just as sense perceptions are the data of a natural science. Just as some of the latter have to be rejected as illusory, so have some of the former; but as the latter are rejected only when they are in conflict with other more accurate sense perceptions, the former are rejected only when they are in conflict with other convictions which stand better the test of reflection. The existing body of moral convictions of the best people is the cumulative product of the moral reflection of many generations, which has developed an extremely delicate power of appreciation of moral distinctions; and this the theorist cannot afford to treat with anything other than the greatest respect. The verdicts of the moral consciousness of the best people are the foundation on which he must build; though he must first compare them with one another and eliminate any contradictions they may contain.

It is worth while to try to state more definitely the nature of the acts that are right. We may try to state first what (if anything) is the universal nature of *all* acts that are right. It is obvious that any of the acts that we do has countless effects, directly or indirectly, on countless people, and the probability is that any act, however right it be, will have adverse effects (though these may be very trivial) on some innocent people. Similarly, any wrong act will probably have beneficial effects on some deserving people. Every act therefore, viewed in some aspects, will be *prima facie* right, and viewed in others, *prima facie* wrong, and right acts can be distinguished from wrong acts only as being those which, of all those possible for the agent in the circumstances, have the greatest balance of *prima facie* rightness, in those respects in which they are *prima facie* right, over their *prima facie* wrongness, in those respects in which they are *prima facie* wrong—*prima facie* rightness and wrongness being understood in the sense previously explained. For the estimation of the comparative stringency of these *prima facie* obligations no general rules can, so far as I can see, be laid down. We can only say that a great deal of stringency belongs to the duties of 'perfect obligation'—the duties of keeping our promises, of repairing wrongs we have done, and of returning the equivalent of services we have received. For the rest, ἐν τῇ αἰσθήσει ἡ κρίσις.[12] This sense of our particular duty in particular circumstances, preceded and informed by the fullest reflection we can bestow on the act in all its bearings, is highly fallible, but it is the only guide we have to our duty. . . .

---

12 'The decision rests with perception'. Arist. *Nic. Eth.* 1109 b 23, 1126 b 4.

Moral Rules

J. D. MABBOTT

We frequently justify a moral decision by referring to a rule. I intend in this paper to discuss the logic of such rules. In recent years the principal interest in moral philosophy has been in attempts to devise alternatives to the objectivist view of moral thinking held in common by writers so different as Mill and Bradley, Ross and Moore. All of them maintained that moral talk stated propositions which were true or false. Recent theories have been alike in attempting a non-propositional analysis of moral language, or of the specifically moral elements in moral language. (For any particular moral judgement—'Jones did wrong in beating his wife'—may include an element of nonmoral factual assertion, that Jones did beat his wife, which is properly expressed in propositional form.) With this controversy I shall not be directly concerned. I shall use the objectivist or propositional language, partly because it is better adapted for discussing my problem and partly because it is the language of those philosophers who have previously discussed it. Yet much of what I say could be restated in terms of any of the half-dozen alternative nonpropositional theories. And I shall occasionally show how this can be done, so as to indicate that the problems with which I shall be concerned face all moral philosophers equally.

MORAL RULES AS SELF-EVIDENT PROPOSITIONS

I am to examine the theory that a particular act is right because it falls under some rule or other, that is, because it is a member of a class or kind of acts all of which are right in virtue of some common character or class membership. Some rules might themselves be particular applications of wider rules. But if this type of explanation of moral experience were to be alone sufficient to clarify moral usage, and if it were not to lead to a self-defeating regress, there would have to be one or more rules for which it would make no sense to ask for a justification, rules which were basic and ultimate, and if these rules were to explain the rightness of particular acts and to validate the truth of particular moral judgements, they would have to be self-evidently true. This is the view maintained by Sir David Ross.

Let me now restate this view in terms of two nonpropositional theories. On an approval theory it would hold that a moral judgment (or the

From Proceedings of the British Academy, *XXXIX (1953), published by Oxford University Press. Reprinted by permission of the author and the publisher.*

specifically moral element in a moral judgment) is the expression, not of an approval of a particular action, but of an *attitude* of approval towards actions of a certain kind, and that the approval would not have been felt towards this particular action unless it had been recognized as being of that kind. On an imperative theory it would maintain that a moral judgment is always a *general* moral imperative, combined (in cases where the judgment seems particular) with the recognition that the general imperative applies in the circumstances in question.

Now what is to be said about the view that all moral judgments rest ultimately on certain self-evident moral rules? There is first the general logical difficulty about recognizing the possibility of any *a priori* synthetic judgments. In some cases indeed the truth of a moral rule may seem merely analytic. 'Debts ought to be repaid' would seem to owe its self-evidence to the word 'debt'. And the same kind of certainty was achieved when the words 'Thou shalt not kill' in the Authorized Version were amended to 'Thou shalt do no murder' by the revisers. But this result cannot always be attained. 'Tell the truth' and 'Honor thy father and thy mother' cannot be shown to be tautologies. There are two further difficulties about the view. First, no rules are binding without exceptions. Promises ought sometimes to be broken and creditors disappointed. It is therefore impossible to hold that any particular act ought to be done because it belongs to a class of acts all of which ought to be done. For there are no such classes of acts, all of which ought to be done. I think the solution of this difficulty put forward by Ross is entirely satisfactory. A moral rule is not binding in all circumstances. It is *relevant* in all circumstances. It is binding unless countered by another moral rule. Even when it is broken it has its force and should be broken with compunction. (The parallel of a physical law or force is a good one. The law of gravity is obeyed by Newton's apple but also by the iron filings which fly up in apparent defiance of gravity to reach the magnet.) The other difficulty, and the fatal one for a theory like that of Ross, is that rules vary. Many people accept as ultimate (and would claim as self-evident) rules which Ross would reject. Ross meets this, following A. E. Taylor,[1] by distinguishing between basic rules and *media axiomata*, the latter being more determinate rules arising from the application of the basic rules to special circumstances. Ross holds that all men agree on basic rules. Their differences arise only over *media axiomata*; and these differences are explicable either by the different special circumstances in which the basic rule is applied, or by differences in the factual beliefs about these circumstances entertained by the different moral agents in question.[2] Thus the duty of a Briton to help the police to arrest a

---

[1] *Mind*, **XXXV** (1926), 289.
[2] *The Foundations of Ethics*, pp. 17–21.

murderer and the duty of a Corsican to kill a member of the murderer's family are basically the same duty of requiting murder, applied to two different sets of circumstances (those with and without an effective legal authority). Or again the North Siberian, when he kills a woman who steps across his shadow, holds the same basic moral rule as we do, that deleterious influences should not be allowed to damage human personalities, along with the mistaken beliefs that a woman is a deleterious influence and that his shadow is part of his personality. Tribesmen who eat their parents combine the universally valid basic rule that men should honor their parents and try to acquire their virtues with the mistaken dietary belief that men come to resemble what they eat.

But, as Taylor himself admitted, it is not possible to reduce all variations in moral rules to variations on agreed themes. To go no farther from home than the Old Bailey, it cannot be shown that the conscientious objector and his judges are agreed on fundamentals or that there is no basic difference between those who hold that suicide is sometimes right and those who hold it is always wrong.

MORAL RULES AS EMPIRICAL GENERALIZATIONS

Those who, for these reasons or others, reject the primacy or self-evidence of moral rules are liable to go in the opposite direction and maintain that particular moral judgments are ultimate and that moral rules are empirical generalizations. Any rule must rest on the apprehended rightness of a number of particular actions. These are observed to resemble each other not only in being right but also in having some other general character. It is then inferred with a certain degree of probability that rightness and this other character will accompany each other always or in the next observed case. This view too can be held and has been held by nonpropositional moral philosophers. If moral language expresses emotions or attitudes of approval then the emotion or attitude is felt primarily towards particular actions. If a man states a moral rule he is either asserting that all actions similar in a certain respect are likely to arouse this particular emotion or attitude, or else he is expressing an acquired habit of feeling this emotion or having this attitude towards actions of this kind. Similarly, on an imperative theory, the basic moral imperatives will be orders to do (or to approve of) particular actions. A moral rule will be either an inductive generalization that future imperatives will resemble past imperatives in a certain respect, or will itself be an imperative ('never kill' or 'always pay') expressing an habitual reaction resulting from the prior particular imperatives 'don't kill Jones', 'don't kill Robinson', 'pay Smith sixpence', 'pay Brown fourpence'.

Now this theory, that moral rules are empirical generalizations, seems to me the one theory about them which is certainly false. To see this all that is needed is to state the theory clearly and draw out its implications. The view was stated with great accuracy by Adam Smith. 'General maxims of morality are formed, like all other general maxims, from experience and induction. We observe in a great variety of particular cases what pleases or displeases our moral faculties, what these approve or disapprove of, and, by induction from this experience, we establish the general rules.'3 But it is echoed, though less clearly, by subsequent moralists down to the present day and including defenders of nonpropositional theories of moral judgment. C. L. Stevenson, for example, maintains that moral attitudes are adopted primarily towards particular actions. The attachment of a moral adjective such as 'right' to a *kind* of action is merely the result of 'habit and rough generalization'. It is due to 'the psychological economy that comes from ordering the objects of attitudes in some sort of classification'.4 What does this involve? In order to establish that acts having a certain character x are right it is necessary first to recognize that a number of particular acts are right independently of their possessing the character x, then to observe that they also possess the character x, and only thus to conclude that rightness and the character x are connected. The same point can be made in the approval or imperative language, as I shall indicate in the two illustrations which follow. How could we justify returning borrowed articles? Someone must approve of handing a certain book to Jones, of delivering a certain umbrella to Brown and of sending a certain bicycle to Robinson. He would have to approve of these particular actions independently of any recognition that these articles had previously been in the possession of Jones and Brown and Robinson respectively. Then, observing this fact about them, he has to conclude inductively that the returning of other borrowed articles is likely to arouse approval, or he would tend to acquire the habit of approving of the return of an article on observing that it had been borrowed. To take an example in the imperative language, a man must find himself dissuading Tom from hitting Jack, dissuading Jill from sticking pins into Jane, dissuading Robert from twisting the arm of Marmaduke. He must then notice that each of these actions involves the infliction of pain, and as a result formulate inductively the expectation that he will find himself dissuading other people who are inflicting pain, or acquire the habit, when observing an infliction of pain, of saying, 'Stop that!' The original approvals or dissuasions on which these two inductions rest must of course have been completely independent of any recognition that articles were borrowed or pain was inflicted. For, if the agent approved of returning the book to Jones *because* it was borrowed or if he dissuaded

---

3 *The Theory of Moral Sentiments*, 1st ed., p. 502. (Selby-Bigge, *British Moralists*, I, para. 344.)
4 *Ethics and Language*, p. 95.

Jill from pin sticking *because* it would cause pain, then the connection between 'right' and returning borrowed articles or between 'wrong' and causing pain would not have been an empirical generalization nor inductively established. It is this feature of the theory, concealed in most statements of it, which makes me hold that it is indubitably false. I suspect, however, that this is not the theory intended by some who say that moral rules are empirical generalizations. Yet this is the only proper and accurate sense of such an assertion.

MORAL RULES AS UTILITARIAN PRECEPTS

What is more often meant by those who say that moral rules are empirical generalizations is some form of utilitarian theory. On this view we discover that a number of particular actions are alike in that each produces the greatest possible good under the circumstances. We find that they also resemble each other in being the keeping of promises or the payment of debts. We conclude that promise keeping or debt paying will be likely in the next case or in most future cases to produce good and therefore to be right.

It is to be noticed, on this version of the theory, that the empirical generalization in question has to be supplemented by two other general statements before it can be taken as relevant to moral conduct at all. First, that certain *kinds* of states of affairs are good, and second, that that action is right which produces most good. Neither of these is an empirical generalization. It follows too that the empirical generalization itself is not a moral generalization but an ordinary factual generalization asserting that certain kinds of action are usually conducive to knowledge or pleasure (or fear or pain) or whatever is the particular result involved. The statement of this generalization is not itself a moral rule. It becomes a rule only with the addition of the two nonempirical propositions noted above. Thus G. E. Moore greatly oversimplifies his own utilitarian theory of moral rules when he says, 'All moral laws are merely statements that certain kinds of actions will have good effects'[5] or again that 'these laws are generalizations'.[6] The statement of the preceding point in approval language is obvious and need not be detailed here.

Now let us consider the utilitarian theory as thus more accurately restated. It rests, as we have seen, on one premise which, for a utilitarian, is not an inductive generalization, namely that the right action is that which produces the most good. Now one of the principal objections to this premise itself arises from the very existence of these moral rules which

---

[5] *Principia Ethica*, p. 146.
[6] Ibid., p. 22.

we have been considering, such as promise keeping and debt paying. Ross has shown, I think convincingly, that every moral agent frequently thinks it right to do an action which would produce less good than some other alternative open to him because this action, which he thinks right, is the fulfillment of a rule. It is right to keep a promise even on certain occasions when we should do more good by breaking it. It is right to pay a debt even on certain occasions when we might give the money to someone in greater need than our creditor.

The usual utilitarian explanation of this is that, when we compare the alternatives and appear forced to the conclusion that we must keep a rule even when it does less good than breaking it, we have not taken all the consequences into account. Full consideration of the consequences will show that, after all, keeping the rule has better consequences. I have promised a nephew to take him to the circus; why should I not take another boy who will enjoy it more? Because, if I do, my nephew will suffer not only circus shortage but also disappointment. But this utilitarian argument may be evaded. Suppose I have promised not my nephew but his parents and he knows nothing of the promise. He will not be disappointed. But, say the utilitarians, the parents will be, if not disappointed, then disillusioned about me and about promises in general. A man who breaks a particular promise weakens the whole system of trust and confidence, even if he does particular good to the particular people directly concerned. So too when I ask whether my money will do more good to my tailor to whom I owe it or to Famine Relief in Europe, I am not stating the case fairly. When I bilk my tailor I attack and weaken the whole credit system. My tailor versus Famine Relief is a one-sided contest. Famine Relief versus the credit system is a much fairer fight. But to meet this further utilitarian defence we need only apply more thoroughly the device we used with the small boy. He was not disappointed because he did not know I had promised. So in general the systems of credit or confidence will not be weakened unless other people know I have broken the rule. I promise a friend who is going to the wars that I will help to look after his children if he does not come back. He has told no one else of this arrangement. If he does not return, why, on utilitarian grounds, should I help his children rather than other children who need help more? If I break my promise no one will know and the system of trust and confidence will be wholly unaffected. All similar cases in which the keeping of a rule is defended by reference to its indirect consequences on the system can be met by the same method—'Break the rule and keep it dark.'[7] If no one else knows, the system cannot suffer.

---

[7] I may be allowed to refer to my article on 'Punishment' in *Mind*, XLVIII (1939), 155–57, where I give further examples to illustrate this point.

It may be said, however, that at least one person knows and that is the agent. The bad consequences on *him* of breaking a promise in order to do good explain why he ought to keep it. But what could these bad consequences be? There are only two alternative suggestions. Breaking the promise may be held to make him a morally worse man or to make him less likely to keep promises in future. The first answer begs the question. If he decides it is right to break the promise in order to do good, breaking it cannot make him a morally worse man. No one is now made morally worse by doing what he believes to be right. As for the second alternative, that it may make him more likely to break promises in future, it must be remembered that for a utilitarian theory promise keeping is a general rule to which there must be exceptions anyhow. It is desirable then that a man should not acquire a rigid habit of keeping promises but should remain capable of breaking the rule on the right occasions. And the right occasion for a utilitarian is one on which more good is done by breaking than by keeping it; and this is precisely one of those occasions. I conclude that these indirect utilitarian arguments fail to explain why it is sometimes right to keep a rule when breaking it would do more good to the parties directly concerned. As against the utilitarians, Ross is right.

Moore admits that we sometimes believe it right to keep a rule when so far as we can see more good will result from breaking it. But he gives a further utilitarian argument for holding this belief is justified. The argument is simply that our opinion that more good will be done by breaking it is very likely to be mistaken.

> For, if it is certain that in a large majority of cases the observance of a certain rule is useful, it follows that there is a large probability that it would be wrong to break the rule in any particular case; and the uncertainty of our knowledge both of effects and of their value, in particular cases, is so great, that it seems doubtful whether the individual's judgment that the effects will probably be good can ever be set against the general probability that that kind of action is wrong. Added to this general ignorance is the fact that, if the question arises at all, our judgment will generally be biased by the fact that we strongly desire one of the results which we hope to attain by breaking the rule. It seems then, with regard to any rule which is *generally* useful, we may assert that it ought *always* to be observed, not on the ground that in *every* particular case it will be useful, but on the ground that in *any* particular case the probability of its being so is greater than that of our being likely to decide rightly that we have before us an instance of its disutility.[8]

---

[8] *Principia Ethica*, p. 162. (Italics original.)

Now this is a very queer theory for a utilitarian to be forced to adopt. It results in imposing a Kantian attitude towards rules on all moral agents. Though it is in fact sometimes right to break a promise, I ought never to break one, because I can never tell when it is right to do so. Though truth telling is only *generally* and not universally useful I must never tell a lie. Again, the crucial cases arise when I have a 'conflict of duties' and when desire is not 'strongly engaged' on one side, as my examples have shown. I have no strong desire to give money to Famine Relief in Europe. This point is therefore irrelevant. Moreover, the whole argument is very queer. If 'in a large majority of cases' the rule is useful, this implies that in some cases it is not. And if 'it is certain that in most cases it is useful' this implies that we can recognize cases in which it is useful and therefore presumably cases in which it is not. But why then should we suppose that the case in point, in which we do seem to ourselves to recognize that it is not useful, is one in which we are probably mistaken? If we are probably mistaken here (because of our uncertainty about effects and about value) then are we not equally likely on all other cases to be mistaken? And then no one could ever establish that any rule is generally useful.

We now return to the difficulty, mentioned earlier, that rules vary from people to people. Other men have felt about hara-kiri, about dueling, and about vendettas just as we feel about debts and promises. They would maintain that it will not do to ask what good will be done if I commit ceremonial suicide, or call out my insulter, or kill a brother of my brother's murderer. It is not a question of doing good; it is a plain duty; honor not utility is at stake.

Faced by this difficulty some may sit back contentedly with a subjectivist or relativist view—and perhaps any nonpropositional theory of ethics (approval, emotive, or imperative) would be committed to this easy way out. There is no more need of explanation here than there is of the fact that men like different kinds of food.

Others will be content with an historical or causal explanation. We approve of debt paying, and Corsicans approve of vendetta, because we and they have been brought up so to approve. Rules are accepted because society imposes them. Get a child young enough and you could give it similar moral scruples about anything whatever. This, however, cannot be the whole truth. If it were, it would be impossible for a man ever to question the rules of his society and therefore impossible for the rules ever to change (unless the man arrived, like the Prince Consort, bringing with him the rules of some society to which he had previously belonged, or one society was absorbed into another by force, as Poland and Czechoslovakia have been—with consequent changes in their moral codes).

It is clear, however, that moral rules are criticized by members of the society whose rules they are and sometimes changed as a result of such criticism. How then can a moral rule be attacked or justified? I think the answer is by using Kant's test but by giving it a utilitarian twist which he carefully avoided. Is the rule justified? What would happen if it were universally observed? Kant held that in some cases universalization would produce a self-contradiction. A lie is a false statement made when it would deceive a hearer expecting the truth. A fairy story is not a lie. But if everyone misstated the truth there could be no expectation. Hence 'universal lying' is a contradiction. Stealing is taking the private property of another. If everyone took what others held, at will, there would be no private property; and thus 'universal stealing' is a contradiction. In other cases universalization involves no contradiction but it involves a state of affairs which his agent could not will universally because he could not will it for his own case. There would be no self-contradiction if all men let their good talents atrophy; but, says Kant, I could not will this universally because I could not will that my own talents should lie unused.[9]

Kant has been accused of utilitarianism in using these arguments, as if he were saying that the world would be a worse place if all men lied or stole or did not develop their talents. This is not so. But the self-contradiction argument, sound as it is so far, leaves a gap. Why should the institutions of communicative language and private property be accepted at all? Why should we not use language (as the Irish are sometimes said to do) to please or to amuse rather than to inform? What about communism as an alternative to private property? And it is not impossible for an agent to will not to use his own talents, for obviously this is just what is done by the lotus-eating South Sea islanders whom Kant meant to condemn.

May we not then use Kant's test but with the utilitarian addition? A rule is worthy of approval if a society in which it was observed would live a better life than one in which no rule in this field or an alternative rule were accepted. This solution seems first to have been put forward by Francis Hutcheson. 'The way of deciding about any disputed *practice* is to enquire whether this conduct or the contrary will most effectively promote the publick good. The morality is immediately adjusted when the natural *tendency* or influence of the action upon the universal natural good of mankind is agreed upon.' And compare his remark on passive obedience, 'The point disputed among men of sense was whether *universal* submission would probably be attended with greater natural evils than temporary insurrections where privileges were invaded.'[10]

---

[9] *Grundlegung* (*Works*, ed. Rosenkranz and Schubert, VIII, 47–50. Abbott, *Kant's Theory of Ethics*, pp. 39–41. Paton, *The Moral Law*, pp. 88–90).

[10] *An Inquiry concerning the Original of our Ideas of Virtue or Moral Good*, sect. ii, para. iii. (Selby-Bigge, *British Moralists*, I, para. 112.) (My italics.)

It is to be noted that there is a crucial difference between accepting the utilitarian validation of a rule and accepting the utilitarian account of the rightness of a particular action. This is sometimes missed or obscured. Even G. E. Moore obscures it, when he says: 'Apart from the immediate evils which murder generally produces, the fact that if it were a common practice the feeling of insecurity thus caused would absorb much time which might be spent to better purpose is perhaps conclusive against it.'[11] The general observance of a rule may have good consequences, while its observance in this particular case has bad consequences. When I approve a rule because its general observance would have good consequences, I approve a particular act which falls under the rule even in some cases where that particular act does less good than some alternative open to me. This is what is called acting on principle. I might well refuse to fight a duel with a man who had pushed me off the pavement even if I were the better swordsman and my adversary a man of whom the world would be well rid. Asked for my reasons I should not appeal to the consequences of this fight (for they would be good) nor to the consequences of my refusal on the general system of dueling (for I should still be right to refuse even if I were regarded as a crank or a coward, and the system remained unshaken). What I should be inclined to say is that dueling is a bad system. When adopted it has the effect of making all injuries equivalent. (This clearly could not be a reason against fighting any particular duel.) It is interesting, as an example of persuasive language, to see how this same point about the system can be described in opposite tones. Hegel speaks of the 'barbarity of the formal code of honor, which found in every injury an unpardonable insult' and Burke of 'that sensibility of principle, that chastity of honor, which felt a stain like a wound'. Moreover the dueling system makes punishment depend on aim or swordsmanship and not on guilt, so that a bully who is good with his weapons would be able (and encouraged by the system) to go about insulting and injuring people and counting on his skill to save him from any unpleasant consequences. (And this argument too cannot be used in the particular case in which I am refusing to fight for I am the better swordsman and the bully would not escape.)

What can be said against this explanation of the superiority of some rules to others? It may be objected[12] that nobody who keeps a promise or pays a debt does so for such recondite reasons. I should agree that many rules are obeyed, in life as in games, by people who have no idea why the rule holds (and 'why' here demands not history but justification). But most of my beliefs on matters of fact have no better basis than authority, and this does not mean that there can be no better evidence for them.

11 *Principia Ethica*, pp. 156–57.
12 Cf. I. Gallic, 'Oxford Moralists', *Philosophy* (1932).

Moral life like the rest of ordinary life is too short for everyone always to obtain or to demand the best kind of evidence possible for his beliefs. But when a belief is challenged it should be possible to ask what would be the right kind of evidence and to have some idea where to look for it.

Second, it may be said[13] that a man has a duty to pay his debts even if he regards the credit system as inferior to other systems (such as barter or loans only on security). Hence the rightness of his payment cannot be derived from the superior good produced by the system. There are two answers to this. First, there is the duty of supporting the existing system, whatever it may be, because of the general trust and confidence placed in it. Second, the man himself accepted the system when he incurred the debt. Perhaps a man who disapproves of the credit system should not incur debts. A parallel case is that of a judge whose obligation to enforce a bad law is due partly to the general good done by the system of law as a whole and partly to his own acceptance of the law as a whole when he took up his appointment.

It may be objected that I have now myself reduced moral rules to empirical generalizations. For a moral rule is validated if its general observance would produce more good than no rule or an alternative rule in the same field. And is not this an empirical generalization? On what could it rest except on the inspection of repeated observances of the rule compared, by inspection, with the working of alternative rules or the absence of a rule in the field in question?

Here the parallel with rules of a game may help. Some of the rules are needed to make the game the game that it is: that each bridge player should have thirteen cards, or that the association footballer should not carry the ball about in his hands. Alterations in these rules would result in a different game altogether. The new game might, of course, be a better game such as some say we owe to Mr. W. W. Ellis who in 1823 'with a fine disregard for the rules of football as played in his time first took the ball in his arms and ran with it'. Other rules, however, are justified by the fact that their observance makes the game in question a better game on the whole. The offside rule in football and the revoke rule in bridge have been altered with this aim and without making the game a different game altogether. Now none of these rules—neither the constitutive rules like the handling rule nor the regulative rules like the offside rule—could plausibly be called empirical generalizations. They are not justified by observing, prior to the formation of any rule, a number of games and discovering that those in which a certain practice was followed were better than those in which it was not and then laying down that practice as a rule. There are shorter cuts to the required conclusion. It does not require

---

[13] N. G. H. Robinson, *The Claim of Morality*, p. 277.

a series of experiments showing a high degree of frequency to establish the conclusion that the reduction of services in tennis from two to one would diminish the present advantage of the service and hence the premium placed on height and strength. No repeated observations are needed to show that the abolition of body-line bowling would improve the spirit of cricket, or that the change from auction to contract bridge would reduce the element of luck and make bidding more important than before in comparison with play. These conclusions are not and never were empirical generalizations. So too in life. No repeated observations are needed to establish that loans on security will be more readily given than credit without it, that a relaxation in the grounds for divorce will result in more divorces, or that the dueling system will encourage a bully who is a good swordsman in his evil ways. It is indeed one reason for some current suspicion of sociology, when practiced as an empirical science, that it takes much trouble to establish, by empirical methods, conclusions which are obvious without them, such as that the children of divorced parents are likely to present special problems, that two juries faced with the same evidence may reach opposite conclusions, or that a visible luxury, such as a car or a television apparatus, will have a prestige value and be bought by some people who cannot afford it and by others who do not use it.

Moral rules vary in the degree to which they are constitutive or merely regulative. There are some rules without which no civilized society could survive and few goods could be achieved. The rules against killing and promise breaking are of this kind (and this may be the reason why they have been supposed to be self-evident). Then there are rules essential to a particular institution or a particular kind of society, as the rule against theft is essential to a society of our kind. The abolition of such rules would involve a complete change (for example to a communist society). Or the abolition of the rules making parents specially responsible for their children would involve a complete change (for example to a Platonic Republic in which children were taken from their parents at birth and brought up in government crèches). These other societies would have their constitutive rules too, the communist society a rule against sabotage and the Platonic State a rule that children should not know who their parents are. Then there are regulative rules, which are alternative to others within a given society or institution and alterable without completely changing its structure, as a family system may be patriarchal or matriarchal, or a property system may rest on entailed inheritance or on free testamentary disposal. But, in regard to all these alternative institutions or rules within institutions, it is always possible and legitimate (and sometimes necessary) to ask which are the best rules.

A further difficulty in considering a rule as an empirical generalization, based on observing the good consequences of particular actions, arises where a rule is one of a number of rules essential *together* for the working of an institution, so that it cannot be said *alone* to have good results, and where its alteration would involve the alteration of other rules. If we admit the justice of opening the professions to women we shall have to alter our views about the duties of parents. If we defend equal pay we may find ourselves having to defend family allowances.

In estimating the general effects of a rule there is an additional complication which removes the process still further from anything plausibly called empirical generalization. For this description to be appropriate it would be necessary for the rule to be kept in a large number of cases and from each case taken by itself (or from each a majority of all cases) good results to follow. But normally the good results of a rule do not follow *seriatim* on the several observances of it. They follow from awareness that the rule has been adopted. A rule is laid down that thefts will be punished. The best results of this rule are achieved not when a series of people are punished for theft but when no one is punished at all, when the threat succeeds. The good produced by a rule that loans are to be repaid is produced by the belief that loans will be repaid, for the good in question comes from resources readily available to those who need them. Actual repayments or punishments come in primarily as applications of the rule and not as themselves sources of good (though they may incidentally achieve some good too).

This may be seen in another way. If the good were produced by the successive repayments or punishments themselves, it would be natural to expect it to vary, roughly at least, with the number of observances, and the harm done by breaking it to vary with the number of breakages. But this is not the case. A few failures to repay or punish may produce no harm at all. People feel no less secure because a few thieves escape justice. People find it no less easy to get credit because of the few actual bad debts which any tradesman expects. But in the increase of breakages there are two danger points, one when the increase affects confidence and another where it breaks the system. When the first point is reached, people who have previously shown no reaction to the rising tide of failures to pay or to punish suddenly take new and special precautions, double locking their doors or looking up customers in the local directory before giving them credit. Then, if the failures mount further, a new crisis may come when the system collapses altogether; tradesmen stop giving credit to anybody, or the people adopt lynch law. Banks know these two danger points. Ordinarily there is no problem; deposits balance withdrawals. Then there may be an increase in withdrawals, as general confidence in saving is weakened by a threat of inflation. At a certain point measures may have to be taken to counter this—perhaps a rise in the rate of interest. But if withdrawals continue to increase there may come a new crisis, a further loss of confidence, a run on the bank, and the system collapses altogether. This shows that the good done by rules is usually a matter of confidence. These successive crises of confidence, with their discontinuity from the steady rise of the tide of actual breakages of the rule, may be even more independent of numbers. A large number of breakages of which people are unaware will do little harm. A whole series of thefts at a single railway terminus or on a single route will do less harm (by doing less to shake confidence) than fewer thefts in a single street or group of streets. A dozen murders poorly publicized or widely distributed will do less harm to confidence than three, given front-page treatment or restricted to one locality.

Another corollary of the importance of confidence and expectation is that a bad rule may produce good results simply because it is a rule and thus makes planning possible. In this respect a bad rule may often be better than none. I may disapprove of the black market; but if a drug essential to save a life is obtainable only on the black market (but attainable there with complete certainty) I may be able to do more good than if there were no reliable source of supply. I may be able to plan my affairs more satisfactorily in a country where every official has his price (and the prices are well known) than in one in which nobody knows whether a service will be rendered without a bribe and I may spend my time insulting the honest or failing to bribe the venal.

These points about confidence and the value of a regular practice are the factors which drove G. E. Moore to his extreme conclusion that the only rules a moral agent ought to observe are rules which are both generally useful *and generally practiced*. For example Moore says: 'In a society in which certain kinds of theft are the common rule the utility of abstinence from such thefts on the part of a single individual is exceedingly doubtful, even though the common rule is a bad one.'[14] Moore admits that this position may be weakened by the possibility that the example given by breaking the bad rule may tend to break down the existing custom and so may have good results. But surely this is not how any moral agent would decide the question. Even if such thefts are common (and bootlegging or promiscuity may provide similar examples) it is surely obvious that anyone who believes that society would be better off without such practices will maintain that it is right for him to abstain from them, even if his example does nothing to weaken the practice. Moore then explicitly rejects the view I am defending, when he says:

> The question whether the general observance of a rule not generally observed, would or would not be desirable, cannot much affect the question how any individual ought to act; since on the one hand

---

[14] *Principia Ethica*, p. 164.

there is a large probability that he will not, by any means, be
able to bring about its general observance, and, on the other hand,
the fact that its general observance would be useful could, in any
case, give him no reason to conclude that he himself ought to
observe it in the absence of such general observance.[15]

IS A MORALITY OF RULES INADEQUATE?

There are various reasons which may be given for maintaining that this appeal to moral rules is inadequate, in addition to the
reason I have been examining, namely that decisions on particular cases
are prior and rules are empirical generalizations.

Some may urge that we sometimes see there is something wrong about
an action or proposed solution to a moral problem without being able in
the least to say what it is. 'It smells bad' we may say, or 'I don't like the
idea of that somehow'. Yet even in these situations there are two points to
be noted. First we are dissatisfied with them. We try to find out what it is
that is wrong and we feel we are on firmer ground if we find it. This would
be otiose on the view that the basic moral judgments are those on particular
cases and that rules are only 'rough generalizations useful for psychological
economy'. Second, even if we fail to find out just what it is that *is* wrong
we are quite sure about a number of things it is *not*. We may be sure
it is not the place or the date or the ages or parentage of the participants
or their education, or their nationality. And here is another general reason
for thinking that moral judgments or approvals are not 'of' particular
actions or situations. For in any moral action or situation (and not only
in the special cases we are now considering) the great majority of the
characteristics of the action or situation are recognized to be *irrelevant* to
the rightness of the decision or the goodness of the situation (if indeed
they are noticed at all).

We do not, of course, go about armed with fully formulated moral
rules which we apply by explicit syllogisms to particular cases. As Ross says:
'Rightness is recognized as belonging to particular acts in virtue of a
particular characteristic they possess.'[16] But this is to say that the general
rule is recognized in the particular case; and it is this recognition which
enables us not only to see what is relevant but to exclude what is irrelevant
also.

A second line of attack on rules as basic to morality comes from those
who contrast the morality of rules with the morality of grace or love or
'supererogation'. Rules are adequate for scribes and pharisees. Christian
morality requires of us more than the rules lay down, and turns away

---

[15] *Op. cit.*, p. 161.
[16] *The Foundations of Ethics*, p. 170.

from rules to personality and personal relationships. But this is surely a misunderstanding. The new morality came to fulfil the law not to destroy it, and issued in rules sterner and more uncompromising than the old rules, in rules which go to the heart of the matter and are not content with mere external observance.

A third type of opposition comes from the existentialists. Their favorite examples of moral decision are chosen to show that in the great crises of life rules are useless. Decisions have then to be made with anguish and desperation which commit the whole personality and involve a creative and unique response. On this I would make three comments. Even if we grant that some difficult and heroic decisions are well described by the existentialists, moral heroism and sublimity are no monopoly of such situations. The return of Regulus to Carthage, Sir Walter Scott's great battle to pay off his debts, Oates walking out into the snow so that he should not handicap his companions: these were all examples of obedience to simple and obvious moral rules and none the less splendid or difficult for being so. Secondly the existentialist himself admits an element of rule making in his moral decisions. He says: 'In committing myself I commit all men. . . . Thus I am responsible for myself and for all men. . . . A man accepts the responsibility not only for being what he chooses to be but of being a legislator choosing at the same time what the whole human race shall be.'[17] Thirdly what makes these typical existentialist decisions choices involving anguish and desperation is that they involve conflicts of rules. If there were no special aspects of situations which challenged the moral self, if the situation simply presented itself in all its complete reality and uniqueness, there would be no problem of moral decision. If there were no such rules as 'stand by your parents,' 'keep faith with your comrades', 'obey the Party' there would be no anguish in making the decision. The only anguish would be that of carrying it out in the face of natural feelings and temptations. Rules are the very stuff of moral life.

It is true, however, that there are features of moral judgment which my account of moral rules leaves unexplained. It does not explain or validate the basic judgments of good on which the rules themselves depend. This is to say that in the last resort moral insight or approval is not acceptance of rules but appreciation of values. Second, it does not explain how a decision between conflicting rules can be justified or validated. But there are two possible mitigations of this difficulty. It is possible to ask what values are achieved by the two conflicting rules, what importance each rule has in the whole fabric of social life, what would be the extent of the damage if either rule were abandoned. This can sometimes be more easily seen in a limited field. For example, as an examiner I may adopt

---

[17] J. Sartre, *L'Existentialisme est un Humanisme*, pp. 124–28.

two rules, one that examiners should not communicate with each other until all papers have been read, and another that an oral examination should be held. Now in some special case (for example a candidate suddenly summoned overseas) it may be impossible to give the candidate an adequate oral examination without consulting my fellow examiners before all the papers have been read by all of us. In this case I can compare the effects of the rules themselves. The nonconsultation rule could be given up altogether without substantial injustice; in fact many boards of examiners do not adopt it. But abolishing oral examinations does involve greater sacrifices; it is true many boards do not require oral examinations, but nevertheless I think they lose more by this than by abolishing the nonconsultation rule. I said earlier that it was vital to distinguish between the good done in general by the adoption of a rule and the good done by following a rule in a particular case. This example illustrates the point. For I could not possibly decide whether to prefer the nonconsultation rule to the oral rule by estimating the results in the particular case. For until we consult each other I cannot guess whether consultation will make any difference; and until the oral examination has been held it is impossible to estimate whether it would make any difference. It is not easy to apply this kind of method to moral rules of a less restricted kind. Yet I think such considerations can be, and sometimes are, taken into account over such debated issues as divorce or birth control. A second point about conflicts of rules is this. Such conflicts may be so frequent and so serious as to make us ask what it is about our whole way of life which appears to render these conflicts inevitable, and thus to attack the conflict at its source. It is one of the principal grounds for holding that war is evil that it is a prolific source of such conflicts of rules. In a modern war there are no 'happy warriors' except those whose sensitivity is so blunted or whose position is so subordinate that they can shut out or devolve their moral responsibilities entirely. Again it is an argument against a 'Pétainist' form of government that it creates moral conflicts for all except the most fanatical or the most self-seeking inhabitants of a conquered country. These considerations support the view which looks for the basis of morality, not in the particular action, nor in the moral rule, but in the kind of life a community will live when such-and-such rules hold within it.

MORAL RULES AND NONPROPOSITIONAL THEORIES

On the view I have been defending, a good reason (and the only good reason) for approving a particular action is that it is the carrying out of a rule; and a good reason (and the only good reason) for approving a rule is that its general adoption would do good on the whole. I now wish to consider, in conclusion, how nonpropositional theories of morals stand in relation to these suggestions.

On the simplest of such theories, the approval theory, these considerations fall outside ethics altogether. Ethical theory is restricted to the single proposition that moral judgments express approval. The various particular actions or sorts of actions which arouse such approval are the concern of the psychologist.[18] He will record the different things of which men approve and the causes which operate to produce these approvals. It will not make sense to ask a man who approves of Oates's action in walking out into the snow whether he has a good reason for doing so, any more than it makes sense to ask a man who likes the taste of rough cider whether he has a good reason for liking it. Moreover, the same action or rule may evoke approval in one man and disapproval in another. This again can only be accepted and recorded. It will not do to ask whether A who approves it or B who disapproves it is on stronger ground. Such attitudes neither require nor can receive any rational support; they are ultimate facts about the situation just as are the differing tastes of people in regard to tripe or garlic or eggs ten years old. If I say 'A's approval is justified' or 'this is worthy of approval, though B disapproves of it' I am simply expressing more emphatically than usual *my own* approval of it. On this consistent and simple version of the approval theory this lecture of mine has been merely a display of the sorts of approvals I myself experience. It is just a peculiarity of mine that I look for rules and approve of particular actions only in virtue of some general character; it is another peculiarity of mine that I approve of rules only in virtue of their general beneficence. And if these approval attitudes are found in others this is probably because they and I share the occupational disease of philosophers of wanting to find general justifications where none are necessary or even possible. If other people approve of actions not exemplifying rules or of rules without justifications these are merely facts about their psychology also.

The same conclusions follow on the simplest versions of the imperative or persuasive theory.[19] It is just a fact to be accepted that people do indulge in different or conflicting persuasions or issue different or conflicting commands.

Some nonpropositional theories, however, have noticed that people frequently maintain that they have good reasons for the ethical judgments they make and that ethical disagreement often does look very like argument. They admit that, so far as ethical judgments embody or imply

---

18 Cf. A. J. Ayer, *Language, Truth and Logic*, 2nd ed., p. 112.
19 Cf. R. Carnap, *Philosophy and Logical Syntax*, p. 24.

ordinary factual judgments, there can be good reason for these, and disagreement on them is argument. But such judgments are not moral nor is the disagreement about them moral disagreement. The moral element in a moral judgment is not a proposition and so cannot stand in a *logical* relation of entailment or implication or verification or probabilification to any proposition. These theorists, then, while they admit the importance of 'reasons' and 'argument' on moral issues have to maintain that moral argument is always merely persuasive rhetoric devoid of logical relevance and justified only by success in persuasion. And a moral agent's 'reason' for his own moral decision can never have any logical relation to the decision but only a causal relation. A 'good reason' means again only a successful persuasive utterance.[20]

Yet these are consistent conclusions for a nonpropositional theory to reach. For any admission that a reason was *required* for a moral imperative, or that it would have to be of a certain kind to be a *good* reason, would import into such a theory an element of objectivity which it is a principal aim of all such theories to banish. To claim that a moral attitude or imperative is justified or that there is a good reason for it has there to be dismissed as only an emphatic reiteration of the imperative itself or a nonrational attempt to persuade a hearer to assent to it.

But none of this is what anyone means to assert when he says that certain states of affairs are worthy of approval, whether in fact approved or not, or that a certain rule is justified and another is not. Thus, while the views I have been defending can be stated in terms of nonpropositional theories, their statement involves certain strains on these theories, interpreted as clarifications of moral usage. If my general line of argument about moral rules and their logical status has anything in it, it would seem to involve one of two results. Either nonpropositional theories of ethics stand in need of substantial revision and development and the crude and simple versions in which they have so far appeared fail to do justice to the complexity of moral experience. Or, perhaps, such theories cannot be revised to take these considerations into account without such radical alteration that they can no longer be regarded as adequate alternatives to a theory which retains an objectivist basis and is therefore more naturally expressed in a propositional language.

---

[20] C. L. Stevenson, *Ethics and Language*, pp. 6, 28, 30, 113, 168.

Two Concepts of Rules

JOHN RAWLS

In this paper I want to show the importance of the distinction between justifying a practice[1] and justifying a particular action falling under it, and I want to explain the logical basis of this distinction and how it is possible to miss its significance. While the distinction has frequently been made,[2] and is now becoming commonplace, there remains the task of explaining the tendency either to overlook it altogether, or to fail to appreciate its importance.

To show the importance of the distinction I am going to defend utilitarianism against those objections which have traditionally been made against it in connection with punishment and the obligation to keep promises. I hope to show that if one uses the distinction in question then one can state utilitarianism in a way which makes it a much better explication of our considered moral judgments than these traditional objections would seem to admit.[3] Thus the importance of the distinction is shown by

---

From The Philosophical Review, *LXIV (1955). Reprinted by permission of the author and* The Philosophical Review.

1 I use the word "practice" throughout as a sort of technical term meaning any form of activity specified by a system of rules which defines offices, roles, moves, penalties, defenses, and so on, and which gives the activity its structure. As examples one may think of games and rituals, trials and parliaments.

2 The distinction is central to Hume's discussion of justice in *A Treatise of Human Nature*, Bk. III, Pt. II, esp. secs. 2–4. It is clearly stated by John Austin in the second lecture of *Lectures on Jurisprudence*, 4th ed. (London, 1873), I, 116 ff (1st ed., 1832). Also it may be argued that J. S. Mill took it for granted in *Utilitarianism*; on this point cf. J. O. Urmson, "The Interpretation of the Moral Philosophy of J. S. Mill," *Philosophical Quarterly*, III (1953). In addition to the arguments given by Urmson there are several clear statements of the distinction in *A System of Logic*, 8th ed. (London, 1872), Bk. VI, Ch. XII, paras. 2, 3, 7. The distinction is fundamental to J. D. Mabbott's important paper, "Punishment," *Mind*, n.s., XLVIII (April, 1939). More recently the distinction has been stated with particular emphasis by S. E. Toulmin in *The Place of Reason in Ethics* (Cambridge, 1950), see esp. Ch. XI, where it plays a major part in his account of moral reasoning. Toulmin doesn't explain the basis of the distinction, nor how one might overlook its importance, as I try to in this paper, and in my review of his book (*Philosophical Review*, LX [October, 1951]), as some of my criticisms show, I failed to understand the force of it. See also H. D. Aiken, "The Levels of Moral Discourse," *Ethics*, LXII (1952), A. M. Quinton, "Punishment," *Analysis*, XIV (June, 1954), and P. H. Nowell-Smith, *Ethics* (London, 1954), pp. 236–39, 271–73.

3 On the concept of explication see the author's paper, *Philosophical Review*, LX (April, 1951).

the way it strengthens the utilitarian view regardless of whether that view is completely defensible or not.

To explain how the significance of the distinction may be overlooked, I am going to discuss two conceptions of rules. One of these conceptions conceals the importance of distinguishing between the justification of a rule or practice and the justification of a particular action falling under it. The other conception makes it clear why this distinction must be made and what is its logical basis.

1

The subject of punishment, in the sense of attaching legal penalties to the violation of legal rules, has always been a troubling moral question.[4] The trouble about it has not been that people disagree as to whether or not punishment is justifiable. Most people have held that, freed from certain abuses, it is an acceptable institution. Only a few have rejected punishment entirely, which is rather surprising when one considers all that can be said against it. The difficulty is with the justification of punishment: various arguments for it have been given by moral philosophers, but so far none of them has won any sort of general acceptance; no justification is without those who detest it. I hope to show that the use of the aforementioned distinction enables one to state the utilitarian view in a way which allows for the sound points of its critics.

For our purposes we may say that there are two justifications of punishment. What we may call the retributive view is that punishment is justified on the grounds that wrongdoing merits punishment. It is morally fitting that a person who does wrong should suffer in proportion to his wrongdoing. That a criminal should be punished follows from his guilt, and the severity of the appropriate punishment depends on the depravity of his act. The state of affairs where a wrongdoer suffers punishment is morally better than the state of affairs where he does not; and it is better irrespective of any of the consequences of punishing him.

What we may call the utilitarian view holds that on the principle that bygones are bygones and that only future consequences are material to present decisions, punishment is justifiable only by reference to the probable consequences of maintaining it as one of the devices of the social order. Wrongs committed in the past are, as such, not relevant considerations for deciding what to do. If punishment can be shown to promote effectively the interest of society it is justifiable, otherwise it is not.

---

[4] While this paper was being revised, Quinton's appeared; footnote 2 supra. There are several respects in which my remarks are similar to his. Yet as I consider some further questions and rely on somewhat different arguments, I have retained the discussion of punishment and promises together as two test cases for utilitarianism.

I have stated these two competing views very roughly to make one feel the conflict between them: one feels the force of *both* arguments and one wonders how they can be reconciled. From my introductory remarks it is obvious that the resolution which I am going to propose is that in this case one must distinguish between justifying a practice as a system of rules to be applied and enforced, and justifying a particular action which falls under these rules; utilitarian arguments are appropriate with regard to questions about practices, while retributive arguments fit the application of particular rules to particular cases.

We might try to get clear about this distinction by imagining how a father might answer the question of his son. Suppose the son asks, "Why was J put in jail yesterday?" The father answers, "Because he robbed the bank at B. He was duly tried and found guilty. That's why he was put in jail yesterday." But suppose the son had asked a different question, namely, "Why do people put other people in jail?" Then the father might answer, "To protect good people from bad people" or "To stop people from doing things that would make it uneasy for all of us; for otherwise we wouldn't be able to go to bed at night and sleep in peace." There are two very different questions here. One question emphasizes the proper name: it asks why J was punished rather than someone else, or it asks what he was punished for. The other question asks why we have the institution of punishment: why do people punish one another rather than, say, always forgiving one another?

Thus the father says in effect that a particular man is punished, rather than some other man, because he is guilty, and he is guilty because he broke the law (past tense). In his case the law looks back, the judge looks back, the jury looks back, and a penalty is visited upon him for something he did. That a man is to be punished, and what his punishment is to be, is settled by its being shown that he broke the law and that the law assigns that penalty for the violation of it.

On the other hand we have the institution of punishment itself, and recommend and accept various changes in it, because it is thought by the (ideal) legislator and by those to whom the law applies that, as a part of a system of law impartially applied from case to case arising under it, it will have the consequence, in the long run, of furthering the interests of society.

One can say, then, that the judge and the legislator stand in different positions and look in different directions: one to the past, the other to the future. The justification of what the judge does, *qua* judge, sounds like the retributive view; the justification of what the (ideal) legislator does, *qua* legislator, sounds like the utilitarian view. Thus both views have a point (this is as it should be since intelligent and sensitive persons have been on both sides of the argument); and one's initial confusion disappears once one sees that these views apply to persons holding different offices with different duties, and situated differently with respect to the system of rules that make up the criminal law.[5]

One might say, however, that the utilitarian view is more fundamental since it applies to a more fundamental office, for the judge carries out the legislator's will so far as he can determine it. Once the legislator decides to have laws and to assign penalties for their violation (as things are there must be both the law and the penalty) an institution is set up which involves a retributive conception of particular cases. It is part of the concept of the criminal law as a system of rules that the application and enforcement of these rules in particular cases should be justifiable by arguments of a retributive character. The decision whether or not to use law rather than some other mechanism of social control, and the decision as to what laws to have and what penalties to assign, may be settled by utilitarian arguments; but if one decides to have laws then one has decided on something whose working in particular cases is retributive in form.[6]

The answer, then, to the confusion engendered by the two views of punishment is quite simple: one distinguishes two offices, that of the judge and that of the legislator, and one distinguishes their different stations with respect to the system of rules which make up the law; and then one notes that the different sorts of considerations which would usually be offered as reasons for what is done under the cover of these offices can be paired off with the competing justifications of punishment. One reconciles the two views by the time-honored device of making them apply to different situations.

But can it really be this simple? Well, this answer allows for the apparent intent of each side. Does a person who advocates the retributive view necessarily advocate, as an *institution*, legal machinery whose essential purpose is to set up and preserve a correspondence between moral turpitude and suffering? Surely not.[7] What retributionists have rightly insisted upon is that no man can be punished unless he is guilty, that is, unless he has broken the law. Their fundamental criticism of the utilitarian account is that, as they interpret it, it sanctions an innocent person's being punished (if one may call it that) for the benefit of society.

On the other hand, utilitarians agree that punishment is to be inflicted only for the violation of law. They regard this much as understood from

[5] Note the fact that different sorts of arguments are suited to different offices. One way of taking the differences between ethical theories is to regard them as accounts of the reasons expected in different offices.

[6] In this connection see Mabbott, op. cit., pp. 163–64.

[7] On this point see Sir David Ross, *The Right and the Good* (Oxford, 1930), pp. 57–60.

the concept of punishment itself.[8] The point of the utilitarian account concerns the institution as a system of rules: utilitarianism seeks to limit its use by declaring it justifiable only if it can be shown to foster effectively the good of society. Historically it is a protest against the indiscriminate and ineffective use of the criminal law.[9] It seeks to dissuade us from assigning to penal institutions the improper, if not sacrilegious, task of matching suffering with moral turpitude. Like others, utilitarians want penal institutions designed so that, as far as humanly possible, only those who break the law run afoul of it. They hold that no official should have discretionary power to inflict penalties whenever he thinks it for the benefit of society; for on utilitarian grounds an institution granting such power could not be justified.[10]

The suggested way of reconciling the retributive and the utilitarian justifications of punishment seems to account for what both sides have wanted to say. There are, however, two further questions which arise, and I shall devote the remainder of this section to them.

First, will not a difference of opinion as to the proper criterion of just law make the proposed reconciliation unacceptable to retributionists? Will they not question whether, if the utilitarian principle is used as the criterion, it follows that those who have broken the law are guilty in a way which satisfies their demand that those punished deserve to be punished? To answer this difficulty, suppose that the rules of the criminal law are

---

8 See Hobbes's definition of punishment in *Leviathan*, Ch. XXVIII; and Bentham's definition in *The Principle of Morals and Legislation*, Ch. XII, para. 36, Ch. XV, para. 28, and in *The Rationale of Punishment* (London, 1830), Bk. I, Ch. I. They could agree with Bradley that: "Punishment is punishment only when it is deserved. We pay the penalty, because we owe it, and for no other reason; and if punishment is inflicted for any other reason whatever than because it is merited by wrong, it is a gross immorality, a crying injustice, an abominable crime, and not what it pretends to be." *Ethical Studies*, 2nd ed. (Oxford, 1927), pp. 26–27. Certainly by definition it isn't what it pretends to be. The innocent can only be punished by mistake; deliberate "punishment" of the innocent necessarily involves fraud.

9 Cf. Leon Radzinowicz, *A History of English Criminal Law: The Movement for Reform 1750–1833* (London, 1948), esp. Ch. XI on Bentham.

10 Bentham discusses how corresponding to a punitory provision of a criminal law there is another provision which stands to it as an antagonist and which needs a name as much as the punitory. He calls it, as one might expect, the *anætiosostic*, and of it he says: "The punishment of guilt is the object of the former one: the preservation of innocence that of the latter." In the same connection he asserts that it is never thought fit to give the judge the option of deciding whether a thief (that is, a person whom he believes to be a thief, for the judge's belief is what the question must always turn upon) should hang or not, and so the law writes the provision: "The judge shall not cause a thief to be hanged unless he have been duly convicted and sentenced in course of law" (*The Limits of Jurisprudence Defined*, ed. C. W. Everett [New York, 1945], pp. 238–39).

justified on utilitarian grounds (it is only for laws that meet his criterion that the utilitarian can be held responsible). Then it follows that the actions which the criminal law specifies as offenses are such that, if they were tolerated, terror and alarm would spread in society. Consequently, retributionists can only deny that those who are punished deserve to be punished if they deny that such actions are wrong. This they will not want to do.

The second question is whether utilitarianism doesn't justify too much. One pictures it as an engine of justification which, if consistently adopted, could be used to justify cruel and arbitrary institutions. Retributionists may be supposed to concede that utilitarians *intend* to reform the law and to make it more humane; that utilitarians do not *wish* to justify any such thing as punishment of the innocent; and that utilitarians may appeal to the fact that punishment presupposes guilt in the sense that by punishment one understands an institution attaching penalties to the infraction of legal rules, and therefore that it is logically absurd to suppose that utilitarians in justifying *punishment* might also have justified punishment (if we may call it that) of the innocent. The real question, however, is whether the utilitarian, in justifying punishment, hasn't used arguments which commit him to accepting the infliction of suffering on innocent persons if it is for the good of society (whether or not one calls this punishment). More generally, isn't the utilitarian committed in principle to accepting many practices which he, as a morally sensitive person, wouldn't want to accept? Retributionists are inclined to hold that there is no way to stop the utilitarian principle from justifying too much except by adding to it a principle which distributes certain rights to individuals. Then the amended criterion is not the greatest benefit of society *simpliciter,* but the greatest benefit of society subject to the constraint that no one's rights may be violated. Now while I think that the classical utilitarians proposed a criterion of this more complicated sort, I do not want to argue that point here.[11] What I want to show is that there is *another* way of preventing the utilitarian principle from justifying too much, or at least of making it much less likely to do so: namely, by stating utilitarianism in a way which accounts for the distinction between the justification of an institution and the justification of a particular action falling under it.

I begin by defining the institution of punishment as follows: a person is said to suffer punishment whenever he is legally deprived of some of the normal rights of a citizen on the ground that he has violated a rule of law, the violation having been established by trial according to the due process of law, provided that the deprivation is carried out by the recognized legal authorities of the state, that the rule of law clearly specifies both the

---

[11] By the classical utilitarians I understand Hobbes, Hume, Bentham, J. S. Mill, and Sidgwick.

offense and the attached penalty, that the courts construe statutes strictly, and that the statute was on the books prior to the time of the offense.[12] This definition specifies what I shall understand by punishment. The question is whether utilitarian arguments may be found to justify institutions widely different from this and such as one would find cruel and arbitrary.

This question is best answered, I think, by taking up a particular accusation. Consider the following from Carritt:

> ... the utilitarian must hold that we are justified in inflicting pain always and only to prevent worse pain or bring about greater happiness. This, then, is all we need to consider in so-called punishment, which must be purely preventive. But if some kind of very cruel crime becomes common, and none of the criminals can be caught, it might be highly expedient, as an example, to hang an innocent man, if a charge against him could be so framed that he were universally thought guilty; indeed this would only fail to be an ideal instance of utilitarian 'punishment' because the victim himself would not have been so likely as a real felon to commit such a crime in the future; in all other respects it would be perfectly deterrent and therefore felicific.[13]

Carritt is trying to show that there are occasions when a utilitarian argument would justify taking an action which would be generally condemned; and thus that utilitarianism justifies too much. But the failure of Carritt's argument lies in the fact that he makes no distinction between the justification of the general system of rules which constitutes penal institutions and the justification of particular applications of these rules to particular cases by the various officials whose job it is to administer them. This becomes perfectly clear when one asks who the "we" are of whom Carritt speaks. Who is this who has a sort of absolute authority on particular occasions to decide that an innocent man shall be "punished" if everyone can be convinced that he is guilty? Is this person the legislator, or the judge, or the body of private citizens, or what? It is utterly crucial to know who is to decide such matters, and by what authority, for all of this must be written into the rules of the institution. Until one knows these things one doesn't know what the institution is whose justification is being challenged; and as the utilitarian principle applies to the institution one doesn't know whether it is justifiable on utilitarian grounds or not.

Once this is understood it is clear what the counter-move to Carritt's argument is. One must describe more carefully what the *institution* is which his example suggests, and then ask oneself whether or not it is likely that

---

[12] All these features of punishment are mentioned by Hobbes; cf. *Leviathan*, Ch. XXVIII.

[13] *Ethical and Political Thinking* (Oxford, 1947), p. 65.

having this institution would be for the benefit of society in the long run. One must not content oneself with the vague thought that, when it's a question of *this* case, it would be a good thing if somebody did something even if an innocent person were to suffer.

Try to imagine, then, an institution (which we may call "telishment") which is such that the officials set up by it have authority to arrange a trial for the condemnation of an innocent man whenever they are of the opinion that doing so would be in the best interests of society. The discretion of officials is limited, however, by the rule that they may not condemn an innocent man to undergo such an ordeal unless there is, at the time, a wave of offenses similar to that with which they charge him and telish him for. We may imagine that the officials having the discretionary authority are the judges of the higher courts in consultation with the chief of police, the minister of justice, and a committee of the legislature.

Once one realizes that one is involved in setting up an *institution*, one sees that the hazards are very great. For example, what check is there on the officials? How is one to tell whether or not their actions are authorized? How is one to limit the risks involved in allowing such systematic deception? How is one to avoid giving anything short of complete discretion to the authorities to telish anyone they like? In addition to these considerations, it is obvious that people will come to have a very different attitude towards their penal system when telishment is adjoined to it. They will be uncertain as to whether a convicted man has been punished or telished. They will wonder whether or not they should feel sorry for him. They will wonder whether the same fate won't at any time fall on them. If one pictures how such an institution would actually work, and the enormous risks involved in it, it seems clear that it would serve no useful purpose. A utilitarian justification for this institution is most unlikely.

It happens in general that as one drops off the defining features of punishment one ends up with an institution whose utilitarian justification is highly doubtful. One reason for this is that punishment works like a kind of price system: by altering the prices one has to pay for the performance of actions it supplies a motive for avoiding some actions and doing others. The defining features are essential if punishment is to work in this way; so that an institution which lacks these features, e.g., an institution which is set up to "punish" the innocent, is likely to have about as much point as a price system (if one may call it that) where the prices of things change at random from day to day and one learns the price of something after one has agreed to buy it.[14]

---

[14] The analogy with the price system suggests an answer to the question how utilitarian considerations insure that punishment is proportional to the offense. It is interesting to note that David Ross, after making the distinction between justifying

If one is careful to apply the utilitarian principle to the institution which is to authorize particular actions, then there is *less* danger of its justifying too much. Carritt's example gains plausibility by its indefiniteness and by its concentration on the particular case. His argument will only hold if it can be shown that there are utilitarian arguments which justify an institution whose publicly ascertainable offices and powers are such as to permit officials to exercise that kind of discretion in particular cases. But the requirement of having to build the arbitrary features of the particular decision into the institutional practice makes the justification much less likely to go through.

2

I shall now consider the question of promises. The objection to utilitarianism in connection with promises seems to be this: it is believed that on the utilitarian view when a person makes a promise the only ground upon which he should keep it, if he should keep it, is that by keeping it he will realize the most good on the whole. So that if one asks the question "Why should I keep *my* promise?" the utilitarian answer is understood to be that doing so in *this* case will have the best consequences. And this answer is said, quite rightly, to conflict with the way in which the obligation to keep promises is regarded.

Now of course critics of utilitarianism are not unaware that one defense sometimes attributed to utilitarians is the consideration involving the practice of promise keeping.[15] In this connection they are supposed to argue some-

---

a penal law and justifying a particular application of it, and after stating that utilitarian considerations have a large place in determining the former, still holds back from accepting the utilitarian justification of punishment on the grounds that justice requires that punishment be proportional to the offense, and that utilitarianism is unable to account for this. Cf. *The Right and the Good*, pp. 61–62. I do not claim that utilitarianism can account for this requirement as Sir David might wish, but it happens, nevertheless, that if utilitarian considerations are followed penalties will be proportional to offenses in this sense: the order of offenses according to seriousness can be paired off with the order of penalties according to severity. Also the absolute level of penalties will be as low as possible. This follows from the assumption that people are rational (i.e., that they are able to take into account the "prices" the state puts on actions), the utilitarian rule that a penal system should provide a motive for preferring the less serious offense, and the principle that punishment as such is an evil. All this was carefully worked out by Bentham in *The Principles of Morals and Legislation*, Chs. XIII–XV.

15 Ross, *The Right and the Good*, pp. 37–39, and *Foundations of Ethics* (Oxford, 1939), pp. 92–94. I know of no utilitarian who has used this argument except W. A. Pickard-Cambridge in "Two Problems about Duty," *Mind*, n.s., XLI (April, 1932), 153–57, although the argument goes with G. E. Moore's version of utilitarianism in *Principia Ethica* (Cambridge, 1903). To my knowledge it does not appear in the classical utilitarians; and if one interprets their view correctly this is no accident.

thing like this: it must be admitted that we feel strictly about keeping promises, more strictly than it might seem our view can account for. But when we consider the matter carefully it is always necessary to take into account the effect which our action will have on the practice of making promises. The promisor must weigh, not only the effects of breaking his promise on the particular case, but also the effect which his breaking his promise will have on the practice itself. Since the practice is of great utilitarian value, and since breaking one's promise always seriously damages it, one will seldom be justified in breaking one's promise. If we view our individual promises in the wider context of the practice of promising itself we can account for the strictness of the obligation to keep promises. There is always one very strong utilitarian consideration in favor of keeping them, and this will insure that when the question arises as to whether or not to keep a promise it will usually turn out that one should, even where the facts of the particular case taken by itself would seem to justify one's breaking it. In this way the strictness with which we view the obligation to keep promises is accounted for.

Ross has criticized this defense as follows:[16] however great the value of the practice of promising, on utilitarian grounds, there must be some value which is greater, and one can imagine it to be obtainable by breaking a promise. Therefore there might be a case where the promisor could argue that breaking his promise was justified as leading to a better state of affairs on the whole. And the promisor could argue in this way no matter how slight the advantage won by breaking the promise. If one were to challenge the promisor his defense would be that what he did was best on the whole in view of all the utilitarian considerations, which in this case *include* the importance of the practice. Ross feels that such a defense would be unacceptable. I think he is right insofar as he is protesting against the appeal to consequences in general and without further explanation. Yet it is extremely difficult to weigh the force of Ross's argument. The kind of case imagined seems unrealistic and one feels that it needs to be described. One is inclined to think that it would either turn out that such a case came under an exception defined by the practice itself, in which case there would not be an appeal to consequences in general on the particular case, or it would happen that the circumstances were so peculiar that the conditions which the practice presupposes no longer obtained. But certainly Ross is right in thinking that it strikes us as wrong for a person to defend breaking a promise by a general appeal to consequences. For a general utilitarian defense is not open to the promisor: it is not one of the defenses allowed by the practice of making promises.

---

[16] Ross, *The Right and the Good*, pp. 38–39.

Ross gives two further counter-arguments:[17] First, he holds that it overestimates the damage done to the practice of promising by a failure to keep a promise. One who breaks a promise harms his own name certainly, but it isn't clear that a broken promise always damages the practice itself sufficiently to account for the strictness of the obligation. Second, and more important, I think, he raises the question of what one is to say of a promise which isn't known to have been made except to the promisor and the promisee, as in the case of a promise a son makes to his dying father concerning the handling of the estate.[18] In this sort of case the consideration relating to the practice doesn't weigh on the promisor at all, and yet one feels that this sort of promise is as binding as other promises. The question of the effect which breaking it has on the practice seems irrelevant. The only consequence seems to be that one can break the promise without running any risk of being censured; but the obligation itself seems not the least weakened. Hence it is doubtful whether the effect on the practice ever weighs in the particular case; certainly it cannot account for the strictness of the obligation where it fails to obtain. It seems to follow that a utilitarian account of the obligation to keep promises cannot be successfully carried out.

From what I have said in connection with punishment, one can foresee what I am going to say about these arguments and counter-arguments. They fail to make the distinction between the justification of a practice and the justification of a particular action falling under it, and therefore they fall into the mistake of taking it for granted that the promisor, like Carritt's official, is entitled without restriction to bring utilitarian considerations to bear in deciding whether to keep *his* promise. But if one considers what the practice of promising is one will see, I think, that it is such as not to allow this sort of general discretion to the promisor. Indeed, the point of the practice is to abdicate one's title to act in accordance with utilitarian and prudential considerations in order that the future may be tied down and plans coordinated in advance. There are obvious utilitarian advantages in having a practice which denies to the promisor, as a defense, any

---

17 Ross, *ibid.*, p. 39. The case of the nonpublic promise is discussed again in *Foundations of Ethics*, pp. 95–96, 104–105. It occurs also in Mabbott, "Punishment," op. cit., pp. 155–57, and in A. I. Melden, "Two Comments on Utilitarianism," *Philosophical Review*, LX (October, 1951), 519–23, which discusses Carritt's example in *Ethical and Political Thinking*, p. 64.

18 Ross's example is described simply as that of two men dying alone where one makes a promise to the other. Carritt's example (cf. n. 17 supra) is that of two men at the North Pole. The example in the text is more realistic and is similar to Mabbott's. Another example is that of being told something in confidence by one who subsequently dies. Such cases need not be "desert island arguments" as Nowell-Smith seems to believe (cf. his *Ethics*, pp. 239–44).

general appeal to the utilitarian principle in accordance with which the practice itself may be justified. There is nothing contradictory, or surprising, in this: utilitarian (or aesthetic) reasons might properly be given in arguing that the game of chess, or baseball, is satisfactory just as it is, or in arguing that it should be changed in various respects, but a player in a game cannot properly appeal to such considerations as reasons for his making one move rather than another. It is a mistake to think that if the practice is justified on utilitarian grounds then the promisor must have complete liberty to use utilitarian arguments to decide whether or not to keep his promise. The practice forbids this general defense; and it is a purpose of the practice to do this. Therefore what the above arguments presuppose—the idea that if the utilitarian view is accepted then the promisor is bound if, and only if, the application of the utilitarian principle to his own case shows that keeping it is best on the whole—is false. The promisor is bound because he promised: weighing the case on its merits is not open to him.[19]

Is this to say that in particular cases one cannot deliberate whether or not to keep one's promise? Of course not. But to do so is to deliberate whether the various excuses, exceptions and defenses, which are understood by, and which constitute an important part of, the practice, apply to one's own case.[20] Various defenses for not keeping one's promise are allowed, but among them there isn't the one that, on general utilitarian grounds, the promisor (truly) thought his action best on the whole, even though there may be the defense that the consequences of keeping one's promise would have been *extremely* severe. While there are too many complexities here to consider all the necessary details, one can see that the general defense isn't allowed if one asks the following question: what would one say of someone who, when asked why he broke his promise, replied simply that breaking it was best on the whole? Assuming that his reply is sincere, and that his belief was reasonable (i.e., one need not consider the possibility that he was mistaken), I think that one would question whether or not he knows what it means to say "I promise" (in the appropriate circumstances). It would be said of someone who used this excuse without further explanation that he didn't understand what defenses the practice, which defines a promise, allows to him. If a child were to use this excuse one would correct him; for it is part of the way one is taught the concept of a promise to be corrected if one uses this excuse. The point of having the practice would be lost if the practice did allow this excuse.

---

[19] What I have said in this paragraph seems to me to coincide with Hume's important discussion in the *Treatise of Human Nature*, Bk. III, Pt. II, sec. 5; and also sec. 6, para. 8.

[20] For a discussion of these, see H. Sidgwick, *The Methods of Ethics*, 6th ed. (London, 1901), Bk. III, Ch. VI.

It is no doubt part of the utilitarian view that every practice should admit the defense that the consequences of abiding by it would have been extremely severe; and utilitarians would be inclined to hold that some reliance on people's good sense and some concession to hard cases is necessary. They would hold that a practice is justified by serving the interests of those who take part in it; and as with any set of rules there is understood a background of circumstances under which it is expected to be applied and which need not—indeed which cannot—be fully stated. Should these circumstances change, then even if there is no rule which provides for the case, it may still be in accordance with the practice that one be released from one's obligation. But this sort of defense allowed by a practice must not be confused with the general option to weigh each particular case on utilitarian grounds which critics of utilitarianism have thought it necessarily to involve.

The concern which utilitarianism raises by its justification of punishment is that it may justify too much. The question in connection with promises is different: it is how utilitarianism can account for the obligation to keep promises at all. One feels that the recognized obligation to keep one's promise and utilitarianism are incompatible. And to be sure, they are incompatible if one interprets the utilitarian view as necessarily holding that each person has complete liberty to weigh every particular action on general utilitarian grounds. But must one interpret utilitarianism in this way? I hope to show that, in the sorts of cases I have discussed, one cannot interpret it in this way.

3

So far I have tried to show the importance of the distinction between the justification of a practice and the justification of a particular action falling under it by indicating how this distinction might be used to defend utilitarianism against two long-standing objections. One might be tempted to close the discussion at this point by saying that utilitarian considerations should be understood as applying to practices in the first instance and not to particular actions falling under them except insofar as the practices admit of it. One might say that in this modified form it is a better account of our considered moral opinions and let it go at that. But to stop here would be to neglect the interesting question as to how one can fail to appreciate the significance of this rather obvious distinction and can take it for granted that utilitarianism has the consequence that particular cases may always be decided on general utilitarian grounds.[21]

---

[21] So far as I can see it is not until Moore that the doctrine is expressly stated in this way. See, for example, *Principia Ethica*, p. 147, where it is said that the statement "I am morally bound to perform this action" is identical with the state-

I want to argue that this mistake may be connected with misconceiving the logical status of the rules of practices; and to show this I am going to examine two conceptions of rules, two ways of placing them within the utilitarian theory.

The conception which conceals from us the significance of the distinction I am going to call the summary view. It regards rules in the following way: one supposes that each person decides what he shall do in particular cases by applying the utilitarian principle; one supposes further that different people will decide the same particular case in the same way and that there will be recurrences of cases similar to those previously decided. Thus it will happen that in cases of certain kinds the same decision will be made either by the same person at different times or by different persons at the same time. If a case occurs frequently enough one supposes that a rule is formulated to cover that sort of case. I have called this conception the summary view because rules are pictured as summaries of past decisions arrived at by the *direct* application of the utilitarian principle to particular cases. Rules are regarded as reports that cases of a certain sort have been found on *other* grounds to be properly decided in a certain way (although, of course, they do not *say* this).

There are several things to notice about this way of placing rules within the utilitarian theory.[22]

---

ment "*This* action will produce the greatest possible amount of good in the Universe" (my italics). It is important to remember that those whom I have called the classical utilitarians were largely interested in social institutions. They were among the leading economists and political theorists of their day, and they were not infrequently reformers interested in practical affairs. Utilitarianism historically goes together with a coherent view of society, and is not simply an ethical theory, much less an attempt at philosophical analysis in the modern sense. The utilitarian principle was quite naturally thought of, and used, as a criterion for judging social institutions (practices) and as a basis for urging reforms. It is not clear, therefore, how far it is necessary to amend utilitarianism in its classical form. For a discussion of utilitarianism as an integral part of a theory of society, see L. Robbins, *The Theory of Economic Policy in English Classical Political Economy* (London, 1952).

22 This footnote should be read after sec. 3 and presupposes what I have said there. It provides a few references to statements by leading utilitarians of the summary conception. In general it appears that when they discussed the logical features of rules the summary conception prevailed and that it was typical of the way they talked about moral rules. I cite a rather lengthy group of passages from Austin as a full illustration.

John Austin in his *Lectures on Jurisprudence* meets the objection that deciding in accordance with the utilitarian principle case by case is impractical by saying that this is a misinterpretation of utilitarianism. Accordng to the utilitarian view "... our conduct would conform to *rules* inferred from the tendencies of actions, but would not be determined by a direct resort to the principle of general utility. Utility would be the test of our conduct, ultimately, but not immediately: the immediate test of the rules to which our conduct would conform, but not the immediate test of specific or individual actions. Our rules would be fashioned on utility; our conduct, on our rules" (Vol. I, p. 116). As to how one decides on the tendency of an action he says: "If we would try the tendency of a specific or individual act, we must not contemplate the act as if it were single and insulated, but must look at the class of acts to which it belongs. We must suppose that acts of the class were generally done or omitted, and consider the probable effect upon the general happiness or good. We must guess the consequences which would follow, if the class of acts were general; and also the consequences which would follow, if they were generally omitted. We must then compare the consequences on the positive and negative sides, and determine on which of the two the *balance* of advantage lies. . . . If we truly try the tendency of a specific or individual act, we try the tendency of the class to which that act belongs. The *particular* conclusion which we draw, with regard to the single act, implies a *general* conclusion embracing all similar acts. . . . To the rules thus inferred, and lodged in the memory, our conduct would conform *immediately* if it were truly adjusted to utility" (*ibid.*, p. 117). One might think that Austin meets the objection by stating the practice conception of rules; and perhaps he did intend to. But it is not clear that he has stated this conception. Is the generality he refers to of the statistical sort? This is suggested by the notion of tendency. Or does he refer to the utility of setting up a practice? I don't know; but what suggests the summary view is his subsequent remarks. He says: "To consider the specific consequences of single or individual acts, would *seldom* [my italics] consist with that ultimate principle" (*ibid.*, p. 117). But would one ever do this? He continues: ". . . this being admitted, the necessity of pausing and calculating, which the objection in question supposes, is an imagined necessity. To preface each act or forbearancy by a conjecture and comparison of consequences, were clearly *superfluous* [my italics] and mischievous. It were clearly superfluous, inasmuch as the *result of that process* [my italics] would be embodied in a known *rule*. It were clearly mischievous, inasmuch as the *true* result would be expressed by that rule, whilst the process would probably be faulty, if it were done on the spur of the occasion" (*ibid.*, pp. 117–18). He goes on: "If our experience and observation of particulars were not *generalized*, our experience and observation of particulars would seldom avail us in *practice.* . . . The inferences suggested to our minds by repeated experience and observation are, therefore, drawn into *principles*, or compressed into *maxims*. These we carry about us ready for use, and apply to individual cases promptly . . . without reverting to the process by which they were obtained; or without recalling, and arraying before our minds, the numerous and intricate considerations of which they are *handy abridgments* [my italics]. . . . True theory is a *compendium* of particular truths. . . . Speaking then, generally, human conduct is inevitably *guided* [my italics] by *rules*, or by *principles* or *maxims*" (*ibid.*, pp. 117–18). I need not trouble to show how all these remarks incline to the summary view. Further, when Austin comes to deal with cases of "comparatively rare occurrence" he holds that specific considerations may outweigh the general. "Looking at the reasons from which we had inferred the rule, it were absurd to think it inflexible. We should therefore dismiss the *rule;* resort directly to the *principle* upon which our rules were fashioned; and calculate *specific* consequences to the best of our knowledge and ability" (ibid., pp. 120–21). Austin's view is interesting because it shows how one may come close to the practice conception and then slide away from it.

In *A System of Logic*, Bk. VI, Ch. XII, para. 2, Mill distinguished clearly between the position of judge and legislator and in doing so suggests the distinction between the two concepts of rules. However, he distinguishes the two positions to

1. The point of having rules derives from the fact that similar cases tend to recur and that one can decide cases more quickly if one records past decisions in the form of rules. If similar cases didn't recur, one would be required to apply the utilitarian principle directly, case by case, and rules reporting past decisions would be of no use.

2. The decisions made on particular cases are logically prior to rules. Since rules gain their point from the need to apply the utilitarian principle to many similar cases, it follows that a particular case (or several cases

---

illustrate the difference between cases where one is to apply a rule already established and cases where one must formulate a rule to govern subsequent conduct. It's the latter case that interests him and he takes the "maxim of policy" of a legislator as typical of rules. In para. 3 the summary conception is very clearly stated. For example, he says of rules of conduct that they should be taken provisionally, as they are made for the most numerous cases. He says that they "point out" the manner in which it is least perilous to act; they serve as an "admonition" that a certain mode of conduct has been found suited to the most common occurrences. In *Utilitarianism*, Ch. II, para. 24, the summary conception appears in Mill's answer to the same objection Austin considered. Here he speaks of rules as "corollaries" from the principle of utility; these "secondary" rules are compared to "landmarks" and "direction posts." They are based on long experience and so make it unnecessary to apply the utilitarian principle to each case. In para. 25 Mill refers to the task of the utilitarian principle in adjudicating between competing moral rules. He talks here as if one then applies the utilitarian principle directly to the particular case. On the practice view one would rather use the principle to decide which of the ways that make the practice consistent is the best. It should be noted that while in para. 10 Mill's definition of utilitarianism makes the utilitarian principle apply to morality, i.e., to the rules and precepts of human conduct, the definition in para. 2 uses the phrase "actions are right in *proportion* as they *tend* to promote happiness" [my italics] and this inclines towards the summary view. In the last paragraph of the essay "On the Definition of Political Economy," *Westminster Review* (October, 1836), Mill says that it is only in art, as distinguished from science, that one can properly speak of exceptions. In a question of practice, if something is fit to be done "in the majority of cases" then it is made the rule. "We may ... in talking of art *unobjectionably* speak of the *rule* and the *exception*, meaning by the rule the cases in which there exists a preponderance ... of inducements for acting in a particular way; and by the exception, the cases in which the preponderance is on the contrary side." These remarks, too, suggest the summary view.

In Moore's *Principia Ethica*, Ch. V, there is a complicated and difficult discussion of moral rules. I will not examine it here except to express my suspicion that the summary conception prevails. To be sure, Moore speaks frequently of the utility of rules as generally followed, and of actions as generally practiced, but it is possible that these passages fit the statistical notion of generality which the summary conception allows. This conception is suggested by Moore's taking the utilitarian principle as applying directly to particular actions (pp. 147–48) and by his notion of a rule as something indicating which of the few alternatives likely to occur to anyone will generally produce a greater total good in the immediate future (p. 154). He talks of an "ethical law" as a prediction, and as a generalization (pp. 146, 155). The summary conception is also suggested by his discussion of exceptions (pp. 162–63) and of the force of examples of breaching a rule (pp. 163–64).

similar to it) may exist whether or not there is a rule covering that case. We are pictured as recognizing particular cases prior to there being a rule which covers them, for it is only if we meet with a number of cases of a certain sort that we formulate a rule. Thus we are able to describe a particular case as a particular case of the requisite sort whether there is a rule regarding *that* sort of case or not. Put another way: what the A's and the B's refer to in rules of the form 'Whenever A do B' may be described as A's and B's whether or not there is the rule 'Whenever A do B', or whether or not there is any body of rules which make up a practice of which that rule is a part.

To illustrate this consider a rule, or maxim, which could arise in this way: suppose that a person is trying to decide whether to tell someone who is fatally ill what his illness is when he has been asked to do so. Suppose the person to reflect and then decide, on utilitarian grounds, that he should not answer truthfully; and suppose that on the basis of this and other like occasions he formulates a rule to the effect that when asked by someone fatally ill what his illness is, one should not tell him. The point to notice is that someone's being fatally ill and asking what his illness is, and someone's telling him, are things that can be described as such whether or not there is this rule. The performance of the action to which the rule refers doesn't require the stage setting of a practice of which this rule is a part. This is what is meant by saying that on the summary view particular cases are logically prior to rules.

3. Each person is in principle always entitled to reconsider the correctness of a rule and to question whether or not it is proper to follow it in a particular case. As rules are guides and aids, one may ask whether in past decisions there might not have been a mistake in applying the utilitarian principle to get the rule in question, and wonder whether or not it is best in this case. The reason for rules is that people are not able to apply the utilitarian principle effortlessly and flawlessly; there is need to save time and to post a guide. On this view a society of rational utilitarians would be a society without rules in which each person applied the utilitarian principle directly and smoothly, and without error, case by case. On the other hand, ours is a society in which rules are formulated to serve as aids in reaching these ideally rational decisions on particular cases, guides which have been built up and tested by the experience of generations. If one applies this view to rules, one is interpreting them as maxims, as "rules of thumb"; and it is doubtful that anything to which the summary conception did apply would be called a *rule*. Arguing as if one regarded rules in this way is a mistake one makes while doing philosophy.

4. The concept of a *general* rule takes the following form. One is pictured as estimating on what percentage of the cases likely to arise a given rule may be relied upon to express the correct decision, that is, the

decision that would be arrived at if one were to correctly apply the utilitarian principle case by case. If one estimates that by and large the rule will give the correct decision, or if one estimates that the likelihood of making a mistake by applying the utilitarian principle directly on one's own is greater than the likelihood of making a mistake by following the rule, and if these considerations held of persons generally, then one would be justified in urging its adoption as a general rule. In this way *general* rules might be accounted for on the summary view. It will still make sense, however, to speak of applying the utilitarian principle case by case, for it was by trying to foresee the results of doing this that one got the initial estimates upon which acceptance of the rule depends. That one is taking a rule in accordance with the summary conception will show itself in the naturalness with which one speaks of the rule as a guide, or as a maxim, or as a generalization from experience, and as something to be laid aside in extraordinary cases where there is no assurance that the generalization will hold and the case must therefore be treated on its merits. Thus there goes with this conception the notion of a particular exception which renders a rule suspect on a particular occasion.

The other conception of rules I will call the practice conception. On this view rules are pictured as defining a practice. Practices are set up for various reasons, but one of them is that in many areas of conduct each person's deciding what to do on utilitarian grounds case by case leads to confusion, and that the attempt to coordinate behavior by trying to foresee how others will act is bound to fail. As an alternative one realizes that what is required is the establishment of a practice, the specification of a new form of activity; and from this one sees that a practice necessarily involves the abdication of full liberty to act on utilitarian and prudential grounds. It is the mark of a practice that being taught how to engage in it involves being instructed in the rules which define it, and that appeal is made to those rules to correct the behavior of those engaged in it. Those engaged in a practice recognize the rules as defining it. The rules cannot be taken as simply describing how those engaged in the practice in fact behave: it is not simply that they act as if they were obeying the rules. Thus it is essential to the notion of a practice that the rules are publicly known and understood as definitive; and it is essential also that the rules of a practice can be taught and can be acted upon to yield a coherent practice. On this conception, then, rules are not generalizations from the decisions of individuals applying the utilitarian principle directly and independently to recurrent particular cases. On the contrary, rules define a practice and are themselves the subject of the utilitarian principle.

To show the important differences between this way of fitting rules into the utilitarian theory and the previous way, I shall consider the differences between the two conceptions on the points previously discussed.

1. In contrast with the summary view, the rules of practices are logically prior to particular cases. This is so because there cannot be a particular case of an action falling under a rule of a practice unless there is the practice. This can be made clearer as follows: in a practice there are rules setting up offices, specifying certain forms of action appropriate to various offices, establishing penalties for the breach of rules, and so on. We may think of the rules of a practice as defining offices, moves, and offenses. Now what is meant by saying that the practice is logically prior to particular cases is this: given any rule which specifies a form of action (a move), a particular action which would be taken as falling under this rule given that there is the practice would not be *described as* that sort of action unless there was the practice. In the case of actions specified by practices it is logically impossible to perform them outside the stage setting provided by those practices, for unless there is the practice, and unless the requisite proprieties are fulfilled, whatever one does, whatever movements one makes, will fail to count as a form of action which the practice specifies. What one does will be described in some *other* way.

One may illustrate this point from the game of baseball. Many of the actions one performs in a game of baseball one can do by oneself or with others whether there is the game or not. For example, one can throw a ball, run, or swing a peculiarly shaped piece of wood. But one cannot steal base, or strike out, or draw a walk, or make an error, or balk; although one can do certain things which appear to resemble these actions such as sliding into a bag, missing a grounder and so on. Striking out, stealing a base, balking, etc., are all actions which can only happen in a game. No matter what a person did, what he did would not be described as stealing a base or striking out or drawing a walk unless he could also be described as playing baseball, and for him to be doing this presupposes the rule-like practice which constitutes the game. The practice is logically prior to particular cases: unless there is the practice the terms referring to actions specified by it lack a sense.[23]

2. The practice view leads to an entirely different conception of the authority which each person has to decide on the propriety of following

---

[23] One might feel that it is a mistake to say that a practice is logically prior to the forms of action it specifies on the grounds that if there were never any instances of actions falling under a practice then we should be strongly inclined to say that there wasn't the practice either. Blueprints for a practice do not make a practice. That there is a practice entails that there are instances of people having been engaged and now being engaged in it (with suitable qualifications). This is correct, but it doesn't hurt the claim that any given particular instance of a form of action specified by a practice presupposes the practice. This isn't so on the summary picture, as each instance must be "there" prior to the rules, so to speak, as something from which one gets the rule by applying the utilitarian principle to it directly.

a rule in particular cases. To engage in a practice, to perform those actions specified by a practice, means to follow the appropriate rules. If one wants to do an action which a certain practice specifies then there is no way to do it except to follow the rules which define it. Therefore, it doesn't make sense for a person to raise the question whether or not a rule of a practice correctly applies to *his* case where the action he contemplates is a form of action defined by a practice. If someone were to raise such a question, he would simply show that he didn't understand the situation in which he was acting. If one wants to perform an action specified by a practice, the only legitimate question concerns the nature of the practice itself ("How do I go about making a will?").

This point is illustrated by the behavior expected of a player in games. If one wants to play a game, one doesn't treat the rules of the game as guides as to what is best in particular cases. In a game of baseball if a batter were to ask "Can I have four strikes?" it would be assumed that he was asking what the rule was; and if, when told what the rule was, he were to say that he meant that on this occasion he thought it would be best on the whole for him to have four strikes rather than three, this would be most kindly taken as a joke. One might contend that baseball would be a better game if four strikes were allowed instead of three; but one cannot picture the rules as guides to what is best on the whole in particular cases, and question their applicability to particular cases as particular cases.

3 and 4. To complete the four points of comparison with the summary conception, it is clear from what has been said that rules of practices are not guides to help one decide particular cases correctly as judged by some higher ethical principle. And neither the quasi-statistical notion of generality, nor the notion of a particular exception, can apply to the rules of practices. A more or less general rule of a practice must be a rule which according to the structure of the practice applies to more or fewer of the kinds of cases arising under it; or it must be a rule which is more or less basic to the understanding of the practice. Again, a particular case cannot be an exception to a rule of a practice. An exception is rather a qualification or a further specification of the rule.

It follows from what we have said about the practice conception of rules that if a person is engaged in a practice, and if he is asked why *he* does what *he* does, or if he is asked to defend what he does, then his explanation, or defense, lies in referring the questioner to the practice. He cannot say of *his* action, if it is an action specified by a practice, that he does it rather than some other because he thinks it is best on the whole.[24] When a man engaged in a practice is queried about his action he must as-

---

[24] A philosophical joke (in the mouth of Jeremy Bentham): "When I run to the other wicket after my partner has struck a good ball I do so because it is best on the whole."

sume that the questioner either doesn't know that he is engaged in it ("Why are you in a hurry to pay him?" "I promised to pay him today") or doesn't know what the practice is. One doesn't so much justify one's particular action as explain, or show, that it is in accordance with the practice. The reason for this is that it is only against the stage setting of the practice that one's particular action is described as it is. Only by reference to the practice can one *say* what one is doing. To explain or to defend one's own action, as a particular action, one fits it into the practice which defines it. If this is not accepted it's a sign that a different question is being raised as to whether one is justified in accepting the practice, or in tolerating it. When the challenge is to the practice, citing the rules (saying what the practice is) is naturally to no avail. But when the challenge is to the particular action defined by the practice, there is nothing one can do but refer to the rules. Concerning particular actions there is only a question for one who isn't clear as to what the practice is, or who doesn't know that it is being engaged in. This is to be contrasted with the case of a maxim which may be taken as pointing to the correct decision on the case as decided on *other* grounds, and so giving a challenge on the case a sense by having it question whether these other grounds really support the decision on this case.

If one compares the two conceptions of rules I have discussed, one can see how the summary conception misses the significance of the distinction between justifying a practice and justifying actions falling under it. On this view rules are regarded as guides whose purpose it is to indicate the ideally rational decision on the given particular case which the flawless application of the utilitarian principle would yield. One has, in principle, full option to use the guides or to discard them as the situation warrants without one's moral office being altered in any way: whether one discards the rules or not, one always holds the office of a rational person seeking case by case to realize the best on the whole. But on the practice conception, if one holds an office defined by a practice, then questions regarding one's actions in this office are settled by reference to the rules which define the practice. If one seeks to question these rules, then one's office undergoes a fundamental change: one then assumes the office of one empowered to change and criticize the rules, or the office of a reformer, and so on. The summary conception does away with the distinction of offices and the various forms of argument appropriate to each. On that conception there is one office and so no offices at all. It therefore obscures the fact that the utilitarian principle must, in the case of actions and offices defined by a practice, apply to the practice, so that general utilitarian arguments are not available to those who act in offices so defined.[25]

---

[25] How do these remarks apply to the case of the promise known only to father and son? Well, at first sight the son certainly holds the office of promisor, and so he isn't allowed by the practice to weigh the particular case on general utilitarian grounds. Suppose instead that he wishes to consider himself in the office of one

Some qualifications are necessary in what I have said. First, I may have talked of the summary and the practice conceptions of rules as if only one of them could be true of rules, and if true of any rules, then necessarily true of *all* rules. I do not, of course, mean this. (It is the critics of utilitarianism who make this mistake insofar as their arguments against utilitarianism presuppose a summary conception of the rules of practices.) Some rules will fit one conception, some rules the other; and so there are rules of practices (rules in the strict sense), and maxims and "rules of thumb."

Secondly, there are further distinctions that can be made in classifying rules, distinctions which should be made if one were considering other questions. The distinctions which I have drawn are those most relevant for the rather special matter I have discussed, and are not intended to be exhaustive.

Finally, there will be many borderline cases about which it will be difficult, if not impossible, to decide which conception of rules is applicable. One expects borderline cases with any concept, and they are especially likely in connection with such involved concepts as those of a practice, institution, game, rule, and so on. Wittgenstein has shown how fluid these notions are.[26] What I have done is to emphasize and sharpen two conceptions for the limited purpose of this paper.

4

What I have tried to show by distinguishing between two conceptions of rules is that there is a way of regarding rules which allows the option to consider particular cases on general utilitarian grounds; whereas there is another conception which does not admit of such discretion except insofar as the rules themselves authorize it. I want to suggest that the tendency while doing philosophy to picture rules in accordance with the summary conception is what may have blinded moral philosophers to the significance of the distinction between justifying a practice and justifying a particular action falling under it; and it does so by misrepresenting the logical force of the reference to the rules in the case of a challenge to a particular action falling under a practice, and by obscuring the fact that where there is a practice, it is the practice itself that must be the subject of the utilitarian principle.

---

empowered to criticize and change the practice, leaving aside the question as to his right to move from his previously assumed office to another. Then he may consider utilitarian arguments as applied to the practice; but once he does this he will see that there are such arguments for not allowing a general utilitarian defense in the practice for this sort of case. For to do so would make it impossible to ask for and to give a kind of promise which one often wants to be able to ask for and to give. Therefore he will not want to change the practice, and so as a promisor he has no option but to keep his promise.

[26] *Philosophical Investigations* (Oxford, 1953), I, paras. 65–71, for example.

It is surely no accident that two of the traditional test cases of utilitarianism, punishment and promises, are clear cases of practices. Under the influence of the summary conception it is natural to suppose that the officials of a penal system, and one who has made a promise, may decide what to do in particular cases on utilitarian grounds. One fails to see that a general discretion to decide particular cases on utilitarian grounds is incompatible with the concept of a practice; and that what discretion one does have is itself defined by the practice (e.g., a judge may have discretion to determine the penalty within certain limits). The traditional objections to utilitarianism which I have discussed presuppose the attribution to judges, and to those who have made promises, of a plenitude of moral authority to decide particular cases on utilitarian grounds. But once one fits utilitarianism together with the notion of a practice, and notes that punishment and promising are practices, then one sees this attribution is logically precluded.

That punishment and promising are practices is beyond question. In the case of promising this is shown by the fact that the form of words "I promise" is a performative utterance which presupposes the stage setting of the practice and the proprieties defined by it. Saying the words "I promise" will only be promising given the existence of the practice. It would be absurd to interpret the rules about promising in accordance with the summary conception. It is absurd to say, for example, that the rule that promises should be kept could have arisen from its being found in past cases to be best on the whole to keep one's promise; for unless there were already the understanding that one keeps one's promises as part of the practice itself there couldn't have been any cases of promising.

It must, of course, be granted that the rules defining promising are not codified, and that one's conception of what they are necessarily depends on one's moral training. Therefore it is likely that there is considerable variation in the way people understand the practice, and room for argument as to how it is best set up. For example, differences as to how strictly various defenses are to be taken, or just what defenses are available, are likely to arise amongst persons with different backgrounds. But irrespective of these variations it belongs to the concept of the practice of promising that the general utilitarian defense is not available to the promisor. That this is so accounts for the force of the traditional objection which I have discussed. And the point I wish to make is that when one fits the utilitarian view together with the practice conception of rules, as one must in the appropriate cases, then there is nothing in that view which entails that there must be such a defense, either in the practice of promising, or in any other practice.

Punishment is also a clear case. There are many actions in the sequence of events which constitute someone's being punished which presuppose a practice. One can see this by considering the definition of punishment which I gave when discussing Carritt's criticism of utilitarianism. The definition there stated refers to such things as the normal rights of a citizen, rules of law, due process of law, trials and courts of law, statutes, etc., none of which can exist outside the elaborate stage setting of a legal system. It is also the case that many of the actions for which people are punished presuppose practices. For example, one is punished for stealing, for trespassing, and the like, which presuppose the institution of property. It is impossible to say what punishment is, or to describe a particular instance of it, without referring to offices, actions, and offenses specified by practices. Punishment is a move in an elaborate legal game and presupposes the complex of practices which make up the legal order. The same thing is true of the less formal sorts of punishment: a parent or guardian or someone in proper authority may punish a child, but no one else can.

There is one mistaken interpretation of what I have been saying which it is worthwhile to warn against. One might think that the use I am making of the distinction between justifying a practice and justifying the particular actions falling under it involves one in a definite social and political attitude in that it leads to a kind of conservatism. It might seem that I am saying that for each person the social practices of his society provide the standard of justification for his actions; therefore let each person abide by them and his conduct will be justified.

This interpretation is entirely wrong. The point I have been making is rather a logical point. To be sure, it has consequences in matters of ethical theory; but in itself it leads to no particular social or political attitude. It is simply that where a form of action is specified by a practice there is no justification possible of the particular action of a particular person save by reference to the practice. In such cases the action is what it is in virtue of the practice and to explain it is to refer to the practice. There is no inference whatsoever to be drawn with respect to whether or not one should accept the practices of one's society. One can be as radical as one likes but in the case of actions specified by practices the objects of one's radicalism must be the social practices and people's acceptance of them.

I have tried to show that when we fit the utilitarian view together with the practice conception of rules, where this conception is appropriate,[27] we can formulate it in a way which saves it from several traditional objec-

---

[27] As I have already stated, it is not always easy to say where the conception is appropriate. Nor do I care to discuss at this point the general sorts of cases to which it does apply except to say that one should not take it for granted that it applies to many so-called "moral rules." It is my feeling that relatively few actions of the moral life are defined by practices and that the practice conception is more relevant to understanding legal and legal-like arguments than it is to the more complex sort of moral arguments. Utilitarianism must be fitted to different conceptions of rules depending on the case, and no doubt the failure to do this has been one source of difficulty in interpreting it correctly.

tions. I have further tried to show how the logical force of the distinction between justifying a practice and justifying an action falling under it is connected with the practice conception of rules and cannot be understood as long as one regards the rules of practices in accordance with the summary view. Why, when doing philosophy, one may be inclined to so regard them, I have not discussed. The reasons for this are evidently very deep and would require another paper.

Extreme and Restricted Utilitarianism

J. J. C. SMART

1

Utilitarianism is the doctrine that the rightness of actions is to be judged by their consequences. What do we mean by 'actions' here? Do we mean particular actions or do we mean classes of actions? According to which way we interpret the word 'actions' we get two different theories, both of which merit the appellation 'utilitarian'.

(1) If by 'actions' we mean particular individual actions we get the sort of doctrine held by Bentham, Sidgwick, and Moore. According to this doctrine we test individual actions by their consequences, and general rules, like 'keep promises', are mere rules of thumb which we use only to avoid the necessity of estimating the probable consequences of our actions at every step. The rightness or wrongness of keeping a promise on a particular occasion depends only on the goodness or badness of the consequences of keeping or breaking the promise on that particular occasion. Of course part of the consequences of breaking the promise, and a part to which we will normally ascribe decisive importance, will be the weakening of faith in the institution of promising. However, if the goodness of the consequences of breaking the rule is *in toto* greater than the goodness of the consequences of keeping it, then we must break the rule, irrespective of whether the goodness of the consequences of *everybody's* obeying the rule is or is not

---

From The Philosophical Quarterly, *VI (1956). Reprinted, with revision, by permission of the author and* The Philosophical Quarterly.

Based on a paper read to the Victorian Branch of the Australasian Association of Psychology and Philosophy, October 1955.

greater than the consequences of *everybody's* breaking it. To put it shortly, rules do not matter, save *per accidens* as rules of thumb and as *de facto* social institutions with which the utilitarian has to reckon when estimating consequences. I shall call this doctrine 'extreme utilitarianism'.

(2) A more modest form of utilitarianism has recently become fashionable. The doctrine is to be found in Toulmin's book *The Place of Reason in Ethics*, in Nowell-Smith's *Ethics* (though I think Nowell-Smith has qualms), in John Austin's *Lectures on Jurisprudence* (Lecture II), and even in J. S. Mill, if Urmson's interpretation of him is correct (*Philosophical Quarterly*, III (1953), 33–39). Part of its charm is that it appears to resolve the dispute in moral philosophy between intuitionists and utilitarians in a way which is very neat. The above philosophers hold, or seem to hold, that moral rules are more than rules of thumb. In general the rightness of an action is *not* to be tested by evaluating its consequences but only by considering whether or not it falls under a certain rule. Whether the rule is to be considered an acceptable moral rule, is, however, to be decided by considering the consequences of adopting the rule. Broadly, then, actions are to be tested by rules and rules by consequences. The only cases in which we must test an individual action directly by its consequences are (a) when the action comes under two different rules, one of which enjoins it and one of which forbids it, and (b) when there is no rule whatever that governs the given case. I shall call this doctrine 'restricted utilitarianism'.

It should be noticed that the distinction I am making cuts across, and is quite different from, the distinction commonly made between hedonistic and ideal utilitarianism. Bentham was an extreme hedonistic utilitarian and Moore an extreme ideal utilitarian, and Toulmin (perhaps) could be classified as a restricted ideal utilitarian. A hedonistic utilitarian holds that the goodness of the consequences of an action is a function only of their pleasurableness and an ideal utilitarian, like Moore, holds that pleasurableness is not even a necessary condition of goodness. Mill seems, if we are to take his remarks about higher and lower pleasures seriously, to be neither a pure hedonistic nor a pure ideal utilitarian. He seems to hold that pleasurableness is a necessary condition for goodness, but that goodness is a function of other qualities of mind as well. Perhaps we can call him a quasi-ideal utilitarian. When we say that a state of mind is good I take it that we are expressing some sort of *rational preference*. When we say that it is pleasurable I take it that we are saying that it is enjoyable, and when we say that something is a higher pleasure I take it that we are saying that it is more truly, or more deeply, enjoyable. I am doubtful whether 'more deeply enjoyable' does not just mean 'more enjoyable, even though not more enjoyable on a first look', and so I am doubtful whether quasi-ideal utilitarianism, and possibly ideal utilitarianism too, would not collapse into hedonistic utilitarianism on a closer scrutiny of the logic of words like 'preference', 'pleasure', 'enjoy', 'deeply enjoy', and so on. However, it is beside the point of the present paper to go into these questions. I am here concerned only with the issue between extreme and restricted utilitarianism and am ready to concede that both forms of utilitarianism can be either hedonistic or nonhedonistic.

The issue between extreme and restricted utilitarianism can be illustrated by considering the remark 'But suppose everyone did the same'. (Cf. A. K. Stout's article in *The Australasian Journal of Philosophy*, XXXII, 1–29.) Stout distinguishes two forms of the universalization principle, the causal forms and the hypothetical form. To say that you ought not to do an action A because it would have bad results if everyone (or many people) did action A may be merely to point out that while the action A would otherwise be the optimific one, nevertheless when you take into account that doing A will probably cause other people to do A too, you can see that A is not, on a broad view, really optimific. If this causal influence could be avoided (as may happen in the case of a secret desert island promise) then we would disregard the universalization principle. This is the causal form of the principle. A person who accepted the universalization principle in its hypothetical form would be one who was concerned only with what would happen *if* everyone did the action A: he would be totally unconcerned with the question of whether in fact everyone would do the action A. That is, he might say that it would be wrong not to vote because it would have bad results if everyone took this attitude, and he would be totally unmoved by arguments purporting to show that my refusing to vote has no effect whatever on other people's propensity to vote. Making use of Stout's distinction, we can say that an extreme utilitarian would apply the universalization principle in the causal form, while a restricted utilitarian would apply it in the hypothetical form.

How are we to decide the issue between extreme and restricted utilitarianism? I wish to repudiate at the outset that milk and water approach which describes itself sometimes as 'investigating what is implicit in the common moral consciousness' and sometimes as 'investigating how people ordinarily talk about morality'. We have only to read the newspaper correspondence about capital punishment or about what should be done with Formosa to realize that the common moral consciousness is in part made up of superstitious elements, of morally bad elements, and of logically confused elements. I address myself to good hearted and benevolent people and so I hope that if we rid ourselves of the logical confusion the superstitious and morally bad elements will largely fall away. For even among good hearted and benevolent people it is possible to find superstitious and morally bad reasons for moral beliefs. These superstitious and morally bad reasons hide behind the protective screen of logical confusion. With people who are not logically confused but who are openly superstitious or morally bad I can of course do nothing. That is, our ultimate pro-attitudes may be different. Nevertheless I propose to rely on *my own* moral consciousness and to appeal to *your* moral consciousness and to forget about what people ordinarily say. 'The obligation to obey a rule', says Nowell-Smith (*Ethics*, p. 239), 'does not, *in the opinion of ordinary men*', (my italics), 'rest on the beneficial consequences of obeying it in a particular case'. What does this prove? Surely it is more than likely that ordinary men are confused here. Philosophers should be able to examine the question more rationally.

2

For an extreme utilitarian moral rules are rules of thumb. In practice the extreme utilitarian will mostly guide his conduct by appealing to the rules ('do not lie', 'do not break promises', etc.) of common sense morality. This is not because there is anything sacrosanct in the rules themselves but because he can argue that probably he will most often act in an extreme utilitarian way if he does not think as a utilitarian. For one thing, actions have frequently to be done in a hurry. Imagine a man seeing a person drowning. He jumps in and rescues him. There is no time to reason the matter out, but usually this will be the course of action which an extreme utilitarian would recommend if he did reason the matter out. If, however, the man drowning had been drowning in a river near Berchtesgaden in 1938, and if he had had the well-known black forelock and moustache of Adolf Hitler, an extreme utilitarian would, if he had time, work out the probability of the man's being the villainous dictator, and if the probability were high enough he would, on extreme utilitarian grounds, leave him to drown. The rescuer, however, has not time. He trusts to his instincts and dives in and rescues the man. And this trusting to instincts and to moral rules can be justified on extreme utilitarian grounds. Furthermore, an extreme utilitarian who knew that the drowning man was Hitler would nevertheless praise the rescuer, not condemn him. For by praising the man he is strengthening a courageous and benevolent disposition of mind, and in general this disposition has great positive utility. (Next time, perhaps, it will be Winston Churchill that the man saves!) We must never forget that an extreme utilitarian may praise actions which he knows to be wrong. Saving Hitler was wrong, but it was a member of a class of actions which are generally right, and the motive to do actions of this class is in general an optimific one. In considering questions of praise and blame it is not the expediency of the praised or blamed action that is at issue, but the expediency of the praise. It can be expedient to praise an inexpedient action and inexpedient to praise an expedient one.

Lack of time is not the only reason why an extreme utilitarian may, on extreme utilitarian principles, trust to rules of common sense morality.

He knows that in particular cases where his own interests are involved his calculations are likely to be biased in his own favor. Suppose that he is unhappily married and is deciding whether to get divorced. He will in all probability greatly exaggerate his own unhappiness (and possibly his wife's) and greatly underestimate the harm done to his children by the breakup of the family. He will probably also underestimate the likely harm done by the weakening of the general faith in marriage vows. So probably he will come to the correct extreme utilitarian conclusion if he does not in this instance think as an extreme utilitarian but trusts to common sense morality.

There are many more and subtle points that could be made in connection with the relation between extreme utilitarianism and the morality of common sense. All those that I have just made and many more will be found in Book IV, Chapters 3–5, of Sidgwick's *Methods of Ethics.* I think that this book is the best book ever written on ethics, and that these chapters are the best chapters of the book. As they occur so near the end of a very long book they are unduly neglected. I refer the reader, then, to Sidgwick for the classical exposition of the relation between (extreme) utilitarianism and the morality of common sense. One further point raised by Sidgwick in this connection is whether an (extreme) utilitarian ought on (extreme) utilitarian principles to propagate (extreme) utilitarianism among the public. As most people are not very philosophical and not good at empirical calculations, it is probable that they will most often act in an extreme utilitarian way if they do not try to think as extreme utilitarians. We have seen how easy it would be to misapply the extreme utilitarian criterion in the case of divorce. Sidgwick seems to think it quite probable that an extreme utilitarian should not propagate his doctrine too widely. However, the great danger to humanity comes nowadays on the plane of public morality—not private morality. There is a greater danger to humanity from the hydrogen bomb than from an increase of the divorce rate, regrettable though that might be, and there seems no doubt that extreme utilitarianism makes for good sense in international relations. When France walked out of the United Nations because she did not wish Morocco discussed, she said that she was within her rights because Morocco and Algiers are part of her metropolitan territory and nothing to do with U.N. This was clearly a legalistic if not superstitious argument. We should not be concerned with the so-called 'rights' of France or any other country but with whether the cause of humanity would be best be served by discussing Morocco in U.N. (I am not saying that the answer to this is 'Yes'. There are good grounds for supposing that more harm than good would come by such a discussion.) I myself have no hesitation in saying that on extreme utilitarian principles we ought to propagate extreme utilitarianism as widely as possible. But Sidgwick had respectable reasons for suspecting the opposite.

The extreme utilitarian, then, regards moral rules as rules of thumb and as sociological facts that have to be taken into account when deciding what to do, just as facts of any other sort have to be taken into account. But in themselves they do not justify any action.

3

The restricted utilitarian regards moral rules as more than rules of thumb for short-circuiting calculations of consequences. Generally, he argues, consequences are not relevant at all when we are deciding what to do in a particular case. In general, they are relevant only to deciding what rules are good reasons for acting in a certain way in particular cases. This doctrine is possibly a good account of how the modern unreflective twentieth-century Englishman often thinks about morality, but surely it is monstrous as an account of how it is most rational to think about morality. Suppose that there is a rule R and that in 99 per cent of cases the best possible results are obtained by acting in accordance with R. Then clearly R is a useful rule of thumb; if we have not time or are not impartial enough to assess the consequences of an action it is an extremely good bet that the thing to do is to act in accordance with R. But is it not monstrous to suppose that if we *have* worked out the consequences and if we have perfect faith in the impartiality of our calculations, and if we *know* that in this instance to break R will have better results than to keep it, we should nevertheless obey the rule? Is it not to erect R into a sort of idol if we keep it when breaking it will prevent, say, some avoidable misery? Is not this a form of superstitious rule worship (easily explicable psychologically) and not the rational thought of a philosopher?

The point may be made more clearly if we consider Mill's comparison of moral rules to the tables in the nautical almanac. (*Utilitarianism*, Everyman Edition, pp. 22–23). This comparison of Mill's is adduced by Urmson as evidence that Mill was a restricted utilitarian, but I do not think that it will bear this interpretation at all. (Though I quite agree with Urmson that many other things said by Mill are in harmony with restricted rather than extreme utilitarianism. Probably Mill had never thought very much about the distinction and was arguing for utilitarianism, restricted or extreme, against other and quite nonutilitarian forms of moral argument.) Mill says: 'Nobody argues that the art of navigation is not founded on astronomy, because sailors cannot wait to calculate the Nautical Almanac. Being rational creatures, they go out upon the sea of life with their minds made up on the common questions of right and wrong, as well as on many of the far more difficult questions of wise and foolish. . . . Whatever we adopt as the fundamental principle of morality, we require subordinate principles to apply it by'. Notice that this is, as it stands, only an argument for subordinate principles as rules of thumb. The example of the nautical almanac is misleading because the information given in the almanac is in all cases the same as the information one would get if one made a long and laborious calculation from the original astronomical data on which the almanac is founded. Suppose, however, that astronomy were different. Suppose that the behavior of the sun, moon, and planets was very nearly as it is now, but that on rare occasions there were peculiar irregularities and, discontinuities, so that the almanac gave us rules of the form 'in 99 per cent of cases where the observations are such and such you can deduce that your position is so and so'. Furthermore, let us suppose that there were methods which enabled us, by direct and laborious calculation from the original astronomical data, not using the rough and ready tables of the almanac, to get our correct position in 100 per cent of cases. Seafarers might use the almanac because they never had time for the long calculations and they were content with a 99 per cent chance of success in calculating their positions. Would it not be absurd, however, if they *did* make the direct calculation, and finding that it disagreed with the almanac calculation, nevertheless they ignored it and stuck to the almanac conclusion? Of course the case would be altered if there were a high enough probability of making slips in the direct calculation: then we might stick to the almanac result, liable to error though we knew it to be, simply because the direct calculation would be open to error for a different reason, the fallibility of the computer. This would be analogous to the case of the extreme utilitarian who abides by the conventional rule against the dictates of his utilitarian calculations simply because he thinks that his calculations are probably affected by personal bias. But if the navigator were sure of his direct calculations would he not be foolish to abide by his almanac? I conclude, then, that if we change our suppositions about astronomy and the almanac (to which there are no exceptions) to bring the case into line with that of morality (to whose rules there are exceptions), Mill's example loses its appearance of supporting the restricted form of utilitarianism. Let me say once more that I am not here concerned with how ordinary men think about morality but with how they ought to think. We could quite well imagine a race of sailors who acquired a superstitious reverence for their almanac, even though it was only right in 99 per cent of cases, and who indignantly threw overboard any man who mentioned the possibility of a direct calculation. But would this behavior of the sailors be rational?

Let us consider a much discussed sort of case in which the extreme utilitarian might go against the conventional moral rule. I have promised to a friend, dying on a desert island from which I am subsequently rescued, that I will see that his fortune (over which I have control) is given to a jockey club. However, when I am rescued I decide that it would be better to give the money to a hospital, which can do more good with it. It may be argued that I am wrong to give the money to the hospital. But why? (a) The hospital can do more good with the money than the jockey club can. (b) The present case is unlike most cases of promising in that no one except me knows about the promise. In breaking the promise I am doing so with complete secrecy and am doing nothing to weaken the general faith in promises. That is, a factor, which would normally keep the extreme utilitarian from promise breaking even in otherwise unoptimific cases, does not at present operate. (c) There is no doubt a slight weakening in my own character as an habitual promise keeper, and moreover psychological tensions will be set up in me every time I am asked what the man made me promise him to do. For clearly I shall have to say that he made me promise to give the money to the hospital, and, since I am an habitual truth teller, this will go very much against the grain with me. Indeed I am pretty sure that in practice I myself would keep the promise. But we are not discussing what my moral habits would probably make me do; we are discussing what I ought to do. Moreover, we must not forget that even if it would be most rational of me to give the money to the hospital it would also be most rational of you to punish or condemn me if you did, most improbably, find out the truth (e.g. by finding a note washed ashore in a bottle). Furthermore, I would agree that though it was most rational of me to give the money to the hospital it would be most rational of you to condemn me for it. We revert again to Sidgwick's distinction between the utility of the action and the utility of the praise of it.

Many such issues are discussed by A. K. Stout in the article to which I have already referred. I do not wish to go over the same ground again, especially as I think that Stout's arguments support my own point of view. It will be useful, however, to consider one other example that he gives. Suppose that during hot weather there is an edict that no water must be used for watering gardens. I have a garden and I reason that most people are sure to obey the edict, and that as the amount of water that I use will be by itself negligible no harm will be done if I use the water secretly. So I do use the water, thus producing some lovely flowers which give happiness to various people. Still, you may say, though the action was perhaps optimific, it was unfair and wrong.

There are several matters to consider. Certainly my action should be condemned. We revert once more to Sidgwick's distinction. A right action may be rationally condemned. Furthermore, this sort of offence is normally found out. If I have a wonderful garden when everybody else's is dry and brown there is only one explanation. So if I water my garden I am weakening my respect for law and order, and as this leads to bad results an extreme utilitarian would agree that I was wrong to water the garden. Suppose now that the case is altered and that I can keep the thing secret: there is a secluded part of the garden where I grow flowers which I give away anonymously to a home for old ladies. Are you still so sure that I did the wrong thing by watering my garden? However, this is still a weaker case than that of the hospital and the jockey club. There will be tensions set up within myself: my secret knowledge that I have broken the rule will make it hard for me to exhort others to keep the rule. These psychologically ill effects in myself may be not inconsiderable: directly and indirectly they may lead to harm which is at least of the same order as the happiness that the old ladies get from the flowers. You can see that on an extreme utilitarian view there are two sides to the question.

So far I have been considering the duty of an extreme utilitarian in a predominantly nonutilitarian society. The case is altered if we consider the extreme utilitarian who lives in a society every member, or most members, of which can be expected to reason as he does. Should he water his flowers now? (Granting, what is doubtful, that in the case already considered he would have been right to water his flowers.)[1] As a first approximation, the answer is that he should not do so. For since the situation is a completely symmetrical one, what is rational for him is rational for others. Hence, by a *reductio ad absurdum* argument, it would seem that watering his garden would be rational for none. Nevertheless, a more refined analysis shows that the above argument is not quite correct, though it is correct enough for practical purposes. The argument considers each person as confronted with the choice either of watering his garden or of not watering it. However there is a third possibility, which is that each person should, with the aid of a suitable randomizing device, such as throwing dice, give himself a certain probability of watering his garden. This would be to adopt what in the theory of games is called 'a mixed strategy'. If we could give numerical values to the private benefit of garden watering and to the public harm done by 1, 2, 3, etc., persons using the water in this way, we could work out a value of the probability of watering his garden that each extreme utilitarian should give himself. Let a be the value which each extreme utilitarian gets from watering his garden, and let $f(1)$, $f(2)$, $f(3)$, etc., be the public harm done by exactly 1, 2, 3, etc., persons respectively watering their gardens. Suppose that p is the probability that each person gives himself of watering his garden. Then we can easily calculate, as functions of p, the probabilities that exactly 1, 2, 3, etc., persons will water their gardens. Let these probabilities be $p_1, p_2, \ldots p_n$. Then the total net probable benefit can be expressed as

$$V = p_1(a - f(1)) + p_2(2a - f(2)) + \ldots p_n(na - f(n))$$

Then if we know the function $f(x)$ we can calculate the value of p for which $(dV/dp) = 0$. This gives the value of p which it would be rational

---

[1] [The author has revised considerably the remainder of this paragraph—Ed.]

for each extreme utilitarian to adopt. The present argument does not of course depend on a perhaps unjustified assumption that the values in question are measurable, and in a practical case such as that of the garden watering we can doubtless assume that p will be so small that we can take it near enough as equal to zero. However the argument is of interest for the theoretical underpinning of extreme utilitarianism, since the possibility of a mixed strategy is usually neglected by critics of utilitarianism, who wrongly assume that the only relevant and symmetrical alternatives are of the form 'everybody does X' and 'nobody does X'.

I now pass on to a type of case which may be thought to be the trump card of restricted utilitarianism. Consider the rule of the road. It may be said that since all that matters is that everyone should do the same it is indifferent which rule we have, 'go on the left hand side' or 'go on the right hand side'. Hence the only *reason* for going on the left hand side in British countries is that this is the rule. Here the rule does seem to be a reason, in itself, for acting in a certain way. I wish to argue against this. The rule in itself is not a reason for our actions. We would be perfectly justified in going on the right hand side if (a) we knew that the rule was to go on the left hand side, and (b) we were in a country peopled by superanarchists who always on principle did the opposite of what they were told. This shows that the rule does not give us a reason for acting so much as an indication of the probable actions of others, which helps us to find out what would be our own most rational course of action. If we are in a country not peopled by anarchists, but by nonanarchist extreme utilitarians, we expect, other things being equal, that they will keep rules laid down for them. Knowledge of the rule enables us to predict their behavior and to harmonize our own actions with theirs. The rule 'keep to the left hand side', then, is not a logical *reason* for action but an anthropological *datum* for planning actions.

I conclude that in every case if there is a rule R the keeping of which is in general optimific, but such that in a special sort of circumstances the optimific behavior is to break R, then in these circumstances we should break R. Of course we must consider all the less obvious effects of breaking R, such as reducing people's faith in the moral order, before coming to the conclusion that to break R is right: in fact we shall rarely come to such a conclusion. Moral rules, on the extreme utilitarian view, are rules of thumb only, but they are not bad rules of thumb. But if we *do* come to the conclusion that we should break the rule and if we have weighed in the balance our own fallibility and liability to personal bias, what good reason remains for keeping the rule? I can understand 'it is optimific' as a reason for action, but why should 'it is a member of a class of actions which are usually optimific' or 'it is a member of a class of actions which as a class are more optimific than any alternative general class' be a good reason? You might as well say that a person ought to be picked to play for Australia just because all his brothers have been, or that the Australian team should be composed entirely of the Harvey family because this would be better than composing it entirely of any other family. The extreme utilitarian does not appeal to artificial feelings, but only to our feelings of benevolence, and what better feelings can there be to appeal to? Admittedly we can have a pro-attitude to anything, even to rules, but such artificially begotten pro-attitudes smack of superstition. Let us get down to realities, human happiness and misery, and make these the objects of our pro-attitudes and anti-attitudes.

The restricted utilitarian might say that he is talking only of *morality*, not of such things as rules of the road. I am not sure how far this objection, if valid, would affect my argument, but in any case I would reply that as a philosopher I conceive of ethics as the study of how it would be *most rational* to act. If my opponent wishes to restrict the word 'morality' to a narrower use he can have the word. The fundamental question is the question of rationality of action *in general*. Similarly if the restricted utilitarian were to appeal to ordinary usage and say 'it might be most rational to leave Hitler to drown but it would surely not be *wrong* to rescue him', I should again let him have the words 'right' and 'wrong' and should stick to 'rational' and 'irrational'. We already saw that it would be rational to praise Hitler's rescuer, even though it would have been most rational not to have rescued Hitler. In ordinary language, no doubt, 'right' and 'wrong' have not only the meaning 'most rational to do' and 'not most rational to do' but also have the meaning 'praiseworthy' and 'not praiseworthy'. Usually to the utility of an action corresponds utility of praise of it, but as we saw, this is not always so. Moral language could thus do with tidying up, for example by reserving 'right' for 'most rational' and 'good' as an epithet of praise for the motive from which the action sprang. It would be more becoming in a philosopher to try to iron out illogicalities in moral language and to make suggestions for its reform than to use it as a court of appeal whereby to perpetuate confusions.

One last defence of restricted utilitarianism might be as follows. 'Act optimifically' might be regarded as itself one of the rules of our system (though it would be odd to say that this rule was justified by its optimificality). According to Toulmin (*The Place of Reason in Ethics*, pp. 146–48) if 'keep promises', say, conflicts with another rule we are allowed to argue the case on its merits, as if we were extreme utilitarians. If 'act optimifically' is itself one of our rules then there will always be a conflict of rules whenever to keep a rule is not itself optimific. If this is so, restricted utilitarianism collapses into extreme utilitarianism. And no one could read

Toulmin's book or Urmson's article on Mill without thinking that Toulmin and Urmson are of the opinion that they have thought of a doctrine which does *not* collapse into extreme utilitarianism, but which is, on the contrary, an improvement on it.

Rules and Utilitarianism

B. J. DIGGS

Although moral rules have had a prominent place in recent moral philosophy, their character is not clear. One reason for this is the vagueness and ambiguity which infect the use of the term "rule": Philosophers tend to conceive of moral rules on some particular model, sometimes in a confused way, often innocently and without a clear view of the alternatives. J. Rawls called attention to one important instance of this: He pointed out that the tendency to regard rules as convenient guides, or as summaries of earlier experiences, seems to have blinded some philosophers "... to the significance of the distinction between justifying a practice and justifying a particular action falling under it...."[1]

Partly as a consequence, utilitarianism has been interpreted in a special way, as asserting that the rightness and wrongness of particular acts is decidable on general utilitarian grounds. This form of utilitarianism, so-called "act utilitarianism," is open to serious and well-known objections.[2]

The appeal of the recently more popular "rule utilitarianism" is that it is able to meet some of these objections, and still retain the tie between morality and "the general welfare," which is one of the most attractive characteristics of utilitarianism. I shall argue in this paper, however, that rule utilitarians (and some of their critics, and many others who view moral rules in the same general way) have also tended unwittingly to adopt a particular kind of rule as the model of a moral rule. When this kind of rule has been delineated, and alternatives noted, I think rule utilitarianism loses much of its initial appeal.

My object in this paper, however, is not so much to refute rule utilitarianism as to contribute to the clarification of moral rules. By distinguishing two kinds of rules I shall try to illuminate one of the fundamental

From American Philosophical Quarterly, *I (1964). Reprinted by permission of the author and* American Philosophical Quarterly.

[1] Two Concepts of Rules," *Philosophical Review,* LXIV (1955), 29–30.

[2] Cf. e.g., R. B. Brandt, *Ethical Theory* (Englewood Cliffs, N.J., 1959), chap. 15.

options (as well as one of the fundamental confusions) open to moral theory. (1) The first kind of rule is exemplified by the rules which workers follow as part of their jobs; these rules may be used to describe a job. (2) The other kind of rule characterizes such common games as baseball, chess, and the like. Both kinds of rule define "practices," but the practices are very different. I think the easy tendency to confuse them may have blinded moral philosophers to significant distinctions between justifying a system of rules designed to contribute to some goal or product, justifying a system of rules which defines a "form of life," and justifying moral rules. Marking these distinctions should help clarify certain steps taken in recent moral philosophy: One should be able to appreciate more fully the point of Baier's assertion that although moral rules are "for the good of everyone alike," they are not designed to promote the greatest good of everyone.[3] One should also be able to see more clearly why Rawls maintains that the decision on the rules of justice is not properly conceived on the utilitarian model, as an administrative decision on how to promote the greatest happiness.[4] The analysis of rules is illuminating, moreover, not only because it helps mark major differences of this kind, but also because it shows what is behind some of the twists and turns of moral theory.

1

1.0 The first kind of rule which I shall describe belongs to a large class of rules which I call "instrumental." All rules in this large class are adopted or followed as a means to an end, in order to "accomplish a purpose" or "get a job done." The simplest of these rules is the "practical maxim" which one ordinarily follows at his own pleasure, such as "Be sure the surface to be painted is thoroughly dry" or "Do not plant tomatoes until after the last frost."[5]

The instrumental rule to which I call attention is more complex. On many occasions when one wants a job done, either he is not in a position or not able or not willing to do the job himself. If he is in a position of power or authority, or if he has money, he may simply order or hire others to "do the job" and leave it to them. In numerous cases, however, he himself lays down rules of procedure, and establishes "jobs" or "roles" in the institutional sense. A "job" in this latter sense is not a job to be "done," but a job to be "offered to" or "given" to a person. If a person "takes" or is "assigned"

3 K. Baier, *The Moral Point of View* (Ithaca, N.Y., 1958), pp. 200–204.

4 "Justice as Fairness," *Philosophical Review*, LXVII (April, 1958), 164–94. It will be clear that Rawls's analysis in "Two Concepts of Rules" does not support a utilitarian theory.

5 Cf. Max Black, "Notes on the Meaning of 'Rule'," *Theoria*, XXIV (1958), 121–22; reprinted in his *Models and Metaphors* (Ithaca, N.Y., 1962), pp. 95–139.

"the job" then we often think of him as under an obligation to "do his job," and this partly consists in his following rules. Instrumental rules of this kind, unlike practical maxims, have a social dimension: It *makes sense* to ask whether a job-holder (or role-taker) is *obligated* to follow a particular rule, or whether this is one of his *duties*, and the penalty attaching to a breach of the rules does not consist simply in his not "getting the job done."

Rules of this kind are found in very different institutions. Some are rules of a "job" in the ordinary sense. Others apply to anyone who voluntarily assumes a "role," such as "automobile driver." Others characterize a position which one is obliged to take by law, for example, that of private in the army. The goals which the rules are designed to serve may be ordinary products of labor, such as houses, steel beams, etc.; or fairly specific social goals such as "getting vehicles to their destinations safely and expeditiously"; or goals as general as "the national defense." In some cases the rules, differing from job to job, mark a division of labor, as the rules which say what factory workers, or the members of a platoon, are to do. In other cases, the same rules apply more or less equally to all, as in the case of (at least some) rules regulating traffic.

Notwithstanding their variety, these rules can be classified together because they share two fundamental characteristics: (1) The rules prescribe action which is thought to contribute to the attainment of a goal. This is the "design" of such rules, at least in the sense that if the prescribed action does not effectively contribute to the attainment of the goal, for the most part, then the rule itself is subject to criticism. (2) The rules are "laid down" or "legislated" or "made the rule" by a party which has power or authority of some kind; one cannot learn "what the rules are" simply by determining what general procedures most effectively promote the goal. This latter characteristic sharply differentiates these rules from what I have called practical maxims, although both share the first characteristic and are "instrumental."[6]

---

[6] Practical maxims should not be dismissed, however, as "mere rules of thumb" on the one hand, or as "simply stating relations between means and ends" on the other. When one follows a maxim the rule *directs* action and is a *criterion* of certain kinds of rightness and wrongness in acting.

In passing note that Rawls's "summary conception," as a whole, does not properly apply to practical maxims, although several features of this conception do apply. Rawls's analysis, admirable as it is, is very apt to mislead. For the "summary view," as he calls it, is a blend of two quite distinct conceptions: In part it is a confused conception or a misconception of a rule, as a summary or report. In other respects it is an accurate conception of what I have called a practical maxim. This may account for an ambivalence in Rawls's article: Cf. ". . . it is doubtful that anything to which the summary conception did apply would be called a *rule*." [(p. 23) "Two Concepts . . . "] with "Some rules will fit one conception, some rules the other; and so there are rules of practices (rules in the strict sense), and maxims and 'rules

I shall now consider each of these two characteristics in turn.

1.1 Since rules of this kind are designed to serve a goal, the "best" set of rules is that set, *other things equal*, which is most effective in promoting the goal. The qualification is important: One ordinarily asks the question, "Is this a good rule?" in order to determine whether or not the action to be prescribed by the rule, together with other acts, will most efficiently produce the goal, without violating certain other rules, and in a way that harmonizes best with other aims, assuming persons can be persuaded to follow the rule.[7]

Consider a factory planner designing an assembly line, or an army officer considering platoon reorganization, or a traffic planning commission trying to decide whether a street should be made a throughway. In each case rules are proposed, but there is no contradiction in saying that action on the rules will not contribute to the goal. Within its context the question "Is this a good rule?" is one of practical fact and experience. This indicates one sense in saying that the goal is "over and beyond" the action and the rules.

There is another sense in saying this: In practice a goal is often described in terms of rules or procedures which are thought to produce it (when, for example, a beam is to be built according to procedural specifications). Moreover, at the time of action one may not be able to say just what he wants in other terms. Nevertheless, there is no contradiction, explicit or implied, in saying that this person got the goal (in the sense that he can truthfully say "This has all the desirable features of what I wanted") without anyone's having laid down or followed rules. Although the beam was not constructed according to specifications, tests may now show that it is as strong as one could have wished for. In this sense it is *logically* possible for one to attain the goal which a set of instrumental rules is designed to serve without these rules having been followed. I shall refer to this characteristic by saying that the goal of any set of instrumental rules is "logically independent" of these rules.

Although an instrumental action is *properly* described in many ways, depending on the context, it can always be *truthfully* described in terms of a goal, as a "trying to get or produce G." For a goal is essential to such action, and to the rules which guide it. Nevertheless, it is clear that it is

---

of thumb'." (p. 29). The point is that maxims are rules in a *different* sense from other kinds of rules, whereas no rule, *qua rule*, is a summary or report.

The importance of this point is that there are two possible confusions here, not one: A person may conceive moral rules as summaries or reports, or he may conceive moral rules on the model of maxims. The texts of Austin and Mill, which Rawls cites, together with Rawls's discussion, suggest that the latter, more than the former, was their mistake. *V.*, however, note 13 below.

[7] Cf. my "Technical Ought," *Mind*, LXIX (1960), July issue.

logically possible to act and follow instrumental rules without attaining the goal, and to attain the goal without following rules.

Moreover, although obviously one cannot act *on* a rule of any kind if there is no rule, one can act *in the way* specified by a set of instrumental rules (as well as attain a desired result) without *these* rules having been adopted. A group of workers, for example, may hit upon certain procedures which are so effective that they are made "the rule"; in such a case we may say, somewhat misleadingly, that one discovered a good rule by observing the actual results of a line of action. In complex cases it is very unlikely that men will act in the way rules would prescribe if the rules have not in fact been enacted. Nevertheless, there is no contradiction in saying that men acted in this way but there were no rules prescribing this course of action.[8]

Thus in the case of instrumental rules the action as well as the goal may be said to be logically independent of the rules.

1.2 Now consider the second major characteristic of rules of this kind, namely, that they are "laid down," "legislated," "made," or "adopted."

It is clear enough that an employer, for example, who "informs" his employee of the rules, is not simply "giving information." Moreover, this act or performance is very different from one's "adopting" a practical maxim or making a rule "a rule for himself." Note that in the case of a maxim the adoption of the rule is "incomplete" so long as one simply resolves to follow it. Rules of the present kind, however, are normally made for others to follow: To make their adoption complete, one must get at least some of these others "to agree," in some sense, to follow the rules.

This is so in spite of our sometimes speaking, in the sense indicated earlier, of one's "discovering a good rule" of this kind. We also speak of an administrator's "thinking of a good rule," "deciding on a rule," and "informing an employee of the rules decided on." It is quite clear, however, that "thinking of a rule" and "deciding on it" are steps taken *in the direction of* adopting a rule; the latter corresponds roughly to the stage of "resolution" in the case of a maxim. They are only steps; the rule will not become effective, and strictly speaking, will not *be* a rule, until it is "put in force" or "made a rule."

Legislation is one way of putting such a rule in force. In this case parents and guardians "teach" their children what the laws are; they do not ask for consent. In other cases the members of a group, working cooperatively, "decide on the rules," or an employer or a sergeant "tells one the rules." By such an act those subject to the rules are "directed to follow them," and the rules are then "in force." The rules serve on the one hand as guides to action—they tell one what to do—and on the other as criteria

---

[8] Cf. Rawls, ibid., p. 22.

of correctness of action—acts in accord with them are said to be *right* and breaches of them are said to be *wrong*. The rules thus tell one both *what* to do, and *that* he should do it. They are useful just on this account: One may lay down rules of this kind to make use of unskilled labor, or to gain the benefits of a division of labor, or simply to coordinate activity as in the case of an efficient traffic system.

The analysis of what the various cases of adopting a rule have in common, and what it is to be subject to rules, takes one to the difficult problem of what constitutes an authority. For our purpose the following will suffice: A party seems to be constituted as a *de facto* authority when one accepts the fact, that this party prescribes an act, as a *reason* for following the prescription (a rule of the present kind being one form of prescription). This indicates the somewhat technical sense of saying that the rule follower "agrees to" follow the rules.[9] In the case of rules of the present kind authority is ordinarily constituted, and agreement to follow the rules obtained, by contract, law, convention, or the like. Some such arrangement is necessary to induce a person to follow rules of this kind, since persons other than the rule-follower "are interested in" the goal, and normally he himself does not get (more than a share of) the product of his labor. The contract, law, or convention both promises some reward to the rule-follower, and at the same time converts others' "being interested in" the goal to their "having an interest in it"—in a legal or quasi-legal sense. This, of course, is why one who follows rules of this kind, unlike one who adopts a maxim as his guide, is not free to alter or follow the rules "at his pleasure."

The point which needs particular emphasis here, however, is that the contract, law, or convention is essential to the rule's being a rule; it is not "external" to the rule, since without it one's "laying down the rules" would be only so much rhetoric. When a contract is simply "to do a job," notice that the criterion of correctness is simply "getting the job done." If I hire a person to paint a house, he has done what he is supposed to do when the house is painted. On the other hand, to the extent to which a contract lays down rules specifying how the job is to be done, the rules are the criterion. If a painter contracts to follow certain procedures, and then fails to follow them, he has not done what he is supposed to do. This should make it quite clear that it is the contract, law, or convention which determines in a given case that rules will be the criterion of correctness. The "agreement" secured by contract, law, or convention thus makes a rule a rule, and without something like it there could be no rules of this kind.

---

9 Cf. Black, pp. 120–21. Black's analysis of the "laying down of rules" in terms of "promulgator activities" and "subject activities" (pp. 139–46) is illuminating, as is H. L. A. Hart's recent analysis of the complex idea of "acceptance" in the case of the law. *V. The Concept of Law* (Oxford, 1961), chaps. IV-VI, esp. pp. 107–14.

1.3 The discussion of the two major characteristics of these rules reveals two criteria of correctness. On the one hand, there is the criterion of a "good" rule. On the other, there are rules *in force* constituting a criterion in certain respects of the *right thing to do*. In the case of these rules there is thus a clear distinction between the justification of a rule or practice and the justification of a particular action falling under it. Perhaps on this very account some have been led to view moral rules as rules of this kind.

1.3.1 Before going on to moral rules let us notice that this distinction is not important simply because acts are judged by rules which are judged in turn in another manner, in this case by reference to a goal. The significance of the distinction derives more from the fact that the two criteria are "independent" in the following way: One may do the thing which most contributes to the goal, yet violate the rules in force; and one may act according to the rule in force when the rule is a poor one.

Moreover, the rules *in force*, not the rules which are *best*, constitute (at least under certain conditions) the criterion of right and wrong acts. This is evident in practice: A worker who does his job is *entitled* to his pay, whether or not the rules he follows in doing his job are *good* rules. This question, whether or not the rules in force are "good," ordinarily does not have to be settled for them to serve as a criterion of right action. Normally it does not even arise.

Of course, one might criticize the rules *in force* as "illegitimate" or as laid down by one who lacks rightful or proper authority, and *on this account* argue that they are not the "true" criterion of right action. However, the question of the "legitimacy" of the rules is not settled by determining which rules are best. To try to have it this way would be to invite disagreement concerning which rules *are* best, and to have no effective rule at all.[10] It would be wholly impractical to accept as authoritative or binding, and as the criterion of right action, only "the rules which are best." Who, for example, would lay down, or contract to follow under penalty, rules characterized only in this way?

Thus, even though rules of the present kind are explicitly designed to promote a goal, the rule follower is not generally at liberty to use the goal as his criterion of the right thing to do. The distinction between the two criteria so far remains firm.

1.3.2 Nevertheless, the independence of these two criteria can be overemphasized. For one thing, the criterion of a good rule, in virtue of its being used by those who adopt rules, is an indirect criterion of right action. The rules which are the criterion of right and wrong action do not prescribe

---

[10] Cf. Hume's remarks on the need of a "determinate rule of conduct," or "general rules," in his discussions of justice, both in the *Treatise* and *Inquiry*. Hume, however, does not make precisely the same point.

action which just *as a matter of fact* contributes or fails to contribute to the goal; the rules are *criticizable* if they are not good rules. Thus it does not "just so happen" that the right act *tends* to contribute to the goal. If it did not generally do this it would not be called "right," for there would be no such rules.

Second, no statement of a rule includes reference to all conditions pertinent to its application; one would not wish so to encumber it, even if every contingency could be foreseen. This implies that every rule follower is expected to know "what he is doing" in a sense larger than "following the rules"; and if the rules are instrumental he is often expected to know the goal to which his rule-directed action supposedly contributes—to know "what he is doing" in this sense. Not always, to be sure, but often he could not make a sound judgment of when and how to apply the rule without this knowledge.

For both of these reasons it is a mistake to say, in a pedestrian and casuistical way, that "the criterion of right acts is the rules." It is a mistake to think of *every* exception and *every* case as somehow included in the rule. The motive for doing so, presumably to preserve the authority of rules, is mistaken: There is an important difference between interpreting a rule, or violating it *in special circumstances*, and deciding each individual case just as if there were no rules. A person subject to rules who follows the latter course merits a special kind of criticism. Although it is difficult to specify conditions in which the violation of an instrumental rule is proper, surely the bare fact, "that by doing so one can better promote the goal," is not sufficient. The rule follower is not the sole or final authority on the propriety of breaking a rule, even when it is for the benefit of the other party.

This brings us back to the independence of the two criteria. However, It should now be clear that these criteria are interrelated and operate together. Moreover, since there are two criteria in the case of rules of the present kind, it always *makes sense* to ask if an action right by the rules is also right in the respect that it is good that a rule prescribes it. It not only *makes sense* to speak of its being proper to violate a rule; "successful violations" tend to be commended.

2

2.0 As soon as rules of the foregoing kind have been described it is rather obvious that many moral theorists, intentionally or not, have cut moral rules to their pattern. Anyone who regards the standard of morally right action as itself a means to an end will have this tendency, and this is typically true of rule utilitarians: The distinctive characteristic of their theory is that a system of rules is the criterion of morally right action, and these rules in turn are to be judged good or bad according to the consequences which action on the rules either generally produces as a matter of fact, or would produce if people could be persuaded to follow them.[11] The consequence which has been thought to be critical in assessing the soundness of a system of rules has been variously identified, as "the happiness of all," "public utility," "security," "the general welfare," etc. Nevertheless, in spite of the difference in name and even in conception, this has been taken to be a consequence, real or possible, and as an end or goal which a good system of rules would first promote and then ensure. The question of which system of rules will be most successful in this respect generally has been thought to be, at least broadly speaking, empirical: Fact and practical experience will decide which system is best. The theory thus implies that the goal, and goal promoting action, both, in senses indicated earlier, are *logically* independent of any system of rules. This fundamentally instrumental and telic character of the system of rules, and indirectly of rule-directed action as well, is a distinctive feature of utilitarianism.[12] Moreover, as I pointed out above, it is an essential feature of rules of the foregoing kind that persons other than the rule follower are "interested" in the product; this "interest" is expressed in some kind of contract, convention, or law which gives the rules authority. In utilitarian theory the "party-in-authority" tends to be "the people"; directly or indirectly they enter conventions, "adopt" rules, then enforce them, so that all may share the fruits

---

[11] See, for example, J. O. Urmson's "The Interpretation of the Moral Philosophy of J. S. Mill," *Philosophical Quarterly*, III (1953), 33–39. By and large I agree with this interpretation of Mill, although Mill showed other tendencies, not only toward a more radical utilitarianism but, in the opposite direction, toward the ethics of Bradley. John Austin is sometimes said to be a good representative of this point of view, but his conception of moral rules as commands, learned in the way we learn practical maxims, is a hodgepodge (see *The Province of Jurisprudence Determined*, Lectures I-III). In *some* respects Hume's discussion of the artificial virtues, especially justice, is a much better (and perhaps the best) classical example of this type of theory.

Among contemporaries (and apart from useful textbook presentations: see Brandt, loc. cit., and J. Hospers, *Human Conduct*). S. Toulmin in *The Place of Reason in Ethics* and P. H. Nowell-Smith in *Ethics* have come closest to an explicit statement of the theory.

An examination of actual cases of this kind of theory, with all the proper qualifications, especially if the theory is extended beyond utilitarianism, would require considerable space. I do not undertake the historical investigation here. In my judgment, the theory has a popularity which exceeds its merit, and some tendencies which are pernicious (see Section 4 below). By isolating the germ, the disease may be better understood—its valuable antibodies notwithstanding.

[12] It would be a mistake to say that utilitarians maintained this deliberately, after considering alternatives, or even that they did so consistently. John Stuart Mill, in Chapter IV of *Utilitarianism*, seems to have been unaware of the issue when he discussed happiness as "a concrete whole" and virtue as one of its "parts." Cf. below 4.5.

of the rule-directed action. The product is shared, the goal is the good of all.

2.1 Moral rules on the rule utilitarian view thus have the basic characteristics of the rules which I discussed in (1). When the two are compared, and the analysis in (1) is brought to bear, it quickly reveals that rule utilitarianism is faced with a fundamental problem. If the position is to have the advantage over act utilitarianism that is claimed for it, then the criterion of right action must be a system of rules and not general utility. Rules are a criterion of right action, however, only on condition that they are "rules-in-force" and in some sense "agreed to." But obviously the rules which are "in force" or "agreed to" may or may not be the rules which maximize utility; and to the extent that they are not, then the "best rules" by the utilitarian standard, not having been "adopted," are not the criterion of right action. The best rules may not even be known. The "rules" and the "utilitarianism" in "rule utilitarianism" thus constitute two independent criteria, and they may not be in much accord.

2.1.1 The analysis in (1) not only clearly shows the nature of this difficulty, but also helps one to understand some of the directions in which utilitarianism has moved in an effort to avoid it. Some good utilitarians, mindful of evil in ordinary conventions, tend to say that just as men *ought* to adopt a rule only if it maximizes utility, so one is *obligated* to follow a rule only if it maximizes utility. This doctrine implies that one may freely disregard a rule if ever he discovers that action on the rule is not maximally felicific, and in this respect makes moral rules like "practical maxims." It deprives social and moral rules of their authority and naturally is in sharp conflict with practice. On this alternative rule utilitarianism collapses into act utilitarianism.[13]

2.1.2 Other rule utilitarians, equally concerned to avoid an ethical conventionalism, either close their eyes to the difficulty or else overlook it. They either just declare an ideal set of rules to be the criterion, or else say that the criterion of right action is the system of rules which, *if* adopted, *would* maximize utility, or something of the sort. Such a formulation clearly does not acknowledge that rules must be adopted if they are to be rules: The "if adopted" is only a way of describing the ideal and actually obscures the necessity of a rule's being adopted.

The fact that it is commonly the case that some moral principles and rules to which a person subscribes are not "in force" in his society raises important issues for *any* moral philosophy of rules. I cannot even try to do them justice here. Nevertheless, surely it is a mistake to maintain that

---

13 For a clear recent statement of this position, see J. J. C. Smart, "Extreme and Restricted Utilitarianism," *Philosophical Quarterly*, VI (1956), 344–54. Notice that Smart argues explicitly that moral rules are "rules of thumb." [this Vol. pp. 249–60.]

a set of rules, thought to be ideally utilitarian or felicific, is the criterion of right action. If the rules are simply described in this way, and are not enumerated, we so far do not have any rules and are not likely to get any.[14] On the other hand, if we are presented with a list, but these are not rules in practice, the most one could reasonably do is to try to get them adopted. A manager in the quiet of his office may dream of a system of rules which will maximize production, and a utilitarian may build a theory around the set of rules which will maximize utility. Surely the latter would be as foolish as the former if he said that these ideal rules are the criterion of right and wrong acts. As previous analysis has shown, acts are not judged by proposed rules, ideal rules, and rules-in-theory: for these do not fully qualify as rules.[15]

2.1.3 Other rule utilitarians show a finer appreciation of the logic of their position: They interpret moral rules on analogy with the rules in (1), even if it forces them to admit that the criterion of right action is not the set of rules which maximizes utility. This alternative seems to be popular with those whose primary allegiance is to a "morality of rules," and who are utilitarian only because they suppose that "welfare" *must* have something to do with morality. (After all, what else *can* serve as a criterion of rules?)

On this alternative it always makes sense to ask whether or not a "moral or social convention" subscribed to in practice is best, and this gives sense to the question, sometimes asked, whether a people who follow their conventions act in the best way they could. At the same time the question, whether an individual ought to do something in particular—for example, repay money borrowed—is quite a different question, to be answered by referring, at least in part, to the practices and conventions of that society. Such a view does not make the blunder of taking an ideal system of rules as the criterion of which particular acts are right, and yet it does not endorse conventions which are obviously questionable. One may seek earnestly to reform the moral conventions of a people, and yet insist that these conventions, some of which are in need of reform, are the general

---

[14] Cf. above, 1.3.1.

[15] See 1.2 and 1.3.1 above. Since utilitarianism is rather often associated with reform, it tends to be formulated in ideal terms. See, for example, J. S. Mill's most explicit statement of his position in Ch. II, paragraph 10 of *Utilitarianism* "... the standard of morality, which may accordingly be defined 'the rules and precepts for human conduct', by the observance of which an existence such as has been described might be, to the greatest extent possible, secured to all mankind. . . ." In this passage, how is "possible" to be taken? Does it mean "possible, within the framework of existing institutions"? For one attempt to avoid in this way the difficulties inherent in an ideal formulation, see R. B. Brandt, op. cit., pp. 396–400. This attempt goes only part of the way in meeting the difficulty. On the difficulty itself cf. H. J. McCloskey, "An Examination of Restricted Utilitarianism," *Philosophical Review*, LXVI (1957), esp. 475–81; and J. Austin, op. cit., Lecture III.

criterion by which a man must decide what in particular he ought to do, and by which his acts are to be judged. At the same time, such a view need not dichotomize the two criteria. As we found above, rules of this kind have an open texture which permits the criterion of the rules to enter into their proper interpretation. I think we may presume, moreover, that there are instances in which one should violate the letter of a moral rule when following it would clearly be to the detriment of the general welfare, or the welfare of all parties concerned. Rule utilitarians could no doubt take instances of this sort to support their theory. As we also found above, one may admit this without depriving rules of their authority.[16]

3

3.0 A careful development and criticism of rule utilitarianism, as just outlined, would be worth while, but it is outside the range of this paper. Even without this development, however, it can be shown that rule utilitarians, by using the kind of rule in (1) as a model, have exercised a definite option, and I want to indicate the general character of this option. To do this, I shall first consider briefly the rules of certain kinds of games.[17]

3.1 Rules of common competitive games, such as baseball, chess, and the like, say how a game is to be played. They state the "object of the game," "the moves," "how the counting should go," etc. Often they are stated in "rule books," and sometimes they are enforced by referees appointed by an acknowledged authority. These formalities, however, are not at all necessary. The rules must be "laid down" or "adopted" in some sense, but all that is required (in the case of those games being discussed) is that

---

16 I think that is the most favorable interpretation which can be given to the utilitarianism of the nineteenth-century reformers: They framed a theory which would make sense of reform, but at the same time had too much practical (if not always philosophical) sense to advocate the use of the criterion of rules as the criterion of acts. It is as if they perceived the importance of moral rules and practices but were unable fully to accommodate these to their theory. I think that the presence of the two criteria, which the analysis of the rules in (1) clearly reveals, explains for example the "tension" between chapter two of Mill's *Utilitarianism* on the one hand, and chapters three and five on the other.

17 I can be brief because rules of this kind have been discussed by others. I shall mostly confine myself to points not previously mentioned, or at least not emphasized. I am perhaps most indebted to Rawls's acute analysis of what he calls the "practice conception," and on the whole agree with it. The name is misleading since very many "practices," as we ordinarily think of them, are defined by rules (e.g. by job rules) which are quite unlike those to which his "practice conception of rules" properly applies. Although unimportant in itself, it is just this kind of thing, I suspect, which has led moral philosophers into serious error. One can sympathize since it is almost impossible to find a conventional expression which is not misleading in some important respect.

a group of players "agree" on a set of rules. This agreement may consist simply in their following and enforcing rules which they all have learned: Think, for example, of a group of small boys playing baseball, and think of the difference between one's knowing the rules and playing the game. In such cases there is no formally agreed-upon authority; each player—in principle—is both rule-follower and rule-enforcer. No player has the authority to modify the rules at will, but the players together can change them in any way they see fit. As one should expect, there are many variations.

In the latter respects game rules of this kind are quite like the rules in (1). These game rules, however, noticeably lack the first major characteristic of those rules: They are not designed to yield a product. More precisely, they are not adopted to promote the attainment of a goal which, in the senses indicated earlier, is "over and beyond" the rules.[18] They do not serve a goal which is "logically independent" of the game which they define.

3.1.1 Of course people who play games do so with various motives, and some of the goals which motivate them are logically independent of the game; for example, exercise, recreation, the opportunity to talk to friends or make a conquest. Undoubtedly games are popular because they serve so many ends. Nevertheless, motives and goals of this kind are not essential. Many players participate (so far as can be determined without psychoanalyzing them) "just because they want to" or simply "from love of the game." Actually this kind of motive, even if it is not typical, is that which is most distinctive of players: One who "loves a game" commonly regards another, who lacks the motive, as poorly appreciating "the quality of the game." This is apt to be missed just because games have been turned into instruments, for exercise, diversion, etc., to such a great degree. The point is, they *need* not be.

Moreover, games qua games do not seem to have a design or goal *different* from the motives of the rule-followers, in the way rules of jobs commonly do. What is this goal? One who most appreciates a game speaks about it rather as if it were an aesthetic object, worth playing on its own account and apart from any product or result; and if he is asked to justify his claim that it is good, he seems to have a problem analogous to that of justifying an aesthetic judgment.[19] Sometimes, to be sure, the rules of games are changed, and in particular instances violated, in order

---

[18] Some games have become instruments to such a considerable degree, and some instrumental activities have become so much like games, that no description will prevent the intrusion of dubious and borderline cases.

[19] This reminds one of the ancient distinctions between "doing" and "making," and between (what the medievals called) "immanent" and "transitive" activity. I do not mean to deny that some jobs are worth doing "on their own account," but even when "one enjoys a job," there is a discernible purpose which it is designed to promote.

to change the consequences. Many official rules, for example, have been changed in order to lessen player injuries; and particular persons may find a game played by the official rules too strenuous, or pursuit of the ball after a bad drive too troublesome. These facts, however, do not imply that the rules are designed to produce consequences, such as the right amount of exercise or exertion, or the good health of the players. Changes of the kind mentioned simply indicate that the rules of a game, like the rules of a job, are adopted in a context by persons who have many desires and many obligations other than "to play the game" and "follow its rules." Games are often altered to make them harmonize better with such contextual features. It is true, of course, that persons who have turned games into instruments change or violate the rules more readily. As we say, these people do not take the game as seriously.

Some philosophers are inclined to say that even when one plays a game "just because he wants to" or "for love of the game," the game is still an instrument—to "his enjoyment" or "pleasure." This stand depends for its cogency on our being able to describe this pleasure or enjoyment without referring to the game, which should be possible if the pleasure or enjoyment really were something separate from playing the game. However, although it is clearly possible to play a game and not enjoy it, the converse does not appear plausible. To be sure, one sometimes says that he gets about the same enjoyment from one game as another, especially when the two are similar. But this is apt to mean that he has no strong preference for one game over another, that he likes one as well as the other, not that there is a kind of pleasurable feeling which in fact results from both, more or less equally, and which *conceivably* could be had from very different activities or even from being acted *on* in some way. (Similarly, when one says that he "likes to talk to one person about as much as another," this clearly does not mean that talking to the two persons produces the same kind of pleasure in him.) Moreover, when we speak of getting about the same enjoyment from two games, sometimes the "enjoyment" does not appear to be, strictly speaking, the enjoyment "of playing the game," but rather the enjoyment of exercising, talking to friends, etc. I do not deny, however, that games can become instruments. I want to argue that they need not be, often are not, and that in calling them games we do not imply that they are instruments.

The kind of goal the pursuit of which to some degree *is* essential to the playing of the game is the "object of the game," as defined by the rules, and the various subgoals which promote this object according to the rules. Such goals as these, for example, "to score the most runs," "to get the batter out at second base," obviously are not logically independent of the rules of the game—if there were no rules it would be logically impossible to try do these things. It is just nonsense to speak of changing the rules so that one can better attain the object of the game.

3.1.2 Since the action within a game is designed to attain goals defined by the rules, the action as well as the goal logically depends on the rules: In important respects a move in the game has the consequences it has because the rules say it has; *in these respects* the rules define the consequences and determine the character of the action.[20] Since the character of instrumental action is fixed at least partly by the goal which the action is designed to serve, the action can be described in this essential respect, as a "trying to get the goal," without referring to or presupposing rules. In the case of play in a game, unless the game has become an instrument, this is not possible; if one describes the action in a game apart from the rules, as a "trying to catch a ball," he leaves out the design. On account of this difference one may feel inclined to say that whereas rules of the kind described in (1) *may* be used to describe an action, game rules by defining new kinds of action just constitute "forms of life."[21]

3.2 However, this is but one side of the story, and if it were the only one it is not likely that the two kinds of rules would be confused. To see the other side, which is equally important, one should attend to the fact that the play in a game is not wholly defined by the rules of the game. "The kind of game he plays" ordinarily does not refer to the game as defined by the rules; "to play a game" ordinarily means more than following the rules. The point is that although the object of the game is defined by the rules, since the action in a game normally consists in "trying to attain that object," and since the game rules do not determine success in this respect, the action in *this* respect is instrumental. Players often develop tactics and strategies and skills in playing. Sometimes they follow what I have called practical maxims, and at other times they follow team rules agreed on among themselves or laid down by the "manager." The latter are, of course, examples of the rules described in (1). Obviously they should not be confused with rules of games, as I have described them. For one can be said to play a game without his following any particular set of instrumental rules.

The point of greatest importance here is that although game rules are not themselves instruments, they support, as it were, a considerable amount of instrumental activity, much of which logically could not be carried on without them. To play a game is typically to follow the rules of the game *and* engage in this instrumental activity; a "good player" does more than just follow the rules. Even one who "loves the game for its own sake" derives his satisfaction from the kind of *instrumental* activity which the rules of the game make possible. Games make new goals, new pursuits, and new skills available to men.

---

[20] This is the point which Rawls emphasized.
[21] Cf. A. I. Melden, "Action," *Philosophical Review*, LXV (1956), 523–41.

In this situation it is not surprising that some should regard games themselves as instruments. To regard them in this way, however, would be to confuse their function.

4

4.0 The rules of games just considered differ most significantly from the rules described in (1) because they are, by our criterion, "non-instrumental." This point of difference between the two kinds of rules is one of the most important to be found. I have been concerned to mark it here to focus attention on the thesis, maintained by many utilitarians, that moral rules and social institutions are instruments designed to promote a goal logically independent of the rules and institutions. The thesis is only rarely discussed, and I think that failure to discuss it helps account for the recurrent popularity of utilitarianism. However, morality is obviously not a game, and if the thesis is to be fully assessed, moral rules must be carefully analyzed and alternatives considered. This is out of the question here. In the remainder of this paper I shall note a complexity which is too often overlooked, and just indicate the critical force of certain recently developed lines of argument. However, the fundamental issue here is not at all new.[22]

---

22 Historically one perhaps first senses the issue in his reading of Plato and Aristotle. Is man's end somehow "writ in his nature" in such a way that it can be determined apart from a determination of virtue? If so, it might be reasonable to regard virtue as a *means* to the end, and instruction in virtue as a matter of learning from practical experience the best means. On the other hand, if man's end cannot be determined without the determination of virtue—if man's end is properly defined in terms of virtue, as activity in accordance with it, and man's nature is defined as potentialities for this end—then virtue is not a means and its discovery in practical experience must be understood differently. Although the second interpretation is the sounder, there were tendencies in medieval thought to favor the first—undoubtedly deriving from the fact that God, who is certainly different from man, was said to be man's end. Moreover, the desire of God was said to be implanted in man's nature. This inclination was said to be a natural participation of the eternal law, and natural virtue was said to be an insufficient means to God. I think myself, however, that the second interpretation gives a sounder account of the ethics not only of Augustine but also of Aquinas. Yet it is not surprising that out of this tradition there should have come the contrary (Lockian) doctrine that natural law applies to man in a "state of nature," and that men by compact make societies as a remedy for natural evils and as a means to natural goals. This doctrine in turn, by way of reaction, stimulated theories according to which the distinction of right and wrong is not founded in nature, but in contract, convention, or rules. In the nineteenth century the opposition between the two general points of view assumed more of its original form when idealists worked out their own interpretation of the social contract, and opposed utilitarianism. (See, for example, Bradley's "Pleasure for Pleasure's Sake" in *Ethical Studies* and Bosanquet's *Philosophical Theory of the State.*) Very recent philosophy in some respects strongly resembles idealism, undoubtedly because it itself is a reac-

4.1 Consider the rule "Do not cheat." Often it is taught in the context of a game, and it acquires a rather specific sense in this context. The rule in this use can be paraphrased as "Do not violate the rules of the game in order to gain an advantage for yourself." In this use the rule logically presupposes games as social institutions; if there were no games, the rule could not have this use and this meaning.

The same general point applies to many other moral rules, such as "Keep your promises," "Do not steal," and "Do not lie." Each of these logically presupposes institutions and practices, such as "promising," "a system of property," "a language." Since these moral rules presuppose such practices, they cannot be understood apart from them; the practice, constituted by its own rules, makes the moral rule meaningful. Philosophical analyses which have attempted to clarify moral rules apart from institutionalized practices have surrounded them with theoretical perplexities and turned them into "mere forms" of morality.[23]

However, the fact that these moral rules presuppose institutions or practices does not *in itself* decide the question whether or not they are instrumental and utilitarian. In some respects the rules "Do not cheat," "Do not lie," etc., are like the rules "Do not violate traffic lights," "Do not drive on the wrong side," etc. These rules obviously presuppose practices, and the rules and practices appear to be primarily instrumental and utilitarian. We can easily conceive of the practices being changed in order to provide a more effective system of traffic control.

On the utilitarian view moral rules and the institutions which they presuppose are rather like a system of this kind. The assumption is that men have various destinations which they want to reach and the social aim is to provide the system of institutions which will be most effective in helping them along. As men together devise such public instruments as roads and bridges, which no one alone could construct, and then regulate the use of these instruments for the "public good," so on this view men together have developed such institutions as "promising," " a system of property," etc. These institutions may not have arisen through deliberate design, although (there often seems to be the assumption that) if an institution or practice has arisen, then it *must* have been rewarding, and consequently *must* have served some purpose. The instrumental character of these institutions is evidenced more directly, however, by the fact that persons hold and dispose of property, make promises, and, quite generally, engage in the life of their

---

tion to a kind of philosophy which arose in reaction to idealism. For one example, cf. Bosanquet, op. cit., with A. I. Melden, *Rights and Right Conduct* (Oxford, 1959).

This is, of course, only a fragmentary account of the historical origins of the issue.

[23] This misinterpretation accounts for some criticisms of a morality of rules. Cf. A Macbeath, *Experiments in Living* (London, 1952), Lecture XIII.

institutions with goals in mind. If these reasons are decisive, moreover, one's language, too, should be viewed as a social tool.[24] Certainly men have purposes in speaking.

As in the case of a traffic system, however, on occasion it is to a person's advantage to break the rules of their institutions. Men must be taught not to; they must be made to realize that temporary advantage is far outweighed by the more permanent benefits to be gained if all can be depended on to follow the rules. Moral rules, such as "Keep your promises," "Do not steal," "Do not lie," like the rules "Always obey traffic signals," "Do not drive on the wrong side," seem to be conceived as deriving from the occasional but recurrent conflict between private advantage and public institutions. Utilitarians commonly make the point that if a person in his own interest is sometimes led to violate a rule, he will nevertheless insist, also in his own interest, that others follow the rule: The "security" which derives from a system of public institutions is given an important place in moral theory. Moral rules of this kind thus seem to be conceived as supports for and ancillary to the public institutions which they presuppose. If these rules could only be made to serve a system of truly *rational* (i.e., utilitarian) institutions, the aforementioned conflict would be minimized, as the happiness of all was promoted. The negative morality of rules would be lost in liberal affection for the general welfare.

4.2 Moral rules of this kind in a sense do *tend* to support the institutions and practices which they presuppose: They *tend* to receive their effective interpretation from the character of the institutions, and they are both taught and reaffirmed most vigorously when persons from self-interest show an inclination to violate the rules of the institutions. As a consequence (and for an additional reason which will soon be apparent[25]) these institutions and practices have, as it were, a "moral dimension" or a "moral part." Nevertheless, in assessing rule utilitarianism it is important to distinguish moral rules on the one hand from other rules which also define and characterize the underlying institutions and practices. For it is possible to learn the rules of a game, and to play the game, without being tempted to cheat, without grasping the concept of "cheating," and without learning the moral rule "Do not cheat." It is not uncommon for children to do this. Children ordinarily also learn to speak correctly, in the sense of learning many rules of the language, without learning the rule "Do not lie," thus without grasping the moral concept of a lie. It may not be so evident, but it is also the case that one can learn many rules governing property, can learn to make a promise, etc., without grasping the moral force of the rules "Do

---

24 Cf. Hume's *Treatise*, Bk. III, Pt. II, Sec. II. Esp. p. 490 in Selby-Bigge edition.
25 See 4.5 below.

not steal," "Keep your promises," etc. There are surely legal experts on property and contract who have, as we say, very little moral understanding.[26]

In considering the soundness of rule utilitarianism, there are thus two interrelated questions. The first is whether or not the institutions of promising, property, language, etc., are instruments serving goals logically independent of these institutions. This bears on the question of the soundness of utilitarianism not only as a *moral* but as a *social* theory. Then there is the more restricted question whether rule utilitarianism offers a sound account of moral rules.

4.3.1 Several lines of thought, some recently developed, bear on these questions. To take one example, primarily as it applies to the first of the questions: Utilitarians, as already indicated, have put considerable emphasis on "security," if not as *the* goal, nevertheless as an important "part" of the goal. A person cannot be "secure," however, without being able to *count on* others to act and refrain from acting in a variety of ways. His counting on others, moreover, is in a great many cases not "an expectation" based on an ordinary induction. For most often the expectation involved in one's counting on another is based on the fact that the action or restraint in question is governed by rules which define rights, obligations, duties, etc.: One can count on another because the other (presumably) is acting on such rules.[27] For this reason the expression "counting on another" in many occasions of its use makes no more sense apart from rules than "deciding to act" or "acting" makes apart from reasons for acting. There is also the related point that the action which one counts on another to do, itself, in many cases presupposes rules; for example, just as one could not count on a person to "play first base" if there were no game of baseball, so one could not count on another to "keep his promise" or "respect property" if there were no practice of promising or institution of property.[28] Although "security" is an ambiguous term, in the sense in which it refers to a signifi-

---

26 Although an adequate description of property and promising in a sense implies that theft and promise breaking are morally wrong, a person may fail to "see" the implication. When we teach a child what property and promising are, we commonly say that it is wrong for him to take what belongs to another and wrong for him not to do what he has promised to do. So far, however, the child is not guilty of theft or promise breaking, and until he has witnessed them, or an inclination thereto, in himself or another (since he has not yet had occasion to *use* the rules "Do not steal" and "Keep your promises"), he will have little practical understanding of these rules. Before he reaches this point, however, he may have learned enough of the underlying rules to exchange property, make promises, etc. Growth in moral understanding is long and complex and participation in ordinary practices does not wait upon it.

27 Cf. Hart, op. cit., pp. 54–57.

28 Cf. Hume, loc. cit. Black and many others make the same point.

cant social goal it could not mean what it does without rules which define institutions and practices.

For both these reasons "security" just does not appear to be a goal which is logically independent of the rules of institutions and practices like property, promising, language, etc. Moreover, it would seem very strange to think of the greatest number having the greatest happiness or pleasure or welfare without being fairly secure. The utilitarian position thus appears to be quite vulnerable, even apart from the fact that its proponents have notoriously failed to give "happiness," "pleasure," "welfare," and the like the clarity of meaning which they must have to function as goals.

4.3.2 Furthermore, as the earlier analysis of games revealed, the fact that one does many things as a means to an end when engaging in a practice gives no support to the claim that the practice itself is a means. The fact that one uses various devices to win a game does not imply that the game is an instrument, and similarly, the fact that one uses words as tools, or makes a promise or deals in property for some purpose, does not support the view that institutions and practices such as language, promising, and property are instruments for the promotion of goals logically independent of these institutions and practices. Nor does this appear plausible: It seems rather to be the case that institutions and practices create or establish most of the goals which men pursue, in the sense that these goals, like the object of a game, would be logically impossible without the institutions and practices. It also appears that persons who engage in business, or make speeches, or follow intellectual pursuits ultimately because "they just enjoy doing these things" are rather like players who enjoy a game for its own sake—in the respect that they derive their enjoyment from instrumental activity which is also made possible by institutions and practices.

At this point, however, it becomes apparent that much requires to be worked out before one can replace the utilitarian view of social institutions with another which is more adequate.

4.4 When one turns to consider utilitarianism as a theory of moral rules, *to some extent* the same arguments apply. For some moral rules *are* in some respects ancillary to the practices and institutions which they presuppose, and in so far as this is the case, then generally speaking moral rules are just as utilitarian as, and no more utilitarian than, these practices and institutions. Notice that the most common uses of the moral rules "Do not lie," "Do not steal," and the like presuppose not only underlying institutions and practices, but also, as suggested above, a tendency or inclination of some persons at some times not to conform to the institutions and practices. This seems to explain why persons living in a law-abiding community use these moral rules so little. This in turn suggests that moral rules are "protective devices," rather like a police system, which also is little used in a law-abiding community and which also presupposes both institutions and an inclination on the part of some persons to violate them. The "police" view of moral rules is partial, but it is also partly true: It helps one see why moral rules are so often conceived as "external" to an individual, imposing restraints on him (and why some philosophers tend to pattern moral rules on rules in a prison!). At the same time it helps one understand why some people "internalize" moral rules in the way they do. For some insist on the importance of following moral rules only because they value a system of institutions and the "happiness and security" which the institutions afford. Seeing that valued institutions would cease to exist if people generally did not act in the way moral rules prescribe, they teach these rules—although morality for them is primarily a matter of promoting individual or public welfare, and it would be better if moral rules had little use. This interest in morality is epitomized in the person who regards moral rules as a protector of life, liberty, and property; breaking the rules breeds fear, ruins business, and disrupts the game. This is the internalization of moral rules as ancillary to institutions; it tends to characterize utilitarians past and present.

4.5 Moral rules, however, may be internalized in quite another way, and on this account utilitarianism as a *moral* theory is open to an additional criticism specific to itself.

For a person who values an institution constituted by rules may come to see that rules by nature apply to all members of a class. One who sees this may then be led to look upon the rules which characterize some particular institutions and practices not simply as "applying to all," but at the same time as constituting "a common standard of correctness." And in this way one may be led to the abstract but practical conception of "a community of men living under the idea of law," of which particular institutions afford so many possible examples. In so far as one thinks that others as well as himself act under this conception, he will no doubt value a particular game or language or any other such institution not only qua game, qua language, etc., but also as a particular instance and a particular form of such a community.

When the idea of such a community is attained and made to govern practice (as it seems to have been, for example, by the Socrates of the *Crito*) then the moral rules "Do not lie," "Do not steal," etc., will appear in a new light. One who acts under such an idea will teach these rules neither as primarily negative and restraining, nor primarily as supports or protections for particular institutions. For although he may view the rules in these ways, he will regard them primarily as affirming in so many different ways the fundamental principle "Live under the idea of law." The principle may be stated negatively, in the form "Do not make an exception of oneself," but his primary aim in teaching the rules will be to raise one to the conception of a moral community. Since such a community potentially includes all men, part of the challenge may be to find particular institutions in which the conception can be realized.

Moral rules regarded in this way of course still presuppose particular institutions and practices. However, they are no longer, properly speaking, "ancillary to" the institutions and practices: They now "add something" to the institutions and practices which they presuppose; the institutions and practices now have a new dimension. Cheating comes to be deplored not primarily because it tends to disrupt a game but because it detracts from the quality which a game can have. If there is cheating, one may simply prefer not to play. In a similar way, lying may be deplored because it detracts from the quality of speech, theft because it detracts from the quality of exchange, etc. Put affirmatively, the idea of a moral community is realizable analogically—only in a variety of forms—in sportsmanship, morally mature speech, honest argument, etc. It should be evident that common institutions and practices are often not in fact logically independent of morality; one has to form a limited or abstract conception of them to make them so.

When moral rules are regarded in this way,[29] then obviously they do not serve a goal logically independent of themselves. In the language of Mill, virtue has now become a "part" of the end, a "part of happiness." Only it is clear that when Mill said this, with his usual willingness to sacrifice theory to good sense, he deserted utilitarianism. The instrumental and utilitarian pattern just will not fit.

5

Further discussion of moral rules is beyond the aim of this paper. My primary purpose has been to contribute to the clarification of moral rules by clarifying a fundamental option open to moral theory. To this end I have both analyzed the general utilitarian view of social rules and practices, along with some variations, and I have tried to lay bare the (largely implicit) utilitarian view of moral rules. I have analyzed moral rules, however, only to the point where the character and significance of the option, and the force of some of the arguments which apply, will be fairly clear. I do not want to suggest that all moral rules are like those which I have considered. The analysis of games, in distinguishing the moral player from the good player, may remind one that there are two traditions in the history of ethics, one emphasizing an exoteric ethic and a moral law known to all, the other an esoteric ethic and a virtue reserved for the wise. I have been concerned, almost exclusively, with the former, and not all of that.

In the course of the discussion attention has been called to the fact that moral rules can be (and thus tend to be) conceived as summaries, reports,

---

29 Cf. K. Baier, op. cit., pp. 200–204, and W. D. Falk's comments on "natural obligation" and "mature moral thinking" in "Morality and Convention," *Journal of Philosophy*, LVII (1960), 675–85.

practical maxims, rules designed to promote a goal, rules which define institutions, rules which protect institutions, and as particular forms of the fundamental principle of justice.[30] Marking the important differences between these alternatives should remove more than one confusion and at the same time provide *some* of the subtlety which will be needed if the discussion of moral rules is to make genuine advances in the future.

---

[30] The list is not meant to be exhaustive. Cf. e.g., D. S. Shwayder, "Moral Rules and Moral Maxims," *Ethics*, LXVII (1957), 269–85.

Some Merits of One Form
of Rule-Utilitarianism

RICHARD B. BRANDT

1. Utilitarianism is the thesis that the moral predicates of an act—at least its objective rightness or wrongness, and sometimes also its moral praiseworthiness or blameworthiness—are functions in some way, direct or indirect, of consequences for the welfare of sentient creatures, and of nothing else. Utilitarians differ about what precise function they are; and they differ about what constitutes welfare and how it is to be measured. But they agree that all one needs to know, in order to make moral appraisals correctly, is the consequences of certain things for welfare.

Utilitarianism is thus a normative ethical thesis and not, at least not necessarily, a metaethical position—that is, a position about the meaning and justification of ethical statements. It is true that some utilitarians have declared that the truth of the normative thesis follows, given the ordinary, or proper, meaning of moral terms such as "right." I shall ignore this further, metaethical claim. More recently some writers have suggested something very similar, to the effect that our concept of "morality" is such that we could not call a system of rules a "moral system" unless it were utilitarian in some sense.

This latter suggestion is of special interest to us, since the general topic of the present conference is "the concept of morality," and I wish to com-

---

From University of Colorado Studies, *1967. Reprinted by permission of the author and the University of Colorado Press.*

A revised version of a paper presented to a conference on moral philosophy held at the University of Colorado in October, 1965.

ment on it very briefly. It is true that there is a connection between utilitarianism and the concept of morality; at least I believe—and shall spell out the contention later—that utilitarianism cannot be explained, at least in its most plausible form, without making use of the concept of "morality" and, furthermore, without making use of an analysis of this concept. But the reverse relationship does not hold: it is not true that the concept "morality" is such that we cannot properly call a system of rules a morality unless it is a thoroughly utilitarian system, although possibly we would not call a system of rules a "morality" if it did not regulate at all the forms of conduct which may be expected to do good or harm to sentient persons. One reason why it is implausible to hold that any morality is necessarily utilitarian is that any plausible form of utilitarianism will be a rather complex thesis, and it seems that the concept of morality is hardly subtle enough to entail anything so complex—although, of course, such reasoning does not exclude the possibility of the concept of morality entailing some simple and unconvincing form of utilitarianism. A more decisive reason, however, is that we so use the term "morality" that we can say consistently that the morality of a society contains some prohibitions which considerations of utility do not support, or are not even thought to support: for example, some restrictions on sexual behavior. (Other examples are mentioned later.) Thus there is no reason to think that only a utilitarian code could properly be called a "moral code" or a "morality," as these are ordinarily used.

In any case, even if "nonutilitarian morality" (or "right, but harmful") were a contradiction in terms, utilitarianism as a normative thesis would not yet be established; for it would be open to a nonutilitarian to advocate changing the meaning of "morality" (or "right") in order to allow for his normative views. There is, of course, the other face of the coin: even if, as we actually use the term "morality" (or "right"), the above expressions are not contradictions in terms, it might be a good and justifiable thing for people to be taught to use words so that these expressions would become self-contradictory. But if there are good reasons for doing the last, presumably there are good and convincing reasons for adopting utilitarianism as a normative thesis, without undertaking such a roundabout route to the goal. I shall, therefore, discuss utilitarianism as a normative thesis, without supposing that it can be supported by arguing that a nonutilitarian morality is a contradiction in terms.

2. If an analysis of concepts like "morally wrong" and "morality" and "moral code" does not enable us to establish the truth of the utilitarian thesis, the question arises what standard a normative theory like utilitarianism has to meet in order for a reasonable presumption to be established in its favor. It is well known that the identity and justification of any such standard can be debated at length. In order to set bounds to the present discussion, I shall state briefly the standard I shall take for granted for

purposes of the present discussion. Approximately this standard would be acceptable to a good many writers on normative ethics. However this may be, it would be agreed that it is worth knowing whether some form of utilitarianism meets this standard better than any other form of utilitarian theory, and it is this question which I shall discuss.

The standard which I suggest an acceptable normative moral theory has to meet is this: The theory must contain no unintelligible concepts or internal inconsistencies; it must not be inconsistent with known facts; it must be capable of precise formulation so that its implications for action can be.determined; and—most important—its implications must be acceptable to thoughtful persons who have had reasonably wide experience, when taken in the light of supporting remarks that can be made, and when compared with the implications of other clearly statable normative theories. It is not required that the implications of a satisfactory theory be consonant with the uncriticized moral intuitions of intelligent and experienced people, but only with those intuitions which stand in the light of supporting remarks, etc. Furthermore, it is not required of an acceptable theory that the best consequences would be produced by people adopting that theory, in contrast to other theories by which they might be convinced. (The theory might be so complex that it would be a good thing if most people did not try their hand at applying it to concrete situations!) It may be a moving *ad hominem* argument, if one can persuade an act-utilitarian that it would have bad consequences for people to try to determine the right act according to that theory, and to live by their conclusions; but such a showing would not be a reasonable ground for rejecting that normative theory.

3. Before turning to the details of various types of utilitarian theory, it may be helpful to offer some "supporting remarks" which will explain some reasons why some philosophers are favorably disposed toward a utilitarian type of normative theory.

(a) The utilitarian principle provides a clear and definite procedure for determining which acts are right or wrong (praiseworthy or blameworthy), by observation and the methods of science alone and without the use of any supplementary intuitions (assuming that empirical procedures can determine when something maximizes utility), for all cases, including the complex ones about which intuitions are apt to be mute, such as whether kleptomanic behavior is blameworthy or whether it is right to break a confidence in certain circumstances. The utilitarian presumably frames his thesis so as to conform with enlightened intuitions which are clear, but his thesis, being general, has implications for all cases, including those about which his intuitions are not clear. The utilitarian principle is like a general scientific theory, which checks with observations at many points, but can also be used as a guide to beliefs on matters inaccessible to observation (like the behavior of matter at absolute zero temperature).

Utilitarianism is not the only normative theory with this desirable property; egoism is another, and, with some qualifications, so is Kant's theory.

(b) Any reasonably plausible normative theory will give a large place to consequences for welfare in the moral assessment of actions, for this consideration enters continuously and substantially into ordinary moral thinking. Theories which ostensibly make no appeal of this sort etiher admit utilitarian considerations by the back door, or have counter-intuitive consequences. Therefore the ideal of simplicity leads us to hope for the possibility of a pure utilitarian theory. Moreover, utilitarianism avoids the necessity of weighing disparate things such as justice and utility.

(c) If a proposed course of action does not raise moral questions, it is generally regarded as rational, and its agent well advised to perform it, if and only if it will maximize expectable utility for the agent. In a similar vein, it can be argued that society's "choice" of an institution of morality is rational and well advised, if and only if having it will maximize expectable social utility—raise the expectable level of the average "utility curve" of the population. If morality is a system of traditional and arbitrary constraints on behavior, it cannot be viewed as a rational institution. But it can be, if the system of morality is utilitarian. In that case the institution of morality can be recommended to a person of broad human sympathies, as an institution which maximizes the expectation of general welfare; and to a selfish person, as an institution which, in the absence of particular evidence about his own case, may be expected to maximize his own expectation of welfare (his own welfare being viewed as a random sample from the population). To put it in other words, a utilitarian morality can be "vindicated" by appeal either to the humanity or to the selfishness of human beings.

To say this is not to deny that nonutilitarian moral principles may be capable of vindication in a rather similar way. For instance, to depict morality as an institution which fosters human equality is to recommend it by appeal to something which is perhaps as deep in man as his sympathy or humanity.[1]

4. The type of utilitarianism on which I wish to focus is a form of rule-utilitarianism, as contrasted with act-utilitarianism. According to the latter type of theory (espoused by Sidgwick and Moore), an act is objectively right if no other act the agent could perform would produce better consequences. (On this view, an act is blameworthy if and only if it is right to perform the act of blaming or condemning it; the principles of blameworthi-

---

[1] It would not be impossible to combine a restricted principle of utility with a morality of justice or equality. For instance, it might be said that an act is right only if it meets a certain condition of justice, and also if it is one which, among all the just actions open to the agent, meets a requirement of utility as well as any other.

ness are a special case of the principle of objectively right actions.) Act-utilitarianism is hence a rather atomistic theory: the rightness of a single act is fixed by its effects on the world. Rule-utilitarianism, in contrast, is the view that the rightness of an act is fixed, not by its relative utility, but by the utility of having a relevant moral rule, or of most or all members of a certain class of acts being performed.

The implications of act-utilitarianism are seriously counter-intuitive, and I shall ignore it except to consider whether some ostensibly different theories really are different.

5. Rule-utilitarianisms may be divided into two main groups, according as the rightness of a particular act is made a function of ideal rules in some sense, or of the actual and recognized rules of a society. The variety of theory I shall explain more fully is of the former type.

According to the latter type of theory, a person's moral duties or obligations in a particular situation are determined, with some exceptions, solely by the moral rules, or institutions, or practices prevalent in the society, and not by what rules (etc.) it would ideally be best to have in the society. (It is sometimes held that actual moral rules, practices, etc., are only a necessary condition of an act's being morally obligatory or wrong.) Views roughly of this sort have been held in recent years by A. MacBeath, Stephen Toulmin, John Rawls, P. F. Strawson, J. O. Urmson, and B. J. Diggs. Indeed, Strawson says in effect that for there to be a moral obligation on one is just for there to be a socially sanctioned demand on him, in a situation where he has an interest in the system of demands which his society is wont to impose on its members, and where such demands are generally acknowledged and respected by members of his society.[2] And Toulmin asserts that when a person asks, "Is this the right thing to do?" what he is normally asking is whether a proposed action "conforms to the moral code" of his group, "whether the action in question belongs to a class of actions generally approved of in the agent's community." In deliberating about the question what is right to do, he says, "there is no more general 'reason' to be given beyond one which related the action . . . to an accepted social practice."[3]

So far the proposal does not appear to be a form of utilitarianism at all. The theory is utilitarian, however, in the following way: it is thought that what is relevant for a decision whether to try to change moral codes, institutions, etc., or for a justification of them, is the relative utility of the

---

[2] P. F. Strawson, "Social Morality and Individual Ideal," *Philosophy*, XXXVI (1961), 1–17.

[3] Stephen Toulmin, *An Examination of the Place of Reason in Ethics* (Cambridge University Press, 1950), pp. 144–45. See various acute criticisms, with which I mostly agree, in Rawls's review, *Philosophical Review*, LX (1951), 572–80.

code, practice, etc. The recognized code or practice determines the individual's moral obligations in a particular case; utility of the code or practice determines whether it is justified or ought to be changed. Furthermore, it is sometimes held that utilitarian considerations have some relevance to the rightness of a particular action. For instance, Toulmin thinks that in case the requirements of the recognized code or practice conflict in a particular case, the individual ought (although strictly, he is not morally obligated) to do what will maximize utility in the situation, and that in case an individual can relieve the distress of another, he ought (strictly, is not morally obligated) to do so, even if the recognized code does not require him to.[4]

This theory, at least in some of its forms or parts, has such conspicuously counter-intuitive implications that it fails to meet the standard for a satisfactory normative theory. In general, we do not believe that an act's being prohibited by the moral code of one's society is sufficient to make it morally wrong. Moral codes have prohibited such things as work on the Sabbath, marriage to a divorced person, medically necessary abortion, and suicide; but we do not believe it was really wrong for persons living in a society with such prohibitions, to do these things.[5]

Neither do we think it a necessary condition of an act's being wrong that it be prohibited by the code of the agent's society, or of an act's being obligatory that it be required by the code of his society. A society may permit a man to have his wife put to death for infidelity, or to have a child put to death for almost any reason; but we still think such actions wrong. Moreover, a society may permit a man absolute freedom in divorcing his wife, and recognize no obligations on his part toward her; but we think, I believe, that a man has some obligations for the welfare of a wife of

4 Toulmin and Rawls sometimes go further, and suggest that a person is morally free to do something which the actual code or practice of his society prohibits, if he is convinced that the society would be better off if the code or practice were rewritten so as to permit that sort of thing, and he is prepared to live according to the ideally revised code. If their theory were developed in this direction, it need not be different from some "ideal" forms of rule-utilitarianism, although, as stated, the theory makes the recognized code the standard for moral obligations, with exceptions granted to individuals who hold certain moral opinions. See Toulmin, op. cit., pp. 151–52, and Rawls, "Two Concepts of Rules," *Philosophical Review*, LXIV (1955), 28–29, especially ftnt. 25. It should be noticed that Rawls's proposal is different from Toulmin's in an important way. He is concerned with only a segment of the moral code, the part which can be viewed as the rules of practices. As he observes, this may be only a small part of the moral code.

5 Does a stranger living in a society have a moral obligation to conform to its moral code? I suggest we think that he does not, unless it is the right moral code or perhaps at least he thinks it is, although we think that offense he might give to the feelings of others should be taken into account, as well as the result his nonconformity might have in weakening regard for moral rules in general.

thirty years' standing (with some qualifications), whatever his society may think.[6]

Some parts of the theory in some of its forms, however, appear to be correct. In particular, the theory in some forms implies that, if a person has a certain recognized obligation in an institution or practice (e.g., a child to support his aged parent, a citizen to pay his taxes), then he morally does have this obligation, with some exceptions, irrespective of whether in an ideal institution he would or would not have. This we do roughly believe, although we need not at the same time accept the reasoning which has been offered to explain how the fact of a practice or institution leads to the moral obligation. The fact that the theory seems right in this would be a strong point in its favor if charges were correct that "ideal" forms of rule-utilitarianism necessarily differ at this point. B. J. Diggs, for instance, has charged that the "ideal" theories imply that:

> one may freely disregard a rule if ever he discovers that action on the rule is not maximally felicific, and in this respect makes moral rules like 'practical maxims.' ... It deprives social and moral rules of their authority and naturally is in sharp conflict with practice. On this alternative rule-utilitarianism collapses into act-utilitarianism. Surely it is a mistake to maintain that a set of rules, thought to be ideally utilitarian or felicific, is the criterion of right action. ... If we are presented with a list [of rules], but these are not rules in practice, the most one could reasonably do is to try to get them adopted.[7]

I believe, however, and shall explain in detail later that this charge is without foundation.

6. Let us turn now to "ideal" forms of rule-utilitarianism, which affirm that whether it is morally obligatory or morally right to do a certain thing in a particular situation is fixed, not by the actual code or practice of the society (these may be indirectly relevant, as forming part of the situation), but by some "ideal" rule—that is, by the utility of having a certain general moral rule, or by the utility of all or most actions being performed which are members of a relevant class of actions.

If the rightness of an act is fixed by the utility of a relevant rule (class), are we to say that the rule (class) which qualifies must be the optimific rule (class), the one which maximizes utility, or must the rule (class) meet only some less stringent requirement (e.g., be better than the absence of any rule regulating the type of conduct in question)? And, if it is to be of the opti-

---

[6] It is a different question whether we should hold offenders in such societies seriously morally blameworthy. People cannot be expected to rise much above the level of recognized morality, and we condemn them little when they do not.

[7] "Rules and Utilitarianism," *American Philosophical Quarterly*, I (1964), 32–44.

mific type, are all utilities to be counted, or perhaps only "negative" utilities, as is done when it is suggested that the rule (class) must be the one which minimizes suffering?[8]

The simplest proposal—that the rule (class) which qualifies is the one that maximizes utility, with all utilities, whether "positive" or "negative," being counted—also seems to me to be the best, and it is the one I shall shortly explain more fully. Among the several possible theories different from this one I shall discuss briefly only one, which seems the most plausible of its kind, and is at least closely similar to the view defended by Professor Marcus Singer.

According to this theory, an action (or inaction) at time *t* in circumstances C is wrong if and only if, were everyone in circumstances C to perform a relevantly similar action, harm would be done—meaning by "doing harm" that affected persons would be made worse off by the action (or inaction) than they already were at time *t*. (I think it is not meant that the persons must be put in a state of "negative welfare" in some sense, but simply made worse off than they otherwise would have been.) Let us suppose a person is deciding whether to do A in circumstances C at *t*. The theory, then, implies the following: (1) If everyone doing A in circumstances C would make people worse off than they already were at *t* (A can be inaction, such as failing to pull a drowning man from the water) whereas some other act would not make them so, then it is wrong for anyone to do A. (2) If everyone doing A would not make people worse off, then even if everyone doing something else would make them better off, it is not wrong to do A. (3) If everyone doing A would make people worse off, but if there is no alternative act, the performance of which by everyone would avoid making people worse off, then it is right to do A, even though doing A would make people relatively much worse off than they would have been made by the performance of some other action instead. The "optimific rule" theory, roughly, would accept (1), but reject (2) and (3).

Implication (3) of the theory strikes me as clearly objectionable; I am unable to imagine circumstances in which we should think it not morally incumbent on one to avoid very bad avoidable consequences for others, even though a situation somewhat worse than the status quo could not be avoided. Implication (2) is less obviously dubious. But I should think we do have obligations to do things for others, when we are not merely avoiding being in the position of making them worse off. For instance, if one sees

<hr/>

8 In a footnote to Chapter 9 of *The Open Society*, Professor Popper suggested that utilitarianism would be more acceptable if its test were minimizing suffering rather than maximizing welfare, to which J. J. C. Smart replied (*Mind*, 1958, pp. 542–43) that the proposal implies that we ought to destroy all living beings, as the surest way to eliminate suffering. It appears, however, that Professor Popper does not seriously advocate what seemed to be the position of the earlier footnote (Addendum to fourth edition, p. 386).

another person at a cocktail party, standing by himself and looking unhappy, I should suppose one has some obligation to make an effort to put him at his ease, even though doing nothing would hardly make him worse off than he already is.

Why do proponents of this view, like Professor Singer, prefer his view to the simpler, "maximize utility" form of rule-utilitarianism? This is not clear. One objection sometimes raised is that an optimific theory implies that every act is morally weighty and none morally indifferent. And one may concede that this is a consequence of some forms of utilitarianism, even rule-utilitarianism of the optimific variety; but we shall see that it is by no means a consequence of the type of proposal described below. For the theory below will urge that an action is not morally indifferent only if it falls under some prescription of an optimific moral code, and, since there are disadvantages in a moral code regulating actions, optimific moral codes will prohibit or require actions of a certain type only when there are significant utilitarian reasons for it. As a consequence, a great many types of action are morally indifferent, according to the theory. Professor Singer also suggests that optimific-type theories have objectionable consequences for state-of-nature situations;[9] we may postpone judgment on this until we have examined these consequences of the theory here proposed, at a later stage. Other objections to the optimizing type of rule-utilitarianism with which I am familiar either confuse rule-utilitarianism with act-utilitarianism, or do not distinguish among the several possible forms of optimizing rule-utilitarianisms.

7. I propose, then, that we tentatively opt for an "ideal" rule-utilitarianism, of the "maximizing utility" variety. This decision, however, leaves various choices still to be made, between theories better or worse fitted to meet various problems. Rather than attempt to list alternatives, and explain why one choice rather than another between them would work out better, I propose to describe in some detail the type of theory which seems most plausible. I shall later show how this theory meets the one problem to which the "actual rule" type theories seemed to have a nice solution; and I shall discuss its merits, as compared with another quite similar type of theory which has been suggested by Jonathan Harrison and others.

The theory I wish to describe is rather similar to one proposed by J. D. Mabbott in his 1953 British Academy lecture, "Moral Rules." It is also very similar to the view defended by J. S. Mill in *Utilitarianism*, although Mill's formulation is ambiguous at some points, and he apparently did not draw some distinctions he should have drawn. (I shall revert to this historical point.)

For convenience I shall refer to the theory as the "ideal moral code"

---

[9] M. G. Singer, *Generalization in Ethics* (New York: Alfred A. Knopf, Inc., 1961), p. 192 [reprinted above, pp. 114–27].

theory. The essence of it is as follows: Let us first say that a moral code is "ideal" if its currency in a particular society would produce at least as much good per person (the total divided by the number of persons) as the currency of any other moral code. (Two different codes might meet this condition, but, in order to avoid complicated formulations, the following discussion will ignore this possibility.) Given this stipulation for the meaning of "ideal," the Ideal Moral Code theory consists in the assertion of the following thesis: *An act is right if and only if it would not be prohibited by the moral code ideal for the society; and an agent is morally blameworthy (praiseworthy) for an act if, and to the degree that, the moral code ideal in that society would condemn (praise) him for it.* It is a virtue of this theory that it is a theory both about objective rightness and about moral blameworthiness (praiseworthiness) of actions, but the assertion about blameworthiness will be virtually ignored in what follows.

8. In order to have a clear proposal before us, however, the foregoing summary statement must be filled out in three ways: (1) by explaining what it is for a moral code to have currency; (2) by making clear what is the difference between the rules of a society's moral code and the rules of its institutions; and (3) by describing how the relative utility of a moral code is to be estimated.

First, then, the notion of a moral code having currency in a society.

For a moral code to have currency in a society, two things must be true. First, a high proportion of the adults in the society must subscribe to the moral principles, or have the moral opinions, constitutive of the code. Exactly how high the proportion should be, we can hardly decide on the basis of the ordinary meaning of " the moral code"; but probably it would not be wrong to require at least ninety per cent agreement. Thus, if at least ninety per cent of the adults subscribe to principle A, and ninety per cent to principle B, etc., we may say that a code consisting of A and B (etc.) has currency in the society, provided the second condition is met. Second, we want to say that certain principles A, B, etc. belong to the moral code of a society only if they are recognized as such. That is, it must be that a large proportion of the adults of the society would respond correctly if asked, with respect to A and B, whether most members of the society subscribed to them. (It need not be required that adults base their judgments on such good evidence as recollection of moral discussions; it is enough if for some reason the correct opinion about what is accepted is widespread.) It is of course possible for certain principles to constitute a moral code with currency in a society even if some persons in the society have no moral opinions at all, or if there is disagreement, e.g., if everyone in the society disagrees with every other person with respect to at least one principle.

The more difficult question is what it is for an individual to subscribe to a moral principle or to have a moral opinion. What is it, then, for someone to think sincerely that any action of the kind F is wrong? (1) He is to some extent motivated to avoid actions which he thinks are F, and often, if asked why he does not perform such an action when it appears to be to his advantage, offers, as one of his reasons, that it is F. In addition, the person's motivation to avoid F-actions does not derive entirely from his belief that F-actions on his part are likely to be harmful to him or to persons to whom he is somehow attached. (2) If he thinks he has just performed an F-action, he feels guilty or remorseful or uncomfortable about it, unless he thinks he has some excuse—unless, for instance, he knows that at the time of action he did not think his action would be an F-action. "Guilt" (etc.) is not to be understood as implying some special origin such as interiorization of parental prohibitions, or as being a vestige of anxiety about punishment. It is left open that it might be an unlearned emotional response to the thought of being the cause of the suffering of another person. Any feeling which must be viewed simply as anxiety about anticipated consequences, for one's self or person to whom one is attached, is not, however, to count as a "guilt" feeling. (3) If he believes that someone has performed an F-action, he will tend to admire him less as a person, unless he thinks that the individual has a good excuse. He thinks that action of this sort, without excuse, reflects on character—this being spelled out, in part, by reference to traits like honesty, respect for the rights of others, and so on. (4) He thinks that these attitudes of his are correct or well justified, in some sense, but with one restriction: it is not enough if he thinks that what justifies them is simply the fact that they are shared by all or most members of his society. This restriction corresponds with our distinction between a moral conviction and something else. For instance, we are inclined to think no moral attitude is involved if an Englishman disapproves of something but says that his disapproval is justified by the fact that it is shared by "well-bred Englishmen." In such cases we are inclined to say that the individual subscribes only to a custom, or to a rule of etiquette or manners. On the other hand, if the individual thinks that what justifies his attitude unfavorable to F-actions is that F-actions are contrary to the will of God (and the individual's attitude is not merely a prudential one), or inconsistent with the welfare of mankind, or contrary to human nature, we are disposed to say the attitude is a moral attitude and the opinion expressed a moral one. And the same if he thinks his attitude justified, but can give no reason. There are perhaps other restrictions we should make on acceptable justifications (perhaps to distinguish a moral code from a code of honor), and other types of justification we should wish to list as clearly acceptable (perhaps an appeal to human equality).

9. It is important to distinguish between the moral code of a society and its institutions, or the rules of its institutions. It is especially important for the Ideal Moral Code theory, for this theory involves the conception of a moral code ideal for a society in the context of its institutions, so that it is

necessary to distinguish the moral code which a society does or might have from its institutions and their rules. The distinction is also one we actually do make in our thinking, although it is blurred in some cases. (For instance, is "Honor thy father and thy mother" a moral rule, or a rule of the family institution, in our society?)[10]

An institution is a set of positions or statuses, with which certain privileges and jobs are associated. (We can speak of these as "rights" and "duties" if we are careful to explain that we do not mean moral rights and duties.) That is, there are certain, usually nameable, positions which consist in the fact that anyone who is assigned to the position is expected to do certain things, and at the same time is expected to have certain things done for him. The individuals occupying these positions are a group of cooperating agents in a system which as a whole is thought to have the aim of serving certain ends. (E.g., a university is thought to serve the ends of education, research, etc.) The rules of the system concern jobs that must be done in order that the goals of the institution be achieved; they allocate the necessary jobs to different positions. Take, for instance, a university. There are various positions in it: the presidency, the professorial ranks, the registrars, librarians, etc. It is understood that one who occupies a certain post has certain duties, say teaching a specified number of classes or spending time working on research in the case of the instructing staff. Obviously the university cannot achieve its ends unless certain persons do the teaching, some tend to the administration, some do certain jobs in the library, and so on. Another such system is the family. We need not speculate on the "purpose" of the family, whether it is primarily a device for producing a new generation, etc. But it is clear that when a man enters marriage, he takes a position to which certain jobs are attached, such as providing support for the family to the best of his ability, and to which also certain rights are attached, such as exclusive sexual rights with his wife, and the right to be cared for should he become incapacitated.

If an "institution" is defined in this way, it is clear that the moral code of a society cannot itself be construed as an institution, nor its rules as rules of an institution. The moral code is society-wide, so if we were to identify its rules as institutional rules, we should presumably have to say that everyone belongs to this institution. But what is the "purpose" of society as a whole?

---

[10] The confusion is compounded by the fact that terms like "obligation" and "duty" are used sometimes to speak about moral obligations and duties, and sometimes not. The fact that persons have a certain legal duty in certain situations is a rule of the legal institutions of the society; a person may not have a moral duty to do what is his legal duty. The fact that a person has an obligation to invite a certain individual to dinner is a matter of manners or etiquette, and at least may not be a matter of moral obligation. See R. B. Brandt, "The Concepts of Duty and Obligation," *Mind*, LXXIII (1964), especially 380–84.

Are there any distinctions of status, with rights and duties attached, which we could identify as the "positions" in the moral system? Can we say that moral rules consist in the assignment of jobs in such a way that the aims of the institution may be achieved? It is true that there is a certain analogy: society as a whole might be said to be aiming at the good life for all, and the moral rules of the society might be viewed as the rules with which all must conform in order to achieve this end. But the analogy is feeble. Society as a whole is obviously not an organization like a university, an educational system, the church, General Motors, etc.; there is no specific goal in the achievement of which each position has a designated role to play. Our answer to the above questions must be in the negative: morality is not an institution in the explained sense; nor are moral rules institutional expectations or rules.

The moral code of a society may, of course, have implications that bear on institutional rules. For one thing, the moral code may imply that an institutional system is morally wrong and ought to be changed. Moreover, the moral code may imply that a person has also a moral duty to do something which is his institutional job. For instance, it may be a moral rule that a person ought to do whatever he has undertaken to do, or that he ought not to accept the benefits of a position without performing its duties. Take for instance the rules, "A professor should meet his classes" or "Wives ought to make the beds." Since the professor has undertaken to do what pertains to his office, and the same for a wife, and since these tasks are known to pertain to the respective offices, the moral rule that a person is morally bound (with certain qualifications) to do what he has undertaken to do implies, in context, that the professor is morally bound to meet his classes and the wife to make the beds, other things being equal (viz., there being no contrary moral obligations in the situation). But these implications are not themselves part of the moral code. No one would say that a parent had neglected to teach his child the moral code of the society if he had neglected to teach him that professors must meet classes, and that wives must make the beds. A person becomes obligated to do these things only by participating in an institution, by taking on the status of professor or wife. Parents do not teach children to have guilt feelings about missing classes, or making beds. The moral code consists only of more general rules, defining what is to be done in certain types of situations in which practically everyone will find himself. ("Do what you have promised!")

Admittedly some rules can be both moral and institutional: "Take care of your father in his old age" might be both an institutional rule of the family organization and also a part of the moral code of a society. (In this situation, one can still raise the question whether this moral rule is optimific in a society with that institutional rule; the answer could be negative.)

It is an interesting question whether "Keep your promises" is a moral rule, an institutional rule (a rule of an "institution" of promises), or both. Obviously it is a part of the moral code of western societies. But is it also a rule of an institution? There are difficulties in the way of affirming that it is. There is no structure of cooperating individuals with special functions, which serves to promote certain aims. Nor, when one steps into the "role" of a promisor, does one commit one's self to any specific duties; one fixes one's own duties by what one promises. Nor, in order to understand what one is committing one's self to by promising, need one have any knowledge of any system of expectations prevalent in the society. A three-year-old, who has never heard of any duties incumbent on promisors, can tell his friends, who wish to play baseball that afternoon, that he will bring the ball and bat, and that they need give no thought to the availability of these items. His invitation to rely on him for something needed for their common enjoyment, and his assurance that he will do something and his encouraging them thereby to set their minds at rest, *is* to make a promise. No one need suppose that the promisor is stepping into a socially recognized position, with all the rights and duties attendant on the same, although it is true he has placed himself in a position where he will properly be held responsible for the disappointment if he fails, and where inferences about his reliability as a person will properly be drawn if he forgets, or worse, if it turns out he was never in a position to perform. The bindingness of a promise is no more dependent on a set of expectations connected with an institution, than is the wrongness of striking another person without justifying reason.

Nevertheless, if one thinks it helpful to speak of a promise as an institution or a practice, in view of certain analogies (promisor and promisee may be said to have rights and duties like the occupants of roles in an institution, and there is the ritual word "promise" the utterance of which commits the speaker to certain performances), there is no harm in this. The similarities and dissimilarities are what they are, and as long as these are understood it seems to make little difference what we say. Nevertheless, even if making a promise is participating in a practice or institution, there is still the *moral* question whether one is morally bound to perform, and in what conditions, and for what reasons. This question is left open, given the institution is whatever it is—as is the case with all rules of institutions.

10. It has been proposed above that an action is right if and only if it would not be prohibited by the moral code ideal for the society in which it occurs, where a moral code is taken to be "ideal" if and only if its currency would produce at least as much good per person as the currency of any other moral code.[11] We must now give more attention to the conception of an ideal

---

[11] Some utilitarians have suggested that the right act is determined by the total

moral code, and how it may be decided when a given moral code will produce as much good per person as any other. We may, however, reasonably bypass the familiar problems of judgments of comparative utilities, especially when different persons are involved, since these problems are faced by all moral theories that have any plausibility. We shall simply assume that rough judgments of this sort are made and can be justified.

(a) We should first notice that, as "currency" has been explained above, a moral code could not be current in a society if it were too complex to be learned or applied. We may therefore confine our consideration to codes simple enough to be absorbed by human beings, roughly in the way in which people learn actual moral codes.

(b) We have already distinguished the concept of an institution and its rules from the concept of a moral rule, or rule of the moral code. (We have, however, pointed out that in some cases a moral rule may prescribe the same thing that is also an institutional expectation. But this is not a necessary situation, and a moral code could condemn an institutional expectation.) Therefore, in deciding how much good the currency of a specific moral system would do, we consider the institutional setting as it is, as part of the situation. We are asking which moral code would produce the most good in the long run in this setting. One good to be reckoned, of course, might be that the currency of a given moral code would tend to change the institutional system.

(c) In deciding which moral code will produce the most per person good, we must take into account the probability that certain types of situation will arise in the society. For instance, we must take for granted that people will make promises and subsequently want to break them, that people will sometimes assault other persons in order to achieve their own ends, that people will be in distress and need the assistance of others, and so on. We may not suppose that, because an ideal moral code might have certain features, it need not have other features because they will not be required; for instance, we may not suppose, on the ground that an ideal moral system would forbid everyone to purchase a gun, that such a moral system needs no provisions about the possession and use of guns—just as our present moral and legal codes have provisions about self-defense, which would be unnecessary if everyone obeyed the provision never to assault anyone.

It is true that the currency of a moral code with certain provisions might bring about a reduction in certain types of situation, e.g., the number of assaults or cases of dishonesty. And the reduction might be substantial, if the moral code were current which prohibited these offenses very strongly.

---

net intrinsic good produced. This view can have embarrassing consequences for problems of population control. The view here advocated is that the right act is determined by the per person, average, net intrinsic good produced.

(We must remember that an ideal moral code might differ from the actual one not only in what it prohibits or enjoins, but also in how strongly it prohibits or enjoins.) But it is consistent to suppose that a moral code prohibits a certain form of behavior very severely, and yet that the behavior will occur, since the "currency" of a moral code requires only ninety per cent subscription to it, and a "strong" subscription, on the average, permits a great range from person to person. In any case there must be doubt whether the best moral code will prohibit many things very severely, since there are serious human costs in severe prohibitions: the burden of guilt feelings, the traumas caused by the severe criticism by others which is a part of having a strong injunction in a code, the risks of any training process which would succeed in interiorizing a severe prohibition, and so on.

(d) It would be a great oversimplification if, in assessing the comparative utility of various codes, we confined ourselves merely to counting the benefits of people doing (refraining from doing) certain things, as a result of subscribing to a certain code. To consider only this would be as absurd as estimating the utility of some feature of a legal system by attending only to the utility of people behaving in the way the law aims to make them behave—and overlooking the fact that the law only reduces and does not eliminate misbehavior, as well as the disutility of punishment to the convicted, and the cost of the administration of criminal law. In the case of morals, we must weigh the benefit of the improvement in behavior as a result of the restriction built into conscience, against the cost of the restriction—the burden of guilt feelings, the effects of the training process, etc. There is a further necessary refinement. In both law and morals we must adjust our estimates of utility by taking into account the envisaged system of excuses. That *mens rea* is required as a condition of guilt in the case of most legal offenses is most important; and it is highly important for the utility of a moral system whether accident, intent, and motives are taken into account in deciding a person's liability to moral criticism. A description of a moral code is incomplete until we have specified the severity of condemnation (by conscience or the criticism of others) to be attached to various actions, along with the excuses to be allowed as exculpating or mitigating.

11. Philosophers have taken considerable interest in the question what implications forms of rule-utilitarianism have for the moral relevance of the behavior of persons other than the agent. Such implications, it is thought, bring into focus the effective difference between any form of rule-utilitarianism, and act-utilitarianism. In particular, it has been thought that the implications of rule-utilitarianisms for two types of situation are especially significant: (a) for situations in which persons are generally violating the recognized moral code, or some feature of it; and (b) for situations in which, because the moral code is generally respected, maximum utility would be produced by violation of the code by the agent. An example of the

former situation (sometimes called a "state of nature" situation) would be widespread perjury in making out income tax declarations. An example of the latter situation would be widespread conformity to the rule forbidding walking on the grass in a park.

What are the implications of the suggested form of rule-utilitarianism for these types of situation? Will it prescribe conduct which is not utility maximizing in these situations? If it does, it will clearly have implications discrepant with those of act-utilitarianism—but perhaps unpalatable to some people.

It is easy to see how to go about determining what is right or wrong in such situations, on the above described form of rule-utilitarianism—it is a question of what an "ideal" moral code would prescribe. But it is by no means easy to see where a reasonable person would come out, after going through such an investigation. Our form of rule-utilitarianism does not rule out, as morally irrelevant, reference to the behavior of other persons; it implies that the behavior of others is morally relevant precisely to the extent to which an optimific moral code (the one the currency of which is optimific) would take it into account. How far, then, we might ask, would an optimific moral code take into account the behavior of other persons, and what would its specific prescriptions be for the two types of situations outlined?

It might be thought, and it has been suggested, that an ideal moral code could take no cognizance of the behavior of other persons, and in particular of the possibility that many persons are ignoring some prohibitions of the code, sometimes for the reason, apparently, that it is supposed that a code of behavior would be self-defeating if it prescribed for situations of its own breach, on a wide scale. It is a sufficient answer to this suggestion, to point out that our actual moral code appears to contain some such prescriptions. For instance, our present code seems to permit, for the case in which almost everyone is understating his income, that others do the same, on the ground that otherwise they will be paying more than their fair share. It is, of course, true that a code simple enough to be learned and applied cannot include prescriptions for all possible types of situation involving the behavior of other persons; but it can contain some prescriptions pertinent to some general features of the behavior of others.

Granted, then, that an ideal moral code may contain some special prescriptions which pay attention to the behavior of other persons, how in particular will it legislate for special situations such as the examples cited above? The proper answer to this question is that there would apparently be no blanket provision for all cases of these general types, and that a moral agent faced with such a concrete situation would have to think out what an ideal moral code would imply for his type of concrete situation. Some things do seem clear. An ideal moral code would not provide that a person is permitted to be cruel in a society where most other persons are cruel; there could only be loss of utility in any special provision permitting that. On the other hand, if there is some form of cooperative activity which enhances utility only if most persons cooperate, and nonparticipation in which does not reduce utility when most persons are not cooperating, utility would seem to be maximized if the moral code somehow permitted all to abstain—perhaps by an abstract formula stating this very condition. (This is on the assumption that the participation by some would not, by example, eventually bring about the participation of most or all.) Will there be any types of situation for which an ideal moral code would prescribe infringement of a generally respected moral code, by a few, when a few infringements (provided there are not many) would maximize utility? The possibility of this is not ruled out. Obviously there will be some regulations for emergencies; one may cut across park grass in order to rush a heart-attack victim to a hospital. And there will be rules making special exceptions when considerable utility is involved; the boy with no other place to play may use the grass in the park. But, when an agent has no special claim which others could not make, it is certainly not clear that ideal moral rules will make him an exception on the ground that some benefit will come to him, and that restraint by him is unnecessary in view of the cooperation of others.

The implications of the above form of rule-utilitarianism, for these situations, are evidently different from those of act-utilitarianism.[12]

12. The Ideal Moral Code theory is very similar to the view put forward by J. S. Mill in *Utilitarianism.*

Mill wrote that his creed held that "actions are right in proportion as they tend to promote happiness; wrong as they tend to produce the reverse of happiness." Mill apparently did not intend by this any form of act-utilitarianism. He was—doubtless with much less than full awareness—writing of act-*types,* and what he meant was that an act of a certain type is morally obligatory (wrong) if and only if acts of that type tend to promote happiness (the reverse). Mill supposed that it is known that certain kinds of acts, e.g., murder and theft, promote unhappiness, and that therefore we can say, with exceptions only for very special circumstances, that murder and theft are wrong. Mill recognized that there can be a discrepancy between the tendency of an act-type, and the probable effects, in context, of an individual act. He wrote: "In the case of abstinences, indeed—of things which people forbear

12 The above proposal is different in various respects from that set forth in the writer's "Toward a Credible Form of Utilitarianism," in Castaneda and Nakhnikian, *Morality and the Language of Conduct,* 1963. The former paper did not make a distinction between institutional rules and moral rules. (The present paper, of course, allows that both may contain a common prescription.) A result of these differences is that the present theory is very much simpler, and avoids some counter-intuitive consequences which some writers have pointed out in criticism of the earlier proposal.

to do from moral considerations, though the consequences in the particular case might be beneficial—, it would be unworthy of an intelligent agent not to be consciously aware that the action is of a class which, if practiced generally, would be generally injurious, and that this is the ground of the obligation to abstain from it."[13] Moreover, he specifically denied that one is morally obligated to perform (avoid) an act just on the ground that it can be expected to produce good consequences; he says that "there is no case of moral obligation in which some secondary principle is not involved." (op. cit., p. 33).

It appears, however, that Mill did not quite think that it is morally obligatory to perform (avoid) an act according as its general performance would promote (reduce) happiness in the world. For he said (p. 60) that "We do not call anything wrong unless we mean to imply that a person ought to be punished in some way or other for doing it—if not by law, by the opinion of his fellow creatures; if not by opinion, by the reproaches of his own conscience. This seems the real turning point of the distinction between morality and simple expediency." The suggestion here is that it is morally obligatory to perform (avoid) an act according as it is beneficial to have a system of sanctions (with what this promises in way of performance), whether formal, informal (criticism by others), or internal (one's own conscience), for enforcing the performance (avoidance) of the type of act in question. This is very substantially the Ideal Moral Code theory.

Not that there are no differences. Mill is not explicit about details, and the theory outlined above fills out what he actually said. Moreover, Mill noticed that an act can fall under more than one secondary principle and that the relevant principles may give conflicting rulings about what is morally obligatory. In such a case, Mill thought, what one ought to do (but it is doubtful whether he believed there is a strict moral obligation in this situation) is what will maximize utility in the concrete situation. This proposal for conflicts of "ideal moral rules" is not a necessary part of the Ideal Moral Code theory as outlined above.

13. It is sometimes thought that a rule-utilitarianism rather like Mill's cannot differ in its implication about what is right or wrong from the act-utilitarian theory. This is a mistake.

The contention would be correct if two dubious assumptions happened to be true. The first is that one of the rules of an optimific moral code will be that a person ought always to do whatever will maximize utility. The second is that, when there is a conflict between the rules of an optimific code, what a person ought to do is to maximize utility. For then either the utilitarian rule is the only one that applies (and it always will be relevant), in which case the person ought to do what the act-utilitarian directs; or

---

[13] *Utilitarianism*, (New York: Library of Liberal Arts, 1957), p. 25.

if there is a conflict among the relevant rules, the conflict resolving principle takes over, and this, of course, prescribes exactly what act-utilitarianism prescribes. Either way, we come out where the act-utilitarian comes out.

But there is no reason at all to suppose that there will be a utilitarian rule in an optimific moral code. In fact, obviously there will not be. It is true that there should be a directive to relieve the distress of others, when this can be done, say at relatively low personal cost; and there should be a directive not to injure other persons, except in special situations. And so on. But none of this amounts to a straight directive to do the most good possible. Life would be chaotic if people tried to observe any such moral requirement.

The second assumption was apparently acceptable to Mill. But a utilitarian principle is by no means the only possible conflict resolving principle. For if we say, with the Ideal Moral Code theory, that what is right is fixed by the content of the moral system with maximum utility, the possibility is open that the utility maximizing moral system will contain some rather different device for resolving conflicts between lowest-level moral rules. The ideal system might contain several higher-level conflict resolving principles, all different from Mill's. Or, if there is a single one, it could be a directive to maximize utility; it could be a directive to do what an intelligent person who had fully interiorized the rest of the ideal moral system would feel best satisfied with doing; and so on. But the final court of appeal need not be an appeal to direct utilities. Hence the argument that Mill-like rule-utilitarianism must collapse into direct utilitarianism is doubly at fault.[14]

In fact, far from "collapsing" into act-utilitarianism, the Ideal Moral Code theory appears to avoid the serious objections which have been leveled at direct utilitarianism. One objection to the latter view is that it implies that various immoral actions (murdering one's elderly father, breaking solemn promises) are right or even obligatory if only they can be kept secret. The Ideal Moral Code theory has no such implication. For it obviously would not maximize utility to have a moral code which condoned secret murders or breaches of promise. W. D. Ross criticized act-utilitarianism on the ground that it ignored the personal relations important in ordinary morality, and he listed a half-dozen types of moral rule which he thought captured the main themes of thoughtful morality: obligations of fidelity, obligations of gratitude, obligations to make restitution for injuries, obligations to help other persons, to avoid injuring them, to improve one's self, and to bring about a just dis-

---

[14] Could some moral problems be so unique that they would not be provided for by the set of rules it is best for the society to have? If so, how should they be appraised morally? Must there be some appeal to rules covering cases most closely analogous, as seems to be the procedure in law? If so, should we say that an act is right if it is not prohibited, either explicitly or by close analogy, by an ideal moral code? I shall not attempt to answer these questions.

tribution of good things in life. An ideal moral code, however, would presumably contain substantially such rules in any society, doubtless not precisely as Ross stated them. So the rule-utilitarian need not fail to recognize the personal character of morality.

14. In contrast to the type of theory put forward by Toulmin and others, the Ideal Moral Code theory has the advantage of implying that the moral rules recognized in a given society are not necessarily morally binding. They are binding only in so far as they maximize welfare, as contrasted with other possible moral rules. Thus if, in a given society, it is thought wrong to work on the Sabbath, to perform socially desirable abortions, or to commit suicide, it does not follow, on the Ideal Moral Code theory, that these things are necessarily wrong. The question is whether a code containing such prohibitions would maximize welfare. Similarly, according to this theory, a person may act wrongly in doing certain things which are condoned by his sociey.

A serious appeal of theories like Toulmin's is, however, their implications for institutional obligations. For instance, if in society A it is a recognized obligation to care for one's aged father, Toulmin's theory implies that it really is a moral obligation for a child in that society to care for his aged parent (with some qualifications); whereas if in society B it is one's recognized obligation not to care for one's aged father, but instead for one's aged maternal uncle, his theory implies that it really is the moral obligation of a person in that society to care for his aged maternal uncle—even if a better institutional system would put the responsibilities in different places. This seems approximately what we do believe.

The Ideal Moral Code theory, however, has much the same implications. According to it, an institutional system forms the setting within which the best (utility maximizing) moral code is to be applied, and one's obligation is to follow the best moral rules in that institutional setting—not to do what the best moral rules would require for some other, more ideal, setting.

Let us examine the implications of the Ideal Moral Code theory by considering a typical example. Among the Hopi Indians, a child is not expected to care for his father (he is always in a different clan), whereas he is expected to care for his mother, maternal aunt, and maternal uncle, and so on up the female line (all in the same clan). It would be agreed by observers that this system does not work very well. The trouble with it is that the lines of institutional obligation and the lines of natural affection do not coincide, and, as a result, an elderly male is apt not to be cared for by anyone.

Can we show that an "ideal moral code" would call on a young person to take care of his maternal uncle, in a system of this sort? (It might also imply he should try to change the system, but that is another point.) One important feature of the situation of the young man considering whether he should care for his maternal uncle is that, the situation including the expectations of others being what it is, if he does nothing to relieve the distress of his maternal uncle, it is probable that it will not be relieved. His situation is very like that of the sole observer of an automobile accident; he is a mere innocent bystander, but the fact is that if he does nothing, the injured persons will die. So the question for us is whether an ideal moral code will contain a rule that, if someone is in a position where he can relieve serious distress, and where it is known that in all probability it will not be relieved if he does not do so, he should relieve the distress. The answer seems to be that it will contain such a rule: we might call it an "obligation of humanity." But there is a second, and more important point. Failure of the young person to provide for his maternal uncle would be a case of unfairness or free riding. For the family system operates like a system of insurance; it provides one with various sorts of privileges or protections, in return for which one is expected to make certain payments, or accept the risk of making certain payments. Our young man has already benefited by the system, and stands to benefit further; he has received care and education as a child, and later on his own problems of illness and old age will be provided for. On the other hand, the old man, who has (we assume) paid such premiums as the system calls on him to pay in life, is now properly expecting, in accordance with the system, certain services from a particular person whom the system designates as the one to take care of him. Will the ideal moral code require such a person to pay the premium in such a system? I suggest that it will, and we can call the rule in question an "obligation of fairness."[15] So, we may infer that our young man will have a moral obliga-

---

[15] See John Rawls, in "Justice as Fairness," *Philosophical Review*, LXVII (1958), 164–94, especially 179–84.

It seems to be held by some philosophers that an ideal moral code would contain no rule of fairness. The line of argument seems to be as follows: Assume we have an institution involving cooperative behavior for an end which will necessarily be of benefit to all in the institution. Assume further that the cooperative behavior required is burdensome. Assume finally that the good results will be produced even if fewer than all cooperate—perhaps ninety per cent is sufficient. It will then be to an individual's advantage to shirk making his contribution, since he will continue to enjoy the benefits. Shirking on the part of some actually maximizes utility, since the work is burdensome, and the burdensome effort of those who shirk (provided there are not too many) is useless.

I imagine that it would be agreed that, in this sort of system, there should be an agreed and known rule for exempting individuals from useless work. (E.g., someone who is ill would be excused.) In the absence of this, a person should feel free to excuse himself for good and special reason. Otherwise, I think we suppose everyone should do his share, and that it is not a sufficient reason for shirking, to know that enough are cooperating to produce the desired benefits. Let us call this requirement, of working except for special reason (etc.) a "rule of fairness."

Would an ideal moral code contain a rule of fairness? At least, there could hardly be a public rule permitting people to shirk while a sufficient number of others

tion to care for his maternal uncle, on grounds both of humanity and fairness.

We need not go so far as to say that such considerations mean that an ideal moral code will underwrite morally every institutional obligation. An institution may be grossly inequitable; or some part of it may serve no purpose at all but rather be injurious (as some legal prohibitions may be). But I believe we can be fairly sure that Professor Diggs went too far in saying that a system of this sort "deprives social and moral rules of their authority and naturally is in sharp conflict with practice" and that it "collapses into act-utilitarianism."

15. It may be helpful to contrast the Ideal Moral Code theory with a rather similar type of rule-utilitarianism, which in some ways is simpler than the Ideal Moral Code theory, and which seems to be the only form of rule-utilitarianism recognized by some philosophers. This other type of theory is suggested in the writings of R. F. Harrod, Jonathan Harrison, perhaps John Hospers and Marcus Singer, although, as I shall describe it, it differs from the exact theory proposed by any of these individuals, in more or less important ways.

The theory is a combination of act-utilitarianism with a Kantian universalizability requirement for moral action. It denies that an act is necessarily right if it will produce consequences no worse than would any other action the agent might perform; rather, it affirms that an act is right if and only if universal action on the "maxim" of the act would not produce worse consequences than universal action on some other maxim on which the agent could act. Or, instead of talking of universal action on the "maxim" of the act in question, we can speak of all members of the class of relevantly similar actions being performed; then the proposal is that an action is right if and only if universal performance of the class of relevantly similar acts would not have worse consequences than universal performance of the class of acts relevantly similar to some alternative action the agent might perform. Evidently it is important how we identify the "maxim" of an act or the class of "relevantly similar" acts.

---

work. For what would the rule be? It would be all too easy for most people to believe that a sufficient number of others were working (like the well-known difficulty in farm planning, that if one plants what sold at a good price the preceding year, one is apt to find that prices for that product will drop, since most other farmers have the same idea). Would it even be a good idea to have a rule to the effect that if one absolutely knows that enough others are working, one may shirk? This seems highly doubtful.

Critics of rule-utilitarianism seem to have passed from the fact that the best system would combine the largest product with the least effort, to the conclusion that the best moral code would contain a rule advising not to work when there are enough workers already. This is a non sequitur.

One proceeds as follows. One may begin with the class specified by the properties one thinks are the morally significant ones of the act in question. (One could as well start with the class defined by all properties of the act, if one practically could do this!) One then enlarges the class by omitting from its definition those properties which would not affect the average utility which would result from all the acts in the class being performed. (The total utility might be affected simply by enlarging the size of the class; merely enlarging the class does not affect the average utility.) Conversely, one must also narrow any proposed class of "relevantly similar" acts if it is found that properties have been omitted from the specification of it, the presence of which would affect the average utility which would result if all the acts in the class were performed. The relevant class must not be too large, because of omission of features which define subclasses with different utilities; or too small, because of the presence of features which make no difference to the utilities.

An obvious example of an irrelevant property is that of the agent having a certain name (in most situations), or being a certain person. On the other hand, the fact that the agent wants (does not want) to perform a certain act normally is relevant to the utility of the performance of that act.

So much by way of exposition of the theory.

For many cases this theory and the Ideal Moral Code theory have identical implications. For, when it is better for actions of type A to be performed in a certain situation than for actions of any other type to be performed, it will often be a good thing to have type A actions prescribed by the moral code, directly or indirectly.

The theory also appears more simple than the Ideal Moral Code theory. In order to decide whether·a given act is right or wrong we are not asked to do anything as grand as decide what some part of an ideal moral code would be like, but merely whether it would be better, or worse, for all in a relevant class of acts to be performed, as compared with some other relevant class. Thus it offers simple answers to questions such as whether one should vote ("What if nobody did?"), pick wildflowers along the road ("What if everyone did?"), join the army in wartime, or walk on the grass in a park.[16]

---

[16] One should not, however, overemphasize the simplicity. Whether one should vote in these circumstances is not decided by determining that it would have bad consequences if no one voted at all. It is a question whether it would be the best thing for all those people to vote (or not vote) in the class of situations relevantly similar to this one. It should be added, however, that if I am correct in my (below) assessment of the identity of this theory with act-utilitarianism, in the end it is simple, on the theory, to answer these questions.

It hardly seems that an ideal moral code would contain prescriptions as specific as rules about these matters. But the implications for such matters would be fairly direct if, as suggested above, an ideal moral code would contain a principle enjoining

Furthermore, the theory has a simple way of dealing with conflicts of rules: one determines whether it would be better, or worse, for all members of the more complex class (about which the rules conflict) of actions to be performed (e.g., promises broken in the situation where the breach would save a life).

In one crucial respect, however, the two theories are totally different. For, in contrast with the Ideal Moral Code theory, this theory implies that exactly those acts are objectively right which are objectively right on the act-utilitarian theory. Hence the implications of this theory for action include the very counter-intuitive ones which led its proponents to seek an improvement over act-utilitarianism.

It must be conceded that this assessment of the implications of the theory is not yet a matter of general agreement,[17] and depends on a rather complex argument. In an earlier paper (loc. cit.) I argued that the theory does have these consequences, although my statement of the theory was rather misleading. More recently Professor David Lyons has come to the same conclusion, after an extensive discussion in which he urges that the illusion of a difference between the consequences of this theory and those of act-utilitarianism arises because of failure to notice certain important features of the context of actions, primarily the relative frequency of similar actions at about the same time, and "threshold effects" which an action may have on account of these features.[18]

It may be worthwhile to draw attention to the features of the Ideal Moral Code theory which avoid this particular result. In the first place, the Ideal Moral Code theory sets a limit to the number and complexity of the properties which define a class of morally similar actions. For, on this theory, properties of an act make a difference to its rightness, only if a moral principle referring to them (directly or indirectly) can be learned as part of the optimific moral code. Actual persons, with their emotional and intellectual limitations, are unable to learn a moral code which incorporates all the distinctions the other theory can recognize as morally relevant; and even if they could learn it, it would not be utility maximizing for them to try to apply it. In the second place, we noted that to be part of a moral code a proscription must be public, believed to be part of what is morally disapproved of by most adults. Thus whereas some actions (e.g., some performed

---

fairness, i.e., commanding persons to do their share in common enterprises (or restraints), when everyone benefits if most persons do their share, when persons find doing their share a burden, and when it is not essential that everyone do his share although it is essential that most do so, for the common benefit to be realized.

[17] See, for instance, the interesting paper by Michael A. G. Stocker, "Consistency in Ethics," *Analysis* Supplement, XXV (January 1965), 116–22.

[18] David Lyons, *Forms and Limits of Utilitarianism* (Oxford: Clarendon Press, 1965).

in secret) would be utility maximizing, the Ideal Moral Code theory may imply that they are wrong, because it would be a bad thing for it to be generally recognized that a person is free to do that sort of thing.

16. I do not know of any reason to think that the Ideal Moral Code theory is a less plausible normative moral theory than any other form of utilitarianism. Other types of rule-utilitarianism are sufficiently like it, however, that it might be that relatively minor changes in formulation would make their implications for conduct indistinguishable from those of the Ideal Moral Code theory.

Two questions have not here been discussed. One is whether the Ideal Moral Code theory is open to the charge that it implies that some actions are right which are unjust in such an important way that they cannot be right. The second question is one a person would naturally wish to explore if he concluded that the right answer to the first question is affirmative: it is whether a rule-utilitarian view could be combined with some other principles like a principle of justice in a plausible way, without loss of all the features which make utilitarianism attractive. The foregoing discussion has not been intended to provide an answer to these questions.

A Comment[1] on "Some Merits of One Form of Rule-Utilitarianism"

B. J. DIGGS

In "Rules and Utilitarianism" I undertook to develop the view that several forms of utilitarianism can be distinguished by virtue of the different conceptions of moral rules which are implicit or explicit in these forms: I wanted principally to show that not only is it the case that act-utilitarianism conceives moral rules on the pattern of a specific kind of rule, as Rawls had suggested, but that rule-utilitarianism does this as well although it uses a different kind of rule as the pattern. In order to clarify the view of rules implicit in what I consider to be the strongest form of rule-utilitarianism, and to show the limitation of this view, I went on to distinguish moral rules from the social or institutional rules which they presuppose. Toward the end of my paper I argued that rule-utilitarianism,

---

[1] I gratefully acknowledge helpful suggestions and comments of my colleague, Louis Werner.

because it conceives moral rules in the way it does, is open to a fundamental line of criticism. In passing I criticized, briefly and highhandedly, the view that the criterion of right action is a set of ideal rules which are, or would be if they were adopted, maximally utilitarian or felicific. Brandt, in undertaking to defend his Ideal Moral Code theory, argues that I went too far in my criticisms. In this reply I shall not discuss many of the interesting points in Brandt's paper. I want to raise one central issue.

The issue is this. Is the criterion of morally right acts a code or a set of rules which is ideal in the sense that "... its currency in a particular society *would* produce at least as much good ... as the currency of any other moral code"? (Section 7, italics mine. For Brandt's sense of 'currency', see section 8). On Brandt's view such an ideal code is the criterion of morally right acts without its having actual currency; his Ideal Moral Code is ideal not only as optimific but as contrasted with actual codes.

In order to clarify the issue we must distinguish Brandt's kind of ideal rule-utilitarianism from another kind with which it may be confused. Since ideal rule-utilitarianism would have us take as the criterion of right action not the set of rules which has currency, but a set of ideally utilitarian rules, one who subscribes to this position might argue that every rule must contain a clause excluding from application of the rule any particular case in which violation of the rule is optimific, for example, a case of optimific theft— otherwise we could conceive a more ideally utilitarian set of rules. Following this line of reasoning some will conclude that the set of optimific rules which is to serve as the criterion will prescribe the optimific act in every individual case. Although it is unlikely that anyone would subscribe to the ideal rule theory presented in this way, one might if it were given universal dress—if, for example, an action were said to be right "... if and only if universal performance of the class of relevantly similar acts [where relevant similarity is determined solely by utilitarian consequences] would not have worse consequences than universal performance of the class of acts relevantly similar to some alternative action the agent might perform" (see Brandt, section 15).

An ideal utilitarianism of this kind, presented in either way, will always agree in its judgments with act-utilitarianism. Moreover, so far as I can see, as a form of rule-utilitarianism it is fatuous, for there is no way of determining what the ideal rule requires until one has determined which act is optimific; certainly it requires one to follow rules having actual currency only if they prescribe the optimific act.[2]

Brandt finds act-utilitarianism counter-intuitive and he rejects this kind

---

[2] Brandt's quotations (see sections 5 and 15) from my paper are a confusing mix taken from sections 2.1.1 and 2.1.2 in which I criticize two quite different views. Insofar as my statements in 2.1.1 are a criticism of "ideal" theories, they

of ideal rule-utilitarianism. His way of protecting his Ideal Moral Code theory from equivalence with this kind of theory is significant: He insists that ideal rules should not be viewed just as "rules in theory" but as rules which can become current in the practice of persons as they are in this world. "Actual persons, with their emotional and intellectual limitations, are unable to learn a moral code which incorporates all the distinctions the other theory can recognize as morally relevant; and even if they could learn it, it would not be utility maximizing for them to try to apply it. In the second place, we noted that to be part of a moral code a prescription must be public, believed to be part of what is morally disapproved of by most adults. Thus whereas some actions (e.g., some performed in secret) would be utility maximizing, the Ideal Moral Code theory may imply that they are wrong..." (section 15, also see section 10).

These comments proceed from a sound intuition of the nature of moral rules. But although Brandt insists that moral rules must be practical, able to be applied, and not theoretical expressions of a divinely omniscient utilitarian Mind, he also insists that the criterion of right action is an Ideal Code, one which *would be* optimific if it *did have* currency in a particular society. In view of this his comments may be puzzling. Since a rule to be part of the Ideal Code must itself be ideal, it is *not* necessary that the rule be subscribed to in practice. It is thus not necessary that the rule *be public* but only necessary that it be the kind of rule which *could be* public. But if it does not have to be public *in fact*, why must it be such that it is *able to be* public? If rules don't have to be learned and generally recognized in order to be criteria of right acts, why must they be learn*able*, and *able to be* generally recognized to be criteria? If they don't have to be actual rules why do they have to be actualizable as rules? Furthermore, if they don't have to be actualized, why would it not be utility maximizing to apply a rule which prescribes the utility maximizing act, however complicated the rule is?

Brandt's answer to this kind of question is not clear. The most cogent answer I can supply from his point of view is that appeal to a rule in justification of an act implies that the rule *ought* to be adopted and have currency, if it does not have currency already; and the complex rules of theoretical rule-utilitarianism are not rules which ought to be adopted because any attempt to give them currency would produce chaos. Thus, for example, if a person violates an accepted practice which deprives persons of a certain race from gainful employment, he must be willing to appeal to a rule which he can propose as productive of a happier state of affairs, *if* it *were* adopted. I am not sure that Brandt would take this tack, but it does give his theory a certain cogency in reply to the above questions. We are still

criticize the kind of ideal utilitarianism which I have just described and which Brandt himself criticizes. He should not have said that I went too far.

confronted, however, with the basic question: Is it reasonable to maintain that a moral rule *is* the criterion of right acts whether or not it is actually subscribed to and *has* currency in Brandt's sense?

Let us approach this question by considering the force of the objection to ideal rule-utilitarianism which I raised in my paper (2.1.2). This kind of theory is often stated very loosely and in a way which obscures an important characteristic of rules. It is said to be the theory which holds that the criterion of morally right acts is the system of rules which either maximizes utility or would maximize utility if followed, or something of the sort. In the first place, this kind of statement fails to mark the distinction between moral rules and institutional or other social rules which have significant utilitarian effects and which many moral rules presuppose. Equally important, it obscures the fact that a rule which is not a rule in practice cannot have the character and utility of a rule in practice. If rules are not in fact generally followed or accepted in some sense, they are not actually used as criteria of right action and thus do not serve as the determinant of acts and expectations. Such "rules" do not enable one person to know how another will act, they do not promote cooperation, allow competition, etc. They simply do not have that utility of rules or conventions to which Hume so strenuously called attention. Moreover, unless they can be shown somehow to follow from principles of natural law, since they lack utility and are not agreed to or accepted in practice, they have no authority. They are about as effective and authoritative a criterion of right acts as a proposed "law" which has not yet been passed and made into law. If a person fails to follow an actual rule because he can think of a more nearly optimific rule, his act is apt to defeat expectations, reduce utility, and lead to gross injustice. To use one of Brandt's examples, it may be the case ideally that children should not provide direct care for the aged and leave this to the state. But if a person followed such an "ideal" rule before it was generally accepted, woe to his aged parent. Quite generally, following ideal rules, unless they are rules in practice, will lead to social chaos.

This was my fundamental criticism of the kind of ideal rule-utilitarianism which is implicit in many formulations of rule-utilitarianism, and in Brandt's formulation of it in *Ethical Theory*,[3] at least on one interpretation. However, as I pointed out in a note (see notes on 2.1.2), Brandt attempted in his book, albeit briefly, to escape the objection by applying ideally optimific rules to persons living under generally accepted institutional and social rules which are not (necessarily) optimific. Recognizing that chaos would result if a person acted on ideal rather than actual *institutional* rules, he takes the criterion of *morally* right action to be an ideal rule applied to a person living under conditions largely determined by actual rules. Thus

---

[3] See pp. 396–97.

he says, for example, "Given a community in which it is established practice for children to support their parents and where there are no other institutional arrangements, would it have maximum net utility for everybody to stop supporting parents? The answer is obviously, 'No' " (p. 399). In the foregoing article Brandt makes explicit and emphasizes this distinction between institutional rules and moral rules. Institutions are one thing, morality another. In order to determine the morally right act, judge by an ideally optimific code applied to a person in a context fixed by commonly accepted institutions.

This is an intricate move. One basic difficulty is with the interpretation of this "context" in which the Ideal Code is to be applied. Brandt says that his ". . . theory involves the conception of a moral code ideal for a society in the context of its institutions . . .", further that ". . . morality is not an institution . . .", and ". . . in deciding how much good the currency of a specific moral system would do, we consider the institutional setting as it is, as part of the situation. We are asking which moral code would produce the most good in the long run in this setting" (sections 9 and 10).

How should this doctrine be interpreted? Let us take an example. It is not unreasonable to think that it would be optimific if all persons were to refuse to bear arms in settling differences between nations. If so, the rule, that it is wrong to bear arms to settle national differences, would seem to be a reasonable candidate for admission in Brandt's Ideal Code. However, until this rule *is* generally accepted and given currency, it surely is not the criterion of morally right acts. It was surely not morally wrong to take up arms against Hitler's armies *because* or *for the reason that* it would be best if persons generally would not bear arms—if it was wrong at all. At the time of the invasion of France, a Frenchman could not have reasonably given as a reason for his refusal to bear arms the fact that the general currency of the rule "Don't bear arms to settle national differences" would be optimific. The ideal rule is not constituted a criterion of right acts because it is ideal, however desirable it would be to have such a rule and thus such a criterion.

I do not think, however, that Brandt would want his Ideal Moral Code theory applied or interpreted to yield the unwelcome conclusion that it was morally wrong to fight against Hitler. His paper suggests three different ways in which he might object to drawing this conclusion. First, he might argue that the rule that I have suggested is not simple or clear enough to be taught, or that the benefits of having the rule do not outweigh the burdens. Since I do not think that Brandt would take this line, except as interpreted below, I shall not discuss it here.

Second, Brandt might argue that the rule that I have proposed is not optimific for our society "in the context of its institutions" or considering "the institutional setting as it is." He might pursue this argument in either of two ways. On the one hand, he might point out that our political institutions as they are presently constituted require one to bear arms, and our rule would thus prescribe that one violate an important political obligation, and this would have decisive undesirable consequences. On the other hand, he might argue that in the present state of our political institutions violation of this rule would not be universally punished, and since the rule would be very unequally enforced, those nations in which it was not enforced would be given an advantage which would not produce very happy results.

These lines of argument introduce considerations which a person may reasonably give as reasons for not refusing to bear arms for his country, even if he thinks that it would be desirable for *all* persons to refuse. It is by no means clear, however, that either line of argument keeps one from drawing the unwelcome conclusion which I proposed. Brandt clearly states that a rule of the Ideal Code can require one to violate an institutional rule of his society —when the currency of the rule requiring the violation *would* maximize welfare or *would* be optimific in that society. And *if* all persons violated their political obligation to bear arms, following the ideal rule, although there would be some undesirable consequences, it is not unreasonable to think that the total consequences *would be* much closer to the optimum than the consequences which will actually ensue. Moreover, granting that a change in law and perhaps in political institutions would be needed if the proposed rule were actually to be equally and universally enforced, it is nevertheless the case that the rule *to be a criterion* on Brandt's view does not need to be enforced. The only requirement which the Ideal Code theory imposes is that the rule is *able* to have currency and *would* be optimific *if* it had currency in our society. Our society's institutions would undoubtedly place hurdles in the way of the rule's gaining currency, as would any institution the rules of which were to be violated by an ideal rule, but *if* the rule had currency—and this does not appear to be a practical impossibility—the results could reasonably be thought favorable. There are persons who actually stand on some such principle.

On such a complex question, however, there is sure to be difference of opinion. Some might argue that currency of the rule would not be optimific because Brandt requires only ninety per cent adherence to a rule in order for it to have currency, and if ten per cent of the world's population, largely concentrated in one industrialized country, bore arms in violation of the rule, then the ninety per cent would be enslaved. Others might present sound arguments *pro* and *con* on the basis of other distributions and percentages. Brandt's theory is thus confronted with a curious problem. If the rule is assumed or required to have a high degree of currency, the rule would be optimific (or more nearly so), and a person is thus morally obliged to refuse to bear arms. On the other hand, if the rule is assumed to have a lesser currency, it would not be optimific and one is not morally obliged in this respect. The morality of my act would thus depend, very oddly, on what degree of currency we require our hypothetical ideal rules to have. How much currency should be required of them? Brandt says, "...we can hardly decide on the basis of the ordinary meaning of 'the moral code', but probably it would not be wrong to require at least ninety per cent agreement" (section 8). Why not ninety-nine per cent? The Ideal Moral Code theory neither gives an answer nor indicates principles by reference to which an answer is to be sought; any answer one gives seems as arbitrary as Brandt's ninety per cent, even though the morality of an act depends on it. However, this is just what we should expect, for we are talking about a purely hypothetical currency. Naturally we can hypothesize any currency we want—the only limit Brandt imposes is that we cannot expect any practicable rule to be followed by everyone. If it be added that the rule proposed cannot reasonably be expected to have ninety-nine per cent currency in this world, I would ask "Why not?" The conditions in which this would be possible seem to be implied by the hypothetical percentage. Since the rule of an actual institution can be rightfully violated, in what respects am I bound by and free from actual conditions in considering hypothetical currencies? So far as I can see the theory does not answer.

Moreover, how does the estimate of consequences of hypothetical currencies of hypothetical rules relate to the moral and practical question whether a person should bear arms? If the theory were correct, this whole line of reasoning, barely sketched above, would have an essential bearing on the morality of one's taking up arms—after all, one should follow the rule the currency of which would be optimific for our society. Actually, however, this line of reasoning seems barely relevant at best. Why is this so? I would say that this hypothetical and so-called rule, having hypothetical currency, rests on and has no authority. It has not been agreed to, it is not useful, benefits have not been derived from persons having followed it, and no claim is made, at least by Brandt, that either Nature or God has prescribed it. Why should one follow it, even if eighty per cent currency would have optimific consequences? The only answer I can see is that it would be optimific. This may be good reason for trying to get the rule adopted, but if there is no likelihood of this, it seems both a poor and an odd reason for following it.

The attempt to show that the rule I proposed is not one the currency of which would be optimific in the context of our society's institutions, and not morally binding on one who accepts the Ideal Moral Code theory, is thus both unsuccessful and ill-advised; unsuccessful, because optimificity of the rule depends on degree of currency, and ill-advised, because it reveals very serious weaknesses in the theory, at least as I so far have interpreted it. Happily, however, Brandt's case against drawing the unwanted conclusion from his theory, that one ought to refuse to bear arms in settling national differences, does not rest on the foregoing argument. His exposition of the theory provides him with a third way of arguing against this conclusion, and one which is much closer to the way in which one would actually argue against following such a rule.

The primary reason why a person does not consider himself morally required to refuse to bear arms for his country, even in face of the great loss to justice and humanity which results from persons generally being willing to bear arms, is that there is no reason to think that persons in other countries will *in fact* join him in refusing to bear arms. If *he* refuses, he is simply giving an advantage to the other side, and usually in circumstances such that the other side's winning is not thought to make for either an increase in justice or other good consequences. Brandt considers this kind of reason indirectly, when he considers "the moral relevance of the behavior of persons other than the agent" (section 11). He says that ". . . if there is some form of cooperative activity which enhances utility only if most persons cooperate, and nonparticipation in which does not reduce utility when most persons are not cooperating, utility would seem to be maximized if the moral code somehow permitted all to abstain—perhaps by an abstract formula stating this very condition." Brandt was considering cases in which most persons are not cooperating in a practice actually recognized, but it seems quite proper to apply his formula to the present case.

This formula gives Brandt a more cogent way of arguing against the rule I proposed: It cannot be said that the Ideal theory requires one to refuse to bear arms for his country, because refusing to bear arms is a kind of "cooperative enterprise" which would be optimific only if almost all "participated." Other persons are not refusing to bear arms and under these actual conditions my not refusing may enhance and does not reduce utility. For these reasons I cannot be said to have an obligation to refuse, and the Ideal theory does not impose this obligation.

However, to say that in cases of this kind a person has a moral obligation to follow the ideal rule only if most persons cooperate, or that one is excepted from application of the rule when most, do not cooperate, is in effect to admit that actual currency is in cases of this kind a necessary condition of the rule's being a criterion. Brandt's only other alternative is to say that a person has *an* obligation to follow the rule in these cases but the obligation is outweighed by the disutility of his doing so. However, there seems to be no ground for this obligation. The fact that in such cases the rule would be optimific *if* it had currency may be a good reason for trying to get the rule accepted, but apart from this consideration, it does not seem to be even *a* reason for following the rule. It is thus more reasonable to say that mutual acceptance of a rule of this kind is a necessary condition of the rule's having authority and being binding. After all, a hypothetical rule, however desirable, can have only hypothetical authority: The rule *would* be binding *only if* persons cooperated, since only then *would* each person who obeyed the rule have a rightful claim to the obedience of all others who fairly share the benefits.[4]

Mutual acceptance, in a weak form at least, is a necessary condition of a number of moral rules having authority, including such rules as "Do not steal" and "Keep your promises." This is not the case, however, with all moral rules. The authority of the rule "One ought not to practice racial discrimination" does not depend on the rule's being generally accepted— this authority is not weakened in a society in which racial discrimination is accepted as the rule. But clearly the authority of this rule also does not depend on the good consequences which the rule *would* have *if* the rule had at least ninety per cent currency. The obligation to follow it is imposed not by a hypothetical optimificity but by a fundamental principle of justice whose authority derives from the moral authority of free persons to pursue goals of their own choice and to legislate for themselves. The principle asserts the right of all persons to be in the moral community of self-legislating persons. The members of our society commonly regard themselves as constituting such a community and implicitly subscribe to the principle even when violating the abovementioned rule; they live under a constitution which includes the principle from which the rule derives. Thus the principle of justice is ideal, not in Brandt's sense, but in the sense that persons often fail to live up to it even while living under it and at least nominally subscribing to it. This is not to say that all persons everywhere subscribe to it; but if they do not, they do not live under the morality which Brandt and I are trying to understand. Obviously at this point much more needs to be said, but this is not the place to say it.

It appears to me that whatever appeal the Ideal Moral Code theory has comes from the following kind of reasoning: Men ought to accept an ideally optimific rule, for example, "Don't bear arms to settle national differences." But if they ought to accept this rule, surely they ought to do what this rule prescribes. Thus the ideally optimific rule is a criterion of morally right acts and men ought to follow it unless there are weightier reasons for not doing so.

This reasoning seems to me defective. If one thinks that men ought to have a rule, he may express this simply by stating the rule, as in the case of the example "Men ought not to bear arms to settle national differences." The assertion of the rule in such a case means that men ought to adopt or subscribe to the rule and follow it. However, before the rule is adopted, unless the action prescribed will contribute to the adoption of the rule, or is

---

[4] Cf. H. L. A. Hart, "Are There Any Natural Rights?" *Philosophical Review*, LXIV (April 1955), 183–86, 188–91.

required on some other authority, a person cannot be criticized for not doing what is prescribed. The mere desirability of a rule does not constitute the rule a criterion.

However, this is only part of the difficulty. One may be repelled by the idea of moral rules being "adopted"—wrongly, I think, since we are not speaking of rules in a rule book, being adopted at a meeting. Moreover, moral rules should be distinguished from moral principles. But perhaps the greatest difficulty of all comes from one's surreptitiously presupposing the' utilitarian principle "Every person ought to promote good to the greatest extent possible." One who accepts this principle will have a source of authority for optimific rules, but a source which he has created.

Brandt's Ideal Code theory can be given a somewhat different interpretation, with perhaps greater cogency and appeal, if one develops his theme that rules in the Code must be practicable and actualizable. I suggested that Brandt may impose this requirement because appeal to a rule as a criterion implies that the rule ought to be adopted and to have currency, if it does not have currency already, and that from a practical point of view, the rules which ought to be adopted are those rules which it would be reasonable to propose for adoption. We might extend this idea and say that only those rules ought to be seriously proposed which it would be reasonable to try to get accepted in a particular society, here and now. Then one could say that those ideal rules for which it is practically possible to get an optimific degree of currency, given not only the institutions but the attitudes, present morality, etc., of the society, and only those rules, constitute the criterion of morally right acts. There is some merit in this extension of the theory, since one reason for a person's following an ideal rule is that by doing so he can promote acceptance.

This reason is not always available, however, and other difficulties appear on the horizon. They cannot be explored here. Without going further it should be clear, at least, that Brandt's Ideal Moral Code theory is in many respects far away from the kind of ideal rule-utilitarianism I criticized in my article. One need only review all the modifications which Brandt introduces: He requires that ideal moral rules be practicable and applicable to a society shaped by nonmoral rules; and in some cases in which they do not have actual currency, he seems to deprive them of their force. These are significant modifications and steps in the right direction (I quite agree with Brandt that we do not want to go so far as to say that the actual moral rules of a society are the criteria of morally right acts). Brandt's new theory, however, presents one fundamental difficulty in common with the ideal rule-utilitarianism which I criticized: It overlooks the fact that ideally optimific rules may have only ideal authority and consequently do not necessarily obligate. The basic trouble with the Ideal Moral Code theory is, I suspect, that it tries to preserve the "ideal character of morality" in not quite the right way, by trying sensibly to modify and bulwark a theory which is just wrong. The resultant theory, moreover, is so complex, and its key terms (like 'currency' and 'the context of a society's institutions') pose such a difficult problem of interpretation, that one is unsure what the theory says or how it is to be applied. Perhaps I have misinterpreted it.[5]

---

[5] The reader may be interested to compare my comments with those of my colleague Alan Donagan on Brandt's earlier paper "Toward a Credible Form of Utilitarianism," *Morality and the Language of Conduct,* Castaneda and Nakhnikian, eds. (1963). See "Is There a Credible Form of Utilitarianism?" forthcoming in a volume edited by Michael Bayles, to be published by Doubleday.

Section Three
Recent Conceptions of Morality

The history of moral philosophy in the first half of the twentieth century reveals a preoccupation with the notions of "good" and "ought." In recent years, however, philosophers have devoted more attention to the concept of morality. This has been due, in large measure, to the realization that some of the various meanings of "good" and "ought" could not be satisfactorily clarified nor the criteria for the correct application of those terms ascertained without a clear understanding of the concept of morality itself.

The question "What is morality?" is an ambigious question. It may, among other things, be a question about the necessary and sufficient conditions for a point of view to be *a* moral point of view. What, in other words, are the essential respects in which a moral point of view differs from, say, a religious or legal point of view? Or the question may be one regarding what point of view is *the* moral point of view. How, in other words, can correct moral principles and rules be distinguished from incorrect ones? These two questions are not always distinguished, nor after being distinguished are they always kept distinct. Perhaps this is because the distinction between the two questions is not always a comfortable one, since what one is likely to count as *a* moral point of view is probably influenced by what one, in the first place, thinks is *the* moral point of view. Moreover, some people tend to disallow a given point of view as a moral one, if it diametrically opposes their own moral view. A case in point is the denial by some that the Nazis even had a morality, much less a correct one.

Although the distinction between "a morality" and "a correct morality" is not always observed in common speech and thought, the distinction is legitimate and important. For people often talk about Christian morality as contrasted with heathen morality and capitalist morality as distinguished from socialist and communist morality without implying that any one of them is a morally correct point of view. What, then, justifies us in saying that Christians and socialists, for example, have *a* morality? The answer to this question centrally involves

319

a descriptive-explanatory account of how the term "a moral-ity" is used and the criteria for its use. However, an inquiry regarding what is *the* moral point of view will also necessarily involve an account of the criteria, necessary and/or sufficient, for distinguishing a morally correct point of view from other allegedly correct moralities. Nevertheless, any moral point of view as well as any correct one will involve the use of practical reason, i.e., a mode of inquiry and reason whose principal aim is to supply action-guidance. But since law and religion also supply action-guidance of a kind, the use of practical reason is not a sufficient ground for distinguishing between morality, law, and religion.

Enlightened ethical egoism, i.e., the view that one ought to do whatever and only whatever is in one's enlightened self-interest, has enjoyed a long and enduring history as a candidate for the morally correct point of view. However, while some would argue that it is not the moral point of view, others would go even further and deny it the status of a morality. Kurt Baier, for example, contends that enlightened egoism is not the moral point of view (though he also appears to disallow egoism the status of a morality), whereas William K. Frankena has on occasion argued that enlightened egoism is not even a morality.

In his paper "The Point of View of Morality" Kurt Baier argues against certifying enlightened egoism as the moral point of view. His argument rests upon the following contentions: That the moral point of view, but not enlightened egoism, contains behavior regulating rules which recognize men as equally important "centers" of desires, needs, aspirations, and the like. Interestingly enough, in his later work *The Moral Point of View*, Baier offers another argument against certifying enlightened egoism as the moral point of view. There he contends that self-interest can never provide a moral solution for conflicts of interest. However, according to Baier, since by "the moral point of view" we mean a point of view that is a court of appeal for conflicts of interest, the point of view of self-interest and the moral point of view cannot logically be identical.

The interesting question regarding the relation between a personal ideal and a morality has been raised by P. F. Strawson in his paper "Social Morality and Individual Ideal." In attempting to ascertain the nature of this relationship, Strawson considers the adequacy of what he calls the minimum conception of morality, i.e., rules the observance of which is a condition for the existence of sociey. Strawson finds that neither the minimal conception nor the conception of morality as what is required of man qua man is satisfactory. The minimal conception, he argues, must be supplemented by the abstract virtue of justice, i.e., the reciprocal acknowledgement of rights and duties.

Perhaps the most important debate concerning the concept of morality is over whether the concept is applicable only where the welfare of others is considered simply because they are sentient beings. In recent years most philosophers have argued that the concept of morality has just such a social or other-regarding feature built into it. Thus, they have declined to allow enlightened egoism even the status of a morality, for an egoist considers the welfare of others only insofar as his own well-being is directly or indirectly promoted. However, W. D. Falk in his paper "Morality, Self, and Others" has called attention to another conception of morality, and a competing one, which requires no such social orientation. This is the conception of moral as any rational, definitive, and authentic commitment of a self-directing person. This conception, which Falk traces back to the Greeks, does not entail that a rational, definitive, and authentic commitment must involve a primary concern for the welfare of others, though it may. Rather than offer a ruling as to which conception of morality is the "genuine" one, Falk concludes that the multiple associations of the concept are a barrier to summing it up in a single way. William K. Frankena in his paper "The Concept of Morality" offers an assessment of Falk's views, further clarifies the debate concerning the concept of morality, and illuminates many aspects of the question "What is morality?" He is, moreover, chiefly concerned with reconciling or combining the "rational" and "social" features associated with the concept of morality.

The Point of View of Morality

KURT BAIER

Philosophical skepticism is often due to and supported by arguments based on confused epistemological theories. Skepticism in ethics is no
exception. Consider skeptical views such as these: that the answers to
moral questions are the unsupportable deliverances of our moral sense or
intuition or flair, deliverances which unfortunately vary from age to age,
from class to class, and even from person to person; or that they are merely
the expressions of personal tastes, opinions, feelings, or attitudes; or that
they are the announcements of personal decisions, affirmations, choices, or
proposals. Philosophers usually come to hold such skeptical views because
they have had before their minds questions which are not genuinely moral
or, when they were genuinely moral, because their investigations of the
ways in which we ordinarily go about answering moral questions were comparatively superficial. Repelled by the transparent attempts of many moral
philosophers to assimilate moral to well-known "safe" questions and answers,
such as mathematical, ordinary empirical, or means-ends questions and
answers, the skeptics overemphasize the obvious differences. Opposition to
the "safe" models leads them to adopt or think in terms of well-known
"unsafe" ones, such as questions and answers in matters of taste, matters of
opinion, expressions of feelings and attitudes, and of decisions. The truth,
however, is much more complicated.

Accordingly, I shall attempt to isolate one type of genuinely moral
question and outline the appropriate procedure for answering it. It will
then be seen that moral questions also have a "method of verification",
although it is not the sort of empirical verification which in recent years
has been taken as the only type deserving the name.

It will be granted that "What shall I do?" is sometimes a moral question. But obviously it is not the mere employment of these words themselves, not the form of the interrogative sentence in which they are employed,
nor the ways in which these various employed words are severally used,
that make it moral. This form of words constitutes a *moral* question only
when it is *intended as* a moral question, i.e. when an answer of a certain
sort is wanted, an answer that can stand up to certain complicated tests;
in other words, when the questioner wants the person questioned first to consider and then to answer the question *from the point of view of morality*.

From Australasian Journal of Philosophy, *XXXII (1954). Reprinted by permission of the author and* Australasian Journal of Philosophy.

Let us be quite clear, in the first place, that not every question asked by means of these words is a moral question.

"What shall I do?" is not, for instance, a moral question when it is a request for instructions, as in the lieutenant's "What shall I do, Sir, shall I attack or wait for reinforcements?" This is not a moral question because the lieutenant, in asking for orders, is attempting to shift responsibility for what he is about to do on to his commanding officer. In moral cases, however, the agent himself is responsible for what he does. He cannot legitimately give the excuse "I acted on orders". Nor is it a moral question when asked by a pupil in the course of being taught. The learner wishing to know how to get on with his parking of the car, might ask the teacher, "What shall I do now?", but this is not necessarily a moral case either. When one asks for moral advice in a moral difficulty, one need not necessarily be a learner at all, not even a moral learner.

Nor is it a moral question when what one wants of the other person is that he should submit suggestions or declare his own preferences in the matter, as when someone asks: "What shall I do? Shall I leave the key in the milk box or what?"

What, then, is it to ask a *moral* question by means of these words? We are nearer the typical case on those occasions when we are driven into raising this question by a practical problem which forces us to choose between alternative courses of action, as when I say "What shall I do? I must pay back. But there were no replies to my advertisement. So where can I get the money?" In such a case I can either answer my own question or I can seek guidance from other people. Both I myself and others must work out the answer by going through the process of deliberation. Everyone is in principle capable of deliberating on his own or on someone else's behalf. There is a symmetrical relation between the person who asks "What shall I do?" and the person whom he asks. Their roles might at any time be exchanged. There is no question of superordination or subordination. Both are surveying and weighing the considerations in favor of and against the possible alternatives. In asking for advice I am not necessarily asking for, and in giving it, I am not necessarily giving orders, instructions, or tuition. When I ask for advice I am asking the person to deliberate on my behalf, i.e. to survey the reasons or considerations relevant to the problem, though I am not necessarily asking him to *give* me these reasons. But I should think that he had not done what I asked him to do, if he had not surveyed and weighed the reasons, had not thought about my problem at all.

But not all advice, not all deliberation, is moral. It is only when I deliberate from the point of view of morality that my deliberation can be said to be moral. I am not considering the problem from this point of view unless I attempt to survey and weigh all the relevant moral considerations. I must here assume an understanding of what is by no means generally understood, namely, the nature of deliberation and of a consideration. All I have space to examine here are the questions, What is deliberation *from the point of view of morality*? and What are *moral* considerations?

Suppose I have wealthy relatives whose son wants a bicycle. Perhaps I could get the money I need by selling my bicycle to them. They would surely be prepared to pay a good price, for my bicycle is as good as new. It is an English racing bicycle and they know the boy would be very happy with it. The cost is of no importance to them.

So far, my deliberation was not from the point of view of morality at all, for I have merely asked myself whether the proposed line of conduct was likely to produce the effect desired. I cannot be said to have considered this question from the former point of view unless I ask myself whether there are *any moral objections to*, i.e. any moral considerations against my proposed line of conduct.

When would we say that there were such objections? There is a moral objection to a proposed line of conduct if it would constitute a breach of a moral rule. Determining whether a particular line of action does or does not constitute such a breach is a complicated business and we must not think that it can be done in one move. There are two main steps: first, finding out whether the contemplated act is forbidden, or incompatible with another act enjoined, by a moral rule of the agent's group; secondly, finding out whether this moral rule of the agent's group can stand up to the appropriate moral criticism.

1

Our first question, then, is whether the planned line of conduct is forbidden by a moral rule of the group, and this involves the further question, when we would say of a rule that it belonged to the morality of a given group.

A few preliminary remarks about the nature of this question will help. A given rule which is part of the way of life of a certain group may belong to its law, its religion, or its mores, and if to the mores, then either to that part of the mores which we call its etiquette, or to its manners, or its fashions and so on. That a rule belongs to the law of the group can be ascertained by a comparatively precise method, namely, by ascertaining whether the rule is a valid part of its legal system. That it belongs to the religion of the group can usually be determined by finding out whether it is contained in any of the sacred books. On the other hand, that a given rule belongs to the mores of the group cannot be determined in any of these comparatively precise and specific ways. The most obvious method of finding out would seem to be to see whether the rule in question is supported by one or the other of the types of social pressure by which the various parts of the mores are supported. For instance, the rule will be said to belong to the manners of the group if the person on account of its breach is called ill-mannered, ill-bred, impolite, rude, or some such epithet, *and is treated accordingly.*

What we want to know is how we can characterize those rules which must be said to belong to the morality of the group.

Now, briefly, my answer to this question is as follows. For a rule to belong to the morality of a given group it is not necessary that, like the Decalogue, it should forbid or enjoin or permit a certain definite line of conduct or one or the other out of a definite range of conduct. What is necessary is rather that it should be: (1) part of the mores of the group, (2) supported by the characteristically moral pressure, (3) universally teachable and therefore universalizable, (4) not merely a taboo, (5) applied in accordance with certain principles of exception and modification, (6) applied in accordance with certain principles of application whose prevalence is a condition of the group being said to have a morality.

If a rule satisfies all these conditions, then it must be said to belong to the morality of the group in question, it is a moral rule *of* that group. I now proceed to discuss these points in detail.

(1) I shall simply assume, without much further argument, that the moral rules of a group belong to its mores and not to its law or religion. Moral rules of a group cannot be laid down, amended, abrogated, abolished. If a legislator were to attempt to do that, the rules he lays down would become part of the law. If the legislator is divine, the law is Divine Law. Of course, a legislator may not actually make new law, but merely declare law what is already existing custom. But then he has made law what was previously custom. And if he declares law what is a moral rule, then the moral rule has received legal backing. The same line of behavior is now forbidden by a moral *and* by a legal rule. If it is morally wrong to break the law, then it is morally wrong to drive on the right, where the law forbids it. If it is morally wrong to disobey God, then it has been morally wrong to play tennis on Sunday ever since God prohibited it. In this sense only can the word of command or of law create moral rules. But no word of command or law can *create* the moral rule that it is morally wrong to break the law or disobey the word of God. A rule is part of the morality of a group in virtue of the moral convictions and pressures of the people of that group. A rule can become part of the morality of a group through propaganda, education, teaching, by hook or by crook, but not by word of command or law. A rule must become part of the living tradition of the group to become a moral rule *of* that group.

(2) That a rule belongs to the mores of the group and not to its law or religion is not, however, sufficient. For it might still be merely a rule

of etiquette or custom. Now it might be thought that all that was necessary was that the rule should be supported by the *specifically moral pressure*. If infringers of the rule are said to be immoral, wicked, wrongdoers, evil, morally bad, or some term implying one of these, and they are treated accordingly, then the rule is supported by the specifically moral pressure. Whatever may be the precise treatment meted out to those we think we rightly say are immoral, evil, wicked, etc., it is plain that we tend to condemn them, dissociate ourselves from them, perhaps would want to see them punished. Again, it is evidence that the rule is part of the morality of the group if rule-breakers feel guilty and experience remorse. It is evidence that the rule is not part of the group morality if group members feel merely regret or pleasure when infringing it. Finally, it is evidence that the rule belongs to the group morality if, on discovering that the rule is not part of the mores of another group, group members are shocked, outraged, indignant, or horrified, and if they feel they must introduce this rule to the other group. Whereas, that they are quite unperturbed about this and don't feel driven to encourage them to adopt this rule, is evidence to the contrary.

Thus we can say that, although support of a rule by this sort of pressure is a necessary, it is not a sufficient condition of the rule belonging to the morality of the group.

(3) A further condition which a rule must satisfy if it is to be said to belong to the morality of a given group, is that it must have been taught in a certain way. Three features of the teaching of moral rules are particularly important here. In the first place, moral rules must be taught to all children. Moral education is not the preserve of a certain privileged or oppressed caste or class within the group, nor of certain privileged or oppressed individuals. Secondly, children are made to understand that the breach of the moral rules is very serious and that infringers of moral rules are peculiary reprehensible, horrible, and despicable. They are also taught that certain circumstances are extenuating and others aggravating and that in certain situations the rules need not be kept. They are taught that everyone is expected to observe them and that everyone will be treated in the same way when breaking or when observing these rules. Lastly, these rules are taught quite openly to everybody and taught in a way which makes it clear that one may be proud of observing these rules, of encouraging others to observe them and teach them to their children, of disapproving of others for not observing them or not teaching them to their children.

From this last point about universal teaching there follow certain principles, often called principles of universalizability, which exclude rules with a certain content from being part of the morality of any group whatever, since they could not be taught in the way in which rules must be capable of being taught if they are to be called moral rules. That this is so, shows that certain rules (logically) could not be said to be moral rules of a group. Hence it is not necessary to invoke any sort of moral intuition to "see" whether they are true or false moral rules. This question does not arise at all.

Notice that these rules are not self-contradictory, but that their content is such that no one who understands the nature of morality could rationally wish them to belong to the morality of any group.

(a) No one could wish a rule to belong to the morality of a group if the rule embodied a principle that was *self-frustrating*. For surely it must be possible for moral rules to be observed by all members of the group. Each member of the group might for instance wish to adopt the rule, When you are down ask for help, but don't ever help another man when he is down. But if all members of the group adopted this principle, then their adopting the second half of it would frustrate what is *obviously* the point of adopting the first half, namely, to *get* help when one is down. Such a principle is not, in itself, self-contradictory. Any one person may for himself consistently adopt it. But it is clearly a parasitic principle. It is useful to anyone only if many people act on the opposite principle.

(b) The same is true of self-defeating rules. A principle is self-defeating if its point is defeated as soon as its adoption by someone is revealed by him, e.g. the principle, Give a promise even when you know or think that you can never keep it, or when you don't intend to keep it. Now, the very point of giving promises is to reassure and give a guarantee to the promisee. Hence any remark that throws doubt on the sincerity of the promisor will defeat the purpose of making a promise. But clearly to *say* that one gives promises even when one knows or thinks one cannot, or when one does not intend to keep them, is to raise such doubts. And to say that one acts on the above principle is to imply that one may well give promises in these cases. Hence to reveal that one acts on this principle will tend to defeat one's own purpose.

But it has already been said that moral rules must be capable of being taught openly. Yet this rule is self-defeating if it is taught openly, for then everyone would be known to act on it. Hence it cannot belong to the morality of any group.

(c) Lastly, there are some rules which it is literally impossible to teach in the way the moral rules of a group must be capable of being taught, e.g. the rule "Always assert what you don't think to be the case". Such *morally impossible* rules differ from self-frustrating and self-defeating rules in that the latter could have been taught in this way, although it would have been quite senseless to do so, whereas the former literally cannot be so taught.

The reason why this rule cannot be taught thus is that the only possible case of acting on this principle, doing so secretly, is ruled out by the conditions of moral teaching.

(1) Consider first someone secretly adopting this principle. His remarks will almost always mislead people, for *he will be taken to be saying what he thinks true*, and in most cases what he thinks true will be true. Thus, it will usually be the case that p when he says "not-p", and that not-p when he says "p", whereas people will take it that p when he says "p", and that not-p when he says "not-p". Thus communication between him and other people breaks down, since they will almost always be misled by him whether he wishes to mislead them or not. The possibility of communication depends on the possibility of a speaker's ability *at will* to say either what he thinks to be the case or what he does not think to be the case. Our speaker cannot communicate because by his principle he is forced to mislead his hearers.

Thus, anyone secretly adopting the principle, Always assert what you don't think to be the case, cannot communicate with others since he is bound to mislead them whether he wants to or not. Hence he cannot possibly teach the principle to anybody. And if he were to teach the principle without having adopted it himself, then although he would be understood, yet those who adopted it would not. At any rate, since moral teaching involves teaching rules such as the taught may openly avow to be observing, this case is ruled out. A principle which is taught for secret acceptance only, cannot be embodied in a *moral* rule of the group.

(2) Of course, people might soon come to realize what is the matter with our man. They may discover that in order not to be misled by what he says, they only have to substitute "p" for "not-p" and vice versa. But if they do this then they have interpreted his way of speaking, not as a reversal of the general presumption that one says what one thinks is the case (not the opposite), but as a change of the use of "not". In his language, it will be said, "not" has become an affirmation sign, negation being effected by omitting it. Thus, if communication is to be possible, we must interpret as a change in usage what is intended as the reversal of the presumption that every assertion conveys what the assertor believes to be the case.

Thus, if everyone were, by accident, to adopt simultaneously and secretly our principle "Always assert what you think is not the case", then, for some time at least, communication would be impossible. If, on the other hand, it were adopted openly, then communication would be possible, but only if the adoption of this principle is accompanied by a change in the use of "not" which completely cancels the effect of the adoption of the principle. In that case, however, it can hardly be said that the principle has been adopted.

(3) However, the case we are considering is neither (1) nor (2). We are considering the case of the open teaching of the principle, Always assert what you don't think is the case, for open acceptance by everybody, which is not to be interpreted as a change in the use of "not". But this is nonsense. We cannot all openly tell one another that we are always going

to mislead one another in a certain way and insist that we must continue to be misled, though we know how we could avoid being misled.

Thus, this principle could not be embodied in a rule belonging to the morality of any group.

These points are of some general interest in that they clarify some valuable points contained in Kant's doctrine of the Categorical Imperative. In particular they clarify the expression "can will" contained in the formulation "Act so that thou *canst will* thy maxim to become a universal law of nature". "Canst will" in one sense means what I have called "morally possible". That is to say, your maxim must be a formula which is morally possible, i.e. which is logically capable of being a rule belonging to the morality of some group, as the maxim "Always lie" is not. No one *can* wish that maxim to be a rule of some morality. To say that one is wishing it, is to contradict oneself. One cannot wish it any more than one can wish that time should move backwards.

The second sense of "can will" is that in which no rational person can will certain things. Self-frustrating and self-defeating moral rules are not morally impossible, they are merely senseless. No rational person could wish such rules to become part of any morality. That is to say, anyone wishing that they should would thereby expose himself to the charge of irrationality, like the person who wishes that he should never attain his ends or that he should (for no reason at all) be plagued by rheumatic pains throughout his life.

But the points made also show the weakness of Kant's doctrine. For while it is true that someone who acts on the maxim "Always lie" acts on a morally impossible one, it is not true that every liar necessarily acts on that maxim. For if he acts on a principle at all, it may e.g. be, Lie when it is the only way to avoid harming someone, or Lie when it is helpful to you and harmful to no one else, or Lie when it is entertaining and harm-less, and so on. Maxims such as these can, of course, be willed in either of the senses explained.

(4) That the rule should be taught in the way explained is a necessary but not a sufficient condition of the rule belonging to the morality of the group.

Suppose that a group had the rule "Don't pick your teeth after a meal" and that this rule was taught in the way explained and supported by the typically moral pressure. But suppose also that, provided you crossed the fingers of your left hand, it was all right to pick your teeth after a meal. I think we would not say that such a rule belonged to the morality of that group.

The reason is not far to seek. We would not call this a rule of their morality, because it is merely a taboo. We do not allow it to be one of their moral rules, because they allow exemption on irrational grounds. Of course, one would have to examine their beliefs further to be sure that this was irrational. It would not necessarily be irrational if they also thought and offered some reason for thinking that crossing one's fingers when picking one's teeth appeased the deity who was incensed by the picking of one's teeth. We would not call a system of taboos a morality, not only because of the frequently odd contents of taboos, but also because of the mechanical and irrational nature of the ways in which members can gain exemption.

(5) It might be thought that I have given the wrong reason for saying that the taboos of a group cannot be moral rules of that group; I should not have said "exemptions on the wrong grounds" but just "exemptions". For it is sometimes held that moral rules do not allow of exceptions at all. "Fiat iustitia ruat caelum." Yet we do not regard a man who kills another in self-defense or executioners carrying out death sentences as murderers or even as wrongdoers. Theirs are justified killings. That we so regard them indicates more precisely the way we apply the rule "Never kill a man" by showing us one or the other of its legitimate exceptions. That we so interpret it does not show, as beginners usually think, that we do not really believe killing is wrong or that we have contradictory moral convictions, but it shows that, to speak technically, we think killing prima facie wrong, wrong other things being equal, wrong in the absence of special justifying factors.

What, then, are the required principles of making exceptions to a moral rule? It has been held that one of the principles is that one must never make an exception in one's own favor. This has been interpreted (and very naturally) as meaning "Never make an exception to a moral rule when doing so would be in your own interest". But this cannot be right, for I am at least as justified in killing a man in my own defense as I am in killing one in someone else's. And often it is just as immoral to make an exception when this is in someone else's interest, e.g. my wife's, my son's or my nephew's. In fact, it is quite unimportant in itself in whose favor the exception operates, so long as it was made legitimately, and it is made legitimately in the case of self-defense. The truth contained in this view is simply this, that I must not make exceptions to a moral rule *on the principle* that I will depart from the rule *whenever and simply because* doing so is in my interest or, for that matter, in that of someone else whom I wish to favor.

Generally speaking, we can say that a man is not treating a rule as moral unless he makes exceptions to the rule only in those cases which are themselves provided for by the rules of the morality of the group; that is to say, in our case, when the killing was by the hangman, in self-defense, of an enemy in war, and perhaps in mercy killing. But this is only rough, for it is not the case that we allow the morality of the group itself to provide for exceptions in any sorts of cases whatever. We would not, for instance, be satisfied to say that the rule, Never kill a human being, did belong to the morality of a group, if the rule was supported by the moral pressure, and if the making of exceptions on the grounds of self-interest was also supported by the moral pressure, as when a man is condemned for not killing another whose fortune he would have acquired.

(6) The question we are trying to answer, "When would we say that a given rule was a moral rule of a given group?" or "When would we say that a given rule belonged to the morality of a given group?", does, of course, presuppose that the group has a morality. For otherwise the question could not arise. On the other hand, having moral rules is one of the conditions of a group being said to have a morality. It might, therefore, be thought that the group needed only one rule of the right sort, say, Thou shalt not kill, or Thou shalt not lie, in order to be said to have a morality.

But I think this would be a mistake. We have already seen that for any such rule to be said to belong to the morality of the group, it must be supported by the right sort of pressure, be taught in the right sort of way, and be applied in accordance with certain principles of exception. But even this is not enough. We would not say of a group that it had a morality, even if it had one or several such rules and had all the practices already mentioned unless, in addition, it applied these rules in accordance with certain very general principles. Only if it did so apply some rules would we say that the group had a morality, and only those which were so applied would be said to belong to the morality of the group. The principles I have in mind might be called principles of *differentiation* and of *priority*.

The supreme principle of the application of moral rules is that in the absence of morally relevant differences between people moral rules must be applied to everyone alike. If a group is to be said to have a morality, it must have certain rules of differentiation, i.e. rules which lay down what are to be regarded by group members as morally relevant differences.

We would be inclined to say of a group that it had no morality if its rules of differentiation deviated more than a certain amount from the true principles of differentiation. Just what these true principles are and just what this maximum amount of deviation is, I cannot say now. All I can do at present is to indicate what are our rules of differentiation. (More about this below, page 341.) Notice also that one of the grounds on which we grade different moralities as less or more civilized, more or less primitive, less or more advanced, is the amount by which they depart from what we regard as the true principles of differentiation.

The most obvious grounds recognized by our morality for differentiating between different people are these:

(1) Breach of a moral rule by someone and consequent forfeiture of the protection of certain moral rules. Thus a man who without provocation is attempting to kill another man cannot claim the protection of the moral rule, Thou shalt not kill. If the other man, in self-defense, kills him, then the killer cannot be said to be a murderer, as he otherwise might have to be.

(2) Special effort (greater than standard) and consequent moral claims to special consideration. Thus a man who has worked hard on a common project is entitled to a greater return from the common proceeds than one who has been idle.

(3) Greater or less need (than standard) and consequently fewer or more tasks, duties, jobs, obligations. Thus, a man with a large family or one who has lost his eyesight is entitled to special consideration, partly because his need is greater and partly because certain duties would be more onerous for him than for others.

(4) Special undertakings freely entered into and consequently special obligations to carry these out. Thus, a man who has a job as a social worker is not entitled to the gratitude and reward to which another is entitled, who does the same thing without having entered into any undertakings.

The supreme *principle of priority* lays it down that when two rules clash, i.e. when a person, by doing one thing, would be breaking one rule and by not doing it, breaking another, he ought to observe the more important rule and break the less important. Rules of priority of a given group provide guidance for the most likely clashes of moral rules.

Thus, when I know that by lying to his pursuers about his whereabouts I can save the life of an innocent man endangered by them, I am in the position of having either to lie or to help increase the danger to someone's life. In making a moral decision on this, I am guided by moral rules of priority. Our morality lays it down, I think, that we should lie in order not to endanger the innocent man's life, rather than vice versa.

If a morality had no rules at all for those cases in which two or more moral rules clash, if people sometimes acted in one way and then in another and felt no need for a uniform settlement, then one would be inclined to say that the group had no morality.

This completes my explanation of the first step in answering the moral question "What shall I do?" Suppose our agent has found, in this way, that his proposed course was not forbidden by any moral rule of the group nor incompatible with any course of action required by such a rule. He has then found a (preliminary) positive answer to his moral question. Speaking in this preliminary way, there are no moral objections to doing what he is proposing to do. He can go ahead. What he is proposing to do is morally all right, is not something he morally ought not to do. If, on the other hand, he finds that this line of action is contrary to a moral rule of the group, then he has found a (preliminary) negative answer.

2

No doubt many people never go further than this. They are like Plato's well-behaved auxiliaries in never challenging the authority of those who have taught them what is right and wrong. But if there is to be moral progress there must be at least some who subject the morality of their group to rational scrutiny and attempt to reform it where it is found wanting. The view that our morality *needs* no criticism because it is the word of God Who revealed it to us is as detrimental to moral advance as the view that there is *no point* in criticizing it because the juggernaut of history is inexorably pushing it forward in its predetermined grooves, anyway.

Let us then try to understand what such criticism of a morality comes to. Suppose our questioner finds that his proposed line of conduct is contrary to a rule of this group morality. Suppose also that he is not satisfied to accept uncritically the morality of his group. He will then go on to ask a question which he might formulate in these words, "Granted that our morality forbids this course of action, is our morality right in forbidding it?" We all understand this question. Most of us have sometimes asked it. We all admit that at least a few of our moral convictions may be misguided. Most of us now suspect that certain views on poverty and private property widely held in England in the eighteenth century were wrong, and also the nineteenth-century views on sex.

What, then, does such a critically minded person ask? What sort of doubt is he raising about the rules of his group morality? In what ways can the rules of a group morality go wrong?

Consider, to begin with, the analogous case of the expression "religious rule". It is well to remember that the two most important senses of "religious rule" are not parallel to the two main senses of "legal rule", namely, "law" and "lawful rule". There is no sense of "religious rule" which corresponds to "lawful rule". We would not say of the rule "Don't pick your teeth in public" that it was in any sense religious, just because it was not irreligious; although we would say that this rule was legal just because it was not illegal, i.e. was lawful. "Moral rule" is in this respect like "religious rule" and *not* like "legal rule". "Don't pick your teeth in public" would no more be called a moral rule (because in our society it is not considered immoral) than it would be called a religious rule (because it is not irreligious).

There is, however, a sense of "religious rule" which is parallel to "legal rule" in the sense of "law". I think it would not be seriously misleading for our purposes if we said that no system of beliefs and rules could be called a religion if it did not contain either supernatural beliefs or prescribed rites or rules of worship. If we know that a group has a certain religion, we can then tell whether a given rule of a group belongs to its religion or not. In the case, for instance, of the Christian religion, it is easy to tell that a rule is religious, namely, if it is contained in one of the sacred books.

Even so, there are rather different sorts of rule in the Holy Scriptures.

(1) Thou shalt not make unto thee any graven image or any likeness of anything that is in the heaven above, or that is in the earth beneath, or that is in the water under the earth.

(2) But if the ox were wont to push with his horn in time past, and it hath been testified to his owner, and he hath not kept him in, but that he hath killed a man or a woman; the ox shall be stoned, and his owner also shall be put to death.

Both these rules are religious rules, in a sense corresponding to that which makes certain rules legal rules, i.e. laws: being part of the system. But we must now take notice that there is another sense of "religious rule" in which they are not both religious rules. Rule (2) about the ox is not, in this sense, religious, whereas clearly rule (1) is. Religious Jews would not feel that they were sinning if they broke the rule concerning the ox, but they would do so if they broke rule (1), even though both these rules are held to have been revealed by God on Mount Sinai.

We thus distinguish between those rules which are, as I shall say, *genuinely religious,* and those which merely happen to be *part of the religion of the group.* We may similarly distinguish between those moral rules of the group which are *genuinely moral* and those which merely happen to be *part of the morality of the group.*

Let us make this distinction a little clearer. As we have seen, a rule will be said to belong to the morality of the group (provided the group has a morality), if it is treated in all the important respects in the way in which a genuinely moral rule ought to be treated: if it is taught in the way indicated, if it is applied in accordance with the moral principles of making exceptions, if it passes the universalization tests, if rule-breakers are dealt with in the specifically moral way, and perhaps some other things.

On the other hand, even if a rule does satisfy all these conditions, we may still have misgivings about it. Take the rule "Don't eat beans" or "Don't walk under ladders". Like the rules "Don't kill a human being" or "Don't lie", these rules might satisfy all the conditions necessary in order to be said to belong to the morality of some group. But even when they satisfy these conditions, we think that they *ought not to* belong to any morality. The first of these rules may perhaps have a place in a treatise on health foods, and the second is a mere superstition. They may belong to, but neither belongs *in* a morality. How, then, do we distinguish the genuine from the spurious, among the rules actually belonging to the morality of a group?

Let us remember that doing this is the task of a *critic* of a morality. Hence we need to lay bare the standards employed in this task. There seem to me to be four ways of getting at these standards. (A) In the first place, we already have some idea of what point of view we actually adopt when we perform this task. We only need to remind ourselves of it and make it explicit. (B) Secondly, we have the paradigms of genuinely moral rules, such as "Don't kill any human being", "Don't lie", "Don't be cruel". With regard to these rules we are more certain to be right than with regard to any other rules and principles. Hence an examination of the characteristics of these rules as opposed to obviously spurious ones, like "Don't eat beans", will help us to work out the principles by which we distinguish between genuinely moral and spurious rules. (C) Thirdly, we already have a fair idea of some of the principles we are using in this job. (D) Lastly, we have some idea of the relative merit of moralities as a whole. We already grade them as primitive and advanced, crude and civilized, lower and higher, and so on. But since these gradings of whole moralities depend, at least to some extent, on whether a morality contains fewer or more of the genuinely moral rules than of the spurious ones, this too helps us to arrive at the truth. Arriving at the truth in this matter consists in following up these beginnings, pressing as far as possible the various implications contained in them, and making them consistent and sensible.

Ad (A). I take the following to be the point of view which we adopt when we perform the task of a critic of a morality. I shall call it the point of view of morality. We are adopting it if we regard the rules belong to the morality of the group as designed to regulate the behavior of people all of whom are to be treated as equally important "centers" of cravings, impulses, desires, needs, aims, and aspirations; as people with ends of their own, all of which are entitled, prima facie, to be attained. (I take this to be the meaning of "treating them as ends in themselves and not merely as means to one's own ends".) The pursuits and wishes and ends of none of these goal-seekers are to be subordinated without special justification to those of any one or any group of them. From this point of view every one of these individuals is required to modify his impulsive behavior, his endeavors, and his plans by observing certain rules, the genuinely moral rules. These forbid any individual's pursuit, even that of his own greatest good, if it is at the expense of the legitimate pursuits of others, at the same time indicating whose pursuit has to be abandoned in the case of conflicts (e.g. "Don't kill anyone except in self-defense, etc."); or they direct or admit him to the performance of certain ministrations to or by others because of his either being in a certain social position (teacher, soldier, etc.), or his finding himself in certain social relations to others (female dependant, beneficiary), or having inflicted certain things on others or suffered them at their hands (maiming, deceiving someone, etc.).

It is worth noting that this point of view differs from that of an Enlightened Egoist. The latter regards other people as complicated and subtle organisms who tend to compete with him for the good things in life but who, if properly handled, can be made to serve him the better to attain his own ends. An Enlightened Egoist must be and is prepared for other people to be similarly engaged in the pursuit of their own good and for each to subordinate the good of others to his own, i.e. to pursue his own good whenever possible, even to the detriment of others.

The job of a critic of morality may also be confused with that of some sort of ideal legislator. For both moral rules and laws are rules for members of groups, both in the ideal case applying to all members alike, both varying from group to group inasmuch as the exigencies of life, the technical means and the social arrangements vary, and both designed to protect each individual in the pursuit of his own good (made possible within the framework of his society) from any interference and abuse of the social devices by others. But while there are these similarities, there also are decisive differences.

There are a number of quite different jobs to be performed in the field of law and in the field of morality. In the field of law a man may perform the task of a legal critic, of a legal reformer, or of a legislator. The job of legal critic is to examine the legal system of his group and to ferret out weaknesses and devise improvements. It is not his job to publicize the weaknesses or to campaign for their removal. That is the job of the legal reformer. The task of the legislator is to create new law. He merely uses the existing machinery of legislation. The job of the critic is the invention of improvements, the job of the reformer is the preparation of public opinion, the job of the legislator is the setting in motion of the legal machinery.

In the field of morality there are only two comparable jobs, that of the critic of a morality and of the moral reformer. For reasons already mentioned there could not be the job of a moral legislator. When public opinion has been swayed, the morality of the group has already been changed. The group is then ready for legal changes, but the actual legal changes have yet to come. Legal authority rests with the legislator, moral authority with the public.

The critic's job differs from that of the reformer in being theoretical rather than practical. A thinker can criticize the law or the morality of the Ancients, he cannot reform it. The critic may consider all sorts of past, present or future possibilities, the reformer considers only immediate practical future possibilities. There is no doubt that the institution of slavery was a shortcoming of the morality of the Ancients. There is considerable doubt whether the abolition of slavery should have been on the program of an ancient moral reformer.

There is a further important difference. Both the legal critic and the critic of morality may and should adopt the point of view of morality. But if the legal critic adopts it, he imposes on himself certain extraneous restrictions; if the critic of morality adopts it, he does not. If the legal critic does not adopt it, he may still be a legal critic; if the critic of morality does not adopt it, he cannot be a critic of morality. If the legal critic correctly criticizes law from the moral point of view, his criticisms will be morally justified, but they may be incompetent from the lawyers' point of view. If the critic of morality criticizes a morality from the point of view of morality, his criticism will be morally justified and that is all it needs to be.

It should now be clear what sort of a task it is to distinguish the genuine from the spurious among the rules actually belonging to the morality of a given group. It is the task of a critic of a morality. We all have this task in that, as moral beings, we are normally guided by the moral convictions of our group which we absorb in the course of our upbringing. It is our task as critics to examine this group morality, our task as moral reformers to attempt to bring about the removal of glaring inadequacies and needed improvements.

Ad (B). I have now completed my discussion of the point of view appropriate for a critic of the morality of his group. If my sketch of that point of view was accurate, it should enable us to say something about the principles governing the critic's work. In particular, if from the point of view of morality we look upon human beings as equally engaged in the pursuit of their legitimate interests, we would expect one of the principles by which we test group moralities to be this, that a genuine moral rule must be *for the good* of human beings. And since, from the point of view of morality, all are to be regarded equally, we would expect that the rules should *affect everyone alike*.

These points are confirmed independently, if we consider such paradigms of moral rules as Thou shalt not kill, Thou shalt not be cruel, Thou shalt not break promises, Thou shalt not lie. It certainly would seem to be for the good of all human beings alike that rules like these are part of the morality of groups.

Ad (C). This can be seen more clearly if we turn to our third way of getting at the standards employed, in criticizing an existing morality, namely, the consideration of the principles which we actually find ourselves using in this job. If we investigated what more exactly is meant by saying that the inclusion of a certain rule in the morality of a given group is for the good of human beings alike, by trying it out in a number of individual cases, we find that the application of this general principle tallies with our actual practice as critics of a morality. When would a rule be said to be *for the good* of human beings?

(a) In the first place, a rule must *not* be harmful. But it will be said to be harmful if (1) acting in accordance with it is harmful to the agent (e.g. "If your eye offends you, pluck it out"); (2) one man's acting on it is harmful to many people, including the agent (e.g. "If you want to have a really pleasant drive, get drunk first"); (3) one man's acting in accordance with it is harmful to others but not to the agent (e.g. "If you can get away with it, cheat in business"); (4) everybody's or many people's, but not a single person's acting in accordance with it, is generally detrimental (e.g. "Turn on the current during the restricted hours").

A few words must be said in explanation of cases (1) and (4). In both cases the tests are tests of *rules*, not of *particular acts*. (1) says that a rule requiring of people behavior harmful to themselves is, other things being equal, not a genuinely moral rule even if it belongs to the morality of a group. But this must not be confused with the question whether a particular act harmful to the agent and known to him to be so, is morally wrong. Such an *act* would be morally wrong only if this sort of act, whether harmful or not, or if harming oneself in any manner whatsoever, were *contrary to* a genuine moral rule of that group. But this is the opposite of the case we are considering, namely, the case of a rule *enjoining* (not forbidding) what is harmful to the agent. A rule which forbids what is harmful to the agent may, of course, belong to the morality of a group.

It is characteristic e.g. of bourgeois morality that certain types of prudent behavior are regarded as virtues (the observation of moral rules) and certain imprudent ones as vices (contrary to moral rules forbidding what is harmful to *oneself*), e.g. taking exercise, saving money, working hard, on the one hand, and smoking, drinking, neglecting one's health on the other. It is not clear whether these types of behavior are so regarded because they tend to be harmful or useful, respectively, to the agent, or because they usually also tend to be harmful or useful to *others*. In my opinion, it is only if they really are harmful to others that these lines of action can rightly be regarded as vices.

An analogous distinction must be borne in mind when considering case (4): there I have mentioned as reason for saying that a *rule* is not genuinely moral that everyone's or many people's acting in accordance with it would be generally detrimental. This too, is quite different from saying that *a particular line of conduct* is wrong because everyone's or many people's doing this sort of thing would be generally detrimental. In the notorious "landlady argument", "You can't use the iron just whenever you like, Miss Thompson; what if everybody were to do that!", the imaginary "universalization" does not test an existing moral rule—no one thinks of the rule, Use the iron whenever you like, as a rule of our morality —rather, it is supposed to be a test of a particular line of action. Let us be quite clear about the difference.

Suppose that there is a power shortage and that it is widely held that restrictions would be necessary if the supply is not to break down.

Take first the case of a society in which there are no regulations to cope with this. The legislator may then consider the imposition of restrictions on the use of electric appliances. Among *his* reasons for *introducing* this sort of legislation could be our argument in case (4), namely, that if everybody or many people were to continue using these appliances at all times, the power supply would break down. If this is true, then it would be an excellent reason for introducing this piece of legislation and, unless there were reasons against doing so, the legislator would be to some extent to blame if he failed to do so.

In the absence of such legislation there would seem to be two possibilities: either the case is already covered by a moral rule of the group or it is not. In the first case it would clearly be morally wrong to use any electric appliances extensively. I am entitled to do so only if I have a special reason, as when I am ill and must have a radiator going continuously. In this case, if I really know that my turning on the radiator will not make any difference to the power supply, my justification for not observing the moral rule gains weight.

It may, of course, be difficult to decide whether the case is already covered by a rule or principle belonging to the morality of a given group. There is no doubt, for instance, that our morality does not contain the specific rule "Do not use electric appliances for more than an hour a day", although it does or did contain other similarly specific rules, such as "It is wrong for women to have careers of their own" or "It is wrong for young girls to use makeup". But it is not quite so obvious that our morality does not contain the rule "It is morally wrong to do that the doing of which by everyone or very many people (but not by one alone) would be harmful", which would cover our case. It may be said that we do have this rule because it is simply a specific case under the principle of fairness and we do have the principle of fairness, which in one of its forms runs as follows: "Take no unfair advantage, that is to say, no advantage which, in the circumstances, it would be harmful to grant to anyone and everyone". That our morality contains this principle can be seen from the fact that words like "shirking", "malingering", "not pulling one's weight" on the one hand and "taking more than one's fair share" on the other have negative "moral tone". It seems, therefore, reasonably certain that our morality contains the principle of fairness and that the general rule covering our example is a special application of it. If this is right, then it would be wrong by our moral standards to use the radiator in periods of known power shortage, whether or not there is a specific regulation prohibiting such use.

It would take too long to consider whether there could be moralities that contained no rules covering our case, and what we would say in such cases (if there were any) about the question whether, in the absence of specific legislation forbidding the use of radiators, it would be morally wrong to use them in times of known power shortage. All that can be said is that even if in such a society it could not be *shown* to be wrong, it would still *be* wrong, if it is true that the rule of fairness *ought* to belong to any morality whatsoever and if our case is covered by that rule.

But now consider the case where the appropriate legislation has already been introduced. Then it is (prima facie) morally wrong to infringe this legislation, since any bona fide law or regulation has the moral backing. One may argue with the legislator about the need for such regulations, but as a citizen one must obey them while they are in force. The reason for this is not that if everyone used his radiator the power supply would break down, but simply that there is a bona fide regulation against it. A citizen can, of course, agitate for the repeal of any piece of legislation, but until then he must (other things being equal) obey them, whether he thinks them necessary or unnecessary, good or bad laws.

It is, therefore, simply irrelevant to this issue that my own use of the radiator will make little or no difference. It is wrong to turn it on, even if I know that, because everybody else is law-abiding, no one will do so and that, therefore, my doing so will make no difference. It is wrong to turn it on even if I know that everybody else will do so and that, therefore, the power supply will break down anyway. I have an excuse for breaking the regulation, if I have a special overriding ground for doing so, as when I am ill and must have warmth, but even then I should try to get a permit to do so. Here again my knowledge (if I know) that my turning on the radiator will make no difference, gives added force to my excuse for breaking the regulations.

Of course, all this holds only for valid bona fide laws and regulations. That a law or regulation is valid is determined by legal tests; that it is bona fide is not a legal matter. If a law enjoins what is known to be immoral because contrary to a moral principle of the group, then the law is not bona fide. In this case it is morally wrong to obey the law unless the consequences of disobeying it are morally worse than the consequences of obeying it. If, on the other hand, a law is willfully unnecessary, i.e. such that everyone can see plainly that the law is unnecessary, as would be the case with the possible law "No women must smoke in the street" or "No New Australians must be served intoxicating liquor", then neither obeying it nor disobeying it while trying to avoid being caught is morally wrong. But this applies only to plainly willfully unnecessary laws or plain chicaneries. If a law is in fact unnecessary, but it is still a highly disputable question whether it is unnecessary or if it is unnecessary, but not at all plainly so, then the law must be regarded as bona fide and, therefore, as morally binding.

(b) A further condition that must be satisfied if a rule is to be said to be for the good of human beings is that it must not impose any *unnecessary restrictions*. "Don't eat beans" is a rule which is unsuitable for inclusion on this score.

(c) Lastly, a rule is for the good of human beings if it promotes the good of some people, provided it does not violate any of the other conditions, especially of unjustifiably and necessarily harming or tending to harm some people. "Be kind to others", "Give to charity", "Be generous", "Help your aged parents" and so on belong in this group.

Here again, the difference between the justification of individual acts and of rules should be noted. It is wrong not to look after one's aged parents because there is in our morality a rule to that effect, and this rule is rightly part of our morality because it promotes the good of certain people and prevents harm to which they are exposed in the special conditions of our society. If the aged were cared for by the state and the rule ceased to be part of our morality, then it would no longer be morally wrong not to assist one's aged parents, although it might still not be wrong or might even be meritorious to do so.

On the other hand, it is not morally wrong not to be generous because no rule of our morality makes generosity compulsory. Generosity is merely meritorious. Or rather, we mean by "generosity" that amount of assistance to others which goes beyond that which is compulsory. As our moral and economic standards rise, more and more in the way of mutual assistance is required of us as a matter of course. Generosity and charity begin after that.

Ad (D). We can now turn to our last approach towards the standards of criticism of a morality: the grading of various different moralities. We say of some moralities that they are higher or lower, more or less advanced, more or less primitive or civilized, more or less developed or evolved than others. What are the standards in accordance with which we grade these?

The most obvious method of weighing moralities is according to the proportion of genuine over spurious moral rules. This is not a matter of mere counting, for some rules are more important than others: the rule "Don't kill any human being" is much more important than the rule "Don't be grumpy".

But there are other methods. We have seen above (p. 331) that a group in order to be clearly said to have a morality must have rules governing the making of exceptions to moral rules. We have distinguished above two sets of such rules, those concerning discrimination between different sets of people, and those governing conflicts between moral rules. We have mentioned the most obvious such rules of our morality, but have said nothing about what are the correct principles that should govern them. For obviously it is particularly in these fields that one morality differs from another. Racial theories, class and caste systems, nationalism, and so on are phenomena in which differences of rules of discrimination play an important part.

Take first the rules of discrimination. These are based on one basic principle, that of nondiscrimination, i.e., the principle that all rules qua moral apply to everyone alike. That is to say, a moral rule must not discriminate between people, i.e. differentiate between them on morally irrelevant grounds, where a morally relevant ground of differentiation is one which reveals differences of moral desert. The system of these grounds of differentiation rests on the principle of equality, that to begin with, all other things being equal, i.e. unless there are some specific grounds for differentiation, all moral rules must, therefore, be equally applied to all.

But what can we say are the *correct* principles in accordance with which a group *should* recognize grounds of differentiation? I think we can say that those are correct which themselves satisfy all the tests which a genuine moral rule must satisfy.

We do, for instance, distinguish between parents and others in respect of what they owe their children because we think it *for the good of human beings* that someone in particular should have the responsibility for the care of the young and we think it most natural and, in our social setup, best that the parents should have this responsibility.

The same thing is true, *mutatis mutandis*, of the rules of priority. These, too, must pass all the tests for genuine moral rules. If they pass these tests, then they are not merely rules of priority belonging to our group morality, but genuine rules of moral priority.

One more point in this connection. We have seen reason to think that if a group did not have any rules of differentiation or priority or if those it had were totally different from, perhaps contrary to the best ones, we would have reason to doubt whether the group in question had a morality at all. On the other hand, it is not necessary that these rules of discrimination and priority should be exactly in accordance with the best ones. Here there is the possibility of a gradual approximation to the ideal. It has often been pointed out that in the history of mankind we find a gradual extension of the application of rules of morality first to ever larger groups and then to people outside any particular group. Christianity, by the introduction of the notion of Equality in the eyes of God, All men being the children of God, All men being brothers, and so on, has contributed much to this spread. But we do not deny that a group has a morality simply because it does not extend the application of its moral rules equally to everyone.

We can thus say that there are certain minimal requirements which must be fulfilled if the group is to be said to have a morality at all. If these are fulfilled, we speak of varying degrees of perfection of a morality, depending on the degree of approximation to a certain ideal.

This completes the answer to our main question. We have seen that "What shall I do?" is a moral question if and only if it is asked with a view to getting an answer that can stand up to certain complicated tests. We have seen what these tests are. We make sure first that the proposed course of action is not contrary to a moral rule of the agent's group, and secondly that, if it is, this rule is not a genuine moral rule. Concerning the first step, we have seen that every member of a group that can be said to have a morality is taught the rules belonging to that morality. I have mentioned tests for telling whether a given rule does or does not belong to the morality of one's group, and tests for telling whether a rule is genuinely moral. With this information it is possible to answer the moral question "What shall I do?" One has to rely on one's moral education for supplying the first answer to whether or not a proposed line of conduct is contrary to a moral rule of the group. If one has found a rule which one has been taught as a moral rule of the group and to which the proposed line of conduct is contrary, then one can, by applying the tests I have mentioned, make sure whether it is *really wrong*. It is really morally wrong if it is contrary to a rule which is really a rule belonging to the morality of the group and which is also genuinely moral. I have said nothing about the more difficult cases when the line of conduct is contrary to a moral rule belonging to the group which is not genuinely moral (e.g. "No sports on Sundays"), and the case when it is contrary to a genuinely moral rule which is not part of the morality of the agent's group (e.g. "Don't discriminate against Jews").

Finally, it should be noticed that "What shall I do?" is a moral question asked by a particular agent belonging to a particular group, and cannot be answered *in abstracto*. On the other hand, the critical testing of moralities is done by means of standards and against principles which are not tied to any group. "What shall I do?", when it is a moral question, is asked from within a culture, but it involves the asking and answering of questions which would be the same in any culture context whatsoever. But this does not mean that these questions would receive the same answers in every culture context. "Parents, not the State, must look after children" may be a genuinely moral rule in one society but not in another, although the principles in accordance with which this is settled are the same in both cases.

How simpleminded it is to look for the one feature that marks off *the* moral judgment or utterance from other sorts. The moral agent asks moral questions and answers them with a view to doing something. The moral critic asks and answers the question whether a particular agent has acted in accordance with or contrary to the moral rules of his society, with a view to judging his moral merit. The critic of a morality, on the other hand, asks and answers the question whether any of its rules are spurious, or whether any genuine moral rules are missing, or perhaps whether this morality is more or less advanced or civilized than certain others. The moral reformer "sees" that certain rules belonging to the morality of his group are not genuinely moral rules, or that certain rules which would be genuinely moral rules, if they were part, are not part of the morality of his group, and advocates the necessary reform. Here "intuition" is the proper word to use.

But while all these people busy with all these different tasks are employing moral terms, moral arguments, and moral reasons, while they all engage in moral talk, it is surely absurd to think that they are all uttering quasi-imperatives or are all expressing or arousing specific emotions or attitudes or feelings, or that they are all trying to persuade someone to change his attitudes, or to give him moral advice, or pass moral judgment on him. Surely, they are sometimes doing one, sometimes another of these things.

Social Morality
and Individual Ideal[1]

P. F. STRAWSON

Men make for themselves pictures of ideal forms of life. Such pictures are various and may be in sharp opposition to each other; and one and the same individual may be captivated by different and sharply conflicting pictures at different times. At one time it may seem to him that he should live—even that *a man* should live—in such-and-such a way; at another that the only truly satisfactory form of life is something totally different, incompatible with the first. In this way, his outlook may vary radically, not only at different periods of his life, but from day to day, even from one hour to the next. It is a function of so many variables: age, experiences, present environment, current reading, current physical state are some of them. As for the ways of life that may thus present themselves at different times as each uniquely satisfactory, there can be no doubt about their variety and opposition. The ideas of self-obliterating devotion to duty

From Philosophy, *XXXVI (1961). Reprinted by permission of the author and* Philosophy.

1 This paper has been read at philosophical societies in a number of British universities. I am grateful to my critics on these occasions for forcing me to make myself at least a little clearer.

or to the service of others; of personal honor and magnanimity; of asceticism, contemplation, retreat; of action, dominance, and power; of the cultivation of "an exquisite sense of the luxurious"; or simple human solidarity and cooperative endeavor; of a refined complexity of social existence; of a constantly maintained and renewed affinity with natural things—any of these ideas, and a great many others too, may form the core and substance of a personal ideal. At some times such a picture may present itself as merely appealing or attractive; at others it may offer itself in a stronger light, as, perhaps, an image of the only sane or nonignoble human reaction to the situation in which we find ourselves. "The nobleness of life is to do thus" or, sometimes, "The sanity of life is to do thus": such may be the devices with which these images present themselves.

Two quite different things may be urged against, or in mitigation of, this picture of a multiplicity of pictures. First, it might be said that the many, apparently conflicting pictures are really different parts or aspects, coming momentarily into misleading prominence, of a single picture; this latter being the composite ideal image of our coolest hours, in which every god is given his due and conflict is avoided by careful arrangement and proper subordination of part to part. And it may be true of some exceptional individuals that they entertain ideal images which exhibit just such a harmonious complexity. I believe this to be rarer than we sometimes pretend; but in any case to describe this situation is not to redescribe the situation I have spoken of, but to describe a different situation. The other mitigating point has more weight. It is that, however great the variety of images which dominate, at one time or another, our ethical imaginations, our individual lives do not, as a matter of fact, exhibit a comparable internal variety. Indeed they scarcely could. Something approaching consistency, some more or less unsteady balance, is usually detectable in the pattern of an individual person's decisions and actions. There are, so to speak, empirical grounds for ordering his ideal images in respect to practical efficacy, even, perhaps, for declaring one of them to be practically dominant. This point I shall grant. I think it is easy to exaggerate it; easy to exaggerate the unity of the personalities of those we say we know, when we really know them only in one or two particular connections; easy to dismiss as phases or moods whatever lacks conformity with our only partly empirical pictures of each other. But I shall not dwell on this. What I shall dwell on is precisely this readiness, which a great many people have, to identify themselves imaginatively at different times with different and conflicting visions of the ends of life, even though these visions may receive the scantiest expression in their actual behavior and would call for the most upsetting personal revolutions if they received more.

This fact about many people—a fact which partly explains, among other things, the enormous charm of reading novels, biographies, histories

—this fact, I say, has important consequences. One consequence is that when some ideal image of a form of life is given striking expression in the words or actions of some person, its expression may evoke a response of the liveliest sympathy from those whose own patterns of life are as remote as possible from conformity to the image expressed. It is indeed impossible that one life should realize all the ideal pictures which may at one time or another attract or captivate the individual imagination. But the owner of one life may with perfect practical consistency wish that his conflicting images should all be realized in different lives. The steadiest adherence to one image may coexist with the strongest desire that other and incompatible images should have their steady adherents too. To one who has such a desire, any doctrine that the pattern of the ideal life should be the same for all is intolerable; as it is to me. The way in which I have just expressed the position makes its practical consistency look more simple than it is. One cannot simply escape the conflict between different ideal images by diffusing their realization over different lives. For different lives interact and one's own is one of them; and there may be conflict in the areas of interaction. One is not forced to welcome this, though one may; it is simply something that in fact goes with the fulfillment of the wish for this kind of diversity in the pursuit of ends. Equally one is not precluded from taking one side in a conflict because one has wished that both sides should exist and has some sympathy with both.

I think there can be no doubt that what I have been talking about falls within the region of the ethical. I have been talking about evaluations such as *can* govern choices and decisions which are of the greatest importance to men. Whether it falls within the region of the moral, however, is something that may be doubted. Perhaps the region of the moral falls within it. Or perhaps there are no such simple inclusion-relations between them. The question is one I shall come back to later. I should like first to say something more about this region of the ethical. It could also be characterized as a region in which there are truths which are incompatible with each other. There exist, that is to say, many profound general statements which are capable of capturing the ethical imagination in the same way as it may be captured by those ideal images of which I spoke. They often take the form of general descriptive statements about man and the world. They can be incorporated into a metaphysical system, or dramatized in a religious or historical myth. Or they can exist—their most persuasive form for many—as isolated statements such as, in France, there is a whole literature of, the literature of the maxim. I will not give examples, but I will mention names. One cannot read Pascal or Flaubert, Nietzsche or Goethe, Shakespeare or Tolstoy, without encountering these profound truths. It is certainly possible, in a coolly analytical frame of mind, to mock at the whole notion of the profound truth; but we are guilty of mildly bad faith if we do. For in most of us the ethical imagination succumbs again and again to *these* pictures of man, and it is precisely as truths that we wish to characterize them while they hold us captive. But these truths have the same kind of relation to each other as those ideal images of which I have already spoken. For pictures of the one kind reflect and are reflected by pictures of the other. They capture our imagination in the same way. Hence it is as wholly futile to think that we could, without destroying their character, systematize these truths into one coherent body of truth as it is to suppose that we could, without destroying their character, form a coherent composite image from these images. This may be expressed by saying that the region of the ethical is the region where there are truths but no truth; or, in other words, that the injunction to see life steadily *and* see it whole is absurd, for one cannot do both. I said I would give no examples, but I will allude to one near contemporary one. Many will remember the recorded encounter between Russell and Lawrence, the attempt at sympathy and the failure to find it. That failure is recorded in such words as: "I thought there might be something in what he said, but in the end I saw there was nothing" on the one hand; and "Get back to mathematics where you can do some good; leave talk about human beings alone" on the other. The clash was a clash of two irreconcilable views of man, two irreconcilable attitudes. The spectator familiar with both may say: Russell is right; he tells the truth; he speaks for civilization. He may also say: Lawrence is right; he tells the truth; he speaks for life. The point is that he may say both things. It would be absurd to hope for a reconcilation of the two conflicting attitudes. It is not absurd to desire that both should exist, in conflict.

The region of the ethical, then, is a region of diverse, certainly incompatible and possibly practically conflicting ideal images or pictures of a human life, or of human life; and it is a region in which many such incompatible pictures may secure at least the imaginative, though doubtless not often the practical, allegiance of a single person. Moreover this statement itself may be seen not merely as a description of what is the case, but as a positive evaluation of evaluative diversity. Any diminution in this variety would impoverish the human scene. The multiplicity of conflicting pictures is itself the essential element in one of one's pictures of man.

Now what are the relations between the region of the ethical and the sphere of morality? One widely accepted account of the latter is in terms of the idea of rules or principles governing human behavior which apply universally within a community or class. The class may be variously thought of as a definite social group or the human species as a whole or even the entire class of rational beings. It is not obvious how these contrasting conceptions, of diversity of ideal and of community of rule, are related to each other; and in fact, I think, the relationship is complicated. One way of trying to harmonize the ideas would be as follows. This way is extremely crude and inadequate, but it may serve as a starting point. It is obvious that many, if not all, of the ideal images of which I spoke demand for their realization the existence of some form of social organization. The demand is in varying degrees logical or empirical. Some ideals only make sense in a complex social context, and even in a particular kind of complex social context. For others, some complexity of social organization seems, rather, a practically necessary condition of the ideal's being realized in any very full or satisfactory way. Now it is a condition of the existence of any form of social organization, of any human community, that certain expectations of behavior on the part of its members should be pretty regularly fulfilled: that some duties, one might say, should be performed, some obligations acknowledged, some rules observed. We might begin by locating the sphere of morality here. It is the sphere of the observance of rules, such that the existence of some such set of rules is a condition of the existence of a society. This is a minimal interpretation of morality. It represents it as what might literally be called a kind of public convenience: of the first importance as a condition of everything that matters, but only as a condition of everything that matters, not as something that matters in itself.

I am disposed to see considerable merit in this minimal conception of morality. By this I mean not that it is really, or nearly, an adequate conception—only that it is a useful analytical idea. There would be objections to claiming that it was an adequate conception. One objection might be simply expressed by saying that, after all, being moral is something that does matter in itself, that it is not simply an affair of complying with rules in a situation where the observance of some such rules is an indirect condition of approximating to ideal forms of life. There is a lot in this objection. But it is not an objection to *using* the minimal idea of morality. We might for example argue that there was an intricate interplay between ideal pictures of man on the one hand and the rule requirements of social organization on the other; and that one's ordinary and vague conception of morality was the product of this interplay. This would be one way—I do not say the right way—of using the minimal idea of morality to try to get clearer about the ordinary idea. I shall come back later to this question too.

Meanwhile there is another objection to be considered. I think there is something in it as well, but that what there is in it is not at all straightforward. It turns on the idea of the universal applicability of moral rules. The idea is that it is a necessary requirement of a *moral* rule that it should at least be regarded as applying to all human beings whatever. Moral behavior is what is demanded of men as such. But we can easily imagine, and even find, different societies held together by the observance of sets of rules which are very different from each other. Moreover we can find or imagine a single society held together by a set of rules which by no means make the same demands on all its members, but make very different demands on different classes or groups within the society. Insofar as the rules which give cohesiveness to a society are acknowledged to have this limited and sectional character, they cannot, in the sense of this objection, be seen as moral rules. But the rules which do give cohesiveness to a society may well have this character, whether asknowledged or not. So the prospect of explaining true morality in terms of what I called the minimal conception of morality is a poor one. Now it is possible to admit the principle of this objection, and then meet it with a formal maneuver. Thus a rule which governs the professional behavior of Samoan witch doctors can be said to apply to all men under the condition that they are witch doctor members of a society with the general characteristics of Samoan society. Or again, a rule which might be held to apply to ten-year old children, namely that they should obey their parents in domestic matters, could be represented as applying to all men without exception, under the condition that they were ten-year old children. Obviously there is a certain futility about this maneuver, and equally obviously there is no compulsion to execute it. We might simply drop the idea of moral rules as universally binding on men as men. Or we might say that though there was something in this idea, it was absurd to try to apply it directly and in detail to the question of what people were required to do in particular situations in particular societies. And here we might be tempted by another maneuver, which we should note as a possible one even if we do not think that it, either, is altogether satisfactory. We might be tempted to say that the relevant universally applicable, and hence moral, rule, was that a human being should conform to the rules which apply to him in a particular situation in a particular society. Here universality is achieved by stepping up an order. A man should perform the duties of his station in his society. This allows for an indefinite variety of societies and of stations within them; and would also seem to allow us, in so far as we regarded the universal rule as a truly moral one, to see at least part of true morality as resting upon and presupposing what I called the minimal social interpretation of morality.

Enough, for the moment, of objections to this minimal idea. Let me set out some of its merits. First we must be clearer about what this minimal interpretation is. The fundamental idea is that of a socially sanctioned demand made on an individual in virtue merely of his membership of the society in question, or in virtue of a particular position which he occupies within it or a particular relation in which he stands to other members of it. I spoke of rules in this connection; and the rules I meant would simply be the generalized statements of demands of this type. The formula I employ for the fundamental idea is deliberately flexible, the notions of a society and of social sanctioning deliberately vague. This flexibility is necessary to do justice to the complexities of social organization and social relationships. For instance, we can regard ourselves as members of many different social groups or communities, some of which fall within others; or again, when I speak of the social sanctioning of a demand which is made on an individual member of a group in virtue of his position in the group, we may think of the social sanction of that demand sometimes as arising only within the limited group in question, sometimes as arising also within a wider group which includes that limited group. A position in a society may or may not also be, so to speak, a position in society. Thus a position in a family generally gives rise to certain demands upon the holder of that position which are recognized both within the family and within some wider group or groups within which the family falls. The same may be true of membership of a profession or even of a professional association. On the other hand, some of the demands of certain class or caste moralities receive little or no extraneous reinforcement from the wider social groupings to which the members of the limited class also belong. Or again what one might call the internal morality of an intimate personal relationship may be as private as the relationship itself. One of the merits I should claim for this approach to morality is precisely that it so easily makes room for many concepts which we habitually employ, but which tend to be neglected in moral philosophy. Thus we talk of medical ethics, of the code of honor of a military caste, of bourgeois morality and of working-class morality. Such ideas fit more easily into an account of morality which sees it as essentially, or at any rate fundamentally, a function of social groupings than they do into the more apparently individualistic approaches which are generally current.

Another merit which I shall claim for the present approach is that it makes it relatively easy to understand such notions as those of conscientiousness, duty and obligation in a concrete and realistic way. These notions have been treated almost entirely abstractly in moral philosophy in the recent past, with the result that they have come to some of our contemporaries[2] to seem to be meaningless survivals of discarded ideas about the government of the universe. But as most ordinarily employed I do not think they are that at all. There is nothing in the least mysterious or metaphysical in the fact that duties and obligations go with offices, positions, and relationships to others. The demands to be made on somebody in virtue of his occupation of a certain position may indeed be, and often are, quite explicitly listed in considerable detail. And when we call someone conscientious or say that he has a strong sense of his obligations or of duty, we do not ordinarily mean that he is haunted by the ghost of the idea of supernatural ordinances; we mean rather such things as this, that he can be counted on for sustained efforts to do what is required of him in definite capacities, to fulfil the demand made on him as student or teacher or parent or soldier or whatever he may be. A certain professor once said: "For me to be moral is to behave like a professor".

---

[2] Cf. G. E. M. Anscombe, "Modern Moral Philosophy", *Philosophy* (January, 1958).

Suppose we now raise that old philosophical question: What interest has the individual in morality? The question may force us to a more adequate conception of morality than the minimal interpretation offers by itself. It certainly forces us to strike, or to try to strike, some delicate balances. The only answer to the question so far suggested is this: that the individual's ethical imagination may be captured or fired by one or more ideal pictures of life which require for their realization the existence of social groupings and social organizations such as could not exist in the absence of a system of social demands made on individual members of these groups or organizations. I have already hinted that this answer is too crude, that the interplay between ethical ideal and social obligation is more intricate than it suggests. The answer is also not crude enough. The picture of the ideal form of life and the associated ethical vision of the world tend to be the products of the refined mind and relatively comfortable circumstances. But when we ask what the interest of the individual is in morality, we mean to ask about all those individuals on whom socially sanctioned demands are made; not just about the imaginatively restless and materially cozy. We need not, perhaps, insist upon just the same answer for all; but, if we take the question seriously, we must insist on *some* answer for all. There may seem to be a broader answer which does not altogether depart from the form of the over-refined answer. For who could exist at all, or pursue any aim, except in some form of society? And there is no form of society without rules, without some system of socially sanctioned demands on its members. Here at least is a common interest in morality as minimally conceived, an interest which can be attributed to all those about whom the question can be raised. Still we may feel that it is not enough. And in this feeling is the germ of the reason why the minimal conception of morality is inadequate to the ordinary notion, at least in its contemporary form; and perhaps, in uncovering the reason for this inadequacy, we may discover too what there is in the notion of the universal applicability of moral rules.

We have arrived at the fact that everyone on whom some form of socially sanctioned demand is made has an interest in the existence of some system of socially sanctioned demands. But this fact seems inadequate to answer the question what the individual's interest in morality is. We can begin to understand this inadequacy by thinking of the different things that might be meant by the social sanctioning of a demand. "Sanction" is related to "permission" and "approval"; and also to "power" and to "penalty". A socially sanctioned demand is doubtless a demand made with the permission and approval of a society; and backed, in some form and degree, with its power. But the idea of a society as the totality of individuals subject to demands may here come apart from the idea of society as the source of sanction of those demands. The sanctioning society may simply be a sub-group of the total society, the dominant subgroup, the group in which power resides. Mere membership of the total society does not guarantee membership of the sanctioning part of the society. Nor does a mere interest in the existence of some system of socially sanctioned demands guarantee an interest in the particular system of socially sanctioned demands to which one is subjected. But unless at least one, and perhaps both, of these nonguaranteed conditions is satisfied, it does not seem that the fulfillment of a socially sanctioned demand comes anywhere near being what we should regard as the fulfillment of a moral obligation. That is to say, if I have no foothold at all in the sanctioning part of society, and if no interest of mine is safeguarded by the system of demands to which I am subject, then, in fulfilling a demand made upon me, I may indeed, in one sense, be doing what I am obliged to do; but scarcely what I am *morally* obliged to do. No wonder, then, that the question "What is the individual's interest in morality"? is not answered by mentioning the general interest in the existence of some system of socially sanctioned demands. The answer now scarcely appears to touch the question.

Suppose, then, that we consider the idea of a society such that all its members have *some* interest, not merely in there being a system of socially sanctioned demands, but in the actual system of demands which obtains in that society. It seems that we can ensure such an interest even to the powerless and enslaved by stipulating that the system includes not only demands made on them in the interest of their masters, but also demands made on their masters in their interests. We might be tempted to say that by thus securing to them an interest in the system of demands, we secure to them also some sort of position or foothold in the sanctioning part of society. Certainly, when the master recognizes moral obligations to his slave, we shall be at least one step nearer to allowing that the slave is not merely subject to the demands of his master, but may recognize a moral obligation to fulfill them. Even in this extreme case, then, we can approach the situation which everyone would agree to regard as characteristically moral, the situation in which there is reciprocal acknowledgement of rights and duties.

Still I think we must admit a distinction of two stages in this approach to the characteristically moral situation. Interest in claims on others and acknowledgement of claims on oneself are connected but not identical. It is a tautology, though not an easy one, that everyone subject to moral demands has some interest in morality. For a demand made on an individual is to be regarded as a moral demand only if it belongs to a system of demands which includes demands made on others in his interest. It would be agreeable, as I just now suggested, to be able to argue strictly that this fact carries with it the conclusion that mere self-conscious membership of a moral community implies at least in some degree extending one's sanction to its system of demands, to the extent of genuinely acknowledging as obligations at least some of the claims which others have on one, even if only provisionally and with the strongest desire that the system should be different. But to argue so would be to equivocate with the phrase "membership of a moral community". There would be nothing self-contradictory about the idea of one who recognized his interest in the system of moral demands and resolved merely to profit by it as much as he could, fulfilling its demands on himself only in so far as his interest calculably required it. He might get away with it successfully if he were subtle enough in his practice of the hypocrisy which this policy would necessarily involve. But it is an important fact that hypocrisy would be necessary. It is connected with the further fact, a fact of human nature which can probably be explained in a number of ways, that quite thoroughgoing egotism of this kind is rare. But for this fact there could be no such thing as a system of moral demands. We cannot argue that it is a tautology that *anyone* subject to moral demands who recognizes his interest in the system of demands must also genuinely acknowledge some obligations under the system. But we can argue that it is a tautology that the *generality* of those subject to moral demands must genuinely recognize some obligations under the system of demands. For if this were not so, there would be no such thing as a system of moral demands and hence no such thing as being subject to a moral demand.

　　These steps from a minimal to a more adequate conception of morality (i.e. to a conception which at least begins to square with what we nowadays vaguely understand by the word) may easily encourage abstract exaggerations and distortions in moral philosophy. For instance, the necessary truth that the members of a moral community in general acknowledge some moral claims upon them may be exaggerated into the idea of a self-conscious choice or adoption of the principle of those claims. So everyone appears, grandly but implausibly, as a moral self-legislator. This is an exaggeration which has appealed, in different forms, to more than one philosopher. Again these steps reveal something genuinely universal in morality: the necessary acceptance of reciprocity of claim. And *one* way in which a demand made on one individual in the interest of others can be balanced by a demand made on others in his interest is through the operation of a general rule or principle having application to all alike. But it does not follow from this that *all* moral claims have, or are seen by those who acknowledge them as having, the character of applications of universal principles holding for all men. There is no reason why a system of moral demands characteristic of one community should, or even could, be found in every other. And even within a single system of reciprocal claims, the moral demand may essentially *not* relate to a situation in which any member of the system could find himself *vis-à-vis* any other. Here are two reasons why it is misleading to say that moral behavior is what is demanded of men as men. It might, in some cases, be essentially what is demanded of Spartans by other Spartans, or of a king by his subjects. What is universally demanded of the members of a moral community is something like the abstract virtue of justice: a man should not insist on a particular claim while refusing to acknowledge any reciprocal claim. But from this formally universal feature of morality no consequences follow as to the universality of application of the particular rules in the observance of which, in particular situations and societies, justice consists.

One must beware, however, of meeting exaggeration with counter-exaggeration. It is important to recognize the diversity of possible systems of moral demands, and the diversity of demands which may be made within any system. But it is also important to recognize that certain human interests are so fundamental and so general that they must be universally acknowledged in some form and to some degree in any conceivable moral community. Of some interests, one might say: a system could scarcely command *sufficient* interest in those subject to its demands for these demands to be acknowledged as obligations, unless it secured to them *this* interest. Thus some claim on human succor, some obligation to abstain from the infliction of physical injury, seem to be necessary features of almost any system of moral demands. Here at least we have types of moral behavior which are demanded *of* men as men because they are demanded *for* and *by* men as men. Another interest which is fundamental to many types of social relation and social grouping is the interest in not being deceived. In most kinds of social grouping for which there obtains any system of moral demand and claim at all this interest is acknowledged as a claim which any member of the group has on any other; and perhaps most such groupings could scarcely exist without this acknowledgement. When all allowance has been made, then, for the possible diversity of moral systems and the possible diversity of demands within a system, it remains true that the recognition of certain general virtues and obligations will be a logically or humanly necessary feature of almost any conceivable moral system: these will include the abstract virtue of justice, some form of obligation to mutual aid and to mutual abstention from injury and, in some form and in some degree, the virtue of honesty. This guarded recognition of the necessary universal applicability of some relatively vague and abstract moral principles is itself a corrective to the idea of unbounded freedom of choice of such principles on the part of the individual.

I spoke earlier of the need for striking some delicate balances, and I hope that the nature of some of these is now apparent. Constant checks are required if these balances are not to be lost. We have seen in what sense it is true that everyone on whom a moral demand is made must have an interest in morality. But we have also seen that the existence of a system of moral demands (at least as we now understand this concept) requires some degree of general readiness to recognize claims made upon one even when this recognition cannot plausibly be said to be in one's own interest. The

existence of some such readiness needs no more to be argued for than the
existence of morality in general. But it is necessary to emphasize it in order
to correct another exaggeration, the exaggeration which would represent all
morality as prudential.[3] To say that this readiness to acknowledge the claims
of others does not need to be argued for is not to say that it does not need to
be explained. We may discuss its natural sources; and the terms in which we
do so will change with the state of our psychological knowledge: the appeal
to the concept of sympathy, for example, will scarcely now seem adequate.
But, however we explain it, there is no need to sophisticate ourselves into
denying altogether the existence or fundamental importance of this recognition of others' claims. Again, we have seen that the fact of acknowledgement of claims may be blown up into the picture of the self-legislating moral
agent; and here we should do well to scale down our pretensions to freedom
by remembering, if nothing else, the importance of the training we receive
and the limited choice we exercise of the moral communities to which we
belong. Finally, we have acknowledged some force in the idea of universally
applicable principles of moral demand and claim. But to keep within bounds
the pretensions of this idea, we must insist again on the flexibility of the
concept of a social group, upon the diversity of groups and upon the
absurdity of the idea that detailed demands could be shifted indifferently
from group to group or apply to all members alike within a group.

There are further important moral phenomena of which the account I
have given makes little or no explicit mention. Some of these it might even
seem, at first sight, to exclude. Is there not such a thing as moral criticism,
from within a society, of the existing moral forms of that society? Cannot
different systems of socially sanctioned demand, under which those subject to
demands genuinely acknowledge obligations, be the subject of relative moral
evaluation? Cannot there be situations in which men may or should recognize
moral obligations to each other, although there is no common society of
which they are members and there is no concept of a "social" relationship
which can be at all plausibly represented as applying to their situation? Any
acceptable account of morality must certainly allow an affirmative answer
to these questions; and there are others which will suggest themselves. But
they no more yield a reason for mistrusting the approach I have adopted
than the inadequacy of what I called the minimal interpretation of morality
gave a reason for wholly discarding that idea. By enriching the minimal
interpretation with certain applications of the notions of interest, and of
acknowledgement of obligation, we obtained what was recognizably a
concept of social morality. It is necessary only to draw out the significance
of certain elements in *this* conception in order to make room for the ideas of

3 Cf. P. R. Foot, "Moral Beliefs", *Proceedings of the Aristotelian Society*,
(1958–59).

moral criticism, and of a morality which transcends standard forms of social relationship. I have remarked already that, because certain human needs and interests are as fundamental and as general as they are, we shall find correspondingly general types of virtue and obligation acknowledged in some form and in some degree in almost any conceivable moral system. Now it is characteristically by analogy with, and extension of, acknowledged forms of these, that moral development proceeds, and that these ideas themselves assume more refined and generous shapes. And moral criticism at its most self-conscious proceeds characteristically by appeal to, and interpretation of, such general moral ideas as those of justice, integrity, and humanity: existing institutions, systems of demand and claim, are criticized as unjust, inhumane, or corrupt. We may say that so far from excluding the idea of moral criticism, the concept of social morality, as I have outlined it, makes fully intelligible the nature and possibility of such criticism. For we can perceive how the seeds of criticism lie in the morality itself; and we may even hope, on this basis, to achieve some understanding of the complex interrelationships between social and economic change, the critical insights of individual moralists, and the actual course of moral evolution. (It is, for instance, an easy consequence of our principles that moral *formalism*—i.e. a rigid adherence to the letter, with no appeal to the spirit, of the rules—will tend to be at a maximum in a static and isolated society, and that moral *disorientation* will tend to be at a maximum when such a morality is suddenly exposed to radical change.) Just as a social morality contains the seeds of moral criticism, so the two together contain the seeds of a morality transcending standard social relationships. It is easy to see how the tendency of at least one type of self-conscious and critical morality is generalizing and antiparochial, as it is antiformalist. Some moralists would maintain that a true concept of morality emerges only at the limit of this generalizing process. This is a judgment in which, as it seems to me, the sense of reality has become quite subordinated to zeal. But wherever we choose to say that "true morality" begins, I have no doubt whatever that our understanding of the concept of morality in general is best served by the kind of approach that I have sketched. Where what we are dealing with is a developing human institution, it is no reproach to an explanation that it may be described as at least partially genetic.

But now it is time to return to the question of the relation between social moralities and those ideal pictures of forms of life which I spoke of at the outset. All I have so far explicitly said about this is that the realization of any such ideal requires the existence of forms of social grouping or organization which in turn require the existence of a system of socially sanctioned demands on their members. We have since remarked that a system of socially sanctioned demands would fall short of being a system of moral demands unless those demands were not merely enforced as demands, but also at least in some degree generally acknowledged as claims by those subject to them; and it follows from this that to be a member of a moral community cannot merely be a matter of convenience, except perhaps for those who can practice a sustained hypocrisy of which few are in fact capable. Yet it may still be true in general to say that the possibility of the pursuit of an ideal form of life quite pragmatically requires membership of a moral community or of moral communities; for it is extremely unlikely in fact that the minimal social conditions for the pursuit of any ethical ideal which anyone is likely to entertain could in practice be fulfilled except through membership of such communities. But of course the relations between these two things are much more intricate and various than this formulation by itself suggests. The possibilities of collision, absorption, and interplay are many. The way I have just expressed the matter perhaps makes most obvious the possibility of collision; and this possibility is worth stressing. It is worth stressing that what one acknowledges or half-acknowledges as obligation may conflict not only, crudely, with interest and, weakly, with inclination but also with ideal aspiration, with the vision that captures the ethical imagination. On the other hand, it may be that a picture of the ideal life is precisely one in which the interests of morality are dominant, are given an ideal, overriding value. To one dominated temporarily or permanently by such a picture the "consciousness of duty faithfully performed" will appear as the supremely satisfactory state, and being moral not merely as something that matters but as the thing that supremely matters. Or again the ideal picture may be, not that in which the interests of morality in general are dominant, but rather one in which the dominating idea operates powerfully to reinforce some, but not perhaps others, of a system of moral demands. So it is with that ideal picture in which obedience to the command to love one another appears as the supreme value.

This is still to draw too simple a picture. Let us remember the diversity of communities to which we may be said to belong, and the diversity of systems of moral demand which belong to them. To a certain extent, though to an extent which we must not exaggerate, the systems of moral relationships into which we enter are a matter of choice—or at least a matter in which there are alternative possibilities; and different systems of moral demand are variously well or ill adapted to different ideal pictures of life. The ideal picture, moreover, may call for membership not merely of communities in which certain interests are safeguarded by a system of moral demands, but for membership of a community or of a system of relationships in which the system of demands reflects in a positive way the nature of the ideal. For one crude instance of this, we may think again of the morality of a military caste in connection with the ideal of personal honor. In general, in a society as complex as ours, it is obvious that there are different moral environments, different subcommunities within the community, different systems of moral relationships, interlocking indeed and overlapping with one another, but offering some possibilities of choice, some possibilities of adjustment of moral demand and individual aspiration. But here again, at least in our time and place, it is the limits of the direct relevance of each to the other that must finally be stressed. Inside a single political human society one may indeed find different, and perhaps widely different, moral environments, social groupings in which different systems of moral demand are recognized. But if the one grouping is to form part of the wider society, its members must be subject too to a wider system of reciprocal demand, a wider common morality; and the relative significance of the wider common morality will grow in proportion as the subgroups of the society are closely interlocked, in proportion as each individual is a member of a plurality of subgroups and in proportion as the society is not rigidly stratified, but allows of relatively free access to, and withdrawal from, its subgroups. In a political society which thus combines a wide variety of social groupings with complex interlocking and freedom of movement between them the dissociation of idiosyncratic ideal and common moral demand will doubtless tend to be at its maximum. On the other hand an ideal picture of man *may* tend, in fact or in fancy, to demand the status of a comprehensive common morality. Thus Coleridgean or Tolstoyan dreamers may play with the thought of self-enclosed ideal communities in which the system of moral demands shall answer exactly, or as exactly as possible, to an ideal picture of life held in common by all their members. Such fancies are bound to strike many as weak and futile; for the price of preserving the purity of such communities is that of severance from the world at large. More seriously, there may be some attempt to make the whole moral climate of an existing national state reflect some ideal image of human solidarity or religious devotion or military honor. In view of the natural diversity of human ideals—to mention only that—such a state (or its members) will evidently be subject to at least some stresses from which a liberal society is free.

    To conclude. I have spoken of those ideal images of life of which one individual may sympathize with many, and desire to see many realized in some degree. I have spoken also of those systems—though the word is too strong—of recognized reciprocal claim that we have on one another as members of human communities, or as terms of human relationships, many of which could scarcely exist or have the character they have but for the existence of such systems of reciprocal claim. I have said something, though too little, of the complex and various relations which may hold between these two things, viz. our conflicting visions of the ends of life and the systems of moral demand which make social living possible. Finally I have glanced at the relations of both to the political societies in which we necessarily live. The field of phenomena over which I have thus loosely ranged is, I think, very much more complex and many-sided than I have been able to suggest; but I have been concerned to suggest something of its complexity. Some implications for moral philosophy I have hinted at in passing, mainly by way of an attempt to correct some typical exaggerations of contemporary theory. But the main practical implications for moral and political philosophy are, I think, that more attention should be concentrated on types of social structure and social relation, and on those complex inter-relationships which I have mentioned as well as others which I have not. For instance, it is hard not to believe that understanding of our secular morality would be enhanced by considering the historical role that religion has played in relation to morality. Or again, I doubt if the nature of morality can be properly understood without some consideration of its relationship to law. It is not merely that the spheres of morality and law are largely over-lapping, or that their demands often coincide. It is also that in the way law functions to give cohesiveness to the most important of all social groupings we may find a coarse model of the way in which systems of moral demand function to give cohesiveness to social groupings in general. Similarly, in the complexity of our attitudes towards existing law we may find a model of the complexity of our attitude towards the systems of moral demand which impinge upon us in our social relations at large—or upon others, in theirs.

Finally, I do not think there is any very definite invitation to moral or political commitment implicit in what I have said. But perhaps one question can be raised, and in part answered. What will be the attitude of one who experiences sympathy with a variety of conflicting ideals of life? It seems that he will be most at home in a liberal society, in a society in which there are variant moral environments but in which no ideal endeavors to engross, and determine the character of, the common morality. He will not argue in favor of such a society that it gives the best chance for the truth about life to prevail, for he will not consistently believe that there is such a thing as the truth about life. Nor will he argue in its favor that it has the best chance of producing a harmonious kingdom of ends, for he will not think of ends as necessarily capable of being harmonized. He will simply welcome the ethical diversity which the society makes possible, and in pro-portion as he values that diversity he will note that he is the natural, though perhaps the sympathetic, enemy of all those whose single intense vision of the ends of life drives them to try to make the requirements of the ideal coextensive with those of common social morality.

Morality, Self, and Others

W. D. FALK

1

In: And how can you say that I never had a moral education? As a child, I was taught that one ought not to maltreat other children, ought to share one's sweets with them, ought to keep tidy and clean; as an adolescent, that one ought to keep one's word, to work, to save, to leave off drink, not to waste the best years of one's life, to let reason govern one's emotions and actions. Nor did I simply learn that one is *called upon* to act in these ways by paternal authority and social custom on pain of censure. I learned to appreciate that one *ought* to do these things *on their merits*, and that what one ought to do on its merits does not depend on the requests or enjoinders of anyone. The facts in the case themselves make one liable, as a reflective person, to act in these ways of one's own accord: they provide one with choice-supporting reasons sufficient to determine one if one knows them and takes diligent account of them.[1]

Out: I know you were taught all this. But why did your teacher say that you ought to act in these ways?

In: Why? For very cogent reasons. My tutor was a student of the Ancients. The moral man, "the man of practical wisdom," he kept quoting Aristotle, "is the man who knows how to deliberate well about what is good and useful for himself." And surely, he would say, you can see for yourself: if you don't act sociably, who will act sociably towards you? Uncleanliness breeds disease. Without work, how are you to live? Without savings, what about your future? Drink leaves one a wreck. Indulging one's sorrows makes them worse. The wasted years, one day you will regret them when it is too late. People who cannot govern themselves are helpless before fortune, without the aid and comfort of inner strength.

Out: And so you think that you had a moral education? Let me tell

---

From Hector-Neri Castaneda and George Nakhnikian, eds., Morality and the Language of Conduct *(Detroit: Wayne State University Press, 1963), pp. 25–67. Copyright © 1963 by Wayne State University Press. Reprinted by permission of the author and Wayne State University Press.*

1 For the use of "ought," compare my " 'Ought' and Motivation" (1947–48) in *Readings in Ethical Theory*, ed. W. S. Sellars and J. Hospers (New York: Appleton-Century-Crofts, 1952), pp. 492–510; "Goading and Guiding," *Mind*, n.s. LXII (1953), 145–71 [reprinted in this volume, pp. 60–83]; and "Morality and Convention," *The Journal of Philosophy*, LVII (1960), 675–85. Parts of the last paper have been incorporated in the present essay.

you, you never even made a start. For what were you taught? That there are things that you ought to do or to avoid on your own account. But one does not learn about morality that way. What one *morally* ought to do is what one ought to do on account of others, or for the sake of some good state of things in general. Now had you been taught to appreciate that you ought to keep clean so as to be pleasing to others, and that you ought to do what moral custom requires for the sake of the general good, then, and then only, would you have learned the rudiments of moral duty.

In: Very well, my upbringing was too narrow. One would hardly be a human being if the good of others, or of society at large, could not weigh with one as a cogent reason for doing what will promote it. So one has not fully learned about living like a rational and moral being unless one has learned to appreciate that one ought to do things out of regard for others, and not only out of regard for oneself.

Out: No, you have still not got my point. I am saying that only insofar as you ought to do things—no matter whether for yourself or for others— for the sake of others, is the reason a moral reason and the ought a moral ought. Reasons of self-regard are not moral reasons at all, and you can forget about them in the reckoning of your *moral* obligations.

In: But this seems artificial. A moral education surely should teach one all about the principles of orderly living and the reasons which tell in their favor. And if there are also perfectly good personal reasons which tell in their favor, why suppress them? To be sure, in talking to people in ordinary life, we do no such thing. If they say 'Why ought I to act sociably?" we say "For the general good as well as your own." If they say "Why ought I to be provident?" we say "For your own good as well as that of others." In short, we offer mixed reasons, and none of these reasons can be spared. One ought not to lie because this is a good social rule, and equally because the habit of evasiveness is destructive of oneself as a person. And one ought not to take to drink or indulge one's sorrows, or waste the best years of one's life primarily out of proper regard for oneself, much as there may be other-regarding reasons as well. If morality were all social service, and one had no moral responsibilities towards oneself or towards others, the moral inconveniences of life would be far less than they are. So I don't see the point of saying "But one has no *moral* commitment to do anything except insofar as one ought to do it on account of others." To say this seems like encouraging people not to bother about doing things insofar as they ought to do them only for personal reasons, as after all this is not a moral ought.

Out: But one does not speak of a moral duty to do things for one's own sake. If one ought to save in order to provide for one's own future, one regards this as a precept not of morals but of prudence. It would be different if one ought to save in order to provide for one's dependents. Moral commitments are those which one has as a moral being, and what makes one a moral being is that one has commitments towards others and does not evade them.

In: Not everyone will agree that as a moral being one has only commitments towards others or that only such commitments are properly "moral." The Greeks, for example, took a wider view. For Plato the equivalent of a moral being was the just or right-living person, and of a moral commitment the right and just course—the one which the right-living person would be led to take. And this right-living person was one who would keep himself in good shape as a sane and self-possessed being, and who would do whatever good and sufficient reasons directed him to do. This is why for Plato and the Greeks temperance and prudence were no less among the just man's commitments than paying his debts and not willfully harming others, and why the one was not treated any less as a moral commitment than the other. The Greeks placed the essence of man as a moral being in his capacity to direct himself on rational grounds; and his commitments as a moral being were therefore all those which he seriously incurred as a properly self-directing being.

Out: Citing the Greeks only shows how distant their concept of morality is from ours. We will not call every rational commitment "moral" or equate the moral with the rational man.

In: This is broadly so, although not entirely. Our concept of morality vacillates between the Greek and the Christian tradition. We associate "moral" with "social" commitment, and the "morally good man" with the "selfless man." But we also speak of man as a "moral agent," of his "moral freedom" and "moral powers"; and here we refer to his whole capacity of self-direction by good and sufficient reasons. One may speak without strain of a personal and a social ethic, and refer to the negligent disregard of oneself as a vice, and a sign of moral defect. We call the improvident man "morally weak," and call the man who can resist drink in company on account of his health or who sticks to his vocation in adversity a man of "moral strength and character." There is certainly little difference in the qualities needed to live up to a social or a personal ought. It takes self-denial to provide for one's future, moral courage to stick to one's vocation. One may show one's mettle as a moral agent here no less than in selfless care for others. There are contemporary moralists who call "moral" any "authentic" commitment of a self-governing person, whether its grounds are social or personal. What justifies them is the broader use of the term which is also part of our language and tradition.

Out: And how eccentric this use is. Our very concept of a moral being is inseparable from the notion of submission of self to a good other than one's own. It is not conceivable that a man should have moral duties on a desert island, devoid of man or beast. Would one say that he still had a moral duty to do what was good for him? You may as well go on and say that if a shipwrecked fellow arrived to share his vegetables, it might be his moral duty to let him starve rather than starve himself.

In: The good of others need not always have the overriding claim on one, if this is what you mean. One could say to a good-hearted and weak-willed person, "For your own sake, you ought to stop neglecting your future, even if this hurts others." This would not be a typically "moral" ought, but one may be giving sound moral advice.

Out: And so, if beneficence had the better of this person, you should call him morally irresponsible and blameworthy. On your showing, he has evaded a moral commitment, and for such evasions one is held morally responsible and liable to censure. But surely, even if I granted your case, one would not call him blameworthy and a morally bad man; as indeed in any case where a person fails to do what his own good requires we do not call him morally bad, but only imprudent, unwise, rash. It is quite a different offense to be slack about brushing one's teeth, than to be negligent about providing dentures for others. And this is so precisely because the second is a moral offense and the first is not and because one is blameworthy for the one and not for the other.

In: I agree that there is a difference. One is only called morally bad and is held answerable to *others* for neglecting what one ought to do out of regard for them. And this is understandable enough. After all, insofar as one fails to do only what one's own good requires, the failing is no one's concern but one's own. But then I should not say that such self-neglect was in no sense morally irresponsible and blameworthy. If it does not call for blame by others, it still calls for self-reproach. A rational person is responsible to himself for not being evasive about anything that he is convinced that he really ought to do. And the lack of moral strength and courage in personal matters, although commonly viewed as an amicable vice, is an amicable vice only in the estimation of others since it is not directly a threat to them.

However, we are not making headway. You find it repugnant to call a commitment "moral" unless its grounds are social and unless its non-observance makes one liable not only to social censure but also to self-reproach; and so be it. Perhaps our disagreement is only verbal, and despite some misgivings, I am ready to settle for your usage. Let us only speak of a moral ought where one ought to do things on account of others. But let us not be misled. For it still does not follow that if one ought to do things on one's own account, this ought may not still be otherwise functioning *like* a moral ought.

Out: How could it be like a moral ought if it is not a moral ought?

In: Because when one thinks of a moral ought, one thinks not only that its grounds are social but also that it has a special force and cogency. A moral ought commits one in all seriousness and in every way, without leaving any reasonable option to act otherwise. Your view comes to saying that if an ought is to be moral it must satisfy two conditions: it must seriously bind one in every way, and it must do so for other-regarding reasons. On your showing, a personal ought cannot be moral, as it cannot satisfy one of these conditions simply by having personal grounds. But it may still satisfy the other condition, and be as cogently binding and action-guiding in its force and function as a moral ought. This is why I can only accept your usage with one proviso: that one may also say that there are other than strictly moral commitments which a right-living person may have to reckon with no less than his strictly moral ones.

Out: Surely you don't expect me to fall for this. When I say "Don't count the purely personal ought as moral" I am not saying "Count it as well, but call it by another name." My point is precisely that it does not function like a moral ought at all. Personal reasons do not commit one to do anything with the same cogency as social reasons. In fact, in calling them reasons of prudence or expediency, we deprecate them. We regard them as inferior, and often disreputable, guides to action. So I won't let you reduce my position to triviality. That only the social commitments are essentially moral must be taken as implying that only they have the characteristic moral force.

In: I thought that this was at the back of our discussion all along. It usually is so with people who are so insistent on your usage, although part of the trouble is that one can never be sure. First one is told that a moral ought is one that commits one on other-regarding grounds and that a personal ought is not a moral ought *for this reason.* But then comes the further suggestion that it is not only different from a moral ought in this way, but is also otherwise inferior. It gives directives, but directives of a somehow shady kind. One way or other, the idea is that a commitment that has personal grounds is either not properly a commitment at all, or, if one in any way, then one that belongs in some limbo of disrepute. But your argument so far has done nothing to prove this point. From your language rule, it only follows that the personal ought must be unlike a moral ought in one essential respect, but not, except by way of confusion, that it must be therefore also unlike a moral ought in other respects too. You might as well say "Surely a lay analyst is not a doctor," as one is not a doctor without a medical degree, and take this to be proof that a lay analyst cannot otherwise cure like a doctor either. "No lay analyst is a doctor" is strictly and trivially true in one way, and may be misleading and tendentiously false in another. And the same with "No personal ought is a *moral* ought." Your language rule makes this strictly and trivially true; but it does not go to show that a personal ought cannot otherwise be *like* a moral ought by being seriously committing or by taking precedence in a conscientious calculus of action-guiding considerations. My point is that, even if this were so, your appeal to usage cannot settle this matter. Logical grammar can decree that only social reasons are properly called "moral." But it cannot decide what reasons can, or cannot, be seriously committing for human beings.

Out: But what I am saying seems substantially true. What one ought to do on account of others is the prototype of the categorically binding ought. Personal reasons have not got the binding cogency of other-regarding reasons, and one deprecates them as inferior and disreputable.

In: And there is some truth in this. Personal and social reasons are not on the same footing in the economy of action-guiding considerations. Personal reasons are very commonly less thoroughly committing, they are often inferior reasons, and not rarely discreditable. But why this is so is a different matter and has not yet been touched on in any way. What is more, personal reasons need not always be in this inferior position. They are often not intrinsically discreditable, and become inferior guides to action only where there are other reasons in the case deserving of prior consideration. Take someone concerned for his health, or future, or self-respect. Surely these are respectable aspirations and there may be things which he ought to do on account of them without violating other claims. His health requires that he be temperate, his self-respect that he live without evasion. Would it not then be positively remiss of him not to act in these ways? If he did not, one would say that he had failed to do what a man in his position really ought to have done, and precisely for the reason which he had. And, if one can say this, what remains of the blemish?

This is why it remains perplexing to me why commitments on personal grounds should be excluded from the orbit of moral teaching, and why modern moralists, unlike the Ancients, should disdain to mention them as an integral part of the moral life. For they may also be cogent and sometimes overridingly cogent commitments to action. And if they are not the whole of morals, why not count them as part of them? For it also seems natural to say that to teach someone all about morality is to teach him about all the valid directives for action; about all those things which he might not otherwise do readily but which, for good and compelling reasons in the nature in the case, he ought to do and would have to break himself into doing whether for the sake of others or his own.

There is, I agree, one tendency to say that the moral man acts in accordance with precepts of selflessness. But there is also another tendency to say that he is the man to organize his life in accordance with all valid precepts. Our disagreement has exhibited the kind of shuttle service between rival considerations better known as the dialectic of a problem. It may be that this shuttle service is maintained by a cleft in the very concept of morality. This concept may have grown from conflicting or only partially overlapping observations, which are not fully reconciled in ordinary thinking.

Out: If this is so, I would have to be shown, for common sense still seems to me right in its disparagement of personal reasons.

In: Very well, then we shall have to consider why personal reasons should function as a less cogent guide to action than social ones. I shall admit that in more ways than one the personal ought presents a special case, but not that it presents a case for disparagement except in special contexts. After this, the question of whether the personal ought is properly called moral or not will appear less important, partly because it will have become plainer why there is a question. Nor shall I try to offer a ruling on this point. With a background of discourse as intricate and full of nuance as in this case, discretion is the better part of valor, and clarification is a safer bet than decision.

2

Whenever one remarks that clearly there are things which one ought to avoid or do if only for one's own sake, someone is sure to say, "No doubt; but any such ought is only a precept of prudence or expediency." It is a textbook cliché against Hobbes that his account of morality comes to just this. And this is said as if it were an obvious truth and enough to discredit all such precepts in one go. This assumes a great deal and settles nothing.

What it assumes is this: that everything that one ever does for one's own sake, one does as a matter of prudence *or* expediency; that there is no difference between these two; that morality always differs from prudence as a scent differs from a bad smell; and that everyone knows how so and why.

None of this will do.

In the first place, not everything done for oneself is done for reasons of prudence. That one ought to insure one's house, save for one's old age, not put all one's money into one venture, are precepts of prudence. But it is not a precept of prudence, though it may be a good precept, that someone ought to undergo a dangerous operation as a long shot to restoring his health rather than linger under a disability forever after.

The point is that prudence is only one way of looking after oneself. To act prudently is to play safe, for near-certain gains at small risks. But some good things one cannot get in this way. To get them at all one has to gamble, taking the risk of not getting them even so, or of coming to harm in the process. If one values them enough, one will do better by oneself to throw prudence to the winds, to play for high stakes, knowing full well the risk and the price of failure. Explorers, artists, scientists, mountaineers are types who may serve themselves better by this course. So will most people at some juncture. Thus, if someone values security, then that he ought to save in order to be secure is a precept of prudence. But that someone ought to stick to his vocation when his heart is in it enough to make it worth risking security or health or life itself is not a precept of *prudence*, but of *courage*.

One says sometimes, "I ought to save, as I *want* to be prudent," but sometimes "as I *ought* to be prudent." One may also decide that in one's own best interests one ought to be prudent rather than daring, or daring rather than prudent, as the case may be. Now, that one ought to do something as it would be prudent is a dictate of prudence. But that one really ought to be prudent, in one's own best interests, would not be a dictate of prudence again. One then ought to play safe in order to serve oneself *best* and not in order to serve oneself *safely*.

A dictate of prudence where one wants to be prudent but ought to be courageous in one's own best interests is a dictate of timidity. A dictate of courage, where one feels reckless but ought to be prudent, is a dictate of foolhardiness. Both will then plainly be morally imperfect precepts. But there is nothing obviously imperfect about a dictate of prudence where one ought to be prudent, or a dictate of courage where one ought to be daring. Such precepts seem near-moral enough to allow one to call the habit of acting on them a virtue. The Ancients considered both prudence and courage as moral virtues. Oddly enough, in our time, one is more ready to view courage on one's own behalf as a moral virtue than prudence. It needs the reminder that precepts of self-protection may be precepts of courage as well as of prudence for one to see that any precept of self-protection may have a moral flavor. I think that the dim view which we take of prudence corresponds to a belief that to be daring is harder than to be level-headed, a belief most likely justified within our own insurance-minded culture. But such belief would have seemed strange to Bishop Butler and the fashionable eighteenth-century gentlemen to whom he addressed himself. Prudence in Butler's time, as throughout the ancient world, was not yet the cheap commodity which it is with us; and the price of virtue varies with the market.

There are other precepts of self-protection which are not "just a matter of prudence" either. That one ought not to take to drugs or drink, indulge oneself in one's sorrows, waste one's talents, commit suicide just in the despair of the moment, are precepts made of sterner stuff. One wants to say, "Surely, it is more than just a matter of prudence that one ought to avoid these things." And rightly so. The effect on oneself of taking to drugs or drink, or of any of the others, is not conjectural, but quite certain. To avoid them is therefore more than a matter of *taking no risks*. Sometimes, when one looks down a precipice, one feels drawn to jump. If one refrains, it will hardly be said of one, "How prudent he is, he takes no chances." The avoidance of excesses of all kinds in one's own best interests is in this class. The habit of avoiding them the Greeks called temperance, a virtue distinct from prudence.

Another error is to equate the prudent with the expedient, and, again, the expedient with everything that is for one's own good. To save may be prudent; but whether it is expedient or convenient to start now is another matter. With a lot of money to spare at the moment it will be expedient; otherwise it will not. But it may be prudent all the same. Again, one marries in the hope of finding happiness; but marriage in this hope is not a marriage of convenience. The point is that reasons of expediency are reasons of a special sort: reasons for doing something on the ground that it is incidentally at hand to serve one's purpose, or because it serves a purpose quite incidental to the purpose for which one would normally be doing this thing. One marries for reasons of expediency when one marries for money, but not when in hope of finding happiness. Hobbes said that "men never act except with a view to some good to themselves." This would be quite different from saying that "they never act except with a view to what is expedient."

There is also this difference between the prudent and the expedient: one can speak of "rules of prudence," but less well of "rules of expediency." The expedient is what happens to serve. It is not therefore easily bottled in rules.

The word "prudence" is used too freely in still one more context. When one wishes to justify the social virtues to people, a traditional and inviting move is to refer them, among other things at least, to their own good. "You ought to hold the peace, be honest, share with others." "Why?" "Because an order in which such practices were universal is of vital concern to you; and your one hope of helping to make such an order is in doing your share." The classical formulation of this standard move is Hooker's, quoted with approval by Locke: "If I cannot but wish to receive good . . . how should I look to have any part of my desire herein satisfied, unless I myself be careful to satisfy the like desire: my desire therefore to be loved of my equals in nature, as much as possible may be, imposes upon me a *natural duty* of bearing to themward fully the like affection."

Now, it is said again, "So defended, the social duties come to no more than precepts of prudence"; and this goes with the veiled suggestion that it is morally improper to use this defense. But, even if so defended, the social duties are not necessarily reduced purely to precepts of prudence. For they may be recommended in this way either as mere *rules* or as *principles* of self-protection; and as principles they would be misdescribed as mere precepts of prudence. The distinction is this: When one says, "People ought to practice the social virtues, if only for their own benefit," one may be saying, "They ought to practice them for this reason as a *rule,* i.e., normally, as much as each time this is likely to be for their own good." Or one may be saying, "They ought to practice them for this reason not merely as a rule but as a *matter of principle*, i.e., every time, whether at that time this is likely to be for their good or not." And one might defend the adoption of this *principle* by saying, "Because your best, even if slim, hope of contributing to a society fit for you to live in lies in adding to the number of principled people who will do their share each time, without special regard for their good at that time."

Now this seems to me a precept of courage rather than one of prudence. The game of attempting by one's actions to make society a place fit for one to live in is a gamble worth the risk only because of the known price of not attempting it. This gamble is a root condition of social living. One is sure to give hostages to fortune, but again, what other hope has one got? Hence, if a man practiced the social virtues, thinking that he ought to as a matter of principle, and on these grounds, one will praise him for his *wisdom*, his firm grasp of vital issues, his steadfastness, his courage. But one will not necessarily congratulate him on his prudence. For many times the prudent course might have been otherwise. It may be wise to persist in being honest with cheats or forbearing with the aggressive, or helpful to those slow to requite helpfulness; but it might have been more prudent to persist for no longer than there was requital, or not even to start before requital was assured.

Now would it be a moral precept or not that, if only out of proper care for oneself, one ought to act on principles of wisdom and courage? That one ought to risk life in order to gain it? And, assuming a society of men acting fixedly on these principles but no others, would it or would it not contain men of moral virtue? One might as well ask, "Is a ski an article of footwear?" There is no more of a straight answer here than there. One may say, "Not quite"; and the point of saying this needs going into. But it would be more misleading to say, "Not at all." For it is part of the meaning of "moral precept" that it prescribes what a man would do in his wisdom—if he were to consider things widely, looking past the immediate concerns of self and giving essentials due weight before incidentals. As it is also part of what is meant by one's moral capacities that one can live by such considerations, it becomes fruitless after a time to press the point whether such precepts are properly called moral.

There are then varieties of the personal ought, differing in the considerations on which they are based and the qualities needed to follow them; and they all seem at least akin to a "moral" ought in their action-guiding force and function. But I grant that one does not want to speak of more than a kinship, and the point of this needs considering. One's hesitancy derives from various sources which have to be traced one by one.

Some of the hesitancy comes from contexts where one can say disparagingly, "He did this *only* for reasons of prudence, *only* for reasons of expediency, *only* for himself." This plainly applies sometimes, but it does not apply always. One would hardly say of someone without dependents, "He thought that he ought to save, but *only* for reasons of prudence"; or of someone, "He thought that he ought to have the carpenter in along with the plumber, but *only* for reasons of expediency or convenience"; or "He thought that he ought to become a doctor, but *only* because the career would suit him." "Only" has no point here. Why else should a man without dependents save, except to be prudent? Why else should anyone have the carpenter in along with the plumber, except for convenience? What better reason is there normally for choosing a career than that it will suit one? On the other hand, there is point in saying, "He held the peace only because it was prudent," "He saved only because it was convenient," "He practices the social virtues only for self-protection." It is plain why "only" applies here and is disparaging. One says "only" because something is done for the wrong or for not quite the right reason—done for *one* reason where there is *another* and nearer reason for doing it anyway. Personal reasons are often in this position, and then they are disparaged as inferior. One saves "only" because it is expedient, if one ought to have saved anyway for reasons of prudence. One holds the peace "only" because it was prudent when one ought to have done so anyway as a matter of principle and even if it had not been prudent. And one practices the social virtues "only" for self-protection when one does not *also* practice them for the general good.

The last case is different from the others. Plainly, one ought to practice the social virtues as principles of general good. But on none but perhaps pure Christian principles would it hold, or necessarily hold, that one ought to practice them on this ground unconditionally, however great the provocation to oneself. The case for the social virtues is weakened when the social environment becomes hostile and intractable by peaceable means; it is correspondingly strengthened where they can also be justified as wise principles of self-protection. That someone practices forbearance "only" as a wise principle of self-protection is not therefore to say that he practices it for a reason which is neither here nor there; but rather for a reason which falls short of all the reason there is. This was, in effect, the view of the old Natural Law moralists—Hooker, Grotius, Puffendorf: the social virtues derive joint support from our natural concern for our own good and for that of society. Hobbes streamlined this account by denying the second, which provoked subsequent moralists to deny the first. Both Hobbes's sophistical toughness and the well-bred innocence of the academic moralists since are distorted visions which are less convincing than the unsqueamish common sense of the philosophers and divines of earlier times.

3

So far we have met no reason for deprecating every personal ought. Men often have cause to be temperate, courageous, wise for their own good. This is often the only, or the nearest, reason why they should. It is then pointless to go on complaining, "But they still only act so for their own sakes." "Only" is a dangerous word.

Even so one feels that somehow a commitment that has only personal grounds is morally inferior. "One ought to risk one's life in order to gain it" seems near-moral enough. But compare it with "One ought to risk one's life in order to save others." This still seems different. And this is so not only because the one has a personal reason and the other has not, but also because where the reason is social rather than personal, the ought itself feels different —more binding, more relentless, and more properly called "moral" for this reason. The real inferiority of the personal ought seems here to lie in a lack of formal stringency.

There are such differences of stringency between "I ought to save, as I *want* to provide for my future" and "I ought to save, as I *ought* to provide for my children." The first prescribes saving as a means to an end which one *is* seeking; the second as a means to an end which in turn one *ought* to seek. The first therefore commits one formally less than the second. It leaves one at liberty to escape the commitment by renouncing the ultimate end, which the second does not. One may, as Kant did, call the first ought hypothetical and nonmoral, and the second categorical and moral on account of this difference. The distinction is made to rest on a formal difference of the binding force and not at all on any material difference in the justifying grounds. The formally "moral" commitment is to an ultimate end or rule of life and to what one ought to do on account of it in any particular case.

Now the personal ought comes more typically as nonmoral and the social ought as moral in form. One says, "You don't *want* to make your misery worse, so you ought not to dwell on it"; "You *want* to secure your future, so you ought to be prudent and save." One might also say "You *want* to provide for your children, so you ought to save"; and then formally this too would be a nonmoral ought although its grounds are other-regarding. But this is the less typical case. One is often more grudging about the needs of others than one's own. So there is here less occasion for saying, "You ought to do this on account of an end which you *are* seeking"; and more for saying, "You ought to do it on account of an end which in turn you *ought* to seek."

This typical difference between the personal and the social ought raises two questions: one, whether it is an inherent feature of the personal ought to be never more than nonmoral in form; the other, whether, even if this were so, it would be any the worse as a possibly serious commitment. Both of these positions have been taken. One's own good one always seeks. It is not therefore among the ends which one ever ought to seek in the absence of a sufficient inclination. But with the good of others, or the avoidance of harm to them, it is different. Here are ends which one does not always seek, but ought to seek all the same: ends which one may still have reason for seeking on their own account; which one would be led to seek on a diligently comprehending and imaginative review of them (of what doing good, or harm, inherently amount to). Only the social ought, therefore, may bind one to the choice of the final end as well as of the means, while the personal ought binds one only to the means on account of an end which one wants already. The personal ought is therefore only nonmoral in form, and "only" once again signifies a defect. But all this is misleading. One does not always seek one's own good as much as one has reasonable ground for seeking it, and about this I shall say more later. But even supposing that one did, then all precepts of self-regard would prescribe what one ought to do consistently with an already desired end. But they would not therefore be negligible or improper all the time.

It is true that what one ought to do consistently with a desired end need not be what one really ought to do at all. The end, or the means towards it, may prove undesirable on further scrutiny either by reason of what it is in itself or of the special circumstances of the case. I ought to save as I wish for security, and there is nothing inherently wrong with the end or the means, and so far so good. But I also ought to support my mother, and I cannot do both. Then maybe I ought not to do *all told* what otherwise I ought to have done. But in this case, the precept of prudence would have been less than "only" nonmoral. It would have been invalid all told, and counter-moral altogether. But surely not every case is like this.

For often there is nothing wrong with the things which one cares for on one's own behalf, and one really does care for them. Even if one had the abstract option to give them up, one has no serious wish to do so. One often does care for one's life or health or career or the regard of others, and one often *may* without violating other claims. And one always *may* care, if one does, for one's peace of mind or self-respect. And so what one ought to do as far as these ends go one really ought to do. As one wants to live, one really ought to look after one's health. As one wants to be liked by others, one really ought to keep a civil tongue. As one wants to live after one's own fashion, one really ought to stick to one's vocation in adversity. As one wants to be able to respect oneself or, in Hume's phrase, "bear one's own survey," one really ought to conduct oneself as one thinks that one has good reasons for doing. All these precepts tell one what one ought to do consistently with a personal end which one actually has at heart; and where they hold after scrutiny, they hold no less validly and conclusively than any fully "moral" precept. The conscientious man would have to take notice of them no less than of the others. They deserve to be called "semimoral" at least.

I keep allowing that a distinction remains. "I ought to work hard, as I *want* to succeed" is still a different kind of commitment from "I ought to work hard as I *ought* to provide for others." The difference is partly in the end, personal in the one case, impersonal in the other. But this quite apart, there is another reason for the difference. The second ought has a quality of sternness which is lacking from the first, and which is a product of its *form*, not of its *content*. For the second is an ought twice over. It says that one ought to take steps for an end which one ought to pursue ultimately. The first is an ought only once; it says that one ought to take steps for an end with regard to which one is at liberty as far as it goes. So the second ought subjects one to a regimen which is complete. It commits one *through and through*, whereas the semimoral ought does not. And this through-and-throughness gives to the moral ought its notoriously stern flavor. It makes it more imposing and often more onerous. One is having one's socks pulled up all over. And additional qualities are required of one for appreciating it and acting on it: not only forethought and consistency, but also the ability to appreciate an end as committing by reason of its own nature, which, among other things, requires sympathetic understanding and imagination. No wonder that a moral ought inspires those confronted with it with awe. The semimoral ought cannot compete with this, though when it comes to the precepts of wisdom and courage on one's own behalf they come near enough.

However, having given the formally moral ought its due, I want to add that respect for it should be no reason for slighting the other. For in the first place, and as a reassurance to those who regard lack of onerousness as a defect, though the semimoral ought is not so bad, it may be bad enough. How hard it is to pull up one's socks does not necessarily depend on their number; two commodious socks may respond more readily than one shrunken one. One semimoral and one moral case may serve as examples. If one really *wants* to do a thing and do it well, one ought to take trouble. And if one really *ought* to do good to the sick, one ought to telephone and inquire how they are getting on. The first requires a lot: putting oneself into harness, forgoing all sorts of things which one would rather do, particularly at that moment, coping with aches and pains and anxieties, playing the endless game of snakes and ladders with achievement, and yet going on, nursing one's purpose. The second, though in form a commitment through and through, requires nothing but getting up and dialing a number. It may need a great deal not to put things off, not to dwell on one's miseries, not to spend improvidently, all simply because one really ought not to in one's own best interest. The ought that lays down the law on these things may be little imposing in form. But such is the bulk of the stuff which compounds the "moral" inconveniences of ordinary life. And one also measures oneself and others by the show that is made on this front.

But then it is not the lack of onerousness as much as that of formal stringency that is felt to discredit the semimoral ought. It still is not binding like the moral ought, simply as it is not committing through and through. Moreover, its very subservience to an end which is only desired seems something amiss, as if a man should rather act always for the sake of ends which he ultimately ought to seek, and not just of ends which he happens to be seeking even if nothing is wrong with them.

This sense of guilt about the nonobligatory rests partly on excessive zeal for original sin. What the natural man in one desires never can be quite as it should. It is always "Tell me what you want to do, and I shall tell you what you ought to do instead." But there is also a failure to see that not every semimoral commitment is renounceable at will. Not every situation need confront one with a commitment through and through, and it is improper to demand that it should or to deplore that it does not.

When one ought to do a thing on account of some desired end, then one need not always be at liberty to escape the commitment by renouncing the end. It depends on whether one is free to give up the end itself, and this is not always so. One says of some ends, "If you want to seek it you may, and if you don't want to you need not." There is here no reason against seeking the end, nor reason enough to tell one to seek it in the absence of a desire for it. And one is free to escape a commitment on account of such an end simply by giving up the end. But in the case of other ends one will say, "If you want to seek it you may, but if you do not want to you still ought to all the same." Again there is no reason against seeking the end if one wants to, but here there would be still reason for seeking it even if one did not want to. A commitment on account of such an end one may not escape at will as one is not here free to give up the end. It is arguable whether commitments on personal grounds are not often in this position. One ought to be temperate as one wants to preserve one's health. And although this is a semimoral ought as far as it goes, one need not be free to get out of it at will. For even if one ceased to care about the end, one might still here have reasonable ground for caring, and ought to care all the same.

An ought of this kind commits one on account of an end which one seeks as well as ought to seek. And this makes it like an ought through and through, but still not quite. There can be ends which one seeks and ought to seek. But insofar as one *is* seeking such an end, it is strained to say that one also *ought* to seek it at the same time. One would rather say that if one were not seeking it already, then one ought to be seeking it all the same. This is why, if someone is perfectly willing about an end, a commitment on account of this end would still not for him have the form of a commitment through and through; and this although it is potentially such a commitment and would turn into one as soon as he ceased to be readily inclined towards the end.

The point is that ought applies only where there is a case for pulling one's socks up. The same action may be viewed in otherwise the same circumstances either as one which one ought to do, or as one which one wants to and may do, according to the psychological starting point. One

normally wants to have one's breakfast, and one would find it improper to
have it put before one with the remark. "You ought to eat this morning."
"Why ought I? Don't I eat every morning anyway?" But if one were con-
valescent, the remark would be in place. Nor would one say to a notoriously
indulgent parent, "You ought not to be harsh with your children" (though
one might wonder whether he *may* be so indulgent). The remark applies to
a parent bad at controlling his temper. If I resolved to become an early riser
and succeeded, I might report in retrospect, "For the first month it was a
duty, but afterwards it ceased to be a duty and became a habit, if not a
pleasure."

None of this should be surprising. Ought is an action-guiding concept.
It expresses the notion that one is liable to direction by reasons in the case
which would motivate one if one gave them due consideration. And one
cannot be *liable* to direction by reasons except in a matter of doing what
one is not fully motivated to do already. This is why it cannot be an obligation for one to do what one wants to do anyway, much as it might become
an obligation for one to do it if one ceased to want to. This is also why, when
one really wants to do something, the natural question to ask is not, "And
ought I to do this thing?" but rather, "And *may* I do it?" or "Would there
be anything wrong with it?" or "Ought I perhaps *not* to do it?" One looks
for possible reasons against, not for possible reasons for. And what point
would there be in doing anything more? When one really wants to do something, one already has, *for* doing it, all the reason one needs. And this is also
why one only says "You ought to" to others when one takes it that there is a
case for changing their present frame of mind. But to wonder whether one
ought to (as distinct from wondering whether one may, or perhaps ought
not to) where one already wants to would be like wondering whether to sit
down when seated; and to say "You ought to" to someone quite ready to,
would be like advising a sitting man to take a seat. *There is no ought for
those blessed with wants which are not wrong.*

One may object: "But surely one can say that everyone ought to do
good, and if there were benevolent people this would not make this false."
And this is correct, but no refutation. What raises a problem are general
statements like "People ought to do good," "One ought to be tolerant." But
one may make a general statement without having to specify all the conditions when it shall or shall not hold. One says in general, "Butter will
melt in the sun"; and if someone interjected, "But *not* when one has just
melted it on the kitchen stove," this would be no rebuttal. "*This* butter will
melt in the sun," when I am bringing it dripping from the kitchen, would be
different. This particular butter is not *liable* to melt, even though it remains
true that butter is. The same with "People ought to do good." This is a
general statement, and one need not state the obvious: that it will not apply
to someone whose heart needs no melting as it is soft already. Nor does one

use "one ought to" directively to people, except for general purposes of propaganda. "I ought to" and "you ought to" are in a logically different class.

One makes general ought-statements about standard ends and practices towards which people commonly have no sufficient inclination. These ought-statements apply particularly to doing things for others, and less so to doing things for oneself. And this alone could explain why one normally does not say that people ought to care for their own good. For the question of whether they *ought* to does not here normally arise. They can be trusted with a modicum of well adjustment towards this end—they seek it, and, within limits, they may seek it. Hence, what one ought to do on account of one's own good is commonly a commitment on account of a desired end, much as it might also turn into a commitment through and through with a loss of immediate interest in the end. Nor could one reasonably hope that such commitments were more imposing in form than they are. On the contrary, one may say that the less imposing the ought, the better designed for living the man.

4

We are nearly out of the woods, but not quite. For the picture now before us still gives *Out* more than he can have. *Out* could say at this point: "By and large you have vindicated me. All your personal oughts are at best semimoral. Only what one ought to do on account of others is in any way like what one morally ought to do. In fact, you have explained why this is so. Men are more immediately and unreflectively drawn towards their own good than towards that of others. So the pursuit of their own good as an end never comes to them as an obligation. But in the matter of considering others they need the full treatment. Here they must learn to care for the end as well as the means, and to care for the end even at cost to themselves. To do what serves social ends therefore comes as obligatory on one through and through. And this is the moral ought, the one that pulls one up without further question all along the line. However, you have convinced me on one point. Personal commitments need not always be negligible or discreditable. Sometimes one really ought to be prudent or courageous in one's own best interest, and the conscientious man ought to take notice of this and to conduct himself accordingly. So in a sense perhaps there is a personal as well as a social morality. But I still insist that the two are not on the same level, that only the social commitments are in every way properly 'moral,' and that only their neglect is a properly 'moral' failing."

This statement calls for two comments. The first is that *Out* is already loosening the hold on his position. He has to speak of morality in a strict and in a broader sense, and of the conscientious man as doing his share by both. And this rightly so. By a conscientious person one understands someone who will not be evasive about anything that he is convinced he really ought to do. He is the right-living man of the Greeks whose first commitment is to the principle of self-guidance by good and sufficient reasons. To observe his socially grounded commitments will be an imposing part of his job. But the whole job will be to conduct himself in line with all valid commitments, no matter whether they are imposing in form or not. One may say if one wishes that his properly "moral" commitments are only those which commit him through and through and out of regard for others. But then it must be granted that there is more to being a right-living person than only observing one's "moral" commitments; and that the neglect of a nonmoral commitment, even if not strictly a "moral" failing, is nevertheless like one by being the evasion of a known commitment supported by valid reasons.

The second comment is that the case against *Out* needs pressing still further. It is also not the case that only the social commitments are ever fully moral in form. Commitments on personal grounds are less commonly so, because of the greater immediate regard which one has for oneself. One's own pain or unhappiness are closer to one than these same states in others. Unless they lie in the future it requires no effort of understanding and imagination to enable one to respond to them. But this immediate regard for oneself has its limits. Men may feel as unreasonably unconcerned for their own good as for that of others. Hume rightly spoke of "that narrowness of soul which makes us prefer the present to the remote"; and there are sick drives towards self-effacement and self-denial, so much so that it has been said that "man's inhumanity towards man is only equalled by his inhumanity towards himself." One meets the suggestion that everyone is at liberty to act as he will in the matter of his own life. But it would be odd if in this matter one were not liable to correction from a reflective appraisal of the nature of what one is doing. Men who are separated from their own good as an end may still have reasonable ground for seeking it in the absence of sufficient inclination. Their own good will then become something that they ought to seek and stand up for more than they are wont to or can readily bring themselves to; and to do the things which their own good requires will for them then become a commitment through and through.

It may also be that in a case like this someone ought to stand up for his own good even to the detriment of another. It could be sound advice to say to a woman in strife with herself and tied to a demanding parent, "You ought to consider yourself, and so break away now, hard as it may be on the parent." One is then saying more than simply, "If you wanted to you would have a right to." One is saying, "I know you are shrinking away from it, but this is what you ought to do, and above all else." In form this is an ought through and through, and an overriding one at that, but its ground is not other-regarding. And even true Christian charity might not here prescribe anything different. One cannot love one's neighbor as oneself if one has not also learned to accept one's own wishes as a proper object of respect and care, as one's own wishes are the paradigm of all wishes. There is a profound sense in which charity begins at home. For some this acceptance of themselves is hard, and it may confront them with a personal commitment as categorical and as onerous as any. Is this then a "moral" commitment or not? Here language fails one. For the usual conjunction between the categorical and the socially grounded commitment has come apart and turned into a clash. It is to strain the usual associations of language to the limit to speak of a moral commitment to put one's own good before that of another. But the unqualified refusal to call this a moral commitment is strained too and may be tendentiously misleading. For apart from not being grounded in regard for others, such a commitment may be precisely like the typical moral commitment in its cogency, its form and its action-guiding relevance.

There is still another type of case. One's own good comprises not only one's states but also the possession of one's self as a mind. One cannot earnestly wish to lose hold of oneself, to be reduced to a shaky mess when in trouble; one needs to be in control and to be able to cope with whatever may come. And this preservation of oneself as a capable ego is also something that one may find that one ought to care for when one is too driven or despondent to be inclined to care for it. Kant spoke of the duties of self-perfection, the commitments which subserve the protection of one's rational nature; and he did not hesitate to include them among one's moral duties along with the social ones. And this quite consistently so, as here is a type of concern for oneself for which one has reasonable ground though one is not always ready for it by inclination. Moreover, this type of personal commitment is morally relevant in a special way. For among the duties of self-perfection is the conscientious man's commitment to live without evading any issue—to seek out and weigh what cogent reasons would lead him to do, and to submit himself without self-deception or evasion to their determination. One cannot derive that one ought to live in this manner from one's special obligations towards others. For one may never duly confront any of one's special obligations unless one is already willing to live that way. All principled conduct which is reasoned practice and not just well-bred habit turns on this commitment as its pivot. It involves the acceptance of the principle of nonescapism as an overall rule of life. And this commitment has the most intimately personal reason. It rests on an individual's inmost concern to preserve himself intact as a living and functioning self: mentally in possession of himself and of his world, able to look at himself and what he is doing without having to hide himself from himself. The penalty for slighting this need is his undoing as a person.

And now is one still to say that only what one ought to do with a view to the good of others can have the *cogency and force* of the "moral" commitment? The claim has been further reduced. Only most commitments which are committing through and through rest on other-regarding considerations. There can also be such commitments which rest on personal considerations, and they may on occasion take precedence over one's social commitments. And there is one commitment whose ground is intimately personal and which comes before any other personal or social commitment whatsoever: the commitment to the principled mode of life as such. One is tempted to call this the supreme moral commitment, but if no commitment may count as "moral" unless one has it on account of others, then the commitment to the practice of nonevasive living cannot properly count as a "moral" commitment at all.

That the social commitments make up the bulk of the formally imposing ones is, of course, a fact which one has no reason to deny. The good of others is the standard case of an end towards which men commonly find themselves less drawn by inclination than committed to on due reflection, through the exercise of understanding and imagination. But it illuminates the logic of the case that this is so as a matter of fact and of none else. Suppose that we were made the opposite of the way we are: that we were concerned about the good of others as immediately as we are now concerned about our own, and were concerned about our own good no more readily than we are now about that of others. Then the whole moral machine would be working busily in reverse. The bulk of the formerly imposing duties would be those which prescribe the subordination of our excessive regard for others to a proper regard for ourselves. Morality, in effect, would no longer serve primarily an order of mutual consideration, but the protection of the individual from being overwhelmed by his social sentiments. Nietzsche's transvaluation of all values was the claim that the hidden facts were such as to make this morality's real task. "Men are too weak-minded to be self-seeking." Their besetting vice is morbid pity, a guilty fear of their own wishes, self-hate, and resentment against others under the guise of concern. The moral machine needs putting into reverse.

I am not saying with Nietzsche that it does, though it may well with some. My point is rather to insist that a morality, if by this we mean a reasoned body of action-guiding principles and commitments, is always a morality for someone; and a morality for humans is one for humans. This is why in our morality, and in spite of Nietzsche, the socially grounded commitments have a special place. They are, even if not the only, the standard case of what reflective human beings meet as committing through and through. But this is so because men are what they are and their situation is what it is: because they do not live alone; because they can identify themselves with the concerns of others and of the communities of which they are members and can care about them; and because they can learn to care as much as they are able to by learning to comprehend. One commonly takes it that materially moral or social reasons are in some measure ought-implying for everyone. And this is fair enough if taken as a regulative principle, or presumption, with a massive, if incomplete, backing in experience. The presumption is that such reasons can be treated as standard reasons; that anyone can be taken to be accessible to them (although to an extent for which there is no standard measure) unless he is willfully uncomprehending, mentally disordered, or immature for reasons of age or cultural background. But there can be no demonstrative certainty of this being so. The case of an otherwise human being congenitally inaccessible to other-regarding considerations may be treated as *incredible*, but not as *inconceivable*.

There is also, however, the suggestion that one means by "moral" reasons more than this. "Moral" reasons are considerations of social good which are always binding, and in case of conflict with personal good, always *overridingly* binding on every reflective human being alike. But while one may *conceive* of moral reasons in these terms, there is nothing gained by doing so. For no conceptual gerrymandering can settle what will then be the crucial question, namely, whether what is here termed a "moral" reason is a concept applicable to human beings; and, if so to any extent, then by way of anything but a massively grounded presumption.

One may still say that the social commitments are the only "moral" ones properly so called. One is then making a *material* criterion a necessary condition for applying "moral" to a commitment. A "moral" commitment must not only be validly action-guiding and committing through and through; it must also be incurred on account of others. By this language rule, "moral" is used to mark off the species of social grounded commitments from the genus of validly action-guiding commitments in general. That there is this language rule is not disputed. The sole point at issue is that one should not be misled by it. The rule entails that none but the socially grounded commitments are properly "moral," but only for a reason which does not imply that they alone are seriously cogent, or committing through and through, or that they alone can take precedence in a proper calculus of action-guiding considerations. No answers to the questions, "How ought one to live?" and "What ought one to do?" must be taken as prejudged by the semantic taboo on calling a personally grounded commitment strictly "moral." No real-life possibility is excluded by the insistence that a Nietzschean "morality" would not properly be a "morality" at all. The question of what can or cannot be validly action-guiding principles and commitments for a reflective and human being is not settled by appeal to a linguistic convention.

5

      I have argued that one may say that only the socially grounded ought is properly "moral"; but that, if the only reason for this is semantic, nothing substantial follows. Personal considerations, though not called "moral," could still be as seriously choice-supporting and binding on one as properly moral ones. But this conclusion may still seem unconvincing. One may object that we simply do not think that doing the right thing by oneself is ever *binding* on one in the same way as doing the right thing by others. In the matter of acting as we ought on our own account we consider ourselves free and not responsible to anyone. But in the matter of acting as we ought on account of others we consider ourselves obligated and responsible to them. This suggests that the personal and the social ought are not after all on the same footing; that the social ought carries with it an added authority which derives from the very fact that it is social, and that this is implied in calling it alone "moral."

It remains to be shown that here is another line of argument for the nonformalist, like *Out*, to follow; that this line of argument is indispensable to the understanding of the complex phenomenon that morality is; but that its ultimate relevance must not be overrated.

One may argue as follows. There is one plain difference between ought-abiding conduct in social and in personal matters. Other people have a stake in the first which they have not in the second. Their legitimate interests are involved in our social conduct; they hold us accountable for doing the right thing by them. This applies particularly to those rules and practices which, in a given society, are regarded as the backbone of the social order. Society credits its mature members with the ability to appreciate that they ought to respect these rules for their social merits. If they violate them without valid excuse they act counter to what others have a stake in their doing; and they are made responsible for their conduct. One may ask them to justify themselves, admonish and censure them. And this is why it may be said that the social ought alone is called moral; not only because it is social, but also because it has a special authority. When it comes to respect for social rules and the good of others, society obligates one to act as one ought on pain of moral sanctions. One is here, as it were, doubly bound; by the voice of reason and by the majesty of the law; by the knowledge that one ought to, and by one's accountability to others for doing it. None of this applies to one's conduct in the matter of acting as one ought on one's own account. One is not here socially obligated; one is a morally bad and socially guilty person for not acting as one ought.

Contemporary writers like Hart[2] are inclined to make this point more strongly. They suggest that the sense in which social ought-abidance is *obligatory*, and personal ought-abidance not, is the only proper sense of this term. Traditional philosophy, it is said, has ignored that "ought" and "obligation" are different concepts. Ought-language is "teleological"; only obligation-language is "deontological." That one ought to do something is to say that it is the "best" or "reasonable" thing to do, but not yet that one is obligated or bound to do it. Words like "obligation" or "duty" are at home in legal or quasi-legal contexts and apply only to social injunctions or prohibitions. Any other use of them is a philosopher's extension of language, a use which is as unwarranted as it is misleading. "Duties" are something assigned to one, "obligations" something imposed on one. Both are liabilities created by a public rule or requirement, or liabilities which one incurs by giving rise to claims against oneself as in giving a promise, or becoming a husband or father. It will then follow that a moral *obligation* can be only a liability created by a social rule or demand on one; and that what makes this liability "moral" is that its force derives from moral sanctions or from an internalized sense of moral propriety. The definitive authority which one associates with moral injunctions and prohibitions will then derive solely from this source. There may be things which one ought to do even on a desert island; but one is not bound, let alone morally bound, to do them outside a social context which alone can create an obligation.

Here, then, seems to be another way of diagnosing the formalist's error. He assumes correctly that moral judgments have a special authoritative role. And he argues from this that every authentic and definitive ought-judgment is a moral judgment. But it now turns out that no ought-judgment, whether its grounds are personal or social, has the characteristic force of a moral judgment. Moral judgments relate to obligations; ought-judgments only to what is "reasonable" or "best." Even what one ought to do on account of others is a *moral* ought only insofar as one is socially answerable for doing it. What falls within morality is only a segment of ought-abiding conduct. And what segment this is, what will count as *morally* obligatory or permissible, will be settled exclusively by our looking over our shoulders for the frowns and smiles of the social order. I doubt that those who press for a sharp distinction between "ought" and "obligation" would wish to go all the way with this conclusion. But this conclusion is implicit,

---

[2] H. L. A. Hart, "Legal and Moral Obligation," *Essays in Moral Philosophy*, ed. A. I. Melden (Seattle: University of Washington Press, 1958), p. 82.

and, given the premises, not easily avoided. If the conclusion seems extreme, the question is, Why?

There is rarely smoke without a fire: social ought-abidance plainly is of social concern, and blame and admonition have a place in it. Equally plainly, personal ought-abidance is treated differently. Our evasions here count as amicable vices, and not as moral turpitude. We may take the censure of others amiss, and require them to mind their own business. And the same with their admonitions. To say "you ought to" to another is always a kind of interference; and the propriety of *saying so* (as distinct from having a judgment about it) varies with the case. Ought-judgments and ought-speech, ought-judgments and judgments of blame or of praise-worthiness have different and variable functions. Again, the language of "ought" and "obligation" is infected with these distinctions. There is a sense in which obligations are social liabilities, and moral obligations such liabilities as are morally sanctioned. In this sense one has no obligation, moral or otherwise, to do the right thing by oneself. Nor has one, in this sense, a moral obligation to do everything that one's social conscience may tell one to do. Society only requires our conscientiousness in standard situations; it treats deeds which only an exceptionally sensitive regard for others would prescribe as acts of superarrogation. To devote one's life to the care of lepers is praiseworthy but "beyond the call of duty." But, true as this may be, this fashionable observation also shows the limitations of the view. We do not conceive of moral obligations as only dependent on social requirements and their external or built-in sanctions. Saints and heroes go beyond these in what they judge they must or ought to do. And it would be farfetched to say that, when they follow their judgment, they are not doing what they think is their duty. "Duty" and "obligation" are not words unequivocally tied to the socially obligatory.

Nor is the "morally permissible" tied only to the socially welcome. There may be occasions when someone may validly judge that he ought to put his own good before that of another. Here others may not readily welcome his ought-abidance. They may have a stake in discouraging it and be tempted to censure. But, granted that one accepts the authenticity of his judgment, one will here forbear censure, and consider him morally justified. The measure of moral justification is here his conviction that he ought to. But it is well to note how this case puts the social orientation of our moral thinking under stress. The upright deviant from social norms and interests is not judged "morally bad," but not "morally good" or "praiseworthy" either. We have to grant to others, as we must insist on for ourselves, that conscientious ought-abidance is the supreme moral rule for any agent in the situation of choice. But, socially, such conduct need not be an unmixed blessing. And if we may not condemn it on moral grounds, we need not bless it either. "Moral goodness" is a term of appraisal so geared to socially welcome conduct that not every morally *correct* choice makes one a morally *good* man.

There seems to be, then, a sense in which "ought" and "moral obligation" are not sharply separable; though there also is another in which they are distinct, and in which social ought-abidance has the added force of an obligation. How then do these two senses relate to one another? The question may be answered by considering the view that what gives to the social ought the force of a special *obligation* adds significantly to its action-guiding authority. For while this view is correct in one way, it is false in another. While social ought-abidance is required of us socially, we are surely not bound to it *only* on this account. The social ought differs in this respect from the obligations created only by law or custom. One has a legal obligation simply by being required by an appropriate public rule. But with the things which one ought to do on social grounds this is not so. What is here socially required of one is moral conduct: conduct in line with what one ought and can be reasonably expected to know that one ought to do. The very requirement presupposes that one has already an antecedent obligation to do it, insofar, namely, as one knows already that one ought to do it.

This would have seemed plain language in the past. What then is at issue in debarring us from using it? The traditional philosopher may have been guilty of an unidiomatic extension of language in speaking here of an antecedent commitment or obligation. He may well have made light of the common or garden use of these terms for a liability created by an external rule. But sometimes an unidiomatic extension of language is less misleading than a narrow insistence on linguistic propriety; and if there is cause for complaint here the cure seems worse than the disease. The traditional philosopher wanted to bring out that if a deliberative person ought to do a thing he is to this extent also bound to do it *in some manner*. He is facing, if not a conventional, then a "natural" duty or obligation. And this extension of language has a warrant. Where one has an obligation or commitment to do something one is up against a characteristic constraint or limitation of one's freedom to act otherwise. And some language is needed to make the point that the demands or assignments of others are neither the only nor the most decisive form in which this constraint can be incurred.

A person who is obligated to do something is under a constraint which is not purely psychological or physical. He need not feel impelled to do it, he is not made to do it by main force, it is not causally impossible for him to act otherwise. The constraint is conceived as latent rather than actual, and as arising not from causes, but from reasons. The situation has features which *tell* for or against some action: they need not determine a person's choice, but they would if he knew them and took careful account of them. A deliberative person who can appreciate that he has such reasons will meet in them a latent limitation of his freedom to act otherwise. Obligations in the common or garden sense are a special case of this. One meets a constraining reason in a social rule or demand on one which one can ill afford to ignore. Such obligations are imposed on one from without. The rule or demand issues from others; their insistence is the feature in the situation which supplies as well as creates the reason which limits one's freedom of action. But not all liability to direction by known reasons is like this. There are choice-guiding considerations which are not first imported into the situation by others with a view to direct one: they exist and can be found in the nature, effects, and implications of actions and principles themselves. A deliberative person need not wait for others to bring them to his notice; nor in being guided by them is he doing their bidding. That he is up against such reasons for doing things is equivalent to saying that he ought to do them, of his own accord and prior to being asked. This is why one may speak of a "natural obligation": of an *obligation* because a person is up against a latent limitation of his freedom by reasons; of a *natural* obligation because the limitation is the work here not of *anyone*, but of reasons to be found antecedently in the nature of the case.

Where one *ought* to do things on account of others, one is therefore *socially obligated* to do only what one has an antecedent natural obligation to do already. One is answerable to others, as someone against whom they have legitimate claims, precisely because one ought, and can know that one ought, to give them consideration to begin with. And this is why one's answerability to them cannot here significantly add to the weight and authority of one's commitment. It may do so *de facto*. When a person hesitates to do what he has no doubt that he ought to do, the reminder that he is accountable to others is a potent consideration. The mere thought of incurring recrimination and blame evokes apprehension and guilt. But these are not considerations to increase the force of a moral commitment *de jure*. A reflective person has no need of coercive reasons for acting as he ought. He does not require the fear of blame as a reason for not evading his own better judgment. And this is also why the absence of coercive reasons, where one ought to do things on one's own account, or on account of others, but beyond the call of conventional duty, could not allow one seriously to breathe a sigh of relief. Whatever one judges that one seriously ought to do, whether the reasons for doing it are ultimately social or personal, whether one is socially blameworthy for the omission or not, one is sufficiently committed to do and responsible to oneself for doing unasked. It is inconsistent with the concepts of mature moral thinking to keep looking for the differentia of the authority of the moral commitments in one's social answerability for observing them.

6

I am saying "with the concepts of mature moral thinking" advisedly. For the complex fabric of moral thinking contains still another notion of the moral bond. And the view that moral commitments have a special authority which derives from the sanctioned demands of the social order keeps drawing support from it. In fact, here is the primary concept of the moral bond, the one from which it derives its name, and the one which comes first, not only in the history of the race, but also in that of the individual. For as one grows up this is what happens. Father says, "Don't lie, don't be slovenly." Mother says, "This is what father says." The world says, "Don't be promiscuous." Father says, "This is what everyone says, this is also what God says." Father also says, "Do what God says," and, he says, "God says, 'Do what father says.'" Here is a mixed barrage of requests made on one or reported to be made on one. They specify what one is to do or not to do. They come from "out there," though their precise imponent is obscure. They are addressed to one not without heat and are backed not by main force, like the law, but by moral suasion —smiles or frowns, approval or disapproval, the promise of bestowing or the threat of withdrawing love. And in these requests everyone first meets the demands of "morality." They are the first model for the notions of "moral law" and "moral duty," the first standard of "moral right" and "moral wrong." They create the moral obligations in their primary sense: as restrictions on one's freedom of action by the "mores" or "manners" of a social group. These obligations are like the legal obligations in being barriers against license maintained by social consensus for the protection of the social order. They only differ from them by the kind of sanctions employed, and by the absence of institutional procedures for their promulgation, codification, and administration.

Confusion keeps arising from the complex relations between the primary moral bond and the commitments of a reflective person by cogent considerations. As one's understanding develops one becomes acquainted and learns to live with both, yet without learning to keep them distinctly apart. One's moral commitments, in the mature sense, may oblige one to defer to the same rules on which the mores insist. In fact, this is how they come to be called "moral" commitments. The notion of the natural moral commitment arrives on the logical scene when it comes to be understood that a person who can use his own judgment does not need the insistence of the mores to defer to the rules which they prescribe. There are reasons why he ought to do so unasked, and, if not, then there are reasons why he ought to defer to other rules more adequate to the underlying social purposes of the moral code. This is how the word "moral" is transferred from the one level to the other. The commitments of a reflective person,

by social considerations especially, are called "moral" because they incor-
porate and supersede the obligations by the mores in their role of protecting
the social order. Social reasons become "moral" reasons, and the powers
of mind and agency on which unforced self-direction by reasons depends,
become "moral powers" on account of their continuity of function with
the purposes of primary morality. But these new connotations are acquired
at the loss of others. The new-style moral commitment is no longer a
creation of the social order. To call it "moral" is no longer to imply that
its *authority* depends on the apprehension of guilt for the violation of a
public rule. It is "moral" as backed by considerations which, while prior
to the demands of primal morality, are favorable to its purposes; and it has
authority if and when these considerations prove cogent on a due appraisal
of the case.

This is how the word "moral" acquires its multiple associations. Such
notions as the "moral order," or "moral rule," may all be viewed in *two
ways:* as a body of rules or a rule publicly maintained by moral force; and
as a body of rules or a rule which the members of a group ought, and can
be expected to know that they ought, to respect unasked. Each time, the
moral commitment to defer to the rule may be said to arise from the
"requirements of the social order." But the ambiguities of this expression
easily pass unnoticed. In the one case, the commitment arises from what
the *will* of society "requires," i.e., insists on. In the other, it arises from what
the *needs* of society "require," i.e., causally presuppose for their satisfaction,
and from what a due appraisal of these needs "requires" one to do, i.e.,
provides one with telling reasons for doing. Both notions are settled parts
of ordinary thought, in which the mind moves hazily from viewing the
morally right or wrong as being so by a rule whose violation makes him
socially guilty to viewing it as being so by a rule to which he ought to
conform anyway. Moreover, the primary associations of "moral" are so
ingrained that it is hard to appreciate that there really is a level on which
public demands and the apprehension of incurring social guilt are irrelevant
to the authority of a commitment considered as "moral." There is a
standing temptation for the philosopher no less than for the ordinary person
to import the quasi-legal features of the primary model into the mature
one and to expect them to persist where they no longer have a place.

What furthers confusion is that even in the mature perspective the
action-guiding role of the mores is not entirely superseded. There is a
presumption (of which one can make too much as well as too little) that
a rule strongly insisted on by the mores will also have valid prior reasons
in its favor. And there is ground for caution in pitting ones' own judgment
too readily against the presumptive wisdom of the moral code. A commitment to a rule of the mores on this ground is still, in a way, created for one
by the moral code. But there is a difference. The existence of the moral

code is here no longer the *ratio essendi* of a moral commitment viewed as primal. It is rather that the moral code has become the *ratio cognoscendi* of a moral commitment on the level of maturity. A moral education is commonly a training in the mores as a first guide to what one is to do or not to do. But it will be a moral education in quite different senses, depending on whether one is introduced to the moral code simply as a body of morally sanctioned demands, or as a first, though by no means the last, ground for the determinations of mature moral thinking.

I have argued that the mature moral commitments are incurred through the unforced appreciation of cogent reasons in the case. Their authority owes nothing to the coercive moral pressures. They are roughly called "moral" because they are commitments which supersede the primary moral law in its action-guiding role. But the question of why and when they strictly deserve this name cannot well be settled.

We are inclined to conceive of morality by the joint application of two criteria. "Moral" principles commit one in a special and cogently authoritative manner; and they commit one in this manner to conduct which is, or is held to be, socially desirable. This concept is applicable well enough to primary morality. The primary moral law (on its own level and by its own means) supplies an authoritative rule of life which obligates everyone alike, and in the social interest. The coincidence between rules with moral force and in the service of social ends can here be counted on: it is contrived, albeit unwittingly, and where it is wanting it can be mended. One can define morality, on the primary level, as authoritative action-guidance whose function is to regulate the social order. But morality, on the mature level, is less well-conceived in this way. There are difficulties in uniting the authoritative and the social associations of "moral" in one concept.

It is plainly not the principal function of mature morality to protect the social order, if by the "function" of a practice is meant the reason why it exists and is carried on. The commitments by cogent reasons in the case are not imposed on one from without for social ends. One incurs them, if through anyone's doing, through one's own: as someone willing to seek direction from the counsel of cogent reasons. The involvement of human beings in this practice is personal: it turns on their stake in the kind of self-preservation which requires that one should be able to bear before oneself the survey of one's own actions. Responsibly reason-guided and ought-abiding living exists, in the first place, for the sake of sane and ordered individual being, and not for the regulation of the social order. Nor is the coincidence between ought-abiding living and the social interest axiomatic.

The fact—which traditional moral philosophy seems almost to exist to dispute away—*is that primary morality has no unequivocal successor on the level of autonomous choice.* The "moral law" (whether the actual law of the tribe, or the ideal law that would best suit its needs) has no identical counterpart in a "law of our own nature." It is true that the commitments by noncoercive reasons (like the primary moral law) supply a *definitive* guide to conduct on their level; and that where they have other-regarding grounds, they are in the *social interest*. But the agreement between the definitive commitments on this level and those typically geared to the social interest is not here guaranteed. The agreement is not contrived; the social order cannot lay down what reflective choice shall bid a mature person do, or for what reasons. Nor is the agreement logically necessary. Valid ought-judgments rest on the backing of choice-supporting reasons: of facts in the case which can dispose those who know and review them in favor of or against the choice. There is therefore no logical limit to what may be a valid ought. The care of others may be a valid ought for one, and so may be the proper care of oneself. Either end may manifestly direct one to seek it on a diligently comprehending view of it. Either, or both, may be valid premises for a particular ought-judgment. One may be conscientiously ought-abiding in serving one's community, or in seeking personal salvation behind the walls of a Buddhist retreat. Considerations of prudence and wisdom may relevantly add to the reasons why one ought to practice the social virtues, along with reasons of humanity and compassion. What is judged a valid ought, on a due appraisal of the facts and their force for one as deciding reasons, may have all manner of grounds; it may protect individual as well as social needs; it need not be the same for everyone alike. Nor need every ought be an ought for one through and through in order to be a seriously cogent ought, and among one's responsibilities as a right-living, reason-guided person. The ought-judgments which are formally imposing and backed by materially moral considerations are the standard case for human beings of the formally imposing ones; but they are no more than a species of the broad genus "definitively action-guiding ought-judgments."

Is one to say then that the mature moral enterprise is the general practice of conscientiously ought-abiding living? Or that it is only the part of it which is socially beneficial and a matter of active social concern? Are the mature moral commitments those which *formally*, or only those which *formally and materially*, continue the job of the primary moral law? Usage here leans uneasily either way. That man is a "moral agent" with "moral freedom" is associated with his power for responsible self-direction. "Moral strength" or "moral weakness" are terms which relate to the exercise of this power. But the "morally good man" connects with the "selfless man." The "moral" commitments of a mature person are conceived as essentially self-incurred through the responsible exercise of his moral powers and also as grounded in regard for others. There are those who insist that mature morality is socially beneficial ought-abidance: that language prescribes a material as well as a formal criterion for the use of "moral." There are others who will call "moral" any definitive and "authentic" commitment of a self-directing person, whether its grounds are social or personal.

Here is a semantic issue which it is far more important to understand than to take sides on. For whatever one says—whether it is the more consonant with ordinary language or not—must be semantically disquieting. Usage (at any rate, current English usage) backs the nonformalist more than the formalist. The mature moral commitments are those to conduct which is of social concern: they are properly called "moral" *as they supersede the primary moral law in its social role.* This usage is unexceptionable as long as its implications are faced. The *moral* and the *definitive* commitments on the mature level need not then coincide. One must grant that "morality" on this level is demoted from its accustomed place of being the sole and final arbiter of right and wrong choice. This is why, much as the nonformalist has semantically a case, the formalist has one too. He is opting for the other horn of the dilemma. The moral commitments on the mature level are *those which supersede the primary moral law in its role of supplying an authoritative and supreme rule of life.* And this rule is in the definitive— but not necessarily only materially moral—commitments which a reflective person incurs on a nonevasive appreciation of all the reasons in the case; and, in the last analysis, in his first commitment to the "authentic" way of life itself.

If both alternatives are repugnant, it is because both fall short of expectations. The unequivocal successor to the primary moral law should be a commitment by noncoercive reasons, manifestly binding on everyone alike, to give precedence always to the claims of beneficence and the requirements of social living. But there is no warrant for assuming such a commitment on the level of autonomous choice. The rules of language cannot furnish it any more than pure reason, or intuition. The hard fact is that the rational and autonomous mode of life overlaps, but no longer necessarily coincides, with the moral mode of life as conceived from the point of view of the social interest. The autonomous agent can be a debatable social asset. It is vain to expect morality on all levels to do the same kind of job as the institution of the law. The concept of morality itself bears the accumulated scars of conceptual evolution. Its multiple associations are a bar to summing it up in any one way.

The Concept of Morality

WILLIAM K. FRANKENA

1

"What is morality?" is a vague and ambiguous question, much discussed by the metamoralists of recent years. Here I shall ask only one of the many questions involved, namely, "When is an individual, group, or society to be said to have a morality or a moral action-guide?", or "When is a code or action-guide to be called a moral one, a morality?"

This question may be and has been answered in many different ways, some monistic (one-concept theories), others pluralistic (two-or-more-concept theories), some definist, others antidefinist. We cannot try to describe or discuss them all now. All may be presented either as descriptive-elucidatory accounts or as normative proposals, conservative or revisionary —one may even hold one theory as a descriptive-elucidatory account and advance another as a normative proposal (revisionary), as I shall—but I am here interested primarily in views that are presented as normative proposals, at least implicitly. Then four of them strike me as being of the greatest pith and moment. In order to state these four views we must distinguish between a *wider* formal concept of morality and a *narrower* material and social one. According to the former, an AG (action-guide) is a morality (a moral AG as opposed to a nonmoral AG) if and only if it satisfies such formal criteria as the following, regardless of its content:

(A) *X* takes it as prescriptive.

(B) *X* universalizes it.

(C) *X* regards it as definitive, final, overriding, or supremely authoritative.

According to the second, narrower concept, *X* has a morality, or moral AG, only if, perhaps in addition to such formal criteria as A and B, his AG also fulfills some such material and social condition as the following:

(D) It includes or consists of judgments (rules, principles, ideals, etc.) that pronounce actions and agents to be right, wrong, good, bad, etc., simply because of the effect they have on the feelings, interests, ideals, etc., of *other* persons or centers of sentient experience, actual or hypothetical (or perhaps simply because of their effects on human-

From The Journal of Philosophy, *LXIII (1966). Reprinted by permission of the author and* The Journal of Philosophy. *Presented in an American Philosophical Association symposium of the same title, December 27, 1966. A longer, earlier version of this paper appears in* University of Colorado Studies, *1965.*

ity, whether in his own person *or* in that of another). Here 'other' may mean "some other" or "all other."

On this conception, a morality must embody some kind of social concern or consideration; it cannot be purely prudential or purely aesthetic.

In these terms, view I is the proposal that we conceive of moralities only in the *wider* way, or use the words 'moral' and 'morality' only in the wider sense. It is a monistic view and is favored, if I understand them, by Hare, Ladd, Falk, the existentialists (perhaps, without criterion B), many religious thinkers, and at least some Aristotelians. View II is the proposal that we conceive of moralities only in the *narrower* way, or use 'moral' and 'morality' only in the narrower sense. It too is a monistic view, but one which regards formal conditions like A, B, and C as insufficient to make an AG a morality and insists on the necessity of building in a condition of the kind indicated by D. In fact, recognizing that an AG satisfying criterion D may not be or be taken as rationally definitive or supremely authoritative —a point forcefully made by Falk (64)[1]—view II rejects criterion C in all its forms, not only as a sufficient, but also as a necessary condition of an AG's being a morality. View II is maintained by Toulmin, Baier, Singer, Strawson, and Kemp, among others. I believe that it was once held by Aiken, but was given up by him in favor of view I, perhaps with criterion B left out. View III contends that we ought to employ *both* the wider and the narrower concepts of morality, using 'moral' and 'morality' in both senses, though perhaps in different contexts. It is at least a dualistic view, but may be more pluralistic. Though Falk usually favors view I, as I said, he seems to settle, rather despairingly, for view III in the last paragraph of the essay already referred to (66). In any case, view III is in effect maintained by some of those who insist that 'moral', even in the sense in which it is opposed to 'nonmoral', is ambiguous, but propose to do nothing about it. View IV represents a rather different kind of attempt to have it *both* ways; it too seeks to preserve both "the authoritative and the social associations of 'moral' " (63), but it does so by trying to build into a single concept both criterion C and criterion D. It is, therefore, like view II in being monistic and in espousing the narrower social concept of morality, but like view I in regarding criterion C as necessary—and perhaps A and B also— though not as sufficient. I myself have suggested view IV in a longer paper, also called "The Concept of Morality," which will appear elsewhere.[2]

---

[1] W. D. Falk, "Morality, Self, and Others," in H.–N. Castaneda and G. Nakhnikian, eds., *Morality and the Language of Conduct* (Detroit: Wayne State University Press, 1963), pp. 25–67; page references will appear in parentheses in the text.

[2] In the *University of Colorado Publications in Philosophy*. Compare also an earlier essay, "Recent Conceptions of Morality," in Castaneda and Nakhnikian, pp. 1–24.

Indeed, it suggests itself to a reader of Falk's last paragraph, referred to a moment ago.

2

About view III I shall not say much. The corresponding descriptive-elucidatory theory seems to me to be true, as it does to Falk, Hare, and others, but view III itself is unsatisfactory because it simply proposes to continue the present state of affairs, in which we use the word 'morality' ambiguously for two or more rather different sorts of AG's. View IV, which I recently proposed myself, I still am not entirely ready to reject. Its most dubious feature, to my mind, is the fact that, although it builds in social criterion D, it also makes it senseless for one to ask, "Why should I be moral?" This is a nice trick if it can be done, but it is bound to seem like a trick, at least to opponents of criterion D.

The remaining issue is between view I and view II. Like Falk (65 f.), I think that a historical and semantic case can be made for both of these views, though I am inclined to believe that such evidence favors view II. I shall not argue this now. Instead, I shall first briefly indicate my other reasons for opposing view I, and then try to rebut some objections to view II.

The reasons for my being unhappy with view I are of various sorts. (1) Falk and Hare regard a social definition of morality as "misleading."[3] To me, however, it seems at least as misleading to say that an AG is a moral one provided only that it satisfies such formal conditions as A, B, and C. If saying that an AG is not a morality suggests that it is wicked or at least negligible, saying that it is a morality suggests that it is respectable and ought to be supported by the moral sanctions of society. If saying that an "ought" is nonmoral suggests that it is questionable or unimportant, saying that it is moral suggests that it is socially important and legitimate. And I am somehow more troubled by the latter misleadingness than by the former. (2) Falk insists that we must not "expect morality on all levels to do the same kind of job as the institution of law," and I agree that a morality is and should be a very different kind of AG from law. But I still share Kemp's conviction that, "if by the 'function' of a practice is meant the reason why it exists and is carried on" (Falk's words; 63), then the function of morality is not just to serve as a supreme AG but to make possible "some kind of cooperation or social activity between human beings,"[4] as law does, though not in the same way. Indeed, I do not see how society can recognize as a morality any AG that does not serve such a function to

---

3 Falk, op. cit., pp. 30, 53; R. M. Hare, *Freedom and Reason* (New York: Oxford University Press, 1963), p. 147.

4 J. Kemp, *Reason, Action and Morality* (New York: Humanities Press, Inc., 1964), p. 196.

at least a certain extent. (3) We generally think that a man who takes prudential or aesthetic considerations as final is living by a nonmoral AG (and perhaps also by an immoral one). But, on view I, his AG will have to be regarded as a morality. (4) If any AG, no matter what its character may be, can become a morality simply by being taken seriously enough, universalized, etc., it becomes very difficult to discuss questions about the relation of morality to other AG's. This is shown by the fact that, though Hare seems to admit the desirability of distinguishing the moral and the aesthetic, he does not actually give us a way of distinguishing them, and ends by counting as fully moral personal ideals he himself describes as "very like aesthetic ones" (146, 150). (5) On view I, a conscientious objector or social critic could claim his objections or criticisms to be made on moral grounds, even if they are made on purely aesthetic or prudential grounds, provided only that he takes such grounds to be finally authoritative (and perhaps also is willing to universalize his judgments). (6) View I makes nonsense of all talk of religion as an AG that is somehow above or beyond morality—such as Kierkegaard, Tillich, and others go in for. I am not sure I want to go in for this talk, but I am reluctant to rule it out by definition. (7) Falk cites the case of a daughter tied to a demanding mother, and points out that we may say to her, "You owe it to yourself to break away, hard as it may be on your mother" (49). Here personal oughts appear to be given precedence *over* moral ones. But, on view I, they would thereby *become* moral. (8) View I makes the question whether morality is socially concerned dependent on what the facts about man and the world are. It seems to me preferable, however, to make this a matter of definition and to make the question whether morality is "the rational and autonomous way of life" contingent upon the nature of man and the universe. In fact, I find it hard to believe that Hare and Falk would favor view I if they were not assuming that all or at least most of us would choose a socially considerate AG to live by "on a nonevasive appreciation of all the reasons in the case." (9) View I also makes nonsense of the question, "Why should I be moral?" For one cannot oneself take an AG as supremely authoritative and still ask, sensibly, "Why should I live by it?" It may, of course, be argued that the question, "Why should I be moral?", is, indeed, nonsense— in fact, this has often been argued—but one may at least reasonably doubt that this is so or should be made so by definition.

Only some of the objections to building criterion D, or any "material" condition, into the definition of a morality can be dealt with here. (1) Hare implies that a social definition of morality builds in "utilitarianism" and begs the question against its opponents (163). But I have stated criterion D in such a way as to allow deontological AG's to be moralities, as well as utilitarian ones. In fact, criterion D allows for nationalistic and class moralities, for Nazism, for inequalitarianism—as far as I can see, for anything that Hare himself is really concerned to allow for. I am not even sure that it rules out sadistic AG's. It does rule out AG's that are basically egoistic or aesthetic, but this at least checks with much actual usage. (2) It is argued that view II reads out of the moral party such AG's as those of the Greeks, Spinoza, Nietzsche, the Navaho, etc. But, first, were their AG's consistently and thoroughly nonsocial in their basis? What, for example, about Artistotle's views on justice or Nietzsche's precept, "Be unto thy neighbor an arrow, and a longing for the Superman"? Second, if they were basically nonsocial, should we call them moralities? (3) It might be thought that view II precludes the possibility of there being moral duties to oneself that are not derivative from one's duties to others. However, criterion D, as I have stated, allows that a moral AG may *include* purely self-referential duties and ideals (though I am in fact inclined to doubt that these are moral) ; it insists only that it must include duties or ideals that are basically other-regarding. (4) There is a sense in which a social definition of morality does not "build out" even egoism or aestheticism. It might be, for instance, that the most effective way for one to serve the welfare of others is to do always what is most to ones' own interest. Then, even though one's basic principle would be social, one might adopt an egoistic AG as one's working guide. In this case, however, one's AG would still be moral on view II.[5]

(5) Falk contends that, if we adopt view II, then we demote morality "from its accustomed place of being the sole and final arbiter of right and wrong choice" (65 f.). We do so, however, only in the sense of not making it part of the *definition* of morality that it is the sole and final arbiter. But, even if criterion D is made part of the definition of morality, and not criterion C, it still may be that morality "prescribes what a man would do in his wisdom"—in short, morality might still be the definitive commitment of the honestly reflective person, his sole and final arbiter. Whether this is so or not would then be up to the facts about man and the world. It does follow from view II that morality *may* not be the sole and final arbiter of right and wrong; it does not follow that it *is* not that arbiter. That is, it follows that "Why should I live by a moral AG?" is a sensible question, which is as it should be. (Isn't it?)

(6) Hare implies that any view that includes a material or social criterion in the definition of morality is guilty of "naturalism," i.e., of "making moral questions depend upon conceptual ones" or setting normative questions by definition (163, 187, 195). This raises hackles, specters, and large issues, but I must say a little. I am inclined to think that Hare, MacIntyre, and others who attack view II are too ready to think that 'moral', even in such phrases as 'moral code', 'moral judgment', 'moral

---

[5] Compare, e.g., the position of R. G. Olson, *The Morality of Self-Interest* (New York: Harcourt, Brace & World, Inc., 1965).

rightness', etc., is a normative term like 'right' or 'good', when it is at least prima facie a term of a very different kind; they, rather than Toulmin, may be failing to distinguish sufficiently between 'moral' in the sense in which it is opposed to 'nonmoral' and 'moral' in the sense in which it is opposed to 'immoral'. Be that as it may, it is not clear that my adopting criterion D commits me to any particular normative judgment of a substantive kind, moral or nonmoral (except the judgment that we ought to adopt this criterion). To begin with, asserting that an AG is a moral AG does not commit one to agreeing that acting on it is morally right or good, for one may regard it as a moral AG without accepting it oneself. Does holding that an AG is not a moral AG unless it sometimes judges actions and agents simply on the basis of their effects on the lives of others commit me to saying that not considering effects on others at all is wrong or bad? Certainly it does not commit me to saying that this is wrong or bad in every sense. Does it commit me to regarding it as *morally* bad or wrong? It is tempting to say so, and in the longer paper referred to earlier I did say so. Now I think this was a mistake on my part. For I may agree that an AG is not a moral AG unless it calls for a consideration of the effects on others as such, without myself accepting any moral AG and, hence, without myself making any judgments about what is right or wrong, good or bad, moral or otherwise. On view II, I simply cannot myself make a moral judgment unless I commit myself to considering the effects of my action on others (at least some of them) as such, and I do not commit myself to this merely by agreeing that an AG is a moral one only if it calls for considering effects on others as such.

The point, I suppose, is that criterion D does not specify *what* effects on others (or on persons as such) are to be avoided or promoted. Only if it did specify these would one be begging any substantive moral issue by building it into the concept of a moral code.

(7) Well, there is always the open-question argument, and "them as likes it" have used it to refute alleged definitions of 'moral'.[6] But, however effective this is in the case of clearly normative terms like 'right' and 'good', one must be cautious about using it in the case of 'moral' (as opposed to 'nonmoral'). It will not do to claim, in objection to view II, that one can sensibly say, "This AG calls for a consideration of effects on others as such; but is it right to act on it?", or even "This AG calls for a consideration of effects on others as such; but is it morally right to act on it?" That this will not do follows from what I have said and also from the fact that our problem is not what 'right' means but what 'moral' means, or should be taken

---

[6] A. McIntyre, "What Morality Is Not," *Philosophy*, XXXII (October, 1957), 325–35; cf. my "MacIntyre on Defining Morality," ibid., XXXIII (April, 1958), 158–62. H. D. Aiken makes a similar use of the argument, "The Concept of Moral Objectivity," in Castaneda and Nakhnikian, pp. 69–105.

to mean. To use the open-question argument against view II, one must claim that the question, "This AG calls for a consideration of effects on others as such, for universalization, etc.; but is it a moral AG?", is a sensible question. And it does not seem obvious to me that it is, even in terms of our actual use of the word 'moral' (in the sense in which it is contrasted with 'nonmoral'). Even if it is a sensible question in these terms, however, this fact would do little to show that we ought not to accept view II, since this is a proposal about our future use of 'moral'.

3

Having made my case, such as it is, for view II—or, more accurately, for a certain form of view II—I wish to finish with a line of thought about the idea of morality which may have a larger import. (1) Although I have been defending view II, I am inclined to think that it can be plausibly maintained only if it is combined with a postulate to the effect that it is rational to live by an AG that is moral or socially considerate in the sense indicated by criterion D. That is, I agree with Kant that a rational man can adopt a moral AG only under the presupposition that it is ulti- mately rational for him to live by it even though, for the reasons given, I am reluctant to build this presupposition into the very concept of a morality (as Kant is). (2) In fact, I believe that views I, III, and IV are also plausi- ble only if they are combined with a postulate to the same effect. Then there are four live options in this part of moral philosophy, namely: view II with the postulate indicated, view I with the postulate that the AG we will find rational to live by if we know what we are about (i.e., moral by its criteria) will turn out to be one that calls for a consideration of others or of persons as such, view III with the postulate that what we take to be moral in the wider will turn out to be moral also in the narrower sense, and view IV with the postulate that criteria C and D will turn out not to pull apart for "a man in his wisdom." (3) One might contend that, with these postulates, which all come to the same thing, the four views are essentially equivalent, and this does appear to be true in some sense, though it still seems to me that view II is preferable to the others on the grounds men- tioned before.

(4) The point, I suggest, is that the idea of morality, as we have known it in our history, is the idea of an AG that is somehow *both* rational and social. The idea of morality represents a wager that man and the world are such that these two desiderata will eventually be found to coincide. That this is so is not something that can be proved in our present state of knowl- edge, but neither is it something that has been disproved. It may and must be *postulated*. Kant thought that this postulate must take the form of a belief that there is a God who sees to it that a life of moral virtue is rewarded by the happiness it deserves. But it need not take this form. In

some form or other it is made by Plato and Aristotle, by Butler and Sidgwick, and by all of the religious and idealistic thinkers who believe that he
who loses his life for morality's sake shall gain it. Even John Dewey postulates a coincidence of a kind between the happy life and the socially considerate and interested one, and, though Reinhold Niebuhr labels Dewey's
faith naive and touching, he himself similarly believes that love is the true
way to self-realization. I have already suggested that Falk and Hare, even
when they are most in favor of view I, may themselves be betting that the
AG a fully rational, informed, and nonevasive man would choose under
its criteria would be a socially considerate one.

I have no wish to sound mystical. It does not seem to me that the
postulate is at all plausible if it is understood as saying that an individual is
never a loser in prudential terms—i.e., in terms of his own interest or happiness—by doing the socially moral thing. But is the finally rational way of
life for the individual to be identified with that which is for his own greatest
happiness? Butler and Kant thought that it was, but Falk seems to me to be
on a better track when he insists that rational personal oughts need not
take a prudential form.[7] The finally rational course, he suggests, is "what
a man would do in his wisdom—if he were to consider things widely, looking past the immediate concerns of self and giving essentials due weight
before incidentals"; and it must not simply be assumed that this is the course
known as egoism. Even if we identify being rational with calm deliberation
in the light of full knowledge about what one wants and how to get it, it
does not follow that the rational life is that of cool self-love. Whether it is
or not depends on what one wants when one is enlightened about himself
and his world. One might then want exactly the kind of world that a socially
considerate AG would call for, even at the cost of some sacrifice on one's
own part. There is some evidence in modern psychology—so Erich Fromm
and others have been arguing—that this is in fact the case. At least it may
be that, as our insight into man, society, and the universe increases, we shall
more and more come to see that the finally rational way of life for the individual is or at least may be precisely the socially considerate one.

---

[7] Falk, op. cit., pp. 33–38. I think Aiken would agree; see op. cit.

Section Four
Why Should I Be Moral?

The main controversy regarding the question "Why should I be moral?" is not over whether a certain answer to it is correct, but whether the question is, in the first place, a meaningful philosophical question. H. A. Prichard, Stephen Toulmin, and J. C. Thornton, among others, have denied the meaningfulness of the question, while Kurt Baier and Kai Nielsen have argued for its meaningfulness. Both the critics and the defenders of the meaningfulness of the question have based their respective cases on a detailed analysis of what the question is asking.

H. A. Prichard, in his classic paper "Does Moral Philosophy Rest on a Mistake?," contends that the history of moral philosophy, as usually understood, rests upon a mistake that is parallel to one made in theory of knowledge. What we want, Prichard says, is a proof that justifies morality, i.e., a proof that we really ought to do what we in our nonreflective consciousness have hitherto believed we morally ought to do. This, Prichard contends, is impossible, impossible because the apprehension of what we morally ought to do is immediate, direct, and self-evident and in that respect similar to our knowledge of mathematical truths. If a proof or any additional support is offered in support of what we morally ought to do, it can, at best, only make us want to do what we morally ought to do. Additional considerations can motivate, but not justify. Thus, on Prichard's view it cannot be proven that we ought to be moral. To ask for a proof of morality is to ask an illegitimate question, illegitimate because a proof is neither necessary nor possible.

Prichard's case against the meaningfulness of the question "Why should I be moral?" rests upon his moral epistemology, namely, his intuitionism, and his interpretation of the question as asking for a proof for morality. However, it is possible to make a case against the meaningfulness of the question without embracing what is for many a very suspect moral epistemology. Stephen Toulmin, for example, in "The Logic of Moral Reasoning, and Reason and Faith," denies the meaningfulness of the question on logical rather than

epistemological grounds. He understands the question as asking "Why ought one to do what is right?" To say that something is right, Toulmin argues, logically implies that one ought
to do it. Hence, the original question is vacuous, for it turns
out to be asking "Why ought one to do what one ought to
do?" Thus, to ask "Why should I be moral?" is to ask a
"limiting" question. Ethical reasoning can provide justification for doing this or doing that, for adopting this social
practice or that, but, on Toulmin's view, providing a justification of morality as opposed to expediency is not a philosophical task.

However, Kurt Baier argues in "Why Should We Be
Moral?" that in asking for the case for morality, one is asking
"Are moral reasons superior to reasons of enlightened self-
interest?" and "What reasons could there be for being moral?"
These questions, Baier maintains, are meaningful and all come
to the same thing. He contends that moral reasons are superior
to reasons of self-interest because the universal obedience to
rules of self-interest must lead to what Thomas Hobbes calls
the state of nature. On the other hand, universal obedience
to moral rules would produce a state of affairs which would
serve everyone's interest. By examining these two alternative
worlds, we can see that the first is the better world. Since
the very purpose of a morality is to provide reasons that
override reasons of self-interest when everyone's following
self-interest would be harmful to everyone, moral reasons
are superior to reasons of self-interest. This shows, in Baier's
opinion, that one ought to be moral. For to ask "What
ought I to do?" is to ask "What course of action is supported
by the best reasons?" Baier acknowledges that even though
someone may maximize his own self-interest by not always
adhering to moral rules, the rules of morality are, nevertheless, in the interest of everyone alike. For to say that rules of
morality are in the interest of everyone alike, means that it
is better for everyone that a morality, rather than self-
interest, should be acknowledged as supplying the decisive
action-guiding considerations.

J. C. Thornton in "Can the Moral Point of View Be
Justified?" remains unconvinced by Baier's case for the moral
point of view. He contends that Baier has shifted the question from "Why should I be moral?" (or, "Should anyone
do what is morally right when doing so is not to his advantage and why?") to "Why should we be moral?" (or, "What

is the case for the institution of morality in general?"). Thornton believes that Baier has, at best, only shown that there are weightier reasons for everyone always doing what is morally right than for everyone always following self-interest. Be this as it may, Thornton argues, this consideration does not touch the question of why any single individual should follow the dictates of morality rather than those of self-interest. Moreover, the question "Why should I be moral?," as Baier poses it, is a pseudo-question. For to say "I should do what is morally right even when it is not in my enlightened self-interest" expresses either a tautology or a contradiction. The statement expresses a tautology if the term "should" means "morally should." For then one would be saying "I morally should do what is morally right, even when doing so is not in my enlightened self-interest." On the other hand, the statement expresses a contradiction if "should" is used in its self-interest sense. For then one would be saying "It is in my enlightened self-interest to do what is morally right, even when doing so is not in my enlightened self-interest." Nevertheless, Thornton contends that questions regarding the ultimate basis for a "rational" justification of an action can be meaningfully raised and answered.

Notwithstanding the kinds of considerations that Thornton has offered, Kai Nielsen still maintains that the question "Why should I be moral?" admits of a meaningful interpretation. An agent may, Nielsen argues, have no doubts about the benefit of morality as a social institution, be aware that his question is not a moral one, and realize that it would be contradictory for someone to give him a reason in accord with his enlightened self-interest for acting counter to his enlightened self-interest. Nevertheless, an agent can intelligibly ask "Why should I be moral?" if he is asking for a reason for his adopting one point of view rather than another. The question here is whether there are any good reasons for an individual to adopt the moral point of view rather than the egoistic point of view. Or does practical reason come to an end here? If it does, then is there nothing left but an arbitrary choice, as the moral subjectivists would argue? Nielsen contends that a choice is involved, but it need not be arbitrary.

Does Moral Philosophy
Rest on a Mistake?

H. A. PRICHARD

Probably to most students of Moral Philosophy there comes a time when they feel a vague sense of dissatisfaction with the whole subject. And the sense of dissatisfaction tends to grow rather than to diminish. It is not so much that the positions, and still more the arguments, of particular thinkers seem unconvincing, though this is true. It is rather that the aim of the subject becomes increasingly obscure. 'What,' it is asked, 'are we really going to learn by Moral Philosophy?' 'What are books on Moral Philosophy really trying to show, and when their aim is clear, why are they so unconvincing and artificial?' And again: 'Why is it so difficult to substitute anything better?' Personally, I have been led by growing dissatisfaction of this kind to wonder whether the reason may not be that the subject, at any rate as usually understood, consists in the attempt to answer an improper question. And in this article I shall venture to contend that the existence of the whole subject, as usually understood, rests on a mistake, and on a mistake parallel to that on which rests, as I think, the subject usually called the Theory of Knowledge.

If we reflect on our own mental history or on the history of the subject, we feel no doubt about the nature of the demand which originates the subject. Any one who, stimulated by education, has come to feel the force of the various obligations in life, at some time or other comes to feel the irksomeness of carrying them out, and to recognize the sacrifice of interest involved; and, if thoughtful, he inevitably puts to himself the question: 'Is there really a reason why I should act in the ways in which hitherto I have thought I ought to act? May I not have been all the time under an illusion in so thinking? Should not I really be justified in simply trying to have a good time?' Yet, like Glaucon, feeling that somehow he ought after all to act in these ways, he asks for a *proof* that this feeling is justified. In other words, he asks '*Why* should I do these things?', and his and other people's moral philosophizing is an attempt to supply the answer, i.e. to supply by a process of reflection a proof of the truth of what he and they have prior to reflection believed immediately or without proof. This frame of mind seems to present a close parallel to the frame of mind which originates the Theory of Knowledge. Just as the recognition that the doing of our duty often vitally interferes with the satisfaction of our inclinations leads us to

From Mind, *XXI (1912). Reprinted by permission of* Mind.

wonder whether we really ought to do what we usually call our duty, so the recognition that we and others are liable to mistakes in knowledge generally leads us, as it did Descartes, to wonder whether hitherto we may not have been always mistaken. And just as we try to find a proof, based on the general consideration of action and of human life, that we ought to act in the ways usually called moral, so we, like Descartes, propose by a process of reflection on our thinking to find a test of knowledge, i.e. a principle by applying which we can show that a certain condition of mind was really knowledge, a condition which *ex hypothesi* existed independently of the process of reflection.

Now, how has the moral question been answered? So far as I can see, the answers all fall, and fall from the necessities of the case, into one of two species. *Either* they state that we ought to do so and so, because, as we see when we fully apprehend the facts, doing so will be for our good, i.e. really, as I would rather say, for our advantage, or, better still, for our happiness; *or* they state that we ought to do so and so, because something realized either in or by the action is good. In other words, the reason 'why' is stated in terms either of the agent's happiness or of the goodness of something involved in the action.

To see the prevalence of the former species of answer, we have only to consider the history of Moral Philosophy. To take obvious instances, Plato, Hutcheson, Paley, Mill, each in his own way seeks at bottom to convince the individual that he ought to act in so-called moral ways by showing that to do so will really be for his happiness. Plato is perhaps the most significant instance, because of all philosophers he is the one to whom we are least willing to ascribe a mistake on such matters, and a mistake on his part would be evidence of the deep-rootedness of the tendency to make it. To show that Plato really justifies morality by its profitableness, it is only necessary to point out (1) that the very formulation of the thesis to be met, viz. that justice is ἀλλότριον ἀγαθόν [someone else's good] implies that any refutation must consist in showing that justice is οἰκεῖον ἀγαθόν [one's own good], i.e., really, as the context shows, one's own advantage, and (2) that the term λυσιτελεῖν [to be profitable] supplies the key not only to the problem but also to its solution.

The tendency to justify acting on moral rules in this way is natural. For if, as often happens, we put to ourselves the question 'Why should we do so and so?', we are satisfied by being convinced either that the doing so will lead to something which we want (e.g. that taking certain medicine will heal our disease), or that the doing so itself, as we see when we appreciate its nature, is something that we want or should like, e.g. playing golf. The formulation of the question implies a state of unwillingness or indifference towards the action, and we are brought into a condition of willingness by the answer. And this process seems to be precisely what we desire

when we ask, e.g., 'Why should we keep our engagements to our own loss?';
for it is just the fact that the keeping of our engagements runs counter to
the satisfaction of our desires which produced the question.

The answer is, of course, not an answer, for it fails to convince us that
we ought to keep our engagements; even if successful on its own lines, it
only makes us *want* to keep them. And Kant was really only pointing out
this fact when he distinguished hypothetical and categorical imperatives,
even though he obscured the nature of the fact by wrongly describing his
so-called 'hypothetical imperatives' as imperatives. But if this answer be no
answer, what other can be offered? Only, it seems, an answer which
bases the obligation to do something on the *goodness* either of something
to which the act leads or of the act itself. Suppose, when wondering whether
we really ought to act in the ways usually called moral, we are told as a
means of resolving our doubt that those acts are right which produce
happiness. We at once ask: 'Whose happiness?' If we are told 'Our own
happiness', then, though we shall lose our hesitation to act in these ways,
we shall not recover our sense that we ought to do so. But how can this
result be avoided? Apparently, only by being told one of two things: *either*
that anyone's happiness is a thing good in itself, and that *therefore* we
ought to do whatever will produce it, *or* that working for happiness is itself
good, and that the intrinsic goodness of such an action is the reason why
we ought to do it. The advantage of this appeal to the goodness of something consists in the fact that it avoids reference to desire, and, instead,
refers to something impersonal and objective. In this way it seems possible
to avoid the resolution of obligation into inclination. But just for this reason
it is of the essence of the answer, that to be effective it must neither include
nor involve the view that the apprehension of the goodness of anything
necessarily arouses the desire for it. Otherwise the answer resolves itself into
a form of the former answer by substituting desire or inclination for the
sense of obligation, and in this way it loses what seems its special advantage.

Now it seems to me that both forms of this answer break down, though
each for a different reason.

Consider the first form. It is what may be called Utilitarianism in the
generic sense, in which what is good is not limited to pleasure. It takes its
stand upon the distinction between something which is not itself an action,
but which can be produced by an action, and the action which will produce
it, and contends that if something which is not an action is good, then we
ought to undertake the action which will, directly or indirectly, originate it.[1]

But this argument, if it is to restore the sense of obligation to act, must
presuppose an intermediate link, viz. the further thesis that what is good
ought to be.[2] The necessity of this link is obvious. An 'ought', if it is to be

----

[1] Cf. Dr. Rashdall's *Theory of Good and Evil*, I, 138.
[2] Dr. Rashdall, if I understand him rightly, supplies this link (cf. ibid., 135–36).

derived at all, can only be derived from another 'ought'. Moreover, this link tacitly presupposes another, viz. that the apprehension that something good which is not an action ought to be involves just the feeling of imperativeness or obligation which is to be aroused by the thought of the action which will originate it. Otherwise the argument will not lead us to feel the obligation to produce it by the action. And, surely, both this link and its implication are false.³ The word 'ought' refers to actions and to actions alone. The proper language is never 'So and so ought to be', but 'I ought to do so and so'. Even if we are sometimes moved to say that the world or something in it is not what it ought to be, what we really mean is that God or some human being has not made something what he ought to have made it. And it is merely stating another side of this fact to urge that we can only feel the imperativeness upon us of something which is in our power; for it is actions and actions alone which, directly at least, are in our power.

Perhaps, however, the best way to see the failure of this view is to see its failure to correspond to our actual moral convictions. Suppose we ask ourselves whether our sense that we ought to pay our debts or to tell the truth arises from our recognition that in doing so we should be originating something good, e.g. material comfort in *A* or true belief in *B*, i.e. suppose we ask ourselves whether it is this aspect of the action which leads to our recognition that we ought to do it. We at once and without hesitation answer 'No'. Again, if we take as our illustration our sense that we ought to act justly as between two parties, we have, if possible, even less hesitation in giving a similar answer; for the balance of resulting good may be, and often is, not on the side of justice.

At best it can only be maintained that there is this element of truth in the Utilitarian view, that unless we recognize that something which an act will originate is good, we should not recognize that we ought to do the action. Unless we thought knowledge a good thing, it may be urged, we should not think that we ought to tell the truth; unless we thought pain a bad thing, we should not think the infliction of it, without special reason, wrong. But this is not to imply that the badness of error is the reason why it is wrong to lie, or the badness of pain the reason why we ought not to inflict it without special cause.⁴

It is, I think, just because this form of the view is so plainly at variance with our moral consciousness that we are driven to adopt the other form of the view, viz. that the act is good in itself and that its intrinsic goodness

³ When we speak of anything, e.g., of some emotion or of some quality of a human being, as good, we never dream in our ordinary consciousness of going on to say that therefore it ought to be.

⁴ It may be noted that if the badness of pain were the reason why we ought not to inflict pain on another, it would equally be a reason why we ought not to inflict pain on ourselves; yet, though we should allow the wanton infliction of pain on ourselves to be foolish, we should not think of describing it as wrong.

is the reason why it ought to be done. It is this form which has always made the most serious appeal; for the goodness of the act itself seems more closely related to the obligation to do it than that of its mere consequences or results, and therefore, if obligation is to be based on the goodness of something, it would seem that this goodness should be that of the act itself. Moreover, the view gains plausibility from the fact that moral actions are most conspicuously those to which the term 'intrinsically good' is applicable.

Nevertheless this view, though perhaps less superficial, is equally untenable. For it leads to precisely the dilemma which faces everyone who tries to solve the problem raised by Kant's theory of the good will. To see this, we need only consider the nature of the acts to which we apply the term 'intrinsically good'.

There is, of course, no doubt that we approve and even admire certain actions, and also that we should describe them as good, and as good in themselves. But it is, I think, equally unquestionable that our approval and our use of the term 'good' is always in respect of the motive and refers to actions which have been actually done and of which we think we know the motive. Further, the actions of which we approve and which we should describe as intrinsically good are of two and only two kinds. They are either actions in which the. agent did what he did because he thought he ought to do it, or actions of which the motive was a desire prompted by some good emotion, such as gratitude, affection, family feeling, or public spirit, the most prominent of such desires in books on Moral Philosophy being that ascribed to what is vaguely called benevolence. For the sake of simplicity I omit the case of actions done partly from some such desire and partly from a sense of duty; for even if all good actions are done from a combination of these motives, the argument will not be affected. The dilemma is this. If the motive in respect of which we think an action good is the sense of obligation, then so far from the sense that we ought to do it being derived from our apprehension of its goodness, our apprehension of its goodness will presuppose the sense that we ought to do it. In other words, in this case the recognition that the act is good will plainly *presuppose* the recognition that the act is right, whereas the view under consideration is that the recognition of the goodness of the act *gives rise* to the recognition of its rightness. On the other hand, if the motive in respect of which we think an action good is some intrinsically good desire, such as the desire to help a friend, the recognition of the goodness of the act will equally fail to give rise to the sense of obligation to do it. For we cannot feel that we ought to do that the doing of which is *ex hypothesi* prompted solely by the desire to do it.[5]

---

[5] It is, I think, on this latter horn of the dilemma that Martineau's view falls; cf. *Types of Ethical Theory*, Part II, Book I.

The fallacy underlying the view is that while to base the rightness of an act upon its intrinsic goodness implies that the goodness in question is that of the motive, in reality the rightness or wrongness of an act has nothing to do with any question of motives at all. For, as any instance will show, the rightness of an action concerns an action not in the fuller sense of the term in which we include the motive in the action, but in the narrower and commoner sense in which we distinguish an action from its motive and mean by an action merely the conscious origination of something, an origination which on different occasions or in different people may be prompted by different motives. The question 'Ought I to pay my bills?' really means simply 'Ought I to bring about my tradesmen's possession of what by my previous acts I explicitly or implicitly promised them?' There is, and can be, no question of whether I ought to pay my debts from a particular motive. No doubt we know that if we pay our bills we shall pay them with a motive, but in considering whether we ought to pay them we inevitably think of the act in abstraction from the motive. Even if we knew what our motive would be if we did the act, we should not be any nearer an answer to the question.

Moreover, if we eventually pay our bills from fear of the county court, we shall still have done *what* we ought, even though we shall not have done it *as* we ought. The attempt to bring in the motive involves a mistake similar to that involved in supposing that we can will to will. To feel that I ought to pay my bills is to be *moved towards* paying them. But what I can be moved towards must always be an action and not an action in which I am moved in a particular way, i.e. an action from a particular motive; otherwise I should be moved towards being moved, which is impossible. Yet the view under consideration involves this impossibility, for it really resolves the sense that I ought to do so and so, into the sense that I ought to be moved to do it in a particular way.[6]

So far my contentions have been mainly negative, but they form, I think, a useful, if not a necessary, introduction to what I take to be the truth. This I will now endeavor to state, first formulating what, as I think, is the real nature of our apprehension or appreciation of moral obligations, and then applying the result to elucidate the question of the existence of Moral Philosophy.

The sense of obligation to do, or of the rightness of, an action of a particular kind is absolutely underivative or immediate. The rightness of an action consists in its being the origination of something of a certain kind *A* in a situation of a certain kind, a situation consisting in a certain

---

6 It is of course not denied here that an action done from a particular motive may be *good*; it is only denied that the *rightness* of an action depends on its being done with a particular motive.

relation *B* of the agent to others or to his own nature. To appreciate its rightness two preliminaries may be necessary. We may have to follow out the consequences of the proposed action more fully than we have hitherto done, in order to realize that in the action we should originate *A*. Thus we may not appreciate the wrongness of telling a certain story until we realize that we should thereby be hurting the feelings of one of our audience. Again, we may have to take into account the relation *B* involved in the situation, which we had hitherto failed to notice. For instance, we may not appreciate the obligation to give *X* a present, until we remember that he has done us an act of kindness. But, given that by a process which is, of course, merely a process of general and not of moral thinking we come to recognize that the proposed act is one by which we shall originate *A* in a relation *B*, then we appreciate the obligation immediately or directly, the appreciation being an activity of *moral* thinking. We recognize, for instance, that this performance of a service to *X*, who has done us a service, just in virtue of its being the performance of a service to one who has rendered a service to the would-be agent, ought to be done by us. This apprehension is immediate, in precisely the sense in which a mathematical apprehension is immediate, e.g. the apprehension that this three-sided figure, in virtue of its being three-sided, must have three angles. Both apprehensions are immediate in the sense that in both insight into the nature of the subject leads us to recognize its possession of the predicate; and it is only stating this fact from the other side to say that in both cases the fact apprehended is self-evident.

The plausibility of the view that obligations are not self-evident but need proof lies in the fact that an act which is referred to as an obligation may be incompletely stated, what I have called the preliminaries to appreciating the obligation being incomplete. If, e.g., we refer to the act of repaying *X* by a present merely as giving *X* a present, it appears, and indeed is, necessary to give a reason. In other words, wherever a moral act is regarded in this incomplete way the question '*Why* should I do it?' is perfectly legitimate. This fact suggests, but suggests wrongly, that even if the nature of the act is completely stated, it is still necessary to give a reason, or, in other words, to supply a proof.

The relations involved in obligations of various kinds are, of course, very different. The relation in certain cases is a relation to others due to a past act of theirs or ours. The obligation to repay a benefit involves a relation due to a past act of the benefactor. The obligation to pay a bill involves a relation due to a past act of ours in which we have either said or implied that we would make a certain return for something which we have asked for and received. On the other hand, the obligation to speak the truth implies no such definite act; it involves a relation consisting in the fact that others are trusting us to speak the truth, a relation the apprehension of which gives rise to the sense that communication of the truth is something owing by us to them. Again, the obligation not to hurt the feelings of another involves no special relation of us to that other, i.e. no relation other than that involved in our both being men, and men in one and the same world. Moreover, it seems that the relation involved in an obligation need not be a relation to another at all. Thus we should admit that there is an obligation to overcome our natural timidity or greediness, and that this involves no relations to others. Still there is a relation involved, viz. a relation to our own disposition. It is simply because we can and because others cannot directly modify our disposition that it is our business to improve it, and that it is not theirs, or, at least, not theirs to the same extent.

The negative side of all this is, of course, that we do not come to appreciate an obligation by an *argument*, i.e. by a process of nonmoral thinking, and that, in particular, we do not do so by an argument of which a premise is the ethical but not moral activity of appreciating the goodness either of the act or of a consequence of the act; i.e. that our sense of the rightness of an act is not a conclusion from our appreciation of the goodness either of it or of anything else.

It will probably be urged that on this view our various obligations form, like Aristotle's categories, an unrelated chaos in which it is impossible to acquiesce. For, according to it, the obligation to repay a benefit, or to pay a debt, or to keep a promise, presupposes a previous act of another; whereas the obligation to speak the truth or not to harm another does not; and, again, the obligation to remove our timidity involves no relations to others at all. Yet, at any rate, an effective *argumentum ad hominem* is at hand in the fact that the various qualities which we recognize as good are equally unrelated; e.g. courage, humility, and interest in knowledge. If, as is plainly the case, ἀγαθά differ ᾗ ἀγαθά [Goods differ qua goods], why should not obligations equally differ *qua* their obligatoriness? Moreover, if this were not so there could in the end be only one obligation, which is palpably contrary to fact.[7]

Certain observations will help to make the view clearer.

---

[7] Two other objections may be anticipated: (1) that obligations cannot be self-evident, since many actions regarded as obligations by some are not so regarded by others, and (2) that if obligations are self-evident, the problem of how we ought to act in the presence of conflicting obligations is insoluble.

To the first I should reply:

(a) That the appreciation of an obligation is, of course, only possible for a developed moral being, and that different degrees of development are possible.

(b) That the failure to recognize some particular obligation is usually due to the fact that, owing to a lack of thoughtfulness, what I have called the preliminaries to this recognition are incomplete.

In the first place, it may seem that the view, being—as it is—avowedly put forward in opposition to the view that what is right is derived from what is good, must itself involve the opposite of this, viz. the Kantian posi-that what is good is based upon what is right, i.e. that an act, if it be good, is good because it is right. But this is not so. For, on the view put forward, the rightness of a right action lies solely in the origination in which the act consists, whereas the intrinsic goodness of an action lies solely in its motive; and this implies that a morally good action is morally good not simply because it is a right action but because it is a right action done because it is right, i.e. from a sense of obligation. And this implication, it may be remarked incidentally, seems plainly true.

In the second place, the view involves that when, or rather so far as, we act from a sense of obligation, we have no purpose or end. By a 'purpose' or 'end' we really mean something the existence of which we desire, and desire of the existence of which leads us to act. Usually our purpose is something which the act will originate, as when we turn round in order to look at a picture. But it may be the action itself, i.e. the origination of something, as when we hit a golf ball into a hole or kill someone out of revenge.[8] Now if by a purpose we mean something the existence of which we desire and desire for which leads us to act, then plainly, so far as we act from a sense of obligation, we have no purpose, consisting either in the action or in anything which it will produce. This is so obvious that it scarcely seems worth pointing out. But I do so for two reasons. (1) If we fail to scrutinize the meaning of the terms 'end' and 'purpose', we are apt to assume un-critically that all deliberate action, i.e. action proper, must have a purpose; we then become puzzled both when we look for the purpose of an action done from a sense of obligation, and also when we try to apply to such an action the distinction of means and end, the truth all the time being that since there is no end, there is no means either. (2) The attempt to base the sense of obligation on the recognition of the goodness of something is really an attempt to find a purpose in a moral action in the shape of something

---

(c) That the view put forward is consistent with the admission that, owing to a lack of thoughtfulness, even the best men are blind to many of their obligations, and that in the end our obligations are seen to be coextensive with almost the whole of our life.

To the second objection I should reply that obligation admits of degrees, and that where obligations conflict, the decision of what we ought to do turns not on the question 'Which of the alternative courses of action will originate the greater good?' but on the question 'Which is the greater obligation?'

[8] It is no objection to urge that an action cannot be its own purpose, since the purpose of something cannot be the thing itself. For, speaking strictly, the purpose is not the *action's* purpose but *our* purpose, and there is no contradiction in holding that our purpose in acting may be the action.

good which, as good, we want. And the expectation that the goodness of something underlies an obligation disappears as soon as we cease to look for a purpose.

The thesis, however, that, so far as we act from a sense of obligation, we have no purpose must not be misunderstood. It must not be taken either to mean or to imply that so far as we so act we have no *motive*. No doubt in ordinary speech the words 'motive' and 'purpose' are usually treated as correlatives, 'motive' standing for the desire which induces us to act, and 'purpose' standing for the object of this desire. But this is only because, when we are looking for the motive of the action, say, of some crime, we are usually presupposing that the act in question is prompted by a desire and not by the sense of obligation. At bottom, however, we mean by a motive what moves us to act; a sense of obligation does sometimes move us to act; and in our ordinary consciousness we should not hesitate to allow that the action we were considering might have had as its motive a sense of obligation. Desire and the sense of obligation are coordinate forms or species of motive.

In the third place, if the view put forward be right, we must sharply distinguish morality and virtue as independent, though related, species of goodness, neither being an aspect of something of which the other is an aspect, nor again a form or species of the other, nor again something deducible from the other; and we must at the same time allow that it is possible to do the same act either virtuously or morally or in both ways at once. And surely this is true. An act, to be virtuous, must, as Aristotle saw, be done willingly or with pleasure; as such it is just not done from a sense of obligation but from some desire which is intrinsically good, as arising from some intrinsically good emotion. Thus, in an act of generosity the motive is the desire to help another arising from sympathy with that other; in an act which is courageous and no more, i.e. in an act which is not at the same time an act of public spirit or family affection or the like, we prevent ourselves from being dominated by a feeling of terror, desiring to do so from a sense of shame at being terrified. The goodness of such an act is different from the goodness of an act to which we apply the term moral in the strict and narrow sense, viz. an act done from a sense of obligation. Its goodness lies in the intrinsic goodness of the emotion and of the consequent desire under which we act, the goodness of this motive being different from the goodness of the moral motive proper, viz. the sense of duty or obligation. Nevertheless, at any rate in certain cases, an act can be done either virtuously or morally or in both ways at once. It is possible to repay a benefit either from desire to repay it, or from the feeling that we ought to do so, or from both motives combined. A doctor may tend his patients either from a desire arising out of interest in his patients or in the exercise of skill, or from a sense of duty, or from a desire and a sense of duty combined. Further, although we recognize that in each case the act possesses an intrinsic goodness, we regard that action as the best in which both motives are combined; in other words, we regard as the really best man the man in whom virtue and morality are united.

It may be objected that the distinction between the two kinds of motive is untenable, on the ground that the *desire* to repay a benefit, for example, is only the manifestation of that which manifests itself as the *sense of obligation* to repay whenever we think of something in the action which is other than the repayment and which we should not like, such as the loss or pain involved. Yet the distinction can, I think, easily be shown to be tenable. For, in the analogous case of revenge, the desire to return the injury and the sense that, we ought not to do so, leading, as they do, in opposite directions, are plainly distinct; and the obviousness of the distinction here seems to remove any difficulty in admitting the existence of a parallel distinction between the desire to return a benefit and the sense that we ought to return it.[9]

Further, the view implies that an obligation can no more be based on or derived from a virtue than a virtue can be derived from an obligation, in which latter case a virtue would consist in carrying out an obligation. And the implication is surely true and important. Take the case of courage. It is untrue to urge that, since courage is a virtue, we ought to act courageously. It is and must be untrue, because, as we see in the end, to feel an obligation to act courageously would involve a contradiction. For, as I have urged before, we can only feel an obligation to *act*; we cannot feel an obligation to *act from a certain desire*, in this case the desire to conquer one's feelings of terror arising from the sense of shame which they arouse. Moreover, if the sense of obligation to act in a particular way leads to an action, the action will be an action done from a sense of obligation, and therefore not, if the above analysis of virtue be right, an act of courage.

The mistake of supposing that there can be an obligation to act courageously seems to arise from two causes. In the first place, there is often an obligation to do that which involves the conquering or controlling of

---

[9] This sharp distinction of virtue and morality as coordinate and independent forms of goodness will explain a fact which otherwise it is difficult to account for. If we turn from books on Moral Philosophy to any vivid account of human life and action such as we find in Shakespeare, nothing strikes us more than the comparative remoteness of the discussions of Moral Philosophy from the facts of actual life. Is not this largely because, while Moral Philosophy has, quite rightly, concentrated its attention on the fact of obligation, in the case of many of those whom we admire most and whose lives are of the greatest interest, the sense of obligation, though it may be an important, is not a dominating factor in their lives?

our fear in the doing of it, e.g. the obligation to walk along the side of a precipice to fetch a doctor for a member of our family. Here the acting on the obligation is externally, though only externally, the same as an act of courage proper. In the second place there is an obligation to acquire courage, i.e. to do such things as will enable us afterwards to act courageously, and this may be mistaken for an obligation to act courageously. The same considerations can, of course, be applied, *mutatis mutandis*, to the other virtues.

The fact, if it be a fact, that virtue is no basis for morality will explain what otherwise it is difficult to account for, viz. the extreme sense of dissatisfaction produced by a close reading of Aristotle's *Ethics*. Why is the *Ethics* so disappointing? Not, I think, because it really answers two radically different questions as if they were one: (1) 'What is the happy life?' (2) 'What is the virtuous life?' It is, rather, because Aristotle does not do what we as moral philosophers want him to do, viz. to convince us that we really ought to do what in our nonreflective consciousness we have hitherto believed we ought to do, or if not, to tell us what, if any, are the other things which we really ought to do, and to prove to us that he is right. Now, if what I have just been contending is true, a systematic account of the virtuous character cannot possibly satisfy this demand. At best it can only make clear to us the details of one of our obligations, viz. the obligation to make ourselves better men; but the achievement of this does not help us to discover what we ought to do in life as a whole, and why; to think that it did would be to think that our only business in life was self-improvement. Hence it is not surprising that Aristotle's account of the good man strikes us as almost wholly of academic value, with little relation to our real demand, which is formulated in Plato's words: οὐ γὰρ περὶ τοῦ ἐπιυχόντος ὁ λόγος, ἀλλὰ περὶ τοῦ ὄντινα τρόπον χρὴ ζῆν [for no light matter is at stake, nothing less than the rule of human life].

I am not, of course, *criticizing* Aristotle for failing to satisfy this demand, except so far as here and there he leads us to think that he intends to satisfy it. For my main contention is that the demand cannot be satisfied, and cannot be satisfied because it is illegitimate. Thus we are brought to the question: 'Is there really such a thing as Moral Philosophy, and, if there is, in what sense?'

We should first consider the parallel case—as it appears to be—of the Theory of Knowledge. As I urged before, at some time or other in the history of all of us, if we are thoughtful, the frequency of our own and of others' mistakes is bound to lead to the reflection that possibly we and others have *always* been mistaken in consequence of some radical defect of our faculties. In consequence, certain things which previously we should have said without hesitation that we *knew*, as e.g. that $4 \times 7 = 28$, become subject to doubt; we become able only to say that we thought we knew these things. We inevitably go on to look for some general procedure by which we can ascertain that a given condition of mind is really one of knowledge. And this involves the search for a criterion of knowledge, i.e. for a principle by applying which we can settle that a given state of mind is really knowledge. The search for this criterion and the application of it, when found, is what is called the Theory of Knowledge. The search implies that instead of its being the fact that the knowledge that A is B is obtained directly by consideration of the nature of A and B, the knowledge that A is B, in the full or complete sense, can only be obtained by first knowing that A is B, and then knowing that we knew it by applying a criterion, such as Descartes's principle that what we clearly and distinctly conceive is true.

Now it is easy to show that the doubt whether A is B, based on this speculative or general ground, could, if genuine, never be set at rest. For if, in order really to know that A is B, we must first know that we knew it, then really, to know that we knew it, we must first know that we knew that we knew it. But—what is more important—it is also easy to show that this doubt is not a genuine doubt but rests on a confusion the exposure of which removes the doubt. For when we *say* we doubt whether our previous condition was one of knowledge, what we *mean*, if we mean anything at all, is that we doubt whether our previous *belief* was *true*, a belief which we should express as the *thinking* that A is B. For in order to doubt whether our previous condition was one of knowledge, we have to think of it not as knowledge but as only belief, and our only question can be 'Was this belief true?' But as soon as we see that we are thinking of our previous condition as only one of belief, we see that what we are now doubting is not what we first *said* we were doubting, viz. whether a previous condition of knowledge was really knowledge. Hence, to remove the doubt, it is only necessary to appreciate the real nature of our consciousness in apprehending, e.g. that $7 \times 4 = 28$, and thereby see that it was no mere condition of believing but a condition of knowing, and then to notice that in our subsequent doubt what we are really doubting is not whether this consciousness was really knowledge, but whether a consciousness of another kind, viz. a belief that $7 \times 4 = 28$, was true. We thereby see that though a doubt based on speculative grounds is possible, it is not a doubt concerning what we believed the doubt concerned, and that a doubt concerning this latter is impossible.

Two results follow. In the first place, if, as is usually the case, we mean by the 'Theory of Knowledge' the knowledge which supplies the answer to the question 'Is what we have hitherto thought knowledge really knowledge?', there is and can be no such thing, and the supposition that there can is simply due to a confusion. There can be no answer to an illegitimate question, except that the question is illegitimate. Nevertheless the question is one which we continue to put until we realize the inevitable immediacy of knowledge. And it is positive knowledge that knowledge is immediate and neither can be, nor needs to be, improved or vindicated by the further knowledge that it was knowledge. This positive knowledge sets at rest the inevitable doubt, and, so far as by the 'Theory of Knowledge' is meant this knowledge, then even though this knowledge be the knowledge that there is no Theory of Knowledge in the former sense, to that extent the Theory of Knowledge exists.

In the second place, suppose we come genuinely to doubt whether, e.g., $7 \times 4 = 28$ owing to a genuine doubt whether we were right in believing yesterday that $7 \times 4 = 28$, a doubt which can in fact only arise if we have lost our hold of, i.e. no longer remember, the real nature of our consciousness of yesterday, and so think of it as consisting in believing. Plainly, the only remedy is to do the sum again. Or, to put the matter generally, if we do come to doubt whether it is true that A is B, as we once thought, the remedy lies not in any process of reflection but in such a reconsideration of the nature of A and B as leads to the knowledge that A is B.

With these considerations in mind, consider the parallel which, as it seems to me, is presented—though with certain differences—by Moral Philosophy. The sense that we ought to do certain things arises in our unreflective consciousness, being an activity of moral thinking occasioned by the various situations in which we find ourselves. At this stage our attitude to these obligations is one of unquestioning confidence. But inevitably the appreciation of the degree to which the execution of these obligations is contrary to our interest raises the doubt whether after all these obligations are really obligatory, i.e. whether our sense that we ought not to do certain things is not illusion. We then want to have it *proved* to us that we ought to do so, i.e. to be convinced of this by a process which, as an argument, is different in kind from our original and unreflective appreciation of it. This demand is, as I have argued, illegitimate.

Hence, in the first place, if, as is almost universally the case, by Moral Philosophy is meant the knowledge which would satisfy this demand, there is no such knowledge, and all attempts to attain it are doomed to failure because they rest on a mistake, the mistake of supposing the possibility of proving what can only be apprehended directly by an act of moral thinking. Nevertheless the demand, though illegitimate, is inevitable until we have carried the process of reflection far enough to realize the self-evidence of our obligations, i.e. the immediacy of our apprehension of them. This realization of their self-evidence is positive knowledge, and so far, and so far only, as the term Moral Philosophy is confined to this knowledge and to the knowledge of the parallel immediacy of the apprehension of the goodness of the various virtues and of good dispositions generally, is there such a thing as Moral Philosophy. But since this knowledge may allay doubts which often affect the whole conduct of life, it is, though not extensive, important, and even vitally important.

In the second place, suppose we come genuinely to doubt whether we ought, for example, to pay our debts, owing to a genuine doubt whether our previous conviction that we ought to do so is true, a doubt which can, in fact, only arise if we fail to remember the real nature of what we now call our past conviction. The only remedy lies in actually getting into a situation which occasions the obligation, or—if our imagination be strong enough—in imagining ourselves in that situation, and then letting our moral capacities of thinking do their work. Or, to put the matter generally, if we do doubt whether there is really an obligation to originate A in a situation B, the remedy lies not in any process of general thinking, but in getting face to face with a particular instance of the situation B, and then directly appreciating the obligation to originate A in that situation.

The Logic of Moral Reasoning, and Reason and Faith

STEPHEN E. TOULMIN

. . . No doubt those philosophers who search for more general rules will not be satisfied. No doubt they will still feel that they want an explicit and unique answer to our central question. And no doubt they will object that, in all this, I have not even 'justified' our using reason in ethics at all. 'It's all very well your laying down the law about particular types of ethical argument', they will say; 'but what is the justification for letting *any* reasoning affect how we decide to behave? Why *ought* one to do what is right, anyway?'

They are sufficiently answered by the peculiarity of their own questions. For let us consider what kind of answer they want when they ask, 'Why ought one to do what is right?' 'There is no room *within* ethics for such a question. Ethical reasoning may be able to show why we ought to do this action as opposed to that, or advocate this social practice as opposed to that, but it is no help where there can be no choice. And their question does not present us with genuine alternatives at all. For, since the notions of

From Stephen E. Toulmin, An Examination of the Place of Reason in Ethics *(Cambridge: Cambridge University Press, 1950), pp. 162–65, 202–9, 217–19. Reprinted by permission of the author and the publisher.*

'obligation' originate in the same situations and serve similar purposes, it is a self-contradiction (taking 'right' and 'ought' in their simplest senses) to suggest that we 'ought' to do anything but what is 'right'. This suggestion is as unintelligible as the suggestion that some emerald objects might not be green, and the philosophers' question is on a level with the question, 'Why are all scarlet things red?' We can therefore parry it only with another question—'What else "ought" one to do?'

Similar oddities are displayed by all their questions—as long as we take them literally. Ethics may be able to 'justify' one of a number of courses of action, or one social practice as opposed to another: but it does not extend to the 'justification' of all reasoning about conduct. One course of action can be opposed to another: one social practice can be opposed to another. But to what are we expected to oppose 'ethics-as-a-whole'? There can be no discussion about the proposition, 'Ethics is ethics'; any argument treating 'ethics' as something other than it is must be false; and, if those who call for a 'justification' of ethics want 'the case for morality', as opposed to 'the case for expediency', etc., then they are giving philosophy a job which is not its own. To show that you ought to choose certain actions is one thing: to make you *want to do* what you ought to do is another, and not a philosopher's task.

11.10 Reason and self-love. Hume ran sharply into this difficulty. He had, in fact, to confess (of a man in whom self-love overpowered the sense of right), 'It would be a little difficult to find any [reasoning] which will appear to him satisfactory and convincing.'[1] This confession of his was, however, a masterpiece of understatement. The difficulty he speaks of is no 'little' one: indeed, it is an 'absolute and insuperable' one, an 'impossibility'. But note the reason: it is not a *practical* impossibility at all, but a *logical* one. A man's ignoring all ethical argument is just the kind of thing which would lead us to say that his self-love *had* overpowered his sense of right. As long, and only as long, as he continued to ignore all moral reasoning, we should say that his self-love continued in the ascendant: but once he began to accept such considerations as a guide to action, we should begin to think that 'the sense of right' had won.

It is always possible that, when faced with a man whose self-love initially overpowered his sense of right, we might hit upon some reasoning which appeared to him 'satisfactory and convincing'. The result, however, would not be 'a man in whom self-love was dominant, but who was satisfied and convinced by ethical reasoning' (for this is a contradiction in terms); it would be 'a man in whom self-love was dominant, until reasoning beat it down and reinstated the sense of right'.

---

1 Hume, *Enquiries*, ed. Selby-Bigge, p. 283.

There is, in this respect, an interesting parallel to be drawn between the notion of 'rational belief' in science, and that of 'reasonable belief' in ethics. We call the belief that (for instance) sulphonamides will control pneumonia a 'rational belief', because it is arrived at by the procedure found reliable in clinical research. The same applies to any belief held as a result of a series of properly conducted scientific experiments. Any such belief is strengthened as a result of further confirmatory observations. These observations (we say) increase the 'probability' of any hypothesis with which they are consistent: that is, they increase the degree of confidence with which it is rational to entertain the hypothesis. In practice, of course, we do not always adopt the most reliable methods of argument—we generalize hastily, ignore conflicting evidence, misinterpret ambiguous observations and so on. We know very well that there are reliable standards of evidence to be observed, but we do not always observe them. In other words, we are not always rational; for to be 'rational' is to employ always these reliable, self-consistent methods of forming one's scientific beliefs, and to fail to be 'rational' is to entertain the hypothesis concerned with a degree of confidence out of proportion to its 'probability'.[2]

As with the 'rational' and the 'probable', so with the 'reasonable' and the 'desirable' (the 'desirable', that is, in its usual sense of what ought to be pursued): the belief that I ought to pay the bill which my bookshop has sent me is a 'reasonable' belief, and the bookseller's demand for payment is a 'reasonable' demand, because they represent a practice which has been found acceptable in such circumstances. Any ethical judgment, held as a result of properly interpreted moral experience, is also 'reasonable'. Any such judgment is strengthened by further experiences which confirm the fecundity of the principle from which the judgment derives. Such experiences increase the 'desirability' of the principle: that is, they increase the degree of conviction with which it is reasonable to advocate and act upon the principle. In practice, of course, we do not always adopt the most satisfactory methods of reaching moral decisions—we jump to conclusions, ignore the suffering of 'inferior' people, misinterpret ambiguous experiences, and so on. We know very well that there are reliable standards to be observed in shaping our principles and institutions, but we do not always observe them. That is to say, we are not always reasonable; for to be 'reasonable' is to employ these reliable, self-consistent methods in reaching all our moral decisions, and to fail to be 'reasonable' is to advocate and act upon our principles with a degree of conviction out of proportion to their desirability.

Consider the light which this parallel throws on Hume's difficulties

<hr />

2 In connection with this discussion, see Ayer (*Language, Truth and Logic*, pp. 99–102), whose argument I paraphrase.

and on the 'justification' of ethics. It is sometimes suggested that the 'probability' of a hypothesis is just a matter of our confidence in it, as measured by our willingness to rely on it in practice. This account is oversimplified, for it would be completely acceptable only if we always related belief to observation in a 'rational' way. 'Probability' is, rather, a matter of the degree of confidence with which it is rational to adopt a hypothesis. In an analogous way, Hume's theory of ethics makes the 'desirability' of a moral principle a matter of the conviction with which all fully informed people do hold to it.[3] This likewise would be true—provided that we always related our moral judgments to experience in a 'reasonable' way. . . .

But this clears up the problem. The truth is that, if different people are to agree in their ethical judgments, it is not enough for them all to be fully informed. They must all be *reasonable,* too. (Even this may not be enough: when it comes to controversial questions, they may reasonably differ.) Unfortunately, people are not always reasonable. And this is a sad fact, which philosophers just have to accept. It is absurd and paradoxical of them to suppose that we need produce a 'reasoned argument' capable of convincing the 'wholly unreasonable', for this would be a self-contradiction.[4]

If, therefore, the request for a 'justification' of ethics is equivalent to this demand, there is no room for a 'justification'; and the question used to express this demand, 'Why ought one to do what is right?', has no literal answer. There may yet be room for answers of a *different* kind: but, if there is, it is certainly not the business of a logician, and probably not the business of any kind of philosopher, to give them. (What kinds of answer might be given, and whose business it would be to give them, are questions I shall return to later.)[5]

REASON AND FAITH

It is the heart which is conscious of God, not the reason. This is
faith—God evident to the heart and not to the reason. . . . Faith is
within the heart, and makes us say not 'Scio', but 'Credo'.

PASCAL[6]

---

3 See Toulmin, op. cit., sec. 2.5.

4 I should have thought it unnecessary to formulate such an obvious truth, had I not found it overlooked, in practice, by eminent philosophers. For instance, I recall a conversation with Bertrand Russell in which he remarked, as an objection to the present account of ethics, that it would not have convinced Hitler. But whoever supposed that it should? We do not prescribe logic as a treatment for lunacy, or expect philosophers to produce panaceas for psychopaths.

5 In Chapter 14.

6 *Les Pensées de Pascal, disposées suivant l'ordre du cahier autographique,* ed. G. Michaut (Fribourg, 1896), no. 13, p. 11, and no. 58, p. 25; tr. Rawlings, in *Selected Thoughts* (The Scott Library), VIII, p. 10 and XXXIV, p. 20.

14.1 The finite scope of reasoning. In all the modes of reasoning analyzed so far, we found that the 'reasons' which could logically be given in support of any statement formed a finite chain. In every case, a point was reached beyond which it was no longer possible to give 'reasons' of the kind given until then; and eventually there came a stage beyond which it seemed that no 'reason' of any kind could be given. As a reminder of what I mean: the question 'Why ought I not to have two wives?' calls to begin with for reasons referring to the existing institutions; secondly, may raise the more general question whether our institution of 'marriage' could be improved by altering it in the direction of polygamy; thirdly, transforms itself into a question about the kind of community in which one would personally prefer to live; and beyond that cannot be reasoned about at all.[7] Now we have been interested throughout in *literal* answers only: so, when faced with requests for reasons of any kind beyond the point at which these ceased to be appropriate we dismissed them as illogical.

In doing so, we were acting on the same principle as the father who, when his child goes on asking, 'Why?', parrot-wise, stops answering its questions and checks him instead. Thus:

> *Child*: Why are you putting your coat on, Daddy?
> *Father*: Because I'm going out.
> *C*: Why are you going out, Daddy?
> *F*: I'm going to see Aunt Matilda.
> *C*: Why?
> *F*: Because she isn't very well today.
> *C*: Why?
> *F*: Because she ate something which disagreed with her.
> *C*: Why?
> *F*: Well, I suppose she was hungry, and didn't realize the food was bad.
> *C*: Why?
> *F*: How should I know?
> *C*: But why, Daddy?
> *F*: Oh, don't ask silly questions!

There are four particularly interesting situations on which we have to adopt this course:

(i) When someone asks, 'How do you explain that?', of something which there is no question of 'explaining', such as the deaths on their birthdays of three children in one family.[8]

(ii) When someone asks, 'But which ought I to do?', of two courses of

---

7 See sec. 11.6.
8 See sec. 7.5.

action between which, morally, there is nothing to choose, and insists
on an answer independent of his personal preferences.[9]

(iii) When someone asks, not just 'What reason is there for accepting this
explanation?'—meaning 'this' one rather than 'that'—but also, 'What
reason is there for accepting any scientific explanation?'[10]

(iv) When someone asks, not just 'Why ought I to do this?'—meaning
'this' course of action rather than 'that' one—but also, 'And why
ought I to do anything that is right?'[11]

In each of these situations, no literal question framed in those particular words can arise. And I mean by this more than that such a question
does not happen to arise, or that it happens not to be able to arise. I mean
that, as a consequence of the ways in which we employ the words concerned, and of the purpose which questions of this form serve, there is
logically no place in such a situation for this question—taken literally. And,
since we have confined ourselves strictly to literal interpretations up till
now, that means no place at all of the kinds that we have been considering.

14.2 'Limiting' questions. Nevertheless, one often wants to go
on asking such questions, even when there is no literal, rational sense in
them. The fact that one does so may be a sign of confusion—a sign that
one has just not got the hang of questions of the type concerned—or it
may not. For example, you may use the 'scientific' questions, 'Why does
this happen?' and 'How is that to be explained?', as expressions of surprise; and then you will probably be satisfied by a genuinely scientific
explanation. Or you may go on asking them after they have ceased to be
appropriate, through failing to realize that there is no further room for a
scientific explanation; and then you will be satisfied when this fact is pointed
out. But you may use the same questions as expressions, not merely of surprise at the unexpected, but also of wonder that there should be any phe
nomenon of this sort. If you do, then when all possible scientific explanations
have been exhausted, when it has been shown that things always happen
so, and that the phenomenon about which you are asking is paralleled by
familiar phenomena in other fields, you may still feel that your desire for
an 'explanation' remains unsatisfied; and, when someone points out that no
further scientific explanation can be given, you may come to the conclusion
that these things are so wonderful as to be 'beyond human understanding'.

Surprise and curiosity at the antics of the wagtail, or at the winged
seeds of the sycamore, may be satisfied by the study of botany or ornithology.
No amount of scientific knowledge, however, will still the feeling that birds

---

9 See sec. 11.8.
10 See sec. 7.6.
11 See sec. 11.9.

and trees are *wonderful* things; it will probably only enhance it. And if this is the feeling which prompts your request for an explanation, it will arise again even when science has done all that can be asked of it.

Other feelings may find expression in the same way. The sad deaths of the Jones children may occasion in us both surprise and distress. We soon come to recognize that the question, 'Why did they have to die so young; and all on their birthdays, too?', cannot arise, as a matter of science —that science can do nothing for us in such a situation. And in the absence of a murderer (about whose motives for killing them we might be enquiring) the question cannot arise in *any* form to which there is a literal answer. All the same, we may still want to ask it, and still feel the need of an answer, as an expression of our distress, rather than of our surprise; and indeed, in such a context, it is in this sense that one would most naturally interpret the question.

It is questions of this kind with which I am concerned in the present chapter—questions expressed in a form borrowed from a familiar mode of reasoning, but not doing the job which they normally do within that mode of reasoning. It is characteristic of them that only a small change is required, either in the form of the question, or in the context in which it is asked, in order to bring it unquestionably back into the scope of its apparent mode of reasoning. But it is equally characteristic of them that the way of answering suggested by the form of words employed will never completely satisfy the questioner, so that he continues to ask the question even after the resources of the apparent mode of reasoning have been exhausted. Questions of this kind I shall refer to as 'limiting questions': they are of particular interest when one is examining the limits and boundaries of any mode of reasoning —and of ethical reasoning in particular.

14.3 The peculiarities of 'limiting questions'. I want to point out three peculiarities of questions of this type, which make the ways of answering them quite different from the ways of answering more literal questions. These peculiarities I shall then illustrate in two instances:

(1) Our usage provides no standard interpretation of such questions. Their form suggests a meaning of a familiar kind, but the situations in which they are asked are such that they cannot have that meaning. The form of words may therefore express any of a varied selection of personal predicaments, and we can only find out as we go along what is 'behind' the question.

(2) If the question were to be interpreted literally—that is, by reference to its apparent logical form—we should expect there to be genuinely alternative answers, each applicable over a limited range of cases. Within the apparent mode of reasoning, all questions require a definite choice to be made—e.g. between two theories or social practices, between one moral

decision and another, or between one scientific prediction and another. A 'limiting question', however, does not present us with genuine alternatives to choose between: it is expressed in such a way that the only reply within the apparent mode of reasoning is (for instance), 'Well, isn't the "right" just what one "ought" to do?'

(3) Finally, a 'limiting question' is not flagrantly 'extrarational' in its form. It is not like the questions in Blake's *Tyger*, which no one would ever dream of trying to answer literally:

> What the hammer? What the chain?
> In what furnace was thy brain?
> What the anvil? What dread grasp
> Dare its deadly terrors clasp?

There is therefore always the urge to give it the kind of answer which its form appears to demand. However, either to answer or to refuse to answer in this way will leave the questioner equally dissatisfied. If you refuse, his desire for such an answer remains unstilled: if you answer, there is nothing to stop the question from arising again about your reply.

Consider a familiar instance. One learns to ask the questions, 'How is it supported?' and 'What does it rest on?', in all kinds of everyday situations; for instance, when talking to a gardener about his peach tree, or to an engineer about some piece of machinery. In these familiar situations, there is always the possibility that the object referred to might collapse if there were nothing to support it, nothing for it to rest on: or, at any rate, in all these instances we can understand what it would mean to say that it had 'collapsed'. But, if you start with a familiar object and ask, 'What does it rest on?', and continue to ask of each new object mentioned, 'And what does that rest on?', you will eventually reach the answer, 'The solid earth', and after that you cannot ask the question any more—in that sense anyway.

In the everyday sense, the question, 'What holds the earth up?',[12] is a 'limiting question', having all the peculiarities I have referred to:

(1) If someone does ask it, it is not at all clear what he wants to know, in the way it is if he asks, 'What holds your peach tree up?' In ordinary cases, the form of the question and the nature of the situation between them determine the meaning of the question: here they cannot do so, and one can only guess at what is prompting it.

(2) The different answers to the question, 'What holds your peach tree up?', are intelligible enough, and one can imagine a peach tree's 'falling

---

12 I recall Wittgenstein's likening the problem of induction to this question; and saying that those philosophers who asked for a 'justification' of science were like the Ancients, who felt there must be an Atlas to support the Earth on his shoulders (Cambridge University Moral Science Club: November 14, 1946).

down': but neither of these things is the case when someone asks, 'What holds the earth up?'

(3) Still, there is a strong desire to take the question literally, in a way in which one would never take Blake's questions literally. But, if we do, it will get us nowhere. If we answer 'An elephant', the questioner can ask, 'And what holds the elephant up?'; if we now answer 'A tortoise', the question arises again; and there is no way of stopping its recurrence this side of infinity.

We might of course answer, 'Nothing', and, when the questioner protested, 'Nothing? But it must be held up by something', we might explain to him his error, pointing out that he was misunderstanding the nature of questions of the form, 'What holds it up?', and failing to see that this form of question cannot be asked of 'the earth' at all. If the question had arisen from such a misunderstanding, the questioner would be satisfied by this; and, to the extent that it did satisfy him, we could conclude that the enquiry had arisen in this way, that the motive prompting the question had been the perplexity of misunderstanding. But he might not be so easily satisfied. The question might be a 'cover' for some other feeling; say, for an hysterical apprehensiveness about the future. This could not be settled by any literal answer to his question, or by any rational analysis of the question itself: in fact, the only type of reasoning likely to make any impression on him would be psychoanalytic reasoning.

As a second instance, the question, 'Why ought one to do what is right?', shares these same peculiarities:

(1) The form of the question and the situation in which it is asked do not determine the meaning of the question, in the way in which they determine the meaning of a question like, 'Why ought I to give this book back to Jones?'

(2) There are no 'alternative answers', in the way in which there are to a typically ethical question.

(3) Still, the question does seem to call for an ethical answer—even though whatever you say can be queried in its turn, and so *ad infinitum*.

Once again we might explain to the questioner how the notions of 'right' and 'obligation' arise, pointing out that their origins are such as to make the sentence, 'One ought to do what is right', a truism. And again this might satisfy him, showing that it had been the perplexity born of misunderstanding which had prompted his question. But again our answer might leave him unmoved: and, when this happened, we should have to conclude that the motive behind this question was only being obliquely expressed.

Since, when one is faced with a 'limiting question', there is this additional uncertainty about the way in which it is to be interpreted—since the possible concealed motives for asking a 'limiting question' are many and varied—one cannot help being at a loss to begin with. The fact that such questions have no fixed, literal meaning means that there is no fixed, literal way of answering them, and one just has to wait and see what it is the questioner wants. If, for example, someone asks, 'Why ought one to do what is right?', the answers which can be given are of two kinds. Either they must be tailor-made to fit the questioner—in which case they have no universal application—or they must abandon all pretence of literalness, and take on the elusive, allusive quality of poetry. In the first case, they can at the best take account of the questioner's professional preoccupations, drawing attention (for instance) to analogies between ethical and biological concepts, if he is a biologist, to analogies between ethical and psychological concepts, if he is a psychologist, and so on.[13] In the second, they are to be judged less like the questions in the mode of reasoning whose form they have borrowed, than like Blake's poems—by their impact, that is, and not by excessively intellectual standards.

If the questioner insists on having an answer which is at the same time literal and unique, there is nothing further one can do. The question, 'What is the intellectual basis of ethics?', posed by Dr. C. H. Waddington in the introduction to his symposium, *Science and Ethics*,[14] is a good example. In substance, this question is similar to 'Why ought one to do what is right?', but the use of the word 'intellectual' reinforces the demand for a rational, literal answer—and the whole of the discussion which follows makes it clear that the questioner wants a straightforward answer to an oblique question. And, faced with this demand, we can only answer as Wittgenstein answered, 'This is a terrible business—just terrible! You can at best stammer when you talk of it.' . . .[15]

14.7 Faith and reason in ethics. These remarks about faith and reason have been very general, and we must not leave the subject without returning to our proper field. Let us therefore examine the boundary between religion and ethics—so as to see how, in this sphere, reason marches upon faith.

We encountered 'limiting questions' in three kinds of ethical situation:

(1) When it has been pointed out that an action conforms unambiguously to a recognized social practice, there is no more room for the justification of the action through ethical reasoning: if someone asks, 'Why

---

13 This would be the peg on which to hang a discussion of the so-called 'scientific' theories of ethics, but this would be too much of a digression.

14 C. H. Waddington, *Science and Ethics* (London: George Allen and Unwin Ltd., 1942), p. 7.

15 Waddington himself quotes this remark (loc. cit.) but he has evidently not appreciated its full force.

ought I to give this back to Jones today?', and is given the answer, 'Because you promised to', there is no room within the ethical mode of reasoning for him to ask, 'But why ought I to *really?*'—this question is a 'limiting question'.

(2) When there is nothing to choose on moral grounds between two courses of action, the only reasoned answer which can be given to the question, 'Which ought I to do?', is one taking account of the agent's own preferences—'If you do A, then so-and-so, if you do B, then such-and-such: and it's up to you to decide which you prefer'— and if someone now insists on a unique answer, independent of his preferences, his question is again 'limiting'.

(3) When someone asks, perfectly generally, 'Why ought one do what is right?', and is not satisfied with the answer that the sentence, 'You ought to do what is right', expresses a truism, his question is also a 'limiting' one.

In each of these cases, the logical pattern is similar. In each, ethical reasoning first does for the questioner all that can be asked of it, exhausting the literal answers to his question, and making it clear how far there is any literal sense in his asking what he 'ought' to do. In each case, when this is finished, it is clear that something remains to be done: that moral reasoning, while showing what ought (literally) to be done, has failed to satisfy the questioner. Although he may come to recognize intellectually what he 'ought' to do, he does not feel like doing it—his heart is not in it.

This conflict is manifested in his use of 'limiting questions'. As long as these are taken literally, they seem nonsensical: whether he says, 'I know I promised to, but ought I to, *really?*', or 'Yes, yes; but which ought I *really* to do, A or B?', or 'But why ought one to do *anything* that is right?', he is ostensibly querying something which it makes no sense to question—literally.

In each case, however, his question comes alive again as soon as one takes it 'spiritually', as a religious question. Over those matters of fact which are not to be 'explained' scientifically, like the deaths in the Jones family, the function of religion is to help us resign ourselves to them—and so feel like accepting them. Likewise, over matters of duty which are not to be justified further in ethical terms, it is for religion to help us embrace them—and so feel like accepting them. In all the three situations referred to, therefore, religious answers may still be appropriate, even when the resources to ethical reasoning are exhausted:

(1) 'Why ought I to give back this book?'
    'Because you promised.'
    'But why ought I to, *really?*'
    'Because it would be sinful not to.'
    'And what if I were to commit such a sin?'
    'That would be to cut yourself off from God', etc.

(2) 'Which ought I to do, A or B?'
  'There's nothing to choose between them, morally speaking; it's up to you, but if I were you I should do B.'
  'But which ought I *really* to do?'
  'You ought to do B: that is the course more pleasing to God, and will bring you the truest happiness in the end.'

(3) 'Why ought one to do what is right, anyway?'
  'That is a question which cannot arise, for it is to query the very definition of "right" and "ought".'
  'But why *ought* one to?'
  'Because it is God's will.'
  'And why should one do His will?'
  'Because it is in the nature of a created being to do the will of its Creator', etc. . . .

Why Should We Be Moral?

KURT BAIER

. . . The examination of the prevailing consideration-making beliefs used at the first stage of our practical deliberations leads naturally to the examination of our rules of superiority used at the second stage. This in turn involves our investigating whether moral reasons are superior to all others and . . . whether and why we should be moral. That opens up the most fundamental issue of all, whether and why we should follow reason.

1 THE TRUTH OF CONSIDERATION-MAKING BELIEFS

Let us begin with our most elementary consideration-making belief: the fact that if I did x I would enjoy doing x is a reason for me to do x. There can be little doubt that this is one of the rules of reason recognized in our society. Most people would use the knowledge of the fact that they would enjoy doing something as a pro in their deliberations whether to do it. When we wonder whether to go to the pictures or to a dinner dance, the fact that we would enjoy the dinner dance but not the pictures is regarded as a reason for going to the dinner dance rather than to the pictures. We are now asking whether this widely held belief is true,

From Kurt Baier, The Moral Point of View: A Rational Basis of Ethics *(Ithaca: Cornell University Press, 1958), pp. 298–320. Copyright © 1958 by Cornell University. Reprinted by permission of the author and the publisher.*

whether this fact really is a reason or is merely and falsely believed to be so.

What exactly are we asking? Is our question empirical? Obviously it cannot be answered by direct inspection. We cannot see, hear, or smell whether this belief is true, whether this fact is a reason or not. The nature of our question becomes clearer if we remind ourselves of the function of consideration-making beliefs, namely, to serve as major premises in practical arguments. These arguments are supposed to yield true answers to questions of the form 'What shall I do?' or 'What is the best course of action open to me?' Premises of an argument are true if the argument is valid and the conclusion is true. We can infer that the premise is true if the argument is valid and if it is true that the course of action recommended in the conclusion of the argument is the best course open to the agent. The matter is considerably simplified by the fact that, at this point, we are dealing merely with prima facie reasons. In order to determine the truth of the conclusion, we have only to find out whether the recommended course of action is the best, *other things being equal*, that is, whether it is better than its contradictory or its contrary.

Our practical argument runs as follows:

(1) The fact that if I did x I would enjoy doing x is a reason for me to to do x.

(2) I would enjoy doing x if I did x.

(3) Therefore I ought to do x (other things being equal).

Hence our consideration-making belief (1) is true (since the argument is valid) if our conclusion (3) is true. As pointed out above, our conclusion is true if the course recommended is the best, other things being equal, that is, if it is better than its contrary and its contradictory—better than (4), I ought *not* to do x, and (5), it is *not* the case that I ought to do x.

The problem of the truth or falsity of consideration-making beliefs is thus reduced to the question whether it is better that they, rather than their contraries or contradictories, should be used as rules of reason, that is, as major premises in practical arguments. How would we tell?

It is not difficult to see that the contrary of our rule of reason is greatly inferior to it. For if, instead of the presently accepted belief (see above (1)), its contrary became the prevailing rule, then anyone trying to follow reason would have to conclude that whenever there is something that he would enjoy doing if he did it then he ought *not* to do it. "Reason" would counsel everyone always to refrain from doing what he enjoys, from satisfying his desires. "Reason" would counsel self-frustration for its own sake.

It is important to note that such an arrangement is possible. To say that we would not now *call* it 'following reason' is not enough to refute it. We can imagine two societies in which English is spoken and which differ only in this, that in one society, (1) is accepted, in the other the contrary of (1). It would then be correct to say in one society that doing what one would enjoy doing was following reason, in the other society that it was acting contrary to it. The "tautologousness" of the first remark *in our society* is not incompatible with the "tautologousness" of the contrary remark *in another society*. From the fact that the proposition 'Faithers are male' is analytic, we can infer that 'fathers are male' is necessarily true. But this is so only because we would not correctly *call* anything 'father' that we would correctly call 'not male.' And it is perfectly in order to say that in any society in which English was spoken but in which the words 'father' and/or 'male' were not used in this way those words did not mean quite the same as in our society. And with this, the matter is ended, for we are not concerned to settle the question which verbal arrangement, ours or theirs, is the better. Nothing at all follows from the fact that a society has our usage of 'father' and 'male' or theirs. But in the case of the use of 'reason,' much depends on which usage is accepted. The real difficulty only begins when we have concluded, correctly, that the word 'reason' is used in a different sense in that other society. For the practical implications of the word 'reason' are the same in both societies, namely, that people are encouraged to follow reason rather than act contrary to it. However, *what* is held in one society to be in accordance with reason is held to be contrary to it in the other. Hence, we must say that in practical matters nothing fundamental can be settled by attention to linguistic proprieties or improprieties.

What, then, is relevant? We must remember what sort of a "game" the game of reasoning is. We ask the question 'What shall I do?' or 'What is the best course of action?' Following reasons is following those hints which are most likely to make the course of action the best in the circumstances. The criteria of 'best course of action' are linked with what we mean by 'the good life.' In evaluating a life, one of the criteria of merit which we use is how much satisfaction and how little frustration there is in that life. Our very purpose in "playing the reasoning game" is to maximize satisfactions and minimize frustrations. Deliberately to frustrate ourselves and to minimize satisfaction would certainly be to go counter to the very purpose for which we deliberate and weigh the pros and cons. These criteria are, therefore, necessarily linked with the very purpose of the activity of reasoning. Insofar as we enter on that "game" at all, we are therefore bound to accept these criteria. Hence we are bound to agree that the consideration-making belief which is prevalent in our society is better than its contrary.

But need we accept that purpose? Is this not just a matter of taste or preference? Could not people with other tastes choose the opposite purpose, namely, self-frustration and self-denial rather than satisfaction of desires and enjoyment? The answer is No, it is not just a matter of taste or preference. Whether we like or don't like oysters, even whether we prefer red ink to claret, is a matter of taste, though to prefer red ink is to exhibit a very eccentric taste. Whether we prefer to satisfy our desires or to frustrate them is not, however, a matter of taste or preference. It is not an eccentricity of taste to prefer whatever one does *not* enjoy doing to whatever one does enjoy doing. It is perverse or crazy if it is done every now and then, mad if it is done always or on principle.

It might be objected that these people would merely be *called* mad by us—this does not prove that they really are, any more than the fact that they might well call us mad proves that we are. This objection seems to take the sting out of the epithet 'mad.' However, it only seems to do so, because it is misconstrued on one of the following two models.

(1) 'They are called artesian wells, but that's only what we call them in this country.' In this case, the distinction is between what we all, quite universally but incorrectly, call them in this country and what they really are, that is, what they are properly and correctly called. The difference is between an established but incorrect usage, and the correct but possibly not established usage. However, people who prefer whatever they do not enjoy doing to whatever they do would not merely generally (though incorrectly) but quite correctly be called mad.

(2) 'When two people quarrel and call each other "bastard," that does not prove that they are bastards.' On this model, it might be argued that the word 'mad' has no established usage, that we use it only in order to insult people who are not average. But this is untenable. Admittedly we often use the word 'mad' to insult people who are not mad, just as we use the word 'bastard' to insult people who were born in wedlock. But we could not use these words for these purposes unless they were correctly used to designate characteristics generally regarded as highly undesirable. When a person is certified insane, this is done not just because he differs from average, but because he is different in certain fundamental and undesirable respects. To prove the undesirability of these differences, it is enough here to point out that no one *wants* to become mad. Our conclusion must be that there is a correct use of the word 'mad' and that people who prefer whatever they do not enjoy doing to whatever they do differ from normal people in just such fundamental and undesirable respects as would make the word 'mad' correctly applicable to them.

The contradictory of our most fundamental consideration-making belief is also less satisfactory than *it* is. If it were to be believed that the fact that one would enjoy doing *x* was not a reason for doing it (a belief which is the contradictory of our most fundamental consideration-making belief), then people wishing to follow reason would be neither advised to do what they would enjoy doing nor advised not to do it. Reason would simply be silent on this issue. Never to do what one would enjoy doing would be as much in accordance with reason (other things being equal) as always to do it. In such a world, "following reason" might be less rewarding than following instinct or inclination. Hence this cannot *be* following reason, for it *must* pay to follow reason at least as much as to follow instinct or inclination, or else it is not reason.

To sum up. People who replace our most fundamental consideration-making belief by its contrary or contradictory will not do as well as those who adhere to it. Those who adopt its contrary must even be said to be mad. This seems to me the best possible argument for the preferability of our fundamental consideration-making belief to its contrary and contradictory. And this amounts to a proof of its truth. I need not waste any further time on examining whether the other consideration-making beliefs prevalent in our society are also true. Everyone can conduct this investigation for himself.

2 THE HIERARCHY OF REASONS

How can we establish rules of superiority? It is a prima facie reason for me to do something not only that *I* would enjoy it if *I* did it, but also that *you* would enjoy it if *I* did it. People generally would fare better if this fact were treated as a pro, for if this reason were followed, it would create additional enjoyment all round. But which of the two prima facie reasons is superior when they conflict? How would we tell?

At first sight it would seem that these reasons are equally good, that there is nothing to choose between them, that no case can be made out for saying that people generally would fare better if the one or the other were treated as superior. But this is a mistake.

Suppose I could be spending half an hour in writing a letter to Aunt Agatha who would enjoy receiving one though I would not enjoy writing it, or alternatively in listening to a lecture which I would enjoy doing. Let us also assume that I cannot do both, that I neither enjoy writing the letter nor dislike it, that Aunt Agatha enjoys receiving the letter as much as I enjoy listening to the lecture, and that there are no extraneous considerations such as that I deserve especially to enjoy myself there and then, or that Aunt Agatha does, or that she has special claims against me, or that I have special responsibilities or obligations toward her.

In order to see which is the better of these two reasons, we must draw a distinction between two different cases: the case in which someone derives pleasure from giving pleasure to others and the case where he does not. Everyone is so related to certain other persons that he derives greater pleasure from doing something together with them than doing it alone because in doing so he is giving them pleasure. He derives pleasure not merely from the game of tennis he is playing but from the fact that in playing he is pleasing his partner. We all enjoy pleasing those we love. Many of us enjoy pleasing even strangers. Some even enjoy pleasing their enemies. Others get very little enjoyment from pleasing their fellow men.

We must therefore distinguish between people with two kinds of natural makeup: on the one hand, those who need not always choose between pleasing themselves and pleasing others, who can please themselves *by* pleasing others, who can please themselves more by not merely pleasing themselves, and, on the other hand, those who always or often have to choose between pleasing themselves and pleasing others, who derive no pleasure from pleasing others, who do not please themselves more by pleasing not merely themselves.

If I belong to the first kind, then I shall derive pleasure from pleasing Aunt Agatha. Although writing her a letter is not enjoyable in itself, as listening to the lecture is, I nevertheless derive enjoyment from writing it because it is a way of pleasing her and I enjoy pleasing people. In choosing between writing the letter and listening to the lecture, I do not therefore have to choose between pleasing her and pleasing myself. I have merely to choose between two different ways of pleasing myself. If I am a man of the second kind, then I must choose between pleasing myself and pleasing her. When we have eliminated all possible moral reasons, such as standing in a special relationship to the person, then it would be strange for someone to prefer pleasing someone else to pleasing himself. How strange this is can be seen if we substitute for Aunt Agatha a complete stranger.

I conclude from this that the fact that I would enjoy it if *I* did *x* is a better reason for doing *x* than the fact that you would enjoy it if *I* did *x*. Similarly in the fact that I would enjoy doing *x* if I did it I have a reason for doing *x* which is better than the reason for doing *y* which I have in the fact that you would enjoy doing *y* as much as I would enjoy doing *x*. More generally speaking, we can say that self-regarding reasons are better than other-regarding ones. Rationally speaking, the old quip is true that everyone is his own nearest neighbor.

This is more obvious still when we consider the case of self-interest. Both the fact that doing *x* would be in my interest and the fact that it would be in someone else's interest are excellent prima facie reasons for me to do *x*. But the self-interested reason is better than the altruistic one. Of course, interests need not conflict, and then I need not choose. I can do what is in both our interests. But sometimes interests conflict, and then it is in accordance with reason (prima facie) to prefer my own interest to someone else's. That my making an application for a job is in *my* interest is a reason for me to apply, which is better than the reason against applying, which I have in the fact that my not applying is in *your* interest.

There is no doubt that this conviction is correct for all cases. It is obviously better that everyone should look after his own interest than that everyone should neglect it in favor of someone else's. For whose interest should have precedence? It must be remembered that we are considering a case in which there are no special reasons for preferring a particular person's interests to one's own, as when there are no special moral obligations or emotional ties. Surely, in the absence of any *special* reasons for preferring someone else's interests, *everyone's* interests are best served if *everyone* puts his own interests first. For, by and large, everyone is himself the best judge of what is in his own best interest, since everyone usually knows best what his plans, aims, ambitions, or aspirations are. Moreover, everyone is more diligent in the promotion of his own interests than that of others. Enlightened egoism is a possible, rational, orderly system of running things, enlightened altruism is not. Everyone can look after himself, no one can look after everyone else. Even if everyone had to look after only two others, he could not do it as well as looking after himself alone. And if he has to look after only one person, there is no advantage in making that person some one other than himself. On the contrary, he is less likely to know as well what that person's interest is or to be as zealous in its promotion as in that of his own interest.

For this reason, it has often been thought that enlightened egoism is a possible rational way of running things. Sidgwick, for instance, says that the principle of egoism, to have as one's ultimate aim one's own greatest happiness, and the principle of universal benevolence, to have as one's ultimate aim the greatest happiness of the greatest number, are equally rational.[1] Sidgwick then goes on to say that these two principles may conflict and anyone who admits the rationality of both may go on to maintain that it is rational not to abandon the aim of one's own greatest happiness. On his view, there is a fundamental and ultimate contradiction in our apparent intuitions of what is reasonable in conduct. He argues that this can be removed only by the assumption that the individual's greatest happiness and the greatest happiness of the greatest number are both achieved by the rewarding and punishing activity of a perfect being whose sanctions would suffice to make it always everyone's interest to promote universal happiness to the best of his knowledge.

The difficulty which Sidgwick here finds is due to the fact that he regards reasons of self-interest as being no stronger and no weaker than moral reasons. This, however, is not in accordance with our ordinary convictions. It is generally believed that when reasons of self-interest conflict with moral reasons, then moral reasons override those of self-interest. It is our common conviction that moral reasons are superior to all others. Sidgwick has simply overlooked that although it is prima facie in accordance with reason to follow reasons of self-interest and also to follow moral reasons nevertheless, when there is a conflict between these two types of reason, when we have a self-interested reason for doing something and a moral

---

[1] Henry Sidgwick, *The Methods of Ethics*, 7th ed. (London: Macmillan & Co., Ltd., 1907), concluding chapter, para.1.

reason against doing it, there need not be an ultimate and fundamental contradiction in what it is in accordance with reason to do. For one type of reason may be *stronger* or *better* than another so that, when two reasons of different types are in conflict, it is in accordance with reason to follow the stronger, contrary to reason to follow the weaker.

3 THE SUPREMACY OF MORAL REASONS

Are moral reasons really superior to reasons of self-interest as we all believe? Do we really have reason on our side when we follow moral reasons against self-interest? What reasons could there be for being moral? Can we really give an answer to 'Why should we be moral?' It is obvious that all these questions come to the same thing. When we ask, 'Should we be moral?' or 'Why should we be moral?' or 'Are moral reasons superior to all others? we ask to be shown the reason for being moral. What is this reason?

Let us begin with a state of affairs in which reasons of self-interest are supreme. In such a state everyone keeps his impulses and inclinations in check when and only when they would lead him into behavior detrimental to his own interest. Everyone who follows reason will discipline himself to rise early, to do his exercises, to refrain from excessive drinking and smoking, to keep good company, to marry the right sort of girl, to work and study hard in order to get on, and so on. However, it will often happen that people's interests conflict. In such a case, they will have to resort to ruses or force to get their own way. As this becomes known, men will become suspicious, for they will regard one another as scheming competitors for the good things in life. The universal supremacy of the rules of self-interest must lead to what Hobbes called the state of nature. At the same time, it will be clear to everyone that universal obedience to certain rules overriding self-interest would produce a state of affairs which serves everyone's interest much better than his unaided pursuit of it in a state where everyone does the same. Moral rules are universal rules designed to override those of self-interest when following the latter is harmful to others. 'Thou shalt not kill,' 'Thou shalt not lie,' 'Thou shalt not steal' are rules which forbid the inflicting of harm on someone else even when this might be in one's interest.

The very *raison d'être* of a morality is to yield reasons which overrule the reasons of self-interest in those cases when everyone's following self-interest would be harmful to everyone. Hence moral reasons are superior to all others.

"But what does this mean?" it might be objected. "If it merely means that we do so regard them, then you are of course right, but your contention is useless, a mere point of usage. And how could it mean any more?

If it means that we not only do so regard them, but *ought* so to regard them, then there must be *reasons* for saying this. But there could not be any reasons for it. If you offer reasons of self-interest, you are arguing in a circle. Moreover, it cannot be true that it is always in my interest to treat moral reasons as superior to reasons of self-interest. If it were, self-interest and morality could never conflict, but they notoriously do. It is equally circular to argue that there are moral reasons for saying that one ought to treat moral reasons as superior to reasons of self-interest. And what other reasons are there?"

The answer is that we are now looking at the world from the point of view of *anyone*. We are not examining particular alternative courses of action before this or that person; we are examining two alternative worlds, one in which moral reasons are always treated by everyone as superior to reasons of self-interest and one in which the reverse is the practice. And we can see that the first world is the better world, because we can see that the second world would be the sort which Hobbes describes as the state of nature.

This shows that I ought to be moral, for when I ask the question 'What ought I to do?' I am asking, 'Which is the course of action supported by the best reasons? But since it has just been shown that moral reasons are superior to reasons of self-interest, I have been given a reason for being moral, for following moral reasons rather than any other, namely, they are better reasons than any other.

But is this always so? Do we have a reason for being moral whatever the conditions we find ourselves in? Could there not be situations in which it is not true that we have reasons for being moral, that, on the contrary, we have reasons for ignoring the demands of morality? Is not Hobbes right in saying that in a state of nature the laws of nature, that is, the rules of morality, bind only *in foro interno*?

Hobbes argues as follows.

(1) To live in a state of nature is to live outside society. It is to live in conditions in which there are no common ways of life and, therefore, no reliable expectations about other people's behavior other than that they will follow their inclination or their interest.

(2) In such a state reason will be the enemy of cooperation and mutual trust. For it is too risky to hope that other people will refrain from protecting their own interests by the preventive elimination of probable or even possible dangers to them. Hence reason will counsel everyone to avoid these risks by preventive action. But this leads to war.

(3) It is obvious that everyone's following self-interest leads to a state of affairs which is desirable from no one's point of view. It is, on the contrary, desirable that everybody should follow rules overriding self-

interest whenever that is to the detriment of others. In other words, it is desirable to bring about a state of affairs in which all obey the rules of morality.

(4) However, Hobbes claims that in the state of nature it helps nobody if a single person or a small group of persons begins to follow the rules of morality, for this could only lead to the extinction of such individuals or groups. In such a state, it is therefore contrary to reason to be moral.

(4) The situation can change, reason can support morality, only when the presumption about other people's behavior is reversed. Hobbes thought that this could be achieved only by the creation of an absolute ruler with absolute power to enforce his laws. We have already seen that this is not true and that it is quite different if people live in a society, that is, if they have common ways of life, which are taught to all members and somehow enforced by the group. Its members have reason to expect their fellows generally to obey its rules, that is, its religion, morality, customs, and law, even when doing so is not, on certain occasions, in their interest. Hence they too have reason to follow these rules.

Is this argument sound? One might, of course, object to step (1) on the grounds that this is an empirical proposition for which there is little or no evidence. For how can we know whether it is true that people in a state of nature would follow only inclinations or, at best, reasons of self-interest, when nobody now lives in that state or has ever lived in it?

However, there is some empirical evidence to support this claim. For in the family of nations, individual states are placed very much like individual persons in a state of nature. The doctrine of the sovereignty of nations and the absence of an effective international law and police force are a guarantee that nations live in a state of nature, without commonly accepted rules that are somehow enforced. Hence it must be granted that living in a state of nature leads to living in a state in which individuals act either on impulse or as they think their interest dictates. For states pay only lip service to morality. They attack their hated neighbors when the opportunity arises. They start preventive wars in order to destroy the enemy before he can deliver his knockout blow. Where interests conflict, the stronger party usually has his way, whether his claims are justified or not. And where the relative strength of the parties is not obvious, they usually resort to arms in order to determine "whose side God is on." Treaties are frequently concluded but, morally speaking, they are not worth the paper they are written on. Nor do the partners regard them as contracts binding in the ordinary way, but rather as public expressions of the belief of the governments concerned that for the time being their alliance is in the interest of the allies. It is well understood that such treaties may be canceled before they reach their predetermined end or simply broken when it suits one partner. In international affairs, there are very few examples of *Nibelungentreue*, although statesmen whose countries have profited from keeping their treaties usually make such high moral claims.

It is, moreover, difficult to justify morality in international affairs. For suppose a highly moral statesman were to demand that his country adhere to a treaty obligation even though this meant its ruin or possibly its extinction. Suppose he were to say that treaty obligations are sacred and must be kept whatever the consequences. How could he defend such a policy? Perhaps one might argue that someone has to make a start in order to create mutual confidence in international affairs. Or one might say that setting a good example is the best way of inducing others to follow suit. But such a defense would hardly be sound. The less skeptical one is about the genuineness of the cases in which nations have adhered to their treaties from a sense of moral obligation, the more skeptical one must be about the effectiveness of such examples of virtue in effecting a change of international practice. Power politics still govern in international affairs.

We must, therefore, grant Hobbes the first step in his argument and admit that in a state of nature people, as a matter of psychological fact, would not follow the dictates of morality. But we might object to the next step that knowing this psychological fact about other people's behavior constitutes a reason for behaving in the same way. Would it not still be immoral for anyone to ignore the demands of morality even though he knows that others are likely or certain to do so, too? Can we offer as a justification for morality the fact that no one is entitled to do wrong just because someone else is doing wrong? This argument begs the question whether it *is* wrong for anyone in this state to disregard the demands of morality. It cannot be wrong to break a treaty or make preventive war if we have no reason to obey the moral rules. For to say that it is wrong to do so is to say that we ought not to do so. But if we have no reason for obeying the moral rule, then we have no reason overruling self-interest, hence no reason for keeping the treaty when keeping it is not in our interest, hence it is not true that we have a reason for keeping it, hence not true that we ought to keep it, hence not true that it is wrong not to keep it.

I conclude that Hobbes's argument is sound. Moralities are systems of principles whose acceptance by everyone as overruling the dictates of self-interest is in the interest of everyone alike, though following the rules of a morality is not of course identical with following self-interest. If it were, there could be no conflict between a morality and self-interest and no point in having moral rules overriding self-interest. Hobbes is also right in saying that the application of this system of rules is in accordance with reason only in social conditions, that is, when there are well-established ways of behavior.

The answer to our question 'Why should we be moral?' is therefore as follows. We should be moral because being moral is following rules designed to overrule self-interest whenever it is in the interest of everyone alike that everyone should set aside his interest. It is not self-contradictory to say this, because it may be in one's interest *not* to follow one's interest at times. We have already seen that enlightened self-interest acknowledges this point. But while enlightened self-interest does not require any genuine sacrifice from anyone, morality does. In the interest of the possibility of the good life for everyone, voluntary sacrifices are sometimes required from everybody. Thus, a person might do better for himself by following enlightened self-interest rather than morality. It is not possible, however, that *everyone* should do better for himself by following enlightened self-interest rather than morality. The best possible life *for everyone* is possible only by everyone's following the rules of morality, that is, rules which quite frequently may require individuals to make genuine sacrifices.

It must be added to this, however, that such a system of rules has the support of reason only where people live in societies, that is, in conditions in which there are established common ways of behavior. Outside society, people have no reason for following such rules, that is, for being moral. In other words, outside society, the very distinction between right and wrong vanishes.

4 WHY SHOULD WE FOLLOW REASON?

But someone might now ask whether and why he should follow reason itself. He may admit that moral reasons are superior to all others, but doubt whether he ought to follow reason. He may claim that this will have to be proved first, for if it is not true that he ought to follow reason, then it is not true that he ought to follow the strongest reason either.

What is it to follow reason? As we have explained, it involves two tasks, the theoretical, finding out what it would be in accordance with reason to do in a certain situation, what contrary to reason, and the practical task, to act accordingly. It was shown in Chapter Three [of *The Moral Point of View*] how this is done. We must also remind ourselves that there are many different ways in which what we do or believe or feel can be contrary to reason. It may be *irrational*, as when, for no reason at all, we set our hand on fire or cut off our toes one by one, or when, in the face of conclusive evidence to the contrary, someone *believes* that her son killed in the war is still alive, or when someone is *seized by fear* as a gun is pointed at him although he knows for certain that it is not loaded. What we do, believe, or feel is called irrational if it is the case not only that there are conclusive or overwhelming reasons against doing, believing, or feeling these things, but also that we must know there are such reasons and we still persist in our action, belief, or feeling.

Or it may be *unreasonable*, as when we make demands which are excessive or refuse without reason to comply with requests which are reasonable. We say of demands or requests that they are excessive if, though we are entitled to make them, the party against whom we make them has good reasons for not complying, as when the landlord demands the immediate vacation of the premises in the face of well-supported pleas of hardship by the tenant.

Being unreasonable is a much weaker form of going counter to reason than being irrational. The former applies in cases where there is a conflict of reasons and where one party does not acknowledge the obvious force of the case of the other or, while acknowledging it, will not modify his behavior accordingly. A person is irrational only if he flies in the face of reason, if, that is, all reasons are on one side and he acts contrary to it when he either acknowledges that this is so or, while refusing to acknowledge it, has no excuse for failing to do so.

Again, someone may be *inconsistent*, as when he refuses a Jew admission to a club although he has always professed strong positive views on racial equality. Behavior or remarks are inconsistent if the agent or author professes principles adherence to which would require him to say or do the opposite of what he says or does.

Or a person may be *illogical,* as when he does something which, as anyone can see, cannot or is not at all likely to lead to success. Thus when I cannot find my glasses or my fountain pen, the logical thing to do is to look for them where I can remember I had them last or where I usually have them. It would be illogical of me to look under the bed or in the oven unless I have special reason to think they might be there. To say of a person that he is a logical type is to say that he always does what, on reflection, anyone would agree is most likely to lead to success. Scatterbrains, people who act rashly, without thinking, are the opposite of logical.

When we speak of following reason, we usually mean 'doing what is supported by the best reasons because it is so supported' or perhaps 'doing what we thing (rightly or wrongly) is supported by the best reasons because we think it is so supported.' It might, then, occur to someone to ask, 'Why should I follow reason?' During the last hundred years or so, reason has had a very bad press. Many thinkers have sneered at it and have recommended other guides, such as the instincts, the unconscious, the voice of the blood, inspiration, charisma, and the like. They have advocated that one should not follow reason but be guided by these other forces.

However, in the most obvious sense of the question 'Should I follow reason?' this is a tautological question like 'Is a circle a circle'; hence the advice 'You should not follow reason' is as nonsensical as the claim 'A circle is not a circle.' Hence the question 'Why should I follow reason?' is as silly as 'Why is a circle a circle?' We need not, therefore, take much notice of the advocates of unreason. They show by their advocacy that they are not too clear on what they are talking about.

How is it that 'Should I follow reason?' is a tautological question like 'Is a circle a circle?' Questions of the form 'Shall I do this?' or 'Should I do this' or 'Ought I to do this?' are, as was shown (in Chapter Three [of *the Moral Point of View*]), requests to someone (possibly oneself) to deliberate on one's behalf. That is to say, they are requests to survey the facts and weigh the reasons for and against this course of action. These questions could therefore be paraphrased as follows. 'I wish to do what is supported by the best reasons. Tell me whether this is so supported.' As already mentioned, 'following reason' means 'doing what is supported by the best reasons.' Hence the question 'Shall (should, ought) I follow reason?' must be paraphrased as 'I wish to do what is supported by the best reasons. Tell me whether doing what is supported by the best reasons is doing what is supported by the best reasons.' It is, therefore, not worth asking.

The question '*Why* should I follow reason?' simply does not make sense. Asking it shows complete lack of understanding of the meaning of 'why questions.' 'Why should I do this?' is a request to be given the reason for saying that I should do this. It is normally asked when someone has already said, 'You should do this' and answered by giving the reason. But since 'Should I follow reason?' means 'Tell me whether doing what is supported by the best reasons is doing what is supported by the best reasons,' there is simply no possibility of adding 'Why?' For the question now comes to this, 'Tell me the reason why doing what is supported by the best reasons is doing what is supported by the best reasons.' It is exactly like asking, 'Why is a circle a circle?'

However, it must be admitted that there is another possible interpretation to our question according to which it makes sense and can even be answered. 'Why should I follow reason?' may not be a request for a reason in support of a tautological remark, but a request for a reason why one should enter on the theoretical task of deliberation. As already explained, following reason involves the completion of two tasks, the theoretical and the practical. The point of the theoretical is to give guidance in the practical task. We perform the theoretical only because we wish to complete the practical task in accordance with the outcome of the theoretical. On our first interpretation, "Should I follow reason?' means 'Is the practical task completed when it is completed in accordance with the outcome of the theoretical task? And the answer to this is obviously 'Yes,' for that is what we mean by 'completion of the practical task.' On our second interpretation, 'Should I follow reason?' is not a question about the practical but about the theoretical task. It is not a question about whether, given that one is prepared to perform both these tasks, they are properly completed in the way indicated. It is a question about whether one should enter on the whole performance at all, whether the "game" is worth playing. And this is a meaningful question. It might be better to "follow inspiration" than to "follow reason," in this sense: better to close one's eyes and wait for an answer to flash across the mind.

But while, so interpreted, 'Should I follow reason?' makes sense, it seems to me obvious that the answer to it is 'Yes, because it pays.' Deliberation is the only reliable method. Even if there were other reliable methods, we could only tell whether they were reliable by checking them against this method. Suppose some charismatic leader counsels, 'Don't follow reason, follow me. My leadership is better than that of reason'; we would still have to check his claim against the ordinary methods of reason. We would have to ascertain whether in following his advice we were doing the best thing. And this we can do only by examining whether he has advised us to do what is supported by the best reasons. His claim to be better than reason can in turn only be supported by the fact that he tells us precisely the same as reason does.

Is there any sense, then, in his claim that his guidance is preferable to that of reason? There may be, for working out what is supported by the best reasons takes a long time. Frequently, the best thing to do is to do something quickly now rather than the most appropriate thing later. A leader may have the ability to "see," to "intuit," what is the best thing to do more quickly than it is possible to work this out by the laborious methods of deliberation. In evaluating the qualities of leadership of such a person, we are evaluating *his ability to perform correctly the practical task of following reason* without having to go through the lengthy operations of the theoretical. Reason is required to tell us whether anyone has qualities of leadership better than ordinary, in the same way that pencil and paper multiplications are required to tell us whether a mathematical prodigy is genuine or a fraud.

Lastly, it must be said that sometimes it may be better even for an ordinary person without charisma not to follow reason but to do something at once, for quick action may be needed.

Can the Moral Point of View
Be Justified?[1]

J. C. THORNTON

In the Introduction to *The Moral Point of View*[2] Professor Baier mentions what he regards as "three fundamental questions of ethics requiring unequivocal and reassuring answers". The first of these questions, which he clearly regards as the most important, is this: "Should anyone do what is right when doing so is not to his advantage and if so why?"[3] Concerning this question he says, "if we could prove that we really *should* do what is right and refrain from doing what is wrong by pointing to a good reason why we should, we could remove the most serious of all our doubts (that is, as far as doubts about ethics are concerned), the doubt whether morality is indeed a sensible 'game', a practice worth preserving and worth conforming to".[4] It is this question, and two of the attempts made to answer it, including Baier's own, that I want to discuss in this article. I shall therefore be concerned with the more difficult task of giving a correct analysis of what "the moral point of view" *is* only in so far as it is necessary to do this in order to discuss the problem of its "justification".

This approach might at once be criticized as putting the cart before the horse. Surely, it will be objected, nothing fruitful can be said about the justification of the moral point of view unless it is preceded by a full discussion as to what is *meant* by this expression. (Plato I think would go further and say that *only* by seeing clearly what the moral point of view is can we understand how its adoption is justified, and in a way this is what I want to argue myself.) Yet sometimes an examination of the cart can tell us quite a lot about the sort of animal that pulls it. What is *logically* a prior question is not always methodological-wise the best question to tackle first.

Furthermore, there is something queer about the question "Why should I adopt the moral point of view?" which is missing in the relatively straightforward but nevertheless more difficult question "What constitutes

---

From Australasian Journal of Philosophy, *XLII (1964). Reprinted by permission of the author and* Australasian Journal of Philosophy.

[1] This is a slightly revised version of a paper read at the N.Z. Philosophy Conference at Wellington, in May, 1963.

[2] Kurt Baier, *The Moral Point of View* (New York: Cornell University Press, 1958).

[3] Op. cit., p. 3.

[4] Op. cit., p. 4.

the moral point of view?" and this queerness gives the former question a certain urgency.

But not everyone would agree that Baier's fundamental question *is* queer. Or, if it is admitted to be queer, it is sometimes thought to be none the less important for being that, and one which still needs answering. On the other hand, others have suspected that its queerness is directly related to its being a pseudo-question, a question which cannot be answered because nothing could logically count as an answer to it; and if we discover that a question is logically impossible to answer this is the same thing as saying that what we were trying to answer could not have been a genuine question after all. That Baier's 'fundamental' question is indeed a psuedo-question is, I think, a view widely held nowadays, and it is also with some qualifications my own view. Nevertheless, Baier's book has attracted a good deal of attention and admiration, not the least of which is directed to the way he has taken seriously this so-called pseudo-question. Furthermore, it seems to me that no one (except perhaps Professor D. H. Monro) has expressed quite so forcibly as Baier has the usual arguments for regarding it as a pseudo-question. Yet both Baier and Monro regard these arguments as less than conclusive. Baier obviously thinks that he has provided a satisfactory answer to this "fundamental question of ethics", and of course if he *has* provided a satisfactory answer to it then the arguments pointing to its being a pseudo-question must all be fallacious. (Pseudo-questions presumably can have pseudo-answers, but not satisfactory answers, or for that matter unsatisfactory answers.) In his Critical Notice of Baier's book[5] Monro argues convincingly that Baier has *not* provided a satisfactory answer to the question, but at the same time he commends Baier for taking it seriously. Monro sees this question as one which was raised and given one sort of answer by Hobbes, and he thinks that if we are not prepared to accept Hobbes' own answer (or Baier's for that matter) we are nevertheless still left with Hobbes' question. "It is time", he says, "that someone realized that Hobbism deserves a more convincing answer than it has yet been given".[6]

The question, of course, is older than Hobbes. Baier's formulation of it, "Should anyone do what is right when doing so is not to his advantage and if so why?", is perhaps not a bad paraphrase of the question which Thrasymachus raised, and which Glaucon and Adeimantus forcibly put to Socrates, in the first two books of Plato's *Republic*. It is often shortened to something like "Why should I be moral?" or "Why should I be just?" or "What is the ultimate justification of morals?" These are all variations on

---

5 See *Australasian Journal of Philosophy*, XXXVII (May, 1959).
6 Loc. cit., p. 78.

the one theme and all of them, I believe, equally suspicious. I propose there-fore to examine some recent attempts to persuade us that our suspicions are unfounded and that these are genuine questions which deserve to be taken seriously.

*   *   *

I have already mentioned that Baier himself is quite well aware that there are arguments which provide a prima facie case against the genuine-ness of his "fundamental question of ethics" (though in his view they provide only a prima facie case). The substance of one such argument is as follows: [7]

> Whenever we are offered reasons why we should adopt a proposed course of action, or why we should do A rather than B, then either it makes sense to ask why we should accept these as good or sufficient reasons or else it does not make sense. In cases where it does make sense to ask why the reasons should be accepted, it will be because more ultimate reasons can be given. If and when these more ultimate reasons *are* given, again it will either make sense to ask why *these* should be accepted or it will not make sense to ask this. Where it does make sense, the same question can be repeated, and so on. Now this process of pushing back to more and more basic reasons for practical choice cannot go on *ad infinitum*. There must always come a point when it just does not make sense to ask, "Why should I accept this as a reason for doing A, or avoiding B, etc.?" When this point has been reached, one has been given an "ultimate reason" why a proposed course of action should be pursued or avoided, and, by definition, one cannot ask for a reason for accepting what is itself an ultimate reason.

Now obviously everything depends, in this argument, on whether we can agree on what sort of reason will count as an "ultimate reason". One plausible candidate for this is "self-interest". That self-interest *is* an ultimate reason in this sense is generally thought to be illustrated by the well-known passage from Hume.

> Ask a man why he uses exercise; he will answer, because he desires to keep his health. If you then enquire why he desires health, he will readily reply, because sickness is painful. If you push your enquiries farther, and desire a reason why he hates pain, it is impos-sible he can give any. This is an ultimate end, and is never referred to any other object.[8]

---

[7] Here I am freely drawing upon and expressing in my own way many of the points which Baier makes in chap. 1, section 1, and elsewhere in his book.

[8] *Enquiries*, Appendix I, V.

It is an ultimate end because, generally speaking, the avoidance of pain is agreed to be in one's best interests, and so, unless there are complicating circumstances, no better reason can be given for doing something than to show that it is in one's best interests to do it.

But, of course, there sometimes *are* complicating circumstances, e.g. when a moral issue is at stake. So it seems that a rival candidate for the position of an ultimate reason is the "moral reason". If A says to B, "Why should I keep my promise to marry Jane?" then on the one hand he *might* be asking B for a justification of the general practice of promise keeping (what is the point of keeping promises anyway?). On the other hand, A might be thinking of his own particular situation and asking B to show him why he should keep his particular promise to Jane, hinting that perhaps his situation should be regarded as exceptional because of special extenuating circumstances. On either of these interpretations his question would be perfectly proper. But if, in the course of further discussion, A says, "Oh I *know* that it would be morally wrong for me to break my promise to marry Jane, but why *should* I keep my promise?" then would not this be a very odd remark to make? Surely once a moral reason for a proposed course of action has been given *and accepted* as relevant, no further justification for doing the action is called for. What *could* be a better reason for doing something than a moral reason?

Thus (the argument runs) we have two kinds of ultimate reasons for action—moral reasons and reasons of self-interest. Moreover, nothing else will be found to function as an ultimate reason apart from these two. Only reasons of self-interest and moral reasons can put a logical stop to a series of questions of the form, "Why should I do *x*?"

Now the really serious complication arises when these two sorts of ultimate reason conflict, i.e. when we have a proposed course of action such that, on the grounds of our best interests, we should do it, but on moral grounds we should refrain from doing it. In such cases the reason which is said to have the greater weight is the moral reason, i.e. we should do what is right even when it is not to our advantage to do so. But it will not make sense to ask "Why?" To ask for a reason for a proposed course of action is to ask to be shown either that the action will be conducive to one's best interests or else that it is demanded by one's moral code. Now in the case in point the action is by definition not in one's best interests, so this prevents 'self-interest' from functioning as an ultimate reason. But we are asking why we should do what our moral code demands for us, so we can't be given a *moral* reason why we should be moral. But there aren't any other kinds of ultimate reasons apart from moral reasons and reasons of self-interest. Therefore, the question "why should I do what is right when it is not in my interests to do so?" is logically impossible to answer and is merely a pseudo-question.

So much for the prima facie case for the logical absurdity of Baier's fundamental question of ethics. How strong an argument is it? Its weakest point would seem to be the apparently arbitrary and dogmatic assertion that in situations where moral duty and self-interest conflict it is the moral reason which has the greater weight. There seems to be some sort of logical slide between how much weight a reason *has* and how much weight a reason is to be *given*. What is it to say that moral reasons are weightier than reasons of self-interest if it is not to say that moral reasons *should be given* greater weight than reasons of self-interest? If this is what is meant, it seems intolerable that this claim cannot be justified rationally. It is all very well to mention that we have been *taught* from childhood to regard the moral reasons as being weightier. This merely makes us demand all the more urgently that we be shown that what we have been taught in childhood has some rational basis, and it is just this that Baier felt called upon to provide. He thinks he can show that there are weightier reasons, that it is more rational, to do what is right than to do what is simply in our own interests. But he argues that if someone were then to ask "Why should we be rational?" then this would be a nonsensical question because following reason is just doing what is supported by the weightiest reasons, and it does not make sense to ask for reasons for doing what is supported by the weightiest reasons.[9]

This looks like a promising move, but, of course, the crucial question is: Does Baier succeed in showing that there are weightier reasons for doing what is right than for following our own interests? In one sense he does, but unfortunately not in the sense required by his orginal "fundamental" question. All he succeeds in showing is Hobbes' point, viz. that there are weightier reasons for everyone doing what is right than for everyone following self-interest.[10] Baier asks us to examine "the two alternative worlds, one in which moral reasons are always treated by everyone as superior to reasons of self-interest and one in which the reverse is the practice. And we can see that the first world is the better world, because we can see that the second world would be the sort which Hobbes describes as the state of nature".[11] Baier concludes that the answer to the question 'Why should we be moral?' is as follows: "We should be moral because being moral is following rules designed to overrule self-interest whenever it is in the interest of everyone alike that everyone should set aside his interest. . . . It is not possible that *everyone* should do better for himself by following enlightened self-interest rather than morality. The best possible lite *for everyone* is attainable only by everyone's following the rules of morality,

---

9 Op. cit., p. 318.
10 See D. H. Monro's "Critical Notice", loc. cit., pp. 77 f.
11 Op. cit., p. 310.

that is, rules which quite frequently may require individuals to make genuine sacrifices".[12]

It is clear, I think, that Baier has not answered his original question. His mistake was to think that what we have to do to answer it is to consider two alternative worlds, the one in which moral rules are universally followed and the one in which the rules of enlightened self-interest are universally followed, and then decide which is the better world to live in, i.e. in our own better interests. But if we are going to answer along these lines his fundamental question of ethics, viz. 'Why should I be moral when doing so is not to my advantage?', then there are not just two alternative worlds which we have to compare but *three*. The third possible world is the one in which moral rules are obeyed by everyone else *except me,* who follow enlightened self-interest. The first world is admittedly, from everyone's point of view, a better alternative to the second, but is not the third world, from *my* point of view, a better alternative to either of the other two? Of course, one can hold that the third world is not a practical possibility, but Baier has made it plain that he does not support this view. He makes it quite clear that following morality entails making "genuine sacrifices" and he is not convinced by those who would argue that following morality is in the long run identical with following enlightened self-interest. Inevitably, then, his attempt to give the moral point of view a rational basis comes to grief because, in spite of what he says to the contrary, he has assumed that the only *really* ultimate reason justifying an action is in fact self-interest, and so he is logically prevented from justifying doing one's moral duty in those situations in which duty and interest really do conflict.

My guess is that he was probably prevented from seeing the glaring self-contradiction in his argument by a simple verbal confusion. It is significant that in the early stages of his book he frequently expresses his "fundamental question of ethics" in the words "Why should *I* be moral?" (my italics). However, at the end of the book, when he is at last ready to try to answer the question, he invariably expresses it in the words "Why should *we* be moral?" This latter question can easily be interpreted as a demand for a rational justification for the institution of morality in general, and, of course, a plausible answer can be given to this question along more or less Hobbist lines. But to answer this general question is not automatically to have answered the particular and very different question, "Why should *I* be moral (in the particular situation *x* at time *t*)?", and yet Baier has tended to use these two ways of expressing his question indifferently as if they meant the same thing.

My conclusion at this point is that Baier has not succeeded in answering his "fundamental question of ethics" and therefore not succeeded in

---

[12] Op. cit., pp. 314 f.

showing that it is a genuine question demanding a serious answer. But, of course, it may still be true that the question is in fact a genuine one.

* * *

Another philosopher who has taken the question seriously and whose articles on moral philosophy have caused much favorable comment is Mrs. Philippa Foot. In an article called "Moral Beliefs"[13] she considers the question 'Why should I be just?' This question, it is true, is not verbally identical with Baier's, but I think the context of her discussion shows that in substance the point at issue is the same. The main purpose of her article, however, is to show that the case for "ethical naturalism" is much stronger than is generally admitted. She argues that not *any* sort of belief can function as a moral belief which is not necessarily related in some way to human welfare, and that what constitutes human welfare is very far from being a wholly arbitrary matter of opinion. For example, she argues that it would be as plausible for someone to hold that prudence, courage, or temperance were not virtues as it would be to hold that the loss of one's hands or eyes were not injuries. With this part of her argument I am not immediately concerned and have no particular quarrel.

But the virtue of 'justice' raises a different problem for, as she says, "While prudence, courage, and temperance are qualities which benefit the man who has them, justice seems rather to benefit others, and to work to the disadvantage of the just man himself. . . . We will be asked", she continues, "how on our theory justice can be a virtue and injustice a vice, since it will surely be difficult to show that any man whatsoever must need to be just as he needs the use of his hands and eyes, or needs prudence, courage, and temperance?"[14] Mrs. Foot believes that Thrasymachus' argument has to be taken with complete seriousness and that if his premise is true, viz. that injustice is more profitable than justice, then his conclusion certainly follows, viz. that a man who has the strength to get away with injustice has reason to follow this as the best way of life. "It is a striking fact about modern moral philosophy", she says, "that no one sees any difficulty in accepting Thrasymachus' premise and rejecting his conclusion".[15]

It is only fair to point out that at least Baier saw this to be a difficulty but, as we have seen, he rejected Thrasymachus' conclusion without being successful in rejecting his premise. I now want to try to show that Mrs. Foot has not fared any better. In fact I believe she is guilty of much the same kind of confusion as Baier. Nevertheless, in her article she makes a number of valuable points relevant to what I believe is the correct con-

---

13 *Proceedings of the Aristotelian Society*, 1958–59.
14 P. 99.
15 P. 100.

clusion to be drawn, but which in fact tend to strengthen the case against her.

Like Baier, she stresses the difficulty in showing that it is always profitable for the good man to be just or moral, and yet at the same time she is convinced that, unless this is done, no reason has been given why the good man *should* be just.

> Given Thrasymachus' premise Thrasymachus' point of view is reasonable; we have no particular reason to admire those who practice justice through timidity or stupidity.[16]

But she tries to have it both ways. From having insisted on the reality of the situation in which justice and self-interest are incompatible, she moves on to make a strong suggestion that the conflict in these situations is more apparent than real and that in most if not all cases it will be found that it really *is* profitable for the good man to be just after all.

> Is it true, however, to say that justice is not something a man needs in his dealings with his fellows, supposing only that he be strong? Those who think that he can get on perfectly well without being just should be asked to say exactly how such a man is supposed to live. We know that he is to practice injustice whenever the unjust act would bring him advantage; but what is he to say? Does he admit that he does not recognize the rights of other people, or does he pretend? In the first case even those who combine with him will know that on a change of fortune, or a shift of affection, he may turn to plunder them, and he must be as wary of their treachery as they are of his. Presumably the happy unjust man is supposed, as in Book II of the *Republic*, to be a very cunning liar and actor, combining complete injustice with the appearance of justice: he is prepared to treat others ruthlessly, but pretends that nothing is further from his mind. Philosophers often speak as if a man could thus hide himself even from those around him, but the supposition is doubtful, and in any case the price in vigilance would be colossal.[17]

Then finally (and here the pendulum swings back once more) Mrs. Foot admits that of course there will be *some* situations in which justice is not profitable, but, because a man has a reason to be just on most occasions, he cannot act differently in these highly exceptional circumstances without forfeiting his right to be called a just man. Here I quote her final paragraph:

> The reason why it seems to some people so impossibly difficult to show that justice is more profitable than injustice is that they con-

---

16 P. 102.
17 P. 103.

sider in isolation particular just acts. It is perfectly true that if a man is just it follows that he will be prepared, in the event of very evil circumstances, even to face death rather than to act unjustly— for instance, in getting an innocent man convicted of a crime of which he has been accused. For him it turns out that his justice brings disaster on him, and yet like anyone else he had good reason to be a just and not an unjust man. He could not have it both ways and while possessing the virtue of justice hold himself ready to be unjust should any great advantage accrue. The man who has the virtue of justice is not ready to do certain things, and if he is too easily tempted we shall say that he was ready after all.

But surely this last point is strictly irrelevant, for it is not disputed that the man who acts unjustly when it suits his long-term interest is anything but unjust. Of course he is unjust and immoral—but is he irrational? And the man who does *not* yield to temptation is quite rightly called a just man. But is he rightly called a rational man? There are the doubts which Thrasymachus raised and these are the doubts which Mrs. Foot set out to remove, but it is quite plain that she has not removed them. Or rather, by the way in which she interprets the term 'rational' she ensures that the doubts are removed (as it were) in the other direction, for on her own premises it indeed follows inevitably that a man has no reason to be *consistently* just, for on some occasions he will see that to act justly will bring disaster upon him.

There is, it is true, an alternative conclusion which can be drawn from her argument, viz. that if nothing is to be allowed to count as a virtue unless it is invariably profitable to its possessor, then justice is not a virtue. But it is clear that this conclusion does not suit her purpose either, because, as she denies the consequent (she is sure that justice *is* a virtue), she is logically committed to denying the antecedent, which asserts that being profitable to its possessor is part of what is *meant* by the term virtue. Yet it was precisely in order to *affirm* this antecedent or something very like it, that she wrote the article I have been discussing.

We are now in a position to ask whether the failure of both Baier and Mrs. Foot to answer the question "Why should I be moral (or just) when it is not to my advantage?" is not after all related to its being a pseudo-question, and clearly it *is* so related. Despite explicit claims to the contrary on Baier's part, both he and Mrs. Foot have in fact treated self-interest as the only really ultimate justifying reason for action. This being so, it follows that it is logically impossible for them to justify any action whatever, moral or otherwise, which is not in the agent's supposed long-term self-interest. Once it is admitted that there are situations in which duty and interest genuinely conflict, then it follows that either following duty in such cases is irrational or self-interest is not the only ultimate justifying reason. Furthermore, it seems likely that both Baier and Mrs. Foot were prevented from seeing that they were attempting the logically impossible principally because they both repeatedly confuse the task of justifying particular moral acts with the very different task of justifying the general institution of morality.

However, though the question which Baier and Mrs. Foot set themselves to answer was, given their particular assumptions, logically unanswerable, it seems it would still have been a pseudo-question even had they assumed that moral reasons are also to be counted as genuinely "ultimate reasons". Just what sort of reason *could* we have in the context of a particular situation for choosing to follow morality rather than enlightened self-interest?

Someone who sees the force of this argument might be tempted to say, "Of course no rational justification can be given for accepting the moral point of view, because to say 'I should do what is right even when it is not to my ultimate advantage' is to express a kind of leap of faith". In fact, however, all that it expresses is either a tautology or a contradiction. If 'should' is being used here in its moral sense (as it often is) then it is tautologous to say that we should be moral even when it is not to our advantage, for this is part of what 'being moral' means. But if 'should' is being used in its self-interest sense (as again it often is) then it is just plain self-contradictory to say that we should be moral even when it is not to our advantage. And it is hard to see what other sense, apart from these two, the word 'should' could have in the context of this expression. (This point, by the way, was first brought home to me by Professor Shorter.)

Yet, in spite of all that has been said, it still remains true, of course, that the point of view of enlightened self-interest is different from the moral point of view. Not merely theoretically different but also different in practice. It seems that it is possible to accept the moral point of view or to reject it, and, according to the choice one makes, there will be some situations in which different courses of action will be followed. The rational egoist[18] will follow the rules of morality only to the extent that doing so will further his long-term interests, and to this extent, of course, the conduct of the rational egoist will be identical with the conduct of the morally good man. But in those Gyges-like situations where there is a genuine conflict between moral duty and long-term self-interest, the rational egoist (provided he does not on these occasions act irrationally) will do one thing and the morally good man (provided he does not on these occasions act im-

---

18 For the purposes of this article it will be sufficient to define "rational egoist" as one who accepts as his own basic guide to action the principles of enlightened self-interest.

morally) will do another. Yet, as we have seen, neither the point of view of rational egoism nor the point of view of morality can be justified rationally without begging questions concerning the meaning of the word 'rational'.

But, it may now be objected, is there not an asymmetry about the contrast which demands some sort of explanation? For in the Gyges-like situation, if the egoist does *not* do what is in his own interests we say he acted irrationally, whereas if in the same situation the morally good man does not do his duty we say he acted *immorally* but we do not say he acted *irrationally*. This suggests that it is only the point of view of rational egoism which is truly rational, and that self-interest is the only genuinely 'ultimate reason' after all.

But let us look again at the reasons why self-interest is thought to put an effective logical stop to the question-series "Why should I do *x*?" In her article, Mrs. Foot correctly observes that "in general anyone is given a reason for acting when he is shown the way to something he wants".[19] If someone wants *x*, and we show that the way to *x* is to do *y*, we have given him a reason for doing *y*. But have we given him an ultimate reason? Only, I think, if we have shown him the way to that which, of all the practical possibilities open to him, he wants most of all in the particular circumstances in which he finds himself. But it may be that what he wants most of all is to do his moral duty. Then if *x* is his moral duty, we *have* given him an ultimate reason for doing *y* once we have shown him that *y* is the particular act which in the circumstances moral duty requires him to do.

Thus it is *what we most want to do,* rather than what is in our own self-interest that provides the basis for the ultimate rational justification for action. Moreover, it just seems to be a brute fact about human nature that we do not all agree as to what we most want to do even when the 'wants' are of a highly general sort. Whereas some people want most of all to do whatever is in their own best interests, there are others, it seems, who, at least from time to time, most want to do whatever is their moral duty, even if this *is* at the cost of their own best interests.

The fact that not all of us want to do our moral duty, and even if most of us do we do not *always* want to, or we do not always want to do it most of all, has misled some philosophers into thinking that if anything is going to function as an ultimate reason it will have to be something which *everyone always* wants most of all. They have seen that unless this is so we can never be sure that we have given a person an ultimate reason for doing an action, for if what we gave as a reason was not something that pointed the way to what that person wanted most of all at that particular time, it would always be sensible for him to reply "But why *should* I do *x*?" This is the point Mrs. Foot is making in the following passage:

---

19 Op. cit., p. 101.

> In general, anyone is given a reason for acting when he is shown
> the way to something he wants; but for some wants the question
> 'Why do you want that?' will make sense, and for others it will not.
> ... This is why it is not true to say that 'it's unjust' gives a reason
> in so far as any reasons can ever be given. 'It's unjust' gives a rea-
> son only if the nature of justice can be shown to be such that it is
> necessarily connected with what a man wants.[20]

The correct conclusion to draw, however, is not that the avoidance of a
particular unjust action will be rationally justified only if we connect it with
something that *everyone* always wants, but rather only if it is connected
with what is wanted most of all *by the particular person concerned* at that
particular time. For there seems to be no highly general 'want' which all of
us always want fulfilled more than anything else, and in particular it is not
true that what all of us at all times most want is whatever is in our own
long-term best interests.

* * *

My general conclusions are as follows:

(1) That the so-called fundamental question of ethics which both Baier
and Mrs. Foot have attempted to answer has not been answered by
either of them because, basically, it is a pseudo-question after all.

(2) That in situations where there is a genuine conflict between moral
duty and enlightened self-interest, whichever course of action is followed
will either be rational or irrational according to whether or not the
agent accepts or rejects the moral point of view.

(3) That it is what a person most wants to do, rather than what is in his
own best interests, that provides the ultimate basis for the rational
justification of an action.

---

20 Op. cit., p. 101.

Why Should I Be Moral?

But now scepticism by its extremity begins to reveal its absurdity.

JOHN WISDOM

KAI NIELSEN

1

Subjectivism as an ethical theory is dead. As a metaethical analysis of what is meant when a moral judgment is made, it claims that all moral judgments are in reality only about the attitudes of the person who makes the judgment. According to this theory, if *A* says 'The execution of Nagy was vile', he simply means 'I disapprove of the execution of Nagy'. But the truth-values of these sentences are obviously not the same. *A* might disapprove of the execution of Nagy but he still could reasonably ask if this execution was vile. Autobiographical reports are not in themselves taken as decisive evidence for the truth of moral claims. But in finding out what *A*'s attitudes really are, we discover whether or not *A* disapproves of the execution of Nagy. Objections of this type have been correctly regarded as decisive objections to such a subjective metaethic.

Yet for newcomers (students, interested onlookers, and the like) and for some professionals, too, there is something too easy about this refutation of subjectivism. Variations of subjectivism have been recurrent in the history of philosophy from Gorgias to Bertrand Russell. Some of them have been foolish, some simply confused, but to suggest that these theories have been *simply* foolish and without point seems to me prima facie implausible. In this essay I shall attempt to show why this is so; I shall attempt to indicate a plausible line of reasoning, a common sense core, in these subjective ethical theories. (Here again the task will be to elicit a really crucial use of "subjectivism" in reflections about human conduct. The view often called "naive subjectivism" is for the most part a strawman of certain philosophical analysts.) Once I have made explicit what the common sense core of this subjectivism is, I shall examine what considerations can be reasonably brought against it. In order to get more directly to the core of my argument I shall assume here the correctness of two major contentions.

First, I shall assume the general correctness of the claim developed at length in Hare's *The Language of Morals* and Nowell-Smith's *Ethics,* that moral and evaluational utterances are parts of practical discourse and that a complete justification of any practical claim involves reference to the

From Methodos, *XV (1963). Reprinted by permisssion of the author.*

attitudes of the parties involved or to the decisions they would make. I am aware that this is a controversial claim and that unless carefully stated, it is likely to be misleading and unless carefully qualified it is wrong. Nevertheless, I believe there are careful formulations of it that are correct, though I shall not argue for its correctness here.

Secondly, I shall assume what I have argued for elsewhere,[1] namely, that it makes sense to ask 'Why should people be moral?' and 'Why should I be moral?' as long as we do not construe the 'should' in the above two questions as a moral 'should'. Only if the 'should' is construed morally, are the above questions like 'Why are all round things circular?'

Without entering into a defense of this second point, let me leave the reminder that there are a multitude of uses of 'should' and 'ought' which are not moral uses, i.e. 'I should fill my fountain pen for it's writing poorly', 'People ought to mix their T.V. viewing with a little theater going', The beam should be placed here', 'The level ought to be longer', etc. The second-mentioned sentence is clearly not a technical injunction but gives advice as to how to act in the sphere of human conduct. Yet it is not distinctively moral, for we would not ordinarily say that it is evil to refuse to obey it, though a person who would seriously assert it would say that peoples' lives would be enhanced if they did follow it. There are clearly standard uses of 'ought' that are not moral uses though they are a part of the practical language of human conduct.

'Why should people be moral?' and 'Why should I be moral?' are indeed unusual questions, but the 'should' in them does not function in an unusual way any more than it does in 'Why should people never wear sports jackets to cocktail parties?' A recognition of intelligibility of the odd question 'Why be Moral?' naturally arises in relation to the old saw, "Egoism and Ethics".

The frequently obscured common sense core of subjectivism can be seen most readily from a natural reaction to a refutation of ethical egoism. It is necessary to recall that ethical egoism is not a psychological doctrine of human motivation, so it is not necessary for the so-called ethical egoist to hold that all men always seek their own good even when it conflicts with the good of others. Rather, the so-called ethical egoist claims each person *ought* always to seek his own good as the sole end worth seeking for its own sake.[2] It is important to note the qualifiers 'always' and 'worth seeking for its own sake'. Many nonegoistic views would claim that we frequently ought to seek our own good or even that we have a prima facie

[1] K. Nielsen, "Is 'Why Should I be Moral?' an Absurdity?" *Australasian Journal of Philosophy*, XXXVI (1958), 25–32.
[2] Charles Baylis, for example, defines 'ethical egoism' in this way in his *Ethics: The Principles of Wise Choice* (New York, 1958), p. 169.

right to seek our own good except in those situations where it conflicts with
the common good. The ethical egoist is distinctive in claiming we always
ought to seek our own good and that we always ought to regard this as
the sole aim worthy of pursuit for its own sake; that is to say, the position
I am concerned with here is that of an ethical egoism of ends or what
Brian Medlin has called a "categorical egoism".[3] But it not only must be a
categorical egoism, it must also be a universal egoism if it is to make a claim
to be a normative ethic or even a way of life. Note I said, 'Each person
ought always to seek his own good', that is, 'Everyone ought always to seek
his own good as the sole end worth seeking for its own sake'. This is very
different from an individual egoism which claims that the person making
the claim should seek his own good as his only rational end.

   Universal categorical ethical egoism will not do as a metaethical theory
purporting to analyze what is meant when people say something is morally
good or obligatory; and if it is offered as a radical normative ethic it likewise gets into intolerable paradoxes. In order to remain intelligible, egoism
must be put forth as an individual and not as a universal egoism. But, as
such, it also fails to meet the minimum conditions necessary for something
to count as a 'morality', as that word is ordinarily and intelligibly used.
However, it is just this individual egoism that is at the heart of the matter
for the subjectivist. He wants to know why *he* shouldn't be an individual
egoist. (Remember the 'shouldn't' here does not have a moral force, though
it does have a normative force.)

   The dogmatic sounding contentions of the above paragraph need to
be established. I do not want to write another essay on the refutation of
egoism.[4] But the following remarks should make the essential points and
prepare the way for what is to follow.

   To count as an ethical doctrine, then, an ethical egoism of ends must
be understood as claiming that everyone ought to seek his own good as an
end and consider the good of others only when this would in his judgment
further his own good. What purports to be our standard of moral appraisal
is personal; that is to say, each of us should always ask ourselves when
deliberating on how we ought to act: 'Is this rule or this action or this
attitude in my rational self-interest?' If it is in one's rational interest then
it ought always to be done, if not, not. But, as Baier has ably argued, such
a standard could not be a moral standard for we have moral standards to
impartially adjudicate the conflicting interests of individuals and groups;
but if each individual's own rational self-interest is taken as the standard,

   [3] Brian Medlin, "Ultimate Principles and Ethical Egoism," *The Australasian
Journal of Philosophy*, XXXV (1957), 111–18.
   [4] See my "Egoism in Ethics," *Philosophy and Phenomenological Research*, XIX
(June, 1959).

in reality we have no standard by which to adjudicate these conflicting interests. The very *raison d'être* of morality has been frustrated. Thus self-interest, no matter how enlightened, cannot be our standard of *moral* appraisal. "Ethical egoism" cannot possibly be an ethical or moral doctrine.

More could be said about this—there are moves and counter-moves that could still be made—but I have given what I take to be the most fundamental reason why egoism is not a possible moral stance.[5] So-called ethical egoism is not a radically different "moral geometry", "a perverse morality", or even an iconoclastic morality. It isn't a morality or even a possible morality at all. If we are to be consistent egoists we must be individual egoists, and this is to simply reject the claims of anything that could conceivably count as a morality. As Medlin puts it such "indifference to morals may be wicked, but it is not a perverse morality".[6]

If individual egoism is not dressed up as a kind of morality—something it can't possibly be—it can be put in a logically impeccable way. It can be a personal, rationally thought out plan or policy of action.

But for a man like Thrasymachus who is willing to question the claims of the whole moral enterprise, why isn't individual egoism a viable alternative? He could admit that Butler is perfectly right—people don't always act egoistically—but he could go on to claim that only a benighted fool insists on trying to be a morally good man. A wise man will not be duped by all the humbug about morality learned at Nannie's knee.

Surely one crucial question that any reflective individual in any age must face is the question. 'What kind of life would be a happy life? What sort of people should we strive to become so that we as individuals can be happy?'. The individual egoist, as well as the moral agent, is (or at least can be) vitally concerned with this question. Such an egoist, if he is wise, has considered the claims of morality and has decided that he will not attain genuine and lasting happiness by striving to be a morally good man, though it may be good tactics usually to be a man of good morals. It is his belief that the way of morality is not usually the way of happiness. And if and when it is, it ought to be pursued only because it will bring the pursuer happiness. To be sure, an intelligent individual egoist will not go around proclaiming that everyone should only look after himself. He may, if he is so *inclined*, pass on his insight to his family and some close friends, but he will not try to become an ethical egoist or try to base conventional morality on egoism. This would be the very epitome of foolishness. In certain contexts, he may even find it expedient to mouth "the high-minded pomposities of this morning's editorial". Such behavior, so to say, gives him

5 Some of these are made by John Hospers in his "Baier and Medlin on Ethical Egoism," *Philosophical Studies*, XII (January–February, 1961).

6 Medlin, op. cit., p. 113.

a good press. But he has decided to act on the personal principle: Always look after yourself and no one else, unless looking after someone else will benefit you.

True, there cannot be an egoistic way of life or *Weltanschaungphiloso-phie* but there could be a deliberate, rationally thought out and consistently adhered to personal policy of individual egoism. Brunton correctly notes, "There can be intelligent, self-controlled people, with a plan of life, who care only for themselves".[7] Egoism cannot be an ethical doctrine but the man committed to individual egoism still has a use for 'I *ought* to consider only my own good' as distinguished from 'I only care about myself'. The former normative (though not moral) sentence indicates a settled policy of action. The latter, by contrast, indicates what may be only a momentary or very impermanent reaction. The token 'ought' when used in such a context has more than just the common mark or noise in common with the token 'ought' used in a moral context. In both instances they are only properly used if in some way they indicate a settled policy as distinct from a momentary whim, emotion or impulse.

Thus, I do not see anything logically inconsistent about individual egoism so long as we don't try to extend it into a new rival morality or into an iconoclastic world view. A view that exhibits a contempt for all moral considerations whatsoever, could not possibly be a moral view, not even a perverse moral view. But a consistent individual egoism, intelligently pursued, is not a doctrine; it is not something that would be articulated by an intelligent egoist. Yet privately a person might adopt it as his policy of life.

Why shouldn't he? (Recall the 'shouldn't' here is not a moral 'shouldn't'.) Why is he (or is he?) irrational or mistaken if he follows this egoistic policy? Surely it is not in our *interest* for him to act immorally, but why shouldn't he or I or even you? Why should the "existing individual" who is trying to decide how to live happily, or significantly, opt for the point of view of morality rather than an intelligent and carefully controlled individual egoism?

Imagine yourself studying all the metaethical treatises, the systems of normative ethics, the sage advice of the wise men, in short, all the claims of morality. Then imagine yourself in the quiet of your own study weighing up—not for others but for yourself alone—these considerations against the considerations in favor of individual egoism. Why should *you* choose to act morally rather than nonmorally?

This question, which is at least as old as Plato, has been traditionally

---

[7] J. A. Brunton, "Egoism and Morality," *Philosophical Quarterly*, VI (1956), 298–99.

imbedded in the thick muck of metaphysics.[8] Often it has been confused with a lot of other questions and recently it has been too lightly dismissed as nonsensical or absurd. The *feeling* emerges that finally there is no real argument here, one way or another; one must just opt for one policy rather than another. Here Sartrean or Kierkegaardian talk about decisions and anxiety *seems* correct. Subjectivism again raises its ugly head. We are tempted to say that here decision or commitment is king. Emotional energy may go into our commitment to morality but in a "cool hour" we cannot discover decisive reasons for acting in either way. There seem to be no decisive reasons for our choice here; nor can we conceive of a nonquestion-begging general procedure that would enable us to decide between these conflicting policies.[9]

Reflective people, uncorrupted by philosophical theories, can be brought by ordinary reflection over morality to recognize the point I have just made. The nonphilosophical idioms 'It's a value judgment' or 'It's finally a matter of what sort of a person you want to be', reflect just this point. The very anxiety that any slight reference to subjectivism arouses in some people's breasts counts (I believe) for rather than against my claim. We do not come to a conclusion of this sort unambivalently. In reflecting about morality and human conduct, we are tempted finally to say that you must just decide what sort of person you want to be. No intellectual considerations will settle the matter for you here.

It is just this belief that seems to me to be the common sense core of subjectivism. But is it a belief that we can and should accept as clear-minded, rational human beings?' Can we rationally defend taking a moral point of view? Are there decisive reasons for accepting the claims of morality such that any rational "unmoved spectator of the actual" would have to assent to them? In the next section I shall turn to this question.

---

8 It received a new coat with Donald Walhout's essay "Why Should I Be Moral? A Reconsideration," *The Review of Metaphysics*, XII (June, 1959), 570–88. Consider only "... the final theoretical answer" to our question is that "... one should be moral because this fits into a pattern of universal harmony of all things ..." and the "universal harmony of all things can be regarded as the ultimate culmination of all existence, not indeed as a description at any particular moment of time, but as an all-pervasive ideal." But such an ideal is not left to the whims of mortal will for we are told "it may be regarded as rooted in the ultimate power of being that produces what is." Apparently it is too much to expect that the days are over when this kind of philosophy could be written. Walhout sees there is a problem about justifying the moral point of view that was not adequately met by Bradley and Prichard but in answering what he calls "the ultimate question" he gives us this nonsense.

9 See W. H. Walsh, "Scepticism About Morals and Scepticism About Knowledge," *Philosophy*, XXXV (July 1960), 218–34.

2

Why then be moral? We need initially to note that this question actually ought to be broken down into two questions, namely, (1) 'Why should people be moral?' or 'Why should there be a morality at all?' and (2) 'Why should I be moral?'. As will become evident, these questions ought not in the name of clarity, to be confused. But they have been run together; in asking for a justification for the institution of morality both questions are relevant and easily confused. 'Why be Moral?' nicely straddles these questions. In this section I shall first examine some traditional, and I believe unhelpful, answers to the above general questions. There the general question is not broken down as it should be and in examining these views I shall not break it down either. After noting the difficulties connected with these approaches, I shall state what I believe to be a satisfactory answer to the question, 'Why should there be a morality at all?' and indicate why it leaves untouched the harder question, 'Why should I be moral?'

There is a prior consideration that we must first dispose of. In considering both of these questions we must be careful to distinguish the *causes* of a man's being moral from the *reasons* be gives for being moral. If one is a little careful about the implications of the word 'likes', Bradley seems perfectly right in saying: "A man is moral because he likes being moral; and he likes it, partly because he has been brought up to the habit of liking it, and partly because he finds it gives him what he wants, while its opposite does not to so".[10] In other words people are moral primarily because they have been conditioned to be moral. The human animal is a social animal and (as Butler and Hume observed) people normally tend to consider the welfare of others as well as their own welfare. People indeed act selfishly but they also take out life insurance, feel anxiety over the troubles of others, and even have moments of mild discomfort at the thought that life on this planet may some day be impossible. People react in this way because they have been taught or conditioned to so react. But, the 'because' here is explanatory and *not* justificatory. It explains in a very general way what makes or *causes* people to be moral. But the question I am concerned with here is a quite different one. In asking 'Why should people be moral?', I am asking the question, 'What good reasons do people have for being moral?'. In asking about the justification for acting morally, I am only incidentally concerned with an explanation of the causes of moral behavior.

What good reasons are there for being moral? And if there are good reasons for being moral are they sufficient or decisive reasons?

There is a short, snappy answer to my question. The plain man might well say: 'People ought to be moral because it is wicked, evil, morally

---

[10] F. H. Bradley, *Ethical Studies* (The Liberal Arts Press, 1951), p. 7.

reprehensible not to be moral. We have the very best reasons for being moral, namely that it is immoral not to be moral'. The plain man (or at the very least the plain Western Man and not *just* the ordinary Oxford Don) would surely agree with Bradley "that consciousness, when unwarped by selfishness and not blinded by sophistry is convinced that to ask for the Why? is simple immorality...".[11] The correct answer to the question: 'Why Be Moral?' is simply that this is what we ought to do.

This short answer will not do, for the plain man has failed to understand the question. A clear-headed individual could not be asking for *moral* justification for being moral. This would be absurd. Rather he is asking the practical question: why should people be bound by the conventions of morality at all? He would not dispute Baier's contention that "it is generally believed that when reasons of self-interest conflict with moral reasons, then moral reasons override those of self-interest".[12] It is perfectly true that the plain man regards moral reasons as superior to all others and it is, of course, in accordance with reason to follow superior or overriding reasons, but if a clear-headed man asks 'Why should we be moral?' he is challenging the very grading criteria those ordinary convictions rest on. He would acknowledge that it is indeed morally reprehensible or wicked not to act morally. But he would ask: 'So what?'. And he might even go on to query: 'What is the good of all this morality anyway? Are not those Marxists and Freudians right who claim that the whole enterprise of morality is nothing but an ideological device to hoodwink people into *not* seeking what they really want? Why should people continue to fall for this conjuring trick? To call someone "wicked" or "evil" is to severely grade them down, but why should people accept any *moral* grading criteria at all?'

There are several traditional replies to this. But all of them are unsatisfactory.

One traditional approach advocated by Plato and Bishop Butler, among others, claims that people should be moral because they will not be happy otherwise. Being moral is at least a necessary condition for being happy.

For Butler the argument takes the following form. Human beings are so constituted that they will, generally speaking, act morally. When they don't act morally they will clearly recognize they were mistaken in not doing so. The human animal has a conscience and this conscience not only causes people to act in a certain way, but is in fact a *norm* of action. Conscience guides as well as goads; the deliverances of conscience are both action-evoking and a source of moral knowledge. Conscience tells the moral

---

11 Bradley, op. cit., p. 6.
12 Kurt Baier, *The Moral Point of View: A Rational Basis of Ethics* (Cornell University Press, 1958), p. 308.

agent what to do even in specific situations. It clearly and unequivocally tells him to always act morally and he is so constituted that if he ignores the dictates of his conscience he will not be happy. In other words, Butler agrees with Plato in claiming that Thrasymachus and other amoralists are fundamentally mistaken about the true interests of a human being.

That it is in the human animal's best interest to live virtuously is no more established by Butler than it is by Plato.[13] Plato is reduced to analogy, myth, and mystagogy and, as Duncan-Jones points out, Butler is finally pushed to concede that "full acceptance of the conclusion that human nature is satisfiable and only satisfiable by virtue depends on revelation".[14] In the face of what clearly seem to be genuine exceptions to the claim that it is in the individual's self-interest always to act morally, Butler is driven to remark: "All shall be set right at the final distribution of things".[15]

Some intuitionist may argue that while this Butlerian move won't do, it still remains the case that Butler could rightly have said that we just directly (in some sense) perceive or see the fittingness or suitability of always acting morally. To meet this point we would have to argue against the whole logical or epistemological machinery of intuitionism. We would need to question (as Toulmin has) such a use of 'intuition', to point out that neither 'see' nor 'apprehend' is at home here, and challenge the notion that ethical words simply refer to qualities or relations. But in view of the incisive literature criticizing this overall intuitonist claim, I believe it is quite unnecessary to refute this intuitionist claim once more. At any rate, I have no new arguments to deploy beyond those offered by Toulmin, MacDonald, Strawson, Robinson, Nowell-Smith, and Edwards.

There is a more defensible answer to the question: 'Why should people be moral?'. It was first urged (in the Western World, at least) by Epicurus; later it was developed and given its classical forceful statement by Hobbes. Bertrand Russell elaborates it in his own way in his *Human Society in Ethics and Politics* (1955) and Kurt Baier has clearly elucidated and defended Hobbes' argument in his *The Moral Point of View* (1958). This Hobbesian argument, which within its proper scope seems to me conclusive, can readily be used to meet the objections of those "tough-minded" Marxists and Freudians who do not want the usual fare of "sweetness and light".

Hobbes points out that as a matter of fact the restless, malcontent,

---

13 John Hospers effectively marshalls the points that need to be made against Plato here. See John Hospers, *Human Conduct: An Introduction to the Problems of Ethics* (New York, 1961), pp. 176–83.

14 Austin Duncan-Jones, *Butler's Moral Philosophy* (Pelican Philosophy Series, 1952), p. 181.

15 Quoted by Duncan-Jones, op. cit., p. 182.

foraging human animal wants "The commodious life"; that is, he wants above all peace, security, freedom from fear. He wants to satisfy his desires to the maximum extent, but one of the very strongest and most persistent of these desires is the desire to be free from the "tooth and claw" of a life in which each man exclusively seeks his own interest and totally neglects to consider the interests of others. In such a situation life would indeed be "nasty, brutish, and short". We could not sleep at night without fear of violent death; we could not leave what we possessed without well-warranted anxiety over its being stolen or destroyed. Impulses and inclinations would be held in check only when they would lead to behavior detrimental to the individual's own interest. Where peoples' interests conflict, each man would (without the institution of morality) resort to subterfuge or violence to gain his own ends. A pervasive Dobuan-like suspicion would be normal and natural . . . even rational in such a situation. Every individual would be struggling for the good things of life and no rule except that of his own self-interest would govern the struggle. The universal reign of the rule of exclusive self-interest would lead to the harsh world that Hobbes called "the state of nature". And, as Baier puts it, "At the same time, it will be clear to everyone that universal obedience to certain rules overriding self-interest would produce a state of affairs which serves everyone's interest much better than his unaided pursuit of it in a state where everyone does the same".[16] Baier goes on to point out that "the very *raison d'être* of a morality is to yield reasons which override the reasons of self-interest in those cases when everyone's following self-interest would be harmful to everyone".[17]

When we ask: why should we have a morality—any morality, even a completely conventional morality—we answer that if everyone acts morally, or generally acts morally, people will be able to attain more of what they want. It is obvious that in a moral community more good will be realized than in a nonmoral collection of people. Yet in the interest of realizing a commodious life for all, voluntary self-sacrifice is sometimes necessary; but the best possible life for everyone is attainable only if people act morally; the greatest possible good is realizable only when everyone puts aside his own self-interest when it conflicts with the common good.

If people ask: 'Why should one choose that course of action which will probably promote the greatest possible good?' we are quite correct in answering as Baylis does: There is probably nothing better one could possibly do instead.[18] I would only add that Baylis' caution here is rhetorical for there is no place at all for the qualifying word 'probably'.

---

16 Baier, op. cit., p. 309.
17 Ibid.
18 Charles Baylis, op. cit., pp. 172–73.

3

Yet an answer to the question 'Why should people be moral?'
does not meet one basic question that the thorough-going sceptic may feel
about the claims of morality. The "existing individual" may want to know
why *he*, as an individual, ought to accept the standards of morality when
it is not in *his* personal interest to do so. He may have no doubt at all about
the general utility of the moral enterprise. But *his* not recognizing the
claims of morality will not greatly diminish the total good. Reflecting on
this, he asks himself: 'Why should *I* be moral when I will not be caught
or punished for not acting morally?'.

Recall how Glaucon and Adeimantus readily agree that Socrates has
established that morality is an indispensable social practice. But their perplexity over morals is not at an end. They want Socrates to go on and
prove that the individual ought to be moral even when he is perfectly safe
in not acting morally. Someone might readily agree that the Hobbesian
arguments presented in Section 2 establish that the greatest total good will
be realized if people act morally, but he still wants to know 'Why should I
be moral in those cases where acting morally will not be in *my* rational
self-interest?' He might say to himself—though certainly if he were wise
he would not proclaim it—'There is no reason why I should act morally'.

Such an individual egoist cannot be refuted by indicating that his
position cannot be a moral position. He may grant the overall social good
of morality and he may be fully aware that 'Why should I do my duty?'
cannot be a moral question—there is indeed no room at all for that question
as a moral question, but an individual egoist is not trying to operate within
the bounds of morality. He is trying to decide whether or not he should
become a moral agent or he may—in a more theoretical frame of mind—
wonder if any *reason* can be given for his remaining a moral agent. Prichard
is quite right in arguing that the *moral* agent has no choice here. To assert
'I'll only be moral when being moral is in my rational interest' is to rule
out, in a quite a priori fashion, the very possibility of one's being moral as
long as one has such an intention. To be a moral agent entails that one
gives up seriously entertaining whether one should deliberately adopt a
policy of individual egoism. 'X is moral' entails 'X will try to do his duty
even when so acting is not in his personal interest'. Thus we must be very
careful how we take the individual egoist's question: his question is, 'Should
I become moral and give up my individual egoism or shall I remain such
an egoist?'. If he decides to remain an individual egoist he will have made
the decision that *he* ought to behave like a man of good morals when and
only when such behavior is in his own personal interest. Now what grounds
(if any) have we for saying that a man who makes such a decision is mistaken or irrational? What (if any) intellectual mistake has he made? Re-

member, he doesn't challenge Prichard's remarks about the logical relations of duty to interest or the Hobbesian argument that morality is an essential social device if we are to have a commodious life. But he still wants to know why *he* should be moral rather than nonmoral.

The individual egoist may well believe that those who insist on being moral even when it is not in their self-interest are really benighted fools duped by the claims of society. A "really clever man" will take as his own personal norm of action the furtherance of his own good. Everything else must give pride of place to this. He will only endeavor to make it seem perfectly obvious that he is a staunch pillar of the community so as to avoid reprisals from his society.

Can such an individual egoist be shown to be wrong or to be asking a senseless question? What arguments can be given for an affirmative answer to the question: 'Should I be moral?'.

Kant recognized as clearly as did Prichard that there is no room for this question within morality, but he felt, in a way Prichard apparently did not, that nonetheless such a question needs answering and that this was one of the main reasons we need Good and the graces of religion. Thus, Kant found it necessary to posit God and immortality as postulates of the practical reason so that there would be a heaven in which the morally good man would be rewarded for doing his duty because it is his duty. But these principles of practical reason are, for Kant, finally based on the demands of the moral will. The universe just couldn't be so bad as to allow evil to go permanently unrequited and the man of good will unrewarded. Sidgwick too (strangely enough) created a theological postulate to provide for a harmony between universal and individual happiness. We assume that God so rewards and punishes that it is always in everyone's interest to seek to further the greatest good for the greatest number.

But it is increasingly difficult for an educated modern even to believe in God, to say nothing of making Him such a *deus ex machina*. As J. J. C. Smart rightly remarks: "More and more it seems that man is just part of nature. In the light of modern science he appears to be a very complicated physico-chemical mechanism, who arose by natural selection from simpler mechanisms, and there may well be millions of planets in the universe with similar, or higher, forms of life on them".[19] Yet for the sake of the argument let us assume (what indeed ought not to be assumed) that we have an appropriate use of 'God' and let us also assume that we have some evidence that there is an X such that X is God. Even making these assumptions, it does take the utmost vanity and the epitome of self-delusion to believe that such a Being could be so concerned with our weal and woe. And to postu-

---

[19] J. J. C. Smart, "Philosophy and Religion," *The Australasian Journal of Philosophy*, XXXVI (1958), 57.

late God *because* of His practical necessity or to postulate inmortality to try to insure a justification of morality is just too convenient. It is deserving of the scorn Bradley heaped upon it.

Medlin does not engage in such rationalization but without further ado plays Dr. Johnson. He comments: "If the good fellow wants to know how he should justify conventional morality to the individual egoist, the answer is that he *shouldn't* and *can't*. Buy your car elsewhere, blackguard him whenever you meet, and let it go at that."[20] A philosopher, Medlin goes on to comment, is "not a rat-catcher" and it is not his "job to dig vermin out of such burrows as individual egoism".[21] Inasmuch as Medlin is pointing out that the individual egoist's position isn't and can't be a moral alternative to conventional morality, he is perfectly right in his strictures; but as an answer to the question as I have posed it, Medlin's reply is simply irrelevent.

Must we say at this juncture that practical reasoning has come to an end and that we must simply *decide* for ourselves how to act? Is it just that, depending on what attitudes I actually happen to have, I strive to be one sort of a person rather than another without any sufficient rational guides to tell me what I am to do ? Does it come to just that—finally? Subjectivists say (at such a juncture) that there are no such guides. And this time there seems to be a strong strand of common sense or hardheaded street wisdom to back up the subjectivists' position.

I do not believe that we are that bad off. There are weighty considerations of a mundane sort in favor of the individual's taking the moral point of view. But I think the subjectivists are right in claiming that it is a mistake to argue that a man is simply irrational if he does not at all times act morally. It is indeed true that if a man deliberately refuses to do what he acknowledges as morally required of him, we do say he is irrational or better unreasonable. But here 'irrational' and 'unreasonable' have a distinctively *moral* use. There are other quite standard employments of the word in which we would not say that such a man is irrational.[22] In all contexts the word 'irrational' has the evaluative force of strongly condemning something or other. In different contexts the criteria for what is to be called 'irrational' differ. In Toulmin's terms the criteria are field-dependent and the force of the world is field-independent. In saying a man acts irrationally in not assenting to any moral considerations whatsoever we need not be claiming that he makes any mistakes in observation or deduction. Rather

---

20 Medlin, op. cit., p. 113, italics mine.
21 Ibid., p. 114.
22 I have discussed this issue in my "Appealing to Reason," *Inquiry*, V (Spring, 1962), 65–84.

we are condemning him for not accepting the moral point of view. But he is asking why he, as an individual in an ongoing community, should always act as a moral agent. He is not asking for *motivation* but for a *reason* for being a morally good man. He wants to know what intellectual mistake the man who acts nonmorally must make. To be told such a man is immoral and in *that sense* is unreasonable or irrational is not to the point.

The subjectivist I am interested in contends that in the nature of the case there can be no reasons here for being moral rather than nonmoral. One must just *decide* to act one way or another without reasons. There is much to be said for the subjectivist's claim here but even here I think there are rational considerations in favor of an individual's opting for morality.

4

Before I state and examine those considerations I would like to show how two recent tantalizingly straightforward answers will not do. Baier has offered one and Hospers the other.

Baier says that when we ask 'Why should I be moral?' we are asking 'Which is the course of action supported by the best reasons?'. Since we can show along Hobbesian lines that men generally have better reasons for being moral than for being nonmoral the individual has "been given a reason for being moral, for following moral reasons rather than any other...". The reason is simply that "they are better reasons than any other". *But in the above type situation*, when I am asking, 'Why should I be moral?'. I am not concerned with which course of action is supported by the best reasons *sans phrase* or with what is the best thing to do for all concerned. I am only concerned with what is a good reason *for me*. I want to know what is the best thing *for me* to do; that is, I want to know what will make for *my* greatest good.

Baier might point out that an individual has the best reasons for acting morally because by each man's acting morally the greatest possible good will be realized. Yet, if the reference is to men severally and not to them as a group, it might well be the case that an individual's acting immorally might in effect further the total good, for his bad example might spur others on to greater acts of moral virtue. But be that as it may, the individual egoist could still legitimately reply to Baier: 'All of what you say is irrelevant unless realization of the greatest total good serves *my* best interests. When and only when the reasons for all involved are also the best reasons for me am I personally justified in adopting the moral point of view'.

We can, of course, criticize a so-called ethical egoist for translating the question 'What is the best thing to do' into the question 'What is the best thing *for me* to do'. In morality we are concerned with what is right, what is good and what is supported by the best reasons, *period*; but recall that the *individual* egoist is challenging the sufficiency of moral reasons which we, as social beings, normally grant to the moral enterprise. (We need to reflect on the sense of 'sufficiency' here. The egoist is not challenging the point of having moral codes. He is challenging the sufficiency of the moral life as a device to enhance *his* happiness. But is this "a goal of morality"? It is not.) He is asking for reasons for *his* acting morally and unfortunately Baier's short answer does not meet the question Baier sets out to answer, though as I have already indicated it does answer the question, 'Why should people be moral?'

Hospers has a different argument which, while wrong, carries a crucial insight that takes us to the very heart of our argument. Like Baier, Hospers does not keep apart the question 'Why should I be moral?' from 'Why should people be moral?'. After giving a psychological explanation of what motivates people to be moral, Hospers considers what *reasons* there are for being moral.

Virtue is its own reward and if an act is indeed right this is a sufficient reason for performing the act. We have been operating on the wrong assumption—an assumption that we inherited from Plato—namely, that if it isn't in our interest to behave morally we have no reason to do it. But it does not follow that if a right action is not in our interest we have no reason for doing it. If we ask 'Why should we do this act rather than other acts we might have done instead?' the answer 'Because it is the right act' is, says Hospers, "the best answer and ultimately the only answer".[22]

It is indeed true that *if we are reasoning from the moral point of view* and if an act is genuinely the right act to do in a given situation, then it is the act we should do. Once a moral agent knows that such and such an action is the right *one to do in* these circumstances he has *eo ipso* been supplied with the reason for doing it. But in asking 'Why should I be moral?' an individual is asking why *he* should (nonmoral sense of 'should') reason as a moral agent. He is asking, and *not* as a moral agent, what reason there is for his doing what is right.

It is at this point that Hospers' reply—and his implicit defense of his simple answer—exhibits insight. It will, Hospers points out, be natural for an individual to ask this question only when "the performance of the act is *not* to his own interest".[23] It is also true that *any* reason we give other than a reason which will show that what is right is in his rational self-interest will be rejected by him. Hospers remarks "What he wants, and he will accept no other answer, is a self-interested reason" for acting as a moral

---

[22] John Hospers, *Human Conduct: An Introduction to the Problems of Ethics*, (New York, 1961), p. 194.
[23] Ibid.

agent.[24] But this is like asking for the taste of pink for "the situation is *ex hypothesi* one in which the act required of him is contrary to his interest. Of course it is impossible to give him a reason *in accordance with his interest for acting contrary* to his interest".[25] 'I have a reason for acting in accordance with my interest which is contrary to my interests' is a contradiction. The man who requests an answer to 'Why should I do what is right when it is not in my interest?' is making a "self-contradictory request". We come back once more to Prichard and Bradley and see that after all our "question" is a logically absurd one—no real question at all. The person asking "the question" cannot "without self-contradiction, accept a reason of self-interest for doing what is contrary to his interest and yet he will accept no reason except one of self-interest".[26]

His "question" is no real question at all but at best a nonrational expression of a personal predicament. Our problem has been dissolved— the "common sense core of subjectivism" has turned out to be the core of the onion.

But has it really? Is any further question here but a confused request for *motivation* to do what we know we have the best reasons for doing? Let us take stock. Hospers has in effect shown us: 1 That x's being right entails *both* x should be done (where 'should' has a moral use) and there is (from the moral point of view) a *sufficient reason* for doing x ('I ought to do what is right' is a tautology where 'ought' is used morally) ; 2 That from the point of view of self-interest the only reasons that can be sufficient reasons for acting are self-interested reasons. This again is an obvious tautology. The man asking 'Why should I do what is right when it is not in my self-interest?' has made a self-contradictory request *when he is asking the question as a self-interested question*.

These two points must be accepted, but what if an individual says: As I see it, there are two alternatives: either I act from the moral point of view, where logically speaking I must try to do what is right, or I act from the point of view of rational self-interest, where again I must seek to act according to my rational self-interest. But is there any *reason* for me always to act from one point of view rather than another when I am a member in good standing in a moral community? True enough, Hospers has shown me that *from the moral point of view* I have no alternative but to try to do what is right and from a *self-interested point of view* I have no rational alternative but to act according to what I judge to be in my rational self-interest. But what I want to know is what I am to do: Why adopt one

---

24 Ibid.
25 Ibid.
26 Ibid., p. 195.

point of view rather than another? Is there a good reason *for me*, placed as I am, to adopt the moral point of view or do I just arbitrarily choose, as the subjectivist would argue?

I do not see that Hospers' maneuver has shown this question to be senseless or an expression of a self-contradictory request. Rather his answer in effect brings the question strikingly to the fore by showing how from the moral point of view 'Because it's right' must be a sufficient answer, and how it cannot possibly be a sufficient answer from the point of view of self-interest or from the point of view of an individual challenging the sufficiency of the whole moral point of view, as a personal guide for his actions. It seems that we have two strands of discourse here with distinct criteria and distinct canons of justification. We just have to make up our minds which point of view we wish to take. The actual effect of Hospers' argument is to display in fine rational order the common sense core of subjectivism: *at this point* we just choose and there can be no reasons for our choice.

It will not do for Hospers to argue that an individual could not rationally choose a nonmoral way of life or ethos, for in choosing to act from a self-interested vantage point an individual is not choosing a way of life; he is, instead, adopting a personal policy of action in a very limited area for himself alone. Such an individual might well agree with Hospers that a rational way of life is one, the choice of which, is (1) free, (2) enlightened, and (3) impartial.[27] This remark, he could contend, is definitive of what we *mean* by 'a rational way of life'. An intelligent egoist would even urge that such a way of life be adopted but he could still ask himself (it wouldn't be prudent to ask others) what *reason* there would be for *him* or any single individual living in a community committed to such a way of life to act in accordance with it. (This need not be a question which logically speaking requires a self-interested answer. An existing individual is trying to make up his mind what he is to do.)

To reply, 'If it's rational then it should be done', is to neglect the context-dependent criteria of both 'rational' and 'should'. There are both moral and non-moral uses of 'should' and 'rational'. In the above example Hospers is using 'rational' in a moralistic sense; as Hospers puts it, "Let me first define 'rationality' with regard to a way of life" and while a way of life is not exhausted by moral consideration it essentially includes them.[28] Only if 'rational' and 'should' belong to the same strand of discourse is 'If it is rational then it should be done' analytic. Something could be rational from the moral point of view (morally reasonable) and yet imprudent (irrational from the point of view of self-interest). If we were asking what

---

[27] Ibid., p. 585.
[28] Ibid.

we should do in terms of self-interest, it would not follow in this case that we should do what is rational in the sense of 'morally reasonable'. Conversely, where 'What is rational' means 'What is prudent' it would not follow that what is rational is what, morally speaking, we ought to do.[29]

Thus, it seems to me that neither Baier's nor Hospers' answers will do. We are left with our original question, now made somewhat more precise, 'Is there a good reason for me as an individual in a moral community to always act morally no matter how I am placed?'. There is no room *in morality* for this question but this question can arise when we think about how to act and when, as individuals, we reflect on what ends of action to adopt. But as a result of Hospers' analysis, must we now say that here we must (1) simply make a choice concerning how to act or (2) where there is no live question concerning how to act it is still the case that there can be no nonquestion begging justification for an individual, were he faced with such a choice, to act one way rather than another? (Of course there is the very best *moral* justification for his acting as a moral agent. But that is not our concern here, for here we are asking: why reason morally?)

Here the pull of subjectivism is strong—and at this point it has an enlightened common sense on its side. But I think there is something more to be said that will take the bite out of such subjectivism. In trying to bring this out, I am in *one sense* going back to Plato. It is, of course, true that we can't ask for a self-interested reason for doing what is right where *ex hypothesi* the action is not in our self-interest. But in actual moral situations it is not so clear what is in our self-interest and what is not, and often what is *apparently* in our self-interest is really not. Part of my counter to the subjectivist, and *here* I am with Plato, is that if a man decides *repeatedly* to act nonmorally where he thinks he can get away with it, he will not, as a very general rule, be happy.

This isn't the whole of my case by any means, but I shall start with this consideration.

5

Suppose that I, in a fully rational frame of mind, am trying to decide whether or not to adopt individual egoism as my personal policy of action. I ask myself: 'Should I pursue a selfish policy or should I consider others as well even when in my best judgment it doesn't profit me?'. In my deliberation I might well ask myself: 'Will I really be happy if I act without regard for others?'. And here it is natural to consider the answer of the ancients. Plato and Aristotle believe that only the man who performs

---

[29] See here William Dennes, "An Appeal to Reason," in *Reason, University of California Publications in Philosophy*, Vol. 27 (Berkeley, California, 1939), 3–42, and *Some Dilemmas of Naturalism* (New York, 1960), Chapter 5.

just actions has a well-ordered soul. And only the man with a well-ordered soul will be "truly happy". If I am thrown off course by impulse and blind action I will not have a well-ordered soul; I will not be genuinely happy. But the alternative I am considering is not between impulsive blind action and rational, controlled action, but between two forms of deliberate, rationally controlled activity. Why is my soul any less well-ordered or why do I realize myself (to shift to Bradley's idiom) any the less if I act selfishly than if I act morally? If it is replied, 'You will "realize yourself more" because most people have found that they are happiest when they are moral', I can again ask: 'But what has that to do with me? Though I am one man among men, I may not in this respect be like other men. Most people have neurotic compulsions about duties and are prey to customary taboos and tribal loyalties. If I can free myself from such compulsions and superstitions will I be any the less happy if I am selfish? I should think that I would be happier by being intelligently selfish. I can forget about others and single mindedly go after what I want'.

To this last statement Plato and Aristotle would reply that by always acting selfishly a man will not fully realize his distinctively human *areté*. By so acting, he simply will not be responding in a fully human way. We say of a man that he is a 'good man, a truly happy man' when he performs his function well, just as we say a tranquilizer is a 'good tranquilizer' when it performs its function well; that is to say, when the tranquilizer relaxes the tense, harrassed individual. But can we properly talk about human beings this way? We do speak of a surgeon as 'a good surgeon' when he cures people by deftly performing operations when and only when people need operations. Similarly, a teacher is 'a good teacher' if he stimulates his students to thought and to assimilate eagerly "the best that has been thought and said in the world". We can indeed speak of the *areté* or "virtue" of the teacher, fireman, preacher, thief, or even (as MacIver reminds us) of the wife or unmarried girl.[30] People have certain social roles and they can perform them ill or well. "In this sense we can speak of 'a good husband', 'a good father', 'a good Chancellor of the Exchequer ...' ", but—MacIver rightly concludes—hardly of "a good man".[31] People, qua human beings, do not seem to have a function, purpose, or role. A child can sensibly ask: 'What are hammers for?', 'What are aspirins for?', 'What are dentists for?', but if a child asks 'What are people for?', we must point out to him that this question is not really like the others. 'Daddie, what are people for?' is foolish or *at the very least*—even for the Theist—an extremely amorphous question. At best we must quickly strike some religious attitude and some disputed cosmology must be quickly brought in, but no such

────────────

[30] A. M. MacIver, "Good and Evil and Mr. Geach," *Analysis*, XVIII (October, 1957), 7–13.

[31] Ibid., 8.

exigency arises for the cosmologically neutral question, 'Daddie, what are napkins for?' or 'Daddie, what are policemen for?'. After all, what is the function of man *as such*? In spite of all his hullabalo about it, is not Sartre correct in claiming that man has no "essence"—no a priori nature—but that human beings are what human beings make of themselves? If a human being acts in an eccentric or nonmoral way are we really entitled to say he is any less of a human being?

If we counter that we are indeed entitled to say this, and we then go on to say, 'By not acknowledging that we are so entitled, we are in effect overriding or ignoring man's "distinctively human qualities"' are we not now using 'distinctively human qualities' primarily as a grading label? In such contexts, isn't its actual linguistic function primarily moral? We are disapproving of a way of acting and attempting to guide people away from patterns of behavior that are like this. If we say the consistently selfish man is less human than the moral man, are we not here using 'less human' as a moral grading label and not just as a phrase to describe men? 'More human', on such a use, would not be used to signify those qualities (if there are any) which are common to and distinctive of the human animal; but would be used as an honorific moral label. And *if* it is used *only* to describe how people have behaved then it is perfectly possible for me to ask, 'Why should I be more human rather than less?'.

Most moderns would not try to meet the question 'Why should I be moral?' in this Greek way, though they still would be concerned with that ancient problem, 'How should I live in order to be truly happy?'. A rational man might make this elementary prudential reflection: 'If I am thoroughly and consistently selfish and get caught people will treat me badly. I will be an outcast, I will be unloved, all hands will be on guard against me. I may even be retaliated against or punished as an "irredeemable moral beast". All of this will obviously make me suffer. Thus, I better not take up such a selfish policy or I will surely be unhappy'.

At this point it is natural to take a step which, if pushed too far, cannot but lead to a "desert island example". It is natural to reply: 'Clearly it would be irrational to *appear* selfish. But I don't at all propose to do that. I only propose to look out for "number one" and only "number one". I will do a good turn for others when it is likely, directly or indirectly, to profit me. I will strive to appear to be a man of good morals and I will do a good deed when and only when it is reasonable to believe there will be some personal profit in it. Surely, a policy of unabashed, outright selfishness would be disastrous to me. Obviously, this is something I will strive to avoid. But I shall keep as the maxim of *my* actions: Always consider yourself first. Only do things for others, when by so acting, it will profit you, and do not be frankly selfish or openly aggressive except in those situations where no harm is likely to befall you for so acting. Take great pains to see that your selfishness is undetected by those who might harm you'.

But, at this point our hypothetical rational egoist would need to consider the reply: 'You will regret acting this way. The pangs of conscience will be severe, your superego will punish you. Like Plato's tyrant you will be a miserable, disordered man. Your very mental health will be endangered'.

Imperceptibly drawing nearer to a desert island example, the egoist might reply: 'But the phrase "mental health" is used to describe those well adjusted people who keep straight on the tracks no matter what. I don't intend to be "healthy" *in that sense*. And, I do not recognize the *authority* of conscience. My conscience is just the internalized demands of Father and Tribe. But why should I assent to those demands, when it doesn't serve my interests? They are irrational, compulsive moralistic demands, and I shall strive to free myself from them'.

To this it might be countered, 'Granted that conscience has no moral or even rational authority over *you*, you unfortunate man, but practically speaking, you cannot break these bonds so easily. Consciously you may recognize their lack of authority but unconsciously they have and always will continue to have—in spite of all your ratiocination—a dominating grip on you. If you flaunt them, go against them, ignore them, it will cost you your peace of mind, you will pay in psychic suffering, happiness will be denied you. But as a rational egoist happiness is supposedly your goal. And it is wishful thinking to think some psychiatrist will or can take you around this corner. Neither psychoanalysis nor any other kind of therapy can obliterate the "voice of the superego". It can at best diminish its demands when they are *excessive*. Your conditioning was too early and too pervasive to turn your back on it now. If you are rational you will not struggle in such a wholesale fashion against these ancient, internalized demands. Thus, you should not act without regard to the dictates of morality if you really want to be happy'.

It is at this stage that the rational egoist is likely to use his visa to Desert Island. He might say: 'But if I had the power of Gyges and that power included the power to still the nagging voice of my superego, would it not then be reasonable for me to always act in my own self-interest no matter what the effect on others? If there were some nonharmful pill— some moral tranquilizer—that I could take that would "kill" my conscience but allow me to retain my prudence and intelligence why then, under those circumstances, should I act morally rather than selfishly? What good reason is there for me in that situation to act morally if I don't *want* to?'

It is not sufficient to be told that if most people had Gyges' ring (or its modern, more streamlined, equivalent) they would go on acting as they do now. The question is not 'What would most people do if they had Gyges' ring?' or even 'What would I do if I had Gyges' ring?' The question is rather, 'What should I do?'. At this point can *reasons* be found which would convince an intelligent person that even in this kind of situation, he ought to act morally? That is, would it serve his "true interests" (as Plato believes) for him to be moral, even in the event these conditions obtained?

It is just here, I believe, that subjectivism quite legitimately raises its ugly head. If the above desert island situation did in fact obtain, I think we would have to say that whether it would or would not be in your "true interests" to be moral or nonmoral would depend on the sort of person you are. With the possible exception of a few St. Anthony's, we are, as a matter *of fact*, partly egoistic and partly other-regarding in our behavior. There can be no complete nonpersonal, objective justification for acting morally (rather) than nonmorally. In certain circumstances a person of one temperament would find it in his interests to act one way and a person of another temperament to act in another. We have two policies of action to choose from, with distinct criteria of appropriateness and which policy of action will make us happy will depend on the sort of person we *happen* to be.

It is here that many of us feel the "existential bite" of our question. Students, who are reasonably bright and not a little versed in the ways of the world, are often (and rightly) troubled by the successive destruction of first psychological egoism and then ethical egoism. They come to see that individual egoism can't be a moral view, but they feel somehow cheated; somehow, in some way, they sense that something has been put over on them. And I think there is a point to this rather common and persistent feeling and I have tried, in effect, to show what this is. I would *not*, of course, claim that it is always the "Why-should-I-be-moral?" question that troubles a reflective student at this juncture but frequently, like Glaucon and Adeimantus, the student wants to know why, as a solitary, flesh and blood individual, he should be moral. He *feels* that he should be moral, but is he somehow being duped? He wants a reason that will be a good and sufficient reason for his being moral, quite apart from *his* feelings or attitudes about the matter. He does not want to be in the position of finally having to decide, albeit after reflection, what sort of person to strive to be. It seems to me that the subjectivists are right in suggesting that this is just what he finally can't avoid doing, that he doesn't have and can't have *the kind* of objectivity he demands here. We need not have existentialist dramatics here, but we do need to recognize the logical and practical force of this point. Most rationalistic and theological ethical theories seem to me myth-making devices to disguise this prima facie uncomfortable fact.

6

But need we despair of the rationality of the moral life once we have dug out and correctly placed this irreducible element of choice in reasoning about human conduct? Perhaps some will despair but since it is

not the job of a philosopher to be a kind of universal Nannie I don't think
he need concern himself to relieve this despair. But, I think, if he will
remind people of the exact point on the logical map where this subjectivism correctly enters and make them once more aware of the map as
a whole they will—now able to see the forest as well as the trees—be less
inclined to despair about the rationality of their acting morally. If one is
willing to reason morally, nothing we have said here need upset the objectivity and rationality of moral grading criteria. More importantly here, to
admit subjectivism at this point does not at all throw into doubt the Hobbesian defense of the value of morality as a social practice. It only indicates
that in the situation in which an *individual* is (1) very unlikely to be
caught, (2) so rationally in control that he will be very unlikely to develop
habits which would lead to his punishment, and (3) is free from the power
of his conscience, it might, just might, (if he were a certain kind of person)
make him happier to be nonmoral than moral. But this is not the usual bad
fellow we meet on the streets and the situation is anything but typical.

A recognition of the irrelevance of desert island examples will provide
further relief from moral anxiety over such subjectivism. Critics of utilitarianism invent situations in which a social practice is, as we use moral
language, regarded as obligatory even though there is no advantage in acting
in accordance with it in this particular kind of circumstance. They construct desert island examples and then crucify the utilitarian with them.
They point out, for example, that promises made on desert islands to a
dying man to dispose of his effects in a certain way are considered obligatory
even if it is clear that (1) some other disposal of his effects would be more
beneficial and (2) that there is no reasonable chance that the breach in trust
would be detected. The usual utilitarian answer is that disregarding promises of this sort would weaken our moral character; and, in addition, we
cannot be quite sure that such a breach in trust would not be detected or
that it would really do more good than harm. Further, to ignore a promise
of this sort is bad, for it would tend to weaken the utility of the social
practice of promise keeping.

Nowell-Smith, however, is quite correct in saying: "The relentless desert islander can always break such utilitarian moves by adding stipulations
to the terms of the original problem".[32] That is, he will say to the utilitarian, 'But what would you say *if* breaking a trust in situations of this type
would not weaken the utility of the practice of promise keeping? Surely it
is *intelligible* to suppose that such acts would not weaken people's moral
fiber, would not be detected, and would not do more total good than harm.
To this the utilitarian can only say that this statement of the desert islander

_____

[32] P. H. Nowell-Smith, *Ethics*, p. 240.

is a very "iffy proposition", indeed. Nowell-Smith rightly remarks: "The force of these desert island arguments . . . depend expressly on the improbability of the case supposed".[33] "It is difficult to assess their force precisely because the case *is* improbable and therefore not catered for in our ordinary language".[34] The language of human conduct has the structure it has because the world is as it is and not otherwise. If people and things were very different, the structure of moral codes and the uses of evaluative language presumably would be different. The very form of our talk about human conduct "reflects empirical truths that are so general and obvious that we can afford to ignore exceptions".[35] If through desert island examples we withdraw that pervasive contextual background it is difficult to know what is the logically proper thing to say. The logic of the language of human conduct did not develop with such wildly improbable situations in view. It, after all, has a wide range of distinct, practical uses, and it only has application in a certain type of setting. If one of these desert island situations were to obtain, we would have a good reason, as Wittgenstein clearly saw, to make a linguistic stipulation, that is, we would have to decide what is to be *said* here and our linguistic decision would indeed be an intervention in the world, it would indeed have normative import. But it is neither possible nor necessary that we make all such stipulations in advance and we can hardly reasonably accuse the language of conduct of inadequacy because it does not cater to desert island cases. It would be like saying that "the language of voting" is inadequate because it does not tell us what to do in a situation in which a senior class, consisting of a thousand, tries to elect a president from four candidates and each time a vote is taken each candidate gets exactly 250 votes. This indeed is a logical possibility, but that *this* logical possibility is not considered in setting out the procedures for voting does not at all indicate an inadequacy in our voting procedures.

Our "Gyges' ring situations" are just such desert island cases. In fact, Nowell-Smith is quite correct in remarking that the Gyges' ring example in the *Republic* is a paradigm of all such desert island arguments.

'Would I be happier if I were intelligently selfish in a situation in which I could free myself from guilt feelings, avoid punishment, loss of love, contempt of family and friends, social ostracism, etc.?'. To ask this is to ask a desert island question. Surely we can and do get away with occasional selfish acts—though again note the usual burden of guilt—but given the world as it is, a deliberate, persistent though cunning policy of

---

[33] Ibid., p. 132.
[34] Ibid.
[35] Ibid.

selfishness is very likely to bring on guilt feelings, punishment, estrange-
ment, contempt, ostracism, and the like. A clever man might avoid one or
another of these consequences but it would be very unlikely that he could
avoid them all or even most of them. And it is truistic to remark that we
all want companionship, love, approval, comfort, security, and recognition.
It is very unlikely that the consistently selfish man can get those things he
wants. At this point, it may be objected: 'But suppose someone doesn't
want those things, then what are we to say?'. But this is only to burgeon
forth with another desert island example. The proper thing to reply is that
people almost universally are not that way and that in reasoning about
whether I should or should not be selfish, I quite naturally appeal to certain very pervasive facts (including facts about attitudes) and do not, and
need not, normally, try to find an answer that would apply to all conceivable worlds and all *possible* human natures. To think that one must do so
is but to exhibit another facet of the genuinely irrational core of rationalism.

7

It seems to me that the above considerations count heavily
against adopting a thoroughly consistent policy of individual egoism. But
do such considerations at all touch the individual who simply, on occasion,
when his need is great, acts in a way that is inconsistent with the dictates
of morality? Will such a person always be happier—in the long run—if he
acts conscientiously or is this a myth foisted on us, perhaps for good social
reasons, by our religions and moralities? Are all the situations desert island
situations in which we can reasonably claim that there could be rational
men who would be happier if they acted nonmorally rather than morally
or in which we would have to say that any decision to act one way rather
than another is a matter of arbitrary choice? Are there paradigm cases
which establish the subjectivist's case—establish that it is altogether likely
that some clear-headed people will be happier if, in some non-desert island
circumstances, they deliberately do what they acknowledge is wrong and
or in some non-desert island circumstances some people must just decide
in such circumstances what they are to do?

Let us examine three prima facie cases.

Suppose a man, believing it to be wrong, decides to be unfaithful to
his wife when it is convenient, nonexplosive, and unlikely to be discovered.
Usually it is not, on the part of the knight-errant husband, a deliberate
and systematic policy but it might be and sometimes is. Bored husbands
sometimes daydream that this is a return to paradise; that is to say, it
might earn, at least in anticipation, a good score in a felicific calculus. In
order to make the example sufficiently relevant to the argument, we must
exclude those cases in which the husband believes there is nothing wrong
in this behavior and/or gives reasons or rationalizations to excuse his be-

havior. I must also exclude the guilty weak-willed man with the Pauline syndrome. The case demands a man who deliberately—though with sufficiently prudent moderation—commits adultery. It is important for our case that he believes adultery to be immoral. Nonetheless, while believing people ought not to be adulterers, he asks himself, 'Should I continue to live this way anyway? Will I really be happier if I go the way of St. Paul?'. He does not try to universalize his decision. He believes that to choose to remain an adulterer is immoral, but the immoral choice remains for him a live option. Though people may not put all this to themselves so explicitly, such a case is not an impossibility. People may indeed behave in this way. My example is not a desert island one. I admit there is something odd about my adulterer that might make him seem like a philosophical *papier-mâché* figure. There is also something conceptually odd about saying that a man believes x to be wrong and yet, without guilt or ambivalence and without excusing conditions, rationally decides to do x. With good reason we say, 'If he knows it to be wrong or really believes it to be wrong, he will (everything else being equal) try to avoid it'. Still there is a sense in which he could say he believes x to be wrong even though he seeks x. The sense is this: he would not wish that people generally choose or seek x. When this is the case he says 'x is wrong' even though he makes a frank exception of himself without attempting to morally justify this exception. It is important to note that this is a *special* though perfectly intelligible use on my part of 'He believes it to be wrong'. While it withdraws one essential feature, namely that nonuniversalizable exceptions are inadmissable, it retains something of the general sense of what we mean by calling something morally wrong.

Yet, for the sake of the argument at least, let us assume that we do not have a desert island case. Assuming then that there are such men, is their doing what is wrong here also for *them* the personally disadvantageous thing? Can any individual who acts in such a way ever be reasonably sure he won't be caught—that one of the girls won't turn up and make trouble, that he won't run into an acquaintance at the wrong time? Even if these seem to be remote possibilities, can he ever be free enough from them in his dream life? And if his dreams are bothersome, if he develops a rather pervasive sense of uneasiness, is it really worth it? He must again consider the power of his conscience (superego) even though he rationally decided to reject its authority. Will it give him peace? Will the fun be worth the nagging of his conscience? It is difficult to *generalize* here. Knowledge of oneself, of people, of human psychology, and of imaginative literature is all extremely relevant here. I think the individual egoist can correctly argue that it is not *always* clear that he would be unhappier in such a situation if he did what was wrong. A great deal depends on the individual and the exact particular circumstance but the moralist who says it is never, or hardly ever, the case that a person will be happier by pursuing a selfish policy certainly overstates his case.

Let me now take a different paradigm for which much the same thing must be said. It is important to consider this new case because most people would label this man a "veritable moral beast" yet he stands to gain very much from acting immorally. The case I have in mind is that of a very intelligent, criminally experienced, well-equipped, nonmasochistic but ruthless kidnapper. He is a familiar type in the movies and thrillers. Now, Hollywood to the contrary, why should it not sometimes be the case that such a kidnapper will be happier if he is successful? Indeed, he may have a murder on his hands but the stakes are very high and when he is successful he can live in luxury for the rest of his life. With good reason our *folklore* teaches he would not be happier. It is of the utmost value to society that such behavior be strenuously disapproved. And given the long years of conditioning we are all subject to, it remains the case that most people (placed in the position of the kidnapper) would not be happier with the successful completion of such a kidnapping if it involved murdering the kidnapped child. But then most people are not kidnappers. They have very different personalities. Such brutalities together with fear of detection would haunt them and it is probably the case that they also haunt many kidnappers. But if the kidnapper were utterly nonmoral, very, very clever, etc., why wouldn't *he* really be happier? He could live in comfort; he could marry, have children and attain companionship, love, approval, etc. 'Well', we would say, 'his conscience would always bother him'. But particularly with modern medical help, which he could now well afford, would it bother him enough? 'Well, there would always be the awful possibility of detection and the punishment that might follow'. But, if the stakes were high enough and if he were clever enough might it not be better than a life of dull routine, poverty, or near poverty? And think of the "kicks" he would get in outwitting the police. We all have a little adventure in our souls. 'But'—the dialogue might go on—'if he were intelligent enough to pull off this job successfully, he would certainly be intelligent enough to avoid poverty and to avoid making his living in a routine, boring way'. The dialogue could go on interminably but I think it is clear enough again that even here there is no one decisive, clear-cut answer to be given. The case for morality here is stronger than in the previous paradigm, but it is still not decisive. Yet there are paradigms in which doing what is clearly wrong (and understood by the individual in question to be wrong) is in the rational self-interest of some individuals. Our first more typical paradigm is not completely clear, but the following third and less typical paradigm given by Hospers is a clearer example of a case in which it is in a man's self-interest not to do what is right.

There is a young bank clerk who decides, quite correctly, that he can embezzle $50,000 without his identity ever being known. He fears that he will be underpaid all his life if he doesn't embezzle, that life is slipping by without his ever enjoying the good things of this world; his fiancée will not marry him unless he can support her in the style to which she is accustomed; he wants to settle down with her in a suburban house, surround himself with books, stereo hi-fi set, and various *objets d'art*, and spend a pleasant life, combining culture with sociability; he never wants to commit a similar act again. He does just what he wanted to do: he buys a house, invests the remainder of the money wisely so as to enjoy a continued income from it, marries the girl, and lives happily ever after; he doesn't worry about detection because he has arranged things so that no blame could fall on him; anyway he doesn't have a worrisome disposition and is not one to dwell on past misdeeds; he is blessed with a happy temperament, once his daily comforts are taken care of. The degree of happiness he now possesses would not have been possible had he not committed the immoral act.[36]

Clearly it was in his rational self-interest to do what is wrong.

Someone might claim that it is too much to expect that he could arrange things so that no blame would fall on him. This could happen only in desert island type situations. But unless we began to have the doubts characteristic of traditional epistemologists about 'the blame could not fall on him', there are plenty of cases in which crimes of this general sort are carried out with success. There is no good reason to think such an individual in such circumstances would not be happier.

But it is also crucial to recall that our cases here only involve certain specific acts that do go against the requirements of morality. The cultured despiser of morals, we described in the last section, is a man who rejects the authority of all moral considerations and systematically pursues a selfish policy in all things. Thus, we would need to project risks similar to those of the wayward husband and the kidnapper through his entire life. But are there really any realistic paradigms for such generalized egoistic behavior that would hold any attraction at all for a rational man? I doubt very much that there are. Yet, our three paradigms indicate that for *limited patterns of behavior*, no decisively good reasons can be given to some individuals that would justify their doing the moral thing in such a context. (It would be another thing again if they repeatedly acted in that way. Here the case for morality would be much stronger.)

In pointing this out, the subjectivist is on solid ground. But it is also

36 John Hospers, *Human Conduct: An Introduction to the Problems of Ethics*, pp. 180–81.

true that even here it is not just a matter of "paying your money and taking your choice", for what it would be rational for you to do depends, in large measure, on what sort of person you are and on the particular circumstances into which you are cast.

There is a further more general and more important consideration. Even if large groups of people read and accepted my argument as correct, even if it got favorable billing by Luce publications, it still remains very unlikely that kidnapping and crime would increase one iota. For the most part, people get their standards not from ethical treatises or even scriptural texts or homely sayings but by idealizing and following the example of some living person or persons. Morality or immorality does not typically (or perhaps even ever) arise from precept or argument but from early living examples. The foundations of one's character are developed through unconscious imitation way before perplexity over morality can possibly arise. Unless a man is already ready to run amuck, he will not be morally derailed by the recognition that in deliberating about how to act one finally must simply decide what sort of a person one wishes to be. Since most people are not ready to go amuck, the truth of my argument will not cause a housing shortage in hell.

There are further considerations that will ameliorate this subjectivism. It seems reasonable to say that in different societies the degree of subjectivism will vary. All societies are interested in preserving morality; they have a quite natural and rationally justifiable vested interest in their moral codes. Now, as societies gain a greater know-how, and particularly as they come to understand man and the structure of society better, it seems reasonable to assume they can more effectively protect their vested interests. In other words, I believe, it is reasonable to assume that it will become increasingly difficult to be successfully nonmoral as a society gains more knowledge about itself and the world.

This also poses a puzzle for the intelligent individual egoist. In such advancing culture-studying cultures, it will become increasingly more difficult for *him* to be nonmoral. But it is in his rational interest for *others* to be moral so he should not oppose this more efficient enforcement of morality. And if he does choose to oppose it, it is very probable that he will suffer a fate not unlike Camus' stranger.

More generally, it will not be in the interest of the individual egoist to oppose morality and even if he, and others like him, do find that it pays to act nonmorally their failure to act morally will of necessity be so moderate that the set of social practices that help make up morality will not be disturbed in any extensive way. (This puts the point very modestly). And, if too many go the way of the rational individual egoist, then it will no longer pay to be nonmoral so that large numbers of individual egoists, if they are rational, will become men of good morals.

Though the plain man committed to the moral point of view will probably not jump with joy over this state of affairs, I think the considerations in the last three paragraphs give him genuine grounds for being sanguine. The subjectivism I have pinpointed need not create a generation of "despairing philosophers" even if my argument is accepted as completely sound.

Section Five

Normative, Religious, and Meta-Ethics

The proper function and province of moral philosophy have been variously conceived throughout its history. As evidenced by this volume, twentieth-century moral philosophers in the analytic tradition have concerned themselves for the most part with problems regarding the nature, uses, or meaning of moral concepts, moral judgments, and moral reasoning. The analysis of these problems has been termed "metaethical" since the philosopher is typically writing *about* ethical discourse rather than either using language to make moral judgments or solving particular moral problems. The latter activities are called "normative," and, in addition, would include systematically setting out and defending a principle of morality, a theory of moral obligation, or a list of intrinsic values.

Many analytic moral philosophers either reject normative ethics as a legitimate *philosophical* enterprise (at times on the grounds that the proper concern of the philosopher is with the logical analysis of language), or they indefinitely postpone normative inquiry. Traditionalists occasionally charge that contemporary philosophers have abdicated the fundamental project of classical moral philosophers, and urge that we must get back to those important normative issues. Aside from the controversy over the philosophical legitimacy of normative ethics, we may ask to what extent the classical writers were concerned with metaethics rather than normative ethics. It may be that some of the most interesting theses about morality, which have been taken to be normative, can be interpreted as metaethical theses. For instance, the basic tenet of the ethical egoist, namely, that one ought to do whatever and only whatever is in one's enlightened self-interest, is usually considered to be a normative thesis. But could the thesis not also be understood as a view about the nature of moral discourse, i.e., the view that "moral" judgments are translatable into prudential judgments?[1]

It would be particularly embarrassing to philosophers

---

1 This is the line of argument taken by E. M. Adams in his "Classical Moral Philosophy and Metaethics," *Ethics*, LXXIV (1964), 97–110.

who restrict their province to a neutral metaethics to discover
that metaethical theories either presuppose or imply specific
normative ethical doctrines. William T. Blackstone reviews
some of the literature on this controversy in "Are Metaethical
Theories Normatively Neutral?", and shows that there are at
least six different interpretations of this question: (1) Do
metaethical analyses affect one's moral life? (2) Are metaethical theories logical entailments of normative ethical positions? (3) Do metaethical theories logically entail certain
normative ethical statements? (4) Do metaethical theories
logically entail certain accounts of moral justification? (5)
Are metaethical theories set forth simply and solely as descriptively true theories rather than as prescriptions concerning
the way moral language ought to be used and interpreted?
(6) Do metaethical theories have a normative function?
Prof. Blackstone offers answers to each of these questions and
then discusses the relations between metaethical theories and a
general theory of meaning. The problem of justifying a general theory of meaning, he argues, is crucial for the metaethicist, for "to speak of a 'valid metaethic' requires that one
speak of a valid theory of meaning."

    In "Thomism and Metaethics," Prof. Blackstone turns to
a metaethical analysis of a popular but not always clearly
understood normative ethics. He provides at least a partial
analysis of the nature and meaning of moral judgments and
the nature of moral reasoning in Thomism. Prof. Blackstone
believes that there are seven principal issues in Thomistic
ethics which require metaethical analysis: (1) specification
of the nature and status of the principle of synderesis ("good
is to be pursued, evil avoided"); (2) the meaning of "good"
in Thomistic ethics; (3) the notions of "natural laws" and
"natural rights"; (4) the role of reason and the relation of
fact and value; (5) the meaning of "contradicting nature";
(6) the relationship of fundamental moral concepts—good,
right, obligation, etc.; and (7) a classification of different
kinds of statements and claims found in moral philosophy.
He concludes his paper with the provocative suggestion that
since a metaethical account of the meaning of ethical terms
and statements entails a particular account of moral justification, the normative theorist who does a complete job will have
to argue for the correctness of a certain metaethical view (a
type of cognitivism and objectivism in the case of Thomism).

    P. H. Nowell-Smith's "Morality: Religious and Secular"

is of interest on several counts: First, by placing his analysis of moral rules in the context of a persuasive account of a child's learning to be moral, or becoming a mature moral agent, he has made a strong case for an "act" utilitarian interpretation of moral rules. The reader would do well to master the ins and outs of Section 2: Rules, Principles, and Utilitarianism, before reading or reaching a final appraisal of Prof. Nowell-Smith's paper. Second, the paper is of interest because of its central thesis that religious morality is infantile. It is noteworthy that A. Boyce Gibson, in his critique of Nowell-Smith's paper, agrees in general with Nowell-Smith's analysis of the nature and function of moral rules, but rejects completely his interpretation of Christian ethics, especially the charge that it resembles the infantile stage of moral development. Prof. Gibson proceeds then to rectify the distortions. Prof. Nowell-Smith's paper is of interest, finally, because of his discussion of the relations between religion and morality. Far from indicating a conceptual dependence of morality on religion, he holds that just the reverse is true.[2]

William K. Frankena, in "Love and Principle in Christian Ethics," develops a number of interesting parallels between forms of utilitarianism (act, rule, and combinations of the two) and forms which a love-ethic (agapism) may take. Prof. Frankena believes that in agapism the "law of love" has the same position that the principle of utility has in utilitarianism. Thus, one may distinguish "pure act-agapism, modified act-agapism, and pure rule-agapism." In addition to distinguishing a variety of possible positions in Christian ethics, Prof. Frankena briefly addresses the question of how one is to decide which of the views outlined is the correct or most tenable one. In general, Prof. Frankena's article amounts to something of a challenge to Christian theologians to say what they mean more precisely and to take advantage of the developments within recent moral philosophy.

---

2 See his fuller statement of the historical and conceptual relations between religion and morality in his article in *The Encyclopedia of Philosophy*, Paul Edwards, Editor-in-Chief (New York: The Macmillan Company and The Free Press, 1967), VII, 150–58.

Are Metaethical Theories Normatively Neutral?

WILLIAM T. BLACKSTONE

A. J. Ayer has argued that "all moral theories, intuitionist, naturalistic, objectivist, emotive, and the rest, insofar as they are philosophical theories, are neutral as regards actual conduct".[1] These analyses of moral concepts or metaethical theories do not dictate or recommend certain kinds of conduct. They entail no normative ethical judgments. Metaethical theories are only analyses of "what people are doing when they make moral judgments".

Since the time of Ayer's statement, a number of philosophers[2] have become concerned with the relation between metaethics and the moral life or the relation between analyses of the meaning of moral concepts and normative ethical judgments. They have asked the question: "Are metaethical theories normatively neutral?" This question has been answered differently by different philosophers. In fact, the question itself has been interpreted as asking different things. The purpose of this paper is to set forth six fundamentally different interpretations of the question, "Are metaethical theories normatively neutral?". We will also propose answers to each of these formulations of the question. It is hoped that this procedure will clarify the relationship between metaethics and normative ethics.

1

The question, "Are metaethical theories normatively neutral?", has been interpreted as "Do metaethical theories affect one's moral life?". Olafson,[3] for example, argues that the acceptance of a metaethical theory does affect our first order moral life and that this effect is observable in a modification of our procedures of moral judgment. He is primarily concerned with the emotive theory and it is his specific contention that the

---

From Australasian Journal of Philosophy, *XXXIX (1961). Reprinted by permission of the author and* Australasian Journal of Philosophy.

[1] A. J. Ayer, *Philosophical Essays*, p. 246.

[2] For example, see Frederick Olafson, "Metaethics and the Moral Life", *Philosophical Review*, LXV (1956); Paul Taylor, "The Normative Function of Metaethics," *Philosophical Review*, LXVII (January, 1958); and S. A. Grave, "Are the Analyses of Moral Concepts Morally Neutral?", *The Journal of Philosophy*, LV (May 22, 1958).

[3] Frederick Olafson, op. cit.

acceptance of the emotive theory changes our conception of what we are doing when we make moral judgments, and further that it changes our view of the justification of such judgments. The emotive theory, as a metaethical theory, forces us to recognize the primacy of emotion in morals. This "performatory analysis of moral judgments generates a performatory moral life".[4] Acceptance of the metaethic of emotivism causes psychological or attitudinal changes in one. It makes one feel that rational principles are not operative for morals and that one's moral judgments are nonlogical acts of preference.

Olafson, I think, is correct in his contention that acceptance of the emotive theory causally affects one's attitudes in morals. Although the emotive theory need not entail nihilism or chaos in ethics,[5] there is good evidence that acceptance of the view that moral judgments are mere expressions of emotion causes one to adopt a different attitude toward justification in ethics, and may in fact cause one to make different normative ethical judgments from those made prior to the acceptance of the metaethic.[6] It seems to me that the acceptance of any theory involving metalinguistic analysis results in such causal effects. Certainly the metalinguistic statement that religious or theological statements are noncognitive has a causal effect upon one who operates within a religious framework. The belief that religious utterances can be neither true nor false has very serious causal effects when entertained by one who has religious beliefs, for such a metalinguistic statement is even more devastating than being told that one's religious beliefs are false. It surely makes one feel as if no rational principles are operative in religion and that one's religious judgments are nonlogical acts of preference.

Our point is that philosophical analysis of any area of discourse has a number of practical causal effects and this certainly includes analyses of moral concepts. It is certainly possible and in fact highly probable (though not logically necessary) that acceptance of a given metaethic, whether it be the emotive theory, the subjectivist theory, or the view of the intuitionist, will have a tendency to modify one's behavior. It may (though it need not) result in one's making different normative ethical judgments from those made prior to the acceptance of the metaethic. Thus our answer to the first formulation of our question, namely, "Do metaethical theories affect one's moral life?", is a probable Yes.

---

4 Ibid., p. 175.

5 See W. T. Blackstone, "Objective Emotivism", *The Journal of Philosophy*, LV (November 20, 1958).

6 See Paul Edwards, *The Logic of Moral Discourse*, p. 240, for an analysis of the consequences of adopting the emotivist metaethic.

2

The question, "Are metaethical theories normatively neutral?", can also be put in this manner: "Do one's normative ethical beliefs logically entail one's metaethical theory?".

A look at the history of ethical theory will convince one that the normative ethical views of some philosophers certainly did dictate their metaethical theories. Let's take one such example. Bentham makes the following statement: "Of an action that is conformable to the principle of utility, one may always say either that it is one that ought to be done, or at least that it is not one that ought not to be done. . . . When thus interpreted the words *ought* and *right* and *wrong*, and others of that stamp, have a meaning: When otherwise, they have none."

Bentham's commitment to the principle of utility has led him here to assert the metaethical thesis that the normative terms "ought", "right", etc., could mean nothing other than that specified by the utilitarian. His thesis here is one about the meaning of ethical terms, not a thesis about what we ought to do. But it is clear that his position in normative ethics—that we should act so as to increase the happiness and welfare of all people—is the foundation or source for his metaethical thesis. Bentham's metaethical analysis of the meaning of "right" or "ought" is a reflection of his own ethical evaluations, and his preclusion of other metaethical theories is a logical consequence of his acceptance of the normative ethical views of utilitarianism. He has so defined the "ethical" that an act *must* conform to the principle of utility to be an ethical act. This makes his metaethics a logical entailment of his normative ethics.

It is no doubt true that the normative ethics of many other historical ethical theorists have dictated their metaethical views. However, a metaethical theory need not be a reflection of one's ethical evaluations. One need not arbitrarily define ethical concepts in terms of one's own normative ethical commitments such that one's normative ethics logically entail one's metaethics. That is, one's metaethics can be morally neutral even though it is a historical fact that many metaethical positions are not. The "ethical" or terms like "ought", "right", etc., could be defined in terms of use and function—in a morally neutral manner. One could view "ethics" as any system of norms for human conduct—a system of rules which function as regulative devices. Viewed in this manner, the subject matter of metaethical analysis would include the codes of behavior advocated by anyone—those of Nietzsche, Kant, Mill, St. Paul, Hitler, etc. A metaethic of this type would be a theory about the meaning of all distinctly ethical terms and statements (any term or statement which functions in this regulative sense) and this metaethic would not be a logical entailment of any given normative ethics or a reflection of one's own ethical evaluations. A metaethic of this morally neutral type would be a result of an analysis of the features and functions of discourse in which terms and statements function in a normative, regulative sense concerning human conduct. A metaethicist may, for example, conclude from his analysis that all terms and statements which function in a normative, regulative sense are noncognitive expressions of emotion (the metaethic of emotivism). This conclusion would apply equally to the normative ethical principles of Nietzsche, Kant, Mill, St. Paul, Hitler, etc., and would not be a logical entailment of any given normative ethics. Our answer, then, to the second formulation of our question, namely, "Do one's normative ethical beliefs logically entail one's metaethical theory?", is that although this has been true of many historical ethicists, one's metaethics can be morally neutral.

3

The question, "Are metaethical theories normatively neutral?", can be and has been interpreted in this manner: "Do metaethical theories entail certain normative ethical statements or moral claims?". For instance, is it the case that the metaethical view that moral judgments are noncognitive expressions of emotion entails any particular normative ethical judgments? Or does the metaethic of subjectivism, the view that moral judgments are statements of individual approval or disapproval, entail any particular normative ethical judgments? Ayer's answer to this question is negative and I agree with him. Any given metaethic, including the emotive theory, aims at showing people what they are doing when they make moral judgments—not at suggesting which moral judgments they are to make. Furthermore, without logical inconsistency, one can be for or against the same sort of actions regardless of whether one adopts the metaethic of the emotivist, the subjectivist, objectivist, or intuitionist. One is not logically committed to capital punishment, trial marriage, or euthanasia—no matter what metaethic one adheres to. This is to say that there is no formal incompatibility between any normative ethical statement and any metaethical theory. This conclusion, however, requires that one's metaethical theory be morally neutral in the manner specified above, namely, that it not be a reflection of one's own normative ethical position. It should be noted, however, that the acceptance of any given metaethic may *cause* or influence one to accept a certain moral position. Our answer, then, to the third formulation of our question, "Do metaethical theories logically entail certain normative ethical statements?", is negative.

4

A fourth formulation of the question, "Are metaethical theories normatively neutral?", is "Do metaethical theories logically entail certain accounts of moral justification?". Metaethical theories are theories about the meaning of ethical terms and ethical statements, and, it seems to me, any given theory about the meaning of ethical terms and statements does logically entail a particular account of moral justification. The metaethic of subjectivism, for example, which views the meaning of ethical statements as autobiographical statements of approval or disapproval, entails a particular account of moral justification, namely, that the only data relevant to the justification of moral judgments are the autobiographical facts of personal approval or disapproval. The metaethic of emotivism, which views ethical judgments as noncognitive expressions of emotion, certainly logically entails that moral judgments cannot be justified as true or false since moral judgments do not *assert* anything. For those who adopt the metaethic of emotivism, if there is disagreement in moral attitude between two persons who agree on the facts of the case, there is no method of resolvement besides persuasion or abuse. On the emotivist's scheme, all the reasons relevant for a *purely* moral disagreement (as opposed to a disagreement in belief) are persuasive reasons, for, as Ayer puts it, moral principles have no "objective validity". Thus one analytic entailment of the emotive metaethic is that all ethically relevant reasons are persuasive reasons. Without noting other metaethical theories, it is clear that the manner in which one is to justify moral judgments depends logically upon what those ethical judgments are interpreted as meaning. Our answer, then, to the fourth formulation of our question is affirmative.

5

A fifth sense of the question, "Are metaethical theories normatively neutral?", is "Are metaethical theories set forth as descriptively true theories or as prescriptions concerning the way moral language ought to be used and interpreted?". (We have already discussed above how a metaethic may be prescriptively set forth in the sense of being a logical entailment of a given normative ethic. We are here concerned with a different manner in which a metaethic may be prescriptive.)

If metaethical theories are set forth as descriptively true theories, the question arises as to what it is that they describe. Quite often a metaethicist maintains that his theory is a descriptively accurate account of the way that moral language is used. The emotivist, for example, often seems to make this appeal to the way that moral language is used. If the emotivist's metaethic is based on this appeal, then it seems that it is descriptively false, for moral discourse certainly employs all the devices characteristic of cognitive discourse. As Glassen[7] points out, moral judgments often take the

---

[7] See Peter Glassen, "The Cognitivity of Moral Judgments", *Mind*, LXVII (January, 1959); and Frederick Olafson, op. cit.

form of indicative sentences just as do other sentences known to be cognitive. Moral judgments also often appear in indirect discourse as the object of a cognitional verb like "know" or "believe". One quite often finds judgments like "I know that x is the right thing to do". Furthermore, appraisal terms like "true", "false", "correct", and "mistaken" are often applied to moral judgments. Thus we find persons saying: "It is true that x is right". This linguistic evidence prima facie supports a cognitive interpretation of moral discourse, and hence the appeal to "use" does not support the emotivist's metaethic.

However, the emotivist also maintains that his analysis is the correct analysis of what moral concepts *really* mean and what these concepts really mean is quite different from what they are taken as meaning in ordinary moral discourse. Ethical expressions are *really* expressions of emotion, not statements which can be true or false. But what are we to make of the emotivist's contention that his view is the correct interpretation of the *real* meaning of ethical concepts? What he appears to be doing is setting forth his metaethic as a prescription of how we should interpret and use moral language. This means that his metaethic is not normatively neutral in one sense of "normative neutrality". His metaethic, requiring that we view moral language as emotive, is based on a norm which states what should be accepted as being cognitively meaningful. The phrase, "real meaning of ethical terms", involves a reference to this norm. In the case of at least some emotivists, that norm is the principle of empirical verifiability. The metaethic of intuitionism rests upon a different criterion of meaning from that of the emotivist, and hence the prescription of the intuitionist concerning the way that moral language ought to be used and interpreted differs from that of the emotivist. In neither the case of the intuitionist's metaethic nor the case of the emotivist's metaethic is an appeal made merely to a descriptive account of the way that moral language is used. Our answer, then, to the fifth formulation of our question, "Are metaethical theories normatively neutral?", is negative.

6

A sixth possible interpretation of the question, "Are metaethical theories normatively neutral?", is "Does metaethical analysis have a normative function?". Paul Taylor[8] has argued for an affirmative answer to this question and I think that he is correct. The normative function of metaethics is to introduce greater rationality into our moral life. This function is fulfilled if it makes "our second order beliefs about our first order moral discourse more clear, coherent, and true. If a metaethical analysis can cor-

---

8 Paul Taylor, op. cit.

rect our second order errors and clear up our second order vagueness and confusion about the nature and logic of our moral experience, then it can in turn help us to be more rational in our first order moral deliberations and judgments".[9] For Taylor the criterion for a valid metaethic is whether that theory has the capacity for making us more rational in our moral life. A metaethic has that capacity if it satisfies the following tests: (1) "Does it increase our factual understanding of what happens when, in the ongoing practical situations of everyday life, we deliberate about moral issues, arrive at moral decisions, make and justify and argue about moral judgments, and in general carry on moral discourse with others?" (2) "Does it provide tools for analyzing moral discourse in such a way that we are better able to recognize the presence of ambiguity and vagueness in moral language, and to identify the ways in which, and the purposes for which, such language is used?" (3) "Does it enable us to carry on first order moral discourse more clearly and intelligently?" (4) "Does it make explicit the rules of valid reasoning which are appropriate to moral argument; and does it make clear in what respects these rules are similar to, and in what respects they differ from, the rules of valid reasoning appropriate to matters of fact and to logically necessary propositions?" (5) "And finally, does it show us clearly how these rules can be applied in the everyday situations in which moral problems arise?"[10]

It seems to me that tests (2), (3), (4), and (5) are all heavily dependent upon one's answer to (1). If we are to be better able to recognize the presence of ambiguity and vagueness in moral language (2), we must have a clear understanding of what really goes on in moral discourse. Carrying on first order moral discourse more clearly and intelligently (3) also requires an answer to (1), namely, a view of what really goes on in moral discourse. Furthermore, knowing what could be meant by "rules of valid reasoning appropriate to moral argument" (4) presupposes an answer to (1). If what really occurs in moral discourse is the expressing of emotion, then the meaning of "valid reasoning" in ethics is radically affected. Finally the application of rules of valid reasoning to moral problems (5) requires an answer to (4) which in turn requires an answer to (1). Taylor's proposed test for the acceptability of a metaethical theory, then, seems to boil down to whether the theory "increases our factual understanding of what happens when, in the ongoing practical situations of everyday life, we deliberate about moral issues, arrive at moral decisions, make and justify and argue about moral judgments, and in general carry on moral discourse with others".

It appears to me to be analytically true that if a metaethical analysis

---

9 Ibid., p. 28.
10 Ibid., p. 29.

provides this "factual understanding", then it fulfills the normative function of providing the *capacity* for making us more rational in our moral life (though not necessarily actually making us more rational). But is it not the case that all metaethical analyses are set forth as "factual understandings" of what really happens in moral discourse? How do we know which meta-ethic fulfills this normative function? In other words, how do we determine what constitutes a "factual understanding" of moral discourse? This question can also be formulated in this manner: What is the test for the "real meaning" of ethical terms and ethical statements?

Would a descriptive account of the way moral language is used tell us what really happens in moral discourse or give us the *real* meaning of ethical terms? Taylor answers this question affirmatively. Speaking of moral concepts, he states: "A metaethic simply tries to get us to be fully aware of what this use is and to know what to do when others challenge our use of moral expressions or when we become doubtful about our own use of them".[11] In becoming aware of the use of moral concepts, one becomes aware of their meaning. A valid metaethic, then, is apparently for Taylor one that correctly describes the way that moral concepts are used for the roles that they perform in language.

Taylor's implicit criterion for judging whether a given metaethic constitutes a "factual understanding" of moral discourse seems to be based upon the implicit acceptance of the identification of meaning with use. We can discover what moral concepts really mean by examining their use or the roles that they perform in language. If this criterion is employed, then it would seem that each of the metaethical theories—subjectivism, objectivism, emotivism, and intuitionism—is partially correct. Moral concepts and moral language have many functions or roles. Moral language often performs the function of expressing one's emotion (the function stressed by emotivism). It quite often performs the function of conveying autobiographical information (the function stressed by subjectivism). It also is quite often used to make assertions which are not autobiographical (the function stressed by the various forms of objectivism). Thus if we accept the Wittgensteinian identification of meaning with the use or roles that expressions play in language, it may well be that intuitionism, objectivism, subjectivism, and emotivism are each correct in describing one role or function of moral language but each is incorrect in viewing that role as the exclusive role or function of moral language. On this procedure, a correct metaethic would be one that displays all the uses or roles performed by moral concepts. A metaethic of this type will be more likely to provide clear, coherent, and true second order beliefs about our first order moral discourse, and help us to be more rational in our first order moral deliberations.

---

11 Ibid., p. 31.

The point I wish to make is that any answer to the question of what constitutes a "factual understanding" of moral discourse is logically related to the general theory of meaning that one accepts. Without arguing the point, it seems to me that the metaethic of emotivism is often logically related to the acceptance of the positivist's theory of meaning. It is also clear that the implicit account of meaning in Platonism produces a quite different metaethic from that which results from the acceptance of the positivist's theory of meaning, that which results from the position which identifies meaning with denotation, or that which results from the acceptance of the Wittgensteinian account of meaning. It seems clear, then, that an answer to the question of whether a given metaethic fulfills the normative function of providing us with the capacity for becoming more rational in our moral life (by providing us with a "factual understanding" of moral discourse) ultimately requires reference to a general theory of meaning. Since this is the case, then it seems to me that metaethicists should pay a great deal more attention to the problem of meaning than they have in the past and to the particular problem of criteria of adequacy for a valid theory of meaning.

In summary, we have examined six different interpretations of the question, "Are metaethical theories normatively neutral?" These interpretations of this question were: (1) Do metaethical analyses affect one's moral life? (2) Are metaethical theories logical entailments of normative ethical positions? (3) Do metaethical theories logically entail certain normative ethical statements? (4) Do metaethical theories logically entail certain accounts of moral justification? (5) Are metaethical theories set forth simply and solely as descriptively true theories rather than as prescriptions concerning the way moral language ought to be used and interpreted? (6) Do metaethical theories have a normative function? Our answers to (1), (4), and (6) were affirmative, while our answers to (3) and (5) were negative. Our answer to (2) was affirmative for some historical cases, but we insisted that a metaethical theory need not be a logical entailment of a normative ethical position. Our discussion of (5) and (6), however, indicated that the acceptability or nonacceptability of a metaethical theory is closely related to the acceptability or nonacceptability of a general theory of meaning. The problem, then, of justifying a general theory of meaning is a paramount task for any metaethicist, for to speak of a "valid metaethic" requires that one speak of a valid theory of meaning.

Thomism and Metaethics

WILLIAM T. BLACKSTONE

1

In his contribution to *An Etienne Gilson Tribute,* Vernon J. Bourke suggests that there is "a possibility that metaethics could be associated with Thomistic ethics." He asks this question: "Is there room and need for an overview of the ethics of Thomism, analogous to the sort of thing that analysts do in metaethics?"[1] He suggests that there is such a need and that the distinction between "writing and thinking *about* ethics, and working out ethical problems" is an important one. Contemporary analysts have described this distinction as that between normative ethics and metaethics. A normative ethic is an actual moral code or system of morality, and normative ethics include the principles of a moral system, the actual making of moral judgments or decisions, and the attempt to justify or support such judgments. For example, the judgment that a given individual should keep a promise or the general maxim that promises should be kept would be instances of moral judgments and these, as well as the attempt to justify them by supporting data, would be classified under normative ethics. Normative ethics would also include other kinds of activities such as preaching, advising, and moralizing. A metaethical statement, on the other hand, is a statement about the nature, uses, or meaning of moral judgments, moral concepts, and moral reasoning. Take these examples: "Moral judgments are expressions of emotion." "Moral judgments are autobiographical statements." "Moral judgments are cognitive and refer to nonnatural properties." These statements are all statements about the meaning or nature of moral judgments. They are not themselves moral claims or attempts to justify moral claims. Although there are borderline cases of judgments which are difficult to classify as ethical or metaethical,[2] in general the distinction is a reasonably clear one.

Although Professor Bourke is primarily concerned with the effect or relation of metaethics on Thomistic moral philosophy and does not pretend to set forth a metaethical analysis of Thomistic ethics, he does to some extent perform metaethical analysis. He observes, for example, that

From The Thomist, *XXVIII (1964). Reprinted by permission of the author and* The Thomist.

[1] Vernon J. Bourke, "Metaethics and Thomism," in *An Etienne Gilson Tribute,* ed. Charles J. O'Neil (Marquette University Press, 1959), p. 22.

[2] See Kai Nielsen, "Speaking of Morals," *The Centennial Review,* II (Fall, 1958), for a discussion of such borderline cases.

the Thomist views ethics as a demonstrative science, although the degree of precision in ethics is less than that of some other parts of philosophy or science. He suggests that it is "a question whether Thomistic ethics should be regarded merely as a demonstrative science. Perhaps it is also a wisdom."[3]

Note that Professor Bourke is talking *about* ethics. He is not prescribing conduct or action, making moral judgments, or attempting to justify such judgments. He is talking *about* the nature of moral reasoning. In talking about moral reasoning (which is not the same thing as to reason morally) he introduces a distinction between ethical reasoning viewed as a "wisdom" and ethical reasoning viewed as demonstration or a "sort of syllogistic." Moral reasoning *may* be viewed as demonstrative, the conclusions of ethical argumentation being logically coercive. Moral reasoning may also be viewed, to use Bourke's works, as a "wisdom," in which case presumably the conclusions of ethical argumentation would not be logically coercive. Or ethical reasoning may be viewed as a combination of these, which is, I think, Bourke's suggestion.

What we want to make clear is that Professor Bourke is doing meta-ethics when he talks about the nature of moral reasoning and that one of the fundamental problems for the metaethicist in Thomism is that of analyzing and clarifying the nature of moral reasoning in the philosophy of Thomism. In this paper we will present at least a partial metaethical analysis of Thomistic moral philosophy. This will involve an analysis of the nature and meaning of moral judgments and the nature of moral reasoning in Thomism. (Of course, the questions and issues raised by the meta-ethicist are not confined to any particular system of ethics such as that found in Thomism but apply to any and all ethical systems or moral discourse.) I do not pretend that this will be a complete and adequate analysis. Such a task would be beyond the scope of this paper. However, a number of aspects of Thomistic ethics will be analyzed to some extent and this will constitute at least a partial metaethical analysis of Thomistic ethics.

2

First, let us address ourselves to the question of the nature or meaning of moral judgments or ethical statements themselves. Bourke correctly observes that a number of contemporary philosophers engaged in metaethical analysis assert that ethical judgments are noncognitive or emotive. Moral judgments do not assert anything that can be true or false. They only *express* one's emotion or feeling and persuade or exhort others to adopt the same moral attitude that the speaker has. For the emotivist, moral judgments do not even *state* that one has certain feelings. To maintain

---

3 Bourke, op. cit., p. 24.

that they do would make one a cognitivist—and a subjectivist on the metaethical plane—for moral judgments would be autobiographical statements
verifiable by reference to autobiographical data (whereas the contention of
the emotivist is that moral judgments are not verifiable at all). Ayer and
other emotivists attempt to draw a sharp line between the metaethic of
emotivism and the metaethic of subjectivism.[4]

Now it is clear that the Thomistic analysis of the meaning of moral
judgments will not agree completely with that of the subjectivist or the
emotivist. *In a sense* the Thomist agrees with the subjectivist, for both the
Thomist and the subjectivist maintain that moral judgments are cognitive.
As Bourke notes, "the Thomistic ethician seems to assume that ethics is a
purely cognitive discipline." However, the Thomist and subjectivist differ on
what moral judgments assert, the former maintaining that they assert something about the objective world whereas the latter maintains that they
assert something about the subject, namely, that he has certain feelings or
attitudes. It is obvious, since the Thomist maintains that moral judgments
assert something about the objective world, that the Thomistic position
differs radically from the metaethic of emotivism. Does the Thomist differ
completely from the emotivist position? I think not. Bourke himself notes
that the noncognitivists may be "partly right." Ethical conclusions are not of
the same character as those of mathematics or physics, for in ethical reasoning a strong attempt is made to influence one's conduct. To this extent the
emotivist is correct. Moral judgments are not "merely abstract or speculative
truths." They also have emotive, exhortative, and persuasive force. Bourke
would agree (and the Thomist would agree) that moral judgments express
emotion, or, in the language of the Thomist, moral judgments have an
affective-appetitive character. But Bourke and the Thomist would also insist
that "there is something wrong with denying all cognitive meaning to
ethical sentences." Furthermore, to insist that moral judgments are cognitive, as the Thomist does, "does not mean that we should ignore the affective-appetitive character of these utterances."[5] Bourke's view (and the
Thomistic view) is that moral judgments have both cognitive and noncognitive components. The emotivist analysis is incorrect in denying any
cognitive component. On the other hand "it must be admitted that Thomistic ethicians often handle value judgments as if they were *nothing but* truths
of fact,"[6] and they too, Bourke implies, are mistaken. Bourke's view is that
ethical statements do have objective import or alio-reference but they "are
not as directly and immediately verifiable as factual assertions."[7] Given

4 A. J. Ayer, *Language, Truth, and Logic* (New York, 1946), p. 109.
5 Bourke, op. cit., p. 26.
6 Ibid., p. 26; my italics.
7 Ibid., p. 27.

these remarks it is clear what Bourke or any Thomistic metaethicist must do. He must make perfectly clear the Thomistic analysis of ethical judgments by specifying the sense in which ethical judgments are referential and have objective import (cognitive meaning) and the sense in which they have an "affective-appetitive character" (noncognitive or emotive meaning).

Bourke himself is opposed to the cognitive analysis of moral judgments set forth by the ethical intuitionist, and he objects to the interpretation that "the concept of intuition, by which moral values are apprehended as objective realities . . . is a distinctive feature of Thomistic moral philosophy."[8] To suggest that all we have to do is "go around intuiting real values is a parody on the thought of Thomas Aquinas." But if the Thomistic metaethic is not the intuitionist version of cognitivism, then precisely what is it? Bouke does not make this clear and we must now attempt to specify more clearly the type of cognitive metaethic to which the Thomist adheres. In doing this we will also present (as we indicated that we would earlier) a metaethical analysis of the nature of moral reasoning in the philosophy of Thomism. These two issues (1) the nature of moral judgments, and (2) the nature of moral reasoning, although distinct, cannot be separated by the metaethicist. In fact there seems to be a relation of logical entailment between one's answer to "1" and one's answer to "2." It is clear, for example, that if moral judgments are interpreted as *purely* emotive, then moral reasoning cannot be viewed as a process of demonstration but rather simply as an attempt to persuade. For on the emotivist view, moral judgments are not *statements* or *propositions*—the sort of thing that can be demonstrated. They are simply occurrences, expressions of emotion.

Now there are a number of different kinds of normative concepts and normative judgments in Thomistic ethics. There are at least the concepts of "good," "right," "materially good," "morally good," "morally obligatory," "objectively right," and the various normative judgments in which these normative concepts occur. Of these concepts "good" and "right" and the judgments in which they occur are the more basic or fundamental ones in Thomistic ethics. Thomistic moral philosophy, then, is complicated by the fact that a number of normative concepts and distinctions are employed and it is further complicated by the fact that these different normative judgments involve reference to a multiplicity of factors including human intentions or motives, consequences, the beatific vision, "right reason," the "mean" between extremes, natural law, natural rights, "essential human nature," God's law, and human law. The task of the metaethicist is that of analyzing moral judgments and moral reasoning in Thomistic moral

---

8 Ibid.; Bourke cites Gerard Esser, S.V.D., "Intuition in Thomistic Moral Philosophy," *Proc. Amer. Cath Philos. Assoc.*, **XXXI** (1957), 176, as maintaining this view.

discourse. This involves not only a classification of the different kinds of normative judgments within the Thomistic scheme, but also an analysis of the meaning and the interrelationships of at least the moral concepts noted above and those factors (natural law, natural rights, consequences, etc.) to which moral judgments refer.

We have suggested that "good" is the basic normative term in Thomism, and many philosophers have recognized that Thomistic ethics is eudaemonistic and teleological. Thomas places Aristotle's eudaemonism and teleology within a Christian setting so that "happiness" and the "end of man" are given somewhat different meanings than those specified by Aristotle. Although both Thomas and Aristotle emphasize the perfection of man as a rational being, Thomas views this perfection and man's real happiness as the vision of God—attainable only in the next life. No matter how the "good" is defined, however, it is clear that Thomistic moral philosophy is basically teleological. As Copleston puts it, "the idea of the good is paramount" for the Thomist.[9] What is meant by the concept of the "good" being paramount is that the concept of a "right" act derives its meaning from the relationship of that act to the "good." What makes an act morally right is the fact that it is a means to the attainment of the good (as defined by the Thomist). This means, it seems to me, that *beatitudo* or the vision of God is that which has intrinsic worth or intrinsic value, whereas morally right acts have extrinsic or instrumental value, to use some distinctions employed by ethicists. Morally right acts derive their value from their relation to man's end or good. Thus one contribution towards clarity (and clarity is one of the basic concerns of the metaethicist) in regard to Thomistic moral philosophy is the specification of the relationship between the two fundamental moral notions of "the good" and "the right."

The specification of this relationship is also of fundamental use in setting forth the cognitive aspects of moral judgment in Thomism. At least part of the meaning of the claim that a given act is morally right is that that act will produce or will probably produce the good for man. Assuming that "the good for man" is given some clear meaning by the Thomist (we will see that there are difficulties in this regard), then it would appear that at least in part moral judgments would be properly analyzed as descriptive, factual claims. To use the language of some metaethicists, the Thomist may turn out to be a "value reductionist"—one who translates or reduces all moral judgments to purely descriptive, factual claims. Note that I say that the Thomist *may* turn out to be a value reductionist. Although there is some evidence for this claim, the fact that so many factors are involved in the Thomistic position (at least the seven factors enumerated above) makes it difficult to substantiate this claim. The fact that for the Thomist moral

9 F. C. Copleston, *Aquinas* (London, 1955), p. 198.

judgments involve in the last analysis a reference to "natural law" or "God's law" *may* further support the claim that Thomistic ethics is value reductionistic. That an act is right may be translated to mean that it is an instance of or that it conforms to "natural law" or "God's law" (the presumption being that acts which conform to natural law or God's law are conducive to or are a means to man's final end or good), and the claim that an act conforms to natural law or God's law may be interpreted as a descriptive factual claim, especially if natural law for the Thomist is, as Meyer states, "an expression of the objective essential relations in things."[10] We have not as yet analyzed the meaning of "natural law" or "God's law" (certainly a task for the metaethicist) so that the meaning of the claim that an act conforms to natural law or God's law is not clear. However if it is made clear and interpreted as a factual claim (we will note later that this interpretation is challenged by some philosophers), then this cognitive interpretation of moral judgments is compatible with the further Thomistic claim that ethics is a demonstrative science. Certainly the metaethicist must analyze and clarify the phrase "demonstrative science," but it is at least clear that one must have *statements* or propositions, not *expressions* of emotion, before one could speak of a thing as a "demonstration" or a "science."

3

Without further specifying at this time what is to be meant by conforming to natural law or God's law, let us turn to an examination of the nature of moral reasoning for the Thomist. At least in part the Thomist sets up what appears to be the deductive model for moral reasoning. As Copleston puts it, "the natural moral law in its totality therefore consists of a multiplicity of precepts of varying degrees of generality. But at the same time all these precepts are virtually contained in the fundamental precept that good is to be pursued and evil avoided."[11] Presumably moral precepts with less generality can be deduced from those with more generality. To use one of Thomas' own examples, from the precept that the species should be propagated and children educated, one can derive the precept of monogamy on the ground that this precept is required for the proper care and upbringing of children: And all moral precepts are in some sense contained in the principle that good is to be pursued and evil avoided (principle of synderesis).

The problem for the metaethicist here is the meaning of "deduce" and

---

10 Hans Meyer, *The Philosophy of St. Thomas Aquinas* (St. Louis, 1945), p. 470.
11 Copleston, op. cit., p. 218.

"derive" as used by the Thomist. Is logical deduction what is meant? Surely, if ethics is to be viewed as a "demonstrative science," then logical deduction must be what the Thomist means. Bourke indicates that this is the case in his reference to the theory of proof originating in Aristotle's *Posterior Analytics* which most Thomists use. But if logical deduction is what is meant, then to refer to Thomas' own example, can we logically deduce the precept of monogamy from the precept that the species should be propagated and children educated? Monogamy as a practice may be a means to the attainment of species propagation and proper child care and education. And there are many other means and practices equally conducive to these ends. But I fail to see the relation of logical entailment between the precept of propagation and child care and the precept of monogamy. Furthermore, as Copleston notes, all moral precepts for the Thomist are "virtually contained in the fundamental precept (the principle of synderesis) that good is to be pursued and evil avoided." But what is meant by "virtually contained"? Again, is what is meant logical entailment? Bourke would say no. He states: "Kant's rule (principle of universalizability) endeavors to offer a way in which one can tell what acts are good. St. Thomas' rule does not; it tells you to do them when they are good, not to do them when they are evil. This indicates the futility of trying to make a rationalistic deduction of specific moral duties from the principle of synderesis."[12] Bourke, I think, interprets Thomas correctly on this point. But if no rationalistic deduction of moral duties can be inferred from the principle of synderesis, then in what sense are the moral rules of varying generality "virtually contained" in that principle? Copleston also suggests that we cannot deduce specific rules or duties from the principle of synderesis. He states that "the word 'deduction' can be very misleading; and what Aquinas actually says is that other precepts of the natural law are 'founded on' or 'based on' the precept that good is to be done and evil avoided. The concrete good for man can be known only by reflection on human nature as known in experience."[13]

We might note that Copleston, in talking about the nature of moral reasoning in Thomistic moral philosophy, is doing metaethics. He is certainly correct that the term "deduction" can be used in misleading ways. But the terms "founded on" and "based on" which Copleston suggests that we substitute for "deduction" in Thomistic moral philosophy are at least as ambiguously used as the term "deduction." They too, then, require considerable analysis and explication. In fact, all the terms used by the Thomist in describing moral reasoning require metaethical analysis. Thomas himself, for

---

[12] Bourke, op. cit., p. 27.
[13] Copleston, op. cit., p. 224.

example, says that "every human law has the nature of law in so far as it is derived from the law of nature. If in any case it is incompatible with the natural law, it will not be law, but a perversion of law."[14] Aside from the need for complete analysis of the notion of "natural law," it is clear that one must analyze the notions of "derive," "incompatible," and "perversion" in order to be clear about the nature of moral reasoning in Thomism. Certainly many Thomists consider the entire Decalogue as conclusions derived from first principles of natural law and possessive of the same immutability as natural law. The natural law itself is viewed as being founded[15] on the transcendent eternal law of God. It is the task of the metaethicist to analyze these claims, to find out what is meant by the claim that "natural law is *founded* on divine law," to find out what is meant when it is said that "the Decalogue is *derived from* first principles," or that the rules of morality are "*virtually contained*" within the principle of synderesis. If logical deduction is not intended, then the meaning of the claim that ethics is a "demonstrative science" must be radically altered.

Although the Thomist sets up the deductive model for moral reasoning and speaks of remote and direct derivations of norms from natural law,[16] he fails to show that any specific norms are actually logical entailments of other norms. There is also the further problem of specifying the manner in which experience or empirical data is related to moral reasoning for the Thomist. Copleston states that for the Thomist "the concrete good for man can be known only by reflecting on human nature as known in experience." But this appeal to experience can mean several different things. It could mean that experience teaches one what sort of consequences follow from certain sorts of acts or what means are conducive to certain ends. This kind of empirical data could well be incorporated into the premises of a moral argument, and if this is what is intended by the appeal to experience, the metaethicist must show how this data fits into moral reasoning. Copleston specifically states, however, that the good for man can be known by "reflecting on human nature as known in experience." The Thomistic contention, here, I think, is that natural law (moral rules governing human conduct) can be discovered by examining human nature. Now a number of questions arise here. Is this process of discovery empirical? Do we infer these rules by watching human beings and their behavior? And if this is what is meant, then surely the problems centering around the "is"–"ought" dichotomy arise. Can we infer (Is it logically permissible?) normative conclusions from purely descriptive premises? And if this kind of inference is not involved, then is the notion of "human nature" itself normative—not

---

14 *Summa Theologica*, Ia, IIae, 95, 2.

15 Copleston, op. cit., p. 214.

16 See Meyer, op. cit., p. 502.

merely descriptive? What of the Thomistic view that there is an "essential human nature"? What is meant by this claim and is there such a thing? These questions are all fundamental ones which the metaethicist in Thomism must ask and answer. All of them involve the two fundamental points of metaethical analysis, the nature of moral judgments and the nature of moral reasoning. A complete analysis of these issues would go well beyond the scope of this paper. I would, however, like to enumerate and briefly discuss at least seven issues in Thomistic ethics which require, it seems to me, metaethical analysis. It is not intended that these seven issues are exhaustive. This brief account could be used as a point of reference for a more detailed analysis.

4

(1) *The principle of synderesis.* Specification of the nature and status of the principle of synderesis ("good is to be pursued, evil avoided") is a task for the metaethicist. Presumably this principle plays an important role in Thomistic ethics. Although the Thomist maintains that no specific duties can be rationally deduced from this principle, nonetheless he claims[17] that all moral precepts are "virtually contained" in this principle. The meaning of this claim and the meaning of the principle itself must be analyzed by the metaethicist. We have already seen the difficulties surrounding the meaning of the phrase "virtually contain." There are also difficulties centering around the meaning of the principle of synderesis itself. Some philosophers, for example, would claim that the sentence "good is to be pursued, evil avoided" turns out on analysis to be the tautology that "we ought to do that which we ought to do, and we ought not to do that which we ought not to do." The Thomist sometimes speaks of the principle as a "habit"[18] or as an "instinct."[19] This leads one to interpret the principle as a psychological generalization similar to the principle of psychological hedonism, the thesis that human beings always pursue that which they consider good and avoid that which they consider evil. On this interpretation the principle of synderesis is not even normative but rather descriptive of man's psychology. Furthermore, on this interpretation the relationship of this principle to morality or moral rules requires elucidation (the relation of "is" to "ought").

(2) *The meaning of "good" in Thomistic ethics.* We have noted that Thomistic ethics is teleological and we have seen that man's final good—that which realizes his potentialities in the highest degree—is *beati-*

---

17 See Copleston, op. cit., p. 218.
18 See Bourke, op. cit., p. 27.
19 See Copleston, op. cit., p. 223.

tudo, vision of God or "possession" of God. Since the concept of "good" is paramount, as Copleston states, in Thomistic ethics, a morally right act being defined as an act which is a means to the attainment of the "good," it is crucially important that the meaning of "good" be clear. The task for the metaethicist is to make this concept (and judgments in which it occurs) clear if possible, and if not, to show the vagueness and ambiguity of it. In the ethics of Thomism, it seems to me, there is a serious problem with the concept of "good," for the Thomist maintains that man's supreme or final end or good can be known only through revelation. To many philosophers the appeal to revelation as a means of *knowing* is objectionable, but a more fundamental objection is that the *meaning* of man's final good—*beatitudo*—is not made clear by the Thomist. What does it mean to be "in possession of God"? Are there any ways of testing for this state of affairs? Although the Thomist maintains that we can have some knowledge of the good for man without revelation, man's final good can really only accrue in the next life. This introduces a serious problem concerning the meaning of the concept "good" (some philosophers would suggest that there is no way in principle of testing for this state of affairs) and equally serious difficulties for the concept of a "right act," since the latter is defined as an act which is conducive to man's good.

(3) *Analysis of "natural law" and "natural rights."* The notions of divine or eternal law, natural law, and natural rights are very important in Thomistic ethical and political philosophy. We have seen that in some sense natural law is "founded upon" divine law, and it is also the case that natural rights are "founded upon" natural law. We have already noted the difficulties centering around these relationships and the notions of "founded upon," "based on," and "derived from." But there is an even more fundamental problem with the meaning of the phrases "divine law," "natural law," and "natural rights." The Thomist views natural law as ontological in character. It is "the complexus of tendencies towards ends and inclinations to actions which are based on the constant essences of things. By these inclinations each thing fulfills its own purposes and establishes the order in the things of nature."[20] The natural law includes all the prescriptions required to fulfill the essence of human nature and man's ultimate end. Natural law has objective and universal validity.

Now the analyst or metaethicist has a number of questions to ask about the claim that there is a natural law or laws. What kind of claim is it that these are natural laws? Is it empirical? And if so, what is the data which supports the existence of moral laws. Furthermore, men have certain natural rights because there is natural law. What are these rights and is it an

---

[20] Meyer, op. cit., p. 464.

empirical claim that we have them? One philosopher says that "propositions about natural law and natural rights are not generalizations from experience nor deductions from observed facts subsequently confirmed by experience."[21] MacDonald's position is that "the theory of natural law and natural rights confounds reason with right and both with matter of fact and existence."[22] Another way of putting this is that the natural law theorists confuse analytic and synthetic propositions in their view. They attempt to extract natural moral laws from *essential* human nature. But essential human nature is that which is expressed in the definition of "human being" and the natural laws would be simply analytic entailments of this definition. However, "by logical fusion of the characteristics of two different types of proposition, statements about natural rights tended in this theory to be represented as statements of necessary natural fact."[23] MacDonald further contends that (1) "men do not share a fixed nature, nor, therefore, are there any ends which they must necessarily pursue in fulfillment of such nature";[24] (2) "standards are determined by human choice, not set by nature independently of men";[25] (3) the reason "natural rights" were considered to exist independently of organized society was "in order to emphasize their basic or fundamental character. For words like freedom, equality, security, represented for the defenders of natural rights what they considered to be the fundamental moral and social values which should be or should continue to be realized in any society fit for intelligent and responsible citizens. ... In short, 'natural rights' are the conditions of a good society;[26] (4) assertions about natural rights are value utterances and value utterances are not analytic or synthetic propositions but "records of decisions." "To assert that 'freedom is better than slavery' or 'all men are of equal worth' is not to state a fact but to *choose a side*. It announces, 'This *is where I stand*.' ";[27] and (5) "there are no certainties in the field of values. For there are no true or false beliefs about values, but only better or worse decisions and choices."[28]

The above are some conclusions drawn by an analyst or metaethicist from a study of the doctrine of natural law and natural rights. I do not pretend that the summary is exhaustive, nor do I intend to express agree-

[21] Margaret MacDonald, "Natural Rights," in *Knowledge and Value*, eds. Elmer Sprague and Paul Taylor (New York, 1959), p. 646. Reprinted from *Proceedings of the Aristotelian Society*, 1947–48.
[22] Ibid.
[23] Ibid., p. 644.
[24] Ibid., p. 649.
[25] Ibid., p. 650.
[26] Ibid., pp. 652–53.
[27] Ibid., p. 654.
[28] Ibid., p. 658.

ment with her conclusions. I simply want to point out the need for metaethical analysis of the doctrine of natural law and natural rights in Thomistic moral philosophy and the far-reaching implications that such an analysis might have. It is clear, for example, that if a Thomist would accept Professor MacDonald's analysis, then the notion that natural law has "objective and universal validity" must be radically altered. Of course, if one accepted Professor MacDonald's analysis, then one would cease to be a Thomist.

(4) *The role of reason and the relation of fact and value.* We have noted the problems centering around the deductive model of moral reasoning used by the Thomist. We have also noted that the Thomist appeals to experience as a factor in moral reasoning. The task of the metaethicist is to clarify the roles of "experience," "deduction," and "reason" in the Thomist moral philosophy. The Thomist claims that "reason" has many roles in relation to ethics. Apparently it cannot only inform us of the means to an end but it can discover and direct man to what is "objectively good." Taking an example from Copleston, "both the burglar and the seducer can be said to be acting 'rationally' if they take the appropriate means to the fulfillment of their respective purposes. But since neither burglary nor seduction is compatible with the attainment of the objective good for man, the activities of the burglar and the seducer are not in accordance with 'right reason.' If it is said that moral conduct is rational conduct, what is meant is that it is conduct in accordance with right reason, reason apprehending the objective good for man and dictating the means to its attainment."[29] One can act rationally, then, without acting in accordance with "right reason." Reason, then, has at least the functions of (1) informing us of the means to certain ends (the sense in which both the burglar and seducer act rationally), (2) informing us of the proper or *right means* to certain ends, and (3) providing knowledge of the natural law or the *proper ends* or goals of man. The appeal to "right reason" involves a reference to reason apprehending and following the natural law. If reason can perform these functions (and perhaps others), then it would appear that for the Thomist rational argument could resolve or settle any ethical dispute—as long as the disputants agreed to proceed rationally. This view, however, has been seriously challenged by many contemporary metaethicists. It is claimed by A. J. Ayer, Paul Edwards, Charles Stevenson, H. Feigl[30]

---

29 Copleston, op. cit., p. 205.

30 See A. J. Ayer, *Language, Truth, and Logic* (New York, 1946); Paul Edwards, *The Logic of Moral Discourse* (Glencoe, Illinois, 1955); Charles Stevenson, *Ethics and Language* (New Haven, 1944); Herbert Feigl, "Validation and Vindication: An Analysis of the Nature and Limits of Ethical Arguments," in *Readings in Ethical Theory*, eds. John Hospers and Wilfred Sellars (New York, 1952).

and others who have investigated the role of reason and rational argument in ethical disputes that reason has an important but a *limited* role. The use of reason can make ethical disputants aware of the facts involved in the circumstances, including various means that can be used to attain certain ends. And to the extent that ethical disagreement is based upon differences in awareness of the facts in the circumstances, then it is probable that the disagreement can be rationally resolved. But if the ethical disagreement is not rooted in factual disagreement or "disagreement in belief," as Stevenson would put it, but rather in "disagreement in attitude" or fundamental normative differences, then resolvement is possible only through persuasion, compromise, or perhaps even abuse or force. Reason (these analysts argue) cannot justify certain ethical norms as correct ones as opposed to others.

Now this is a very serious challenge to the claim of the Thomist that reason (with the exception of the need for revelation at a certain point) has an almost unrestricted role in resolving ethical disputes. Certainly the Thomist allows that many men will not proceed rationally, but if they do, the Thomistic position is that reason can resolve ethical disputes, even those rooted in disagreements on fundamental norms—for reason can discover the *correct* norms. It seems to me to be a very crucial issue on the metaethical level that the Thomist analyze, explicate, and support his position on the role of reason in ethics. This would also involve saying something about the relation of "is" to "ought" and perhaps something about the relationship between ethics and epistemology.

(5) *The meaning of "contradicting nature."* Another point requiring metaethical analysis in the ethics of Thomism can be shown by drawing a parallel with Kantian ethics. In Kantian ethics the notions of "consistency" and "contradiction" play a key role in the basic moral principle, the principle of universalizability. Kant tells us that we must be able to *consistently* will that the maxim of one's action be a universal law if one's act is to be moral. He further speaks of certain acts or maxims of action *contradicting* or violating nature. An important problem for the metaethicist in Kantian ethics is to make clear the meaning of Kant's use of the notions of "consistency" and "contradiction." Only when this is done can the basic principle of Kantian ethics—the principle of universalizability—itself be clear. Kant himself sometimes can be interpreted as using "contradiction" in the formal logical sense, sometimes not.

Now there is a similar problem in Thomistic ethics. The Thomist speaks of "reason seeing the irrationality" of certain actions, meaning by this that reason sees that certain actions or maxims of action "contradict" nature or a "natural impulse implanted by God."[31] The problem for the

31 Copleston, op. cit., p. 213.

metaethicist here, as in Kantian ethics, is to find out the meaning of "contradicting nature." Is formal contradiction intended? Or is the term being used in a much looser sense? A similar problem arises when the Thomist says that "God would deny Himself if He were to relinquish His order of justice."[32] What does the term "deny" mean in this claim?

(6) *Analysis of the relationship of fundamental moral concepts—good, right, obligatory, etc.* We noted earlier that "good" is the fundamental normative term for the Thomist and the term "right" derives its meaning from its relationship to "good." A right act is an act which is conducive to man's good. Now in fact there is an entire host of normative concepts or phrases in Thomistic ethics which require analysis by the metaethicist not only concerning their meaning but also concerning their interrelationships with one another. For example, an act may be "materially good" without being "morally good." In fact a "materially good" act may be a "morally bad" act. Furthermore a "morally good" act need not be a "morally obligatory" act, although it may be. It is also possible for one to do that act which is "objectively right" and yet act immorally in doing it. The metaethicist, in giving an analysis of the meaning and relationship of these normative concepts, would introduce a great deal of clarity.

(7) *Classification of different kinds of statements and claims found in moral philosophy.* Another contribution which the metaethicist can make concerning Thomistic moral philosophy or any system of ethics is that of providing a scheme of classification for the various kinds of statements and claims found in moral discourse. Very important in this classification scheme would be the distinction between ethical statements and metaethical statements. But many other kinds of statements or activities take place in moral discourse and it is important to be able to distinguish the differences between these various kinds of statements and activities. Aside from (1) the making of actual moral decisions or utterances and (2) the making of statements' about the logic and meaning of moral utterances (metaethical statements), one finds (3) empirical statements about the means to attain the good life, (4) descriptions and explanations of moral experience, (5) a great deal of preaching and advising, and (6) the attempt to justify or validate moral ideas and practices. There are probably other kinds of statements and activities found in moral discourse, and I do not pretend that the above is an adequate classificatory scheme. But the importance of having such a scheme should now be clear. Such a scheme would enable one to discern and classify the kind of claim being made

---

[32] Meyer, op. cit., p. 494.

and ascertain the kind of evidence, if any, relevant to it. For example, if one claims that certain means will produce certain ends, we know this is an empirical claim verifiable or falsifiable by the use of the scientific method. But if one is preaching or advising, the scientific method is not relevant in the same sense. A different kind of data would also be relevant to a description or explanation of moral experience than that relevant to determining means-ends relationships. Certainly the kind of data relevant to a metaethical claim would be different from that relevant to an ethical claim. Our point is that if one is able to classify the kind of claim being made in moral discourse, one can determine the kind of data relevant to it, if any, and thereby avoid a great deal of confusion which might (and does) accrue without such a classificatory scheme.

5

Let me repeat that I do not claim that the seven areas designated above are the only ones requiring metaethical analysis in Thomistic moral philosophy (or in any moral philosophy). I would argue, however, that they are key points for analysis. Let me also say I have not attempted to set forth a complete metaethical analysis of Thomistic moral philosophy. That is far too large a task for one paper. However, I do think that our discussion about the nature of moral judgments and of moral reasoning along with our brief discussion of the seven factors enumerated above constitute in part a metaethical analysis of Thomistic moral philosophy. Each of the seven factors enumerated (as well as others) requires much more analysis and detail.

Without introducing a meta-metaethical level of discussion, I would like to close by suggesting another issue which requires careful analysis. That issue is the relationship between metaethical theories and normative ethics. I have addressed myself to this issue in some detail elsewhere[33] and I refer the reader to that essay. I will make only one or two observations. A number of contemporary metaethicists claim that metaethical theories are morally neutral. This may well be the case in the sense that a given metaethic does not entail any particular normative views or judgments. For example the metaethic of emotivism—the view that moral judgments are noncognitive expressions of emotion—does not commit one or entail any moral view such as euthanasia or trial marriage. However, there are other relationships between metaethical views and normative ethics which might well affect the moral life. The metaethic of emotivism, for example, changes our conception of what we are doing when we make moral judg-

---

33 See W. T. Blackstone, "Are Metaethical Theories Normatively Neutral?," *The Australasian Journal of Philosophy*, XXXIX (1961), 65–74.

ments and our view of justification in ethics. As Frederick Olafson[34] puts it, acceptance of the emotive metaethic makes one feel that rational principles are not operative for morals and that one's moral judgments are nonlogical acts of preference. The case can be put, I think, even stronger than that stated by Olafson. It appears that one's metaethical account of the meaning of ethical terms and statements actually logically entails a particular account of moral justification. Take the metaethic of subjectivism which views the meaning of ethical statements as autobiographical statements of approval or disapproval. This metaethic would entail a particular account of moral justification, namely, that the only data relevant to the justification of moral judgments are the autobiographical facts of personal approval or disapproval. Or take the metaethic of emotivism. This metaethic views ethical judgments as noncognitive expressions of emotion and such a view certainly logically entails that moral judgments cannot be justified as true or false since moral judgments do not assert anything. For those who adopt the metaethic of emotivism, if there is disagreement in moral attitude between two disputants who agree on the facts of the case, there is no method of resolvement beside persuasion, compromise, or abuse. On the emotivist scheme, all the reasons relevant to a *purely* moral disagreement (as opposed to a disagreement in belief) are persuasive reasons, for, as Ayer puts it, moral principles have "no objective validity." Thus one analytic entailment of the emotivist metaethic is that all ethically relevant reasons are persuasive reasons. Without noting other metaethical theories, our point should be clear: The manner in which one is to justify moral judgments depends logically upon what those judgments are interpreted as meaning.

The point we wished to make is that there are important relations between metaethics and normative ethics, and since there are a number of different metaethical theories (subjectivism, emotivism, objecticism, etc.), then the question arises as to which metaethic is correct. What are the criteria or tests whereby it can be shown that a given metaethic is correct and others incorrect?[35] This question would certainly involve the Thomistic moral philosopher. The Thomistic metaethic is a type of cognitivism and objectivism, and the Thomist must, if he is to be consistent with his emphasis upon the role of reason, show that his metaethic is the correct one. Not only is there need then, for a metaethical analysis of Thomistic moral philosophy, there is also need for a discussion of the validity and criteria for the validity of metaethical theories themselves.

---

[34] Frederick Olafson, "Metaethics and the Moral Life," *Philosophical Review*, LXV (1956).
[35] See W. T. Blackstone, op. cit., for *some* discussion of this issue.

Morality:
Religious and Secular

P. H. NOWELL-SMITH

1

The central thesis of this paper is that religious morality is infantile. I am well aware that this will sound absurd. To suggest that Aquinas and Kant—to say nothing of millions of Christians of lesser genius —never grew up is surely to put oneself out of court as a philosopher to be taken seriously. My thesis is not so crude as that; I shall try to show that, in the moralities of adult Christians, there are elements which can be set apart from the rest and are, indeed, inconsistent with them, that these elements can properly be called 'religious' and that just these elements are infantile.

I shall start by making some assumptions that I take to be common ground between Christians and secular humanists. I propose to say almost nothing about the *content* of morality; that love, sympathy, loyalty, and consideration are virtues, and that their opposites, malice, cruelty, treachery, and callousness, are vices, are propositions that I shall assume without proof. One can't do everything at the same time, and my job now is not to refute Thrasymachus. Secondly, I propose to occupy, as common ground, some much more debatable territory; I shall assume in broad outline the metaphysical view of the nature of man that we have inherited from Plato and Aristotle. The basis of this tradition is that there is something called 'Eudaimonia' or 'The Good Life', that this consists in fulfilling to the highest possible degree the nature of Man, and that the nature of Man is to be a rational, social animal. Love, I shall assume, is the supreme virtue because the life of love is, in the end, the only life that is fully rational and fully social. My concern will be, not with the content of morality, but with its form or structure, with the ways in which the manifold concepts and affirmations of which a moral system is composed hang together; not with rival views of what conduct is moral and what is immoral, but with rival views of what morality *is*.

This contrast between form and content is not difficult to grasp, but experience has taught me that it is often ignored. When they discover that I have moral views but no religious beliefs, people often ask me this question: 'Where do you get your moral ideas from?' Faced with this question, my

From The Rationalist Annual, *1961. Reprinted by permission of the author and The Rationalist Press Association.*

habit is to take it literally and to answer it truthfully. 'From my father and mother,' I say, 'from the companions of my boyhood and manhood, from teachers and from books, from my own reflections on the experience I have had of the sayings and doings of myself and others, an experience similar in countless ways to that of other people born of middle-class English parents some forty-five years ago, but in its totality unique.' This boring and auto-biographical answer never satisfies the questioner; for, though it is the right answer to the question he actually asked, it is not, as I very well knew, the answer to the question he really had in mind. He did not want to know *from whom* I learnt my moral views; he wanted to know what *authority* I have for holding them. But why, if this is what he wanted to know, did he not ask me? He has confused two different questions; and it is natural enough that he should have confused them, since it is often the case that to point to the source of an opinion or claim is to show the authority on which it is based. We appeal to the dictionary to vindicate an assertion about the spelling of a word, and the policeman's production of a warrant signed by a magistrate is a necessary and sufficient condition of his authority to enter my house. But even a dictionary can make mistakes, and one may doubt whether one *ought* to admit the policeman even after his legal title to enter has been satisfactorily made out. 'He certainly has a legal right,' one might say, 'but even so, things being as they are, ought I to admit him?'

Those who put this question to me have made an assumption that they have not examined because they have not reflected sufficiently on the form of morality. They have simply assumed that just as the legal propriety of an action is established by showing it to emanate from an authoritative source, so also the moral propriety of an action must be established in the same way; that legal rightness has the same form as moral rightness, and may there-fore be used to shed light on it. This assumption made, they naturally suppose that, even when I agree with them—for example, about the im-morality of murder—I have no right to hold this impeccable view unless I can show that I have received it from an authoritative source. My autobio-graphical answer clearly fails to do this. My parents may have had a right to my obedience, but no right to make the moral law. Morality, on this view, is an affair of being commanded to behave in certain ways by some person who has a right to issue such commands; and, once this premise is granted, it is said with some reason that only God has such a right. Morality must be based on religion, and a morality not so based, or one based on the wrong religion, lacks all validity.

It is this premise, that being moral consists in obedience to commands, that I deny. There is an argument, familiar to philosophers but of which the force is not always appreciated, which shows that this premise cannot be right. Suppose that I have satisfied myself that God has commanded me to do this or that thing—in itself a large supposition, but I will waive objections on this score in order to come quickly to the main point—it still makes *sense* for me to ask whether or not I *ought* to do it. God, let us say, is an omnipotent, omniscient creator of the universe. Such a creator might have evil intentions and might command me to do wrong; and if that were the case, though it would be imprudent to disobey, it would not be wrong. There is nothing in the idea of an omnipotent, omniscient creator which, by itself, entails his goodness or his right to command, unless we are prepared to assent to Hobbes' phrase, 'God, who by right, *that is by irresistible power, commandeth all things.*' Unless we accept Hobbes' consistent but repugnant equation of God's right with his might, we must be persuaded *independently* of his goodness before we admit his right to command. We must judge for ourselves whether the Bible is the inspired word of a just and benevolent God or a curious amalgam of profound wisdom and gross superstition. To judge this is to make a moral decision, so that in the end, so far from morality being based on religion, religion is based on morality.

Before passing to my main theme, I must add two cautions about what this argument does *not* prove. It does not prove that we should in no case take authority as a guide. Suppose that a man's aim is to make money on the Stock Exchange. He decides that it would be most profitable to invest his money in company A; but his broker prefers company B. He will usually be well advised to accept the verdict of his broker, even if the broker is, as they often are, inarticulate in giving his reasons. He might decide to put all his financial affairs in the hands of a broker, and to do nothing but what the broker tells him to do. But *this* decision, even if it is the only financial decision he ever makes in his life, is still his own. In much the same way, a man might decide to put his conscience wholly into the hands of a priest or a Church, to make no moral decisions of his own but always to do what the priest tells him. Even he, though he makes but one moral decision in his life, must make and continually renew that one. Those who accept the authority of a priest or a Church on what to do are, in accepting that authority, deciding for themselves. They may not fully comprehend that this is so; but that is another matter.

Secondly, to deny that morality need or can have an external nonmoral basis on which to stand is by no means to deny that it can have an internal basis, in the sense of one or a few moral beliefs that are fundamental to the other beliefs of the system. A man's views on gambling or sex or business ethics may (though they need not) form a coherent system in which some views are held *because* certain others views are held. Utilitarianism is an example of such a system in which all moral rules are to be judged by their tendency to promote human happiness. A moral system of this kind is like a system of geometry in which some propositions appear as axioms, others as theorems owing their place in the system to their derivability from the axioms. Few of us are so rationalistic as to hold all our moral beliefs in this way, but to move towards this goal is to begin to think seriously about morals.

2

In any system of morality we can distinguish between its content and its form. By its 'content' I mean the actual commands and prohibitions it contains, the characteristics it lists as virtues and as vices; by its 'form' I mean the sort of propositions it contains and the ways in which these are thought of as connected with each other. The basic distinction here is between a teleological morality in which moral rules are considered to be subordinate to ends, to be rules *for* achieving ends and consequently to be judged by their tendency to promote those ends, and a deontological system in which moral rules are thought of as absolute, as categorical imperatives in no way depending for their validity on the good or bad consequences of obedience, and in which moral goodness is thought to lie in conformity to these rules for their own sake. The first of these ways of looking at morality as a whole derives from the Greeks, so I shall call it the Greek view of morality; it can be summed up in the slogan 'the Sabbath was made for man, not man for the Sabbath.' The second, deriving mainly from Jewish sources, I shall call the Hebrew view. This involves a serious oversimplification, since we find deontological elements in the Greek New Testament and teleological elements in the Hebrew Old Testament; but, taken broadly, the contrast between the deontological character of the Old and the teleological character of the New Testaments is as striking as the difference of language. I shall also indulge in another serious oversimplification in speaking of Christianity as a morality of the Hebrew type while it is, of course, an amalgam of both with different elements predominating in different versions. This oversimplification would be quite unjustifiable if my task were to give an account of Christian morality; but it is legitimate here because my task is to contrast those elements in the Christian tradition which secular humanists accept with those which they reject, and these are broadly coterminous with the Greek and the Hebrew elements in Christianity respectively.

How there can be these two radically different ways of looking at morality, one which sees it as a set of recipes to be followed for the achievement of ends, the other which sees it as a set of commands to be obeyed, can best be understood if we consider the way in which we learn what it is to be moral. For a man's morality is a set of habits of choice, of characteristic responses to his environment, in particular to his social environment, the people among whom he lives; and habits are learnt in childhood. Growing up morally is learning to cope with the world into which we find ourselves pitched, and especially to cope with our relations with other human beings. In the course of living we learn to reflect on our responses, to find in some of them sources of satisfaction, in others sources of regret, and 'coping with the world' means coping with it in a manner ultimately satisfactory to our-selves. Philosophers such as Aristotle and Hobbes who boldly and crudely identified 'good' with 'object of desire' may have made a technical mistake; but they were certainly on the right lines. If men had no desires and aver-sions, if they felt no joy and no remorse, if they were totally indifferent to everything in the universe, there would be no such thing as choice and we should have no concept of morality, of good and evil.

The baby is born with some desires, not many; others it acquires as time goes on. Learning to cope with the world is learning how to satisfy and to modify these desires in a world that is partly propitious and partly hostile. For the world does not leap to gratify my desires like an assiduous flunkey; I do not get fed by being hungry. My desires are incompatible with each other and they come into conflict with those of other people. We have to learn both to bend the world to our wills and to bend our wills to the world. A man's morality is the way in which, in important matters, he does this.

Men are by nature rational and social animals, but only potentially so; they become actually rational and social only in a suitable environment, an environment in which they learn to speak a language. Learning how to cope with one's environment goes on side by side with learning to talk. The child's concepts, the meanings which, at every stage, words have for him, change as his horizon becomes wider, as he learns to grasp ideas that are more and more complicated, more and more remote from the primitive actions and passions that initially constitute his entire conscious life. It is not therefore surprising that the *form* of his morality, the meanings which moral words have and the ways in which they hang together, reflect at each stage the kind of experience he has. To babies who cannot yet talk we can-not, without serious error, attribute any thoughts at all; but though they cannot think, they can certainly feel, experience pleasure and pain, satisfac-tion and frustration. It is in these preverbal experiences that the origin of the ideas of 'good' and 'bad,' even of 'right' and 'wrong,' must be found; for their later development I turn to Piaget. My case for saying that religious morality is infantile cannot be conclusively made out without a much more detailed study of Piaget's researches than I have space for; I shall con-centrate on a few points that seem to me to bear directly on the issue be-tween the religious morality of law and the secular morality of purpose.

Piaget made a detailed study of the attitudes of children of different ages to the game of marbles, and he found three distinct stages. A very small child handles the marbles and throws them about as his humor takes him; he is playing, but not playing a *game*; for there are no rules governing his actions, no question of anything being done right or wrong. Towards the end of this stage he will, to some extent, be playing according to rules; for he will imitate older children who are playing a rule-governed game. But the child himself is not conscious of obeying rules; he has not yet grasped the concept of a 'rule,' of what a rule *is*. We may call this the premoral attitude to rules.

The second type of attitude is exhibited by children from five to nine. During this stage, says Piaget, 'the rules are regarded as sacred and inviolable, emanating from adults and lasting for ever. Every suggested alteration in the rules strikes the child as a transgression.' Piaget calls this attitude to rules 'heteronomous' to mark the fact that the children regard the rules as coming, as indeed they do, from the outside, as being imposed on them by others. We might also call this the 'deontological stage', to mark the fact that the rules are not questioned; they just *are* the rules of marbles, and that's that. At this stage the child has the concept of a rule, he knows what a rule is; but he has not yet asked what a rule is *for*. This deontological character is obviously connected with the unchangeability of the rules. Like laws in a primitive society, they are thought of as having been handed down from time immemorial, as much a part of the natural order of things as sunrise and sunset. The child may chafe at obedience and may sometimes disobey; but he does not question the authority of the rules.

Finally, at the third stage, the child begins to learn what the rules are for, what the point of having any rules is, and why it is better to have this rule rather than that. 'The rule,' says Piaget, 'is now looked upon as a law due to mutual consent, which you must respect if you want to be loyal, but which it is permissible to alter on condition of enlisting the general opinion on your side.' He calls this type of attitude 'autonomous' to mark the fact that the children now regard themselves, collectively, as the authors of the rules. This is not to say that they falsely suppose themselves to have invented them; they know well enough that they received them from older children. But they are the authors in the sense of being the final authorities; what tradition gave them they can change; from 'this is how we learnt to play' they no longer pass unquestioningly to 'this is how we ought to play.' We might also call this stage 'teleological' to mark the fact that the rules are no longer regarded as sacred, as worthy of obedience simply because they are what they are, but as serving a purpose, as rules for playing a game that they want to play. Rules there must certainly be; and in one sense they are sacred enough. Every player must abide by them; he cannot pick and choose. But in another sense there is nothing sacred about them; they are, and are known to be, a *mere* device, to be molded and adapted in the light of the purpose which they are understood by all the players to serve.

To illustrate the transition between the second and the third stages I should like to refer to a case from my own experience. Last summer I was with one other adult and four children on a picnic, and the children wanted to play rounders. We had to play according to the rules they had learnt at school because those just were the rules of rounders. This involved having two teams, and you can well imagine that, with only three players in each team, the game quickly ran on the rocks. When I suggested adapting the rules to our circumstances all the children were scandalized at first. But the two older children soon came round to the idea that, situated as we were, we should have to change the rules or not play at all and to the idea that it would not be wicked to change the rules. The two younger children were troubled, one might say, in their consciences about the idea of changing the rules. In Piaget's words, they thought of an alteration of rules as a transgression against them, having as yet no grasp of the distinction between an alteration of the rules by common consent to achieve a common purpose and the unilateral breach or defiance of them. In the eyes of these younger children we were not proposing to play a slightly different game, one better adapted to our situation; we were proposing to play the old game, but to play it wrong, almost dishonestly.

In another of Piaget's researches, this time directly concerned with moral attitudes, he told the children pairs of stories in each of which a child does something in some sense 'bad' and asked which of the children was naughtier, which deserved most punishment. In one such story a child accidently breaks fifteen cups while opening a door, and in the companion story a child breaks one cup while stealing jam. The replies of the very young children are mixed, some saying that the first child was naughtier; older children are unanimous in calling the second child naughtier. They have got beyond the primitive level of assessing moral guilt by the extent of the damage done.

Some of the youngest children do not recognize an act as wrong unless it is actually found out and punished, and we may call these last two points taken together 'moral realism,' because they display an attitude of mind that makes questions of morality questions of external fact. The inner state of the culprit—his motives and intentions—have nothing to do with it. To break crockery is wrong; therefore to break more crockery is more wrong. Moral laws are like laws of Nature, and Nature gives no marks for good or bad intentions and accepts no excuses. The fire will burn you if you touch it, however careful you were to avoid it. But if you are careless and, by good luck, avoid it, you will not be burnt; for Nature gives no bad marks for carelessness either. In the same way, if you lie and are punished, that is bad; but if you lie and are not punished, that is not bad at all. The fact that retribution did not follow *shows* that the lie was not, in this case, wrong.

3

I want now to compare the religious with the secular attitude towards the moral system which, in its content, both Christians and

Humanists accept. I shall try to show that the religious attitude retains these characteristics of deontology, heteronomy and realism which are proper and indeed necessary in the development of a child, but not proper to an adult: But I must repeat the caution with which I began. The views which I called 'moral realism,' which make intentions irrelevant, were expressed by very young children. No doubt many of these children were Christians and I do not wish to suggest that they never grew up, that they never adopted a more mature and enlightened attitude. This would be absurd. My thesis is rather that these childish attitudes survive in the moral attitudes of adult Christians—and of some secular moralists—as an alien element, like an outcrop of igneous rock in an alluvial plain. When Freud says of someone that he is fixated at the oral stage of sexuality he does not mean that he still sucks his thumb; he means rather that some of his characteristic attitudes and behavior patterns can be seen as an adult substitute for thumb sucking. In the same way, I suggest that some elements characteristic of Christian morality are substitutes for childish attitudes. In the course of this comparison I shall try to show how these infantile attitudes belong to a stage that is a *necessary* stage on the way to the fully adult, a stage which we must have passed through in order to reach maturity.

It needs little reflection to see that deontology and heteronomy are strongly marked features of all religious moralities. First for deontology. For some Christians the fundamental sin, the fount and origin of all sin, is disobedience to God. It is not the nature of the act of murder or of perjury that makes it wrong; it is the fact that such acts are transgressions of God's commands. On the other hand, good acts are not good in themselves, good in their own nature, but good only *as* acts of obedience to God. 'I give no alms only to satisfy the hunger of my brother, but to accomplish the will and command of my God; I draw not my purse for his sake that demands it, but his that enjoined it' (Sir Thomas Browne, *Religio Medici* II, 2). Here charity itself is held to be good *only because* God has told us to be charitable. It is difficult not to see in this a reflection of the small child's attitude towards his parents and the other authorities from whom he learns what it is right to do. In the first instance little Tommy learns that it is wrong to pull his sister's hair, not because it hurts her, but because Mummy forbids it.

The idea of heteronomy is also strongly marked in Christian morality. 'Not as I will, but as thou wilt.' The demand made by Christianity is that of surrendering self, not in the ordinary sense of being unselfish, of loving our neighbor and even our enemy. It is the total surrender of the *will* that is required; Abraham must be prepared to sacrifice Isaac at God's command, and I take this to mean that we must be prepared to sacrifice our most deeply felt moral concerns if God should require us to do so. If we dare to ask why, the only answer is 'Have faith'; and faith is an essentially heteronomous idea; for it is not a reasoned trust in someone in whom we have good grounds for reposing trust; it is blind faith, utter submission of our own reason and will.

Now, to the small child morality is necessarily deontological and heteronomous in form; he must learn *that* certain actions are right and others wrong before he can begin to ask *why* they are, and he learns this from other people. The child has his own spontaneous springs of action; there are things he wants to do off his own bat; morality is a curb, at first nothing but a curb on his own volition. He comes up against parental discipline, even if only in the form of the giving and withdrawing of love, long before he can have any compassion, long before he has any conception of others as sentient beings. When he begins to learn language, words like 'bad' must mean simply 'what hurts me; what I don't like'; through the mechanism of parental discipline they come to mean 'what adults forbid and punish me for.' It is only because actions which cause suffering to others figure so largely among parental prohibitions that the child learns to connect the word 'bad' with them at all.

If we consider the foundations of Christian ethics in more detail we shall find in them moral realism as well. Christianity makes much of charity and the love of our neighbor; but it does not say, as the Greeks did, that this is good because it is what befits the social animal, Man. We ought to be charitable because this is laid on us as a duty and because this state of the soul is the proper state for it during its transient mortal life. We must be charitable because (we are told) only so can we arrive at the soul's goal, the right relation to God. This fundamental isolation of the individual soul with God seems clearly to reflect what one supposes must be the state of mind of the small baby for whom, at the dawn of consciousness, there is only himself on the one side and the collective world of adults, represented largely by his parents, on the other, for whom the idea of others as individuals, as beings like himself, does not yet exist.

This impression is increased when we consider some accounts of what this right relationship between the soul and God is. Granted that to achieve this is the object of right living, just *what* relationship is it that we are to try to achieve? The terms of the relation are an omnipotent creator and his impotent creature, and between such terms the only relation possible is one of utter one-sided dependence, in which the only attitude proper to the creature must be one of adoration, a blend of love and fear. Surely this is just how the world must appear to the young child; for he really *is* impotent, wholly dependent on beings whose ways he cannot understand, beings sometimes loving, sometimes angry, but always omnipotent, always capricious—in short, gods. 'As for Dr. Wulicke himself personally, he had all the awful mystery, duplicity, obstinacy, and jealousy of the Old Testament God. He was as frightful in his smiles as in his anger.'[1]

Consider in this connection the ideas of original sin and grace. Every son of Adam is, of his own nature, utterly corrupt, redeemable only by divine grace. Once more, the conditions in which the child learns morality provide an obvious source for this remarkable conception. Parents are not only omniscient and omnipotent; they are also necessarily and always morally in the right. This must be so, since they are, as the child sees it, the authors of the moral law. Morality, the idea of something being right or wrong, enters the horizon of the child only at those points at which he has, so to speak, a dispute with authority, only on those occasions on which he is told or made to do something that he does not spontaneously want to do. From these premises that, at the time when the meanings of 'right' and 'wrong' are being learnt, the child must disagree with its parents and that they must be right he naturally passes to the conclusion that he must always be wrong. To have the sense of actual sin is to have the sense that one has, on this occasion, done wrong; to have the sense of original sin is simply to feel that one must be always and inevitably wrong. This sense of sin has often been deliberately and cruelly fostered; John Bunyan is not the only man to have left on record the agony of his childhood; but the point I wish to make is that the infantile counterpart of the sense of sin is a necessity at a certain stage of moral development, the stage at which moral words are being learnt and moral rules accepted as necessarily what parents say they are.

On the other side of the picture there is the doctrine of grace. Each individual soul is either saved or damned; but its fate, at least according to some versions, is wholly out of its own control. In these extreme versions, grace is absolutely necessary and wholly sufficient for salvation; and grace is the *free* gift of God. As far as the creature is concerned, there is absolutely nothing that he can do or even try to do either to merit or to obtain it.[2] From his point of view the giving or withholding of the means of salvation must be wholly capricious.

Once more, this is how parental discipline must seem to the child who cannot yet understand its aims and motives. Consider, for example, how

---

1 Thomas Mann, *Buddenbrooks*, referring to the headmaster whom Hanno and Kai nicknamed 'The Lord God.' The whole chapter, Part XI, ch. 2, illustrates this point.

2 This is, I know, heretical; yet I cannot see in the subtle palliatives offered by Catholic theologians anything but evasions, vain attempts to graft a more enlightened moral outlook on to a theological tree which will not bear them. The reformers seem to me to have been right in the sense that they were restoring the original doctrine of the Church.

even the most careful and consistent parents react towards what they call
the clumsiness of a child. He knocks things over; he fumbles with his
buttons. Though most parents do not think of themselves as punishing a
child for such things, their behavior is, from the child's point of view,
indistinguishable from punishment. They display more irritation when the
child knocks over a valuable vase than when he knocks over a cheap cup,
when the button-fumbling happens to occur at a moment when they are
in a hurry than when it does not. If a father takes from a small child
something that is dangerous to play with or stops him hurting himself by
a movement necessarily rough, that to the child is indistinguishable from
punishment; it is a thwarting of his inclination for no reason that he can
see. Children often say things that they know to be untrue; sometimes they
are reprimanded for lying, sometimes complimented on their imagination.
How can the child know under which heading, the good or the bad, a piece
of invention will come, except by observing whether it is punished or
rewarded? The child, by this time, is beginning to make efforts to try to
please his parents, to do what, in his childish mind, he thinks right. The
parents, not being expert child psychologists, will often fail to notice this;
more often they will disregard it. To the child, therefore, there is little
correlation between his own intentions and the reactions he evokes from
the adult world. Salvation in the form of parental smiles and damnation
in the form of parental frowns will come to him, like grace, in a manner
that both seems and is wholly unconnected with any inwardly felt guilt.
The mystery of God's ways to Man is the mystery of a father's ways to his
children.

This characterization of religious morality as essentially infantile may
seem to be unnecessary; for do not Christians themselves liken their relationship to God as that of child to father? In so doing they do not seem to
me always to realize how incompatible this father–child relationship is with
the Greek conception of the good life which they recognize as one of the
sources of their moral doctrine. Aristotle says that children, like animals,
have no share in the good life (a remark which always sounds so odd when
people translate it as 'children have no share in happiness'), and the reason
he gives is that children do not *act*. This is a deep furrow to begin to plough
at this stage—what is meant by 'action'; but briefly it is motion that is
self-initiated and responsible. The prime difference between the adult and
the child is that the adult has freedom to choose for himself and has, what
goes with freedom, responsibility for his actions. In the life of a child there
is always, in the last resort, the parent or some substitute for a parent to
turn to. The father is responsible at law for the actions of his child; he
will undo what harm the child has done; he will put things right, will save
the child from the consequences of his mistakes. To pass from childhood
into adulthood is essentially to pass from dependence into freedom, and the

price we pay is responsibility. As adults we make our own choices and must accept their consequences; the shield that in our childish petulance we once thought so irksome is no longer there to protect us. To many of us this is a matter of life-long regret, and we search endlessly for a father substitute. Surely 'they' will get us out of the mess; there ought to be a law; why doesn't somebody. . . . These, in this godless age, are the common secular substitutes; religion, when it is not a patent substitute, is only a more profound, a more insinuating one.

4

The postulation of a god as the author of the moral law solves no more problems in ethics than the postulation of a god as first cause solves problems in metaphysics. Nor need we base morality, as I have done, on the metaphysical conception of Man as a rational, social animal, though we shall do so if we care to maintain the link with the old meaning of the word 'humanist.' To me, as a philosopher, some systematic view of the whole of my experience, some metaphysic, is essential, and this conception of the nature of Man makes more sense of my experience than any other I know. But I certainly should not argue that *because* the species Man has such and such a nature, *therefore* each and every man ought to act in such and such ways. In trying to sketch a humanist morality I shall start simply with the idea that a morality is a set of habits of choice ultimately determined by the question 'What life is most satisfactory to me as a whole?' and I start with this because I simply do not *understand* the suggestion that I ought to do anything that does not fit into this conception. Outside this context the word 'ought' has for me no meaning; and here at least I should expect Christians to agree with me.

If we start in this way, inquiries into my own nature and into the nature of Man at once become relevant. For my nature is such that there are some things that are impossible for me to do. Some hopes must be illusory, and nothing but frustration could come of indulging them. I could not, for example, become an operatic tenor or a test cricketer. Inquiries into the nature of Man are relevant in two ways; first, because I have to live as a man among men, secondly, because all men are to some degree alike and some of my limitations are common to us all. None of us can fly or witness past events. It is only insofar as men are alike that we can even begin to lay down rules as to how they should (all) behave; for it is only insofar as they are alike that they will find satisfaction and frustration in the same things. Prominent among the similarities among men are the animal appetites, the desire for the love and companionship of their own species, and the ability to think; and it is these three similarities that make us all 'moral' beings. Morality consists largely, if not quite wholly, in the attempt to realize these common elements in our nature in a coherent way, and we have found that this cannot be done without adopting moral rules and codes of law. Humanism does not imply the rejection of all moral rules, but it does imply the rejection of a deontological attitude towards them. Even Piaget's older children could not have played marbles without rules; but they treated them as adaptable, as subservient to the purpose of playing a game, which is what they wanted to do. They treated the rules as a wise man treats his motor car, not as an object of veneration but as a convenience.

This, I suggest, is how we, as adults, should regard moral rules. They are necessary, in the first place, because one man's aim in life often conflicts with the aims of others and because most of our aims involve the cooperation of others, so that, even for purely selfish reasons, we must conform to rules to which others also conform. Most moral rules, from that prohibiting murder to that enjoining punctuality, exist for this purpose. But morality is not wholly an affair of regulating our dealings with others; each man has within himself desires of many different kinds which cannot all be fully satisfied; he must establish an order of priorities. Here I think almost all moralists, from Plato to D. H. Lawrence, have gone astray; for they have overemphasized the extent to which men are like each other and consequently been led to embrace the illusory concept of a 'best life' that is the same for all of us. Plato thought this was a life dominated by the pursuit of knowledge, Lawrence one dominated by the pursuit of sensual experience and animal activity. I do not happen to enjoy lying naked on the grass; but I should not wish to force my preference for intellectual endeavor on anyone who did. Why should we not, within the framework of uniformity required for any life to be satisfactory to anyone at all, seek satisfaction in our own different ways?

The word 'morality' is usually understood in a sense narrower than that in which I have been using it, to refer to just this necessary framework, to the rules to which we must all conform in order to make our aims, however diverse, realizable in a world which we all have to share. In Hobbes' words, the sphere of morality is limited to 'those qualities of mankind that concern their living together in peace and unity' (*Leviathan*, ch. xi). If this is the purpose of moral rules, we must be willing to keep them under review and to discard or modify those that, in the light of experience, we find unnecessary or obstructive. But they must retain a certain inflexibility, since, in our casual contacts, it is important that people should be reliable, should conform so closely to a publicly agreed code that, even if we do not know them as individuals, we know what to expect of them. 'That men perform their covenants made' is an adequate summary of morality in this limited sense.

But, though morality in this sense is necessary, it is not all. Rules belong to the superficial periphery of life. Like the multiplication table and other thought-saving dodges, they exist to free us for more important activities. It is beyond the power of any man to regulate all his dealings with all the people with whom he comes in casual contact by love; for love requires a depth of understanding that cannot be achieved except in close intimacy. Rules have no place in marriage or in friendship. This does not mean that a man must keep his word in business but may break promises made to his wife or to a friend; it is rather that the notion of keeping a promise made to a wife or friend from a sense of duty is utterly out of place, utterly foreign to the spirit of their mutual relationship. For what the sense of duty requires of us is always the commission or omission of specific acts.

That friends should be loyal to one another I take for granted; but we cannot set out a list of acts that they should avoid as disloyal with the sort of precision (itself none too great) with which we could list the things a man should not do in business. Too much will depend on the particular circumstances and the particular natures of the people concerned. Rules must, of their very nature, be general; that is their virtue and their defect. They lay down what is to be done or not done in *all* situations of a certain general kind, and they do this because their function is to ensure reliability in the absence of personal knowledge. But however large we make the book of rules, however detailed we try to make its provisions, its complexity cannot reach to that of a close personal relationship. Here what matters is not the commission or omission of specific acts but the spirit of the relationship as a whole. A man thinks, not of what his obligation to his wife or his friend requires of him, but of what it is best for his wife or his friend that he should do. A personal relationship does indeed consist of specific acts; the spirit that exists between husband and wife or between friends is nothing over and above the specific things they do together. But each specific act, like each brush stroke in a picture or each note in a symphony, is good or bad only as it affects the quality of the relationship as a whole. The life of love is, like a work of art, not a means to an end, but an end in itself. For this reason in all close human relationships there should be a flexibility in our attitude to rules characteristic to the expert artist, craftsman, or games player.

The expert moves quickly, deftly, and, to the untutored eye, even carelessly. It takes me hours to prune an apple tree, and I have to do it book in hand; the expert goes over the tree in a few minutes, snipping here and slashing there, with the abandonment of a small boy who has neither knowledge of pruning nor intention to prune. Indeed, to someone who does not know what he is about, his movements must seem more like those of Piaget's youngest children who just threw the marbles about. But the similarity is superficial. For one thing, the master craftsman's movements do mostly follow the book for all that he never refers to it; and for another he does know what he is about and it is just this knowledge that entitles him to flout the rules when it is suitable to do so. No apple tree is exactly like the drawing in the book, and expertise lies in knowing when and how to deviate from its instructions.

This analogy must not be pressed too far. The conduct of life is more complicated and more difficult than any such task as pruning a tree and few of us could claim, without improper pride, the master craftsman's licence. But I should like to press it some way, to suggest that, in all important matters, our chief consideration should be, not to conform to any code of rules, but simply how we can produce the best results; that we should so act that we can say in retrospect, not 'I did right,' but 'I did what befitted the pattern of life I have set myself as a goal.'

As a philosopher, I cannot but speak in abstract generalities, and it is central to my thesis that at this point the philosopher must give way to the novelist. Tolstoy, Thomas Mann, and Forster have given us many examples of the contrast between the rule-bound and the teleological attitudes to life. But I should like to end by descending one level, not to the particular, but to the relatively specific, and to consider as an example one moral rule, the prohibition of adultery.

By 'adultery' I understand the act of sexual intercourse with someone other than one's spouse. It is expressly forbidden in the Bible, absolutely and without regard to circumstances; it is a crime in some countries and many would make it a crime in this. Until very recently it was almost the only ground for civil divorce. A marriage is supposed to be a life-long union. It could be entirely devoid of love—some married couples have not spoken to each other for years, communicating by means of a blackboard; yet no grounds for divorce existed. Or the husband might insist on sexual intercourse with his wife against her will and yet commit no sin. But let him once go out, get drunk, and have a prostitute and the whole scene changes. He has sinned; his wife has a legal remedy and, in the eyes of many who are not Christians but have been brought up in a vaguely Christian tradition, he has now done a serious wrong. This is a rule-and-act morality according to which what is wrong is a specific act; and it is wrong in all circumstances even, for example, if the wife is devoid of jealousy or so devoid of love that she would rather have her husband lie in any bed but hers.

If we look at this rule against adultery from a teleological standpoint it must appear wholly different. A humanist may, of course, reject the whole conception of monogamy; but if, like myself, he retains it, he will do so only because he believes that the life-long union of a man and a woman in the intimacy of marriage is a supreme form of love. Copulation has its part to play in such a union; but, for the species Man, it cannot be its essence. If someone who holds this view still thinks adultery is wrong, he will do so because it appears to him to be an act of disloyalty, an act likely to break the union which he values. Two consequences follow from this. The first is that if a marriage is, for whatever reason, devoid of love, there is now no union to break; so neither adultery nor any other act can break it. The second is that since adultery is now held to be wrong, not in itself, but only *as* an act of disloyalty, it will not *be* wrong when it is *not* an act of disloyalty. An adultery committed with the full knowledge and consent of the spouse will not be wrong at all. A so-called 'platonic' friendship, even too assiduous an attendance at the local pub or sewing circle, anything that tends to weaken the bonds of love between the partners will be far more damaging to the marriage and consequently far more deeply immoral. Just *what* specific acts are immoral must, on this view, depend on the particular circumstances and the particular people concerned. Christians also insist on the uniqueness of individual people; but since law is, of its nature, general, this insistence seems wholly incompatible with the morality of law to which they are also committed.

Discussion of "Morality: Religious and Secular"

A. BOYCE GIBSON

Having used Professor Nowell-Smith's work on *Ethics* for four years as a textbook for Honors students, I know perhaps better than most how difficult he is to argue with. There is a flexibility, an open-mindedness, one might almost say a Janus quality about him, which ensures that any criticism one wishes to direct to him has been forestalled in the text. This quality, evident in his book, is bountifully exhibited also in this recent article, 'Morality: Religious and Secular'. His main theme, which he bases on the findings of Piaget and his own observations of parent-child behavior, is that 'religious morality is infantile'. Yet for the most part he does not question the content of Christian morality, and even quotes, in the act of expelling religion from morals, 'the Sabbath was made for man, not man for the Sabbath'. This time, however, the scale is small enough to permit

From Journal of Theological Studies, *1962. Reprinted by permission of the author and* Journal of Theological Studies.

of detailed dissection, and the prejudices show out strongly enough to be understood for what they are. I am therefore emboldened to attempt a Christian reply.

1

      As we have noticed, Nowell-Smith carefully distinguishes between the form and the content of religious morality. The content, however, he regards as not specifically religious, being the property of humanists also. What he objects to, and finds specifically religious, and treats as a form of infantilism, is the *formal* aspect of Christian behavior, and by that he means primarily (though, as we shall see, not exclusively) its reliance on rules. And this view of the matter I find extraordinary. It is not that I wish to question his views on the place of rules in the good life: by the time that he has had time for his accustomed qualifications, the sharp edge of his distinction between rule and end is considerably blunted, and the result is one which a Christian would not wish to challenge. No: what is extraordinary is what Nowell-Smith believes Christians to believe. For if there ever was a religion which challenged the morality of rules, it was Christianity. Right from the beginning, Christ preached that the 'rules' of the Jewish law were not enough: 'Except your righteousness shall exceed the righteousness of the scribes and Pharisees, ye shall in no case enter into the kingdom of heaven.' It is the character of rules to apply impartially: it is the character of Christian morality to do more than any rule could demand, in a spirit of love and service. 'The wind bloweth where it listeth: so is every one that is born of the Spirit.' Could Nowell-Smith demand a looser texture than that? 'He maketh his sun to rise on the evil and on the good, and sendeth rain on the just and on the unjust.' By all the canons of rules-morality this is grossly unfair, and many justice fans have said so, and given it as a moral reason for being atheists. And what about that ex-rules-moralist, the apostle Paul? 'But now the righteousness of God without the law is manifested.' 'That no man is justified by the law in the sight of God, it is evident; for the just shall live by faith.' These texts are indeed the scaffolding of Christian history. The Gospel has confronted and confounded Roman rules, Nordic rules, Shinto rules, Confucian rules, and not least Greek rules; and the common charge against Christians among responsible Eastern conservatives today is that by breaking down rules they produce anarchy and pave the way to communism—a charge more disconcerting, because better grounded, than Nowell-Smith's. Only twice has Christianity been philosophically entangled with rules: once when it was infiltrated by the Stoic doctrine (a Greek doctrine) of natural law, and once again when, in the time of the Calvinist ascendancy, it lapsed into Old Testament primitivism. Certainly the basic Christian texts are as hostile to mere rules as Nowell-Smith himself. If Christian behavior has impressed him otherwise, that is not because it is Christian, but because it is not Christian enough.

There is, of course, a place for rules in Christian behavior: as may be seen if we complete some of the passages quoted above. 'Think not I am come to destroy the law, or the prophets: I am not come to destroy, but to fulfill.... Till heaven and earth pass, one jot or one tittle shall in no wise pass from the law, till all be fulfilled.' 'The righteousness of God without the law is manifested, being witnessed by the law and the prophets.' 'The law was our schoolmaster to bring us unto Christ, that we might be justified by faith.' These are the passages which should prevent Christians from running off into antinomianism; but each one of them represents the law as a stage on the journey and not as a destination. And this is exactly what Nowell-Smith wants. He understands the part played by rules in the education of children; he merely protests that they should not continue to play the same part in adult life. Paul's analogy of the schoolmaster should surely suit him admirably. For Paul's schoolmaster (the law) knows that when his pupils are fully grown they will freely confront their future in his spirit, but in their own new way.

There is, it is true, a foothold for misunderstanding, and Nowell-Smith has built it up into a platform. As he says, in the more intimate and affectionate relations such as marriage and friendship, one does not stop behind with the rules; and this is the reason why these relations are so much more central than those which require of us only justice. But even here, and elsewhere much more, sitting loose to the rules can be a perilous adventure for the unprepared; it so often means not rising above them, but sinking below them. We are not all of us all the time moral aristocrats like Aristotle (who, by the way, did not pretend to be moralizing for the vulgar). We are constantly pricked by desire or enraged by opposition; and the best thing we can do is to sit on ourselves till we come round. To that end rules are a great stand-by, and they are most serviceable when most inflexible: otherwise we shall make exceptions in our own favor. If Nowell-Smith has never felt like that, he is to be congratulated, but he is not in a position to speak to the multitude. However, as a matter of fact, he consents to 'certain inflexibilities', mainly for the social ground that people must know what they may expect from each other. This is an urbane common room commutation for 'what I would, that I do not, but what I hate, that I do'; but at least it provides some sort of frame for his open-texture weaving. Nowell-Smith proposes to treat rules as a wise man treats his car, 'not as an object of veneration but as a convenience'. 'Convenience' is an understatement resulting from his underplaying of evil (one *can* do without a car) ; but substitute 'necessary second best' and there is nothing to distinguish him from a Gospel Christian. I hope he will not be disappointed.

As much of the nursery lore which is the mainspring of his paper is introduced to show how the morality of rules is a prolongation of childhood, there is no need to examine it in detail. We can be sure that Piaget saw straight and that Nowell-Smith is a faithful reporter. The trouble is that the whole episode supports the specifically Christian and religious element in Christian morality against the Pharisee, the Roman, and the modern rationalist pagan.[1] On the subject of rules orthodox Christianity is, from Nowell-Smith's point of view, on the side of the angels; and we may pass to another issue.

2

There are, however, other matters, also pointing back to the nursery, on which Nowell-Smith dissents from 'religious' morality. Though he gives far less space to these considerations than he mistakenly gives to rules, I shall develop them at greater length, for it is in canvassing them that he shows the real cause of his irritation.

The first is his subordination of deontology to teleology. On this I shall only observe that he assumes that attention to duty means attention to rules. Against it I should urge that attention to duty can never be attention to rules only, because what is in question, whenever one does one's duty, is what one ought to do in a particular case, and every particular case is a meeting place of rules at least potentially in conflict. For duty, as for Nowell-Smith's alternative, 'coping with the world in a manner satisfactory to ourselves', rules are in the category of ways and means. In another context, I should press this point, because the association between duty and universalizability seems to have been far too easily accepted. Here I pass it by, because duty is not the end-product of a Christian life, any more than it is for Nowell Smith's eudaemonists: and I proceed to the alleged infantilism of the concepts of faith and grace. It is at this point that the collision occurs: though even here the main cause is Nowell-Smith's teen-age (I will not say infantile) translation of these cardinal theological concepts.

The subject is introduced by a discussion of heteronomy, by which Nowell-Smith, following Kant for once, means the determination of the will by reference to some external authority. It is clear that this does happen in the nursery, and also that the answer 'Because I tell you' may be unreasonably perpetuated beyond its proper age limit. Nowell-Smith calls heteronomy infantile because it means that in adult life we defer to

---

[1] One has only to think of the ferocious justice of French atheists like Clemenceau, so self-standing and self-sufficient that he left instructions that he should be buried upright—clearly it does not take a Christian to be implacable, though it does take a Christian to deactivate the more far-reaching implacabilities.

authority instead of deciding for ourselves. The authority which he is concerned to challenge is the will of God. ('Not as I will, but as thou wilt', he quotes with disparagement—forgetting not only the divine compassion of it but also the agonizing effort of a human decision.) There are many other authorities which he might have challenged, especially the political mass movements which have been in the past most effectively withstood by men who appealed to the will of God. However, it is the most liberating authority which most disturbs him, so let us follow where he leads.

To appeal to the will of God, then, even against tyrants, is to submit oneself *and not to decide*. If that assertion is mistaken, the whole argument breaks down. I propose to argue that this view of the matter is both untenable and bad theology.

The first qualm induced in the reader is set in motion, in his usual Janus fashion, by Nowell-Smith himself. He observes that 'those who accept the authority of a priest or a church on what they are to do, are, in accepting that authority, deciding for themselves'. This is surely true, and it shows that authority and deciding are not incompatible. And if it is true of a priest or a church, a fortiori it is true of the decision to follow God's will. It is indeed a decision, not a mere slide from one allegiance to another. Many of us have taken it without the advantage of a religious training, and maintain it despite the pressure of a pagan environment, e.g. in universities. It is not at all a natural or easy continuation of obedience to parents.

It might be replied that it is a decision, but a decision to end decisions; but Nowell-Smith sees that this account will not do. He realizes that the decision has constantly to be reaffirmed. His objection must therefore be either to the content of the decision, or to the reasons for the decision. But he has already conceded that the content is common ground between himself and his opponents. It must be the reasons for the decision which he finds fault with. But, supposing he were right on this issue, it would still be wrong to confuse it with the quite different issue, whether doing the will of God entails the total obliteration of decision.

The objection which Nowell-Smith takes to the will of God as a *reason* for moral action is that it is not a reason. The decision is taken on the strength of an unsocial and unsharable intimation. It is not even based on 'a reasoned trust in someone in whom we have good grounds for reposing trust'; it is 'blind faith, utter submission of our own reason and will'. And one effect of this attitude is to cut away all the good social reasons even for such of our actions as the will of God also commends to us, substituting for them the sole requirement of 'the right relation to God'.

We may begin with the corollary because it illustrates graphically the underlying misrepresentation. Nowell-Smith quotes Sir Thomas Browne, *Religio Medici* II, 2, as saying: 'I give no alms only to satisfy the hunger of my brother, but to accomplish the will and command of my God: I draw not my purse for his sake that demands it, but his that enjoined it.' He interprets this to mean that 'charity itself is held to be good *only because* God has enjoined us to be charitable'. He has certainly misinterpreted Browne by displacing the word 'only': he has made it appear that in Browne's view reference to the will of God *excludes* reference to the man's hunger, whereas all Browne said was that the expressed will of God is a further reason for relieving it. The man's hunger is one of the things the will of God is about. This tendency to depict religion as a set of dichotomies is persistent in Nowell-Smith. If Browne had meant what Nowell-Smith thinks he meant, he would have been much to blame, but he would not have been talking Christianity. I remember vividly how the first Lord Lindsay of Birker, speaking as a Christian, used to declaim against that Victorian classic for children, *The Fairchild Family*, in which the author takes exactly the point of view ascribed to Browne by Nowell-Smith. ' "He that giveth to the poor lendeth to the Lord, and shall be repaid", said Mrs Fairchild, hastily slipping a shilling into the poor woman's hand.' Here the poor woman *is* treated heteronomously, and without Christian charity: it is just that sort of thing which launched the word 'charity' on its downward path. The heteronomy, it may be remarked, though hardly Christian, is not the worst thing about this utterance: what is really evil in it is the teleological tag. To obey God without regarding one's neighbor is only half of the Christian vocation; to obey God with an eye to one's own advantage is to subtract the other half as well. Some teleological arguments, it would seem, are worse than any sort of deontology.

Let us, however, admit that to appeal to the will of God as *opposed to* the welfare of one's neighbor is morally insensitive, and that when the quality of religion declines this is the way the issue is apt to be presented. It is still not what the Christian is expected to do. Love of God and love of neighbor are presented as complementary and collateral, but not as cause and consequence. Text for text, it would actually be possible to argue the other way round. 'If a man loveth not the brother whom he hath seen, how shall he love the God whom he hath not seen?' 'Blessed are the pure in heart, for they shall see God'—not vice versa. The Christian God cannot be loved by high-minded self-centered people, and this is why Jesus kept up the barrage against the Pharisees. In doing what we can for others, we are *ipso facto* doing it for God; God is not so other than others, that we can serve them without serving him. It is the will of God that we should love our neighbor *because he is our neighbor*; only so do we do it for his greater glory.

Thus Christian heteronomy is always qualified. Obedience to the will of God is never pure and simple. It is always in respect of some act or kind of act specifiable in other terms. It is always to be rendered but not to arbitrary command. It is true that Christian morality is through and through religious, and is not primarily concerned with 'what befits the social animal, Man'. But it is concerned with what befits *men* (not man), as children of one Father. If we sometimes think the will of God commands us to do to others what does not befit children of God, we can be sure we have got it wrong: as Abraham discovered in the nick of time, and as Jephthah tragically forgot. The tradition of the Church, as well as human affections, warns us to be on our guard against diabolical simulations of the will of God; and if it is wholly heteronomous there is no way of telling the one from the other. So far from disagreeing with Nowell-Smith on this point, I entirely endorse him. But whatever it is he is attacking—I should call it popular Calvinism desiccating into deism—it is not, as he seems to think, Christian morality.

It may be replied that in that case the will of God is being subjected to the demands of human nature and will thus fade away into a ghostly double. But that is to forget two of the main features of a distinctively Christian philosophy: creation and incarnation. As a creature, man is made, and as God's creature, he is made in God's image. His demands are therefore at the same time God's demands on him. Further, the will of God was made manifest on earth in specific form and under specific conditions, and it was actually exhibited in human form as a human will. Philosophers may find this belief incredible, though it brought life (and sense) into the bloodless abstractions of later Greek philosophy, and wherever it has gone has dispersed a whole cloud of local superstitions. But they should not write about some highest common factor God-in-general and expect Christians to understand them. If incarnation is taken seriously, the whole contrast between autonomy and heteronomy in respect of God goes by the board. The will of man is all the more autonomous for a heteronomy which, flowing up from inside it, in no way constrains it from without. The distinction is between an autonomy thus continually reinforced and the humanist autonomy which locks itself up and declines reinforcement.

But, to return to the immediate issue, once again Nowell-Smith's charge of infantilism—of maintaining in adult life attitudes proper to the early learning process—rests on a wrong diagnosis. All religion celebrates the process of growing up—from aboriginal initiation ceremonies to confirmation services and experiences of conversion—and the Christian religion certainly follows the course of nature in celebrating and emphasizing the passage from childhood to maturity. Moreover, being an incarnational religion it is not immaterialist and assigns a proper value to the humanist enterprises of personal and social improvement. It includes everything that Nowell-Smith wants to include, but in a richer and more resonant context. The reason he misses the point is that he mistakes incarnational Christians for Cathari or Manichees, and plants upon them, in place of an ordered hierarchy, an implacable and unreasonable Either/Or.

3

I have devoted some time to the theme of Christianity and heteronomy, because it is the source of other mistakes, notably with regard to sin and grace. Nowell-Smith points out, justly enough, that from the child's point of view 'right' and 'wrong' must seem to be arbitrary expressions of parental approval or disapproval, and that the alternation of smiles and frowns must seem inexplicable and fortuitous. He goes on to say that the experience of sin and grace in adult life perpetrates this incomprehension and perplexity of childhood. 'The mystery of God's ways to man is the mystery of a father's ways with his children'.

In setting out the comparison, Nowell-Smith states the classical doctrine of sin and grace in what he admits to be an extreme form: 'grace is the *free* gift of God, and . . . there is absolutely nothing that (the creature) can do, or even try to do, either to merit or to obtain it'. This Calvinist deviation is, however, presented deliberately as the model on the ground that it is the original doctrine of the Church, and that 'the subtle palliatives offered by Catholic theologians' are nothing but 'evasions'. This could be disputed, and not only by Catholics: Arminians, Methodists and Quakers, and individuals from other communions, would also insist on the 'subtleties', and their effect on the doctrine of God and man. If I do not stress them here, it is because Nowell-Smith is correct in thinking that they are not the main point at issue.

The point of his analogy between the grace of God and the favors of a father is that both are inexplicable and both are substitutes for human effort. In the extreme form of the doctrine, this is obvious. In its moderate forms, for example, when it is stated that 'sufficient grace' is given to us to improve ourselves by our own efforts, and that if they are successful they are crowned by the 'efficacious grace' which has power to save, a limited field of operations is left for human effort, and the sense of sheer arbitrariness is alleviated; but the fact remains that the first and the final moves rest entirely in God's hands. Even if (as I think we should) we accumulate the subtleties and alleviations, we are still not reassured about human effort. There is (it will be said) less of it than there would be if people rejected the whole conception of grace, and with it the alternative secular father-substitutes: 'they', 'the law', or the welfare state.

But traditionally too much emphasis has been placed on the mechanism of grace and too little on its effects. What matters is that grace *saves*: it does not keep men dangling for the sake of ensuring their dependence. It sets them on their own feet and keeps them there. '*Stand fast* in the liberty wherein Christ has made us free, and be not entangled again in the yoke of bondage.' The effect of grace is exactly like the effect of those parents whom

Nowell-Smith approves. It intervenes to foster independence. It meets every creature in his own style: the radicals by subverting and reconstructing them, the gradualists by building them up and luring them on. The end of it all is that they all grow up; grace is the perfecting of our nature, not its destruction: *naturam non tollit gratia sed perficit*, as Thomas Aquinas so admirably observed; and our decisions grow in grace along with the rest of us. The descent of grace upon us is known by the presence of grace in us. By grace we are stronger, more resolute, more creative and imaginative, than we could possibly be without it. This we *know*—especially those of us to whom it comes as a wholly unexpected glory and not as part of our system of expectations.

Once again, Nowell-Smith has taken an external view of the operation of God on man; and he has failed to note the difference brought about in one's experience of God by the traditional but (among philosophers) neglected doctrines of the Incarnation and the Holy Spirit. And, once again, the objection is not to his theories of education but to his backwoods rendering of Christian belief.

In assessing Nowell-Smith's central passages on the will and the grace of God, I hope it will not seem flippant, and believe that it is consonant with his own attitude, to suggest that coming of age should be celebrated by a ceremonial parricide.

Anthropologists relate that fathers in some communities are ceremonially slaughtered, with every appearance of genuine regret, at about the age of forty-five. The reasons are economic; but that may be the work of a Freudian censor. It could be (and here I simply speculate) that the younger generation feels it cannot grow up until the elder has been finally disposed of. If that is so, we should have an exact parallel to Nowell-Smith's account of the religious and secular elements in morality. As long as anyone has a filial feeling for a father-substitute, as long as he attempts to direct his actions in accordance with his will, he is playing truant from his manhood. At least, so the argument demands: though, as we have seen, it is sometimes quite proper to take authority as a guide in our personal decisions. But this open-minded back door is an escape hatch for the religious moralist. He has only to say that he *chooses* to abide by the will of God and the thing is done. Family analogies would even point to that conclusion. Adult sons *do* go to their fathers for advice. True, they need not and often do not take it; but then men often do not take it from God, even those who consult him. It would be safer for Nowell-Smith's argument if he closed the escape hatch. But if he does, he will have to say, in an authoritarian tone of voice, Thou shalt not consult authorities: which is neither his intention, nor good sense. And if he does not, he must allow the moral adult the adult option of doing the will of the Father which is in Heaven.

I trust that I have not essentially misrepresented Nowell-Smith's argument, though I have hardly done justice to his numerous qualifications. Of these I can only say in general that they reassure me about Nowell-Smith but do not save the argument. And I trust I have shown where the error lies: in presenting a picture of God and man in which there is no mention of incarnation. According to the view attacked by Nowell-Smith God is on one side of the line and man (collectively) is on the other; the will of God is something outside us, to be conformed to; the grace of God descends upon us and does not grow up in us. According to Christian morality God is on both sides of the line; the will of God works *in* the wills of those who love him; and the grace of God is made known in the ability to love him. Once more we are reminded of the observation in Dostoevsky's *Idiot* that 'the atheist is always talking about something else'.

4

It would be neater and more satisfactory to conclude at this point. It would, however, be evasive. Nowell-Smith, in his conclusion discusses a practical moral problem; and it is right that anyone joining issue with him should do the same.

Nowell-Smith takes as his special case the moral rule prohibiting adultery. It is in fact a trump card. Adultery is the only kind of activity with specific and overt characteristics which the Sermon on the Mount condemns without exception or qualification. And he attacks the rule, qua rule, as he attacks rules in general, on the ground that 'just *what* specific acts are immoral must depend on the particular circumstances and the particular people concerned'. Now we have argued that Christianity is not a religion of rules; I have rejected on that account his imputation of 'infantilism'. But here it would seem that we have as bleak and categorical a rule as ever existed. No wonder it is this example that Nowell-Smith has kept for his final throw.

Nowell-Smith proposes to look at the rule against adultery from a 'teleological standpoint', as opposed to the 'rule-and-act' morality of the traditionalists. Now to give consequences as a reason for a rule does not destroy the working efficacy of a rule: it destroys only its absoluteness. Nowell-Smith's teleological morality condemns adultery, because he thinks highly of loyalty as a principle of action and accepts 'life-long union in the intimacy of marriage' as 'a supreme form of love'. Now this means that adultery is to be avoided only because it conduces to the breakdown of loyalties. In that case, where adultery is consented to by the other party, or where there is no love left in the partnership, the rule against it no longer applies.

The question for a Christian who has offered the defence that Christianity is not a religion of rules is how he can avoid Nowell-Smith's conclusion; or, if he insists on unqualified condemnation of adultery, how he can avoid Nowell-Smith's premise, i.e. that Christianity *is* a religion of rules.

1. The first oddity in the argument is the tie-up between 'teleology' and 'loyalty'. Loyalty in itself is not in any sense a matter of consequences. It may be one consideration in a predicament in which consequences have also to be taken into account; but *insofar* as they are done from loyalty actions are not motivated by consequences at all. One is tempted to suggest that Nowell-Smith has conflated two types whose only point in common is that they do not live by rules. If that *is* so, there will be confusion as soon as rules cease to be the center of discussion, e.g. as soon as Christianity appears on the scene. If it is *not* so, Nowell-Smith must be saying that not committing adultery is praiseworthy if it leads, instrumentally, to the maintenance of loyalties (which is normally the case); but ceases to be of moral importance if there are no loyalties to maintain. This second alternative is more in line with his general position.

2. The second oddity in the argument is the extremely subjective interpretation of 'loyalty'. It is read off as 'feeling loyal', and not as 'having loyalties'. But it is a part of the morals of loyalty that one *has* loyalties whether one *feels* loyal or not—and the overruling of disloyal feelings is not a reversion to the morality of rules. Loyalty is mainly a matter of status and certainly not only a matter of contract. It far transcends the mere promise which can be set aside by agreement. Even if neither party feels like observing it, they owe it to their families, their neighbors, their country, and themselves to work themselves back into wanting to observe it. An overt breach such as adultery makes the task harder. And if we are talking about consequences, it is necessary to consider the effect of adultery by consent on unilateral adultery, which stands condemned as cheating on Nowell-Smith's own formula. Human nature being what it is, i.e. rather more fascinated by wickedness than Nowell-Smith thinks it is, it is to be suspected that the effect would be considerable.

3. It begins to be apparent that loyalties are nearly as exacting as rules; but they have the great advantage of being owed to persons and not to principles. If Nowell-Smith takes his stand on loyalties, he may have to go farther than he intends. And he makes it quite clear that he does want to stand on loyalties. He thinks it a good thing that there should be loyalties (and therefore no adultery) even if he sees nothing wrong about adultery in the absence of loyalties. But loyalties don't just happen: they have to be sustained by example and environment. They are hardly encouraged by a mutual agreement that they need not be observed.

4. It is now clear why adultery has no place in the Christian life. The Christian *agape* is a liberal and flexible kind of loyalty, not restricted to the demands of justice, willing to take the initiative in reconciliation, and centered, not on society, but on people's relation with each other. If this attitude is displayed by the parties to a marriage, adultery will be incon-

ceivable. This is not the result of external rules (the breach of which is only too easily conceivable), but the internal and necessary expression of a way of life. And if it be asked why, then, the prohibition? the answer is that the way of life is practiced by men who in its despite sometimes relapse into unsanctified imaginings; and then it is surely appropriate that they should be snapped out of them by a stiff injunction. The injunction, however, is not the reason for their loyalties, but merely the measure of their failure. If that is what Nowell-Smith finds distasteful in the New Testament, in view of his evident concern about loyalties, I cannot see why.

5. It may be thought that I have been pressing too hard Nowell-Smith's incidental reference to loyalties, and have taken too little note of his official profession of teleology. The fact remains, however, that he uses no other test than that of loyalties to distinguish humanist believers in monogamy like himself from other humanists who reject monogamy; and the critic is entitled to explore the implications of his criterion. If it is taken seriously, it is not consistent with adultery by mutual consent: loyalty is shown by what people do, and even if they agree to do what is disloyal, it is disloyal all the same.

I agree, of course, that adultery is not the only offence against married loyalties; I agree even that some unstigmatized offences may well be deadlier. And I do not believe that the ordinary ban on adultery is simply a taboo or arbitrary rule. But it does not follow that it is merely 'one of a set of recipes' 'for the achievement of an end'—even though it is admitted to be a good recipe, and the end the generally laudable end of maximum and integral satisfaction. The fact is that Nowell-Smith accepts too easily the fashionable dichotomy between rule and end, and, rightly understanding that the ban on adultery is not merely a matter of rules, presents in the guise of teleology an alternative theory which being outside the ordinary categories of means and end is far from teleological. It is because his epilogue on adultery forces him to recognize a third possibility which his official theory does not allow for that it has more than an epilogue's significance.

In conclusion, we may summarize as follows:

1. Christian morality is not a set of rules.

2. The will of God is not an external agency, but works on men from within.

3. The grace of God is not arbitrarily bestowed, and in any case, when it has been bestowed, it produces independence of character.

4. The suggestion that the religious element in morality is 'infantile' rests on the view that those who appeal to it are perpetuating the attitude of dependence which is inevitable in childhood but should be outgrown. This is just not the case with Christian morality.

5. Nowell-Smith propounds, instead, a goal of integral human satisfaction. As a counter-proposal to a morality of rules, this has its attractions. But teleological morality does not have to be humanistic (Aquinas is as teleological as Nowell-Smith) ; and Nowell-Smith's detailed discussion of a moral issue does not rest on his teleology. The concept of loyalties, so unexpectedly introduced, would bear further investigation.

For the rest, Nowell-Smith may be assured that his kind of morality is one that Christians can feel at home with, much more so than with Kant or Nietzsche or Sartre; he is a consoling and comfortable fellow citizen. But he misunderstands the autonomy which we both value, because he overlooks what is specifically Christian in Christian theology. Only in the enjoyment of God's love are we finally autonomous; and that is why, on his own criterion, no one is adult but the saints.

Love and Principle
in Christian Ethics

WILLIAM K. FRANKENA

1

A philosopher reading about in the literature of Christian ethics, especially if he is steeped in that of recent philosophical ethics, is bound to be struck, not only by the topics discussed and the claims made, but by the relative absence of careful definition, clear statement, or cogent and rigorous argument, as these are judged by the standards with which he is familiar in his own field (even if he does not himself always conform to them). It seems all too seldom to occur to its writers that they should seriously try to expound and defend Christian ethics in terms of what Matthew Arnold called culture—"the best which has been thought and said in the world"—and in particular in terms of the best philosophical thinking of the time. As H. D. Lewis has put it,

> Much that is peculiarly instructive has been written about these matters by notable ethical thinkers of the present day, and the progress that has been made recently in ethics is one of the most

From Alvin Plantinga, ed., Faith and Philosophy *(Grand Rapids: Wm. B. Eerdmans Publishing Co., 1964), pp. 203–25. Reprinted by permission of the author and the publisher.*

distinctive and promising features of modern thought. But religious thinkers, in the main, have been curiously indifferent to these important advances in a field closely akin to their own.[1]

Indeed, they have not only been "curiously indifferent" to the work of the philosophers; many of them take the position, at least implicitly, that any recognition of its importance would be dangerous—a sinful concession to the intellectual pride of the natural man or the old Adam. At any rate, they reflect the same attitude and manner of thought and expression that were castigated by ancient Celsus, and by Arnold after him, as "the want of intellectual seriousness of the Christians." The issues they are dealing with are all too rarely clearly formulated or rigorously reasoned about. It may be that the philosopher who criticizes them can also be charged with some kind of want of intellectual seriousness, or even with spiritual pride, but his criticism may be correct nevertheless.

This essay represents an attempt, by a philosopher who feels that its theological proponents may be selling Christian ethics short by their manner of expounding and defending it, to do something toward remedying the situation. In it I shall make only a beginning, however, hoping that others who can speak with more authority will follow suit. I shall only try to state what seem to me to be some of the main issues and positions in Christian ethical theory, keeping away from practical issues of the sort that theologians have been writing about so much (more, I admit, than philosophers have). And I shall limit myself to issues and positions in Christian normative ethics, leaving for another occasion the problems and points of view of Christian metaethics, if there is such a thing.[2] As for answers—in stating the issues and positions I shall be indicating those that are possible, but I shall not be doing much to settle on any of them. To do so would involve my venturing farther into theology than I can go with anything like the kind of intellectual seriousness which I am advocating. Anyway, one can only try to throw a certain amount of light at any given time.

In doing what I am doing I make an assumption—that the function of reason and philosophy for the Christian is not simply to serve as an instrument for refuting or otherwise disposing of gentiles, pagans, and unbelievers, but also and especially to serve as a colleague in helping him to understand and deepen the faith that is in him. Some may say, on reading what

---

[1] *Morals and Revelation* (New York, 1951), p. 14. In writing this Lewis had in mind the work of the intuitionists before World War II, but the remark holds equally well if one has in mind the work of the nonintuitionists after the war.

[2] By "normative ethics" I mean the endeavor to propound and defend ethical judgments, rules, or standards; by "metaethics" I mean a theory about the meaning or nature of such rules and principles or about the method and possibility of justifying them.

follows, "Why should we bother to think in such terms as these? What is good but to do justly, and to love mercy, and to walk humbly with thy God? And what is pure religion and undefiled but to visit the fatherless and the widows in their affliction, and to keep oneself unspotted from the world?" But the writers on Christian ethics that I have in mind can themselves hardly make this reply, for they have already ventured out beyond the fold of such simple faith and duty into the forum of rational formulation and defense. My only complaint is that they have not been as careful as they should be if they are going to venture out in this way. As for those who would decry even such venturing into the forum, I can only remind them that the same Book that says,

> We are fools for Christ's sake....

also says,

> Buy . . . also wisdom, and instruction, and understanding,

and

> . . . whatsoever things are true, whatsoever things are honest, whatsoever things are just, whatsoever things are pure, whatsoever things are lovely, whatsoever things are of good report, . . . think on these things.

2

Actually, as I have indicated, there has been a good deal of thinking on these things by Christians. But we cannot consider it all here, and, in fact, I shall limit myself to one of its main themes. Much of this thinking has been about the role of moral rules and principles in Christian ethics. The ensuing debate is especially lively in Protestant circles, but Pope Pius XII and Dietrich von Hildebrand found it necessary not long ago to admonish young Catholics to beware of a "new morality" which they call "circumstance ethics" and which seeks to eliminate general principles from Christian morality, declaring "every moral decision to be based on a unique situation and to be the result of a confrontation of the 'I' of the person with the 'I' of God."[3] No doubt the debate is also present in Jewish ethics. At the one extreme are views variously referred to as antinomian, nominalist, existentialist, situationalist, or contextualist, which hold that each moral decision about what to do is to be a direct function of faith, love or the experience of God together with a knowledge of the facts in the case, with no ethical principles coming into the matter. At the other, apparently, is the Thomist or near-Thomist view that many, if not all, moral decisions should

---

3 See von Hildebrand, *True Morality and Its Counterfeits* (New York, 1955). The quotation is from p. 135.

involve, at least in part, an appeal to certain moral principles whose validity does not depend on faith, love, revelation, or the knowledge of God. It is with the topic of this debate that I wish to deal here, first, because it seems to me to be most unclearly dealt with by theologians, and, second, because philosophers have been discussing somewhat similar subjects with a good deal more clarity and in terms which may, it seems to me, be of some use in the debate in question.

Before we begin, however, five preliminary remarks must be made. (1) A distinction is often made by philosophers and theologians alike between moral rules and ethical principles. A rule is relatively concrete and small, like "We ought to tell the truth," a principle relatively abstract and big, like "We ought to promote the general happiness." This distinction is important in certain contexts, but may here be kept in the background. Unless otherwise specified, then, I shall use "rule" and "principle" synonymously, to mean any general judgments about what is *morally* right, wrong, obligatory, or good, whether abstract or concrete, formal or material. (2) One may speak of love or "the law of love" as a rule or principle in the sense just indicated. Indeed, some of the debate has been on precisely the question whether this way of speaking of love is proper or not. But what interests me here is not so much the question whether love or the love-command is itself a rule or principle as the question whether there are *other* rules or principles which do not mention love, what their status is, and how they are related to the ethic of love (whether this is conceived as a principle or not). (3) The term "law" we may take here as meaning a rule or principle or a set of rules or principles, except perhaps when it is used in the phrase "the law of love." (4) I shall disregard the question whether the "law of love" enjoins or excludes love of self and the question how love of neighbor is related to love of God. It will be convenient to take it simply as enjoining love. We must also leave open the question whether the love enjoined is "an emotion or affection" or "primarily an active determination of the will,"[4] trying so to express what we say that it may be true either way. The main point is that, either way, love is aimed at an object and seeks it or its good. (5) Some may take faith or commitment to God as the basic virtue or posture of Christian ethics, rather than love, but even then most of what I shall say will hold with "faith" or "commitment to God" substituted where I say "love."

3

Our subject, then, is the theological debate about the relation of love and principles in Christian (and similar religious) ethics. To deal

---

4 See C. H. Dodd, *Gospel and Law* (London, 1951), p. 42.

with it we must first look at the parallel debate which I indicated was going on among philosophers. Here the issue is not love versus principle or love versus natural law. Roughly speaking, where theologians talk about love, philosophers talk about beneficence or general utility. At any rate, among the latter, the main debate in normative ethics (as vs. metaethics) has been between the deontologists or formalists on one side, and the teleologists on the other. The latter hold that all rights and duties, particular or general, are to be determined directly or indirectly by looking to see what is conducive to the greatest balance of good over evil, and they are ethical egoists, nationalists, or universalists (utilitarians) depending on whose good they say is to be promoted, that of the agent, that of his nation, or that of the universe as a whole. The deontologists insist that there are rights and duties, general or particular, which hold independently of any conduciveness they may have to promote a balance of good over evil for agent, nation, or universe. Among the deontologists the main issues are whether beneficence or utility is a duty at all or not, whether all moral rules of right and duty fall under justice, and whether the basic judgments of right and duty are formal or material, general or particular. Most teleologists lately have been utilitarians of one sort or another, and here there has been a particularly lively debate between the extreme or act-utilitarians and the restricted or rule-utilitarians (also in another dimension, not directly relevant here, between the hedonistic and the "ideal" utilitarians). This needs a brief explanation here.

We may, in fact, distinguish three utilitarian positions for our purposes, according to the view taken about moral rules. (1) Pure act-utilitarianism is the view which has no place whatsoever for such rules, holding that one is to tell what is one's right or duty in a particular situation simply by an appeal to the principle of utility, that is, by looking to see what action will produce or probably produce the greatest general balance of good over evil, counting all of the consequences which it itself causes or will probably cause and no others, and in particular ignoring the consequences which might be brought about if the same thing were done in similar situations (i.e., if it were made a rule to do that act in such situations). (2) Pure rule-utilitarianism holds that one is to tell what is one's right or duty in a particular situation by appeal to some set of rules like "Keep promises," "Tell the truth," etc., and not by appeal to the principle of utility. In this respect it is like extreme deontological theories. But, as against all deontological theories, it holds that we are to determine what rules should govern our lives by an appeal to the principles of utility, i.e., by looking to see what rules are such that always acting on them is for the greatest general good. That is, we are never to ask what act will have the best consequences in a particular situation, but either what the rules call for or what rule it is most useful always to follow in that kind of a situation. And it may be obligatory to follow the rule in a particular situation even if following it is known not to have the best possible consequences in this particular case. (3) Modified act-utilitarianism would allow us to formulate rules and to use them as guides, but they would be rules which say, not that always-acting in such and such a way in such and such a kind of situation is socially more useful than always-acting on any other rule would be, but that it is always or generally for the greatest good to act in a certain way in such situations. Take

> Keeping-promises-always is for the greatest general good

and

> Keeping promises is always for the greatest general good.

The first is the rule-utilitarian's way of formulating his rules, the second that of the modified act-utilitarian. The main difference is that the latter cannot allow that a rule may ever be followed in a particular situation when following it is known not to have the best possible consequences in this particular case.

Of course, one may combine two of these forms of utilitarianism in one way or another; one might maintain, for instance, that in particular situations we are to appeal to rules justified by their utility in certain kinds of cases and directly to the principle of utility in certain other kinds of cases. I think it will also be clear that ethical egoism may take similar forms: pure act-egoism, modified act-egoism, pure rule-egoism, etc. What concerns me now, however, is to point out that a love-ethic, which I shall call agapism, may take parallel forms. Agapism is the view which assigns to the "law of love" the same position that utilitarianism assigns to the principle of utility; it allows no *basic* ethical principles other than or independent of the "law of love." It can take any of three main forms: pure act-agapism, modified act-agapism, and pure rule-agapism. These will be described more fully in the next section.

One might ask here whether there really is any difference between the ethics of love or agapism and utilitarianism. Theologians generally assume that there is, without discussing the point very carefully. Philosophers, on the other hand, seem to assume that there is no basic difference between them—see, for example, J. S. Mill or A. C. Garnett. This is an important question, and the answer is not very obvious, not at least until one has made some distinctions, and then it seems to me the answer is yes or no depending—.[5] But we must leave it to one side here, and rest with pointing out parallels. Even if the parallels turn out to be identities, however, all that we shall be saying about them will still be true.

But Christian "schemes of morality," as ethical systems were called in

---

[5] There is, for instance, the question of the relation of the love of God to the love of neighbor and mankind (or to the promotion of the general welfare).

the eighteenth century before the word "scheme" came to mean something nefarious, need not be wholly agapistic. Just as a philosopher may hold that some or all rights and duties are independent of utility, so a theologian may hold that some or all rights and duties are independent of the "law of love," or, in other words, that love is not enough to give us all of morality even when taken together with all relevant factual belief or knowledge (empirical or theological).[6] If he does hold this, then his position is like those of the deontologists rather than like those of the utilitarians. In fact, there would be a position for him to take parallel to each of the various deontological positions. And here again we may distinguish three pure positions: pure act-deontologism, modified act-deontologism, and pure rule-deontologism. The first will say that every moral decision is somehow to be a function of a knowledge of the particular situation without any appeal to rules or to utility. The second would allow us to use rules, but would insist that the rules are mere inductions from particular cases and so may never contravene a clear direct verdict in any such case. What Henry Sidgwick called "perceptual intuitionism" might take either of these forms. Pure rule-deontologism would assert that we are always to tell what is right or wrong wholly by appeal to a set of rules or principles, insisting, of course, that these rules and principles are not mere problematic inductions, and that their validity does not depend on their utility. Both what Sidgwick called "dogmatic intuitionism" and what he called "philosophical intuitionism" would be forms of this view, differing only in the number and abstractness of the rules or principles regarded as basic. Again, of course, one might combine two of these forms of deontologism; one might, for example, combine perceptual and dogmatic intuitionism as Sir David Ross does. These are all pure forms of deontologism, and, apart from questions of orthodoxy, positions of all these sorts are open to the theologian who is not being an agapist. If, however, one regards the principle of utility as one of the principles to be used in making moral decisions, though not the only basic one, then one is still a deontologist (not a teleologist) but an impure one. Similarly, if a theologian regards the "law of love" as one of the principles to be used, but not as the only basic one, then he is holding an impure or mixed view, only it will be more convenient in this case to call it an impure form of agapism or mixed agapism.

4

Now, against this background and using my fragmentary knowledge of the literature of Judeo-Christian ethics, I can try to characterize various possible views about the place of principles and their

---

[6] When I say a theologian may hold a certain position, I mean that it is logically open to him, not that he can hold it and be orthodox.

relation to love—various "schemes" of Christian or religious ethics—and do something to relate them to positions actually taken in the literature. In fact, the following outline of positions will be my main contribution to the discussion I am trying to help along. For my conviction is that theologians would be much clearer and much more cogent if they were to state their issues and positions in such terms as these, and then make evident precisely why we should accept their answers. It may be that the Christian ethical thinker cannot be wholly content with the terms, methods, or conclusions of the mere "moral philosopher," as G. F. Thomas and many others before him have urged; but, even so, one may perhaps insist that his thinking ought at least to meet the standards which such a moral philosopher, at his best, sets himself.

It should be pointed out here that, whichever of the following schemes of morality a Christian thinker adopts (if any), there will be a question about just what he is claiming for it. (1) He might be claiming only that said scheme is *the* proper form for Christian or Judeo-Christian ethics to take, or at least that it is *a* proper form for it to take. (2) He may also be claiming, as H. Rashdall does in *Conscience and Christ,* that the Christian normative ethics, as he conceives it, is a satisfactory one in the eyes of the most enlightened moral consciousness and so is tenable by modern man. But if he makes only these claims, he may still be allowing that there are other valid schemes of morality (even of Christian morality) or part-schemes of morality, such as St. Paul seems to ascribe to the Gentiles. Hence a Christian may and often seems to make a stronger claim, namely, (3) that the normative ethics he subscribes to, or something very close to it, is the only adequate and tenable scheme of morality there is. This claim would be harder to defend, but theologians have been known to rush in where angels (not to mention philosophers) would be wary of treading. However this may be, let us get on with our outline. I merely wanted to point out that different claims may be made for the scheme adopted—and to add that theologians do not always make clear just what claim they are making or on what grounds they are making it, just as they do not always make clear precisely what the scheme is that they are adopting in the first place.

The first group of positions I shall call *pure agapism.* They all hold that the "law of love" is the sole basis of morality—that on it hang "the whole law and the prophets," i.e., that the rest of the moral law can and must be derived from love together with relevant nonethical beliefs and knowledge, empirical, metaphysical, or theological. In Bertrand Russell's words, pure agapism holds that "the [morally] good life is a life inspired by love and guided by knowledge."[7] Its most extreme form is *pure act-agapism.*

---

[7] *What I Believe* (London, 1925), Ch. 2.

This admits no rules or principles other than the "law of love" itself, and it also does not allow that there are any "perceptual intuitions" about what is right or wrong in particular situations independently of the dictates of love. It insists that one is to discover or decide what one's right or duty in a particular situation is solely by confronting one's loving will with the facts about that situation, whether one is an individual or a group. Facts about other situations and ethical conclusions arrived at in other situations are, for this extreme view, simply irrelevant, if not misleading. It adopts with complete literalness, as the whole story, St. Augustine's dictum, "Love, and do as you please." Here belong at least the more drastic of the views sometimes referred to as antinomian, nominalist, existentialist, situationalist, simplistic, or contextualist. Thomas ascribes such a view to Emil Brunner, if I understand him, though he correctly points out that Brunner sometimes seems to hold one of the views to be described later.[8] Paul Ramsey, like Thomas and von Hildebrand, has been attacking such theories lately, but in *Basic Christian Ethics* he appeared to come very close to agreeing with them.

The other forms of pure agapism all take rules or principles to be necessary or at least helpful in guiding the loving Christian individual (or group) in the determination of his (its) rights and duties in particular cases. But, being forms of pure agapism, they regard all such rules or principles as somehow derivative from love. First of these forms is *modified act-agapism* or "summary rule" agapism.[9] This admits rules but regards them as summaries of past experience, useful, perhaps almost indispensable, but only as rules of thumb. It cannot allow that a rule may ever be followed in a situation when it is seen to conflict with what love dictates in that situation. For, if rules are to be followed only in so far as they are helpful as aids to love, they cannot constrain or constrict love in any way. But they may and perhaps should be used. I am not sure I know of any good cases of this modified act-agapism, but perhaps some of the so-called contextualists or "circumstance" moralists belong here; some of them at any rate do mention rules or principles on occasion without making clear just how they conceive of them, e.g., J. Sittler in *The Structure of Christian Ethics*.[10]

---

[8] G. E. Thomas, *Christian Ethics and Moral Philosophy* (New York, 1955), pp. 381–88.

[9] Here and in connection with this entire section, see J. Rawls, "Two Concepts of Rules," *Philosophical Review*, LXIV (1955), 3–32; J. D. Mabbott, "Moral Rules," *Proceedings of the British Academy*, XXXIX (1953), 97–118; J. J. C. Smart, "Extreme and Restricted Utilitarianism," *Philosophical Quarterly*, VI (1956); R. B. Brandt, *Ethical Theory* (New York, 1959), Ch. 15.

[10] Baton Rouge, 1958. What Sittler means by "structure" here is hard to make out; as he represents it, Christian ethics has almost none. But he is both for and against principles, and this may mean that he is trying to be a modified act-agapist

Pure rule-agapism is analogous to pure rule-utilitarianism; it maintains that we are always to tell what we are to do in particular situations by referring to a set of rules, and that what rules are to prevail and be followed is to be determined by seeing what rules (not what acts) best or most fully embody love. For modified act-agapism the proper way to state a rule is to say, for example,

> Keeping promises is always love-fulfilling.

For pure rule-agapism one must say, rather,

> Keeping-promises-always is love-fulfilling.

The difference is that on the latter view we may and sometimes must obey a rule in a particular situation even though the action it calls for is seen not to be what love itself would directly require. For pure rule-agapism, in other words, the rules may in a sense constrict the direct expression of love. For if love is, in fact, constrained to fulfill itself through acting according to rules, as Ramsey puts it in his more recent writings,[11] love must be "in-principled," or, as philosophers would now say, it must be "rule-governed."

If we ask here why love is thus constrained to express itself through rules or principles rather than by doing in each case the act which is most loving in that case,[12] the rule-agapist may answer in three apparently different ways which are usually not distinguished. (1) He may argue that love is constrained to cloak itself in principles, not by anything outside of itself, but by its own nature or "inner dialectic," as some might prefer to say. This is not an easy view to get clear—I am not even sure it can be made out—but it is suggested by 1 John 3:17,

> But whoso hath this world's good, and seeth his brother have need, and shutteth up his bowels of compassion from him, how dwelleth the love of God in him?

This suggests that it follows from the very nature of love that the rich should help the poor, and one might argue that all the rules of Christian morality can be derived from the nature of love in this direct way. Rashdall seems to try to follow this course in deducing the "corollaries and consequences" of the law of love: love to enemies, forgiveness, self-sacrifice, purity, repentance, etc.[13] In a somewhat similar way J. S. Mill reasoned (mistakenly, I think)

(or perhaps act-fideist, since he stresses faith rather than love). On the other hand, he may be trying, confusedly, to state one of the forms of rule agapism or even mixed agapism yet to be described.

11 See *War and the Christian Conscience* (New York, 1961), p. 14.

12 A parallel question may be asked in the case of rule-utilitarianism.

13 Op. cit., pp. 119–33.

that justice and equality are entailed by the principle of utility as such; a theologian might claim the same for love, possibly with more justice.[14]

(2) The second possibility is to claim, not that the rules are somehow contained in the very nature of love, but that love must act through rules because the world is so constituted that it can fulfill itself or attain its object more fully if it conforms its actions to rules than if it does not. On this view love is constrained to adopt rules, not by its own nature alone, but by its nature together with the facts about the world in which it is seeking to fulfill itself or reach its object. In a similar way a rule-utilitarian might contend that, although no rules are contained in the principle of utility, rules must be followed if the greatest general good is to be achieved, which rules to follow being determined by a consideration of the relative utility of certain rules as against others.

(3) On the third view, the fact that love must adopt rules is due neither to its own nature nor to the nature of the world, but to the nature of reason or of morality. The argument would be that if love is to be the matrix of *moral* life, then it must follow maxims which it wills to be universally acted on (i.e., embody itself in a set of "universal laws"), since this is a necessary condition of rationality, or of morality, or of both. The affinities of such a position with Kant's is obvious, for both insist that reason and morality require rules which are willed to be universal laws; the difference is in the method of determining which rules make up the moral law—for Kant the method is to see what rules we can will to be universal laws independently of whatever motives or ends we may have, but for the present view it is to see what rules we can or must will to be universal laws when our motivation is *love*. That it is to be rule-governed is required if it is to take the form of reason or morality, but what the rules shall be is still for it to say. They will still be determined as in (1) or (2).

Of these three views the third is suggested, to my mind at least, by some passages in Reinhold Niebuhr,[15] but, in general, they have not been distinguished by the more rule-agapistically minded writers. Presumably what Ramsey calls "in-principled love-ethics" falls under one of them, but I have not been able to tell which. I do not have labels for these three forms of rule-agapism. Enough is enough, and I am doing enough labelling here as it is. What matters is that the three views should not be confused by either friend or foe. I should point out, however, that it is only the second that is strictly analogous to what is usually called rule-utilitarianism, though rule-utilitarianism could also take forms analogous to (1) and (3).

The remaining forms of pure agapism are *combinations* of act-agapism

---

[14] *Utilitarianism*, near the end.

[15] Especially, *An Interpretation of Christian Ethics* (New York, 1935), Ch. 7; *Moral Man and Immoral Society* (New York, 1932), Ch. II.

and rule-agapism. Here would fall, for instance, the view that, while we may and should appeal to rules when we can in deciding what should be done in a particular case, as the rule-agapist holds, we may and should appeal to the "law of love" directly in cases for which there are no rules or in which the rules conflict, just as the act-agapist does. Such combinations may, in fact, be more plausible than either pure act-agapism or pure rule-agapism by themselves.

5

We may now look at what I shall call *pure nonagapistic theories*. These hold that *all* of the basic judgments of morality proper, whether these are particular or general, are independent of any "law of love"—that any such law of love, if it is valid at all, is neither necessary nor helpful in morality, and, in fact, does not belong to morality at all. These views are analogous to (or identical with) the forms of pure deontologism described in Section 3, which do not recognize any moral obligation to be beneficent or to follow the principle of utility. There will be a purely nonagapistic theory corresponding to each of the purely deontological theories mentioned there. Speaking roughly, they all identify morality with justice and regard justice as determinable independently of either the principle of utility or the "law of love." It might seem that no such scheme of morality can be accepted by a Christian, since these schemes all regard the entire substance of morality as coming from some source other than love. But even Christians have "sought out many inventions," and there are at least two types of pure nonagapism which are approximated by what some of them have invented. One is a view which agrees that "love is the fulfilment of the [moral] law," but holds that the whole content of the law is discernible independently of love. In effect, it takes acting in accordance with an independently ascertainable moral code as the criterion or perhaps even as the definition of what love is. Thus it is only verbally and not in any substantive way agapistic.[16] It may therefore turn out to be a wolf in sheep's clothing, but at least some intuitionistic moralists of the past, Samuel Clarke, for example, have meant to be Christians while holding a view which can be described in some such terms as these. The other purely nonagapistic conception of morality to be mentioned here has a rather different character. It involves making a distinction between the moral life or "mere morality" and the religious way of life, adding that morality is to be conceived in a nonagapistic way, and then proposing that it should be supplanted by the religious way of life, this being conceived as a life of love and as transcending "mere morality." Like

---

16 One who holds this view may also be an agapist in the sense of holding that the *motive* for fulfilling the moral law is or should be love.

Nietzsche it goes "beyond good and evil" in the moral sense; unlike him it does so in the interest of religion. Its drift is agapistic, since it advocates a life of love (and its agapism may take any of the forms described in Section 4), but its conception of morality is not. Something of this sort is suggested in different ways by at least some passages in Kierkegaard and Brunner.[17]

Very similar in substance is the *"two morality" theory* variously intimated or proposed by Henri Bergson, Lord Lindsay, and Eliseo Vivas. According to it there are two independent moralities, one the morality of love, the other that of social pressure, one's station and its duties, claims and counter-claims, or what have you. Each is complete and valid in its fashion, but the first is superior to and should supplant the second. This view thus combines a purely agapistic conception of one morality with a purely non-agapistic conception of the other. And, of course, it may conceive the former in any of the ways described in Section 4 and the latter after the fashion of any of the forms of pure deontologism distinguished in Section 3. Yet it is in a sense still a form of agapism since it proposes to replace the nonagapistic morality, where feasible, with that of love. Its ideal is the ethics of love. The only difference between it and the previous theory is that it speaks of two moralities where that theory speaks of two ways of life but calls one of them morality and the other religion.

6

There are also, as I indicated earlier, mixed theories which I shall call *impure or mixed agapisms*. They are combinations of agapism and nonagapism but not along the lines of the "two morality" theory. For them there is only one morality by which we are to live but it has two parts. One of its parts is the "law of love," the other consists of judgments about right and wrong which are independent of the "law of love," judgments which may be either general (rules) or particular. It should be noted here that saying these judgments are independent of the "law of love" means only that they are not derivative from the "law of love" in any such way as agapists think they are (see Section 4); it does not mean that they are knowable apart from revelation, grace, or religion. Confusion here is easy and frequent, but the two points are distinct. The "law of love" may or may not be revealed, and the alleged independent ethical insights also may or may not be revealed. Whether they are or not is a question, not of normative ethics, but of metaethics or, if you will, of the epistemology of ethics.

---

17 See, e.g., Kierkegaard's *Three Stages on Life's Way;* Brunner as quoted by H. D. Lewis, op. cit., p. 18. On Brunner see also N. H. G. Robinson, *Christ and Conscience* (New York, 1956), pp. 72 ff.

Impure agapism is analogous to Ross' impure deontological theory. Ross holds that the principle of utility (nonhedonistically conceived) is one of the valid principles of ethics, but that there are others also whose validity is independent of the principle of utility. Substitute the law of love for the principle of utility here and you get impure or mixed agapism. But Sir David also holds (1) that the principle of utility and the other principles may conflict on occasion, (2) that in that case the former does not always take precedence over the others, and (3) that, partly for this reason, both are necessary for the guidance of our actions. Similarly, an impure agapist might take the position (1) that the "law of love" and the other principles of ethics may conflict, (2) that in such cases the former does not always take precedence, and (3) that, partly for this reason, both the "law of love" and the independent principles are necessary.[18] But he need not accept such an impure form of impure agapism. He may deny that the other principles can conflict with the law of love; or he may agree that they do conflict with it on occasion but contend that then it always takes precedence over them. In either case he would be maintaining that the other principles, while valid, are not necessary for the guidance of our conduct, though they may be helpful. Or he may argue that they are not even helpful—except to those who do not know the "law of love." If he takes any of these three lines, he remains pretty much an agapist in effect though not in strict theory. But he may—and some theologians do—go even farther. While admitting that there *are* ethical insights which are independent of the law of love, he may contend that, though they leave natural man "without excuse," they are so far from being helpful as to be positively misleading—that they are unclear, inaccurate, incomplete, corrupted, etc., and hence not standards of any "true virtue" at all and so not to be relied on by anyone who knows the law of love. For him then the ethics to work by is even more imperatively that of love, at least for those to whom it is available.

There are other, rather different, possible theories for which it is hard to find a label, but which must be mentioned because theologians do sometimes seem to subscribe to them. In all of the above theories, if the law of love is recognized at all (in a nonverbal way), it is regarded as a *basic* norm. But it is not necessary so to regard it if one recognizes it; one may consider it to be derived from some other more basic principle which is in itself nonagapistic. Some thinkers, among them theologians, take as the ultimate norm of our conduct the requirement of realizing ourselves, completing our natures, or fulfilling our beings, and then argue that the (or at least *a*) way to do this is through love. A. C. Garnett reasons thus in his little book *Can Ideals and Norms Be Justified?*

---

18 *See The Right and the Good* (London, 1930). Ross is an intuitionist, but one need not take an intuitionist view of "independent principles."

> ... this discussion ... has shown that utilitarianism (in its non-hedonistic form) [which he identifies with Christian agapism] has correctly pointed to the *end* at which ethical right conduct must aim, while the self-realization theory has correctly stated the *ground* or *reason* why conduct aiming at that end is ethically required.[19]

Similar lines of thought may be found in Tillich and in both Niebuhrs, though less clearly and explicitly expressed.[20] Here the ideal of love is derived in one way or another from what is basically a form of ethical egoism. But the outcome may still be a working agapism, depending on whether or not love is taken to be the only avenue to self-realization or fulfilment of being. If it is, then, of course, the resulting *derived pure agapism* may take any of the forms described in Section 4. If it is not, the outcome will be some kind of *derived impure agapism*.

There are, however, other schemes of morality in which the "law of love" is derivative and not basic. Suppose we hold, as some religious people do, that we have one and only one basic duty, namely, to obey God's commands. Then we might well go on to argue that God has summed up His will in the command to love, and thus again come out with a working agapism to live by (which again can take any of the forms described in Section 4). This line of thought appears in Reinhold Niebuhr's characterization of the ethics of Jesus. It is, he says, "oriented by only one vertical religious reference, to the will of God; and the will of God is defined in terms of all-inclusive love."[21] Here, too, agapism is deduced from a principle which in itself is nonagapistic. We might also, however, reason in one of the following ways, both familiar to Christians:

(a) We ought to imitate God ("Be ye perfect as I am perfect"). God loves us.
   Therefore we ought to love one another.
(b) We ought to be grateful to our benefactors.
   God has sent His Son into the world to save us, etc.
   Therefore we ought to love Him.

If I remember correctly, Niebuhr suggests both of these lines of thought too.[22] In all such patterns of reasoning, however, the law of love is derivative from some principle which is independent of and basic to it. Whether the result is a working agapism or not depends again on whether one holds

---

[19] Pp. 91–92.

[20] See Tillich, *Love, Power, and Justice* (New York, 1954), pp. 76–77; Reinhold Niebuhr, *The Nature and Destiny of Man* (New York, 1941), Vol. I, Ch. 10; H. R. Niebuhr, "The Center of Value," in *Moral Principles of Action*, ed. R. Anshen (New York, 1952).

[21] *An Interpretation of Christian Ethics*, p. 51.

[22] For (a) see ibid., pp. 46, 49.

that there are other duties coordinate with or more basic than love (besides the one stated in the first premise). If one does not, one is a derived agapist of one of the kinds described in Section 4; if one does, one is some kind of a mixed agapist.

7

Well, there in all its, I fear, boring but, I hope, clarifying detail is my outline of possible schemes of Christian ethics considered as bearing on the debate about love and principle. I am sure, to parody one of my favorite texts again, that some will say at this point, "God made man upright, but Frankena has sought out many inventions." Even so, I have no doubt missed some possibilities. No doubt also, in my quest for philosophical clarity, I have blurred some theological refinements and subtleties. Nevertheless, I do think that it would help greatly if theologians and religious thinkers were to use some such table of views as I have sketched, and some such terms as I have employed, in stating their issues, their positions, and their arguments for their positions—all without trying to preach to us at the same time (though there is a time for that too). Throughout, in the interest of relevance, I have sought to relate the positions described to positions actually taken or suggested in the literature, and now, before going on, I should like to add a little along this line. I have mentioned Ramsey, but am not clear just what his position is. It seems to be a form of pure agapism—or possibly of derived agapism—but it is not clear just what kind of pure agapism it is, and it may even be a kind of impure or mixed agapism. G. F. Thomas' position too is not entirely clear. In arguing against Brunner he is certainly rejecting act-agapism, but whether he is a pure rule-agapist or a mixed agapist of some sort I cannot tell for sure. It depends on what he means when he talks about "principles derived from an analysis of the various kinds of human needs and relationships and the best methods of dealing with them"[23] and whether he takes the principle of love as one of the premises needed in deriving them. The position of St. Thomas, with its emphasis on natural law, is, on the other hand, pretty clearly what I have called a mixed theory, though it may involve a rule-utilitarian conception of "human law." Brunner's position I have referred to in one or two connections. It seems to me quite ambiguous; sometimes it looks like a form of act-agapism, but at others like a form of mixed agapism or even like a species of non-agapism. As for Reinhold Niebuhr, he appears to me to suggest, in one place or another, almost every one of the positions I have described; whether this spells richness or confusion of mind I shall leave for others to judge. As for me and my house, the most plausible position seems to me to be a

---

[23] Op. cit., p. 387.

certain kind of mixed theory—roughly, one which takes as basic in ethics
(1) the "law of love" and (2) the "principles of justice"—conceived as
independently arrived at.

Here I must also notice the position of A. C. Garnett, one of the few
philosophers who have taken part in the debate which is our topic. In the
last chapter of *Religion and the Moral Life* he contends that Jesus did not
conceive the agapistic point of view in ethics as "devoid of principles," for
(1) He built "the principles of universality and impartiality" into the injunction to love—the former by interpreting "neighbor" to include enemies, and
the latter by specifying that one is to love each neighbor *as oneself.* Garnett
also argues (2) that Jesus "implies a place for principles of secondary generality," viz., "the moral laws that 'hang upon' the law of love" or which
spell out "the implications of the law of love for certain specific human
relations." Now, in our terms, which position is it that Garnett is thus ascrib-
ing to Jesus and accepting for himself? So far as (1) is concerned, it looks
like a pure rule-agapism of the first sort distinguished in Section 4, for the
two principles involved are represented as being contained in the injunction
to love itself. And this does seem to be true for the principle of universality.
But what about the principle of impartiality or justice? It is not clear
whether it is being thought of as analytically entailed by the bare command
to love our neighbors or as being added as a qualification of that command.
It seems to me it must be the latter, and, in that case, the injunction to love
really is equivalent to "Thou shalt love all men and thou shalt do so justly."
And, then, it seems to me, the position is a form of impure or mixed agapism
of the sort I myself have just proposed. As for (2)—here, so far as "principles of secondary generality" go, the position seems to be a rule-agapism of
the second kind described in Section 4, though it may still be simply a
modified act-agapism. Incidentally, Garnett's proposed view shows, in any
case, that one may hold one kind of theory for some ethical principles and
another kind of theory for others—a point I did not make clear before.

I should also like to take this occasion to say a little about two well-
known and relevant dicta of Christian and other religious moralists. The
first is, "Love is the *fulfillment* of the law." I cannot try here to interpret
St. John and St. Paul, both of whom use this formula. I wish, however, to
point out that the formula can be interpreted in various ways, and may be
accepted by all or almost all of the above views, even by nonagapistic ones.
Thus, (1) the dictum may be taken to say that the moral law is simply to
love, that the content of the moral law is wholly given by love. Agapists,
pure or derived, accept it in this sense. (2) The dictum may also be understood as saying that the moral law is incomplete without the "law of love,"
that this law is necessary to make the moral standard complete. Impure,
pure, and derived agapists may all understand it in this sense, though each
will do so in his own way. (3) Again, the dictum may be conceived as

meaning that loving is *formally* (in Descartes' sense) equivalent to fulfilling the law, i.e., not that the criterion of fulfilling the moral law is loving (agapism) but that the criterion or definition of loving is fulfilling the law. This view, which was introduced earlier, presupposes that the content of the moral law consists of principles and particular judgments which are arrived at independently of love, though not necessarily independently of Scripture or of special revelation. Only a nonagapist can interpret the formula in this sense. (4) But one may also interpret the formula as meaning that love or loving *eminently* (again in Descartes' sense) fulfills the law— that if one loves one fulfills the law and more, one does not fulfill it literally, one fulfills it or overfulfills it but at a higher level and in a different mode. Here again the content of the law itself is independent of the requirement to love, and a nonagapist therefore can accept the dictum in this sense, while an agapist cannot. But it is also implied that one may live by love alone and need not literally (formally) live by the law. In this sense this interpretation yields a working agapism; in fact, this interpretation yields the view, mentioned before, that there are two ways of life, the moral and the religious, the latter being the better in some way. It adds only that following the latter also "fulfills" the former. (5) Our first dictum may, however, also be construed as saying that love is to the law as Jesus Christ is to John Baptist, as is suggested by Jesus' words, "I am not come to destroy [the law] but to fulfill [it]." But this is neither clear nor unambiguous. One might say this and hold that love is to *supplant* the law. Or one might say it and hold only that love fulfills the law in the sense of completing it [i.e., in sense (2)], or that it fulfills the law eminently in the sense just explained.

The second dictum I wish to say something about is, "Love is the *spirit* of the law." This is also vague and ambiguous, though in a different way. (1) It may mean that love is the motive with which one should obey the law. This does not make love the source of the content of the moral law, and hence nonagapists and mixed agapists can agree that love is the spirit of the law in this sense. (2) It may mean, however, that the rest of the moral law is or may be derived from the "law of love" and corrected in the light of it. In this sense it will, of course, be accepted by agapists (except perhaps derived agapists). If all that is claimed is only that "the whole law and the prophets" *can* be derived from the "law of love," then even mixed or nonagapists may agree (for then it may still be that some or all of "the law and the prophets" can also be independently derived). (3) Or it may mean that love fulfills the law eminently in the manner explained a moment ago. (4) Finally, it may mean that love is not a principle which can serve as a major premise for deriving the rest of morality, but a spirit of approaching questions about what to do which also somehow helps us to answer them though it cannot be encapsuled in any verbal formula—i.e., it is a conative and directive attitude or disposition. As indicated at the beginning, I have tried to avoid the issue about whether love is a principle or an attitude. I believe that with the proper distinctions, it can be both. All that needs to be said here, however, is that one can agree that love is the spirit of morality in this fourth sense on any of the views described above.

8

The end cometh, but it is not even yet. For we must still look, at least briefly, at the question how one is to decide which of the above schemes of Christian morality is the correct or most tenable one. How or by what method is the Christian thinker to tell whether he must admit principles in addition to love, how is he to conceive these principles, and which principles is he to admit, if any? By what means is the debate we have taken as our topic to be settled? This methodological matter the theologians have also been none too clear about, perhaps in part because they have not been very clear about the issues and possible positions involved. We must, therefore, consider it before we can close.

There are at least two questions here: (1) whether or not there are any ethical rules or principles (or any particular ethical judgments, for that matter) which do not merely repeat the "law of love" and which are authoritative, necessary, or helpful, (2) whether these ethical rules or principles (or particular judgments) are ascertainable independently of the "law of love" or not, and, in either case how they may be or are to be ascertained. In dealing with the first question, we must note that it is important to be clear just what one is claiming about the rules or principles (or particular judgments) in question. For they may be helpful without being necessary, and they may be authoritative or valid without being either necessary or helpful. But, whatever is being claimed, one method of settling the question at once suggests itself to the Christian thinker, namely, a direct appeal to Scripture, especially the teachings of Jesus and the Apostles. Thus Lindsay Dewar argues directly from the New Testament that Jesus did in fact "legislate certain rules or principles."[24] This sort of appeal seems to me to show only that there are some rules and principles other than the "law of love" (though perhaps not independent of it) which are authoritative or valid, not that they are necessary or helpful, unless it is assumed that Jesus would not have legislated them if they were not necessary or at least helpful (and the Bible does not tell us *this*). Indeed, it seems to me that such appeals do show, to the extent that they show said principles to be authorita-

---

[24] See *A Short Introduction to Moral Theology* (London, 1956), Ch. 1. Dewar does not go on to show just how they are related to the "law of love," but he seems to be holding a mixed theory, for he speaks of "natural law" as well as "divine law." C. H. Dodd in *Gospel and Law* also appeals directly to revelation to show that Christian ethics includes certain "ethical precepts."

tive, that a Christian cannot be satisfied with pure act-agapism as a normative *theory*—in practice, however, unless the principles in question are necessary or at least helpful as well as authoritative, he may still proceed as a pure act-agapist would. But this seems to me the most that an appeal to revelation can show; in principle it can establish anything for a Christian, of course, but in fact it establishes only what is actually revealed, and Scripture does not actually tell us that the disputed rules or principles are necessary or helpful as well as authoritative (and this it tells only to one who accepts it as a divine revelation). To show (or refute) this, therefore, one must resort to "moral philosophy," for example, to a logico-empirical argument calculated to prove (or disprove) that the bare injunction to love, even taken together with relevant factual knowledge about particular situations, is insufficient to give us adequate guidance of a moral kind.

In connection with the second question, we must first observe that whether the alleged ethical rules and judgments are independent of the "law of love" or not, there are various possible alternative theories about how they may or are to be ascertained. If they are not independent of the "law of love," we must still try to decide between modified act-agapism and the various forms of rule-agapism; if they are independent we still have to decide between various possible kinds of mixed agapisms and nonagapisms —and here all sorts of theories are possible: natural law theories, intuitionism, revelationism, social approval theories, etc. In effect, the second question is how to decide between the various normative theories described above. And, again, a Christian theologian may seek to do so by appeal to Scripture; if Scripture were full enough in what it says, this would for him be decisive. But the texts are not full enough in a philosophical sense; some point one way, some another. Perhaps the most crucial is Romans 2:14–15, in which St. Paul says that the Gentiles, who presumably do not have the "law of love," yet have a moral law "written in their hearts." This appears to show that there is moral insight which is independent both of special revelation and the "law of love"—and so to establish the correctness of some kind of mixed or nonagapistic theory. Yet even this passage is hardly explicit and elaborate enough to settle such a theoretical point, and the same is still more true of all the other texts—they are not theoretical enough in their message to help the Christian to decide with any conclusiveness between the rival theories open to him, except perhaps to rule out pure act-agapism (*if* they can be claimed to do even this). Here again the theologian must resort to "moral philosophy" as well as to revelation, if he means to try to settle such points of theory at all on anything like intellectually sufficient grounds, as he seems to.[25]

---

[25] I am not arguing here that moral philosophy is "omnicompetent" or even "sufficient."

If, however, the theologian does resort to moral philosophy, how is he to decide between rival normative schemes? Unfortunately, contemporary moral philosophers are no more in agreement on this point than the theologians are. But I believe that, at their best at any rate, they debate about it more clearly and more rigorously than theologians ever do, perhaps in part because they are not tempted to preach or to fall back on any scriptural or ecclesiastical revelation. In any case, the thinking theologian has no alternative but to become more adequately acquainted with "the best that has been thought and said in the world" of moral philosophy and then try to draw his own conclusions. In particular, he must make himself at home in the most rarified reaches of recent metaethical discussion, for his problem is not merely one within normative ethics; it includes the question how one scheme of normative ethics can be justified as against another, or if it can be justified at all. At this level I think theologians and Christian moralists have been much too unclear and much too unrigorous in their thinking. They almost invariably maintain that morality depends on religion or theology but they are rarely, if ever, very careful in their formulation of this claim or in their arguments in support of it. I myself doubt that it can be established, except perhaps in some greatly and carefully qualified sense, and believe that there are at least some "principles of justice" which are logically independent of the "law of love," of revelation, and of religion and theology. But that is another story which cannot be told now.[26]

It may be objected here that Jesus had no metaethics and hence that we need none. And it is, no doubt, true that the ethics of Jesus, and even of the Bible as a whole, is compatible with a variety of metaethical theories; the history of Judeo-Christian thought seems to show this. But, as I said at the outset, I am assuming that the theologians I have had in mind are right in feeling impelled to "think on [all] these things." If this is a mistake —and it too is a point which Christians have debated—then the mistake is as much theirs as mine.

---

[26] For parts of the story see my "Public Education and the Good Life," *Harvard Educational Review*, Fall Issue, 1961.

Bibliography

BOOKS

Adams, E. M. *Ethical Naturalism and the Modern World-View*. Chapel Hill: University of North Carolina Press, 1960.

Aiken, Henry David. *Reason and Conduct*. New York: Alfred A. Knopf, Inc., 1962.

Ayer, A. S. *Language, Truth, and Logic*. London: Victor Gollancz Ltd., 1948. Ch. 6.

Baier, Kurt. *The Moral Point of View: A Rational Basis of Ethics*. Ithaca: Cornell University Press, 1958.

Blanshard, Brand. *Reason and Goodness*. London: George Allen and Unwin Ltd., 1961.

Brandt, Richard B. *Ethical Theory*. Englewood Cliffs, N.J.: Prentice-Hall, Inc., 1961.

Castaneda, H., and G. Nakhnikian, eds. *Morality and the Language of Conduct*. Detroit: Wayne State University Press, 1963.

Dewey, John. *Theory of Valuation*. Chicago: University of Chicago Press, 1939.

Edel, Abraham. *Ethical Judgment*. New York: The Free Press, 1955.

———. *Method in Ethical Theory*. London: Routledge & Kegan Paul Ltd., 1963.

Edwards, Paul. *The Logic of Moral Discourse*. New York: The Free Press 1955.

Ewing, A. C. *The Definition of Good*. New York: The Macmillan Company, 1947.

———. *Ethics*. London: English Universities Press, 1953.

———. *Second Thoughts in Moral Philosophy*. New York: The Macmillan Company, 1959.

Frankena, William K. *Ethics*. Englewood Cliffs, N.J.: Prentice-Hall, Inc., 1963.

Gauthier, D. *Practical Reasoning*. London: Oxford University Press, 1963.

Ginsberg, Morris. *On The Diversity of Morals*. New York: The Macmillan Company, 1956.

Hall, E. *What Is Value?* London: Routledge & Kegan Paul Ltd., 1952.

Hampshire, Stuart. *Thought and Action*. London: Chatto & Windus Ltd., 1959.

Hare, R. M. *The Language of Morals*. Oxford: The Clarendon Press, 1952.

———. *Freedom and Reason.* Oxford: The Clarendon Press, 1963.

Hart, H. L. A. *The Concept of Law.* Oxford: The Clarendon Press, 1961.

Hartland-Swann, John. *An Analysis of Morals.* London: George Allen and Unwin Ltd., 1960.

Hay, William H., Marcus G. Singer, and Arthur E. Murphy, eds. *Reason and the Common Good. Selected Essays of Arthur E. Murphy.* Englewood Cliffs, N.J.: Prentice-Hall, Inc., 1963.

Hospers, John. *Human Conduct.* New York: Harcourt, Brace & World, Inc., 1961.

Kemp, G. *Reason, Action, and Morality.* London: Routledge & Kegan Paul Ltd., 1964.

Kerner, George C. *The Revolution in Ethical Theory.* London: Oxford University Press, 1966.

Ladd, John. *The Structure of a Moral Code.* Cambridge, Mass.: Harvard University Press, 1957.

Lewis, C. I. *An Analysis of Knowledge and Valuation.* LaSalle, Ill.: Open Court Publishing Co., 1946.

———. *The Ground and Nature of the Right.* New York: Columbia University Press, 1955.

Lyons, David. *Forms and Limits of Utilitarianism.* London: Oxford University Press, 1965.

Mackinnon, D. M. *A Study in Ethical Theory.* London: A. & C. Black, Limited, 1957.

Melden, A. I., ed. *Essays in Moral Philosophy.* Seattle: University of Washington Press, 1958.

———. *Rights and Right Conduct.* Oxford: Basil Blackwell, 1959.

———. *Free Action.* London: Routledge & Kegan Paul Ltd., 1961.

Montefiore, Alan. *A Modern Introduction to Moral Philosophy.* London: Routledge & Kegan Paul Ltd., 1958.

Moore, G. E. *Principia Ethica.* Cambridge: Cambridge University Press, 1903.

———. *Ethics.* London: Oxford University Press, 1912.

Murphy, Arthur E. *The Theory of Practical Reason.* LaSalle, Ill.: Open Court Publishing Co., 1964.

Nowell-Smith, P. H. *Ethics.* Harmondsworth: Penguin Books Ltd., 1954.

Pepper, Stephen C. *Ethics.* New York: Appleton-Century-Crofts, 1960.

———. *The Sources of Value.* Berkeley: University of California Press, 1958.

Perry, R. B. *General Theory of Value*. London: Longmans, Green & Co. Ltd., 1926.

———. *Realms of Value*. Cambridge, Mass.: Harvard University Press, 1954.

Prichard, H. A. *Moral Obligation*. Oxford: The Clarendon Press, 1949.

Prior, A. N. *Logic and the Basis of Ethics*. London: Oxford University Press, 1949. Ch. I.

Rice, Philip Blair. *On the Knowledge of Good and Evil*. New York: Random House, Inc., 1955.

Ross, W. D. *The Right and the Good*. Oxford: The Clarendon Press, 1930.

———. *Foundations of Ethics*. Oxford: The Clarendon Press, 1939.

Schilpp, Paul Arthur, ed. *The Philosophy of G. E. Moore*. Evanston, Ill.: Northwestern University Press, 1942.

Sellars, Wilfrid, and John Hospers, eds. *Readings in Ethical Theory*. New York: Appleton-Century-Crofts, 1952.

Sesonske, Alexander. *Value and Obligation*. Berkeley: University of California Press, 1957.

Shirk, Evelyn. *The Ethical Dimension*. New York: Appleton-Century-Crofts, 1965.

Singer, Marcus George. *Generalization in Ethics*. New York: Alfred A. Knopf, Inc., 1961.

Smart, J. J. C. *An Outline of a System of Utilitarian Ethics*. Melbourne: Melbourne University Press, 1961.

Sparshott, F. E. *An Enquiry into Goodness*. Chicago: University of Chicago Press, 1958.

Stevenson, C. L. *Ethics and Language*. New Haven: Yale University Press, 1944.

———. *Facts and Values*. New Haven: Yale University Press, 1963.

Taylor, Paul. *Normative Discourse*. Englewood Cliffs, N.J.: Prentice-Hall, Inc., 1961.

Toulmin, Stephen E. *An Examination of the Place of Reason in Ethics*. Cambridge: Cambridge University Press, 1950.

von Wright, G. H. *The Varieties of Goodness*. London: Routledge & Kegan Paul Ltd., 1963.

———. *Norm and Action*. London: Routledge & Kegan Paul Ltd., 1963.

Warnock, Mary. *Ethics Since 1900*. London: Oxford University Press, 1960.

Wellman, Carl. *The Language of Ethics*. Cambridge, Mass.: Harvard University Press, 1961.

Wilson, J. *Reason and Morals*. Cambridge: Cambridge University Press, 1961.

Ziff, Paul. *Semantic Analysis*. Ithaca: Cornell University Press, 1960. Ch. 6.

Zink, S. *The Concepts of Ethics*. New York: St. Martin's Press, Inc., 1962.

ARTICLES

Selected articles of principal interest to section One:
Moral Reasoning and the Is–Ought Controversy.

Aiken, Henry David, "Emotive 'Meanings' and Ethical Terms," *Journal of Philosophy*, XLI (1944), 456–70.

———, "Evaluation and Obligation: Two Functions of Judgments in the Language of Conduct," *Journal of Philosophy*, XLVII (1950), 5–22.

Ayer, A. J., "On the Analysis of Moral Judgments," in *Philosophical Essays* (New York: St. Martin's Press, Inc., 1954), pp. 231–49.

Baier, K., "Proving a Moral Judgment," *Philosophical Studies*, IV (1953), 33–44.

———, and S. E. Toulmin, "On Describing," *Mind*, LXI (1952), 13–38.

Barnes, W. H. F., "Ethics Without Propositions," *Proceedings of the Aristotelian Society*, Suppl. XXII (1948), 1–30.

Bennett, J., "Moral Argument," *Mind*, LXIX (1960), 544–49.

Binkley, Robert, "A Theory of Practical Reason," *Philosophical Review*, LXXIV (1965), 423–48.

Black, Max, "The Gap Between 'Is' and 'Should'," *Philosophical Review*, LXXIII (1964), 165–81.

———, "Some Questions About Emotive Meaning," *Philosophical Review*, LXIII (1964), 165–81.

Brandt, R. B., "The Emotive Theory of Ethics," *Philosophical Review*, LIX (1950), 305–18.

———, "The Status of Empirical Assertion Theories in Ethics," *Mind*, LXI (1952), 458–79.

Castaneda, Hector-Neri, "Imperative Reasonings," *Philosophy and Phenomenological Research*, XXI (1960), 21–49.

———, "The Logic of Change, Action, and Norms," *Journal of Philosophy*, LXII (1965), 333–44.

Caton, Charles E., "In What Sense and Why 'Ought'-Judgments Are Universalizable," *Philosophical Quarterly*, XIII (1963), 48–55.

Cohen, M. F., " 'Is and Should': An Unbridged Gap," *Philosophical Review*, LXXIV (1965), 220–28.

Edgley, R., "Practical Reason," *Mind*, LXXIV (1965), 174–91.

Falk, W. D., "Action-Guiding Reasons," *The Journal of Philosophy*, LX (1963), 702–18

Findlay, J. N., "Morality and Convention," *Mind*, LIII (1944), 142–69.

Firth, R., "Ethical Absolutism and the Ideal Observer," *Philosophy and Phenomenological Research*, XII (1952), 317–45.

Flew, Antony, 'On Not Deriving 'Ought' from 'Is'," *Analysis*, XXV (1964), 25–32.

Foot, P. R., "Moral Beliefs," *Proceedings of the Aristotelian Society*, LIX (1958–1959), 83–104.

————, and A. R. Montefiore, "Goodness and Choice" (Symposium), *Proceedings of the Aristotelian Society*, Suppl. XXXV (1961), 45–80.

Frankena, W. K., "Ethical Naturalism Renovated," *Review of Metaphysics*, X (1957), 459–73.

————, "On Saying the Ethical Thing," *Proceedings and Addresses of the American Philosophical Association*, XXXIX (1965–1966), 21–42.

Geach, P. T., "Good and Evil," *Analysis*, XVII (1957), 33–42.

————, "Ascriptivism," *Philosophical Review*, LXIX (1960), 221–25.

Gewirth, A., "Categorial Consistency in Ethics," *The Philosophical Quarterly*, XVII (1967), 289–300.

————, "Meanings and Criteria in Ethics," *Philosophy*, XXXVIII (1963), 329–45.

Hall, E., "Practical Reasons and the Deadlock in Ethics," *Mind*, LXIV (1955), 319–32.

Hampshire, Stuart, "Fallacies in Moral Philosophy," *Mind*, LVIII (1949), 466–82.

Hancock, Roger, "The Refutation of Naturalism in Moore and Hare," *Journal of Philosophy*, LVII (1960), 326–34.

Hare, R. M., "Descriptivism," *British Academy Proceedings*, XLIX (1964), 115–34.

————, "Geach: Good and Evil," *Analysis*, XVII (1957), 103–12.

————, "Some Alleged Differences Between Imperatives and Indicatives," *Mind*, LXVI (1967), 309–26.

————, "Universalizability," *Proceedings of the Aristotelian Society*, IV (1954–1955), 295–312.

Harrison, J., "Can Ethics Do Without Propositions?" *Mind*, LIX (1950), 358–71.

————, "Empiricism in Ethics," *Philosophical Quarterly*, II (1952), 289–306.

Holland, R., and H. D. Lewis, "The Autonomy of Ethics" (Symposium), *Proceedings of the Aristotelian Society*, Suppl. XXXII (1958), 25–74.

Hungerland, Isabel C., "Contextual Implication," *Inquiry*, III (1960), 211–58.

Jarvis, J., "In Defense of Moral Absolutes," *Journal of Philosophy*, LV (1958), 1043–53.

———, "Practical Reasoning," *Philosophical Quarterly*, XII (1962), 316–28.

Kerner, George C., "Approvals, Reasons, and Moral Argument," *Mind*, LXXI (1962), 474–86.

Ladd, John, "Value Judgments, Emotive Meaning, and Attitudes," *Journal of Philosophy*, XLVI (1949), 119–29.

Locke, Don, "The Trivializability of Universalizability," *Philosophical Review*, LXXVII (1968), 25–45.

Macdonald, Margaret, "Ethics and the Ceremonial Use of Language," in Max Black, ed., *Philosophical Analysis* (Ithaca, N.Y.: Cornell University Press, 1950), pp. 211–29.

MacIntyre, A., "Hume on 'Is' and 'Ought'," *Philosophical Review*, LXVIII (1959), 451–68.

Montague, Roger, " 'Ought' from 'Is'," *Australasian Journal of Philosophy*, XXXV (1957), 111–18.

Montefiore, A., "Fact, Value, and Ideology," in *British Analytical Philosophy*, Bernard Williams and Alan Montefiore, eds. (New York: The Humanities Press, 1966), pp. 192–203.

———, "The Meaning of 'Good' and the Act of Commendation," *Philosophical Quarterly*, XVII (1967), 115–29.

Mothersill, Mary, "Anscombe's Account of the Practical Syllogism," *Philosophical Review*, LXXI (1962), 448–61.

Nielson, Kai, "Justification and Moral Reasoning," *Methodos*, IX (1957), 1–35.

———, "The Functions of Moral Discourse," *Philosophical Quarterly*, VII (1957), 236–48.

———, "Conventionalism in Morals and the Appeal to Human Nature," *Philosophy and Phenomenological Research*, XXIII (1962–1963), 217–31.

———, "On Human Needs and Moral Appraisals," *Inquiry*, VI (1963), pp. 170–83.

———, "Ethical Naturalism Once Again," *Australasian Journal of Philosophy*, XLI (1963), 313–17.

Nowell-Smith, P. H., "Contextual Implication and Ethical Theory," *Proceedings of the Aristotelian Society*, Suppl. XXXVI (1962), 1–18.

Nowell-Smith, P. H., and E. J. Lemmon, "Escapism," *Mind*, LXIX (1960), 289–300.

Pahel, K. R., "Stephen Pepper's Ethical Empiricism and the Myth of Analytic Naturalism," *The Southern Journal of Philosophy*, V (1967), 48–58.

Patton, T. E., and P. Ziff, "On Vendler's Grammar of 'Good'," *Philosophical Review*, LXXIII (1964), 528–37.

Phillips, Griffiths A., "Acting with Reason," *Philosophical Quarterly*, VII (1958), 289–99.

Prior, A. N., "The Autonomy of Ethics," *Australasian Journal of Philosophy*, XXXVIII (1960), 199–206.

Robinson, R., "The Emotive Theory of Ethics," *Proceedings of the Aristotelian Society*, Suppl. XXII (1948), 79–106.

Russell, Bertrand, "The Elements of Ethics," in *Philosophical Essays* (London: George Allen & Unwin Ltd. 1910), pp. 13–59.

Searle, J., "Meaning and Speech Acts," *Philosophical Review*, LXI (1962), 423–32.

Slote, M. A., "Value Judgments and the Theory of Important Criteria," *Journal of Philosophy*, LXV (1968), 94–112.

Smart, J. J. C., "The Methods of Ethics and the Methods of Science," *Journal of Philosophy*, LXII (1965), 344–49.

Stevenson, C. L., "Brandt's Questions about Emotive Ethics," *Philosophical Review*, LIX (1950), 528–34.

————, "Persuasive Definitions," *Mind*, XLVII (1938), 331–50.

Taylor, Paul, "Prescribing and Evaluating," *Mind*, LXXI (1962), 213–30.

Thomson, J. and J., "How Not to Derive 'Ought' from 'Is'," *Philosophical Review*, LXXIII (1964), 512–16.

Urmson, J. O., "On Grading," *Mind*, LIX (1950), 145–59.

Vendler, Z., "The Grammar of Goodness," *Philosophical Review*, LXXII (1963), 446–65.

von Wright, G. H., "Practical Inference," *Philosophical Review*, LXXII (1963), 159–79.

Winch, Peter, "The Universalizability of Moral Judgments," *The Monist*, XLIX (1965), 196–214.

Wittgenstein, L., "A Lecture on Ethics," *Philosophical Review*, LXXIV (1965), 3–12.

Selected articles of principal interest to section Two:
Rules, Principles, and Utilitarianism.

Acton, H. B., and J. W. N. Watkins, "Negative Utilitarianism," *Proceedings of the Aristotelian Society*, Suppl. XXXVII (1963), pp. 83–114.

Black, Max, "Notes on the Meaning of 'Rule'," *Theoria*, XXIV (1958), 131–32.

Bradley, M. C., "Professor Smart's 'Extreme and Restricted Utilitarianism,' " *Philosophical Quarterly*, VII (1957), 264–66.

Britton, Karl, "Utilitarianism: The Appeal to a First Principle," *Proceedings of the Aristotelian Society*, LX (1959–1960), 141–54.

Duncan-Jones, A., "Kant and Universalization," *Analysis*, XVI (1955), 12–14.

———, "Utilitarianism and Rules," *Philosophical Quarterly*, VII (1957), 364–67.

Ewing, A. C., "Utilitarianism," *Ethics*, LVIII (1947), 100–111.

———, "What Would Happen If Everybody Acted Like Me?" *Philosophy*, XXVIII (1953), 16–29.

Feinberg, J., "The Forms and Limits of Utilitarianism," *Philosophical Review*, LXXVI (1967), 368–81.

Harrison, J., "Utilitarianism, Universalization and Our Duty to Be Just," *Proceedings of the Aristotelian Society*, LIII (1952–1953), 105–34.

Horsburgh, H. J. N., "Criteria of Assent to a Moral Rule," *Mind*, LXII (1954), 345–68.

Kaplan, Morton A., "Some Problems of the Extreme Utilitarian Position," *Ethics*, LXX (1960), 228–32.

Mabbott, J. D., "Interpretations of Mill's 'Utilitarianism'," *Philosophical Quarterly*, VI (1956), 115–20.

———, "Punishment," *Mind*, XLCIII (1939), 152–67.

McCloskey, H. J., "An Examination of Restricted Utilitarianism," *Philosophical Review*, LXIV (1957), 466–65.

Melden, A. I., "Two Comments on Utilitarianism," *Philosophical Review*, LX (1951), 519–23.

Miller, Leonard G., "Rules and Exceptions," *Ethics*, LXIV (1956), 262–70.

Narveson, Jan, "Utilitarianism and Formalism," *Australasian Journal of Philosophy*, XLIII (1965), 58–72.

Phillips, Griffiths A., "Justifying Moral Principles," *Proceedings of the Aristotelian Society*, LVII (1957–1958), 103–24.

Rawls, John, "Justice as Fairness," *The Journal of Philosophy*, LIV (1957), 653–62.

———, "Outline of a Decision Procedure for Ethics," *Philosophical Review*, LX (1951), 177–97.

———, "Review of S. Toulmin's *An Examination of the Place of Reason in Ethics*," *Philosophical Review*, LX (1951), 572–80.

Rawls, John, "The Sense of Justice," *Philosophical Review*, LXXXII (1963), 281–305.

Rees, W. J., "Moral Rules and the Analysis of 'Ought'," *Philosophical Review*, LXII (1953), 23–40.

Runciman, W. G., and A. K. Sen, "Games, Justice, and the General Will," *Mind*, LXXXIV (1965), 554–62.

Shwayder, D. S., "Moral Rules and Moral Maxims," *Ethics*, LXVII (1957), 269–85.

Singer, Marcus G., "Negative and Positive Duties," *Philosophical Quarterly*, XV (1965), 97–103.

Smart, J. J. C., "Extreme Utilitarianism: A Reply to M. A. Kaplan," *Ethics*, LXXI (1961), 133–34.

Sobel, J. Howard, " 'Everyone,' Consequences, and Generalization Arguments," *Inquiry*, X (1967), 373–404.

Stout, A. K., "But Suppose Everybody Did the Same," *Australasian Journal of Philosophy*, XXXII (1954), 1–29.

Urmson, J. O., "The Interpretation of the Moral Philosophy of J. S. Mill," *Philosophical Quarterly*, III (1953), 33–39.

Selected articles of principal interest to section Three: Recent Conceptions of Morality.

Brunton, J. A., "Egoism and Morality," *Philosophical Quarterly*, VI (1956), 289–303.

———, "Restricted Moralities," *Philosophy*, XLI (1966), 113–26.

Campbell, C. A., "Moral Values and Non-Moral Values," *Mind*, XLIV (1935)', 237–99.

Cooper, Neil, "Two Concepts of Morality," *Philosophy*, XLI (1966), 19–33.

Durrant, R. G., "Moral Neutrality and the Analysis of Morality," *Australasian Journal of Philosophy*, XXXVI (1958), 169–88.

Findlay, J. N., "Morality by Convention," *Mind*, LIII (1944), 142–69.

Foot, P. R., and Jonathan Harrison, "When Is a Principle a Moral Principle?" (a symposium), *Proceedings of the Aristotelian Society*, Suppl. XXVIII (1954), pp. 95–134.

Frankena, W. K., "MacIntyre on Defining Morality," *Philosophy*, XXXIII (1958), 158–62.

———, "The Concept of Morality," *University of Colorado Studies*, (1965), pp. 1–22.

———, "Recent Conceptions of Morality," in *Morality and the Language of Conduct*, eds. H. Castaneda and G. Nakhnikian (Detroit: Wayne State University Press, 1961), pp. 1–24.

Gallie, W. B., "Liberal Morality and Socialist Morality," *Philosophy*, XXIV (1949), 318–34.

Gauthier, David P., "Morality and Advantage," *The Philosophical Review*, LXXVI (1967), 460–75.

Gellner, E. A., "Ethics and Logic," *Proceedings of the Aristotelian Society*, LV (1954–1955), 157–78.

———, "Morality and *Je Ne Sais Quoi* Concepts," *Analysis*, XVI (1956), 97–103.

Griffiths, A. P., and R. S. Peters, "The Autonomy of Prudence," *Mind*, LXXI (1962), 161–80.

Harrison, Jonathan, "Self-Interest and Duty," *Australasian Journal of Philosophy*, XXXI (1953), 22–29.

Hart, H. L. A., "Legal and Moral Obligation," in *Essays in Moral Philosophy*, ed. A. I. Melden (Seattle: The University of Washington Press, 1958), pp. 82–107.

Mabbott, J. D., and H. J. N. Horsburgh, "Prudence" (symposium), *Proceedings of the Aristotelian Society*, XXXVI (1962), 51–76.

MacIntyre, Alasdair, "What Morality Is Not," *Philosophy*, XXXII (1957), 325–35.

Medlin, B., "Ultimate Principles and Ethical Egoism," *Australasian Journal of Philosophy*, XXXV (1957), 111–18.

Meiland, J. W., "Duty and Interest," *Analysis*, XXIII (1963), 106.

Rees, W. J., "Moral Rules and the Analysis of 'Ought'," *The Philosophical Review*, LXII (1953), 23–40.

Sprigge, Timothy L. S., "Definition of a Moral Judgment," *Philosophy*, XXXIX (1964), 301–22.

Taylor, Paul, "The Ethnocentric Fallacy," *The Monist*, XLVII (1963), 563–84.

Toulmin, S. E., "Principles of Morality," *Philosophy*, XXXI (1956), 142–53.

Urmson, J. O., "Saints and Heroes," in *Essays in Moral Philosophy*, ed. A. I. Melden (Seattle: The University of Washington Press, 1958), 198–216.

Wertheim, Peter, "Morality and Advantage," *Australasian Journal of Philosophy*, XLII (1964), 375–87.

Selected articles of principal interest to section Four:
Why Should I Be Moral?

Bradley, F. H., "Why Should I Be Moral?" Essay II in his *Ethical Studies* (Oxford: The Clarendon Press, 1927), 58–81.

Foot, P. R., "Moral Beliefs," *Proceedings of the Aristotelian Society*, LIX (1958-1959), 83-104.

Ladd, J., "The Desire to Do One's Duty for Its Own Sake," in *Morality and the Language of Conduct*, H. Castaneda and G. Nakhnikian, eds. (Detroit: Wayne State University Press, 1963), 301-49.

Melden, A. I., "Why Be Moral?" *Journal of Philosophy*, XLV (1948), 449-56.

Nielsen, K., "Is 'Why Should I Be Moral?' an Absurdity?" *Australasian Journal of Philosophy*, XXXVI (1958), 25-32.

Phillips, D. Z., "Does It Pay to Be Good?" *Proceedings of the Aristotelian Society*, LXV (1964-1965), 45-60.

Stace, W. T., "Why Should I Be Moral?" chapters 11 and 12 in his *The Concept of Morals* (New York: The Macmillan Company, 1937), 250-94.

Wadia, P. A., "Why Should I Be Moral?" *Australasian Journal of Philosophy*, XLII (1964), 216-26.

Winch, P., "Can a Good Man Be Harmed?" *Proceedings of the Aristotelian Society*, LXVI (1965-1966), pp. 55-70.

Selected articles of principal interest to section Five:
Normative, Religious, and Meta-Ethics

Adams, E. M., "Classical Moral Philosophy and Metaethics," *Ethics*, LXXIV (1964), 97-110.

Aiken, Henry, "Morality and Ideology," in *Ethics and Society*, ed. R. T. deGeorge (Garden City: Doubleday & Company, Inc., 1966), pp. 149-72.

Anscombe, G. E. M., "Modern Moral Philosophy," *Philosophy*, XXXIII (1958), 1 19.

Blackstone, W. T., "On Justifying a Metaethical Theory," *Australasian Journal of Philosophy*, XLI (1963), 57-66.

Brown, P., "Religious Morality," *Mind*, LXXII (1963), 235-44.

Ewing, A. C., "The Autonomy of Ethics," in *Prospects for Metaphysics*, ed. I. T. Ramsey (London: George Allen and Unwin Ltd., 1961), pp. 33-49.

Findlay, J. N., "The Methodology of Normative Ethics," *Journal of Philosophy*, LVIII (1961), 757-64.

Gewirth, Alan, "Metaethics and Moral Neutrality," *Ethics*, LXXVIII (1968), 214-25. [A reply to Sumner]

———, "Metaethics and Normative Ethics," *Mind*, LXIX (1960), 187-205.

Harrison, Jonathan, "Moral Talking and Moral Living," *Philosophy*, XXXVIII (1963), 315-28.

Hepburn, Ronald W., "Secular Ethics and Moral Seriousness," in *Christianity and Paradox* (New York: Humanities Press, Inc., 1958), pp. 128–54.

Hick, John, "Belief and Life: The Fundamental Nature of Christian Ethics," *Encounter*, XX (Fall 1959), 494–516. Also appears in John Hick, *Faith and Knowledge*, 2nd ed. (Ithaca: Cornell University Press, 1966), Chapter II, "Faith and Works," pp. 237–63.

Holland, R., and H. D. Lewis, "The Autonomy of Ethics" (a symposium), *Proceedings of the Aristotelian Society*, Suppl. XXXII (1958), 25–74.

Moore, G. E., "The Nature of Moral Philosophy," in *Philosophical Studies* (London: Routledge & Kegan Paul Ltd., 1922), pp. 310–39.

Mosher, D., "A Reply to Mr. Wheatley," *Theoria*, XXVIII (1952), 308–12.

Nielsen, Kai, "An Examination of an Alleged Theological Basis of Morality," *The Iliff Review*, XXI (1964), 39–49.

————, "Problems of Ethics," in *Encyclopedia of Philosophy*, ed. Paul Edwards (New York: The Macmillan Company and The Free Press, 1967), III, 117–32.

————, "Some Remarks on the Independence of Morality from Religion," *Mind*, LXX (1961), 175–86.

Olafson, Frederick A., "Metaethics and the Moral Life," *The Philosophical Review*, LXV (1956), 159–78.

Phillips, D. Z., "Moral and Religious Conceptions of Duty: An Analysis," *Mind*, LXXIII (1964), 406–12.

Quinton, A., S. Hampshire, I. Murdoch, and I. Berlin, "Philosophy and Beliefs," *The Twentieth Century*, CLVII (1955), 495–521.

Rynin, D., "The Autonomy of Ethics," *Mind*, LXVI (1957), 308–17.

Sumner, L. W., "Normative Ethics and Metaethics," *Ethics*, LXXVII (1967), 95–106. [A reply to Gewirth]

Taylor, Paul W., "The Normative Function of Metaethics," *The Philosophical Review*, LXVII (1958), 16–32.

Wheatley, John, "The Logical Status of Metaethical Theories," *Theoria*, XXVI (1960), 71–82.

Wick, Warner A., "Moral Problems, Moral Philosophy, and Metaethics," *The Philosophical Review*, LXII (1953), 3–22.

Wilcox, John T., "Blackstone on Metaethical Neutrality," *Australasian Journal of Philosophy*, XLI (May, 1963), 89–91.